Revised Common Lectionary in NRSV

Sundays and Festivals

Principal Service Lectionary of the Church of England

Personal Edition

MOWBRAY

Mowbray
A Cassell imprint
Wellington House
125 Strand
London
WC2R 0BB

In this edition the Scriptures are shown as prose or as verse according to whether they are
prose or verse in the NRSV. Paragraph divisions are as in the NRSV, except in the Psalms.

The division into paragraphs follows that of the NRSV, except in the Psalms

The Psalms are from the Standard Book of Common Prayer of the Episcopal Church
in the USA adjusted to comply with British orthography and inclusivized with
reference to human beings by the Society of Saint Francis.

The sources and details of the copyright holders of the individual Collects and Post Communion Prayers are
given on pages xii–xvi.

Translations of the Magnificat (Luke 1.46b–55) and Benedictus (Luke 1.68–79) prepared by the
English Language Liturgical Consultation (ELLC), © 1988.

Psalm responses for saints' days by Br Tristam SSF were published in *Exciting Holiness* by
The Canterbury Press Norwich, and are used by permission.

Personal edition first published 1998, based on the Green edition

British Library Cataloguing-in-Publication Data
A catalogue record for this book is available from the British Library.

ISBN	0-264-67494-4
Pew Edition Red Readers' Hardback	0-264-67470-7
Pew Edition Green Solid Text Hardback	0-264-67469-3
ISBN (Limp)	0-264-67475-X
ISBN (Lectern edition)	0-304-33697-1
ISBN for CD-ROM	0-264-67456-1

Cover design: Sr Regina Rynja OSB

Typeset by Pantek Arts, Maidstone, Kent
Printed and bound in Great Britain by The Bath Press, Bath

CONTENTS

Sundays and Festivals

	Year A	Year B	Year C	Collect and Post Communion Prayer

★ For these Sundays the Collect and Post Communion Prayers are those of the appropriate Sunday after Trinity: see pages x and 910–922.

Festivals

★ For these Sundays the Collect and Post Communion Prayers are those of the appropriate Sunday after Trinity: see pages x and 919–923.

CONTENTS

INTRODUCTION
HOW TO USE THE LECTIONARY

The orderly reading of scripture is at the heart of Christian worship. A lectionary clothes the cycle of the Christian year with the stories that tell the story of divine activity and human response to it and makes it possible for Christians to celebrate the mystery of faith the more effectively. When they use a common lectionary, and read the scriptures 'in step', they are also enabled to celebrate their essential unity in Christ.

The Revised Common Lectionary (RCL) is an international and ecumenical lectionary without rivals. Based on the 1969 Roman Lectionary, but modified and developed in an ecumenical setting, it emerged as the Revised Common Lectionary in 1992 and is being adopted by many churches, by some just as it stands, by others with some modification to meet their own needs, particularly in relation to calendar.

The Church of England has adopted this lectionary and made it its own as the main constituent of its Principal Service Lectionary for Sundays, Principal Feasts and Festivals. That lectionary is almost identical with the RCL, from which it is derived, but there are a number of deviations and much of the festival material is additional to the RCL. Its provision for the large majority of Sundays is absolutely identical with RCL.

Among the churches that have adopted the RCL are the Episcopal Church of Scotland, the (Anglican) Church in Wales and the (Anglican) Church of Ireland. Their provisions also draw to a greater or lesser extent on the Church of England's deviations from and additions to the RCL. Their precise local variations are not listed within the lectionary, but users of this lectionary within those churches should, by reference to their tables of readings, be able to deduce whether, on a particular day, they follow the RCL provision or the English variations from it. A supplement provides the texts of the few lections for Ireland, Scotland and Wales that are not included in the main text. These are a series of Old Testament Readings in Eastertide and the readings for specifically Irish, Scottish and Welsh saints.

The variations between the RCL and the Church of England provision include some differences in the ways Sundays are described. This applies particularly on the Sundays after Epiphany and before Lent, and in the time between Trinity Sunday and the First Sunday of Advent. In each case the alternative designations are given. Exclusively Church of England variations and designations are indicated by a † in the margin.

One particular feature of the RCL, reproduced in the Church of England lectionary, is the provision of alternative Old Testament readings for the period of Ordinary Time (the Sundays after Trinity). In Track 1 the approach to the Old Testament is 'semi-continuous'. In other words, one biblical book is followed through in a series of readings over a number of weeks, without any pre-determined relationship with the other readings that day. The

Psalm following it reflects that reading. In Track 2, the Old Testament readings are chosen to relate to the Gospel reading and therefore move around the Old Testament without any sequence from on week to another. A different Psalm is provided to reflect that different Old Testament reading. Users are free to choose which track to follow in any particular year (though the Church of England abandons Track 1 during the four weeks before Advent), but, during any given year, there should be no movement from one track into another.

The Psalms provided for use after the Old Testament reading are in the American Episcopal translation to be found in Britain in the office book, *Celebrating Common Prayer*. The Canticles that replace the Psalms on a small number of days are given in the same biblical translation as the readings, the New Revised Standard Version, except for the Benedictus and Magnificat, which follow the agreed ELLC translation. Because the verse numberings in the American psalter differ slightly from those in the NRSV, some variation from the denominational lectionary tables, which follow the NRSV even for the Psalms, may be noted.

The Psalms are so printed that they may be spoken or sung in a number of different ways. They may be sung to plainchant or Anglican chant. They may be recited with the verses alternating between a reader and the congregation. But they may be used responsorially. The response printed at the beginning of each Psalm (sometimes with a longer and shorter version) is for use by the congregation at all the points where the letter ℟ is printed, in response to the words of the Psalm spoken or sung by a single voice or sung by a choir. Where a verse of a Psalm is bracketed, it should be omitted in a responsorial version, normally because it is a verse occurring several times in the text that has been employed as the response itself. But the bracketed verses should only be omitted when the Psalm is being used responsorially.

Neither RCL nor the Church of England provision gives a text for Psalm responses. The texts included in this book, nearly always from the Psalm itself, have been provided by members of the Inter-Provincial Group, but have not been submitted for approval to any denomination.

In this edition of the Lectionary the Collects and Post Communion Prayers have been added at the end. Other than those for Scottish, Welsh and Irish saints, they were drawn up in the Inter-Provincial Group and have been authorized for use in the Church of England alongside the Lectionary. In the period of Ordinary Time after Pentecost Collects are attached to Sunday names (such and such Sunday after Trinity) rather than to particular readings set by calendar date.

The Collects and Post Communion Prayers may be used in the Episcopal Church of Scotland as alternatives to those included in *Scottish Liturgy (Eucharist)*.

The publishers offer this Lectionary to the churches in the hope that it may help the Church in the public liturgical proclamation of the scriptures, in the discovery of the strengths of the new lectionaries that will bring freshness to that proclamation, and in the recovery of unity among those who find in reading the Hebrew and Christian scriptures the word of God for every generation.

CALENDAR

THE SEASONS

	1997/8	1998/9	1999/2000	2000/1	2001/2
Advent					
First Sunday of Advent	30 Nov[1]	29 Nov	28 Nov	3 Dec	2 Dec
Second Sunday of Advent	7 Dec	6 Dec	5 Dec	10 Dec	9 Dec
Third Sunday of Advent	14 Dec	13 Dec	12 Dec	17 Dec	16 Dec
Fourth Sunday of Advent	21 Dec	20 Dec	19 Dec	24 Dec	23 Dec
Christmas					
Christmas Day	25 Dec	25 Dec	25 Dec	25 Dec	25 Dec
First Sunday of Christmas	28 Dec[2]	27 Dec[7]	26 Dec[11]	31 Dec	30 Dec
Second Sunday of Christmas	(4 Jan)	(3 Jan)	2 Jan	–	–
Epiphany					
The Epiphany	6 (or 4) Jan	6 (or 3) Jan	6 (or 2) Jan	6 Jan	6 Jan
The Baptism of Christ	11 Jan	10 Jan	9 Jan	7 Jan	7 Jan
Second Sunday of Epiphany	18 Jan	17 Jan	16 Jan	14 Jan	13 Jan
Third Sunday of Epiphany	25 Jan[3]	24 Jan	23 Jan	21 Jan	20 Jan
Fourth Sunday of Epiphany	(1 Feb)	(31 Jan)	(30 Jan)	(28 Jan)	27 Jan
The Presentation of Christ					
in the Temple (Candlemas)	2 (or 1) Feb	2 Feb (or 31 Jan)	2 Feb (or 30 Jan)	2 Feb (or 28 Jan)	2 (or 3) Feb
Ordinary Time					
which begins on the day					
following The Presentation					
Fifth Sunday before Lent	–	–	6 Feb (Pr 1)	–	–
Fourth Sunday before Lent	–	–	13 Feb (Pr 2)	4 Feb (Pr 1)	–
Third Sunday before Lent	8 Feb (Pr 1)	–	20 Feb (Pr 3)	11 Feb (Pr 2)	–
Second Sunday before Lent	15 Feb	7 Feb	27 Feb	18 Feb	(3 Feb)
Sunday next before Lent	22 Feb	14 Feb	5 Mar	15 Feb	10 Feb
Lent					
Ash Wednesday	25 Feb	17 Feb	8 Mar	28 Feb	13 Feb
First Sunday of Lent	1 Mar	21 Feb	12 Mar	4 Mar	17 Feb
Second Sunday of Lent	8 Mar	28 Feb	19 Mar[12]	11 Mar	24 Feb
Third Sunday of Lent	15 Mar	7 Mar	26 Mar	18 Mar	3 Mar
Fourth Sunday of Lent –					
Mothering Sunday	22 Mar	14 Mar	2 Apr	25 Mar[17]	10 Mar
Fifth Sunday of Lent –					
(Passiontide begins)	29 Mar	21 Mar	9 Apr	1 Apr	17 Mar

CALENDAR

	1997/8	1998/9	1999/2000	2000/1	2001/2
Palm Sunday	5 Apr	28 Mar	16 Apr	8 Apr	24 Mar
Maundy Thursday	9 Apr	1 Apr	20 Apr	12 Apr	28 Mar
Good Friday	10 Apr	2 Apr	21 Apr	13 Apr	29 Mar
Easter Eve	11 Apr	3 Apr	22 Apr	14 Apr	30 Mar
Easter					
Easter Day	12 Apr	4 Apr	23 Apr[13]	15 Apr	31 Mar
Second Sunday of Easter	19 Apr	11 Apr	30 Apr	22 Apr	7 Apr
Third Sunday of Easter	26 Apr	18 Apr	7 May	29 Apr	14 Apr
Fourth Sunday of Easter	3 May	25 Apr[8]	14 May[14]	6 May	21 Apr
Fifth Sunday of Easter	10 May	2 May	21 May	13 May	28 Apr
Sixth Sunday of Easter	17 May	9 May	28 May	20 May	5 May
Ascension Day	21 May	13 May	1 Jun	24 May	9 May
Seventh Sunday of Easter –					
Sunday after Ascension Day	24 May	16 May	4 Jun	27 May	12 May
Pentecost (Whitsunday)	31 May[4]	23 May	11 Jun[15]	3 Jun	19 May

Ordinary Time
which is resumed on the Monday
following the Day of Pentecost

	1997/8	1998/9	1999/2000	2000/1	2001/2
Trinity Sunday	7 Jun	30 May	18 Jun	10 Jun	26 May
The Day of Thanksgiving for the					
Institution of Holy Communion –					
Thursday after Trinity Sunday	11 Jun[5]	3 Jun	22 Jun	14 Jun	30 May
First Sunday after Trinity	14 Jun (Pr 6)	6 Jun (Pr 5)	25 Jun (Pr 7)	17 Jun (Pr 6)	2 Jun (Pr 4)
Second Sunday after Trinity	21 Jun (Pr 7)	13 Jun (Pr 6)	2 Jul (Pr 8)	24 Jun (Pr 7)[18]	9 Jun (Pr 5)
Third Sunday after Trinity	28 Jun (Pr 8)	20 Jun (Pr 7)	9 Jul (Pr 9)	1 Jul (Pr 8)	16 Jun (Pr 6)
Fourth Sunday after Trinity	5 July (Pr 9)	27 Jun (Pr 8)	16 Jul (Pr 10)	8 Jul (Pr 9)	23 Jun (Pr 7)
Fifth Sunday after Trinity	12 Jul (Pr 10)	4 Jul (Pr 9)	23 Jul (Pr 11)	15 Jul (Pr 10)	30 Jun (Pr 8)
Sixth Sunday after Trinity	19 Jul (Pr 11)	11 Jul (Pr 10)	30 Jul (Pr 12)	22 Jul (Pr 11)[19]	7 Jul (Pr 9)
Seventh Sunday after Trinity	26 Jul (Pr 12)	18 Jul (Pr 11)	6 Aug (Pr 13)[16]	29 Jul (Pr 12)	14 Jul (Pr 10)
Eighth Sunday after Trinity	2 Aug (Pr 13)	25 Jul (Pr 12)[9]	13 Aug (Pr 14)	5 Aug (Pr 13)	21 Jul (Pr 11)
Ninth Sunday after Trinity	9 Aug (Pr 14)	1 Aug (Pr 13)	20 Aug (Pr 15)	12 Aug (Pr 14)	28 Jul (Pr 12)
Tenth Sunday after Trinity	16 Aug (Pr 15)	8 Aug (Pr 14)	27 Aug (Pr 16)	19 Aug (Pr 15)	4 Aug (Pr 13)
Eleventh Sunday after Trinity	23 Aug (Pr 16)	15 Aug (Pr 15)[10]	3 Sept (Pr 17)	26 Aug (Pr 16)	11 Aug (Pr 14)
Twelfth Sunday after Trinity	30 Aug (Pr 17)	22 Aug (Pr 16)	10 Sept (Pr 18)	2 Sept (Pr 17)	18 Aug (Pr 15)
Thirteenth Sunday after Trinity	6 Sept (Pr 18)	29 Aug (Pr 17)	17 Sept (Pr 19)	9 Sept (Pr 18)	25 Aug (Pr 16)
Fourteenth Sunday after Trinity	13 Sept (Pr 19)	5 Sept (Pr 18)	24 Sept (Pr 20)	16 Sept (Pr 19)	1 Sept (Pr 17)
Fifteenth Sunday after Trinity	20 Sept (Pr 20)	12 Sept (Pr 19)	1 Oct (Pr 21)	23 Sept (Pr 20)	8 Sept (Pr 18)
Sixteenth Sunday after Trinity	27 Sept (Pr 21)	19 Sept (Pr 20)	8 Oct (Pr 22)	30 Sept (Pr 21)	15 Sept (Pr 19)
Seventeenth Sunday after Trinity	4 Oct (Pr 22)	26 Sept (Pr 21)	15 Oct (Pr 23)	7 Oct (Pr 22)	22 Sept (Pr 20)[21]
Eighteenth Sunday after Trinity	11 Oct (Pr 23)[6]	3 Oct (Pr 22)	22 Oct (Pr 24)	14 Oct (Pr 23)	29 Sept (Pr 21)
Nineteenth Sunday after Trinity	18 Oct (Pr 24)	10 Oct (Pr 23)	–	21 Oct (Pr 24)	6 Oct (Pr 22)
Twentieth Sunday after Trinity	–	17 Oct (Pr 24)	–	–	13 Oct (Pr 23)
Twenty-First Sunday after Trinity	–	–	–	–	20 Oct (Pr 24)
Last Sunday after Trinity	25 Oct (Pr 25)	24 Oct (Pr 25)	29 Oct (Pr 25)	28 Oct (Pr 25)[20]	27 Oct (Pr 25)

All Saints' Day	1 Nov	(31 Oct) or 1 Nov	1 (or 5) Nov	1 (or 4) Nov
Fourth Sunday before Advent	–	(31 Oct)	(5 Nov)	(4 Nov)
Third Sunday before Advent	8 Nov	7 Nov	12 Nov	11 Nov
Second Sunday before Advent	15 Nov	14 Nov	19 Nov	18 Nov
Christ the King –				
Sunday next before Advent	22 Nov	21 Nov	26 Nov	25 Nov

1997–98

1. St Andrew is transferred to Monday 1 December
2. Kept as Holy Innocents' Day unless transferred to Monday 29 December
3. Kept as The Conversion of St Paul unless transferred to Monday 26 January
4. Visit of Mary to Elizabeth is transferred to Monday 1 June
5. If Corpus Christi is celebrated, St Barnabas is transferred to Friday 12 June
6. Kept as St Luke unless transferred to Monday 17 October

1998–99

7. Kept as St John the Evangelist unless transferred to Tuesday 29 December
8. St Mark is transferred to Monday 26 April
9. Kept as St James unless transferred to Monday 26 July
10. Kept as the Blessed Virgin Mary unless transferred to Monday 16 August

1999–2000

11. Kept as St Stephen unless transferred to Wednesday 29 December
12. St Joseph is transferred to Monday 20 March
13. St George is transferred to Tuesday 2 May
14. St Matthias is transferred to Monday 15 May
15. St Barnabas is transferred to Monday 12 June
16. Kept as the Transfiguration unless transferred to Monday 7 August

2000–1

17. The Annunciation is transferred to Monday 26 March
18. Kept as the Birth of John the Baptist unless transferred to Monday 25 June
19. Kept as St Mary Magdalene unless transferred to Monday 23 July
20. Kept as St Simon and St Jude unless transferred to Monday 29 October

2001–2

21. Kept as St Michael and All Angels unless transferred to Monday 30 September

SOURCES AND COPYRIGHT INFORMATION

The copyright owners and administrators of texts included in *Calendar, Lectionary and Collects* have consented to the use of their material in local reproductions on a non-commercial basis which must conform to the terms laid down in the CBF's booklet of guidance, *Liturgical Texts for Local Use*. This is available from the Copyright Manager, Central Board of Finance, Church House, Great Smith Street, London SW1P 3NZ (tel: 0171 340 0274; fax: 0171 340 0281; e-mail: info@chp.u-net.com). A reproduction which meets the conditions stated in the booklet can be made without application or fee.

Permission must be obtained in advance from the appropriate copyright owner or administrator for any reproduction not covered by *Liturgical Texts for Local Use*. The List of Sources will help to identify the copyright holder for each text. The Copyright Manager of the CBF is able to help with addresses of the copyright owners or administrators of this material.

Abbreviations

ACC	Anglican Church of Canada
ASB	*The Alternative Service Book 1980*
BCP	*The Book of Common Prayer*
CPSA	Church of the Province of Southern Africa (Anglican)
CSI	*The Book of Common Worship of the Church of South India*
ECUSA	Episcopal Church of the USA
PB 1928	*The Book of Common Prayer as Proposed in 1928*

List of sources

Every effort has been made to identify the source for each prayer. If there are any inadvertent omissions we apologize to those concerned. An * indicates that the prayer has been amended.

Advent 1
C   ASB, BCP adapted*
PC   *Gelasian Sacramentary*

Advent 2
C   BCP*
PC   *The Promise of His Glory*, from David Silk, *Prayers for use at the Alternative Services**

Advent 3
C   BCP*
PC   Westcott House, Cambridge*

Advent 4
C   *The Promise of His Glory*, based on a prayer from the Scottish Episcopal Church, *Book of Common Prayer* (also ASB Franciscan)*
PC   ASB, adapted from Frank Colquhoun, *Parish Prayers* (author unknown)*

Christmas Night
C   ASB, translation from the *Latin Missal*
PC   *The Promise of His Glory**

Christmas Day
C   BCP*
PC   ACC, *Book of Alternative Services**

Christmas 1
C   ASB, adapted from PB 1928
PC   ASB*

Christmas 2
C   Church of Ireland, *Collects and Post-Communion Prayers*
PC   ASB, BCP adapted

Epiphany
C   BCP*
PC   *The Promise of His Glory**

Baptism of Christ
C   ASB, based on CSI*
PC   New composition*
Epiphany 2
C   ASB, adapted from CPSA, *Modern Collects*
     (based on CSI)*
PC   *The Promise of His Glory*
Epiphany 3
C   ASB, adapted from CPSA, *Modern Collects*
PC   ACC, *Book of Alternative Services*
Epiphany 4
C   *The Promise of his Glory*, from David Silk,
     Prayers for use at the Alternative Services
PC   *The Promise of His Glory*
Presentation of Christ
C   BCP*
PC   *The Promise of His Glory*, adapted from *The
     Roman Missal*
5 before Lent
C   ASB, based on PB 1928
PC   ACC, *Book of Alternative Services*
4 before Lent
C   BCP*
PC   BCP*
3 before Lent
C   BCP*
PC   New composition
2 before Lent
C   ASB, new composition based on CSI*
PC   *The Promise of His Glory*, from David Silk,
     Prayers for use at the Alternative Services
Next before Lent
C   ASB, adapted from PB 1928
PC   ACC, *Book of Alternative Services*
Ash Wednesday
C   BCP*
PC   BCP*
Lent 1
C   ASB, adapted from BCP
PC   Westcott House, Cambridge*
Lent 2
C   BCP*
PC   BCP*
Lent 3
C   ASB, adapted from ECUSA, *Book of Common
     Prayer*
PC   BCP*
Lent 4
C   BCP*
PC   ASB, adapted from ECUSA, *Book of Common
     Prayer*
Mothering Sunday
C   Michael Perham, in *Enriching the Christian Year*
PC   Michael Perham, in *Enriching the Christian Year*
Lent 5
C   ASB, adapted from CPSA, *Modern Collects* and
     Scottish Episcopal Church, *Book of Common
     Prayer*

PC   ASB, new composition based on a prayer
     attributed to St Augustine*
Palm Sunday
C   BCP*
PC   Church of Ireland, *Alternative Prayer Book*
Maundy Thursday
C   *Lent, Holy, Week, Easter*
PC   ASB, adapted from PB 1928*
Good Friday
C   BCP*
Easter Eve
C   BCP*
Easter Day
C   ASB
PC   PB 1928*
Easter 2
C   BCP*
PC   ASB
Easter 3
C   ASB
PC   ACC, *Book of Alternative Services*
Easter 4
C   ASB, new composition based on BCP*
PC   Church of Ireland, *Collects and Post-
     Communion Prayers*
Easter 5
C   BCP*
PC   ASB
Easter 6
C   *Lent, Holy Week, Easter*
PC   ACC, *Book of Alternative Services*
Ascension Day
C   BCP*
PC   Charles MacDonnell, *After Communion*
Easter 7
C   BCP*
PC   ACC, *Book of Alternative Services*
Pentecost
C   BCP*
PC   ACC, *Book of Alternative Services*
Trinity Sunday
C   BCP*
PC   ASB, adapted from CSI*
Thanksgiving for Holy Communion
C   ASB, adapted from PB 1928*
PC   Charles MacDonnell, *After Communion*
1 after Trinity
C   BCP*
PC   *The Promise of His Glory*
2 after Trinity
C   BCP*
PC   *Lent, Holy Week, Easter*
3 after Trinity
C   ASB*
PC   Janet Morley, *All Desires Known*
4 after Trinity
C   BCP*
PC   ACC, *Book of Alternative Services*

5 after Trinity
C   BCP*
PC   BCP*
6 after Trinity
C   BCP*
PC   ACC, *Book of Alternative Services**
7 after Trinity
C   BCP*
PC   *Lent, Holy Week, Easter*
8 after Trinity
C   BCP*
PC   Liturgy of Malabar, in *Enriching the Christian Year*
9 after Trinity
C   ASB
PC   *Patterns for Worship**
10 after Trinity
C   BCP*
PC   Kenneth Stevenson*
11 after Trinity
C   BCP*
PC   Charles Macdonnell, *After Communion**
12 after Trinity
C   BCP*
PC   ACC, *Book of Alternative Services**
13 after Trinity
C   ASB*
PC   David Silk, *Prayers for use at the Alternative Services**
14 after Trinity
C   ASB
PC   ACC, *Book of Alternative Services*
15 after Trinity
C   David Silk, *Prayers for use at the Alternative Services*, from the *Gelasian Sacramentary**
PC   BCP*
16 after Trinity
C   BCP*
PC   ASB, adapted from the *Leonine Sacramentary**
17 after Trinity
C   ASB*
PC   BCP*
18 after Trinity
C   ASB
PC   Ancient prayer*
19 after Trinity
C   BCP*
PC   *Patterns for Worship**
20 after Trinity
C   New composition
PC   David Silk, *Prayers for use at the Alternative Services*
21 after Trinity
C   BCP*
PC   New composition
Last after Trinity
C   BCP*
PC   ACC, *Book of Alternative Services**

All Saints' Day
C   BCP*
PC   *The Promise of His Glory*
4 before Advent
C   David Silk, *Prayers for use at the Alternative Services*, from the *Gothic Missal*
PC   Ancient prayer, in David Silk, *Prayers for use at the Alternative Services*
3 before Advent
C   ASB
PC   ASB, adapted from CPSA, *Modern Collects**
2 before Advent
C   BCP*
PC   *The Promise of His Glory*, from Charles Macdonnell, *After Communion**
Christ the King
C   ASB*
PC   BCP*
Dedication Festival
C   ASB
PC   Westcott House, Cambridge
The Naming and Circumcision of Jesus
C   ASB, new composition, based on BCP*
PC   New composition
Conversion of St Paul
C   ASB, adapted from BCP*
PC1 ASB*
PC2 ACC, *Book of Alternative Services*
St Joseph
C   Michael Perham, in *Celebrating Common Prayer*
PC   New composition
The Annunciation
C   BCP*
PC   New composition
St George
C   Michael Perham, in *Celebrating Common Prayer*
PC1 *The Roman Missal**
PC2 New composition
St Mark
C   ASB, adapted from BCP*
PC1 ASB*
PC2 ACC, *Book of Alternative Services*
St Philip and St James
C   BCP*
PC1 ASB*
PC2 ACC, *Book of Alternative Services*
St Matthias
C   BCP*
PC1 ASB*
PC2 ACC, *Book of Alternative Services*
The Visit of Mary to Elizabeth
C   ASB*
PC   New composition
St Barnabas
C   ASB*
PC1 ASB*
PC2 ACC, *Book of Alternative Services*

The Birth of St John the Baptist
C   BCP*
PC   New composition
St Peter and St Paul
C   ASB, based on *Leonine Sacramentary*
C2   ASB
PC1 ASB*
PC2 ACC, *Book of Alternative Services*
St Thomas
C   ASB, adapted from CPSA, *Modern Collects*
PC1 ASB*
PC2 ACC, *Book of Alternative Services*
St Mary Magdalene
C   ASB, adapted from PB 1928*
PC   New composition
St James
C   BCP*
PC1 ASB*
PC2 ACC, *Book of Alternative Services*
The Transfiguration
C   Church of Ireland, *Collects and Post-Communion Prayers*
PC   ACC, *Book of Alternative Services*
The Blessed Virgin Mary
C   ASB, adapted from CPSA, *Modern Collects*
PC   New composition
St Bartholomew
C   BCP*
PC1 ASB
PC2 ACC, *Book of Alternative Services*
Holy Cross Day
C   ASB, adapted from PB 1928*
PC   ACC, *Book of Alternative Services*
St Matthew
C   BCP*
PC1 ASB*
PC2 ACC, *Book of Alternative Services*
Michaelmas
C   BCP*
PC   Ancient prayer, in David Silk, *Prayers for use at the Alternative Services*
St Luke
C   BCP*
PC1 ASB*
PC2 ACC, *Book of Alternative Services*
St Simon and St Jude
C   BCP*
PC1 ASB*
PC2 ACC, *Book of Alternative Services*
St Andrew
C   BCP*
PC1 ASB*
PC2 ACC, *Book of Alternative Services*

St Stephen
C   BCP*
PC   The *Promise of His Glory*, from *The Roman Missal*

St John
C   BCP*
PC   *The Promise of His Glory*, from *The Roman Missal*
Holy Innocents
C   ASB*
PC   New composition*
Harvest
C   CPSA, *An Anglican Prayer Book*
PC   New composition
St Kentigern (Mungo)
C   Scottish Episcopal Church, adapted from ASB*, adapted from PB 1928*
PC   Scottish Episcopal Church, adapted from *Patterns for Worship*
St Brigid
C   Church of Ireland, *Alternative Prayer Book*
PC   Church of Ireland, *Collects and Post Communion Prayers*
St David
C   *Celebrating Common Prayer*, adapted from Church in Wales, *Book of Common Prayer*
PC   New composition
St Patrick
C   Church of Ireland, *Alternative Prayer Book*
PC   *Irish Prayer Book, Appendix, 1933*
St Columba (Ireland)
C   Church of Ireland, *Alternative Prayer Book*
PC   Church of Ireland, new composition
St Columba (Scotland)
C   Church of Ireland, *Collects and Post Communion Prayers*
PC   Church of Ireland. *Collects and Post Communion Prayers*, adapted from *Patterns for Worship*
St Ninian
C   ECUSA, *Book of Common Prayer*
PC   Scottish Episcopal Church, adapted from *Patterns for Worship*
St Margaret of Scotland
C   *Celebrating Common Prayer*, based on a prayer from the Scottish Episcopal Church, *Book of Common Prayer*
PC   New composition

ACKNOWLEDGEMENTS

The publisher gratefully acknowledges permission to reproduce copyright material in this book. Every effort has been made to trace and contact copyright holders. If there are any inadvertent omissions we apologize to those concerned.

The Consultation on Common Texts: *The Revised Common Lectionary* is copyright © The Consultation on Common Texts 1992. The Church of England adaptations to the Principal Service lectionary are copyright © The Central Board of Finance of the Church of England, as are the Second and Third Service lectionaries.

Cambridge University Press: Extracts adapted from *The Book of Common Prayer* (1662), the rights in which are vested in the Crown in the United Kingdom, are reproduced by permission of the Crown's Patentee, Cambridge University Press.

The Central Board of Finance of the Church of England: *The Alternative Service Book 1980; Lent, Holy Week, Easter,* 1986; *The Promise of His Glory,* 1991; *Patterns for Worship,* 1995; *The Prayer Book as Proposed in 1928* (additions and deviations); new compositions by the Liturgical Commission of the General Synod of the Church of England are copyright © The Central Board of Finance of the Church of England.

General Synod of the Anglican Church of Canada: Based on (or excerpted from) *The Book of Alternative Services of the Anglican Church of Canada,* copyright © 1985. Used with permission.

Scottish Episcopal Church. Used with permission

Catholic Bishops' Conference of England and Wales. Used with permission.

International Committee on English in the Liturgy: The English translation of the collects and the post communion prayers from *The Roman Missal* © 1973, International Committee on English in the Liturgy, Inc. All rights reserved.

General Synod of the Church of Ireland, *Irish Prayer Book, Appendix,* 1933: *Alternative Prayer Book,* 1984; *Collects and Post Communion Prayers,* 1995. Reproduced with permission.

Church of the Province of Southern Africa: *An Anglican Prayer Book 1989* © Provincial Trustees of the Church of the Province of Southern Africa (includes material from *Modern Collects,* 1972 and *Liturgy 75,* 1975).

Episcopal Church of the USA, *The Book of Common Prayer* according to the use of the Episcopal Church of the USA, 1979. The ECUSA Prayer Book is not subject to copyright.

Church in Wales Publications: *The Book of Common Prayer for use in the Church in Wales,* Vol. 1, 1984. Used with permission.

Cassell plc: C. L. MacDonnell, *After Communion,* 1985; David Silk (ed.), *Prayers for use at the Alternative Services,* 1980; revised 1986; The Society of St Francis: *Celebrating Common Prayer: A version of The Daily Office SSF,* 1992 are copyright © Mowbray, an imprint of Cassell.

Hodder and Stoughton *Publishers:* Frank Colquhoun (ed.), *Parish Prayers,* Hodder and Stoughton, 1967.

Oxford University Press: from *The Book of Common Worship of the Church of South India* (adapted by permission). © 1963 Oxford University Press; used by permission.

Janet Morley: *All Desires Known,* SPCK, 1992.

Michael Perham (ed.): *Enriching the Christian Year,* SPCK/Alcuin Club, 1993.

The Right Reverend Kenneth Stevenson.

Wescott House, Cambridge.

PRINCIPAL SERVICE YEAR A

FIRST READING   Isaiah 2.1–5

A reading from the book of the prophet Isaiah.

The word that Isaiah son of Amoz saw concerning Judah and Jerusalem.

In days to come the mountain of the Lord's house shall be established as the highest of the mountains, and shall be raised above the hills; all the nations shall stream to it. Many peoples shall come and say, 'Come, let us go up to the mountain of the LORD, to the house of the God of Jacob; that he may teach us his ways and that we may walk in his paths.' For out of Zion shall go forth instruction, and the word of the LORD from Jerusalem. He shall judge between the nations, and shall arbitrate for many peoples; they shall beat their swords into ploughshares, and their spears into pruning-hooks; nation shall not lift up sword against nation, neither shall they learn war any more. O house of Jacob, come, let us walk in the light of the LORD!

PSALM   Psalm 122

℟ I was glad when they said to me,
   'Let us go to God's house'.

I was glad when they said to me,
'Let us go to the house of the Lord.'
Now our feet are standing
within your gates, O Jerusalem. ℟

Jerusalem is built as a city
that is at unity with itself.
To which the tribes go up, the tribes of the Lord,
the assembly of Israel, to praise the name of the Lord.
For there are the thrones of judgement,
the thrones of the house of David. ℟

Pray for the peace of Jerusalem:
'May they prosper who love you.
Peace be within your walls
and quietness within your towers. ℟

For my family and companions' sake,
I pray for your prosperity.
Because of the house of the Lord our God,
I will seek to do you good.' ℞

SECOND READING   Romans 13.11–14

A reading from the letter of Paul to the Romans.

Brothers and sisters, you know what time it is, how it is now the moment for you to wake from sleep. For salvation is nearer to us now than when we became believers; the night is far gone, the day is near. Let us then lay aside the works of darkness and put on the armour of light; let us live honourably as in the day, not in revelling and drunkenness, not in debauchery and licentiousness, not in quarrelling and jealousy. Instead, put on the Lord Jesus Christ, and make no provision for the flesh, to gratify its desires.

GOSPEL   Matthew 24.36–44

Hear the gospel of our Lord Jesus Christ according to Matthew.

Jesus spoke to his disciples: 'About that day and hour no one knows, neither the angels of heaven, nor the Son, but only the Father. For as the days of Noah were, so will be the coming of the Son of Man. For as in those days before the flood they were eating and drinking, marrying and giving in marriage, until the day Noah entered the ark, and they knew nothing until the flood came and swept them all away, so too will be the coming of the Son of Man. Then two will be in the field; one will be taken and one will be left. Two women will be grinding meal together; one will be taken and one will be left. Keep awake, therefore, for you do not know on what day your Lord is coming. But understand this: if the owner of the house had known in what part of the night the thief was coming, he would have stayed awake and would not have let his house be broken into. Therefore you also must be ready, for the Son of Man is coming at an unexpected hour.'

ADVENT 2   YEAR A

FIRST READING   **Isaiah 11.1-10**

A reading from the b ook of the prophet Isaiah.

A shoot shall come out from the stock of Jesse,
and a branch shall grow out of his roots.
The spirit of the LORD shall rest on him,
the spirit of wisdom and understanding,
the spirit of counsel and might,
the spirit of knowledge and the fear of the LORD.
His delight shall be in the fear of the LORD.

He shall not judge by what his eyes see,
or decide by what his ears hear;
but with righteousness he shall judge the poor,
and decide with equity for the meek of the earth;
he shall strike the earth with the rod of his mouth,
and with the breath of his lips he shall kill the wicked.
Righteousness shall be the belt around his waist,
and faithfulness the belt around his loins.
The wolf shall live with the lamb,
the leopard shall lie down with the kid,
the calf and the lion and the fatling together,
and a little child shall lead them.
The cow and the bear shall graze,
their young shall lie down together;
and the lion shall eat straw like the ox.
The nursing child shall play over the hole of the asp,
and the weaned child shall put its hand on the adder's den.
They will not hurt or destroy
on all my holy mountain;
for the earth will be full of the knowledge of the LORD
as the waters cover the sea.

On that day the root of Jesse shall stand as a signal to the peoples; the
nations shall inquire of him, and his dwelling shall be glorious.

PSALM   Psalm 72.1–7, 18–19

℟ **In his time shall the righteous flourish,**
  [and peace till the moon shall be no more].

Give the king your justice, O God,
and your righteousness to the king's son;
That he may rule your people righteously
and the poor with justice;
That the mountains may bring prosperity to the people,
and the little hills bring righteousness. ℟

He shall defend the needy among the people;
he shall rescue the poor and crush the oppressor.
He shall live as long as the sun and moon endure,
from one generation to another. ℟

He shall come down like rain upon the mown field,
like showers that water the earth.
In his time shall the righteous flourish;
there shall be abundance of peace
till the moon shall be no more. ℟

Blessèd be the Lord God, the God of Israel,
who alone does wondrous deeds!
And blessèd be his glorious name for ever!
and may all the earth be filled with his glory.
Amen. Amen. ℟

SECOND READING   Romans 15.4–13

A reading from the letter of Paul to the Romans.

Whatever was written in former days was written for our instruction, so that
by steadfastness and by the encouragement of the scriptures we might have
hope. May the God of steadfastness and encouragement grant you to live in
harmony with one another, in accordance with Christ Jesus, so that together
you may with one voice glorify the God and Father of our Lord Jesus Christ.

Welcome one another, therefore, just as Christ has welcomed you, for the
glory of God. For I tell you that Christ has become a servant of the
circumcised on behalf of the truth of God in order that he might confirm the
promises given to the patriarchs, and in order that the Gentiles might glorify
God for his mercy. As it is written,

'Therefore I will confess you among the Gentiles,
and sing praises to your name';
and again he says,
'Rejoice, O Gentiles, with his people';
and again,
'Praise the Lord, all you Gentiles,
and let all the peoples praise him';
and again Isaiah says,
'The root of Jesse shall come,
the one who rises to rule the Gentiles;
in him the Gentiles shall hope.'
May the God of hope fill you with all joy and peace in believing, so that you
may abound in hope by the power of the Holy Spirit.

GOSPEL   **Matthew 3.1–12**

Hear the gospel of our Lord Jesus Christ according to Matthew.

In those days John the Baptist appeared in the wilderness of Judea,
proclaiming, 'Repent, for the kingdom of heaven has come near.' This is the
one of whom the prophet Isaiah spoke when he said,
'The voice of one crying out in the wilderness:
"Prepare the way of the Lord,
make his paths straight."'
Now John wore clothing of camel's hair with a leather belt around his waist,
and his food was locusts and wild honey. Then the people of Jerusalem and
all Judea were going out to him, and all the region along the Jordan, and
they were baptized by him in the river Jordan, confessing their sins.

But when he saw many Pharisees and Sadducees coming for baptism, he said
to them, 'You brood of vipers! Who warned you to flee from the wrath to
come? Bear fruit worthy of repentance. Do not presume to say to yourselves,
"We have Abraham as our ancestor"; for I tell you, God is able from these
stones to raise up children to Abraham. Even now the axe is lying at the root
of the trees; every tree therefore that does not bear good fruit is cut down
and thrown into the fire.

I baptize you with water for repentance, but one who is more powerful than I
is coming after me; I am not worthy to carry his sandals. He will baptize you
with the Holy Spirit and fire. His winnowing-fork is in his hand, and he will
clear his threshing-floor and will gather his wheat into the granary; but the
chaff he will burn with unquenchable fire.'

ADVENT 3 YEAR A

FIRST READING Isaiah 35.1–10

A reading from the book of the prophet Isaiah.

The wilderness and the dry land shall be glad,
the desert shall rejoice and blossom;
like the crocus it shall blossom abundantly,
and rejoice with joy and singing.
The glory of Lebanon shall be given to it,
the majesty of Carmel and Sharon.
They shall see the glory of the LORD,
the majesty of our God.

Strengthen the weak hands,
and make firm the feeble knees.
Say to those who are of a fearful heart,
'Be strong, do not fear!
Here is your God.
He will come with vengeance,
with terrible recompense.
He will come and save you.'

Then the eyes of the blind shall be opened,
and the ears of the deaf unstopped;
then the lame shall leap like a deer,
and the tongue of the speechless sing for joy.
For waters shall break forth in the wilderness,
and streams in the desert;
the burning sand shall become a pool,
and the thirsty ground springs of water;
the haunt of jackals shall become a swamp,
the grass shall become reeds and rushes.

A highway shall be there,
and it shall be called the Holy Way;
the unclean shall not travel on it,
but it shall be for God's people;
no traveller, not even fools, shall go astray.
No lion shall be there,
nor shall any ravenous beast come up on it;
they shall not be found there,

but the redeemed shall walk there.
And the ransomed of the LORD shall return,
and come to Zion with singing;
everlasting joy shall be upon their heads;
they shall obtain joy and gladness,
and sorrow and sighing shall flee away.

PSALM OR CANTICLE

Either   Psalm 146.4–9

℟ **Happy are they**
   who have the God of Jacob for their help.
   or
℟ **Come, Lord, and save us.**

Happy are they who have the God of Jacob for their help!
Whose hope is in the Lord their God;
Who made heaven and earth, the seas,
and all that is in them;
who keeps his promise for ever;
Who gives justice to those who are oppressed,
and food to those who hunger. ℟

The Lord sets the prisoners free;
the Lord opens the eyes of the blind;
the Lord lifts up those who are bowed down;
The Lord loves the righteous;
the Lord cares for the stranger;
he sustains the orphan and widow,
but frustrates the way of the wicked. ℟

The Lord shall reign for ever,
your God, O Zion, throughout all generations.
Alleluia! ℟

Or   Luke 1.46b–55

℟ **My spirit rejoices in God my Saviour,**

My soul proclaims the greatness of the Lord;
My spirit rejoices in God my Saviour,

For he has looked with favour on his lowly servant;
from this day all generations will call me blessèd.
The Almighty has done great things for me,
and holy is his name. ℟

He has mercy on those who fear him
in every generation.
He has shown the strength of his arm;
he has scattered the proud in their conceit. ℟

He has cast down the mighty from their thrones
and has lifted up the lowly.
He has filled the hungry with good things
and the rich he has sent away empty. ℟

He has come to the help of his servant, Israel,
for he has remembered his promise of mercy.
The promise he made to our forebears:
to Abraham and his children for ever. ℟

SECOND READING   James 5.7–10

A reading from the letter of James.

Be patient, beloved, until the coming of the Lord. The farmer waits for the
precious crop from the earth, being patient with it until it receives the early
and the late rains. You also must be patient. Strengthen your hearts, for the
coming of the Lord is near. Beloved, do not grumble against one another, so
that you may not be judged. See, the Judge is standing at the doors! As an
example of suffering and patience, beloved, take the prophets who spoke in
the name of the Lord.

GOSPEL   Matthew 11.2–11

Hear the gospel of our Lord Jesus Christ according to Matthew.

When John heard in prison what the Messiah was doing, he sent word by his
disciples and said to Jesus, 'Are you the one who is to come, or are we to wait
for another?' Jesus answered them, 'Go and tell John what you hear and see:
the blind receive their sight, the lame walk, the lepers are cleansed, the deaf
hear, the dead are raised, and the poor have good news brought to them. And
blessed is anyone who takes no offence at me.'

As they went away, Jesus began to speak to the crowds about John: 'What did you go out into the wilderness to look at? A reed shaken by the wind? What then did you go out to see? Someone dressed in soft robes? Look, those who wear soft robes are in royal palaces. What then did you go out to see? A prophet? Yes, I tell you, and more than a prophet. This is the one about whom it is written,
"See, I am sending my messenger ahead of you,
who will prepare your way before you."
Truly I tell you, among those born of women no one has arisen greater than John the Baptist; yet the least in the kingdom of heaven is greater than he.'

ADVENT 4   YEAR A

FIRST READING   Isaiah 7.10–16

A reading from the book of the prophet Isaiah.

The LORD spoke to Ahaz, saying, 'Ask a sign of the LORD your God; let it be deep as Sheol or high as heaven.' But Ahaz said, 'I will not ask, and I will not put the LORD to the test.' Then Isaiah said: 'Hear then, O house of David! Is it too little for you to weary mortals, that you weary my God also? Therefore the Lord himself will give you a sign. Look, the young woman is with child and shall bear a son, and shall name him Immanuel. He shall eat curds and honey by the time he knows how to refuse the evil and choose the good. For before the child knows how to refuse the evil and choose the good, the land before whose two kings you are in dread will be deserted.'

PSALM   Psalm 80.1–7, 16–18

℟ Restore us, O God of hosts;
   show the light of your countenance and we shall be saved.

Hear, O Shepherd of Israel, leading Joseph like a flock;
shine forth, you that are enthroned upon the cherubim.
In the presence of Ephraim, Benjamin and Manasseh,
stir up your strength and come to help us. ℟

[Restore us, O God of hosts;
show the light of your countenance
and we shall be saved.]

O Lord God of hosts,
how long will you be angered
despite the prayers of your people?
You have fed them with the bread of tears;
you have given them bowls of tears to drink.
You have made us the derision of our neighbours,
and our enemies laugh us to scorn. ℟

[Restore us, O God of hosts;
show the light of your countenance
and we shall be saved.]

Let your hand be upon the man of your right hand,
the son of man you have made so strong for yourself.
And so will we never turn away from you;
give us life, that we may call upon your name. ℟

[Restore us, O Lord God of hosts;
show the light of your countenance
and we shall be saved.]

SECOND READING   Romans 1.1-7

A reading from the letter of Paul to the Romans.

Paul, a servant of Jesus Christ, called to be an apostle, set apart for the gospel
of God, which he promised beforehand through his prophets in the holy
scriptures, the gospel concerning his Son, who was descended from David
according to the flesh and was declared to be Son of God with power
according to the spirit of holiness by resurrection from the dead, Jesus Christ
our Lord. Through Christ we have received grace and apostleship to bring
about the obedience of faith among all the Gentiles for the sake of his name,
including yourselves who are called to belong to Jesus Christ,

To all God's beloved in Rome, who are called to be saints: Grace to you and
peace from God our Father and the Lord Jesus Christ.

GOSPEL   Matthew 1.18-25

Hear the gospel of our Lord Jesus Christ according to Matthew.

The birth of Jesus the Messiah took place in this way. When his mother Mary
had been engaged to Joseph, but before they lived together, she was found to

be with child from the Holy Spirit. Her husband Joseph, being a righteous man and unwilling to expose her to public disgrace, planned to dismiss her quietly. But just when he had resolved to do this, an angel of the Lord appeared to him in a dream and said, 'Joseph, son of David, do not be afraid to take Mary as your wife, for the child conceived in her is from the Holy Spirit. She will bear a son, and you are to name him Jesus, for he will save his people from their sins.' All this took place to fulfil what had been spoken by the Lord through the prophet:

'Look, the virgin shall conceive and bear a son,
and they shall name him Emmanuel,'
which means, 'God is with us.'
When Joseph awoke from sleep, he did as the angel of the Lord commanded him; he took her as his wife,
but had no marital relations with her until she had borne a son; and he named him Jesus.

CHRISTMAS DAY

25 December

Any of the following sets of readings may be used on the evening of Christmas Eve and on Christmas Day. Set III should be used at some service during the celebration.

CHRISTMAS, SET I   YEARS A B C

FIRST READING   Isaiah 9.2–7

A reading from the book of the prophet Isaiah.

The people who walked in darkness
have seen a great light;
those who lived in a land of deep darkness –
on them light has shined.
You have multiplied the nation,
you have increased its joy;
they rejoice before you
as with joy at the harvest,
as people exult when dividing plunder.
For the yoke of their burden,
and the bar across their shoulders,
the rod of their oppressor,

you have broken as on the day of Midian.
For all the boots of the tramping warriors
and all the garments rolled in blood
shall be burned as fuel for the fire.
For a child has been born for us,
a son given to us;
authority rests upon his shoulders;
and he is named
Wonderful Counsellor, Mighty God,
Everlasting Father, Prince of Peace.
His authority shall grow continually,
and there shall be endless peace
for the throne of David and his kingdom.
He will establish and uphold it
with justice and with righteousness
from this time onwards and for evermore.
The zeal of the LORD of hosts will do this.

PSALM

Psalm 96

℟ **To you is born this day a saviour;**
   who is Christ the Lord.
   or
℟ **Great is the Lord and greatly to be praised.**

Sing to the Lord a new song;
sing to the Lord, all the whole earth.
Sing to the Lord and bless his name;
proclaim the good news of his salvation from day to day.
Declare his glory among the nations
and his wonders among all peoples. ℟

For great is the Lord and greatly to be praised;
he is more to be feared than all gods.
As for all the gods of the nations, they are but idols;
but it is the Lord who made the heavens.
O the majesty and magnificence of his presence!
O the power and the splendour of his sanctuary! ℟

Ascribe to the Lord, you families of the peoples;
ascribe to the Lord honour and power.
Ascribe to the Lord the honour due to his name;
bring offerings and come into his courts.

Worship the Lord in the beauty of holiness;
let the whole earth tremble before him. ℟

Tell it out among the nations: 'The Lord is king!
he has made the world so firm that it cannot be moved;
he will judge the peoples with equity.'
Let the heavens rejoice and let the earth be glad;
let the sea thunder and all that is in it;
let the field be joyful and all that is therein. ℟

Then shall all the trees of the wood shout for joy
before the Lord when he comes,
when he comes to judge the earth.
He will judge the world with righteousness
and the peoples with his truth. ℟

SECOND READING   Titus 2.11–14

A reading from the letter of Paul to Titus.

The grace of God has appeared, bringing salvation to all, training us to
renounce impiety and worldly passions, and in the present age to live lives
that are self-controlled, upright, and godly, while we wait for the blessed
hope and the manifestation of the glory of our great God and Saviour, Jesus
Christ. He it is who gave himself for us that he might redeem us from all
iniquity and purify for himself a people of his own who are zealous for good
deeds.

GOSPEL (Short or long reading)   Luke 2.1–14, (15–20)

Hear the gospel of our Lord Jesus Christ according to Luke.

In those days a decree went out from Emperor Augustus that all the world
should be registered. This was the first registration and was taken while
Quirinius was governor of Syria. All went to their own towns to be registered.
Joseph also went from the town of Nazareth in Galilee to Judea, to the city of
David called Bethlehem, because he was descended from the house and
family of David. He went to be registered with Mary, to whom he was
engaged and who was expecting a child. While they were there, the time
came for her to deliver her child. And she gave birth to her firstborn son and
wrapped him in bands of cloth, and laid him in a manger, because there was
no place for them in the inn.

13

In that region there were shepherds living in the fields, keeping watch over their flock by night. Then an angel of the Lord stood before them, and the glory of the Lord shone around them, and they were terrified. But the angel said to them, 'Do not be afraid; for see – I am bringing you good news of great joy for all the people: to you is born this day in the city of David a Saviour, who is the Messiah, the Lord. This will be a sign for you: you will find a child wrapped in bands of cloth and lying in a manger.' And suddenly there was with the angel a multitude of the heavenly host, praising God and saying,
'Glory to God in the highest heaven,
and on earth peace among those whom he favours!'

[When the angels had left them and gone into heaven, the shepherds said to one another, 'Let us go now to Bethlehem and see this thing that has taken place, which the Lord has made known to us.' So they went with haste and found Mary and Joseph, and the child lying in the manger. When they saw this, they made known what had been told them about this child; and all who heard it were amazed at what the shepherds told them. But Mary treasured all these words and pondered them in her heart. The shepherds returned, glorifying and praising God for all they had heard and seen, as it had been told them.]

CHRISTMAS, SET II   YEARS A B C

FIRST READING   Isaiah 62.6–12

A reading from the book of the prophet Isaiah.

Thus says the LORD:
Upon your walls, O Jerusalem,
I have posted sentinels;
all day and all night they shall never be silent.
You who remind the LORD, take no rest,
and give him no rest until he establishes Jerusalem
and makes it renowned throughout the earth.
The LORD has sworn by his right hand
and by his mighty arm:
I will not again give your grain to be food for your enemies,
and foreigners shall not drink the wine
for which you have laboured;
but those who garner it shall eat it

and praise the LORD,
and those who gather it shall drink it
in my holy courts.

Go through, go through the gates,
prepare the way for the people;
build up, build up the highway,
clear it of stones, lift up an ensign over the peoples.
The LORD has proclaimed to the end of the earth:
Say to daughter Zion,
'See, your salvation comes;
his reward is with him,
and his recompense before him.'
They shall be called, 'The Holy People,
The Redeemed of the LORD';
and you shall be called, 'Sought Out,
A City Not Forsaken.'

PSALM

Psalm 97

℟ **Zion hears and is glad
and the cities of Judah rejoice.**

The Lord is king; let the earth rejoice;
let the multitude of the isles be glad.
Clouds and darkness are round about him,
righteousness and justice
are the foundations of his throne. ℟

A fire goes before him
and burns up his enemies on every side.
His lightnings light up the world;
the earth sees it and is afraid. ℟

The mountains melt like wax
at the presence of the Lord,
at the presence of the Lord of the whole earth.
The heavens declare his righteousness,
and all the peoples see his glory. ℟

Confounded be all who worship carved images
and delight in false gods!
Bow down before him, all you gods.

Zion hears and is glad and the cities of Judah rejoice,
because of your judgements, O Lord. ℟

For you are the Lord: most high over all the earth;
you are exalted far above all gods.
The Lord loves those who hate evil;
he preserves the lives of his saints
and delivers them from the hand of the wicked. ℟

Light has sprung up for the righteous,
and joyful gladness for those who are true-hearted.
Rejoice in the Lord, you righteous,
and give thanks to his holy name. ℟

SECOND READING   Titus 3.4–7

A reading from the letter of Paul to Titus.

When the goodness and loving-kindness of God our Saviour appeared, he
saved us, not because of any works of righteousness that we had done, but
according to his mercy, through the water of rebirth and renewal by the Holy
Spirit. This Spirit he poured out on us richly through Jesus Christ our Saviour,
so that, having been justified by his grace, we might become heirs according
to the hope of eternal life.

GOSPEL (Short or long reading)   Luke 2.(1–7), 8–20

Hear the gospel of our Lord Jesus Christ according to Luke.

[In those days a decree went out from Emperor Augustus that all the world
should be registered. This was the first registration and was taken while
Quirinius was governor of Syria. All went to their own towns to be registered.
Joseph also went from the town of Nazareth in Galilee to Judea, to the city of
David called Bethlehem, because he was descended from the house and
family of David. He went to be registered with Mary, to whom he was
engaged and who was expecting a child. While they were there, the time
came for her to deliver her child. And she gave birth to her firstborn son and
wrapped him in bands of cloth, and laid him in a manger, because there was
no place for them in the inn.]

In that region there were shepherds living in the fields, keeping watch over
their flock by night. Then an angel of the Lord stood before them, and the
glory of the Lord shone around them, and they were terrified. But the angel

said to them, 'Do not be afraid; for see – I am bringing you good news of great joy for all the people: to you is born this day in the city of David a Saviour, who is the Messiah, the Lord. This will be a sign for you: you will find a child wrapped in bands of cloth
and lying in a manger.' And suddenly there was with the angel a multitude of the heavenly host, praising God and saying,
'Glory to God in the highest heaven,
and on earth peace among those whom he favours!'

When the angels had left them and gone into heaven, the shepherds said to one another, 'Let us go now to Bethlehem and see this thing that has taken place, which the Lord has made known to us.' So they went with haste and found Mary and Joseph, and the child lying in the manger. When they saw this, they made known what had been told them about this child; and all who heard it were amazed at what the shepherds told them. But Mary treasured all these words and pondered them in her heart. The shepherds returned, glorifying and praising God for all they had heard and seen, as it had been told them.

CHRISTMAS, SET III   YEARS A B C

FIRST READING   Isaiah 52.7–10

A reading from the book of the prophet Isaiah.

How beautiful upon the mountains
are the feet of the messenger who announces peace,
who brings good news,
who announces salvation,
who says to Zion, 'Your God reigns.'
Listen! Your sentinels lift up their voices,
together they sing for joy;
for in plain sight they see
the return of the LORD to Zion.
Break forth together into singing,
you ruins of Jerusalem;
for the LORD has comforted his people,
he has redeemed Jerusalem.
The LORD has bared his holy arm
before the eyes of all the nations;
and all the ends of the earth shall see the salvation of our God.

PSALM   Psalm 98

℟ **All the ends of the earth have seen
   the victory of our God.**

Sing to the Lord a new song,
for he has done marvellous things.
With his right hand and his holy arm
has he won for himself the victory. ℟

The Lord has made known his victory;
his righteousness has he openly shown
in the sight of the nations.
He remembers his mercy and faithfulness
to the house of Israel,
and all the ends of the earth have seen
the victory of our God. ℟

Shout with joy to the Lord, all you lands;
lift up your voice, rejoice and sing.
Sing to the Lord with the harp,
with the harp and the voice of song.
With trumpets and the sound of the horn
shout with joy before the King, the Lord. ℟

Let the sea make a noise and all that is in it,
the lands and those who dwell therein.
Let the rivers clap their hands,
and let the hills ring out with joy before the Lord,
when he comes to judge the earth.
In righteousness shall he judge the world,
and the peoples with equity. ℟

SECOND READING (Short or long reading)

Hebrews 1.1–4, (5–12)

A reading from the letter to the Hebrews.

Long ago God spoke to our ancestors in many and various ways by the
prophets, but in these last days he has spoken to us by a Son, whom he
appointed heir of all things, through whom he also created the worlds. He is
the reflection of God's glory and the exact imprint of God's very being, and
he sustains all things by his powerful word. When he had made purification

for sins, he sat down at the right hand of the Majesty on high, having become as much superior to angels as the name he has inherited is more excellent than theirs.

[For to which of the angels did God ever say,
'You are my Son;
today I have begotten you'?
Or again,
'I will be his Father, and he will be my Son'?
And again, when he brings the firstborn into the world, he says,
'Let all God's angels worship him.'
Of the angels he says,
'He makes his angels winds, and his servants flames of fire.'
But of the Son he says,
'Your throne, O God, is for ever and ever,
and the righteous sceptre is the sceptre of your kingdom.
You have loved righteousness and hated wickedness;
therefore God, your God,
has anointed you with the oil of gladness beyond your companions.'
And, 'In the beginning, Lord, you founded the earth,
and the heavens are the work of your hands;
they will perish, but you remain;
they will all wear out like clothing;
like a cloak you will roll them up, and like clothing they will be changed.
But you are the same, and your years will never end.']

GOSPEL   John 1.1–14

Hear the gospel of our Lord Jesus Christ according to John.

In the beginning was the Word, and the Word was with God, and the Word was God. He was in the beginning with God. All things came into being through him, and without him not one thing came into being. What has come into being in him was life, and the life was the light of all people. The light shines in the darkness, and the darkness did not overcome it.

There was a man sent from God, whose name was John. He came as a witness to testify to the light, so that all might believe through him. He himself was not the light, but he came to testify to the light. The true light, which enlightens everyone, was coming into the world.

He was in the world, and the world came into being through him; yet the world did not know him. He came to what was his own, and his own people did not accept him. But to all who received him, who believed in his name, he gave power to become children of God, who were born, not of blood or of the will of the flesh or of the will of man but of God.

And the Word became flesh and lived among us, and we have seen his glory, the glory as of a father's only son, full of grace and truth.

CHRISTMAS 1   YEAR A

FIRST READING   Isaiah 63.7–9

A reading from the book of the prophet Isaiah.

I will recount the gracious deeds of the LORD,
the praiseworthy acts of the LORD,
because of all that the LORD has done for us,
and the great favour to the house of Israel
that he has shown them according to his mercy,
according to the abundance of his steadfast love.
For he said, 'Surely they are my people,
children who will not deal falsely';
and he became their saviour in all their distress.
It was no messenger or angel
but his presence that saved them;
in his love and in his pity he redeemed them;
he lifted them up and carried them all the days of old.

PSALM   Psalm 148

℟ **Praise, O praise the name of the Lord.**

Alleluia!
Praise the Lord from the heavens;
praise him in the heights.
Praise him, all you angels of his;
praise him, all his host.
Praise him, sun and moon;
praise him, all you shining stars. ℟

Praise him, heaven of heavens,
and you waters above the heavens.

Let them praise the name of the Lord;
for he commanded and they were created.
He made them stand fast for ever and ever;
he gave them a law which shall not pass away. ℟

Praise the Lord from the earth,
you sea-monsters and all deeps;
Fire and hail, snow and fog,
tempestuous wind, doing his will;
Mountains and all hills,
fruit trees and all cedars; ℟

Wild beasts and all cattle,
creeping things and winged birds;
Kings of the earth and all peoples,
princes and all rulers of the world;
Young men and maidens,
old and young together. ℟

Let them praise the name of the Lord,
for his name only is exalted,
his splendour is over earth and heaven.
He has raised up strength for his people
and praise for all his loyal servants,
the children of Israel, a people who are near him.
Alleluia! ℟

SECOND READING   Hebrews 2.10–18

A reading from the letter to the Hebrews.

It was fitting that God, for whom and through whom all things exist, in
bringing many children to glory, should make the pioneer of their salvation
perfect through sufferings. For the one who sanctifies and those who are
sanctified all have one Father. For this reason Jesus is not ashamed to call
them brothers and sisters, saying,
'I will proclaim your name to my brothers and sisters,
in the midst of the congregation I will praise you.'
And again,
'I will put my trust in him.'
And again, 'Here am I
and the children whom God has given me.'

Since the children share flesh and blood, he himself likewise shared the same things, so that through death he might destroy the one who has the power of death, that is, the devil, and free those who all their lives were held in slavery by the fear of death. For it is clear that he did not come to help angels, but the descendants of Abraham. Therefore he had to become like his brothers and sisters in every respect, so that he might be a merciful and faithful high priest in the service of God, to make a sacrifice of atonement for the sins of the people. Because he himself was tested by what he suffered, he is able to help those who are being tested.

GOSPEL   **Matthew 2.13–23**

Hear the gospel of our Lord Jesus Christ according to Matthew.

After the wise men had left, an angel of the Lord appeared to Joseph in a dream and said, 'Get up, take the child and his mother, and flee to Egypt, and remain there until I tell you; for Herod is about to search for the child, to destroy him.' Then Joseph got up, took the child and his mother by night, and went to Egypt, and remained there until the death of Herod. This was to fulfil what had been spoken by the Lord through the prophet, 'Out of Egypt I have called my son.'

When Herod saw that he had been tricked by the wise men, he was infuriated, and he sent and killed all the children in and around Bethlehem who were two years old or under, according to the time that he had learned from the wise men. Then was fulfilled what had been spoken through the prophet Jeremiah:
'A voice was heard in Ramah,
wailing and loud lamentation,
Rachel weeping for her children;
she refused to be consoled,
because they are no more.'

When Herod died, an angel of the Lord suddenly appeared in a dream to Joseph in Egypt and said, 'Get up, take the child and his mother, and go to the land of Israel, for those who were seeking the child's life are dead.' Then Joseph got up, took the child and his mother, and went to the land of Israel. But when he heard that Archelaus was ruling over Judea in place of his father Herod, he was afraid to go there. And after being warned in a dream, he went away to the district of Galilee. There he made his home in a town called Nazareth, so that what had been spoken through the prophets might be fulfilled, 'He will be called a Nazorean.'

CHRISTMAS 2   YEARS A B C

FIRST READING (Alternative readings)

Either   Jeremiah 31.7–14

A reading from the book of the prophet Jeremiah.

Thus says the LORD:
Sing aloud with gladness for Jacob,
and raise shouts for the chief of the nations;
proclaim, give praise, and say,
'Save, O LORD, your people,
the remnant of Israel.'
See, I am going to bring them from the land of the north,
and gather them from the farthest parts of the earth,
among them the blind and the lame,
those with child and those in labour, together;
a great company, they shall return here.
With weeping they shall come,
and with consolations I will lead them back,
I will let them walk by brooks of water
in a straight path in which they shall not stumble;
for I have become a father to Israel,
and Ephraim is my firstborn.

Hear the word of the LORD, O nations,
and declare it in the coastlands far away; say,
'He who scattered Israel will gather him,
and will keep him as a shepherd a flock.'
For the LORD has ransomed Jacob,
and has redeemed him from hands too strong for him.
They shall come and sing aloud on the height of Zion,
and they shall be radiant over the goodness of the LORD,
over the grain, the wine, and the oil,
and over the young of the flock and the herd;
their life shall become like a watered garden,
and they shall never languish again.
Then shall the young women rejoice in the dance,
and the young men and the old shall be merry.
I will turn their mourning into joy,
I will comfort them, and give them gladness for sorrow.

I will give the priests their fill of fatness,
and my people shall be satisfied with my bounty,
says the LORD.

PSALM (if Jeremiah 31.7–14 is read)   Psalm 147.13–21

℟ **The Word became flesh
and lived among us.**
  or
℟ **Sing to the Lord with thanksgiving;
make music to our God.**

Worship the Lord, O Jerusalem;
praise your God, O Zion;
For he has strengthened the bars of your gates;
he has blessed your children within you. ℟

He has established peace on your borders;
he satisfies you with the finest wheat.
He sends out his command to the earth,
and his word runs very swiftly. ℟

He gives snow like wool;
he scatters hoarfrost like ashes.
He scatters his hail like bread crumbs;
who can stand against his cold?
He sends forth his word and melts them;
he blows with his wind and the waters flow. ℟

He declares his word to Jacob,
his statutes and his judgements to Israel.
He has not done so to any other nation;
to them he has not revealed his judgements. ℟

Or   **Ecclesiasticus 24.1–12**

A reading from the book of Ecclesiasticus.

Wisdom praises herself,
and tells of her glory in the midst of her people.
In the assembly of the Most High she opens her mouth,
and in the presence of his hosts she tells of her glory:
'I came forth from the mouth of the Most High,

and covered the earth like a mist.
I dwelt in the highest heavens,
and my throne was in a pillar of cloud.
Alone I compassed the vault of heaven
and traversed the depths of the abyss.
Over waves of the sea
over all the earth,
and over every people and nation I have held sway.
Among all these I sought a resting-place;
in whose territory should I abide?
Then the Creator of all things gave me a command,
and my Creator chose the place for my tent.
He said, "Make your dwelling in Jacob,
and in Israel receive your inheritance."
Before the ages, in the beginning, he created me,
and for all the ages I shall not cease to be.
In the holy tent I ministered before him,
and so I was established in Zion.
Thus in the beloved city he gave me a resting-place,
and in Jerusalem was my domain.
I took root in an honoured people,
in the portion of the Lord, his heritage.'

CANTICLE (if Ecclesiasticus 24.1–12 is read)

Wisdom of Solomon 10.15–21

℟ **The righteous sing hymns to your name.**

Wisdom led the Israelites out of Egypt
A holy people and blameless race
wisdom delivered from a nation of oppressors.
She entered the soul of a servant of the Lord,
and withstood dread kings with wonders and signs. ℟

She gave to holy people the reward of their labours;
she guided them along a marvellous way,
and became a shelter to them by day,
and a starry flame through the night.
She brought them over the Red Sea,
and led them through deep waters;
but she drowned their enemies,
and cast them up from the depths of the sea. ℟

Therefore the righteous plundered the ungodly;
they sang hymns, O Lord, to your holy name,
and praised with one accord your defending hand;
for wisdom opened the mouths of those who were mute,
and made the tongues of infants speak clearly. ℞

SECOND READING   Ephesians 1.3–14

A reading from the letter of Paul to the Ephesians.

Blessed be the God and Father of our Lord Jesus Christ, who has blessed us in
Christ with every spiritual blessing in the heavenly places, just as he chose us
in Christ before the foundation of the world to be holy and blameless before
him in love. God destined us for adoption as his children through Jesus
Christ, according to the good pleasure of God's will, to the praise of his
glorious grace that he freely bestowed on us in the Beloved. In him we have
redemption through his blood, the forgiveness of our trespasses according to
the riches of his grace that he lavished on us. With all wisdom and insight he
has made known to us the mystery of his will, according to his good pleasure
that he set forth in Christ, as a plan for the fullness of time, to gather up all
things in Christ, things in heaven and things on earth. In Christ we have also
obtained an inheritance, having been destined according to the purpose of
God who accomplishes all things according to his counsel and will, so that
we, who were the first to set our hope on Christ, might live for the praise of
his glory. In him you also, when you had heard the word of truth, the gospel
of your salvation, and had believed in him, were marked with the seal of the
promised Holy Spirit; this is the pledge of our inheritance towards
redemption as God's own people to the praise of his glory.

GOSPEL (Long or short reading)   John 1.(1–9), 10–18

Either (Long version)

Hear the gospel of our Lord Jesus Christ according to John.

In the beginning was the Word, and the Word was with God, and the Word
was God. He was in the beginning with God. All things came into being
through him, and without him not one thing came into being. What has
come into being in him was life and the life was the light of all people. The
light shines in the darkness, and the darkness did not overcome it.

There was a man sent from God, whose name was John. He came as a witness to testify to the light, so that all might believe through him. He himself was not the light, but he came to testify to the light. The true light, which enlightens everyone, was coming into the world.

He was in the world, and the world came into being through him; yet the world did not know him. He came to what was his own, and his own people did not accept him. But to all who received him, who believed in his name, he gave power to become children of God, who were born, not of blood or of the will of the flesh or of the will of man, but of God.

And the Word became flesh and lived among us, and we have seen his glory, the glory as of a father's only son, full of grace and truth. (John testified to him and cried out, 'This was he of whom I said, "He who comes after me ranks ahead of me because he was before me."') From his fullness we have all received, grace upon grace. The law indeed was given through Moses; grace and truth came through Jesus Christ. No one has ever seen God. It is God the only Son, who is close to the Father's heart, who has made him known.

Or (Short version)

Hear the gospel of our Lord Jesus Christ according to John.

The true light, which enlightens everyone, was in the world, and the world came into being through him; yet the world did not know him. He came to what was his own, and his own people did not accept him. But to all who received him, who believed in his name, he gave power to become children of God, who were born, not of blood or of the will of the flesh or of the will of man, but of God.

And the Word became flesh and lived among us, and we have seen his glory, the glory as of a father's only son, full of grace and truth. (John testified to him and cried out, 'This was he of whom I said, "He who comes after me ranks ahead of me because he was before me."') From his fullness we have all received, grace upon grace. The law indeed was given through Moses; grace and truth came through Jesus Christ. No one has ever seen God. It is God the only Son, who is close to the Father's heart, who has made him known.

EPIPHANY OF THE LORD   YEARS A B C

6 January

FIRST READING   Isaiah 60.1–6

A reading from the book of the prophet Isaiah.

Arise, shine; for your light has come,
and the glory of the LORD has risen upon you.
For darkness shall cover the earth,
and thick darkness the peoples;
but the LORD will arise upon you,
and his glory will appear over you.
Nations shall come to your light,
and kings to the brightness of your dawn.

Lift up your eyes and look around;
they all gather together, they come to you;
your sons shall come from far away,
and your daughters shall be carried on their nurses' arms.
Then you shall see and be radiant;
your heart shall thrill and rejoice,
because the abundance of the sea shall be brought to you,
the wealth of the nations shall come to you.
A multitude of camels shall cover you,
the young camels of Midian and Ephah;
all those from Sheba shall come.
They shall bring gold and frankincense,
and shall proclaim the praise of the LORD.

PSALM   Psalm 72.1–7, 10–14

℟ **Kings bow down before him;**
   all the nations do him service.

Give the king your justice, O God,
and your righteousness to the king's son;
That he may rule your people righteously
and the poor with justice;
That the mountains may bring prosperity to the people,
and the little hills bring righteousness. ℟

He shall defend the needy among the people;
he shall rescue the poor and crush the oppressor.
He shall live as long as the sun and moon endure,
from one generation to another. ℟

He shall come down like rain upon the mown field,
like showers that water the earth.
In his time shall the righteous flourish;
there shall be abundance of peace
till the moon shall be no more. ℟

The kings of Tarshish and of the isles shall pay tribute,
and the kings of Arabia and Saba offer gifts.
All kings shall bow down before him,
and all the nations do him service. ℟

For he shall deliver the poor who cries out in distress,
and the oppressed who has no helper.
He shall have pity on the lowly and poor;
he shall preserve the lives of the needy.
He shall redeem their lives from oppression and violence,
and dear shall their blood be in his sight. ℟

SECOND READING   Ephesians 3.1–12

A reading from the letter of Paul to the Ephesians.

I, Paul, am a prisoner for Christ Jesus for the sake of you Gentiles – for surely
you have already heard of the commission of God's grace that was given me
for you, and how the mystery was made known to me by revelation, as I
wrote above in a few words, a reading of which will enable you to perceive
my understanding of the mystery of Christ. In former generations this
mystery was not made known to humankind, as it has now been revealed to
his holy apostles and prophets by the Spirit: that is, the Gentiles have
become fellow-heirs, members of the same body, and sharers in the promise
in Christ Jesus through the gospel.

Of this gospel I have become a servant according to the gift of God's grace
that was given me by the working of his power. Although I am the very least
of all the saints, this grace was given to me to bring to the Gentiles the news
of the boundless riches of Christ, and to make everyone see what is the plan
of the mystery hidden for ages in God who created all things; so that
through the church the wisdom of God in its rich variety might now be

made known to the rulers and authorities in the heavenly places. This was in accordance with the eternal purpose that he has carried out in Christ Jesus our Lord, in whom we have access to God in boldness and confidence through faith in him.

GOSPEL   Matthew 2.1–12

Hear the gospel of our Lord Jesus Christ according to Matthew.

In the time of King Herod, after Jesus was born in Bethlehem of Judea, wise men from the East came to Jerusalem, asking, 'Where is the child who has been born king of the Jews? For we observed his star at its rising, and have come to pay him homage.' When King Herod heard this, he was frightened, and all Jerusalem with him; and calling together all the chief priests and scribes of the people, he inquired of them where the Messiah was to be born. They told him, 'In Bethlehem of Judea; for so it has been written by the prophet:
"And you, Bethlehem, in the land of Judah,
are by no means least among the rulers of Judah;
for from you shall come a ruler
who is to shepherd my people Israel."'
Then Herod secretly called for the wise men and learned from them the exact time when the star had appeared. Then he sent them to Bethlehem, saying, 'Go and search diligently for the child; and when you have found him, bring me word so that I may also go and pay him homage.' When they had heard the king, they set out; and there, ahead of them, went the star that they had seen at its rising, until it stopped over the place where the child was. When they saw that the star had stopped, they were overwhelmed with joy. On entering the house, they saw the child with Mary his mother; and they knelt down and paid him homage. Then, opening their treasure-chests, they offered him gifts of gold, frankincense, and myrrh. And having been warned in a dream not to return to Herod, they left for their own country by another road.

THE BAPTISM OF CHRIST   YEAR A

FIRST READING   **Isaiah 42.1–9**

A reading from the book of the prophet Isaiah.

Thus says the LORD:

Here is my servant, whom I uphold,
my chosen, in whom my soul delights;
I have put my spirit upon him;
he will bring forth justice to the nations.
He will not cry or lift up his voice,
or make it heard in the street;
a bruised reed he will not break,
and a dimly burning wick he will not quench;
he will faithfully bring forth justice.
He will not grow faint or be crushed
until he has established justice in the earth;
and the coastlands wait for his teaching.
Thus says God, the LORD,
who created the heavens and stretched them out,
who spread out the earth and what comes from it,
who gives breath to the people upon it
and spirit to those who walk in it:
I am the LORD, I have called you in righteousness,
I have taken you by the hand and kept you;
I have given you as a covenant to the people,
a light to the nations,
to open the eyes that are blind,
to bring out the prisoners from the dungeon,
from the prison those who sit in darkness.
I am the LORD, that is my name;
my glory I give to no other,
nor my praise to idols.
See, the former things have come to pass,
and new things I now declare;
before they spring forth, I tell you of them.

PSALM   Psalm 29

℟ **The Lord shall give his people**
  the blessing of peace.
  or
℟ **The voice of the Lord is**
  upon the mighty waters.

Ascribe to the Lord, you gods,
ascribe to the Lord glory and strength.
Ascribe to the Lord the glory due to his name;
worship the Lord in the beauty of holiness. ℟

The voice of the Lord is upon the waters;
the God of glory thunders;
the Lord is upon the mighty waters.
The voice of the Lord is a powerful voice;
the voice of the Lord is a voice of splendour. ℟

The voice of the Lord breaks the cedar trees;
the Lord breaks the cedars of Lebanon;
He makes Lebanon skip like a calf,
and Mount Hermon like a young wild ox. ℟

The voice of the Lord splits the flames of fire;
the voice of the Lord shakes the wilderness;
the Lord shakes the wilderness of Kadesh.
The voice of the Lord makes the oak trees writhe
and strips the forests bare.
And in the temple of the Lord
all are crying, 'Glory!' ℟

The Lord sits enthroned above the flood;
the Lord sits enthroned as king for evermore.
The Lord shall give strength to his people;
the Lord shall give his people the blessing of peace. ℟

SECOND READING   Acts 10.34–43

A reading from the Acts of the Apostles.

Peter began to speak to those assembled in the house of Cornelius. 'I truly
understand that God shows no partiality, but in every nation anyone who
fears him and does what is right is acceptable to him. You know the message

he sent to the people of Israel, preaching peace by Jesus Christ – he is Lord of all. That message spread throughout Judea, beginning in Galilee after the baptism that John announced: how God anointed Jesus of Nazareth with the Holy Spirit and with power; how he went about doing good and healing all who were oppressed by the devil, for God was with him. We are witnesses to all that he did both in Judea and in Jerusalem. They put him to death by hanging him on a tree; but God raised him on the third day and allowed him to appear, not to all the people but to us who were chosen by God as witnesses, and who ate and drank with him after he rose from the dead. He commanded us to preach to the people and to testify that he is the one ordained by God as judge of the living and the dead. All the prophets testify about him that everyone who believes in him receives forgiveness of sins through his name.'

GOSPEL   Matthew 3.13–17

Hear the gospel of our Lord Jesus Christ according to Matthew.

Jesus came from Galilee to John at the Jordan, to be baptized by him. John would have prevented him, saying, 'I need to be baptized by you, and do you come to me?' But Jesus answered him, 'Let it be so now; for it is proper for us in this way to fulfil all righteousness.' Then he consented. And when Jesus had been baptized, just as he came up from the water, suddenly the heavens were opened to him and he saw the Spirit of God descending like a dove and alighting on him. And a voice from heaven said, 'This is my Son, the Beloved, with whom I am well pleased.'

EPIPHANY 2   YEAR A

FIRST READING   Isaiah 49.1–7

A reading from the book of the prophet Isaiah.

Listen to me, O coastlands,
pay attention, you peoples from far away!
The LORD called me before I was born,
while I was in my mother's womb he named me.
He made my mouth like a sharp sword,
in the shadow of his hand he hid me;
he made me a polished arrow,
in his quiver he hid me away.

And he said to me, 'You are my servant, Israel,
in whom I will be glorified.'
But I said, 'I have laboured in vain,
I have spent my strength for nothing and vanity;
yet surely my cause is with the LORD,
and my reward with my God.'

And now the LORD says,
who formed me in the womb to be his servant,
to bring Jacob back to him,
and that Israel might be gathered to him,
for I am honoured in the sight of the LORD,
and my God has become my strength.
The LORD says,
'It is too light a thing that you should be my servant
to raise up the tribes of Jacob
and to restore the survivors of Israel;
I will give you as a light to the nations,
that my salvation may reach to the end of the earth.'

Thus says the LORD,
the Redeemer of Israel and his Holy One,
to one deeply despised, abhorred by the nations, the slave of rulers,
'Kings shall see and stand up,
princes, and they shall prostrate themselves,
because of the LORD, who is faithful,
the Holy One of Israel, who has chosen you.'

PSALM   Psalm 40.1–11

℟ **I love to do your will, O God,**
   [your law is in my heart].

I waited patiently upon the Lord;
he stooped to me and heard my cry.
He lifted me out of the desolate pit,
out of the mire and clay;
he set my feet upon a high cliff and made my footing sure. ℟

He put a new song in my mouth,
a song of praise to our God;
many shall see and stand in awe
and put their trust in the Lord.

Happy are they who trust in the Lord!
they do not resort to evil spirits or turn to false gods. ℟

Great things are they that you have done, O Lord my God!
how great your wonders and your plans for us!
there is none who can be compared with you.
O that I could make them known and tell them!
but they are more than I can count. ℟

In sacrifice and offering you take no pleasure
you have given me ears to hear you;
Burnt-offering and sin-offering you have not required,
and so I said, 'Behold, I come.
In the roll of the book it is written concerning me:
"I love to do your will, O my God;
your law is deep in my heart."' ℟

I proclaimed righteousness in the great congregation;
behold, I did not restrain my lips;
and that, O Lord, you know.
Your righteousness have I not hidden in my heart;
I have spoken of your faithfulness and your deliverance;
I have not concealed your love and faithfulness
from the great congregation. ℟

SECOND READING   1 Corinthians 1.1–9

A reading from the first letter of Paul to the Corinthians.

From Paul, called to be an apostle of Christ Jesus by the will of God, and our
brother Sosthenes, To the church of God that is in Corinth, to those who are
sanctified in Christ Jesus, called to be saints, together with all those who in
every place call on the name of our Lord Jesus Christ, both their Lord and
ours: Grace to you and peace from God our Father and the Lord Jesus Christ.

I give thanks to my God always for you because of the grace of God that has
been given you in Christ Jesus, for in every way you have been enriched in
him, in speech and knowledge of every kind – just as the testimony of Christ
has been strengthened among you – so that you are not lacking in any
spiritual gift as you wait for the revealing of our Lord Jesus Christ. He will
also strengthen you to the end, so that you may be blameless on the day of
our Lord Jesus Christ. God is faithful; by him you were called into the
fellowship of his Son, Jesus Christ our Lord.

GOSPEL   John 1.29–42

Hear the gospel of our Lord Jesus Christ according to John.

John the Baptist saw Jesus coming towards him and declared, 'Here is the Lamb of God who takes away the sin of the world! This is he of whom I said, "After me comes a man who ranks ahead of me because he was before me." I myself did not know him; but I came baptizing with water for this reason, that he might be revealed to Israel.' And John testified, 'I saw the Spirit descending from heaven like a dove, and it remained on him. I myself did not know him, but the one who sent me to baptize with water said to me, "He on whom you see the Spirit descend and remain is the one who baptizes with the Holy Spirit." And I myself have seen and have testified that this is the Son of God.' The next day John again was standing with two of his disciples, and as he watched Jesus walk by, he exclaimed, 'Look, here is the Lamb of God!' The two disciples heard him say this, and they followed Jesus. When Jesus turned and saw them following, he said to them, 'What are you looking for?' They said to him, 'Rabbi' (which translated means Teacher), 'where are you staying?' He said to them, 'Come and see.' They came and saw where he was staying, and they remained with him that day. It was about four o'clock in the afternoon. One of the two who heard John speak and followed him was Andrew, Simon Peter's brother. He first found his brother Simon and said to him, 'We have found the Messiah' (which is translated Anointed). He brought Simon to Jesus, who looked at him and said, 'You are Simon son of John. You are to be called Cephas' (which is translated Peter).

EPIPHANY 3   YEAR A

FIRST READING   Isaiah 9.1–4

A reading from the book of the prophet Isaiah.

There will be no gloom for those who were in anguish. In the former time he brought into contempt the land of Zebulun and the land of Naphtali, but in the latter time he will make glorious the way of the sea, the land beyond the Jordan, Galilee of the nations.
The people who walked in darkness have seen a great light;
those who lived in a land of deep darkness –
on them light has shined.
You have multiplied the nation,

you have increased its joy;
they rejoice before you
as with joy at the harvest,
as people exult when dividing plunder.
For the yoke of their burden,
and the bar across their shoulders,
the rod of their oppressor,
you have broken as on the day of Midian.

PSALM   Psalm 27.1, 5–13

℟ **The Lord is my light and my salvation;
[whom then shall I fear?]**

The Lord is my light and my salvation;
whom then shall I fear?
the Lord is the strength of my life;
of whom then shall I be afraid? ℟

One thing have I asked of the Lord;
one thing I seek;
that I may dwell in the house of the Lord
all the days of my life;
To behold the fair beauty of the Lord
and to seek him in his temple. ℟

For in the day of trouble
he shall keep me safe in his shelter;
he shall hide me in the secrecy of his dwelling
and set me high upon a rock. ℟

Even now he lifts up my head
above my enemies round about me;
Therefore I will offer in his dwelling an oblation
with sounds of great gladness;
I will sing and make music to the Lord. ℟

Hearken to my voice, O Lord, when I call;
have mercy on me and answer me.
You speak in my heart and say, 'Seek my face.'
Your face, Lord, will I seek. ℟

Hide not your face from me,
nor turn away your servant in displeasure.
You have been my helper;
cast me not away;
do not forsake me, O God of my salvation. ℟

SECOND READING   1 Corinthians 1.10–18

A reading from the first letter of Paul to the Corinthians.

I appeal to you, brothers and sisters, by the name of our Lord Jesus Christ,
that all of you be in agreement and that there be no divisions among you,
but that you be united in the same mind and the same purpose. For it has
been reported to me by Chloe's people that there are quarrels among you, my
brothers and sisters. What I mean is that each of you says, 'I belong to Paul,'
or 'I belong to Apollos,' or 'I belong to Cephas,' or 'I belong to Christ.' Has
Christ been divided? Was Paul crucified for you? Or were you baptized in the
name of Paul? I thank God that I baptized none of you except Crispus and
Gaius, so that no one can say that you were baptized in my name. I did
baptize also the household of Stephanas; beyond that, I do not know
whether I baptized anyone else. For Christ did not send me to baptize but to
proclaim the gospel, and not with eloquent wisdom, so that the cross of
Christ might not be emptied of its power.

For the message about the cross is foolishness to those who are perishing, but
to us who are being saved it is the power of God.

GOSPEL   Matthew 4.12–23

Hear the gospel of our Lord Jesus Christ according to Matthew.

When Jesus heard that John had been arrested, he withdrew to Galilee. He
left Nazareth and made his home in Capernaum by the sea, in the territory of
Zebulun and Naphtali, so that what had been spoken through the prophet
Isaiah might be fulfilled:
'Land of Zebulun, land of Naphtali,
on the road by the sea, across the Jordan,
Galilee of the Gentiles –
the people who sat in darkness
have seen a great light,
and for those who sat in the region and shadow of death
light has dawned.'

From that time Jesus began to proclaim, 'Repent, for the kingdom of heaven has come near.'

As he walked by the Sea of Galilee, he saw two brothers, Simon, who is called Peter, and Andrew his brother, casting a net into the lake – for they were fishermen. And he said to them, 'Follow me, and I will make you fish for people.' Immediately they left their nets and followed him. As he went from there, he saw two other brothers, James son of Zebedee and his brother John, in the boat with their father Zebedee, mending their nets, and he called them. Immediately they left the boat and their father, and followed him.

Jesus went throughout Galilee, teaching in their synagogues and proclaiming the good news of the kingdom and curing every disease and every sickness among the people.

EPIPHANY 4   YEAR A

The Revised Common Lectionary and the Church of England make different provision for today. For Church of England provision see pages 42–44.

REVISED COMMON LECTIONARY

FIRST READING   Micah 6.1–8

A reading from the book of the prophet Micah.

Hear what the LORD says:
Rise, plead your case before the mountains,
and let the hills hear your voice.
Hear, you mountains, the controversy of the LORD,
and you enduring foundations of the earth;
for the LORD has a controversy with his people,
and he will contend with Israel.

'O my people, what have I done to you?
In what have I wearied you? Answer me!
For I brought you up from the land of Egypt,
and redeemed you from the house of slavery;
and I sent before you Moses, Aaron, and Miriam.
O my people, remember now what King Balak of Moab devised,
what Balaam son of Beor answered him,
and what happened from Shittim to Gilgal,
that you may know the saving acts of the LORD.'

'With what shall I come before the LORD,
and bow myself before God on high?
Shall I come before him with burnt-offerings, with calves a year old?
Will the LORD be pleased with thousands of rams,
with ten thousands of rivers of oil?
Shall I give my firstborn for my transgression,
the fruit of my body for the sin of my soul?'
He has told you, O mortal, what is good;
and what does the LORD require of you
but to do justice, and to love kindness,
and to walk humbly with your God?

PSALM   Psalm 15

℞ **The Lord is my light and my salvation;**
[whom then shall I fear?]

Lord, who may dwell in your tabernacle?
who may abide upon your holy hill?
Whoever leads a blameless life and does what is right,
who speaks the truth from his heart. ℞

There is no guile upon his tongue;
he does no evil to his friend;
he does not heap contempt upon his neighbour.
In his sight the wicked are rejected,
but he honours those who fear the Lord. ℞

He has sworn to do no wrong
and does not take back his word.
He does not give his money in hope of gain,
nor does he take a bribe against the innocent.
Whoever does these things
shall never be overthrown. ℞

SECOND READING   1 Corinthians 1.18–31

A reading from the first letter of Paul to the Corinthians.

The message about the cross is foolishness to those who are perishing, but to
us who are being saved it is the power of God.

For it is written, 'I will destroy the wisdom of the wise,
and the discernment of the discerning I will thwart.'
Where is the one who is wise? Where is the scribe? Where is the debater of
this age? Has not God made foolish the wisdom of the world? For since, in
the wisdom of God, the world did not know God through wisdom, God
decided, through the foolishness of our proclamation, to save those who
believe. For Jews demand signs and Greeks desire wisdom, but we proclaim
Christ crucified, a stumbling-block to Jews and foolishness to Gentiles, but to
those who are the called, both Jews and Greeks, Christ the power of God and
the wisdom of God. For God's foolishness is wiser than human wisdom, and
God's weakness is stronger than human strength. Consider your own call,
brothers and sisters: not many of you were wise by human standards, not
many were powerful, not many were of noble birth. But God chose what is
foolish in the world to shame the wise; God chose what is weak in the world
to shame the strong; God chose what is low and despised in the world,
things that are not, to reduce to nothing things that are, so that no one
might boast in the presence of God. He is the source of your life in Christ
Jesus, who became for us wisdom from God, and righteousness and
sanctification and redemption, in order that, as it is written, 'Let the one
who boasts, boast in the Lord.'

GOSPEL   Matthew 5.1–12

Hear the gospel of our Lord Jesus Christ according to Matthew.

When Jesus saw the crowds, he went up the mountain; and after he sat
down, his disciples came to him. Then he began to speak, and taught them,
saying: 'Blessed are the poor in spirit, for theirs is the kingdom of heaven.
Blessed are those who mourn, for they will be comforted. Blessed are the
meek, for they will inherit the earth. Blessed are those who hunger and thirst
for righteousness, for they will be filled. Blessed are the merciful, for they will
receive mercy. Blessed are the pure in heart, for they will see God. Blessed are
the peacemakers, for they will be called children of God. Blessed are those
who are persecuted for righteousness' sake, for theirs is the kingdom of
heaven. Blessed are you when people revile you and persecute you and utter
all kinds of evil against you falsely on my account. Rejoice and be glad, for
your reward is great in heaven, for in the same way they persecuted the
prophets who were before you.'

Or

✝ CHURCH OF ENGLAND

FIRST READING   1 Kings 17.8–16

A reading from the first book of Kings.

Then the word of the LORD came to Elijah, saying, 'Go now to Zarephath,
which belongs to Sidon, and live there; for I have commanded a widow there
to feed you.' So he set out and went to Zarephath. When he came to the gate
of the town, a widow was there gathering sticks; he called to her and said,
'Bring me a little water in a vessel, so that I may drink.' As she was going to
bring it, he called to her and said, 'Bring me a morsel of bread in your hand.'
But she said, 'As the LORD your God lives, I have nothing baked, only a
handful of meal in a jar, and a little oil in a jug; I am now gathering a couple
of sticks, so that I may go home and prepare it for myself and my son, that
we may eat it, and die.' Elijah said to her, 'Do not be afraid; go and do as you
have said; but first make me a little cake of it and bring it to me, and
afterwards make something for yourself and your son. For thus says the
LORD the God of Israel: The jar of meal will not be emptied and the jug of oil
will not fail until the day that the LORD sends rain on the earth.' She went
and did as Elijah said, so that she as well as he and her household ate for
many days. The jar of meal was not emptied, neither did the jug of oil fail,
according to the word of the LORD that he spoke by Elijah.

PSALM   Psalm 36.5–10

℟ **With you is the well of life**
   [and in your light we see light].

Your love, O Lord, reaches to the heavens,
and your faithfulness to the clouds.
Your righteousness is like the strong mountains,
your justice like the great deep;
you save both human and beast, O Lord. ℟

How priceless is your love, O God!
your people take refuge under the shadow of your wings.
They feast upon the abundance of your house;
you give them drink from the river of your delights. ℟

For with you is the well of life,
and in your light we see light.
Continue your loving-kindness to those who know you,
and your favour to those who are true of heart. ℟

SECOND READING   1 Corinthians 1.18–31

A reading from the first letter of Paul to the Corinthians.

The message about the cross is foolishness to those who are perishing, but to
us who are being saved it is the power of God.
For it is written, 'I will destroy the wisdom of the wise,
and the discernment of the discerning I will thwart.'
Where is the one who is wise? Where is the scribe? Where is the debater of
this age? Has not God made foolish the wisdom of the world? For since, in
the wisdom of God, the world did not know God through wisdom, God
decided, through the foolishness of our proclamation, to save those who
believe. For Jews demand signs and Greeks desire wisdom, but we proclaim
Christ crucified, a stumbling-block to Jews and foolishness to Gentiles, but to
those who are the called, both Jews and Greeks, Christ the power of God and
the wisdom of God. For God's foolishness is wiser than human wisdom, and
God's weakness is stronger than human strength.

Consider your own call, brothers and sisters: not many of you were wise by
human standards, not many were powerful, not many were of noble birth.
But God chose what is foolish in the world to shame the wise; God chose
what is weak in the world to shame the strong; God chose what is low and
despised in the world, things that are not, to reduce to nothing things that
are, so that no one might boast in the presence of God. He is the source of
your life in Christ Jesus, who became for us wisdom from God, and
righteousness and sanctification and redemption, in order that, as it is
written, 'Let the one who boasts, boast in the Lord.'

GOSPEL   John 2.1–11

Hear the gospel of our Lord Jesus Christ according to John.

On the third day there was a wedding in Cana of Galilee, and the mother of
Jesus was there. Jesus and his disciples had also been invited to the wedding.
When the wine gave out, the mother of Jesus said to him, 'They have no
wine.' And Jesus said to her, 'Woman, what concern is that to you and to
me? My hour has not yet come.' His mother said to the servants, 'Do

whatever he tells you.' Now standing there were six stone water-jars for the Jewish rites of purification, each holding twenty or thirty gallons. Jesus said to them, 'Fill the jars with water.' And they filled them up to the brim. He said to them, 'Now draw some out, and take it to the chief steward.' So they took it. When the steward tasted the water that had become wine, and did not know where it came from (though the servants who had drawn the water knew), the steward called the bridegroom and said to him, 'Everyone serves the good wine first, and then the inferior wine after the guests have become drunk. But you have kept the good wine until now.' Jesus did this, the first of his signs, in Cana of Galilee, and revealed his glory; and his disciples believed in him.

THE PRESENTATION OF CHRIST   YEARS A B C

2 February

> *Church of England provision allows only Psalm 24. Revised Common Lectionary provides Psalm 84 as an alternative.*

FIRST READING   Malachi 3.1-5

A reading from the book of the prophet Malachi.

Thus says the LORD God:

See, I am sending my messenger to prepare the way before me, and the Lord whom you seek will suddenly come to his temple. The messenger of the covenant in whom you delight – indeed, he is coming, says the LORD of hosts. But who can endure the day of his coming, and who can stand when he appears? For he is like a refiner's fire and like fullers' soap; he will sit as a refiner and purifier of silver, and he will purify the descendants of Levi and refine them like gold and silver, until they present offerings to the LORD in righteousness. Then the offering of Judah and Jerusalem will be pleasing to the LORD as in the days of old and as in former years.

Then I will draw near to you for judgement; I will be swift to bear witness against the sorcerers, against the adulterers, against those who swear falsely, against those who oppress the hired workers in their wages, the widow, and the orphan, against those who thrust aside the alien, and do not fear me, says the LORD of hosts.

PSALM   **Psalm 24.(1–6), 7–10**

Either

℞ **The Lord of hosts,**
   he is the king of glory.
   or
℞ **The Lord whom you seek**
   will suddenly come.

[The earth is the Lord's and all that is in it,
the world and all who dwell therein.
For it is he who founded it upon the seas
and made it firm upon the rivers of the deep. ℞

'Who can ascend the hill of the Lord?
and who can stand in his holy place?'
'Those who have clean hands and a pure heart,
who have not pledged themselves to falsehood,
nor sworn by what is a fraud. ℞

They shall receive a blessing from the Lord
and a just reward from the God of their salvation.'
Such is the generation of those who seek him,
of those who seek your face, O God of Jacob. ℞]

Lift up your heads, O gates;
lift them high, O everlasting doors;
and the King of glory shall come in.
'Who is this King of glory?'
'The Lord, strong and mighty,
the Lord, mighty in battle.' ℞

Lift up your heads, O gates;
lift them high, O everlasting doors;
and the King of glory shall come in.
'Who is he, this King of glory?'
'The Lord of hosts,
he is the King of glory.' ℞

Or (Revised Common Lectionary only)   Psalm 84

℞ **Happy are they who dwell in your house!**
   or
℞ **Lord God of hosts, hear my prayer**
   [hearken, O God of Jacob].

How dear to me is your dwelling, O Lord of hosts!
My soul has a desire and longing
for the courts of the Lord;
my heart and my flesh rejoice in the living God. ℞

The sparrow has found her a house
and the swallow a nest where she may lay her young;
by the side of your altars, O Lord of hosts,
my King and my God. ℞

Happy are they who dwell in your house!
they will always be praising you.
Happy are the people whose strength is in you!
whose hearts are set on the pilgrims' way. ℞

Those who go through the desolate valley
will find it a place of springs,
for the early rains have covered it with pools of water.
They will climb from height to height,
and the God of gods will reveal himself in Zion.
Lord God of hosts, hear my prayer;
hearken, O God of Jacob. ℞

Behold our defender, O God;
and look upon the face of your anointed.
For one day in your courts
is better than a thousand in my own room,
and to stand at the threshold of the house of my God
than to dwell in the tents of the wicked. ℞

For the Lord God is both sun and shield;
he will give grace and glory;
No good thing will the Lord withold
from those who walk with integrity.
O Lord of hosts,
happy are they who put their trust in you! ℞

SECOND READING   **Hebrews 2.14–18**

A reading from the letter to the Hebrews.

Since the children share flesh and blood, Jesus himself likewise shared the same things, so that through death he might destroy the one who has the power of death, that is, the devil, and free those who all their lives were held in slavery by the fear of death. For it is clear that he did not come to help angels, but the descendants of Abraham. Therefore he had to become like his brothers and sisters in every respect, so that he might be a merciful and faithful high priest in the service of God, to make a sacrifice of atonement for the sins of the people. Because he himself was tested by what he suffered, he is able to help those who are being tested.

GOSPEL   **Luke 2.22–40**

Hear the gospel of our Lord Jesus Christ according to Luke.

When the time came for their purification according to the law of Moses, Mary and Joseph brought Jesus up to Jerusalem to present him to the Lord. (as it is written in the law of the Lord, 'Every firstborn male shall be designated as holy to the Lord'), and they offered a sacrifice according to what is stated in the law of the Lord, 'a pair of turtle-doves or two young pigeons.'

Now there was a man in Jerusalem whose name was Simeon; this man was righteous and devout, looking forward to the consolation of Israel, and the Holy Spirit rested on him. It had been revealed to him by the Holy Spirit that he would not see death before he had seen the Lord's Messiah. Guided by the Spirit, Simeon came into the temple; and when the parents brought in the child Jesus, to do for him what was customary under the law, Simeon took him in his arms and praised God, saying,
'Master, now you are dismissing your servant in peace,
according to your word;
for my eyes have seen your salvation,
which you have prepared in the presence of all peoples,
a light for revelation to the Gentiles
and for glory to your people Israel.'

And the child's father and mother were amazed at what was being said about him. Then Simeon blessed them and said to his mother Mary, 'This child is destined for the falling and the rising of many in Israel, and to be a sign that will be opposed so that the inner thoughts of many will be revealed – and a sword will pierce your own soul too.'

There was also a prophet, Anna the daughter of Phanuel, of the tribe of Asher. She was of a great age, having lived with her husband seven years after her marriage, then as a widow to the age of eighty-four. She never left the temple but worshipped there with fasting and prayer night and day. At that moment she came, and began to praise God and to speak about the child to all who were looking for the redemption of Jerusalem.

When they had finished everything required by the law of the Lord, they returned to Galilee, to their own town of Nazareth. The child grew and became strong, filled with wisdom; and the favour of God was upon him.

ORDINARY TIME

In the weeks between now and Lent the Revised Common Lectionary designates Sundays 'Sundays after Epiphany'. The Church of England provision designates them 'Sundays before Lent' with readings according to calendar date.

EPIPHANY 5   YEAR A
† SUNDAY BETWEEN 3 AND 9 FEBRUARY
(if earlier than 2 before Lent)

FIRST READING (Short or long reading)   Isaiah 58.1–9a, (9b–12)

A reading from the book of the prophet Isaiah.

Thus says the LORD:

Shout out, do not hold back!
Lift up your voice like a trumpet!
Announce to my people their rebellion,
to the house of Jacob their sins.
Yet day after day they seek me
and delight to know my ways,
as if they were a nation that practised righteousness
and did not forsake the ordinance of their God;
they ask of me righteous judgements,
they delight to draw near to God.
'Why do we fast, but you do not see?
Why humble ourselves, but you do not notice?'
Look, you serve your own interest on your fast-day,
and oppress all your workers.

Look, you fast only to quarrel and to fight
and to strike with a wicked fist.
Such fasting as you do today
will not make your voice heard on high.
Is such the fast that I choose,
a day to humble oneself?
Is it to bow down the head like a bulrush,
and to lie in sackcloth and ashes?
Will you call this a fast,
a day acceptable to the LORD?

Is not this the fast that I choose:
to loose the bonds of injustice,
to undo the thongs of the yoke,
to let the oppressed go free,
and to break every yoke?
Is it not to share your bread with the hungry,
and bring the homeless poor into your house;
when you see the naked, to cover them,
and not to hide yourself from your own kin?
Then your light shall break forth like the dawn,
and your healing shall spring up quickly;
your vindicator shall go before you,
the glory of the LORD shall be your rearguard.
Then you shall call, and the LORD will answer;
you shall cry for help, and he will say, Here I am.

[If you remove the yoke from among you,
the pointing of the finger, the speaking of evil,
if you offer your food to the hungry
and satisfy the needs of the afflicted,
then your light shall rise in the darkness
and your gloom be like the noonday.
The LORD will guide you continually,
and satisfy your needs in parched places,
and make your bones strong;
and you shall be like a watered garden,
like a spring of water, whose waters never fail.
Your ancient ruins shall be rebuilt;
you shall raise up the foundations of many generations;
you shall be called the repairer of the breach,
the restorer of streets to live in.]

PSALM   **Psalm 112.1–9, (10)**

℟ **Light shines in the darkness for the upright.**
   or
℟ **The righteous are merciful and full of compassion.**

Alleluia!
Happy are they who fear the Lord
and have great delight in his commandments!
Their descendants will be mighty in the land;
the generation of the upright will be blessed. ℟

Wealth and riches will be in their house,
and their righteousness will last for ever.
Light shines in the darkness for the upright;
the righteous are merciful and full of compassion. ℟

It is good for them to be generous in lending
and to manage their affairs with justice.
For they will never be shaken;
the righteous will be kept in everlasting remembrance. ℟

They will not be afraid of any evil rumours;
their heart is right;
they put their trust in the Lord.
Their heart is established and will not shrink,
until they see their desire upon their enemies. ℟

They have given freely to the poor,
and their righteousness stands fast for ever;
they will hold up their head with honour.
[The wicked will see it and be angry;
they will gnash their teeth and pine away;
the desires of the wicked will perish.] ℟

SECOND READING (Short or long reading)
1 Corinthians 2.1–12, (13–16)

A reading from the first letter of Paul to the Corinthians.

When I came to you, brothers and sisters, I did not come proclaiming the
mystery of God to you in lofty words or wisdom. For I decided to know
nothing among you except Jesus Christ, and him crucified. And I came to

you in weakness and in fear and in much trembling. My speech and my proclamation were not with plausible words of wisdom, but with a demonstration of the Spirit and of power, so that your faith might rest not on human wisdom but on the power of God.

Yet among the mature we do speak wisdom, though it is not a wisdom of this age or of the rulers of this age, who are doomed to perish. But we speak God's wisdom, secret and hidden, which God decreed before the ages for our glory. None of the rulers of this age understood this; for if they had, they would not have crucified the Lord of glory.
But, as it is written,
'What no eye has seen, nor ear heard,
nor the human heart conceived,
what God has prepared for those who love him' –
these things God has revealed to us through the Spirit; for the Spirit searches everything, even the depths of God. For what human being knows what is truly human except the human spirit that is within? So also no one comprehends what is truly God's except the Spirit of God. Now we have received not the spirit of the world, but the Spirit that is from God, so that we may understand the gifts bestowed on us by God. [And we speak of these things in words not taught by human wisdom but taught by the Spirit, interpreting spiritual things to those who are spiritual.

Those who are unspiritual do not receive the gifts of God's Spirit, for they are foolishness to them, and they are unable to understand them because they are discerned spiritually. Those who are spiritual discern all things, and they are themselves subject to no one else's scrutiny.
'For who has known the mind of the Lord
so as to instruct him?'
But we have the mind of Christ.]

GOSPEL   Matthew 5.13–20

Hear the gospel of our Lord Jesus Christ according to Matthew.

Jesus went up the mountain and was joined by his disciples. Then he began to teach them: 'You are the salt of the earth; but if salt has lost its taste, how can its saltiness be restored? It is no longer good for anything, but is thrown out and trampled under foot.

You are the light of the world. A city built on a hill cannot be hidden. No one after lighting a lamp puts it under the bushel basket, but on the lampstand, and it gives light to all in the house. In the same way, let your light shine before others, so that they may see your good works and give glory to your Father in heaven.

Do not think that I have come to abolish the law or the prophets; I have come not to abolish but to fulfil. For truly I tell you, until heaven and earth pass away, not one letter, not one stroke of a letter, will pass from the law until all is accomplished. Therefore, whoever breaks one of the least of these commandments, and teaches others to do the same, will be called least in the kingdom of heaven; but whoever does them and teaches them will be called great in the kingdom of heaven. For I tell you, unless your righteousness exceeds that of the scribes and Pharisees, you will never enter the kingdom of heaven.'

EPIPHANY 6   YEAR A
† SUNDAY BETWEEN 10 AND 16 FEBRUARY
(if earlier than 2 before Lent)

FIRST READING (Alternative readings)

Either   **Deuteronomy 30.15-20**

A reading from the book of Deuteronomy.

See, I have set before you today life and prosperity, death and adversity. If you obey the commandments of the LORD your God that I am commanding you today, by loving the LORD your God, walking in his ways, and observing his commandments, decrees, and ordinances, then you shall live and become numerous, and the LORD your God will bless you in the land that you are entering to possess. But if your heart turns away and you do not hear, but are led astray to bow down to other gods and serve them, I declare to you today that you shall perish; you shall not live long in the land that you are crossing the Jordan to enter and possess. I call heaven and earth to witness against you today that I have set before you life and death, blessings and curses. Choose life so that you and your descendants may live, loving the LORD your God, obeying him, and holding fast to him; for that means life to you and length of days, so that you may live in the land that the LORD swore to give to your ancestors, to Abraham, to Isaac, and to Jacob.

Or   **Ecclesiasticus 15.15–20**

A reading from the book of Ecclesiasticus.

If you choose, you can keep the commandments,
and to act faithfully is a matter of your own choice.
He has placed before you fire and water;
stretch out your hand for whichever you choose.
Before each person are life and death,
and whichever one chooses will be given.
For great is the wisdom of the Lord;
he is mighty in power and sees everything;
his eyes are on those who fear him,
and he knows every human action.
He has not commanded anyone to be wicked,
and he has not given anyone permission to sin.

PSALM   **Psalm 119.1–8**

℟ **Happy are they who walk in the law of the Lord.**

Happy are they whose way is blameless,
who walk in the law of the Lord!
Happy are they who observe his decrees
and seek him with all their hearts! ℟

Who never do any wrong,
but always walk in his ways.
You laid down your commandments,
that we should fully keep them. ℟

O that my ways were made so direct
that I might keep your statutes!
Then I should not be put to shame,
when I regard all your commandments. ℟

I will thank you with an unfeigned heart,
when I have learned your righteous judgements.
I will keep your statutes;
do not utterly forsake me. ℟

SECOND READING   **1 Corinthians 3.1-9**

A reading from the first letter of Paul to the Corinthians.

Brothers and sisters, I could not speak to you as spiritual people, but rather as people of the flesh, as infants in Christ. I fed you with milk, not solid food, for you were not ready for solid food. Even now you are still not ready, for you are still of the flesh. For as long as there is jealousy and quarrelling among you, are you not of the flesh, and behaving according to human inclinations? For when one says, 'I belong to Paul,' and another, 'I belong to Apollos,' are you not merely human? What then is Apollos? What is Paul? Servants through whom you came to believe, as the Lord assigned to each. I planted, Apollos watered, but God gave the growth. So neither the one who plants nor the one who waters is anything, but only God who gives the growth. The one who plants and the one who waters have a common purpose, and each will receive wages according to the labour of each. For we are God's servants, working together; you are God's field, God's building.

GOSPEL   **Matthew 5.21-37**

Hear the gospel of our Lord Jesus Christ according to Matthew.

On the mountain, Jesus gathered his disciples around him and taught them, saying: 'You have heard that it was said to those of ancient times, "You shall not murder"; and "whoever murders shall be liable to judgement." But I say to you that if you are angry with a brother or sister, you will be liable to judgement; and if you insult a brother or sister, you will be liable to the council; and if you say, "You fool," you will be liable to the hell of fire. So when you are offering your gift at the altar, if you remember that your brother or sister has something against you, leave your gift there before the altar and go; first be reconciled to your brother or sister, and then come and offer your gift. Come to terms quickly with your accuser while you are on the way to court with him, or your accuser may hand you over to the judge, and the judge to the guard, and you will be thrown into prison. Truly I tell you, you will never get out until you have paid the last penny.

You have heard that it was said, "You shall not commit adultery." But I say to you that everyone who looks at a woman with lust has already committed adultery with her in his heart. If your right eye causes you to sin, tear it out and throw it away; it is better for you to lose one of your members than for your whole body to be thrown into hell. And if your right hand causes you to sin, cut it off and throw it away; it is better for you to lose one of your members than for your whole body to go into hell.

It was also said, "Whoever divorces his wife, let him give her a certificate of divorce." But I say to you that anyone who divorces his wife, except on the ground of unchastity, causes her to commit adultery; and whoever marries a divorced woman commits adultery.

Again, you have heard that it was said to those of ancient times, "You shall not swear falsely, but carry out the vows you have made to the Lord." But I say to you, Do not swear at all, either by heaven, for it is the throne of God, or by the earth, for it is his footstool, or by Jerusalem, for it is the city of the great King. And do not swear by your head, for you cannot make one hair white or black. Let your word be "Yes, Yes" or "No, No"; anything more than this comes from the evil one.'

EPIPHANY 7   YEAR A
† SUNDAY BETWEEN 17 AND 23 FEBRUARY
(if earlier than 2 before Lent)

FIRST READING   Leviticus 19.1–2, 9–18

A reading from the book of Leviticus.

The LORD spoke to Moses, saying: Speak to all the congregation of the people of Israel and say to them: You shall be holy, for I the LORD your God am holy.

When you reap the harvest of your land, you shall not reap to the very edges of your field, or gather the gleanings of your harvest. You shall not strip your vineyard bare, or gather the fallen grapes of your vineyard; you shall leave them for the poor and the alien: I am the LORD your God.

You shall not steal; you shall not deal falsely; and you shall not lie to one another. And you shall not swear falsely by my name, profaning the name of your God: I am the LORD.

You shall not defraud your neighbour; you shall not steal; and you shall not keep for yourself the wages of a labourer until morning. You shall not revile the deaf or put a stumbling-block before the blind; you shall fear your God: I am the LORD.

You shall not render an unjust judgement; you shall not be partial to the poor or defer to the great: with justice you shall judge your neighbour. You shall not go around as a slanderer among your people, and you shall not profit by the blood of your neighbour: I am the LORD.

You shall not hate in your heart anyone of your kin; you shall reprove your neighbour, or you will incur guilt yourself. You shall not take vengeance or bear a grudge against any of your people, but you shall love your neighbour as yourself: I am the LORD.

PSALM   **Psalm 119.33–40**

℞ **Give me understanding and I shall keep your law.**

Teach me, O Lord, the way of your statutes,
and I shall keep it to the end.
Give me understanding and I shall keep your law;
I shall keep it with all my heart. ℞

Make me go in the path of your commandments,
for that is my desire.
Incline my heart to your decrees
and not to unjust gain. ℞

Turn my eyes from watching what is worthless;
give me life in your ways.
Fulfil your promise to your servant,
which you make to those who fear you. ℞

Turn away the reproach which I dread,
because your judgements are good.
Behold, I long for your commandments;
in your righteousness preserve my life. ℞

SECOND READING   **1 Corinthians 3.10–11, 16–23**

A reading from the first letter of Paul to the Corinthians.

According to the grace of God given to me, like a skilled master builder I laid a foundation, and someone else is building on it. Each builder must choose with care how to build on it. For no one can lay any foundation other than the one that has been laid; that foundation is Jesus Christ.

Do you not know that you are God's temple and that God's Spirit dwells in you? If anyone destroys God's temple, God will destroy that person. For God's temple is holy, and you are that temple.

Do not deceive yourselves. If you think that you are wise in this age, you should become fools so that you may become wise. For the wisdom of this world is foolishness with God.
For it is written,
'He catches the wise in their craftiness,'
and again,
'The Lord knows the thoughts of the wise,
that they are futile.'
So let no one boast about human leaders. For all things are yours, whether Paul or Apollos or Cephas or the world or life or death or the present or the future – all belong to you, and you belong to Christ, and Christ belongs to God.

GOSPEL   Matthew 5.38–48

Hear the gospel of our Lord Jesus Christ according to Matthew.

On the mountain, Jesus continued to teach his disciples. 'You have heard that it was said, "An eye for an eye and a tooth for a tooth." But I say to you, Do not resist an evildoer. But if anyone strikes you on the right cheek, turn the other also; and if anyone wants to sue you and take your coat, give your cloak as well; and if anyone forces you to go one mile, go also the second mile. Give to everyone who begs from you, and do not refuse anyone who wants to borrow from you.

You have heard that it was said, "You shall love your neighbour and hate your enemy." But I say to you, Love your enemies and pray for those who persecute you, so that you may be children of your Father in heaven; for he makes his sun rise on the evil and on the good, and sends rain on the righteous and on the unrighteous. For if you love those who love you, what reward do you have? Do not even the tax-collectors do the same? And if you greet only your brothers and sisters, what more are you doing than others? Do not even the Gentiles do the same? Be perfect, therefore, as your heavenly Father is perfect.'

EPIPHANY 8   YEAR A
† SECOND SUNDAY BEFORE LENT

The Revised Common Lectionary and the Church of England make different provision for today
For Church of England provision see pages 60–64.

REVISED COMMON LECTIONARY

FIRST READING   Isaiah 49.8–16a

A reading from the book of the prophet Isaiah.

Thus says the LORD:
In a time of favour I have answered you,
on a day of salvation I have helped you;
I have kept you and given you as a covenant to the people,
to establish the land,
to apportion the desolate heritages;
saying to the prisoners,
'Come out,'
to those who are in darkness,
'Show yourselves.'
They shall feed along the ways,
on all the bare heights shall be their pasture;
they shall not hunger or thirst,
neither scorching wind nor sun shall strike them down,
for he who has pity on them will lead them,
and by springs of water will guide them.
And I will turn all my mountains into a road,
and my highways shall be raised up.
Lo, these shall come from far away,
and lo, these from the north and from the west,
and these from the land of Syene.
Sing for joy, O heavens,
and exult, O earth;
break forth, O mountains, into singing!
For the LORD has comforted his people,
and will have compassion on his suffering ones.

But Zion said, 'The LORD has forsaken me,
my Lord has forgotten me.'
Can a woman forget her nursing-child,
or show no compassion for the child of her womb?

Even these may forget,
yet I will not forget you.
See, I have inscribed you on the palms of my hands.

PSALM   Psalm 131

℟ **I still my soul and make it quiet.**

O Lord, I am not proud;
I have no haughty looks.
I do not occupy myself with great matters,
or with things that are too hard for me. ℟

But I still my soul and make it quiet,
like a child upon its mother's breast;
my soul is quieted within me.
O Israel, wait upon the Lord,
from this time forth for evermore. ℟

SECOND READING   1 Corinthians 4.1–5

A reading from the first letter of Paul to the Corinthians.

My brothers and sisters: Think of us in this way, as servants of Christ and
stewards of God's mysteries. Moreover, it is required of stewards that they be
found trustworthy. But with me it is a very small thing that I should be
judged by you or by any human court. I do not even judge myself. I am not
aware of anything against myself, but I am not thereby acquitted. It is the
Lord who judges me. Therefore do not pronounce judgement before the
time, before the Lord comes, who will bring to light the things now hidden
in darkness and will disclose the purposes of the heart. Then each one will
receive commendation from God.

GOSPEL   Matthew 6.24–34

Hear the gospel of our Lord Jesus Christ according to Matthew.

Jesus taught his disciples, saying. 'No one can serve two masters; for a slave
will either hate the one and love the other, or be devoted to the one and
despise the other. You cannot serve God and wealth.

Therefore I tell you, do not worry about your life, what you will eat or what
you will drink, or about your body, what you will wear. Is not life more than

food, and the body more than clothing? Look at the birds of the air; they neither sow nor reap nor gather into barns, and yet your heavenly Father feeds them. Are you not of more value than they? And can any of you by worrying add a single hour to your span of life? And why do you worry about clothing? Consider the lilies of the field, how they grow; they neither toil nor spin, yet I tell you, even Solomon in all his glory was not clothed like one of these. But if God so clothes the grass of the field, which is alive today and tomorrow is thrown into the oven, will he not much more clothe you – you of little faith? Therefore do not worry, saying, "What will we eat?" or "What will we drink?" or "What will we wear?" For it is the Gentiles who strive for all these things; and indeed your heavenly Father knows that you need all these things. But strive first for the kingdom of God and his righteousness, and all these things will be given to you as well.

So do not worry about tomorrow, for tomorrow will bring worries of its own. Today's trouble is enough for today.'

Or

† CHURCH OF ENGLAND

FIRST READING   Genesis 1.1 – 2.3

A reading from the book of Genesis.

In the beginning when God created the heavens and the earth, the earth was a formless void and darkness covered the face of the deep, while a wind from God swept over the face of the waters. Then God said, 'Let there be light'; and there was light. And God saw that the light was good; and God separated the light from the darkness. God called the light Day, and the darkness he called Night. And there was evening and there was morning, the first day.

And God said, 'Let there be a dome in the midst of the waters, and let it separate the waters from the waters.' So God made the dome and separated the waters that were under the dome from the waters that were above the dome. And it was so. God called the dome Sky. And there was evening and there was morning, the second day.

And God said, 'Let the waters under the sky be gathered together into one place, and let the dry land appear.' And it was so. God called the dry land Earth, and the waters that were gathered together he called Seas. And God saw that it was good. Then God said, 'Let the earth put forth vegetation: plants yielding seed, and fruit trees of every kind on earth that bear fruit with the seed in it.' And it was so. The earth brought forth vegetation: plants yielding seed of every kind, and trees of every kind bearing fruit with the seed in it. And God saw that it was good. And there was evening and there was morning, the third day.

And God said, 'Let there be lights in the dome of the sky to separate the day from the night; and let them be for signs and for seasons and for days and years, and let them be lights in the dome of the sky to give light upon the earth.' And it was so. God made the two great lights – the greater light to rule the day and the lesser light to rule the night – and the stars. God set them in the dome of the sky to give light upon the earth, to rule over the day and over the night, and to separate the light from the darkness. And God saw that it was good. And there was evening and there was morning, the fourth day.

And God said, 'Let the waters bring forth swarms of living creatures, and let birds fly above the earth across the dome of the sky.' So God created the great sea monsters and every living creature that moves, of every kind, with which the waters swarm, and every winged bird of every kind. And God saw that it was good. God blessed them, saying, 'Be fruitful and multiply and fill the waters in the seas, and let birds multiply on the earth.' And there was evening and there was morning, the fifth day.

And God said, 'Let the earth bring forth living creatures of every kind: cattle and creeping things and wild animals of the earth of every kind.' And it was so. God made the wild animals of the earth of every kind, and the cattle of every kind, and everything that creeps upon the ground of every kind. And God saw that it was good.

Then God said, 'Let us make humankind in our image, according to our likeness; and let them have dominion over the fish of the sea, and over the birds of the air, and over the cattle, and over all the wild animals of the earth, and over every creeping thing that creeps upon the earth.'

So God created humankind in his image,
in the image of God he created them;
male and female he created them.

God blessed them, and God said to them, 'Be fruitful and multiply, and fill the earth and subdue it; and have dominion over the fish of the sea and over the birds of the air and over every living thing that moves upon the earth.' God said, 'See, I have given you every plant yielding seed that is upon the face of all the earth, and every tree with seed in its fruit; you shall have them for food. And to every beast of the earth, and to every bird of the air, and to everything that creeps on the earth, everything that has the breath of life, I have given every green plant for food.' And it was so. God saw everything that he had made, and indeed, it was very good. And there was evening and there was morning, the sixth day.

Thus the heavens and the earth were finished, and all their multitude. And on the seventh day God finished the work that he had done, and he rested on the seventh day from all the work that he had done. So God blessed the seventh day and hallowed it, because on it God rested from all the work that he had done in creation.

PSALM   **Psalm 136.1–9, (10–22), 23–26**

Give thanks to the Lord, for he is good,
for his mercy endures for ever.
Give thanks to the God of gods,
for his mercy endures for ever.
Give thanks to the Lord of lords,
for his mercy endures for ever.

Who only does great wonders,
for his mercy endures for ever;
Who by his wisdom made the heavens,
for his mercy endures for ever;
Who spread out the earth upon the waters,
for his mercy endures for ever;
Who created great lights,
for his mercy endures for ever;
The sun to rule the day,
for his mercy endures for ever;
The moon and the stars to govern the night,
for his mercy endures for ever.
[Who struck down the first-born of Egypt,
for his mercy endures for ever;
And brought out Israel from among them,
for his mercy endures for ever;
With a mighty hand and a stretched-out arm,
for his mercy endures for ever;
Who divided the Red Sea in two,
for his mercy endures for ever;
And made Israel to pass through the midst of it,
for his mercy endures for ever;

But swept Pharaoh and his army into the Red Sea,
for his mercy endures for ever;
Who led his people through the wilderness,
for his mercy endures for ever.
Who struck down great kings,
for his mercy endures for ever;
And slew mighty kings,
for his mercy endures for ever;
Sihon, king of the Amorites,
for his mercy endures for ever;
And Og, the king of Bashan,
for his mercy endures for ever;
And gave away their lands of an inheritance,
for his mercy endures for ever;
An inheritance for Israel his servant,
for his mercy endures for ever.]

It is he who remembered us in our low estate,
for his mercy endures for ever;
And delivered us from our enemies,
for his mercy endures for ever;
Who gives food to all creatures,
for his mercy endures for ever;

Give thanks to the God of heaven,
for his mercy endures for ever.

SECOND READING   Romans 8.18–25

A reading from the letter of Paul to the Romans.

I consider that the sufferings of this present time are not worth comparing
with the glory about to be revealed to us. For the creation waits with eager
longing for the revealing of the children of God; for the creation was
subjected to futility, not of its own will but by the will of the one who
subjected it, in hope that the creation itself will be set free from its bondage
to decay and will obtain the freedom of the glory of the children of God.
We know that the whole creation has been groaning in labour pains until
now; and not only the creation, but we ourselves, who have the first fruits of
the Spirit, groan inwardly while we wait for adoption, the redemption of our
bodies. For in hope we were saved. Now hope that is seen is not hope. For
who hopes for what is seen? But if we hope for what we do not see, we wait
for it with patience.

GOSPEL   **Matthew 6.25-34**

Hear the gospel of our Lord Jesus Christ according to Matthew.

Jesus taught his disciples, saying: 'Therefore I tell you, do not worry about your life, what you will eat or what you will drink, or about your body, what you will wear. Is not life more than food, and the body more than clothing? Look at the birds of the air; they neither sow nor reap nor gather into barns, and yet your heavenly Father feeds them. Are you not of more value than they? And can any of you by worrying add a single hour to your span of life? And why do you worry about clothing? Consider the lilies of the field, how they grow; they neither toil nor spin, yet I tell you, even Solomon in all his glory was not clothed like one of these. But if God so clothes the grass of the field, which is alive today and tomorrow is thrown into the oven, will he not much more clothe you – you of little faith? Therefore do not worry, saying, "What will we eat?" or "What will we drink?" or "What will we wear?" For it is the Gentiles who strive for all these things; and indeed your heavenly Father knows that you need all these things. But strive first for the kingdom of God and his righteousness, and all these things will be given to you as well. So do not worry about tomorrow, for tomorrow will bring worries of its own. Today's trouble is enough for today.'

EPIPHANY 9   YEAR A
† SUNDAY NEXT BEFORE LENT

On this Sunday the Church of England allows only one of the two options in the Revised Common Lectionary. Both provisions are given below. The Church of England provision is the first set.

FIRST READING   **Exodus 24.12-18**

A reading from the book of Exodus.

The LORD said to Moses, 'Come up to me on the mountain, and wait there; and I will give you the tablets of stone, with the law and the commandment, which I have written for their instruction.' So Moses set out with his assistant Joshua, and Moses went up into the mountain of God. To the elders he had said, 'Wait here for us, until we come to you again; for Aaron and Hur are with you; whoever has a dispute may go to them.'

Then Moses went up on the mountain, and the cloud covered the mountain. The glory of the LORD settled on Mount Sinai, and the cloud covered it for six days; on the seventh day he called to Moses out of the cloud. Now the appearance of the glory of the LORD was like a devouring fire on the top of the mountain in the sight of the people of Israel. Moses entered the cloud, and went up on the mountain. Moses was on the mountain for forty days and forty nights.

PSALM

Either Psalm 2

℟ **You are my Son;**
  this day have I begotten you.

Why are the nations in an uproar?
Why do the peoples mutter empty threats?
Why do the kings of the earth rise up in revolt
and the princes plot together,
against the Lord and against his anointed? ℟

'Let us break their yoke', they say;
'let us cast off their bonds from us.'
He whose throne is in heaven is laughing;
the Lord has them in derision. ℟

Then he speaks to them in his wrath
and his rage fills them with terror.
'I myself have set my king
upon my holy hill of Zion.'
Let me announce the decree of the Lord:
he said to me, 'You are my Son;
this day have I begotten you. ℟

Ask of me and I will give you the nations
for your inheritance
and the ends of the earth for your possession.
You shall crush them with an iron rod
and shatter them like a piece of pottery.' ℟

And now, you kings, be wise;
be warned, you rulers of the earth.
Submit to the Lord with fear,
and with trembling bow before him;
Lest he be angry and you perish;
for his wrath is quickly kindled.
Happy are they all
who take refuge in him! ℟

Or   **Psalm 99**

℞ **He spoke to them out of the pillar of cloud.**

The Lord is king; let the people tremble;
he is enthroned upon the cherubim; let the earth shake.
²The Lord is great in Zion;
he is high above all peoples.
³Let them confess his name, which is great and awesome;
he is the Holy One. ℞

⁴'O mighty King, lover of justice,
you have established equity;
you have executed justice and righteousness in Jacob.'
⁵Proclaim the greatness of the Lord our God
and fall down before his footstool;
he is the Holy One. ℞

Moses and Aaron among his priests,
and Samuel among those who call upon his name,
they called upon the Lord and he answered them.
He spoke to them out of the pillar of cloud;
they kept his testimonies
and the decree that he gave them. ℞

'O Lord our God, you answered them indeed;
you were a God who forgave them,
yet punished them for their evil deeds.'
Proclaim the greatness of the Lord our God
and worship him upon his holy hill;
for the Lord our God is the Holy One. ℞

SECOND READING   **2 Peter 1.16–21**

A reading from the second letter of Peter.

We did not follow cleverly devised myths when we made known to you the power and coming of our Lord Jesus Christ, but we had been eyewitnesses of his majesty. For he received honour and glory from God the Father when that voice was conveyed to him by the Majestic Glory, saying, 'This is my Son, my Beloved, with whom I am well pleased.' We ourselves heard this voice come from heaven, while we were with him on the holy mountain.

So we have the prophetic message more fully confirmed. You will do well to be attentive to this as to a lamp shining in a dark place, until the day dawns and the morning star rises in your hearts. First of all you must understand this, that no prophecy of scripture is a matter of one's own interpretation, because no prophecy ever came by human will, but men and women moved by the Holy Spirit spoke from God.

GOSPEL   Matthew 17.1–9

Hear the gospel of our Lord Jesus Christ according to Matthew.

Jesus took with him Peter and James and his brother John and led them up a high mountain, by themselves. And he was transfigured before them, and his face shone like the sun, and his clothes became dazzling white. Suddenly there appeared to them Moses and Elijah, talking with him. Then Peter said to Jesus, 'Lord, it is good for us to be here; if you wish, I will make three dwellings here, one for you, one for Moses, and one for Elijah.' While he was still speaking, suddenly a bright cloud overshadowed them, and from the cloud a voice said, 'This is my Son, the Beloved; with him I am well pleased; listen to him!' 6 When the disciples heard this, they fell to the ground and were overcome by fear. But Jesus came and touched them, saying, 'Get up and do not be afraid.' And when they looked up, they saw no one except Jesus himself alone.

As they were coming down the mountain, Jesus ordered them, 'Tell no one about the vision until after the Son of Man has been raised from the dead.'

Or

REVISED COMMON LECTIONARY ONLY

FIRST READING   Deuteronomy 11.18–21, 26–28

A reading from the book of Deuteronomy.

You shall put these words of mine in your heart and soul, and you shall bind them as a sign on your hand, and fix them as an emblem on your forehead. Teach them to your children, talking about them when you are at home and when you are away, when you lie down and when you rise. Write them on the doorposts of your house and on your gates, so that your days and the days of your children may be multiplied in the land that the LORD swore to your ancestors to give them, as long as the heavens are above the earth.

See, I am setting before you today a blessing and a curse: the blessing, if you obey the commandments of the LORD your God that I am commanding you

today; and the curse, if you do not obey the commandments of the LORD
your God, but turn from the way that I am commanding you today, to follow
other gods that you have not known.

PSALM   Psalm 31.1–5, 19–24

℞ **Let your face shine on your servants**
  [and we shall be saved].

In you, O Lord, have I taken refuge;
let me never be put to shame;
deliver me in your righteousness.
Incline your ear to me;
make haste to deliver me. ℞

Be my strong rock, a castle to keep me safe,
for you are my crag and my stronghold;
for the sake of your name, lead me and guide me. ℞
Take me out of the net
that they have secretly set for me,
for you are my tower of strength.
Into your hands I commend my spirit,
for you have redeemed me,
O Lord, O God of truth. ℞

How great is your goodness, O Lord,
which you have laid up for those who fear you;
which you have done in the sight of all
for those who put their trust in you.
You hide them in the covert of your presence
from those who slander them;
you keep them in your shelter from the strife of tongues. ℞

Blessèd be the Lord!
for he has shown me the wonders of his love
in a besieged city.
Yet I said in my alarm,
'I have been cut off from the sight of your eyes.'
Nevertheless, you heard the sound of my entreaty
when I cried out to you. ℞

Love the Lord, all you who worship him;
the Lord protects the faithful,
but repays to the full those who act haughtily.
Be strong and let your heart take courage,
all you who wait for the Lord. ℟

SECOND READING (Short or long reading)
Romans 1.16-17; 3.22b-28, (29-31)

A reading from the letter of Paul to the Romans.

I am not ashamed of the gospel; it is the power of God for salvation to everyone who has faith, to the Jew first and also to the Greek. For in it the righteousness of God is revealed through faith for faith; as it is written, 'The one who is righteous will live by faith.'

For there is no distinction, since all have sinned and fall short of the glory of God; they are now justified by his grace as a gift, through the redemption that is in Christ Jesus, whom God put forward as a sacrifice of atonement by his blood, effective through faith. He did this to show his righteousness, because in his divine forbearance he had passed over the sins previously committed; it was to prove at the present time that he himself is righteous and that he justifies the one who has faith in Jesus.

Then what becomes of boasting? It is excluded. By what law? By that of works? No, but by the law of faith. For we hold that a person is justified by faith apart from works prescribed by the law. [Or is God the God of Jews only? Is he not the God of Gentiles also? Yes, of Gentiles also, since God is one; and he will justify the circumcised on the ground of faith and the uncircumcised through that same faith. Do we then overthrow the law by this faith? By no means! On the contrary, we uphold the law.]

GOSPEL   Matthew 7.21-29

Hear the gospel of our Lord Jesus Christ according to Matthew.

Jesus taught his disciples, saying: 'Not everyone who says to me, "Lord, Lord," will enter the kingdom of heaven, but only the one who does the will of my Father in heaven. On that day many will say to me, "Lord, Lord, did we not prophesy in your name, and cast out demons in your name, and do many deeds of power in your name?" Then I will declare to them, "I never knew you; go away from me, you evildoers."

Everyone then who hears these words of mine and acts on them will be like a wise man who built his house on rock. The rain fell, the floods came, and the winds blew and beat on that house, but it did not fall, because it had been founded on rock. And everyone who hears these words of mine and does not act on them will be like a foolish man who built his house on sand. The rain fell, and the floods came, and the winds blew and beat against that house, and it fell – and great was its fall!'

Now when Jesus had finished saying these things, the crowds were astounded at his teaching, for he taught them as one having authority, and not as their scribes.

ASH WEDNESDAY   YEARS A B C

FIRST READING (Alternative readings)

Either   Joel 2.1-2, 12-17

A reading from the book of the prophet Joel.

Blow the trumpet in Zion;
sound the alarm on my holy mountain!
Let all the inhabitants of the land tremble,
for the day of the LORD is coming, it is near –
a day of darkness and gloom,
a day of clouds and thick darkness!
Like blackness spread upon the mountains
a great and powerful army comes;
their like has never been from of old,
nor will be again after them in ages to come.

Yet even now, says the LORD,
return to me with all your heart,
with fasting, with weeping, and with mourning;
rend your hearts and not your clothing.
Return to the LORD, your God,
for he is gracious and merciful,
slow to anger, and abounding in steadfast love,
and relents from punishing.
Who knows whether he will not turn and relent,
and leave a blessing behind him,

a grain-offering and a drink-offering
for the LORD, your God?

Blow the trumpet in Zion;
sanctify a fast;
call a solemn assembly;
gather the people.
Sanctify the congregation;
assemble the aged;
gather the children, even infants at the breast.
Let the bridegroom leave his room,
and the bride her canopy.

Between the vestibule and the altar
let the priests, the ministers of the LORD, weep.
Let them say, 'Spare your people, O LORD,
and do not make your heritage a mockery,
a byword among the nations.
Why should it be said among the peoples,
"Where is their God?"'

Or   **Isaiah 58.1–12**

A reading from the book of the prophet Isaiah.

Thus says the LORD:

Shout out, do not hold back!
Lift up your voice like a trumpet!
Announce to my people their rebellion,
to the house of Jacob their sins.
Yet day after day they seek me
and delight to know my ways,
as if they were a nation that practised righteousness
and did not forsake the ordinance of their God;
they ask of me righteous judgements,
they delight to draw near to God.
'Why do we fast, but you do not see?
Why humble ourselves, but you do not notice?'
Look, you serve your own interest on your fast-day
and oppress all your workers.
Look, you fast only to quarrel and to fight

and to strike with a wicked fist.
Such fasting as you do today
will not make your voice heard on high.
Is such the fast that I choose,
a day to humble oneself?
Is it to bow down the head like a bulrush,
and to lie in sackcloth and ashes?
Will you call this a fast,
a day acceptable to the LORD?

Is not this the fast that I choose:
to loose the bonds of injustice,
to undo the thongs of the yoke,
to let the oppressed go free,
and to break every yoke?
Is it not to share your bread with the hungry,
and bring the homeless poor into your house
when you see the naked, to cover them,
and not to hide yourself from your own kin?
Then your light shall break forth like the dawn,
and your healing shall spring up quickly;
your vindicator shall go before you,
the glory of the LORD shall be your rearguard.
Then you shall call, and the LORD will answer;
you shall cry for help, and he will say, Here I am.

If you remove the yoke from among you,
the pointing of the finger, the speaking of evil,
if you offer your food to the hungry
and satisfy the needs of the afflicted,
then your light shall rise in the darkness
and your gloom be like the noonday.
The LORD will guide you continually,
and satisfy your needs in parched places,
and make your bones strong;
and you shall be like a watered garden,
like a spring of water, whose waters never fail.
Your ancient ruins shall be rebuilt;
you shall raise up the foundations of many generations;
you shall be called the repairer of the breach,
the restorer of streets to live in.

PSALM   **Psalm 51.1–18**

℟ **Have mercy on me, O God,**
  [and cleanse me from my sin].

Have mercy on me, O God,
according to your loving-kindness;
in your great compassion blot out my offences.
Wash me through and through from my wickedness
and cleanse me from my sin.
For I know my transgressions,
and my sin is ever before me.
Against you only have I sinned
and done what is evil in your sight. ℟

And so you are justified when you speak
and upright in your judgement. ℟

Indeed, I have been wicked from my birth,
a sinner from my mother's womb.
For behold, you look for truth deep within me,
and will make me understand wisdom secretly.
Purge me from my sin and I shall be pure;
wash me and I shall be clean indeed. ℟

Make me hear of joy and gladness,
that the body you have broken may rejoice.
Hide your face from my sins
and blot out all my iniquities.
Create in me a clean heart, O God,
and renew a right spirit within me. ℟

Cast me not away from your presence
and take not your holy Spirit from me.
Give me the joy of your saving help again
and sustain me with your bountiful Spirit.
I shall teach your ways to the wicked,
and sinners shall return to you. ℟

Deliver me from death, O God,
and my tongue shall sing of your righteousness,
O God of my salvation. ℟

Open my lips, O Lord,
and my mouth shall proclaim your praise. ℟

Had you desired it, I would have offered sacrifice,
but you take no delight in burnt-offerings.
The sacrifice of God is a troubled spirit;
a broken and contrite heart, O God, you will not despise. ℟

SECOND READING   2 Corinthians 5.20b – 6.10

A reading from the second letter of Paul to the Corinthians.

We entreat you on behalf of Christ, be reconciled to God. For our sake he
made him to be sin who knew no sin, so that in him we might become the
righteousness of God. As we work together with him, we urge you also not to
accept the grace of God in vain.
For the Lord says,
'At an acceptable time I have listened to you,
and on a day of salvation I have helped you.'
See, now is the acceptable time;
see, now is the day of salvation!
We are putting no obstacle in anyone's way, so that no fault may be found
with our ministry, but as servants of God we have commended ourselves in
every way: through great endurance, in afflictions, hardships, calamities,
beatings, imprisonments, riots, labours, sleepless nights, hunger; by purity,
knowledge, patience, kindness, holiness of spirit, genuine love, truthful
speech, and the power of God; with the weapons of righteousness for the
right hand and for the left; in honour and dishonour, in ill repute and good
repute. We are treated as impostors, and yet are true; as unknown, and yet are
well known; as dying, and see – we are alive; as punished, and yet not killed;
as sorrowful, yet always rejoicing; as poor, yet making many rich; as having
nothing, and yet possessing everything.

GOSPEL (Alternative readings)

*The Church of England provides an alternative (John 8.1–11) to the Revised Common
Lectionary Gospel.*

Either   Matthew 6.1–6, 16–21

Hear the gospel of our Lord Jesus Christ according to Matthew.

Jesus said to the disciples, 'Beware of practising your piety before others in
order to be seen by them; for then you have no reward from your Father
in heaven.

So whenever you give alms, do not sound a trumpet before you, as the hypocrites do in the synagogues and in the streets, so that they may be praised by others. Truly I tell you, they have received their reward. But when you give alms, do not let your left hand know what your right hand is doing, so that your alms may be done in secret; and your Father who sees in secret will reward you.

And whenever you pray, do not be like the hypocrites; for they love to stand and pray in the synagogues and at the street corners, so that they may be seen by others. Truly I tell you, they have received their reward. But whenever you pray, go into your room and shut the door and pray to your Father who is in secret; and your Father who sees in secret will reward you.

And whenever you fast, do not look dismal, like the hypocrites, for they disfigure their faces so as to show others that they are fasting. Truly I tell you, they have received their reward. But when you fast, put oil on your head and wash your face, so that your fasting may be seen not by others but by your Father who is in secret; and your Father who sees in secret will reward you.

Do not store up for yourselves treasures on earth, where moth and rust consume and where thieves break in and steal; but store up for yourselves treasures in heaven, where neither moth nor rust consumes and where thieves do not break in and steal. For where your treasure is, there your heart will be also.'

† **Or**   **John 8.1–11**

Hear the gospel of our Lord Jesus Christ according to John.

Jesus went to the Mount of Olives. Early in the morning he came again to the temple. All the people came to him and he sat down and began to teach them. The scribes and the Pharisees brought a woman who had been caught in adultery; and making her stand before all the people, they said to Jesus, 'Teacher, this woman was caught in the very act of committing adultery. Now in the law Moses commanded us to stone such women. Now what do you say?' They said this to test Jesus, so that they might have some charge to bring against him. Jesus bent down and wrote with his finger on the ground. When they kept on questioning him, he straightened up and said to them, 'Let anyone among you who is without sin be the first to throw a stone at her.' And once again he bent down and wrote on the ground. When they heard it, they went away, one by one, beginning with the elders; and Jesus was left alone with the woman standing before him. Jesus straightened up and said to her, 'Woman, where are they? Has no one condemned you?' She said, 'No one, sir.' And Jesus said, 'Neither do I condemn you. Go your way, and from now on do not sin again.'

LENT 1 YEAR A

FIRST READING Genesis 2.15–17; 3.1–7

A reading from the book of Genesis.

The LORD God took the man and put him in the garden of Eden to till it and keep it. And the LORD God commanded the man, 'You may freely eat of every tree of the garden; but of the tree of the knowledge of good and evil you shall not eat, for in the day that you eat of it you shall die.'

Now the serpent was more crafty than any other wild animal that the LORD God had made. He said to the woman, 'Did God say, "You shall not eat from any tree in the garden"?' The woman said to the serpent, 'We may eat of the fruit of the trees in the garden; but God said, "You shall not eat of the fruit of the tree that is in the middle of the garden, nor shall you touch it, or you shall die."' But the serpent said to the woman, 'You will not die; for God knows that when you eat of it your eyes will be opened, and you will be like God, knowing good and evil.' So when the woman saw that the tree was good for food, and that it was a delight to the eyes, and that the tree was to be desired to make one wise, she took of its fruit and ate; and she also gave some to her husband, who was with her, and he ate. Then the eyes of both were opened, and they knew that they were naked; and they sewed fig leaves together and made loincloths for themselves.

PSALM Psalm 32

℞ **I will confess my transgressions to the Lord.**

Happy are they whose transgressions are forgiven,
and whose sin is put away!
Happy are they to whom the Lord imputes no guilt,
and in whose spirit there is no guile! ℞

While I held my tongue, my bones withered away,
because of my groaning all day long.
For your hand was heavy upon me day and night;
my moisture was dried up as in the heat of summer. ℞

Then I acknowledged my sin to you,
and did not conceal my guilt.
I said, 'I will confess my transgressions to the Lord';
then you forgave me the guilt of my sin. ℟

Therefore all the faithful will make their prayers to you
in time of trouble;
when the great waters overflow, they shall not reach them.
You are my hiding-place;
you preserve me from trouble;
you surround me with shouts of deliverance. ℟

'I will instruct you and teach you
in the way that you should go;
I will guide you with my eye.
Do not be like horse or mule,
which have no understanding;
who must be fitted with bit and bridle,
or else they will not stay near you.' ℟

Great are the tribulations of the wicked;
but mercy embraces those who trust in the Lord.
Be glad, you righteous, and rejoice in the Lord;
shout for joy, all who are true of heart. ℟

SECOND READING   Romans 5.12–19

A reading from the letter of Paul to the Romans.

Just as sin came into the world through one man, and death came through
sin, and so death spread to all because all have sinned – sin was indeed in the
world before the law, but sin is not reckoned when there is no law. Yet death
exercised dominion from Adam to Moses, even over those whose sins were
not like the transgression of Adam, who is a type of the one who was to
come.

But the free gift is not like the trespass. For if the many died through the one
man's trespass, much more surely have the grace of God and the free gift in
the grace of the one man, Jesus Christ, abounded for the many. And the free
gift is not like the effect of the one man's sin. For the judgement following
one trespass brought condemnation but the free gift following many
trespasses brings justification. If, because of the one man's trespass, death
exercised dominion through that one, much more surely will those who

receive the abundance of grace and the free gift of righteousness exercise dominion in life through the one man, Jesus Christ.

Therefore just as one man's trespass led to condemnation for all, so the act of righteousness of one leads to justification and life for all. For just as by the one person's disobedience the many were made sinners, so by the one man's obedience the many will be made righteous.

GOSPEL   Matthew 4.1–11

Hear the gospel of our Lord Jesus Christ according to Matthew.

Jesus was led up by the Spirit into the wilderness to be tempted by the devil. He fasted forty days and forty nights, and afterwards he was famished. The tempter came and said to him, 'If you are the Son of God, command these stones to become loaves of bread.'
But he answered, 'It is written,
"One does not live by bread alone,
but by every word that comes from the mouth of God."'
Then the devil took him to the holy city and placed him on the pinnacle of the temple, saying to him, 'If you are the Son of God, throw yourself down; for it is written,
"He will command his angels concerning you,"
and "On their hands they will bear you up,
so that you will not dash your foot against a stone."'
Jesus said to him, 'Again it is written, "Do not put the Lord your God to the test."' Again, the devil took him to a very high mountain and showed him all the kingdoms of the world and their splendour; and he said to him, 'All these I will give you, if you will fall down and worship me.' Jesus said to him, 'Away with you, Satan! for it is written,
"Worship the Lord your God,
and serve only him."'
Then the devil left him, and suddenly angels came and waited on him.

LENT 2   YEAR A

FIRST READING   Genesis 12.1–4a

A reading from the book of Genesis.

The LORD said to Abram, 'Go from your country and your kindred and your father's house to the land that I will show you. I will make of you a great nation, and I will bless you, and make your name great, so that you will be a blessing. I will bless those who bless you, and the one who curses you I will curse; and in you all the families of the earth shall be blessed.'

So Abram went, as the LORD had told him; and Lot went with him.

PSALM   Psalm 121

℟ My help comes from the Lord,
[the maker of heaven and earth].

¹I lift up my eyes to the hills;
from where is my help to come?
²My help comes from the Lord,
the maker of heaven and earth. ℟

He will not let your foot be moved
and he who watches over you will not fall asleep.
Behold, he who keeps watch over Israel
shall neither slumber nor sleep; ℟

The Lord himself watches over you;
the Lord is your shade at your right hand,
So that the sun shall not strike you by day,
nor the moon by night. ℟

The Lord shall preserve you from all evil;
it is he who shall keep you safe.
The Lord shall watch over your going out
and your coming in,
from this time forth for evermore. ℟

SECOND READING   Romans 4.1–5, 13–17

A reading from the letter of Paul to the Romans.

What are we to say was gained by Abraham, our ancestor according to the flesh? For if Abraham was justified by works, he has something to boast about, but not before God. For what does the scripture say? 'Abraham believed God, and it was reckoned to him as righteousness.' Now to one who works, wages are not reckoned as a gift but as something due. But to one who without works trusts him who justifies the ungodly, such faith is reckoned as righteousness.

For the promise that he would inherit the world did not come to Abraham or to his descendants through the law but through the righteousness of faith. If it is the adherents of the law who are to be the heirs, faith is null and the promise is void. For the law brings wrath; but where there is no law, neither is there violation.

For this reason it depends on faith, in order that the promise may rest on grace and be guaranteed to all his descendants, not only to the adherents of the law but also to those who share the faith of Abraham (for he is the father of all of us, as it is written, 'I have made you the father of many nations') – Abraham believed in the presence of the God who gives life to the dead and calls into existence the things that do not exist.

GOSPEL

The Revised Common Lectionary provides alternative Gospel readings. Church of England provision allows only the first of these (John 3.1–17).

Either   **John 3.1-17**

Hear the gospel of our Lord Jesus Christ according to John.

There was a Pharisee named Nicodemus, a leader of the Jews. He came to Jesus by night and said to him, 'Rabbi, we know that you are a teacher who has come from God; for no one can do these signs that you do apart from the presence of God.' Jesus answered him, 'Very truly, I tell you, no one can see the kingdom of God without being born from above.' Nicodemus said to him, 'How can anyone be born after having grown old? Can one enter a second time into the mother's womb and be born?' Jesus answered, 'Very truly, I tell you, no one can enter the kingdom of God without being born of water and Spirit. What is born of the flesh is flesh, and what is born of the Spirit is spirit. Do not be astonished that I said to you, "You must be born from above." The wind blows where it chooses, and you hear the sound of it, but you do not know where it comes from or where it goes. So it is with everyone who is born of the Spirit.' Nicodemus said to him, 'How can these things be?' Jesus answered him, 'Are you a teacher of Israel, and yet you do not understand these things?

Very truly, I tell you, we speak of what we know and testify to what we have seen; yet you do not receive our testimony. If I have told you about earthly things and you do not believe, how can you believe if I tell you about heavenly things? No one has ascended into heaven except the one who descended from heaven, the Son of Man. And just as Moses lifted up the serpent in the wilderness, so must the Son of Man be lifted up, that whoever believes in him may have eternal life.

For God so loved the world that he gave his only Son, so that everyone who believes in him may not perish but may have eternal life.

Indeed, God did not send the Son into the world to condemn the world, but in order that the world might be saved through him.'

Or (Revised Common Lectionary only)   Matthew 17.1–9

Hear the gospel of our Lord Jesus Christ according to Matthew.

Jesus took with him Peter and James and his brother John and led them up a high mountain, by themselves. And he was transfigured before them, and his face shone like the sun, and his clothes became dazzling white. Suddenly there appeared to them Moses and Elijah, talking with him. Then Peter said to Jesus, 'Lord, it is good for us to be here; if you wish, I will make three dwellings here, one for you, one for Moses, and one for Elijah.' While he was still speaking, suddenly a bright cloud overshadowed them, and from the cloud a voice said, 'This is my Son, the Beloved; with him I am well pleased; listen to him!' When the disciples heard this, they fell to the ground and were overcome by fear. But Jesus came and touched them, saying, 'Get up and do not be afraid.' And when they looked up, they saw no one except Jesus himself alone.

As they were coming down the mountain, Jesus ordered them, 'Tell no one about the vision until after the Son of Man has been raised from the dead.'

LENT 3   YEAR A

FIRST READING   Exodus 17.1–7

A reading from the book of Exodus.

From the wilderness of Sin the whole congregation of the Israelites journeyed by stages, as the LORD commanded. They camped at Rephidim, but there was no water for the people to drink. The people quarrelled with Moses, and said, 'Give us water to drink.' Moses said to them, 'Why do you quarrel with me? Why do you test the LORD?' But the people thirsted there for water; and the people complained against Moses and said, 'Why did you bring us out of Egypt, to kill us and our children and livestock with thirst?' So Moses cried out to the LORD, 'What shall I do with this people? They are almost ready to stone me.' The LORD said to Moses, 'Go on ahead of the people, and take some of the elders of Israel with you; take in your hand the staff with which you struck the Nile, and go. I will be standing there in front of you on the rock at Horeb. Strike the rock, and water will come out of it, so that the people may drink.' Moses did so, in the sight of the elders of Israel. He called the place Massah and Meribah, because the Israelites quarrelled and tested the LORD, saying, 'Is the LORD among us or not?'

PSALM   Psalm 95

℟ O that today you would hearken to his voice!
   Harden not your hearts.

Come, let us sing to the Lord;
let us shout for joy to the rock of our salvation.
Let us come before his presence with thanksgiving
and raise a loud shout to him with psalms.
For the Lord is a great God,
and a great king above all gods. ℟

In his hand are the depths of the earth,
and the heights of the hills are his also.
The sea is his, for he made it,
and his hands have moulded the dry land. ℟

Come, let us bow down and bend the knee,
and kneel before the Lord our Maker.
For he is our God,
and we are the people of his pasture
and the sheep of his hand.
O that today you would hearken to his voice! ℟

'Harden not your hearts,
as your forebears did in the wilderness,
at Meribah, and on that day at Massah,
when they tempted me.
They put me to the test,
though they had seen my works. ℟

Forty years long I detested that generation and said,
"This people are wayward in their hearts;
they do not know my ways."
So I swore in my wrath,
"They shall not enter into my rest."' ℟

SECOND READING   **Romans 5.1–11**

A reading from the letter of Paul to the Romans.

Since we are justified by faith, we have peace with God through our Lord
Jesus Christ, through whom we have obtained access to this grace in which
we stand; and we boast in our hope of sharing the glory of God. And not
only that, but we also boast in our sufferings, knowing that suffering
produces endurance, and endurance produces character, and character
produces hope, and hope does not disappoint us, because God's love has
been poured into our hearts through the Holy Spirit that has been given to us.

For while we were still weak, at the right time Christ died for the ungodly.
Indeed, rarely will anyone die for a righteous person – though perhaps for a
good person someone might actually dare to die. But God proves his love for
us in that while we still were sinners Christ died for us. Much more surely
then, now that we have been justified by his blood, will we be saved through
him from the wrath of God. For if while we were enemies, we were
reconciled to God through the death of his Son, much more surely, having
been reconciled, will we be saved by his life. But more than that, we even
boast in God through our Lord Jesus Christ, through whom we have now
received reconciliation.

GOSPEL   **John 4.5–42**

Hear the gospel of our Lord Jesus Christ according to John.

Jesus came to a Samaritan city called Sychar, near the plot of ground that
Jacob had given to his son Joseph. Jacob's well was there, and Jesus, tired out
by his journey, was sitting by the well. It was about noon.

A Samaritan woman came to draw water, and Jesus said to her, 'Give me a
drink.' (His disciples had gone to the city to buy food.) The Samaritan
woman said to him, 'How is it that you, a Jew, ask a drink of me, a woman of
Samaria?' (Jews do not share things in common with Samaritans.) Jesus
answered her, 'If you knew the gift of God, and who it is that is saying to
you, "Give me a drink," you would have asked him, and he would have
given you living water.' The woman said to him, 'Sir, you have no bucket,
and the well is deep. Where do you get that living water? Are you greater
than our ancestor Jacob, who gave us the well, and with his sons and his
flocks drank from it?' Jesus said to her, 'Everyone who drinks of this water
will be thirsty again, but those who drink of the water that I will give them
will never be thirsty. The water that I will give will become in them a spring
of water gushing up to eternal life.' The woman said to him, 'Sir, give me

this water, so that I may never be thirsty or have to keep coming here to draw water.'

Jesus said to her, 'Go, call your husband, and come back.' The woman answered him, 'I have no husband.' Jesus said to her, 'You are right in saying, "I have no husband"; for you have had five husbands, and the one you have now is not your husband. What you have said is true!' The woman said to him, 'Sir, I see that you are a prophet. Our ancestors worshipped on this mountain, but you say that the place where people must worship is in Jerusalem.' Jesus said to her, 'Woman, believe me, the hour is coming when you will worship the Father neither on this mountain nor in Jerusalem. You worship what you do not know; we worship what we know, for salvation is from the Jews. But the hour is coming, and is now here, when the true worshippers will worship the Father in spirit and truth, for the Father seeks such as these to worship him. God is spirit, and those who worship him must worship in spirit and truth.' The woman said to him, 'I know that Messiah is coming' (who is called Christ). 'When he comes, he will proclaim all things to us.' Jesus said to her, 'I am he, the one who is speaking to you.'

Just then his disciples came. They were astonished that he was speaking with a woman, but no one said, 'What do you want?' or, 'Why are you speaking with her?' Then the woman left her water-jar and went back to the city. She said to the people, 'Come and see a man who told me everything I have ever done! He cannot be the Messiah, can he?' They left the city and were on their way to him.

Meanwhile the disciples were urging him, 'Rabbi, eat something.' But he said to them, 'I have food to eat that you do not know about.' So the disciples said to one another, 'Surely no one has brought him something to eat?' Jesus said to them, 'My food is to do the will of him who sent me and to complete his work. Do you not say, "Four months more, then comes the harvest"? But I tell you, look around you, and see how the fields are ripe for harvesting. The reaper is already receiving wages and is gathering fruit for eternal life, so that sower and reaper may rejoice together. For here the saying holds true, "One sows and another reaps." I sent you to reap that for which you did not labour. Others have laboured, and you have entered into their labour.'

Many Samaritans from that city believed in Jesus because of the woman's testimony, 'He told me everything I have ever done.' So when the Samaritans came to him, they asked him to stay with them; and he stayed there for two days. And many more believed because of his word. They said to the woman, 'It is no longer because of what you said that we believe, for we have heard for ourselves, and we know that this is truly the Saviour of the world.'

LENT 4   YEAR A

Provision for Lent 4 is included in the Revised Common Lectionary and the Church of England provision, but the Church of England adds alternative readings for Mothering Sunday (see pages 88–92).

FIRST READING   1 Samuel 16.1–13

A reading from the first book of Samuel.

The LORD said to Samuel, 'How long will you grieve over Saul? I have rejected him from being king over Israel. Fill your horn with oil and set out; I will send you to Jesse the Bethlehemite, for I have provided for myself a king among his sons.' Samuel said, 'How can I go? If Saul hears of it, he will kill me.' And the LORD said, 'Take a heifer with you, and say, "I have come to sacrifice to the LORD." Invite Jesse to the sacrifice, and I will show you what you shall do; and you shall anoint for me the one whom I name to you.' Samuel did what the LORD commanded, and came to Bethlehem. The elders of the city came to meet him trembling, and said, 'Do you come peaceably?' He said, 'Peaceably; I have come to sacrifice to the LORD; sanctify yourselves and come with me to the sacrifice.' And he sanctified Jesse and his sons and invited them to the sacrifice.

When they came, he looked on Eliab and thought, 'Surely the Lord's anointed is now before the LORD.' But the LORD said to Samuel, 'Do not look on his appearance or on the height of his stature, because I have rejected him; for the LORD does not see as mortals see; they look on the outward appearance, but the LORD looks on the heart.' Then Jesse called Abinadab, and made him pass before Samuel. He said, 'Neither has the LORD chosen this one.' Then Jesse made Shammah pass by. And he said, 'Neither has the LORD chosen this one.' Jesse made seven of his sons pass before Samuel, and Samuel said to Jesse, 'The LORD has not chosen any of these.' Samuel said to Jesse, 'Are all your sons here?' And he said, 'There remains yet the youngest, but he is keeping the sheep.' And Samuel said to Jesse, 'Send and bring him; for we will not sit down until he comes here.' He sent and brought David in. Now he was ruddy, and had beautiful eyes, and was handsome. The LORD said, 'Rise and anoint him; for this is the one.' Then Samuel took the horn of oil, and anointed him in the presence of his brothers; and the spirit of the LORD came mightily upon David from that day forward. Samuel then set out and went to Ramah.

PSALM

℟ **The Lord is my shepherd,
I shall not be in want.**

The Lord is my shepherd;
I shall not be in want.
He makes me lie down in green pastures
and leads me beside still waters. ℟

He revives my soul
and guides me along right pathways for his name's sake.
Though I walk through the valley of the shadow of death,
I shall fear no evil;
for you are with me;
your rod and your staff, they comfort me. ℟

You spread a table before me
in the presence of those who trouble me;
you have anointed my head with oil,
and my cup is running over.
Surely your goodness and mercy shall follow me
all the days of my life,
and I will dwell in the house of the Lord for ever. ℟

SECOND READING

A reading from the letter of Paul to the Ephesians.

Once you were darkness, but now in the Lord you are light. Live as children of light – for the fruit of the light is found in all that is good and right and true. Try to find out what is pleasing to the Lord. Take no part in the unfruitful works of darkness, but instead expose them. For it is shameful even to mention what such people do secretly; but everything exposed by the light becomes visible, for everything that becomes visible is light.
Therefore it says,
'Sleeper, awake!
Rise from the dead, and Christ will shine on you.'

GOSPEL   **John 9.1–41**

Hear the gospel of our Lord Jesus Christ according to John.

As Jesus walked along, he saw a man blind from birth. His disciples asked
him, 'Rabbi, who sinned, this man or his parents, that he was born blind?'
Jesus answered, 'Neither this man nor his parents sinned; he was born blind
so that God's works might be revealed in him. We must work the works of
him who sent me while it is day; night is coming when no one can work. As
long as I am in the world, I am the light of the world.' When he had said
this, he spat on the ground and made mud with the saliva and spread the
mud on the man's eyes, saying to him, 'Go, wash in the pool of Siloam'
(which means Sent). Then he went and washed and came back able to see.
The neighbours and those who had seen him before as a beggar began to ask,
'Is this not the man who used to sit and beg?' Some were saying, 'It is he.'
Others were saying, 'No, but it is someone like him.' He kept saying, 'I am
the man.' But they kept asking him, 'Then how were your eyes opened?' He
answered, 'The man called Jesus made mud, spread it on my eyes, and said to
me, "Go to Siloam and wash." Then I went and washed and received my
sight.' They said to him, 'Where is he?' He said, 'I do not know.'

They brought to the Pharisees the man who had formerly been blind. Now it
was a sabbath day when Jesus made the mud and opened his eyes. Then the
Pharisees also began to ask him how he had received his sight. He said to
them, 'He put mud on my eyes. Then I washed, and now I see.' Some of the
Pharisees said, 'This man is not from God, for he does not observe the
sabbath.' But others said, 'How can a man who is a sinner perform such
signs?' And they were divided. So they said again to the blind man, 'What do
you say about him? It was your eyes he opened.' He said, 'He is a prophet.'

The Jews did not believe that he had been blind and had received his sight
until they called the parents of the man who had received his sight and asked
them, 'Is this your son, who you say was born blind? How then does he now
see?' His parents answered, 'We know that this is our son, and that he was
born blind; but we do not know how it is that now he sees, nor do we know
who opened his eyes. Ask him; he is of age. He will speak for himself.' His
parents said this because they were afraid of the Jews; for the Jews had
already agreed that anyone who confessed Jesus to be the Messiah would be
put out of the synagogue. Therefore his parents said, 'He is of age; ask him.'

So for the second time they called the man who had been blind, and they
said to him, 'Give glory to God! We know that this man is a sinner.' He

answered, 'I do not know whether he is a sinner. One thing I do know, that though I was blind, now I see.' They said to him, 'What did he do to you? How did he open your eyes?' He answered them, 'I have told you already, and you would not listen. Why do you want to hear it again? Do you also want to become his disciples?' Then they reviled him, saying, 'You are his disciple, but we are disciples of Moses. We know that God has spoken to Moses, but as for this man, we do not know where he comes from.' The man answered, 'Here is an astonishing thing! You do not know where he comes from, and yet he opened my eyes. We know that God does not listen to sinners, but he does listen to one who worships him and obeys his will. Never since the world began has it been heard that anyone opened the eyes of a person born blind. If this man were not from God, he could do nothing.' They answered him, 'You were born entirely in sins, and are you trying to teach us?' And they drove him out.

Jesus heard that they had driven him out, and when he found him, he said, 'Do you believe in the Son of Man?' He answered, 'And who is he, sir? Tell me, so that I may believe in him.' Jesus said to him, 'You have seen him, and the one speaking with you is he.' He said, 'Lord, I believe.' And he worshipped him. Jesus said, 'I came into this world for judgement so that those who do not see may see, and those who do see may become blind.' Some of the Pharisees near him heard this and said to him, 'Surely we are not blind, are we?' Jesus said to them, 'If you were blind, you would not have sin. But now that you say, "We see," your sin remains.'

Or

† MOTHERING SUNDAY   YEARS A B C

FIRST READING (Alternative readings)

Either   **Exodus 2.1–10**

A reading from the book of Exodus.

A man from the house of Levi went and married a Levite woman. The woman conceived and bore a son; and when she saw that he was a fine baby, she hid him for three months. When she could hide him no longer she got a papyrus basket for him, and plastered it with bitumen and pitch; she put the child in it and placed it among the reeds on the bank of the river. His sister stood at a distance, to see what would happen to him.

The daughter of Pharaoh came down to bathe at the river, while her attendants walked beside the river. She saw the basket among the reeds and sent her maid to bring it. When she opened it, she saw the child. He was crying, and she took pity on him, 'This must be one of the Hebrews' children,' she said. Then his sister said to Pharaoh's daughter, 'Shall I go and get you a nurse from the Hebrew women to nurse the child for you?' Pharaoh's daughter said to her, 'Yes.' So the girl went and called the child's mother. Pharaoh's daughter said to her, 'Take this child and nurse it for me, and I will give you your wages.' So the woman took the child and nursed it. When the child grew up, she brought him to Pharaoh's daughter, and she took him as her son. She named him Moses, 'because,' she said, 'I drew him out of the water.'

Or   **1 Samuel 1.20–28**

A reading from the first book of Samuel.

Hannah conceived and bore a son. She named him Samuel, for she said, 'I have asked him of the LORD.'

The man Elkanah and all his household went up to offer to the LORD the yearly sacrifice, and to pay his vow. But Hannah did not go up, for she said to her husband, 'As soon as the child is weaned, I will bring him, that he may appear in the presence of the LORD, and remain there for ever; I will offer him as a nazirite for all time.' Her husband Elkanah said to her, 'Do what seems best to you, wait until you have weaned him; only – may the LORD establish his word.' So the woman remained and nursed her son, until she weaned him. When she had weaned him, she took him up with her, along with a three-year-old bull, an ephah of flour, and a skin of wine. She brought him to the house of the LORD at Shiloh; and the child was young. Then they slaughtered the bull, and they brought the child to Eli. And she said, 'Oh, my lord! As you live, my lord, I am the woman who was standing here in your presence, praying to the LORD. For this child I prayed; and the LORD has granted me the petition that I made to him. Therefore I have lent him to the LORD; as long as he lives, he is given to the LORD.' She left him there for the LORD.

PSALM

Either   **Psalm 34.11–20**

℟ **[Come, children, and listen to me:]**
  I will teach you the fear of the Lord.

Come, children, and listen to me;
I will teach you the fear of the Lord.
Who among you loves life
and desires long life to enjoy prosperity? ℟

Keep your tongue from evil-speaking
and your lips from lying words.
Turn from evil and do good;
seek peace and pursue it. ℟

The eyes of the Lord are upon the righteous,
and his ears are open to their cry.
The face of the Lord is against those who do evil,
to root out the remembrance of them from the earth. ℟

The righteous cry and the Lord hears them
and delivers them from all their troubles.
The Lord is near to the brokenhearted
and will save those whose spirits are crushed. ℟

Many are the troubles of the righteous,
but the Lord will deliver him out of them all.
He will keep safe all his bones;
not one of them shall be broken. ℟

Or   **Psalm 127.1–4**

℟ **It is the Lord who builds the house.**

Unless the Lord builds the house,
their labour is in vain who build it.
Unless the Lord watches over the city,
in vain the guard keeps vigil. ℟

It is in vain that you rise so early
and go to bed so late;
vain, too, to eat the bread of toil,
for he gives to his belovèd sleep.
Children are a heritage from the Lord,
and the fruit of the womb is a gift. ℟

SECOND READING (Alternative readings)

Either   **2 Corinthians 1.3–7**

A reading from the second letter of Paul to the Corinthians.

Blessed be the God and Father of our Lord Jesus Christ, the Father of mercies
and the God of all consolation, who consoles us in all our affliction, so that
we may be able to console those who are in any affliction with the
consolation with which we ourselves are consoled by God. For just as the
sufferings of Christ are abundant for us, so also our consolation is abundant
through Christ. If we are being afflicted, it is for your consolation and
salvation; if we are being consoled, it is for your consolation, which you
experience when you patiently endure the same sufferings that we are also
suffering. Our hope for you is unshaken; for we know that as you share in
our sufferings, so also you share in our consolation.

Or   **Colossians 3.12–17**

A reading from the letter of Paul to the Colossians.

As God's chosen ones, holy and beloved, clothe yourselves with compassion,
kindness, humility, meekness, and patience. Bear with one another and, if
anyone has a complaint against another, forgive each other; just as the Lord
has forgiven you, so you also must forgive. Above all, clothe yourselves with
love, which binds everything together in perfect harmony. And let the peace
of Christ rule in your hearts, to which indeed you were called in the one
body. And be thankful. Let the word of Christ dwell in you richly; teach and
admonish one another in all wisdom; and with gratitude in your hearts sing
psalms, hymns, and spiritual songs to God. And whatever you do, in word or
deed, do everything in the name of the Lord Jesus, giving thanks to God the
Father through him.

GOSPEL (Alternative readings)

Either   Luke 2.33–35

Hear the gospel of our Lord Jesus Christ according to Luke.

The child's father and mother were amazed at what was being said about
Jesus. Then Simeon blessed them and said to his mother Mary, 'This child is
destined for the falling and the rising of many in Israel, and to be a sign that
will be opposed so that the inner thoughts of many will be revealed – and a
sword will pierce your own soul too.'

Or   John 19.25b–27

Hear the gospel of our Lord Jesus Christ according to John.

Standing near the cross of Jesus were his mother, and his mother's sister,
Mary the wife of Clopas, and Mary Magdalene. When Jesus saw his mother
and the disciple whom he loved standing beside her, he said to his mother,
'Woman, here is your son.' Then he said to the disciple, 'Here is your
mother.' And from that hour the disciple took her into his own home.

LENT 5   YEAR A

FIRST READING   Ezekiel 37.1–14

A reading from the book of the prophet Ezekiel.

The hand of the LORD came upon me, and he brought me out by the spirit
of the LORD and set me down in the middle of a valley; it was full of bones.
He led me all around them; there were very many lying in the valley, and
they were very dry. He said to me, 'Mortal, can these bones live?' I answered,
'O Lord GOD, you know.' Then he said to me, 'Prophesy to these bones, and
say to them: O dry bones, hear the word of the LORD. Thus says the Lord
GOD to these bones: I will cause breath to enter you, and you shall live. I will
lay sinews on you, and will cause flesh to come upon you, and cover you
with skin, and put breath in you, and you shall live; and you shall know that
I am the LORD.'

So I prophesied as I had been commanded; and as I prophesied, suddenly
there was a noise, a rattling, and the bones came together, bone to its bone. I
looked, and there were sinews on them, and flesh had come upon them, and

skin had covered them; but there was no breath in them. Then he said to me, 'Prophesy to the breath, prophesy, mortal, and say to the breath: Thus says the Lord GOD: Come from the four winds, O breath, and breathe upon these slain, that they may live.' I prophesied as he commanded me, and the breath came into them, and they lived, and stood on their feet, a vast multitude.

Then he said to me, 'Mortal, these bones are the whole house of Israel. They say, "Our bones are dried up, and our hope is lost; we are cut off completely." Therefore prophesy, and say to them, Thus says the Lord GOD: I am going to open your graves, and bring you up from your graves, O my people; and I will bring you back to the land of Israel. And you shall know that I am the LORD, when I open your graves, and bring you up from your graves, O my people. I will put my spirit within you, and you shall live, and I will place you on your own soil; then you shall know that I, the LORD, have spoken and will act, says the LORD.'

PSALM   Psalm 130

℟ **With the Lord there is mercy
and plenteous redemption.**
or
℟ **You shall know that I am the Lord
when I open your graves.**

Out of the depths have I called to you, O Lord;
Lord, hear my voice;
let your ears consider well the voice of my supplication.
If you, Lord, were to note what is done amiss,
O Lord, who could stand?
For there is forgiveness with you;
therefore you shall be feared. ℟

I wait for the Lord; my soul waits for him;
in his word is my hope.
My soul waits for the Lord,
more than the night-watch for the morning,
more than the night-watch for the morning. ℟

O Israel, wait for the Lord,
for with the Lord there is mercy;
With him there is plenteous redemption,
and he shall redeem Israel from all their sins. ℟

SECOND READING   Romans 8.6-11

A reading from the letter of Paul to the Romans.

To set the mind on the flesh is death, but to set the mind on the Spirit is life and peace. For this reason the mind that is set on the flesh is hostile to God; it does not submit to God's law – indeed it cannot, and those who are in the flesh cannot please God.

But you are not in the flesh; you are in the Spirit, since the Spirit of God dwells in you. Anyone who does not have the Spirit of Christ does not belong to him. But if Christ is in you, though the body is dead because of sin, the Spirit is life because of righteousness. If the Spirit of him who raised Jesus from the dead dwells in you, he who raised Christ from the dead will give life to your mortal bodies also through his Spirit that dwells in you.

GOSPEL   John 11.1-45

Hear the gospel of our Lord Jesus Christ according to John.

A certain man was ill, Lazarus of Bethany, the village of Mary and her sister Martha. Mary was the one who anointed the Lord with perfume and wiped his feet with her hair; her brother Lazarus was ill. So the sisters sent a message to Jesus, 'Lord, he whom you love is ill.' But when Jesus heard it, he said, 'This illness does not lead to death; rather it is for God's glory, so that the Son of God may be glorified through it.' Accordingly, though Jesus loved Martha and her sister and Lazarus, after having heard that Lazarus was ill, he stayed two days longer in the place where he was.

Then after this he said to the disciples, 'Let us go to Judea again.' The disciples said to him, 'Rabbi, the Jews were just now trying to stone you, and are you going there again?' Jesus answered, 'Are there not twelve hours of daylight? Those who walk during the day do not stumble, because they see the light of this world. But those who walk at night stumble, because the light is not in them.' After saying this, he told them, 'Our friend Lazarus has fallen asleep, but I am going there to awaken him.' The disciples said to him, 'Lord, if he has fallen asleep, he will be all right.' Jesus, however, had been speaking about his death, but they thought that he was referring merely to sleep. Then Jesus told them plainly, 'Lazarus is dead. For your sake I am glad I was not there, so that you may believe. But let us go to him.' Thomas, who was called the Twin, said to his fellow-disciples, 'Let us also go, that we may die with him.'

When Jesus arrived, he found that Lazarus had already been in the tomb four days. Now Bethany was near Jerusalem, some two miles away, and many of the Jews had come to Martha and Mary to console them about their brother. When Martha heard that Jesus was coming, she went and met him, while Mary stayed at home. Martha said to Jesus, 'Lord, if you had been here, my brother would not have died. But even now I know that God will give you whatever you ask of him.' Jesus said to her, 'Your brother will rise again.' Martha said to him, 'I know that he will rise again in the resurrection on the last day.' Jesus said to her, 'I am the resurrection and the life. Those who believe in me, even though they die, will live, and everyone who lives and believes in me will never die. Do you believe this?' She said to him, 'Yes, Lord, I believe that you are the Messiah, the Son of God, the one coming into the world.'

When she had said this, she went back and called her sister Mary, and told her privately, 'The Teacher is here and is calling for you.' And when she heard it, she got up quickly and went to him. Now Jesus had not yet come to the village, but was still at the place where Martha had met him. The Jews who were with her in the house, consoling her, saw Mary get up quickly and go out. They followed her because they thought that she was going to the tomb to weep there. When Mary came where Jesus was and saw him, she knelt at his feet and said to him, 'Lord, if you had been here, my brother would not have died.' When Jesus saw her weeping, and the Jews who came with her also weeping, he was greatly disturbed in spirit and deeply moved. He said, 'Where have you laid him?' They said to him, 'Lord, come and see.' Jesus began to weep. So the Jews said, 'See how he loved him!' But some of them said, 'Could not he who opened the eyes of the blind man have kept this man from dying?'

Then Jesus, again greatly disturbed, came to the tomb. It was a cave, and a stone was lying against it. Jesus said, 'Take away the stone.' Martha, the sister of the dead man, said to him, 'Lord, already there is a stench because he has been dead four days.' Jesus said to her, 'Did I not tell you that if you believed, you would see the glory of God?' So they took away the stone. And Jesus looked upwards and said, 'Father, I thank you for having heard me. I knew that you always hear me, but I have said this for the sake of the crowd standing here, so that they may believe that you sent me.' When he had said this, he cried with a loud voice, 'Lazarus, come out!' The dead man came out, his hands and feet bound with strips of cloth, and his face wrapped in a cloth. Jesus said to them, 'Unbind him, and let him go.'

Many of the Jews therefore, who had come with Mary and had seen what Jesus did, believed in him.

PALM SUNDAY (LENT 6)   YEAR A

LITURGY OF PALMS

GOSPEL   Matthew 21.1–11

Hear the gospel of our Lord Jesus Christ according to Matthew.

When they had come near Jerusalem and had reached Bethphage, at the
Mount of Olives, Jesus sent two disciples, saying to them, 'Go into the village
ahead of you, and immediately you will find a donkey tied, and a colt with
her; untie them and bring them to me. If anyone says anything to you, just
say this, "The Lord needs them." And he will send them immediately.' This
took place to fulfil what had been spoken through the prophet, saying,
'Tell the daughter of Zion,
Look, your king is coming to you,
humble, and mounted on a donkey,
and on a colt, the foal of a donkey.'
The disciples went and did as Jesus had directed them; they brought the
donkey and the colt, and put their cloaks on them, and he sat on them. A
very large crowd spread their cloaks on the road, and others cut branches
from the trees and spread them on the road. The crowds that went ahead of
him and that followed were shouting, 'Hosanna to the Son of David! Blessed
is the one who comes in the name of the Lord! Hosanna in the highest
heaven!' When he entered Jerusalem, the whole city was in turmoil, asking,
'Who is this?' The crowds were saying, 'This is the prophet Jesus from
Nazareth in Galilee.'

PSALM   Psalm 118.1–2, 19–29

℟ **This is the day that the Lord has made.**
  We will rejoice and be glad in it.

Give thanks to the Lord, for he is good;
his mercy endures for ever.
Let Israel now proclaim,
'His mercy endures for ever.' ℟

Open for me the gates of righteousness;
I will enter them; I will offer thanks to the Lord.
'This is the gate of the Lord;
whoever is righteous may enter.' ℟

I will give thanks to you, for you answered me
and have become my salvation.
The same stone which the builders rejected
has become the chief corner-stone. ℟

This is the Lord's doing,
and it is marvellous in our eyes.
On this day the Lord has acted;
we will rejoice and be glad in it. ℟

Hosanna, Lord, hosanna!
Lord, send us now success.
Blessèd is he who comes in the name of the Lord;
we bless you from the house of the Lord. ℟

God is the Lord; he has shined upon us;
form a procession with branches
up to the horns of the altar.
'You are my God and I will thank you;
you are my God and I will exalt you.'
Give thanks to the Lord, for he is good;
his mercy endures for ever. ℟

LITURGY OF THE PASSION

FIRST READING   Isaiah 50.4–9a

A reading from the book of the prophet Isaiah.

The servant of the LORD said:
The Lord GOD has given me the tongue of a teacher,
that I may know how to sustain the weary with a word.
Morning by morning he wakens –
wakens my ear to listen as those who are taught.
The Lord GOD has opened my ear,
and I was not rebellious,
I did not turn backwards.
I gave my back to those who struck me,
and my cheeks to those who pulled out the beard;
I did not hide my face
from insult and spitting.

The Lord GOD helps me;
therefore I have not been disgraced;

therefore I have set my face like flint,
and I know that I shall not be put to shame;
he who vindicates me is near.
Who will contend with me?
Let us stand up together.
Who are my adversaries?
Let them confront me.
It is the Lord GOD who helps me;
who will declare me guilty?

PSALM

Psalm 31.9–16

℟ **My God, my God, why have you forsaken me?**
or
℟ **I have trusted in you.**
You are my God.

Have mercy on me, O Lord, for I am in trouble;
my eye is consumed with sorrow,
and also my throat and my belly.
For my life is wasted with grief,
and my years with sighing;
my strength fails me because of affliction,
and my bones are consumed. ℟

I have become a reproach to all my enemies
and even to my neighbours,
a dismay to those of my acquaintance;
when they see me in the street they avoid me.
I am forgotten like the dead, out of mind;
I am as useless as a broken pot. ℟

For I have heard the whispering of the crowd;
fear is all around;
they put their heads together against me;
they plot to take my life.
But as for me, I have trusted in you, O Lord.
I have said, 'You are my God.
My times are in your hand;
rescue me from the hand of my enemies,
and from those who persecute me.
Make your face to shine upon your servant,
and in your loving-kindness save me.' ℟

SECOND READING   Philippians 2.5–11

A reading from the letter of Paul to the Philippians.

Let the same mind be in you that was in Christ Jesus,
who, though he was in the form of God,
did not regard equality with God
as something to be exploited,
but emptied himself,
taking the form of a slave,
being born in human likeness.
And being found in human form,
he humbled himself
and became obedient to the point of death –
even death on a cross.

Therefore God also highly exalted him
and gave him the name that is above every name,
so that at the name of Jesus every knee should bend,
in heaven and on earth and under the earth,
and every tongue should confess that Jesus Christ is Lord,
to the glory of God the Father.

PASSION (Long or short reading)
Matthew 26.14 – 27.66 or Matthew 27.11–54

Hear the passion of our Lord Jesus Christ according to Matthew.

[One of the twelve, who was called Judas Iscariot, went to the chief priests and said, 'What will you give me if I betray him to you?' They paid him thirty pieces of silver. And from that moment he began to look for an opportunity to betray him.

On the first day of Unleavened Bread the disciples came to Jesus, saying, 'Where do you want us to make the preparations for you to eat the Passover?' He said, 'Go into the city to a certain man, and say to him, "The Teacher says, My time is near; I will keep the Passover at your house with my disciples."' So the disciples did as Jesus had directed them, and they prepared the Passover meal. When it was evening, he took his place with the twelve; and while they were eating, he said, 'Truly I tell you, one of you will betray me.' And they became greatly distressed and began to say to him one after another, 'Surely not I, Lord?' He answered, 'The one who has dipped his hand into the bowl with me will betray me. The Son of Man goes as it is written of him, but woe to that one by whom the Son of Man is betrayed! It would have been better for that one not to have been born.' Judas, who betrayed him, said, 'Surely not I, Rabbi?' He replied, 'You have said so.'

While they were eating, Jesus took a loaf of bread, and after blessing it he broke it, gave it to the disciples, and said, 'Take, eat; this is my body.' Then he took a cup, and after giving thanks he gave it to them, saying, 'Drink from it, all of you; for this is my blood of the covenant, which is poured out for many for the forgiveness of sins. I tell you, I will never again drink of this fruit of the vine until that day when I drink it new with you in my Father's kingdom.'

When they had sung the hymn, they went out to the Mount of Olives. Then Jesus said to them, 'You will all become deserters because of me this night; for it is written,
"I will strike the shepherd,
and the sheep of the flock will be scattered."
But after I am raised up, I will go ahead of you to Galilee.' Peter said to him, 'Though all become deserters because of you, I will never desert you.' Jesus said to him, 'Truly I tell you, this very night, before the cock crows, you will deny me three times.' Peter said to him, 'Even though I must die with you, I will not deny you.' And so said all the disciples.

Then Jesus went with them to a place called Gethsemane; and he said to his disciples, 'Sit here while I go over there and pray.' He took with him Peter and the two sons of Zebedee, and began to be grieved and agitated. Then he said to them, 'I am deeply grieved, even to death; remain here, and stay awake with me.' And going a little farther, he threw himself on the ground and prayed, 'My Father, if it is possible, let this cup pass from me; yet not what I want but what you want.' Then he came to the disciples and found them sleeping; and he said to Peter, 'So, could you not stay awake with me one hour? Stay awake and pray that you may not come into the time of trial; for the spirit indeed is willing, but the flesh is weak.' Again he went away for the second time and prayed, 'My Father, if this cannot pass unless I drink it, your will be done.' Again he came and found them sleeping, for their eyes were heavy. So leaving them again, he went away and prayed for the third time, saying the same words. Then he came to the disciples and said to them, 'Are you still sleeping and taking your rest? See, the hour is at hand, and the Son of Man is betrayed into the hands of sinners. Get up, let us be going. See, my betrayer is at hand.'

While he was still speaking, Judas, one of the twelve, arrived; with him was a large crowd with swords and clubs, from the chief priests and the elders of the people. Now the betrayer had given them a sign, saying, 'The one I will kiss is the man; arrest him.' At once he came up to Jesus and said, 'Greetings, Rabbi!' and kissed him. Jesus said to him, 'Friend, do what you are here to do.' Then they came and laid hands on Jesus and arrested him. Suddenly, one of those with Jesus put his hand on his sword, drew it, and struck the slave of the high priest, cutting off his ear. Then Jesus said to him, 'Put your sword back into its place; for all who take the sword will perish by the sword. Do you think that I cannot appeal to my Father, and he will at once send me more than twelve legions of angels? But how then would the scriptures be fulfilled, which say it must happen in this way?' At that hour Jesus said to the crowds, 'Have you come out with swords and clubs to arrest me as though I were a bandit? Day after day I sat in the temple teaching, and you did not arrest me. But all this has taken place, so that the scriptures of the prophets may be fulfilled.' Then all the disciples deserted him and fled.

Those who had arrested Jesus took him to Caiaphas the high priest, in whose house the scribes and the elders had gathered. But Peter was following him at a distance, as far as the courtyard of the high priest; and going inside, he sat with the guards in order to see how this would end. Now the chief priests and the whole council were looking for false testimony against Jesus so that they might put him to death, but they found none, though many false witnesses came forward. At last two came forward and said, 'This fellow said, "I am able to destroy the temple of God and to build it in three days."' The high priest stood up and said, 'Have you no answer? What is it that they testify against you?' But Jesus was silent. Then the high priest said to him, 'I put you under oath before the living God, tell us if you are the Messiah, the Son of God.' Jesus said to him, 'You have said so. But I tell you,
From now on you will see the Son of Man
seated at the right hand of Power
and coming on the clouds of heaven.'
Then the high priest tore his clothes and said, 'He has blasphemed! Why do we still need witnesses? You have now heard his blasphemy. What is your verdict?' They answered, 'He deserves death.' Then they spat in his face and struck him; and some slapped him, saying, 'Prophesy to us, you Messiah! Who is it that struck you?'

Now Peter was sitting outside in the courtyard. A servant-girl came to him and said, 'You also were with Jesus the Galilean.' But he denied it before all of them, saying, 'I do not know what you are talking about.' When he went out to the porch, another servant-girl saw him, and she said to the bystanders, 'This man was with Jesus of Nazareth.' Again he denied it with an oath, 'I do not know the man.' After a little while the bystanders came up and said to

Peter, 'Certainly you are also one of them, for your accent betrays you.' Then he began to curse, and he swore an oath, 'I do not know the man!' At that moment the cock crowed. Then Peter remembered what Jesus had said: 'Before the cock crows, you will deny me three times.' And he went out and wept bitterly.

When morning came, all the chief priests and the elders of the people conferred together against Jesus in order to bring about his death. They bound him, led him away, and handed him over to Pilate the governor.

When Judas, his betrayer, saw that Jesus was condemned, he repented and brought back the thirty pieces of silver to the chief priests and the elders. He said, 'I have sinned by betraying innocent blood.' But they said, 'What is that to us? See to it yourself.' Throwing down the pieces of silver in the temple, he departed; and he went and hanged himself. But the chief priests, taking the pieces of silver, said, 'It is not lawful to put them into the treasury, since they are blood money.' After conferring together, they used them to buy the potter's field as a place to bury foreigners. For this reason that field has been called the Field of Blood to this day. Then was fulfilled what had been spoken through the prophet Jeremiah, 'And they took the thirty pieces of silver, the price of the one on whom a price had been set, on whom some of the people of Israel had set a price, and they gave them for the potter's field, as the Lord commanded me.']

Now Jesus stood before the governor; and the governor asked him, 'Are you the King of the Jews?' Jesus said, 'You say so.' But when he was accused by the chief priests and elders, he did not answer. Then Pilate said to him, 'Do you not hear how many accusations they make against you?' But he gave him no answer, not even to a single charge, so that the governor was greatly amazed.

Now at the festival the governor was accustomed to release a prisoner for the crowd, anyone whom they wanted. At that time they had a notorious prisoner, called Jesus Barabbas. So after they had gathered, Pilate said to them, 'Whom do you want me to release for you, Barabbas or Jesus who is called the Messiah?' For he realized that it was out of jealousy that they had handed him over. While he was sitting on the judgement seat, his wife sent word to him, 'Have nothing to do with that innocent man, for today I have suffered a great deal because of a dream about him.' Now the chief priests and the elders persuaded the crowds to ask for Barabbas and to have Jesus killed. The governor again said to them, 'Which of the two do you want me to release for you?' And they said, 'Barabbas.' Pilate said to them, 'Then what should I do with Jesus who is called the Messiah?' All of them said, 'Let him be crucified!' Then he asked, 'Why, what evil has he done?' But they shouted all the more, 'Let him be crucified!'

So when Pilate saw that he could do nothing, but rather that a riot was beginning, he took some water and washed his hands before the crowd, saying, 'I am innocent of this man's blood; see to it yourselves.' Then the people as a whole answered, 'His blood be on us and on our children!' So he released Barabbas for them; and after flogging Jesus, he handed him over to be crucified.

Then the soldiers of the governor took Jesus into the governor's headquarters, and they gathered the whole cohort around him. They stripped him and put a scarlet robe on him, and after twisting some thorns into a crown, they put it on his head. They put a reed in his right hand and knelt before him and mocked him, saying, 'Hail, King of the Jews!' They spat on him, and took the reed and struck him on the head. After mocking him, they stripped him of the robe and put his own clothes on him. Then they led him away to crucify him.

As they went out, they came upon a man from Cyrene named Simon; they compelled this man to carry his cross. And when they came to a place called Golgotha (which means Place of a Skull), they offered him wine to drink, mixed with gall; but when he tasted it, he would not drink it. And when they had crucified him, they divided his clothes among themselves by casting lots; then they sat down there and kept watch over him. Over his head they put the charge against him, which read, 'This is Jesus, the King of the Jews.'

Then two bandits were crucified with him, one on his right and one on his left. Those who passed by derided him, shaking their heads and saying, 'You who would destroy the temple and build it in three days, save yourself! If you are the Son of God, come down from the cross.' In the same way the chief priests also, along with the scribes and elders, were mocking him, saying, 'He saved others; he cannot save himself. He is the King of Israel; let him come down from the cross now, and we will believe in him. He trusts in God; let God deliver him now, if he wants to; for he said, "I am God's Son."' The bandits who were crucified with him also taunted him in the same way.

From noon on, darkness came over the whole land until three in the afternoon. And about three o'clock Jesus cried with a loud voice, 'Eli, Eli, lema sabachthani?' that is, 'My God, my God, why have you forsaken me?' When some of the bystanders heard it, they said, 'This man is calling for Elijah.' At once one of them ran and got a sponge, filled it with sour wine, put it on a stick, and gave it to him to drink. But the others said, 'Wait, let us see whether Elijah will come to save him.' Then Jesus cried again with a loud voice and breathed his last. At that moment the curtain of the temple was torn in two, from top to bottom. The earth shook, and the rocks were split. The tombs also were opened, and many bodies of the saints who had fallen asleep were raised. After his resurrection they came out of the tombs and entered the holy city and appeared to many. Now when the centurion and those with him, who were keeping watch over Jesus, saw the earthquake and what took place, they were terrified and said, 'Truly this man was God's Son!'

[Many women were also there, looking on from a distance; they had followed Jesus from Galilee and had provided for him. Among them were Mary Magdalene, and Mary the mother of James and Joseph, and the mother of the sons of Zebedee.

When it was evening, there came a rich man from Arimathea, named Joseph, who was also a disciple of Jesus. He went to Pilate and asked for the body of Jesus; then Pilate ordered it to be given to him. So Joseph took the body and wrapped it in a clean linen cloth and laid it in his own new tomb, which he had hewn in the rock. He then rolled a great stone to the door of the tomb and went away. Mary Magdalene and the other Mary were there, sitting opposite the tomb.

The next day, that is, after the day of Preparation, the chief priests and the Pharisees gathered before Pilate and said, 'Sir, we remember what that impostor said while he was still alive, "After three days I will rise again." Therefore command the tomb to be made secure until the third day; otherwise his disciples may go and steal him away, and tell the people, "He has been raised from the dead," and the last deception would be worse than the first.' Pilate said to them, 'You have a guard of soldiers; go, make it as secure as you can.' So they went with the guard and made the tomb secure by sealing the stone.]

MONDAY OF HOLY WEEK   YEARS A B C

FIRST READING   Isaiah 42.1-9

A reading from the book of the prophet Isaiah.

Thus says the LORD:
Here is my servant, whom I uphold,
my chosen, in whom my soul delights;
I have put my spirit upon him;
he will bring forth justice to the nations.
He will not cry or lift up his voice,

or make it heard in the street;
a bruised reed he will not break,
and a dimly burning wick he will not quench;
he will faithfully bring forth justice.
He will not grow faint or be crushed
until he has established justice in the earth;
and the coastlands wait for his teaching.
Thus says God, the LORD,
who created the heavens and stretched them out,
who spread out the earth and what comes from it,
who gives breath to the people upon it and spirit to those who walk in it:
I am the LORD,
I have called you in righteousness,
I have taken you by the hand and kept you;
I have given you as a covenant to the people,
a light to the nations,
to open the eyes that are blind,
to bring out the prisoners from the dungeon,
from the prison those who sit in darkness.
I am the LORD, that is my name;
my glory I give to no other, nor my praise to idols.
See, the former things have come to pass,
and new things I now declare;
before they spring forth, I tell you of them.

PSALM   Psalm 36.5–11

℟ **With you is the well of life,
     and in your light we see light.**

Your love, O Lord, reaches to the heavens,
and your faithfulness to the clouds.
Your righteousness is like the strong mountains,
your justice like the great deep;
you save both human and beast, O Lord. ℟

How priceless is your love, O God!
your people take refuge under the shadow of your wings.
They feast upon the abundance of your house;
you give them drink from the river of your delights.
For with you is the well of life,
and in your light we see light. ℟

Continue your loving-kindness to those who know you,
and your favour to those who are true of heart.
Let not the foot of the proud come near me,
nor the hand of the wicked push me aside. ℟

SECOND READING   Hebrews 9.11–15

A reading from the letter to the Hebrews.

Christ came as a high priest of the good things that have come, then through
the greater and perfect tent (not made with hands, that is, not of this
creation). He entered once for all into the Holy Place, not with the blood of
goats and calves, but with his own blood, thus obtaining eternal redemption.
For if the blood of goats and bulls, with the sprinkling of the ashes of a heifer,
sanctifies those who have been defiled so that their flesh is purified, how
much more will the blood of Christ, who through the eternal Spirit offered
himself without blemish to God, purify our conscience from dead works to
worship the living God! For this reason he is the mediator of a new covenant,
so that those who are called may receive the promised eternal inheritance,
because a death has occurred that redeems them from the transgressions
under the first covenant.

GOSPEL   John 12.1–11

Hear the gospel of our Lord Jesus Christ according to John.

Six days before the Passover Jesus came to Bethany, the home of Lazarus,
whom he had raised from the dead. There they gave a dinner for him. Martha
served, and Lazarus was one of those at the table with him. Mary took a
pound of costly perfume made of pure nard, anointed Jesus' feet, and wiped
them with her hair. The house was filled with the fragrance of the perfume.
But Judas Iscariot, one of his disciples (the one who was about to betray him),
said, 'Why was this perfume not sold for three hundred denarii and the
money given to the poor?' (He said this not because he cared about the poor,
but because he was a thief; he kept the common purse and used to steal what
was put into it.) Jesus said, 'Leave her alone. She bought it so that she might
keep it for the day of my burial. You always have the poor with you, but you
do not always have me.'

When the great crowd of the Jews learned that he was there, they came not
only because of Jesus but also to see Lazarus, whom he had raised from the
dead. So the chief priests planned to put Lazarus to death as well, since it was
on account of him that many of the Jews were deserting and were believing
in Jesus.

TUESDAY OF HOLY WEEK   YEARS A B C

FIRST READING   Isaiah 49.1–7

A reading from the book of the prophet Isaiah.

Listen to me, O coastlands,
pay attention, you peoples from far away!
The LORD called me before I was born,
while I was in my mother's womb he named me.
He made my mouth like a sharp sword,
in the shadow of his hand he hid me;
he made me a polished arrow,
in his quiver he hid me away.
And he said to me, 'You are my servant, Israel,
in whom I will be glorified.'
But I said, 'I have laboured in vain,
I have spent my strength for nothing and vanity;
yet surely my cause is with the LORD,
and my reward with my God.'

And now the LORD says,
who formed me in the womb to be his servant,
to bring Jacob back to him,
and that Israel might be gathered to him,
for I am honoured in the sight of the LORD,
and my God has become my strength.
The LORD says,
'It is too light a thing that you should be my servant
to raise up the tribes of Jacob
and to restore the survivors of Israel;
I will give you as a light to the nations,
that my salvation may reach to the end of the earth.'

Thus says the LORD,
the Redeemer of Israel and his Holy One,
to one deeply despised, abhorred by the nations, the slave of rulers,
'Kings shall see and stand up, princes,
and they shall prostrate themselves,
because of the LORD, who is faithful,
the Holy One of Israel, who has chosen you.'

PSALM   Psalm 71.1–14

℞ **You are my hope, O Lord my God,**
   [my mouth shall be full of your praise].

In you, O Lord, have I taken refuge;
let me never be ashamed.
In your righteousness, deliver me and set me free;
incline your ear to me and save me.
Be my strong rock, a castle to keep me safe;
you are my crag and my stronghold. ℞

Deliver me, my God, from the hand of the wicked,
from the clutches of the evildoer and the oppressor.
For you are my hope, O Lord God,
my confidence since I was young.
I have been sustained by you ever since I was born;
from my mother's womb you have been my strength;
my praise shall be always of you. ℞

I have become a portent to many;
but you are my refuge and my strength.
Let my mouth be full of your praise
and your glory all the day long.
Do not cast me off in my old age;
forsake me not when my strength fails. ℞

For my enemies are talking against me,
and those who lie in wait for my life
take counsel together.
They say, 'God has forsaken him;
go after him and seize him;
because there is none who will save.'
O God, be not far from me;
come quickly to help me, O my God. ℞

Let those who set themselves against me
be put to shame and be disgraced;
let those who seek to do me evil
be covered with scorn and reproach.
But I shall always wait in patience,
and shall praise you more and more. ℞

SECOND READING   **1 Corinthians 1.18–31**

A reading from the first letter of Paul to the Corinthians.

The message about the cross is foolishness to those who are perishing, but to
us who are being saved it is the power of God. For it is written,
'I will destroy the wisdom of the wise,
and the discernment of the discerning I will thwart.'
Where is the one who is wise? Where is the scribe? Where is the debater of
this age? Has not God made foolish the wisdom of the world? For since, in
the wisdom of God, the world did not know God through wisdom, God
decided, through the foolishness of our proclamation, to save those who
believe. For Jews demand signs and Greeks desire wisdom, but we proclaim
Christ crucified, a stumbling-block to Jews and foolishness to Gentiles, but to
those who are the called, both Jews and Greeks, Christ the power of God and
the wisdom of God. For God's foolishness is wiser than human wisdom, and
God's weakness is stronger than human strength.

Consider your own call, brothers and sisters: not many of you were wise by
human standards, not many were powerful, not many were of noble birth.
But God chose what is foolish in the world to shame the wise; God chose
what is weak in the world to shame the strong; God chose what is low and
despised in the world, things that are not, to reduce to nothing things that
are, so that no one might boast in the presence of God. He is the source of
your life in Christ Jesus, who became for us wisdom from God, and
righteousness and sanctification and redemption, in order that, as it is
written, 'Let the one who boasts, boast in the Lord.'

GOSPEL   **John 12.20–36**

Hear the gospel of our Lord Jesus Christ according to John.

Among those who went up to worship at the festival were some Greeks. They
came to Philip, who was from Bethsaida in Galilee, and said to him, 'Sir, we
wish to see Jesus.' Philip went and told Andrew; then Andrew and Philip
went and told Jesus. Jesus answered them, 'The hour has come for the Son of
Man to be glorified. Very truly, I tell you, unless a grain of wheat falls into
the earth and dies, it remains just a single grain; but if it dies, it bears much
fruit. Those who love their life lose it, and those who hate their life in this
world will keep it for eternal life. Whoever serves me must follow me, and
where I am, there will my servant be also. Whoever serves me, the Father
will honour.

Now my soul is troubled. And what should I say – "Father, save me from this hour"? No, it is for this reason that I have come to this hour. Father, glorify your name.' Then a voice came from heaven, 'I have glorified it, and I will glorify it again.' The crowd standing there heard it and said that it was thunder. Others said, 'An angel has spoken to him.' Jesus answered, 'This voice has come for your sake, not for mine. Now is the judgement of this world; now the ruler of this world will be driven out.

And I, when I am lifted up from the earth, will draw all people to myself.' He said this to indicate the kind of death he was to die. The crowd answered him, 'We have heard from the law that the Messiah remains for ever. How can you say that the Son of Man must be lifted up? Who is this Son of Man?' Jesus said to them, 'The light is with you for a little longer. Walk while you have the light, so that the darkness may not overtake you. If you walk in the darkness, you do not know where you are going. While you have the light, believe in the light, so that you may become children of light.'

After Jesus had said this, he departed and hid from them.

WEDNESDAY OF HOLY WEEK — YEARS A B C

FIRST READING — Isaiah 50.4–9a

A reading from the book of the prophet Isaiah.

The servant of the LORD said:
The Lord GOD has given me the tongue of a teacher,
that I may know how to sustain the weary with a word.
Morning by morning he wakens –
wakens my ear to listen as those who are taught.
The Lord GOD has opened my ear,
and I was not rebellious,
I did not turn backwards.
I gave my back to those who struck me,
and my cheeks to those who pulled out the beard;
I did not hide my face
from insult and spitting.

The Lord GOD helps me;
therefore I have not been disgraced;
therefore I have set my face like flint,
and I know that I shall not be put to shame;

he who vindicates me is near.
Who will contend with me?
Let us stand up together.
Who are my adversaries?
Let them confront me.
It is the Lord GOD who helps me;
who will declare me guilty?

PSALM   Psalm 70

℟ [As for me, I am poor and needy;]
   Lord, make haste to help me.

Be pleased, O God, to deliver me;
O Lord, make haste to help me.
Let those who seek my life
be ashamed and altogether dismayed;
let those who take pleasure in my misfortune
draw back and be disgraced. ℟

Let those who say to me 'Aha!'
and gloat over me turn back,
because they are ashamed.
Let all who seek you rejoice and be glad in you;
let those who love your salvation say for ever,
'Great is the Lord!' ℟

But as for me, I am poor and needy;
come to me speedily, O God.
You are my helper and my deliverer;
O Lord, do not tarry. ℟

SECOND READING   Hebrews 12.1-3

A reading from the letter to the Hebrews.

Since we are surrounded by so great a cloud of witnesses, let us also lay aside
every weight and the sin that clings so closely, and let us run with
perseverance the race that is set before us, looking to Jesus the pioneer and
perfecter of our faith, who for the sake of the joy that was set before him
endured the cross, disregarding its shame, and has taken his seat at the right
hand of the throne of God.

Consider him who endured such hostility against himself from sinners, so that you may not grow weary or lose heart.

GOSPEL   John 13.21–32

Hear the gospel of our Lord Jesus Christ according to John.

Jesus was troubled in spirit, and declared, 'Very truly, I tell you, one of you will betray me.' The disciples looked at one another, uncertain of whom he was speaking. One of his disciples – the one whom Jesus loved – was reclining next to him; Simon Peter therefore motioned to him to ask Jesus of whom he was speaking. So while reclining next to Jesus, he asked him, 'Lord, who is it?' Jesus answered, 'It is the one to whom I give this piece of bread when I have dipped it in the dish.' So when he had dipped the piece of bread, he gave it to Judas son of Simon Iscariot.

After he received the piece of bread, Satan entered into him. Jesus said to him, 'Do quickly what you are going to do.' Now no one at the table knew why he said this to him. Some thought that, because Judas had the common purse, Jesus was telling him, 'Buy what we need for the festival'; or, that he should give something to the poor. So, after receiving the piece of bread, he immediately went out. And it was night.

When he had gone out, Jesus said, 'Now the Son of Man has been glorified, and God has been glorified in him. If God has been glorified in him, God will also glorify him in himself and will glorify him at once.'

MAUNDY THURSDAY   YEARS A B C

FIRST READING (Short or long reading)
                          Exodus 12.1–4, (5–10), 11–14

A reading from the book of Exodus.

The LORD said to Moses and Aaron in the land of Egypt: This month shall mark for you the beginning of months; it shall be the first month of the year for you. Tell the whole congregation of Israel that on the tenth of this month they are to take a lamb for each family, a lamb for each household. If a household is too small for a whole lamb, it shall join its closest neighbour in obtaining one; the lamb shall be divided in proportion to the number of people who eat of it. [Your lamb shall be without blemish, a year-old male; you may take it from the sheep or from the goats. You shall keep it until the fourteenth day of this month; then the whole assembled congregation of

Israel shall slaughter it at twilight. They shall take some of the blood and put it on the two doorposts and the lintel of the houses in which they eat it. They shall eat the lamb that same night; they shall eat it roasted over the fire with unleavened bread and bitter herbs. Do not eat any of it raw or boiled in water, but roasted over the fire, with its head, legs, and inner organs. You shall let none of it remain until the morning; anything that remains until the morning you shall burn.] This is how you shall eat it: your loins girded, your sandals on your feet, and your staff in your hand; and you shall eat it hurriedly. It is the passover of the LORD. For I will pass through the land of Egypt that night, and I will strike down every firstborn in the land of Egypt, both human beings and animals; on all the gods of Egypt I will execute judgements: I am the LORD. The blood shall be a sign for you on the houses where you live: when I see the blood, I will pass over you, and no plague shall destroy you when I strike the land of Egypt.

This day shall be a day of remembrance for you. You shall celebrate it as a festival to the LORD; throughout your generations you shall observe it as a perpetual ordinance.

PSALM   Psalm 116.1, 10–17

℟ **The cup of blessing that we bless,**
  is it not a sharing in the blood of Christ?
  or
℟ **I will lift up the cup of salvation.**

I love the Lord,
because he has heard the voice of my supplication,
because he has inclined his ear to me
whenever I called upon him. ℟

How shall I repay the Lord
for all the good things he has done for me?
I will lift up the cup of salvation
and call upon the name of the Lord.

I will fulfil my vows to the Lord
in the presence of all his people. ℟

Precious in the sight of the Lord
is the death of his servants.
O Lord, I am your servant;
I am your servant and the child of your handmaid;
you have freed me from my bonds. ℟

I will offer you the sacrifice of thanksgiving
and call upon the name of the Lord.
I will fulfil my vows to the Lord
in the presence of all his people.
In the courts of the Lord's house,
in the midst of you, O Jerusalem. ℟

SECOND READING   1 Corinthians 11.23-26

A reading from the first letter of Paul to the Corinthians.

Beloved: I received from the Lord what I also handed on to you, that the Lord
Jesus on the night when he was betrayed took a loaf of bread,
and when he had given thanks, he broke it and said, 'This is my body that is
for you. Do this in remembrance of me.'
In the same way he took the cup also, after supper, saying, 'This cup is the
new covenant in my blood. Do this, as often as you drink it, in remembrance
of me.'
For as often as you eat this bread and drink the cup, you proclaim the Lord's
death until he comes.

GOSPEL   John 13.1-17, 31b-35

Hear the gospel of our Lord Jesus Christ according to John.

Now before the festival of the Passover, Jesus knew that his hour had come to
depart from this world and go to the Father. Having loved his own who were
in the world, he loved them to the end. The devil had already put it into the
heart of Judas son of Simon Iscariot to betray him. And during supper Jesus,
knowing that the Father had given all things into his hands, and that he had
come from God and was going to God, got up from the table, took off his
outer robe, and tied a towel around himself. Then he poured water into a
basin and began to wash the disciples' feet and to wipe them with the towel
that was tied around him. He came to Simon Peter, who said to him, 'Lord,
are you going to wash my feet?' Jesus answered, 'You do not know now what
I am doing, but later you will understand.' Peter said to him, 'You will never
wash my feet.' Jesus answered, 'Unless I wash you, you have no share with
me.' Simon Peter said to him, 'Lord, not my feet only but also my hands and
my head!' Jesus said to him, 'One who has bathed does not need to wash,
except for the feet, but is entirely clean. And you are clean, though not all of

you.' For he knew who was to betray him; for this reason he said, 'Not all of you are clean.'

After he had washed their feet, had put on his robe, and had returned to the table, he said to them, 'Do you know what I have done to you? You call me Teacher and Lord – and you are right, for that is what I am. So if I, your Lord and Teacher, have washed your feet, you also ought to wash one another's feet. For I have set you an example, that you also should do as I have done to you. Very truly, I tell you, servants are not greater than their master, nor are messengers greater than the one who sent them. If you know these things, you are blessed if you do them.

Now the Son of Man has been glorified, and God has been glorified in him. If God has been glorified in him, God will also glorify him in himself and will glorify him at once. Little children, I am with you only a little longer. You will look for me; and as I said to the Jews so now I say to you, "Where I am going, you cannot come." I give you a new commandment, that you love one another. Just as I have loved you, you also should love one another. By this everyone will know that you are my disciples, if you have love for one another.'

GOOD FRIDAY   YEARS A B C

FIRST READING   Isaiah 52.13 – 53.12

A reading from the book of the prophet Isaiah.

See, my servant shall prosper;
he shall be exalted and lifted up,
and shall be very high.
Just as there were many who were astonished at him –
so marred was his appearance, beyond human semblance,
and his form beyond that of mortals –
so he shall startle many nations;
kings shall shut their mouths because of him;
for that which had not been told them they shall see,
and that which they had not heard they shall contemplate.
Who has believed what we have heard?
And to whom has the arm of the LORD been revealed?
For he grew up before him like a young plant,
and like a root out of dry ground;
he had no form or majesty that we should look at him,

nothing in his appearance that we should desire him.
He was despised and rejected by others;
a man of suffering and acquainted with infirmity;
and as one from whom others hide their faces
he was despised,
and we held him of no account.

Surely he has borne our infirmities and carried our diseases;
yet we accounted him stricken,
struck down by God, and afflicted.
But he was wounded for our transgressions,
crushed for our iniquities;
upon him was the punishment that made us whole,
and by his bruises we are healed.
All we like sheep have gone astray;
we have all turned to our own way,
and the LORD has laid on him
the iniquity of us all.

He was oppressed, and he was afflicted,
yet he did not open his mouth;
like a lamb that is led to the slaughter,
and like a sheep that before its shearers is silent,
so he did not open his mouth.
By a perversion of justice he was taken away.
Who could have imagined his future?
For he was cut off from the land of the living,
stricken for the transgression of my people.
They made his grave with the wicked
and his tomb with the rich,
although he had done no violence,
and there was no deceit in his mouth.

Yet it was the will of the LORD to crush him with pain.
When you make his life an offering for sin,
he shall see his offspring, and shall prolong his days;
through him the will of the LORD shall prosper.
Out of his anguish he shall see light;
he shall find satisfaction through his knowledge.
The righteous one, my servant, shall make many righteous,
and he shall bear their iniquities.
Therefore I will allot him a portion with the great,

and he shall divide the spoil with the strong;
because he poured out himself to death,
and was numbered with the transgressors;
yet he bore the sin of many,
and made intercession for the transgressors.

PSALM

℞ **My God, my God, why have you forsaken me?**

My God, my God, why have you forsaken me?
and are so far from my cry
and from the words of my distress?
O my God, I cry in the daytime,
but you do not answer;
by night as well, but I find no rest.
Yet you are the Holy One,
enthroned upon the praises of Israel. ℞

Our forebears put their trust in you;
they trusted and you delivered them.
They cried out to you and were delivered;
they trusted in you and were not put to shame. ℞

But as for me, I am a worm and no man,
scorned by all and despised by the people.
All who see me laugh me to scorn;
they curl their lips and wag their heads, saying,
'He trusted in the Lord; let him deliver him;
let him rescue him, if he delights in him.' ℞

Yet you are he who took me out of the womb,
and kept me safe upon my mother's breast.
I have been entrusted to you ever since I was born;
you were my God
when I was still in my mother's womb. ℞

Be not far from me, for trouble is near,
and there is none to help.
Many young bulls encircle me;
strong bulls of Bashan surround me.
They open wide their jaws at me,
like a ravening and a roaring lion. ℞

I am poured out like water;
all my bones are out of joint;
my heart within my breast is melting wax.
My mouth is dried out like a pot-sherd;
my tongue sticks to the roof of my mouth;
and you have laid me in the dust of the grave. ℞

Packs of dogs close me in,
and gangs of evildoers circle around me;
they pierce my hands and my feet;
I can count all my bones.
They stare and gloat over me;
they divide my garments among them;
they cast lots for my clothing. ℞

Be not far away, O Lord;
you are my strength; hasten to help me.
Save me from the sword,
my life from the power of the dog.
Save me from the lion's mouth,
my wretched body from the horns of wild bulls. ℞

I will declare your name to my people;
in the midst of the congregation I will praise you.
Praise the Lord, you that fear him;
stand in awe of him, O offspring of Israel;
all you of Jacob's line, give glory. ℞

For he does not despise nor abhor
the poor in their poverty;
neither does he hide his face from them;
but when they cry to him he hears them.
My praise is of him in the great assembly;
I will perform my vows
in the presence of those who worship him. ℞

The poor shall eat and be satisfied,
and those who seek the Lord shall praise him:
'May your heart live for ever!'
All the ends of the earth
shall remember and turn to the Lord,

and all the families of the nations
shall bow before him.
For kingship belongs to the Lord;
he rules over the nations. ℟

To him alone all who sleep in the earth
bow down in worship;
all who go down to the dust fall before him.
My soul shall live for him;
my descendants shall serve him;
they shall be known as the Lord's for ever.
They shall come and make known to a people yet unborn
the saving deeds that he has done. ℟

SECOND READING (Alternative readings)

Either   Hebrews 10.16–25

A reading from the letter to the Hebrews.

The Holy Spirit testifies to us, for after saying,

'This is the covenant that I will make with them after those days,
says the Lord:
I will put my laws in their hearts,
and I will write them on their minds,'
he also adds,
'I will remember their sins and their lawless deeds no more.'
Where there is forgiveness of these, there is no longer any offering for sin.

Therefore, my friends, since we have confidence to enter the sanctuary by
the blood of Jesus, by the new and living way that he opened for us through
the curtain (that is, through his flesh), and since we have a great priest over
the house of God, let us approach with a true heart in full assurance of faith,
with our hearts sprinkled clean from an evil conscience and our bodies
washed with pure water. Let us hold fast to the confession of our hope
without wavering, for he who has promised is faithful. And let us consider
how to provoke one another to love and good deeds, not neglecting to meet
together, as is the habit of some, but encouraging one another, and all the
more as you see the Day approaching.

Or   **Hebrews 4.14–16; 5.7–9**

A reading from the letter to the Hebrews.

Since we have a great high priest who has passed through the heavens, Jesus, the Son of God, let us hold fast to our confession. For we do not have a high priest who is unable to sympathize with our weaknesses, but we have one who in every respect has been tested as we are, yet without sin. Let us therefore approach the throne of grace with boldness, so that we may receive mercy and find grace to help in time of need.

In the days of his flesh, Jesus offered up prayers and supplications, with loud cries and tears, to the one who was able to save him from death, and he was heard because of his reverent submission. Although he was a Son, he learned obedience through what he suffered; and having been made perfect, he became the source of eternal salvation for all who obey him.

PASSION   **John 18.1 – 19.42**

Hear the passion of our Lord Jesus Christ according to John.

After they had eaten the supper, Jesus went out with his disciples across the Kidron valley to a place where there was a garden, which he and his disciples entered. Now Judas, who betrayed him, also knew the place, because Jesus often met there with his disciples. So Judas brought a detachment of soldiers together with police from the chief priests and the Pharisees, and they came there with lanterns and torches and weapons. Then Jesus, knowing all that was to happen to him, came forward and asked them, 'For whom are you looking?' They answered, 'Jesus of Nazareth.' Jesus replied, 'I am he.' Judas, who betrayed him, was standing with them. When Jesus said to them, 'I am he,' they stepped back and fell to the ground. Again he asked them, 'For whom are you looking?' And they said, 'Jesus of Nazareth.' Jesus answered, 'I told you that I am he. So if you are looking for me, let these men go.' This was to fulfil the word that he had spoken, 'I did not lose a single one of those whom you gave me.'

Then Simon Peter, who had a sword, drew it, struck the high priest's slave, and cut off his right ear. The slave's name was Malchus. Jesus said to Peter, 'Put your sword back into its sheath. Am I not to drink the cup that the Father has given me?'

So the soldiers, their officer, and the Jewish police arrested Jesus and bound him. First they took him to Annas, who was the father-in-law of Caiaphas, the high priest that year. Caiaphas was the one who had advised the Jews that it was better to have one person die for the people.

Simon Peter and another disciple followed Jesus. Since that disciple was known to the high priest, he went with Jesus into the courtyard of the high priest, but Peter was standing outside at the gate. So the other disciple, who was known to the high priest, went out, spoke to the woman who guarded the gate, and brought Peter in. The woman said to Peter, 'You are not also one of this man's disciples, are you?' He said, 'I am not.' Now the slaves and the police had made a charcoal fire because it was cold, and they were standing around it and warming themselves. Peter also was standing with them and warming himself.

Then the high priest questioned Jesus about his disciples and about his teaching. Jesus answered, 'I have spoken openly to the world; I have always taught in synagogues and in the temple, where all the Jews come together. I have said nothing in secret. Why do you ask me? Ask those who heard what I said to them; they know what I said.' When he had said this, one of the police standing nearby struck Jesus on the face, saying, 'Is that how you answer the high priest?' Jesus answered, 'If I have spoken wrongly, testify to the wrong. But if I have spoken rightly, why do you strike me?' Then Annas sent him bound to Caiaphas the high priest.

Now Simon Peter was standing and warming himself. They asked him, 'You are not also one of his disciples, are you?' He denied it and said, 'I am not.' One of the slaves of the high priest, a relative of the man whose ear Peter had cut off, asked, 'Did I not see you in the garden with him?' Again Peter denied it, and at that moment the cock crowed.

Then they took Jesus from Caiaphas to Pilate's headquarters. It was early in the morning. They themselves did not enter the headquarters, so as to avoid ritual defilement and to be able to eat the Passover. So Pilate went out to them and said, 'What accusation do you bring against this man?' They answered, 'If this man were not a criminal, we would not have handed him over to you.' Pilate said to them, 'Take him yourselves and judge him according to your law.' The Jews replied, 'We are not permitted to put anyone to death.' (This was to fulfil what Jesus had said when he indicated the kind of death he was to die.)

Then Pilate entered the headquarters again, summoned Jesus, and asked him, 'Are you the King of the Jews?' Jesus answered, 'Do you ask this on your own, or did others tell you about me?' Pilate replied, 'I am not a Jew, am I? Your own nation and the chief priests have handed you over to me. What have you done?' Jesus answered, 'My kingdom is not from this world. If my kingdom were from this world, my followers would be fighting to keep me from being handed over to the Jews. But as it is, my kingdom is not from here.' Pilate asked him, 'So you are a king?' Jesus answered, 'You say that I am a king. For this I was born, and for this I came into the world, to testify to the truth. Everyone who belongs to the truth listens to my voice.' Pilate asked him, 'What is truth?'

After he had said this, he went out to the Jewish leaders again and told them, 'I find no case against him. But you have a custom that I release someone for you at the Passover. Do you want me to release for you the King of the Jews?' They shouted in reply, 'Not this man, but Barabbas!' Now Barabbas was a bandit.

Then Pilate took Jesus and had him flogged. And the soldiers wove a crown of thorns and put it on his head, and they dressed him in a purple robe. They kept coming up to him, saying, 'Hail, King of the Jews!' and striking him on the face. Pilate went out again and said to them, 'Look, I am bringing him out to you to let you know that I find no case against him.' So Jesus came out, wearing the crown of thorns and the purple robe. Pilate said to them, 'Here is the man!' When the chief priests and the police saw him, they shouted, 'Crucify him! Crucify him!' Pilate said to them, 'Take him yourselves and crucify him; I find no case against him.' The Jews answered him, 'We have a law, and according to that law he ought to die because he has claimed to be the Son of God.'

Now when Pilate heard this, he was more afraid than ever. He entered his headquarters again and asked Jesus, 'Where are you from?' But Jesus gave him no answer. Pilate therefore said to him, 'Do you refuse to speak to me? Do you not know that I have power to release you, and power to crucify you?' Jesus answered him, 'You would have no power over me unless it had been given you from above; therefore the one who handed me over to you is guilty of a greater sin.' From then on Pilate tried to release him, but the Jews cried out, 'If you release this man, you are no friend of the emperor. Everyone who claims to be a king sets himself against the emperor.' When Pilate heard these words, he brought Jesus outside and sat on the judge's bench at a place called The Stone Pavement, or in Hebrew Gabbatha. Now it was the day of Preparation for the Passover; and it was about noon. He said to the Jews, 'Here is your King!' They cried out, 'Away with him! Away with him! Crucify him!' Pilate asked them, 'Shall I crucify your King?' The chief priests answered, 'We have no king but the emperor.' Then he handed him over to them to be crucified.

So they took Jesus; and carrying the cross by himself, he went out to what is called The Place of the Skull, which in Hebrew is called Golgotha. There they crucified him, and with him two others, one on either side, with Jesus between them. Pilate also had an inscription written and put on the cross. It read, 'Jesus of Nazareth, the King of the Jews.' Many of the Jews read this inscription, because the place where Jesus was crucified was near the city; and it was written in Hebrew, in Latin, and in Greek. Then the chief priests of the Jews said to Pilate, 'Do not write, "The King of the Jews," but, "This man said, I am King of the Jews."' Pilate answered, 'What I have written I have written.' When the soldiers had crucified Jesus, they took his clothes and divided them into four parts, one for each soldier. They also took his tunic; now the tunic was seamless, woven in one piece from the top. So they said to one another, 'Let us not tear it, but cast lots for it to see who will get it.' This was to fulfil what the scripture says, 'They divided my clothes among themselves, and for my clothing they cast lots.' And that is what the soldiers did.

Meanwhile, standing near the cross of Jesus were his mother, and his mother's sister, Mary the wife of Clopas, and Mary Magdalene. When Jesus saw his mother and the disciple whom he loved standing beside her, he said to his mother, 'Woman, here is your son.' Then he said to the disciple, 'Here is your mother.' And from that hour the disciple took her into his own home.

After this, when Jesus knew that all was now finished, he said (in order to fulfil the scripture), 'I am thirsty.' A jar full of sour wine was standing there. So they put a sponge full of the wine on a branch of hyssop and held it to his mouth. When Jesus had received the wine, he said, 'It is finished.' Then he bowed his head and gave up his spirit.

Since it was the day of Preparation, the Jews did not want the bodies left on the cross during the sabbath, especially because that sabbath was a day of great solemnity. So they asked Pilate to have the legs of the crucified men broken and the bodies removed. Then the soldiers came and broke the legs of the first and of the other who had been crucified with him. But when they came to Jesus and saw that he was already dead, they did not break his legs. Instead, one of the soldiers pierced his side with a spear, and at once blood and water came out. (He who saw this has testified so that you also may believe. His testimony is true, and he knows that he tells the truth.) These things occurred so that the scripture might be fulfilled, 'None of his bones shall be broken.' And again another passage of scripture says, 'They will look on the one whom they have pierced.'

After these things, Joseph of Arimathea, who was a disciple of Jesus, though a secret one because of his fear of the Jews, asked Pilate to let him take away the body of Jesus. Pilate gave him permission; so he came and removed his body. Nicodemus, who had at first come to Jesus by night, also came, bringing a mixture of myrrh and aloes, weighing about a hundred pounds. They took the body of Jesus and wrapped it with the spices in linen cloths, according to the burial custom of the Jews. Now there was a garden in the place where he was crucified, and in the garden there was a new tomb in which no one had ever been laid. And so, because it was the Jewish day of Preparation, and the tomb was nearby, they laid Jesus there.

EASTER EVE   YEARS A B C

These readings are for use at services other than the Easter Vigil.

FIRST READING (Alternative readings)

Either   Job 14.1–14

A reading from the book of Job.

Job said to the LORD:
'A mortal, born of woman,
few of days and full of trouble,
comes up like a flower and withers,
flees like a shadow and does not last.
Do you fix your eyes on such a one?
Do you bring me into judgement with you?
Who can bring a clean thing out of an unclean?
No one can.
Since their days are determined,
and the number of their months is known to you,
and you have appointed the bounds that they cannot pass,
look away from them, and desist,
that they may enjoy, like labourers, their days.

For there is hope for a tree, if it is cut down,
that it will sprout again, and that its shoots will not cease.
Though its root grows old in the earth,
and its stump dies in the ground,
yet at the scent of water it will bud and put forth branches like a young plant.
But mortals die, and are laid low;

humans expire, and where are they?
As waters fail from a lake, and a river wastes away and dries up,
so mortals lie down and do not rise again;
until the heavens are no more,
they will not awake or be roused out of their sleep.
Oh that you would hide me in Sheol,
that you would conceal me until your wrath is past,
that you would appoint me a set time, and remember me!
If mortals die, will they live again?
All the days of my service I would wait until my release should come.'

Or   **Lamentations 3.1–9, 19–24**

A reading from the book of Lamentations.

I am one who has seen affliction
under the rod of God's wrath;
he has driven and brought me into darkness without any light;
against me alone he turns his hand,
again and again, all day long.

He has made my flesh and my skin waste away, and broken my bones;
he has besieged and enveloped me with bitterness and tribulation;
he has made me sit in darkness like the dead of long ago.

He has walled me about so that I cannot escape;
he has put heavy chains on me;
though I call and cry for help,
he shuts out my prayer;
he has blocked my ways with hewn stones,
he has made my paths crooked.

The thought of my affliction and my homelessness
is wormwood and gall!
My soul continually thinks of it
and is bowed down within me.
But this I call to mind, and therefore I have hope:

The steadfast love of the LORD never ceases,
his mercies never come to an end;
they are new every morning;
great is your faithfulness.
'The LORD is my portion,' says my soul,
'therefore I will hope in him.'

125

PSALM

Psalm 31.1–4, 15–16

℞ **Let your face shine on your servants
[and we shall be saved].**

In you, O Lord, have I taken refuge;
let me never be put to shame;
deliver me in your righteousness.
Incline your ear to me;
make haste to deliver me. ℞

Be my strong rock, a castle to keep me safe,
for you are my crag and my stronghold;
for the sake of your name, lead me and guide me.

Take me out of the net
that they have secretly set for me,
for you are my tower of strength. ℞

My times are in your hand;
rescue me from the hand of my enemies,
and from those who persecute me.
Make your face to shine upon your servant,
and in your loving-kindness save me. ℞

SECOND READING

1 Peter 4.1–8

A reading from the first letter of Peter.

Since Christ suffered in the flesh, arm yourselves also with the same
intention (for whoever has suffered in the flesh has finished with sin), so as
to live for the rest of your earthly life no longer by human desires but by the
will of God. You have already spent enough time in doing what the Gentiles
like to do, living in licentiousness, passions, drunkenness, revels, carousing,
and lawless idolatry. They are surprised that you no longer join them in the
same excesses of dissipation, and so they blaspheme. But they will have to
give an account to him who stands ready to judge the living and the dead.
For this is the reason the gospel was proclaimed even to the dead, so that,
though they had been judged in the flesh as everyone is judged, they might
live in the spirit as God does.

The end of all things is near; therefore be serious and discipline yourselves for
the sake of your prayers. Above all, maintain constant love for one another,
for love covers a multitude of sins.

GOSPEL (Alternative readings)

Either   **Matthew 27.57–66**

Hear the gospel of our Lord Jesus Christ according to Matthew.

When it was evening, there came a rich man from Arimathea, named Joseph, who was also a disciple of Jesus. He went to Pilate and asked for the body of Jesus; then Pilate ordered it to be given to him. So Joseph took the body and wrapped it in a clean linen cloth and laid it in his own new tomb, which he had hewn in the rock. He then rolled a great stone to the door of the tomb and went away. Mary Magdalene and the other Mary were there, sitting opposite the tomb.

The next day, that is, after the day of Preparation, the chief priests and the Pharisees gathered before Pilate and said, 'Sir, we remember what that impostor said while he was still alive, "After three days I will rise again." Therefore command the tomb to be made secure until the third day; otherwise his disciples may go and steal him away, and tell the people, "He has been raised from the dead," and the last deception would be worse than the first.' Pilate said to them, 'You have a guard of soldiers; go, make it as secure as you can.' So they went with the guard and made the tomb secure by sealing the stone.

Or   **John 19.38–42**

Hear the gospel of our Lord Jesus Christ according to John.

Joseph of Arimathea, who was a disciple of Jesus, though a secret one because of his fear of the Jews, asked Pilate to let him take away the body of Jesus. Pilate gave him permission; so he came and removed his body. Nicodemus, who had at first come to Jesus by night, also came, bringing a mixture of myrrh and aloes, weighing about a hundred pounds.

They took the body of Jesus and wrapped it with the spices in linen cloths, according to the burial custom of the Jews. Now there was a garden in the place where he was crucified, and in the garden there was a new tomb in which no one had ever been laid. And so, because it was the Jewish day of Preparation, and the tomb was nearby, they laid Jesus there.

EASTER VIGIL   YEARS A B C

YEARS A B C

The following readings and psalms are provided for use at the Easter Vigil.
A minimum of three Old Testament readings should be chosen.
The reading from Exodus 14 should always be used.

OLD TESTAMENT READINGS AND PSALMS

FIRST READING   Genesis 1.1 – 2.4a

A reading from the book of Genesis.

In the beginning when God created the heavens and the earth, the earth was a formless void and darkness covered the face of the deep, while a wind from God swept over the face of the waters. Then God said, 'Let there be light'; and there was light. And God saw that the light was good; and God separated the light from the darkness. God called the light Day, and the darkness he called Night. And there was evening and there was morning, the first day.

And God said, 'Let there be a dome in the midst of the waters, and let it separate the waters from the waters.' So God made the dome and separated the waters that were under the dome from the waters that were above the dome. And it was so. God called the dome Sky. And there was evening and there was morning, the second day.

And God said, 'Let the waters under the sky be gathered together into one place, and let the dry land appear.' And it was so. God called the dry land Earth, and the waters that were gathered together he called Seas. And God saw that it was good. Then God said, 'Let the earth put forth vegetation: plants yielding seed, and fruit trees of every kind on earth that bear fruit with the seed in it.' And it was so. The earth brought forth vegetation: plants yielding seed of every kind, and trees of every kind bearing fruit with the seed in it. And God saw that it was good. And there was evening and there was morning, the third day.

And God said, 'Let there be lights in the dome of the sky to separate the day from the night; and let them be for signs and for seasons and for days and years, and let them be lights in the dome of the sky to give light upon the earth.' And it was so. God made the two great lights – the greater light to rule the day and the lesser light to rule the night – and the stars. God set them in the dome of the sky to give light upon the earth, to rule over the day and over the night, and to separate the light from the darkness. And God saw that it was good. And there was evening and there was morning, the fourth day.

And God said, 'Let the waters bring forth swarms of living creatures, and let birds fly above the earth across the dome of the sky.' So God created the great sea monsters and every living creature that moves, of every kind, with which the waters swarm, and every winged bird of every kind. And God saw that it was good. God blessed them, saying, 'Be fruitful and multiply and fill the waters in the seas, and let birds multiply on the earth.' And there was evening and there was morning, the fifth day.

And God said, 'Let the earth bring forth living creatures of every kind: cattle and creeping things and wild animals of the earth of every kind.' And it was so. God made the wild animals of the earth of every kind, and the cattle of every kind, and everything that creeps upon the ground of every kind. And God saw that it was good.

Then God said, 'Let us make humankind in our image, according to our likeness; and let them have dominion over the fish of the sea, and over the birds of the air, and over the cattle, and over all the wild animals of the earth, and over every creeping thing that creeps upon the earth.' So God created humankind in his image, in the image of God he created them; male and female he created them. God blessed them, and God said to them, 'Be fruitful and multiply, and fill the earth and subdue it; and have dominion over the fish of the sea and over the birds of the air and over every living thing that moves upon the earth.' God said, 'See, I have given you every plant yielding seed that is upon the face of all the earth, and every tree with seed in its fruit; you shall have them for food. And to every beast of the earth, and to every bird of the air, and to everything that creeps on the earth, everything that has the breath of life, I have given every green plant for food.' And it was so. God saw everything that he had made, and indeed, it was very good. And there was evening and there was morning, the sixth day.

Thus the heavens and the earth were finished, and all their multitude. And on the seventh day God finished the work that he had done, and he rested on the seventh day from all the work that he had done. So God blessed the seventh day and hallowed it, because on it God rested from all the work that he had done in creation. These are the generations of the heavens and the earth when they were created.

PSALM   Psalm 136.1–9, 23–26

Give thanks to the Lord, for he is good,
for his mercy endures for ever.
Give thanks to the God of gods,
for his mercy endures for ever.
Give thanks to the Lord of lords,
for his mercy endures for ever.
Who only does great wonders,
for his mercy endures for ever;
Who by his wisdom made the heavens,
for his mercy endures for ever;
Who spread out the earth upon the waters,
for his mercy endures for ever;
Who created great lights,
for his mercy endures for ever;
The sun to rule the day,
for his mercy endures for ever;
The moon and the stars to govern the night,
for his mercy endures for ever.
It is he who remembered us in our low estate,
for his mercy endures for ever;
And delivered us from our enemies,
for his mercy endures for ever;
Who gives food to all creatures,
for his mercy endures for ever;

Give thanks to the God of heaven,
for his mercy endures for ever.

SECOND READING   Genesis 7.1–5, 11–18; 8.6–18; 9.8–13

A reading from the book of Genesis.

The LORD said to Noah, 'Go into the ark, you and all your household, for I have seen that you alone are righteous before me in this generation. Take with you seven pairs of all clean animals, the male and its mate; and a pair of the animals that are not clean, the male and its mate; and seven pairs of the birds of the air also, male and female, to keep their kind alive on the face of all the earth. For in seven days I will send rain on the earth for forty days and forty nights; and every living thing that I have made I will blot out from the face of the ground.' And Noah did all that the LORD had commanded him.

In the six-hundredth year of Noah's life, in the second month, on the seventeenth day of the month, on that day all the fountains of the great deep burst forth, and the windows of the heavens were opened. The rain fell on the earth forty days and forty nights. On the very same day Noah with his sons, Shem and Ham and Japheth, and Noah's wife and the three wives of his sons entered the ark, they and every wild animal of every kind, and all domestic animals of every kind, and every creeping thing that creeps on the earth, and every bird of every kind – every bird, every winged creature. They went into the ark with Noah, two and two of all flesh in which there was the breath of life. And those that entered, male and female of all flesh, went in as God had commanded him; and the LORD shut him in. The flood continued for forty days on the earth; and the waters increased, and bore up the ark, and it rose high above the earth. The waters swelled and increased greatly on the earth; and the ark floated on the face of the waters.

At the end of forty days Noah opened the window of the ark that he had made and sent out the raven; and it went to and fro until the waters were dried up from the earth. Then he sent out the dove from him, to see if the waters had subsided from the face of the ground; but the dove found no place to set its foot, and it returned to him to the ark, for the waters were still on the face of the whole earth. So he put out his hand and took it and brought it into the ark with him. He waited another seven days, and again he sent out the dove from the ark; and the dove came back to him in the evening, and there in its beak was a freshly plucked olive leaf; so Noah knew that the waters had subsided from the earth. Then he waited another seven days, and sent out the dove; and it did not return to him any more. In the six hundred and first year, in the first month, the first day of the month, the waters were dried up from the earth; and Noah removed the covering of the ark, and looked, and saw that the face of the ground was drying. In the second month, on the twenty-seventh day of the month, the earth was dry. Then God said to Noah, 'Go out of the ark, you and your wife, and your sons and your sons' wives with you. Bring out with you every living thing that is with you of all flesh – birds and animals and every creeping thing that creeps on the earth – so that they may abound on the earth, and be fruitful and multiply on the earth.' So Noah went out with his sons and his wife and his sons' wives.

Then God said to Noah and to his sons with him, 'As for me, I am establishing my covenant with you and your descendants after you, and with every living creature that is with you, the birds, the domestic animals, and every animal of the earth with you, as many as came out of the ark. I establish my covenant with you, that never again shall all flesh be cut off by the waters of a flood, and never again shall there be a flood to destroy the

earth.' God said, 'This is the sign of the covenant that I make between me
and you and every living creature that is with you, for all future generations:
I have set my bow in the clouds, and it shall be a sign of the covenant
between me and the earth.'

PSALM   Psalm 46

℟ **The Lord of hosts is with us;**
   the God of Jacob is our stronghold.

God is our refuge and strength,
a very present help in trouble;
Therefore we will not fear, though the earth be moved,
and though the mountains be toppled
into the depths of the sea;
Though its waters rage and foam,
and though the mountains tremble at its tumult. ℟

[The Lord of hosts is with us;
the God of Jacob is our stronghold.]

There is a river whose streams
make glad the city of God,
the holy habitation of the Most High.
God is in the midst of her; s
he shall not be overthrown;
God shall help her at the break of day.
The nations make much ado
and the kingdoms are shaken;
God has spoken and the earth shall melt away. ℟

[The Lord of hosts is with us;
the God of Jacob is our stronghold.]

Come now and look upon the works of the Lord,
what awesome things he has done on earth.
It is he who makes war to cease in all the world;
he breaks the bow and shatters the spear
and burns the shields with fire.
'Be still, then, and know that I am God;
I will be exalted among the nations;
I will be exalted in the earth.' ℟

[The Lord of hosts is with us;
the God of Jacob is our stronghold.]

THIRD READING   **Genesis 22.1–18**

A reading from the book of Genesis.

God tested Abraham. He said to him, 'Abraham!' And Abraham said, 'Here I am.' God said, 'Take your son, your only son Isaac, whom you love, and go to the land of Moriah, and offer him there as a burnt-offering on one of the mountains that I shall show you.' So Abraham rose early in the morning, saddled his donkey, and took two of his young men with him, and his son Isaac; he cut the wood for the burnt-offering, and set out and went to the place in the distance that God had shown him.

On the third day Abraham looked up and saw the place far away. Then Abraham said to his young men, 'Stay here with the donkey; the boy and I will go over there; we will worship, and then we will come back to you.' Abraham took the wood of the burnt-offering and laid it on his son Isaac, and he himself carried the fire and the knife. So the two of them walked on together. Isaac said to his father Abraham, 'Father!' And Abraham said, 'Here I am, my son.' Isaac said, 'The fire and the wood are here, but where is the lamb for a burnt-offering?' Abraham said, 'God himself will provide the lamb for a burnt-offering, my son.' So the two of them walked on together. When they came to the place that God had shown him, Abraham built an altar there and laid the wood in order. He bound his son Isaac, and laid him on the altar, on top of the wood. Then Abraham reached out his hand and took the knife to kill his son. But the angel of the LORD called to him from heaven, and said, 'Abraham, Abraham!' And he said, 'Here I am.' The angel said, 'Do not lay your hand on the boy or do anything to him; for now I know that you fear God, since you have not withheld your son, your only son, from me.' And Abraham looked up and saw a ram, caught in a thicket by its horns. Abraham went and took the ram and offered it up as a burnt-offering instead of his son.

So Abraham called that place 'The LORD will provide'; as it is said to this day, 'On the mount of the LORD it shall be provided.' The angel of the LORD called to Abraham a second time from heaven, and said, 'By myself I have sworn, says the LORD: Because you have done this, and have not withheld your son, your only son, I will indeed bless you, and I will make your offspring as numerous as the stars of heaven and as the sand that is on the seashore. And your offspring shall possess the gate of their enemies, and by your offspring shall all the nations of the earth gain blessing for themselves, because you have obeyed my voice.'

PSALM   Psalm 16

℟ **O Lord, you are my portion and my cup.**

Protect me, O God, for I take refuge in you;
I have said to the Lord, 'You are my Lord,
my good above all other.'
All my delight is upon the godly that are in the land,
upon those who are noble among the people. ℟

But those who run after other gods
shall have their troubles multiplied.
Their libations of blood I will not offer,
nor take the names of their gods upon my lips. ℟

O Lord, you are my portion and my cup;
it is you who uphold my lot.
My boundaries enclose a pleasant land;
indeed, I have a goodly heritage. ℟

I will bless the Lord who gives me counsel;
my heart teaches me, night after night.
I have set the Lord always before me;
because he is at my right hand I shall not fall. ℟

My heart, therefore, is glad and my spirit rejoices;
my body also shall rest in hope.
For you will not abandon me to the grave,
nor let your holy one see the Pit.
You will show me the path of life;
in your presence there is fullness of joy,
and in your right hand are pleasures for evermore. ℟

FOURTH READING   Exodus 14.10–31; 15.20–21

A reading from the book of Exodus.

As Pharaoh drew near, the Israelites looked back, and there were the
Egyptians advancing on them. In great fear the Israelites cried out to the
LORD. They said to Moses, 'Was it because there were no graves in Egypt that
you have taken us away to die in the wilderness? What have you done to us,
bringing us out of Egypt? Is this not the very thing we told you in Egypt, "Let
us alone and let us serve the Egyptians"? For it would have been better for us
to serve the Egyptians than to die in the wilderness.' But Moses said to the
people, 'Do not be afraid, stand firm, and see the deliverance that the LORD

will accomplish for you today; for the Egyptians whom you see today you shall never see again. The LORD will fight for you, and you have only to keep still.'

Then the LORD said to Moses, 'Why do you cry out to me? Tell the Israelites to go forward. But you lift up your staff, and stretch out your hand over the sea and divide it, that the Israelites may go into the sea on dry ground. Then I will harden the hearts of the Egyptians so that they will go in after them; and so I will gain glory for myself over Pharaoh and all his army, his chariots, and his chariot drivers. And the Egyptians shall know that I am the LORD, when I have gained glory for myself over Pharaoh, his chariots, and his chariot drivers.'

The angel of God who was going before the Israelite army moved and went behind them; and the pillar of cloud moved from in front of them and took its place behind them. It came between the army of Egypt and the army of Israel. And so the cloud was there with the darkness, and it lit up the night; one did not come near the other all night.

Then Moses stretched out his hand over the sea. The LORD drove the sea back by a strong east wind all night, and turned the sea into dry land; and the waters were divided. The Israelites went into the sea on dry ground, the waters forming a wall for them on their right and on their left. The Egyptians pursued, and went into the sea after them, all of Pharaoh's horses, chariots, and chariot drivers. At the morning watch the LORD in the pillar of fire and cloud looked down upon the Egyptian army, and threw the Egyptian army into panic. He clogged their chariot wheels so that they turned with difficulty. The Egyptians said, 'Let us flee from the Israelites, for the LORD is fighting for them against Egypt.'

Then the LORD said to Moses, 'Stretch out your hand over the sea, so that the water may come back upon the Egyptians, upon their chariots and chariot drivers.' So Moses stretched out his hand over the sea, and at dawn the sea returned to its normal depth. As the Egyptians fled before it, the LORD tossed the Egyptians into the sea. The waters returned and covered the chariots and the chariot drivers, the entire army of Pharaoh that had followed them into the sea; not one of them remained. But the Israelites walked on dry ground through the sea, the waters forming a wall for them on their right and on their left.

Thus the LORD saved Israel that day from the Egyptians; and Israel saw the Egyptians dead on the seashore. Israel saw the great work that the LORD did against the Egyptians. So the people feared the LORD and believed in the LORD and in his servant Moses. Then the prophet Miriam, Aaron's sister, took a tambourine in her hand; and all the women went out after her with tambourines and with dancing. And Miriam sang to them: 'Sing to the LORD, for he has triumphed gloriously; horse and rider he has thrown into the sea.'

CANTICLE   **Exodus 15.1b–13, 17–18**

℞ **Sing to the Lord, for he has triumphed gloriously.**

'I will sing to the LORD, for he has triumphed gloriously;
horse and rider he has thrown into the sea.
The LORD is my strength and my might,
and he has become my salvation;
this is my God, and I will praise him,
my father's God, and I will exalt him.
The LORD is a warrior;
the LORD is his name. ℞

Pharaoh's chariots and his army he cast into the sea;
his picked officers were sunk in the Red Sea.
The floods covered them;
they went down into the depths like a stone.
Your right hand, O LORD, glorious in power –
your right hand, O LORD, shattered the enemy. ℞

In the greatness of your majesty you overthrew your adversaries;
you sent out your fury, it consumed them like stubble.
At the blast of your nostrils the waters piled up,
the floods stood up in a heap;
the deeps congealed in the heart of the sea. ℞

The enemy said,
"I will pursue, I will overtake, I will divide the spoil,
my desire shall have its fill of them.
I will draw my sword, my hand shall destroy them."
You blew with your wind, the sea covered them;
they sank like lead in the mighty waters. ℞

Who is like you, O LORD, among the gods?
Who is like you, majestic in holiness,
awesome in splendour, doing wonders?
You stretched out your right hand,
the earth swallowed them. ℞

In your steadfast love you led the people whom you redeemed;
you guided them by your strength to your holy abode.
You brought them in
and planted them on the mountain of your own possession,
the place, O LORD, that you made your abode,
the sanctuary, O LORD, that your hands have established.
The LORD will reign for ever and ever.' ℟

FIFTH READING   Isaiah 55.1–11

A reading from the book of the prophet Isaiah.

The LORD says this:
Everyone who thirsts,
come to the waters;
and you that have no money,
come, buy and eat!
Come, buy wine and milk
without money and without price.
Why do you spend your money for that which is not bread,
and your labour for that which does not satisfy?
Listen carefully to me, and eat what is good,
and delight yourselves in rich food.
Incline your ear, and come to me;
listen, so that you may live.
I will make with you an everlasting covenant,
my steadfast, sure love for David.
See, I made him a witness to the peoples,
a leader and commander for the peoples.
See, you shall call nations that you do not know,
and nations that do not know you shall run to you,
because of the LORD your God, the Holy One of Israel,
for he has glorified you.

Seek the LORD while he may be found,
call upon him while he is near;
let the wicked forsake their way,
and the unrighteous their thoughts;
let them return to the LORD, that he may have mercy on them,
and to our God, for he will abundantly pardon.
For my thoughts are not your thoughts,

nor are your ways my ways, says the LORD.
For as the heavens are higher than the earth,
so are my ways higher than your ways
and my thoughts than your thoughts.

For as the rain and the snow come down from heaven,
and do not return there until they have watered the earth,
making it bring forth and sprout,
giving seed to the sower and bread to the eater,
so shall my word be that goes out from my mouth;
it shall not return to me empty,
but it shall accomplish that which I purpose
and succeed in the thing for which I sent it.

CANTICLE   Isaiah 12.2-6

℟ **Shout aloud and sing for joy,**
   for great in your midst is the Holy One of Israel.

Surely God is my salvation;
I will trust, and will not be afraid,
for the LORD GOD is my strength and my might;
he has become my salvation.
With joy you will draw water
from the wells of salvation. ℟

And you will say in that day:
Give thanks to the LORD,
call on his name;
make known his deeds among the nations;
proclaim that his name is exalted. ℟

Sing praises to the LORD,
for he has done gloriously;
let this be known in all the earth.
Shout aloud and sing for joy, O royal Zion,
for great in your midst
is the Holy One of Israel. ℟

SIXTH READING

Either   **Baruch 3.9–15, 32–36; 4.1–4**

A reading from the book of the prophet Baruch.

Hear the commandments of life, O Israel;
give ear, and learn wisdom!
Why is it, O Israel,
why is it that you are in the land of your enemies,
that you are growing old in a foreign country,
that you are defiled with the dead,
that you are counted among those in Hades?
You have forsaken the fountain of wisdom.
If you had walked in the way of God,
you would be living in peace for ever.
Learn where there is wisdom,
where there is strength,
where there is understanding,
so that you may at the same time discern
where there is length of days, and life,
where there is light for the eyes, and peace.

Who has found her place?
And who has entered her storehouses?
But the one who knows all things knows her,
he found her by his understanding.
The one who prepared the earth for all time
filled it with four-footed creatures;
the one who sends forth the light, and it goes;
he called it, and it obeyed him, trembling;
the stars shone in their watches, and were glad;
he called them, and they said, 'Here we are!'
They shone with gladness for him who made them.
This is our God;
no other can be compared to him.
He found the whole way to knowledge,
and gave her to his servant Jacob
and to Israel, whom he loved.

She is the book of the commandments of God,
the law that endures for ever.

All who hold her fast will live,
and those who forsake her will die.
Turn, O Jacob, and take her;
walk towards the shining of her light.
Do not give your glory to another,
or your advantages to an alien people.
Happy are we, O Israel,
for we know what is pleasing to God.

Or   **Proverbs 8.1–8, 19–21; 9.4b–6**

A reading from the book of Proverbs.

Does not wisdom call,
and does not understanding raise her voice?
On the heights, beside the way,
at the crossroads she takes her stand;
beside the gates in front of the town,
at the entrance of the portals she cries out:
'To you, O people, I call,
and my cry is to all that live.
O simple ones, learn prudence;
acquire intelligence, you who lack it.
Hear, for I will speak noble things,
and from my lips will come what is right;
for my mouth will utter truth;
wickedness is an abomination to my lips.
All the words of my mouth are righteous;
there is nothing twisted or crooked in them.
My fruit is better than gold, even fine gold,
and my yield than choice silver.
I walk in the way of righteousness,
along the paths of justice,
endowing with wealth those who love me,
and filling their treasuries.'
To those without sense she says,
'Come, eat of my bread
and drink of the wine I have mixed.
Lay aside immaturity, and live,
and walk in the way of insight.'

PSALM   **Psalm 19**

℟ **The law of the Lord is perfect and revives the soul.**

The heavens declare the glory of God,
and the firmament shows his handiwork.
One day tells its tale to another,
and one night imparts knowledge to another.
Although they have no words or language,
and their voices are not heard,
Their sound has gone out into all lands,
and their message to the ends of the world. ℟

In the deep has he set a pavilion for the sun;
it comes forth like a bridegroom out of his chamber;
it rejoices like a champion to run its course.
It goes forth from the uttermost edge of the heavens
and runs about to the end of it again;
nothing is hidden from its burning heat. ℟

The law of the Lord is perfect
and revives the soul;
the testimony of the Lord is sure
and gives wisdom to the innocent.
The statutes of the Lord are just
and rejoice the heart;
the commandment of the Lord is clear
and gives light to the eyes. ℟

The fear of the Lord is clean
and endures for ever;
the judgements of the Lord are true
and righteous altogether.
More to be desired are they than gold,
more than much fine gold,
sweeter far than honey,
than honey in the comb. ℟

By them also is your servant enlightened,
and in keeping them there is great reward.
Who can tell how often he offends?
Cleanse me from my secret faults. ℟

Above all, keep your servant from presumptuous sins;
let them not get dominion over me;
then shall I be whole and sound,
and innocent of a great offence.
Let the words of my mouth and the meditation of my heart
be acceptable in your sight,
O Lord, my strength and my redeemer. ℟

SEVENTH READING   Ezekiel 36.24–28

A reading from the book of the prophet Ezekiel.

The word of the LORD came to me: I will take you from the nations, and
gather you from all the countries, and bring you into your own land. I will
sprinkle clean water upon you, and you shall be clean from all your
uncleannesses, and from all your idols I will cleanse you. A new heart I will
give you, and a new spirit I will put within you; and I will remove from your
body the heart of stone and give you a heart of flesh. I will put my spirit
within you, and make you follow my statutes and be careful to observe my
ordinances. Then you shall live in the land that I gave to your ancestors; and
you shall be my people, and I will be your God.

PSALM   Psalms 42 and 43

℟ **Why are you so full of heaviness, O my soul?**
  and why are you so disquieted within me?

As the deer longs for the water-brooks,
so longs my soul for you, O God.
My soul is athirst for God, athirst for the living God;
when shall I come to appear before the presence of God?
My tears have been my food day and night,
while all day long they say to me,
'Where now is your God?' ℟

I pour out my soul when I think on these things:
how I went with the multitude
and led them into the house of God,
With the voice of praise and thanksgiving,
among those who keep holy-day. ℟

[Why are you so full of heaviness, O my soul?
and why are you so disquieted within me?]

Put your trust in God;
for I will yet give thanks to him,
who is the help of my countenance, and my God.
My soul is heavy within me;
therefore I will remember you from the land of Jordan,
and from the peak of Mizar among the heights of Hermon.
One deep calls to another in the noise of your cataracts;
all your rapids and floods have gone over me. ℟

The Lord grants his loving-kindness in the daytime;
in the night season his song is with me,
a prayer to the God of my life.
I will say to the God of my strength,
'Why have you forgotten me?
and why do I go so heavily
while the enemy oppresses me?' ℟

While my bones are being broken,
my enemies mock me to my face;
All day long they mock me, say to me,
'Where now is your God?' ℟

[Why are you so full of heaviness, O my soul?
and why are you so disquieted within me?]
Put your trust in God;
for I will yet give thanks to him,
who is the help of my countenance, and my God. ℟

Give judgement for me, O God,
and defend my cause against an ungodly people;
deliver me from the deceitful and the wicked.
For you are the God of my strength;
why have you put me from you?
and why do I go so heavily
while the enemy oppresses me? ℟

Send out your light and your truth,
that they may lead me,
and bring me to your holy hill
and to your dwelling;
That I may go to the altar of God,
to the God of my joy and gladness;
and on the harp I will give thanks to you,
O God my God. ℟

[Why are you so full of heaviness, O my soul?
and why are you so disquieted within me?]
Put your trust in God;
for I will yet give thanks to him,
who is the help of my countenance, and my God. ℞

EIGHTH READING   Ezekiel 37.1–14

A reading from the book of the prophet Ezekiel.

The hand of the LORD came upon me, and he brought me out by the spirit
of the LORD and set me down in the middle of a valley; it was full of bones.
He led me all around them; there were very many lying in the valley, and
they were very dry. He said to me, 'Mortal, can these bones live?' I answered,
'O Lord GOD, you know.' Then he said to me, 'Prophesy to these bones, and
say to them: O dry bones, hear the word of the LORD. Thus says the Lord
GOD to these bones: I will cause breath to enter you, and you shall live. I will
lay sinews on you, and will cause flesh to come upon you, and cover you
with skin, and put breath in you, and you shall live; and you shall know that
I am the LORD.'

So I prophesied as I had been commanded; and as I prophesied, suddenly
there was a noise, a rattling, and the bones came together, bone to its bone. I
looked, and there were sinews on them, and flesh had come upon them, and
skin had covered them; but there was no breath in them. Then he said to me,
'Prophesy to the breath, prophesy, mortal, and say to the breath: Thus says
the Lord GOD: Come from the four winds, O breath, and breathe upon these
slain, that they may live.' I prophesied as he commanded me, and the breath
came into them, and they lived, and stood on their feet, a vast multitude.

Then he said to me, 'Mortal, these bones are the whole house of Israel. They
say, "Our bones are dried up, and our hope is lost; we are cut off completely."
Therefore prophesy, and say to them, Thus says the Lord GOD: I am going to
open your graves, and bring you up from your graves, O my people; and I
will bring you back to the land of Israel. And you shall know that I am the
LORD, when I open your graves, and bring you up from your graves, O my
people. I will put my spirit within you, and you shall live, and I will place
you on your own soil; then you shall know that I, the LORD, have spoken
and will act, says the LORD.'

PSALM   **Psalm 143**

℟ **Let me hear of your loving-kindness in the morning.**

Lord, hear my prayer,
and in your faithfulness heed my supplications;
answer me in your righteousness.
Enter not into judgement with your servant,
for in your sight shall no one living be justified.
For my enemy has sought my life
and has crushed me to the ground;
making me live in dark places
like those who are long dead. ℟

My spirit faints within me;
my heart within me is desolate.
I remember the time past;
I muse upon all your deeds;
I consider the works of your hands.
I spread out my hands to you;
my soul gasps to you like a thirsty land. ℟

O Lord, make haste to answer me; my spirit fails me;
do not hide your face from me
or I shall be like those who go down to the Pit.
Let me hear of your loving-kindness in the morning,
for I put my trust in you;
show me the road that I must walk,
for I lift up my soul to you.
Deliver me from my enemies, O Lord,
for I flee to you for refuge. ℟

Teach me to do what pleases you, for you are my God;
let your good Spirit lead me on level ground.
Revive me, O Lord, for your name's sake;
for your righteousness' sake, bring me out of trouble.
Of your goodness, destroy my enemies
and bring all my foes to naught,
for truly I am your servant. ℟

NINTH READING   Zephaniah 3.14–20

A reading from the book of the prophet Zephaniah.

Sing aloud, O daughter Zion; shout, O Israel!
Rejoice and exult with all your heart,
O daughter Jerusalem!
The LORD has taken away the judgements against you,
he has turned away your enemies.
The king of Israel, the LORD, is in your midst;
you shall fear disaster no more.
On that day it shall be said to Jerusalem:
Do not fear, O Zion;
do not let your hands grow weak.
The LORD, your God, is in your midst,
a warrior who gives victory;
he will rejoice over you with gladness,
he will renew you in his love;
he will exult over you with loud singing
as on a day of festival.
I will remove disaster from you,
so that you will not bear reproach for it.
I will deal with all your oppressors at that time.
And I will save the lame and gather the outcast,
and I will change their shame into praise and renown in all the earth.
At that time I will bring you home, at the time when I gather you;
for I will make you renowned
and praised among all the peoples of the earth,
when I restore your fortunes before your eyes, says the LORD.

PSALM   Psalm 98

℟ **The Lord has made known his victory
in the sight of the nations.**

Sing to the Lord a new song,
for he has done marvellous things.
With his right hand and his holy arm
has he won for himself the victory. ℟

The Lord has made known his victory;
his righteousness has he openly shown
in the sight of the nations.
He remembers his mercy and faithfulness
to the house of Israel,
and all the ends of the earth have seen
the victory of our God. ℟

Shout with joy to the Lord, all you lands;
lift up your voice, rejoice and sing.
Sing to the Lord with the harp,
with the harp and the voice of song.
With trumpets and the sound of the horn
shout with joy before the King, the Lord. ℟

Let the sea make a noise and all that is in it,
the lands and those who dwell therein.
Let the rivers clap their hands,
and let the hills ring out with joy before the Lord,
when he comes to judge the earth.
In righteousness shall he judge the world,
and the peoples with equity. ℟

NEW TESTAMENT READING   Romans 6.3–11

A reading from the letter of Paul to the Romans.

Do you not know that all of us who have been baptized into Christ Jesus
were baptized into his death? Therefore we have been buried with him by
baptism into death, so that, just as Christ was raised from the dead by the
glory of the Father, so we too might walk in newness of life.

For if we have been united with him in a death like his, we will certainly be
united with him in a resurrection like his. We know that our old self was
crucified with him so that the body of sin might be destroyed, and we might
no longer be enslaved to sin. For whoever has died is freed from sin. But if we
have died with Christ, we believe that we will also live with him. We know
that Christ, being raised from the dead, will never die again; death no longer
has dominion over him. The death he died, he died to sin, once for all; but
the life he lives, he lives to God.So you also must consider yourselves dead to
sin and alive to God in Christ Jesus.

PSALM   Psalm 114

℟ **Alleluia! Alleluia! Alleluia!**

Alleluia!
When Israel came out of Egypt,
the house of Jacob from a people of strange speech,
Judah became God's sanctuary
and Israel his dominion. ℟

The sea beheld it and fled;
Jordan turned and went back.
The mountains skipped like rams,
and the little hills like young sheep. ℟

What ailed you, O sea, that you fled?
O Jordan, that you turned back?
You mountains, that you skipped like rams?
you little hills like young sheep? ℟

Tremble, O earth, at the presence of the Lord,
at the presence of the God of Jacob,
Who turned the hard rock into a pool of water
and flint-stone into a flowing spring. ℟

GOSPEL   **YEAR A**   **Matthew 28:1–10**

Years B and C have their own Gospels: see pages 375 and 598 respectively.

Hear the gospel of our Lord Jesus Christ according to Matthew.

After the sabbath, as the first day of the week was dawning, Mary Magdalene
and the other Mary went to see the tomb. And suddenly there was a great
earthquake; for an angel of the Lord, descending from heaven, came and
rolled back the stone and sat on it. His appearance was like lightning, and his
clothing white as snow. For fear of him the guards shook and became like
dead men. But the angel said to the women, 'Do not be afraid; I know that
you are looking for Jesus who was crucified. He is not here; for he has been
raised, as he said. Come, see the place where he lay. Then go quickly and tell
his disciples, "He has been raised from the dead, and indeed he is going
ahead of you to Galilee; there you will see him." This is my message for you.'
So they left the tomb quickly with fear and great joy, and ran to tell his
disciples. Suddenly Jesus met them and said, 'Greetings!' And they came to

him, took hold of his feet, and worshipped him. Then Jesus said to them, 'Do not be afraid; go and tell my brothers to go to Galilee; there they will see me.'

EASTER DAY   YEAR A

The following readings and psalms are provided for use at the principal Easter Day Service. Acts 10.34–43 should be read as either the First or Second Reading.

FIRST READING (Alternative readings)

Either   **Acts 10.34–43**

A reading from the Acts of the Apostles.

Peter began to speak to those assembled in the house of Cornelius. 'I truly understand that God shows no partiality, but in every nation anyone who fears him and does what is right is acceptable to him. You know the message he sent to the people of Israel, preaching peace by Jesus Christ – he is Lord of all. That message spread throughout Judea, beginning in Galilee after the baptism that John announced: how God anointed Jesus of Nazareth with the Holy Spirit and with power; how he went about doing good and healing all who were oppressed by the devil, for God was with him. We are witnesses to all that he did both in Judea and in Jerusalem. They put him to death by hanging him on a tree; but God raised him on the third day and allowed him to appear, not to all the people but to us who were chosen by God as witnesses, and who ate and drank with him after he rose from the dead. He commanded us to preach to the people and to testify that he is the one ordained by God as judge of the living and the dead. All the prophets testify about him that everyone who believes in him receives forgiveness of sins through his name.'

Or   **Jeremiah 31.1–6**

A reading from the book of the prophet Jeremiah.

At that time, says the LORD,
I will be the God of all the families of Israel,
and they shall be my people.
Thus says the LORD:
The people who survived the sword found grace in the wilderness;
when Israel sought for rest,

the LORD appeared to him from far away.
I have loved you with an everlasting love;
therefore I have continued my faithfulness to you.
Again I will build you,
and you shall be built, O virgin Israel!
Again you shall take your tambourines,
and go forth in the dance of the merrymakers.
Again you shall plant vineyards on the mountains of Samaria;
the planters shall plant, and shall enjoy the fruit.
For there shall be a day
when sentinels will call in the hill country of Ephraim:
'Come, let us go up to Zion, to the LORD our God.'

PSALM   Psalm 118.1-2, 14-24

℟ **On this day the Lord has acted;**
  we will rejoice and be glad in it.
       or
℟ **Alleluia! Alleluia! Alleluia!**
  This is the day the Lord has made.

Give thanks to the Lord, for he is good;
his mercy endures for ever.
Let Israel now proclaim,
'His mercy endures for ever.' ℟

The Lord is my strength and my song,
and he has become my salvation.
There is a sound of exultation and victory
in the tents of the righteous:
'The right hand of the Lord has triumphed!
the right hand of the Lord is exalted!
the right hand of the Lord has triumphed!' ℟

I shall not die, but live,
and declare the works of the Lord.
The Lord has punished me sorely,
but he did not hand me over to death.
Open for me the gates of righteousness;
I will enter them; I will offer thanks to the Lord. ℟

'This is the gate of the Lord;
whoever is righteous may enter.'

I will give thanks to you, for you answered me
and have become my salvation.
The same stone which the builders rejected
has become the chief corner-stone. ℟

This is the Lord's doing,
and it is marvellous in our eyes.
On this day the Lord has acted;
we will rejoice and be glad in it. ℟

SECOND READING (Alternative readings)

Either   Colossians 3.1–4

A reading from the letter of Paul to the Colossians.

If you have been raised with Christ, seek the things that are above, where
Christ is, seated at the right hand of God. Set your minds on things that are
above, not on things that are on earth, for you have died, and your life is
hidden with Christ in God. When Christ who is your life is revealed, then
you also will be revealed with him in glory.

Or   Acts 10.34–43

A reading from the Acts of the Apostles.

For text see page 149.

GOSPEL (Alternative readings)

Either   John 20.1–18

Hear the gospel of our Lord Jesus Christ according to John.

Early on the first day of the week, while it was still dark, Mary Magdalene
came to the tomb and saw that the stone had been removed from the tomb.
So she ran and went to Simon Peter and the other disciple, the one whom
Jesus loved, and said to them, 'They have taken the Lord out of the tomb,
and we do not know where they have laid him.' Then Peter and the other
disciple set out and went towards the tomb. The two were running together,
but the other disciple outran Peter and reached the tomb first. He bent down
to look in and saw the linen wrappings lying there, but he did not go in.

Then Simon Peter came, following him, and went into the tomb. He saw the linen wrappings lying there, and the cloth that had been on Jesus' head, not lying with the linen wrappings but rolled up in a place by itself. Then the other disciple, who reached the tomb first, also went in, and he saw and believed; for as yet they did not understand the scripture, that he must rise from the dead. Then the disciples returned to their homes.

But Mary stood weeping outside the tomb. As she wept, she bent over to look into the tomb; and she saw two angels in white, sitting where the body of Jesus had been lying, one at the head and the other at the feet. They said to her, 'Woman, why are you weeping?' She said to them, 'They have taken away my Lord, and I do not know where they have laid him.' When she had said this, she turned around and saw Jesus standing there, but she did not know that it was Jesus. Jesus said to her, 'Woman, why are you weeping? For whom are you looking?' Supposing him to be the gardener, she said to him, 'Sir, if you have carried him away, tell me where you have laid him, and I will take him away.' Jesus said to her, 'Mary!' She turned and said to him in Hebrew, 'Rabbouni!' which means Teacher. Jesus said to her, 'Do not hold on to me, because I have not yet ascended to the Father. But go to my brothers and say to them, "I am ascending to my Father and your Father, to my God and your God."' Mary Magdalene went and announced to the disciples, 'I have seen the Lord'; and she told them that he had said these things to her.

Or   **Matthew 28.1–10**

Hear the gospel of our Lord Jesus Christ according to Matthew.

After the sabbath, as the first day of the week was dawning, Mary Magdalene and the other Mary went to see the tomb. And suddenly there was a great earthquake; for an angel of the Lord, descending from heaven, came and rolled back the stone and sat on it. His appearance was like lightning, and his clothing white as snow. For fear of him the guards shook and became like dead men. But the angel said to the women, 'Do not be afraid; I know that you are looking for Jesus who was crucified. He is not here; for he has been raised, as he said. Come, see the place where he lay. Then go quickly and tell his disciples, "He has been raised from the dead, and indeed he is going ahead of you to Galilee; there you will see him." This is my message for you.' So they left the tomb quickly with fear and great joy, and ran to tell his disciples. Suddenly Jesus met them and said, 'Greetings!' And they came to him, took hold of his feet, and worshipped him. Then Jesus said to them, 'Do not be afraid; go and tell my brothers to go to Galilee; there they will see me.'

OLD TESTAMENT READINGS FOR SUNDAYS IN EASTERTIDE

For those who require an Old Testament reading on the Sundays in Eastertide, provision is made in the Supplement, pages 831–844 (Church of England) or 844–857 (Church of Ireland/Church in Wales). If these are used, the reading from Acts must be used as the Second Reading.

EASTER 2   YEAR A

FIRST READING   Acts 2.14a, 22–32

A reading from the Acts of the Apostles.

On the day of Pentecost, Peter, standing with the eleven, raised his voice and addressed the crowd,

'You that are Israelites, listen to what I have to say: Jesus of Nazareth, a man attested to you by God with deeds of power, wonders, and signs that God did through him among you, as you yourselves know – this man, handed over to you according to the definite plan and foreknowledge of God, you crucified and killed by the hands of those outside the law. But God raised him up, having freed him from death, because it was impossible for him to be held in its power.
For David says concerning him,
"I saw the Lord always before me,
for he is at my right hand so that I will not be shaken;
therefore my heart was glad, and my tongue rejoiced;
moreover my flesh will live in hope.
For you will not abandon my soul to Hades,
or let your Holy One experience corruption.
You have made known to me the ways of life;
you will make me full of gladness with your presence."

Fellow Israelites, I may say to you confidently of our ancestor David that he both died and was buried, and his tomb is with us to this day. Since he was a prophet, he knew that God had sworn with an oath to him that he would put one of his descendants on his throne. Foreseeing this, David spoke of the resurrection of the Messiah, saying,
"He was not abandoned to Hades,
nor did his flesh experience corruption."
This Jesus God raised up, and of that all of us are witnesses.'

PSALM

℟ O Lord, you are my portion and my cup.

Protect me, O God, for I take refuge in you;
I have said to the Lord, 'You are my Lord,
my good above all other.'
All my delight is upon the godly that are in the land,
upon those who are noble among the people. ℟

But those who run after other gods
shall have their troubles multiplied.
Their libations of blood I will not offer,
nor take the names of their gods upon my lips. ℟

O Lord, you are my portion and my cup;
it is you who uphold my lot.
My boundaries enclose a pleasant land; indeed,
I have a goodly heritage. ℟

I will bless the Lord who gives me counsel;
my heart teaches me, night after night.
I have set the Lord always before me;
because he is at my right hand I shall not fall. ℟

My heart, therefore, is glad and my spirit rejoices;
my body also shall rest in hope.
For you will not abandon me to the grave,
nor let your holy one see the Pit.
You will show me the path of life;
in your presence there is fullness of joy,
and in your right hand are pleasures for evermore. ℟

SECOND READING

A reading from the first letter of Peter.

Blessed be the God and Father of our Lord Jesus Christ! By his great mercy he has given us a new birth into a living hope through the resurrection of Jesus Christ from the dead, and into an inheritance that is imperishable, undefiled, and unfading, kept in heaven for you, who are being protected by the power of God through faith for a salvation ready to be revealed in the last time. In this you rejoice, even if now for a little while you have had to suffer various trials, so that the genuineness of your faith – being more precious than gold that, though perishable, is tested by fire – may be found to result in praise and glory and honour when Jesus Christ is revealed. Although you have not seen him, you love him; and even though you do not see him now, you believe in him and rejoice with an indescribable and glorious joy, for you are receiving the outcome of your faith, the salvation of your souls.

GOSPEL   John 20.19–31

Hear the gospel of our Lord Jesus Christ according to John.

When it was evening on the first day of the week, and the doors of the house where the disciples had met were locked for fear of the Jews, Jesus came and stood among them and said, 'Peace be with you.' After he said this, he showed them his hands and his side. Then the disciples rejoiced when they saw the Lord. Jesus said to them again, 'Peace be with you. As the Father has sent me, so I send you.' When he had said this, he breathed on them and said to them, 'Receive the Holy Spirit. If you forgive the sins of any, they are forgiven them; if you retain the sins of any, they are retained.'

But Thomas (who was called the Twin), one of the twelve, was not with them when Jesus came. So the other disciples told him, 'We have seen the Lord.' But he said to them, 'Unless I see the mark of the nails in his hands, and put my finger in the mark of the nails and my hand in his side, I will not believe.'

A week later his disciples were again in the house, and Thomas was with them. Although the doors were shut, Jesus came and stood among them and said, 'Peace be with you.' Then he said to Thomas, 'Put your finger here and see my hands. Reach out your hand and put it in my side. Do not doubt but believe.' Thomas answered him, 'My Lord and my God!' Jesus said to him, 'Have you believed because you have seen me? Blessed are those who have not seen and yet have come to believe.'

Now Jesus did many other signs in the presence of his disciples, which are not written in this book. But these are written so that you may come to believe that Jesus is the Messiah, the Son of God, and that through believing you may have life in his name.

EASTER 3   YEAR A

FIRST READING   **Acts 2.14a, 36–41**

A reading from the Acts of the Apostles.

On the day of Pentecost, Peter, standing with the eleven, raised his voice and addressed the crowd,

'Let the entire house of Israel know with certainty that God has made him both Lord and Messiah, this Jesus whom you crucified.'

Now when they heard this, they were cut to the heart and said to Peter and to the other apostles, 'Brothers, what should we do?' Peter said to them, 'Repent, and be baptized every one of you in the name of Jesus Christ so that your sins may be forgiven; and you will receive the gift of the Holy Spirit. For the promise is for you, for your children, and for all who are far away, everyone whom the Lord our God calls to him.' And he testified with many other arguments and exhorted them, saying, 'Save yourselves from this corrupt generation.' So those who welcomed his message were baptized, and that day about three thousand persons were added to their number.

PSALM   **Psalm 116.1–3, 10–17**

℟ **Gracious is the Lord and righteous;
[our God is full of compassion].**

I love the Lord, because he has heard the voice of my supplication,
because he has inclined his ear to me
whenever I called upon him. ℟

The cords of death entangled me;
the grip of the grave took hold of me;
I came to grief and sorrow.
Then I called upon the name of the Lord:
'O Lord, I pray you, save my life.' ℟

How shall I repay the Lord
for all the good things he has done for me?
I will lift up the cup of salvation
and call upon the name of the Lord.
I will fulfil my vows to the Lord
in the presence of all his people. ℟

Precious in the sight of the Lord
is the death of his servants.
O Lord, I am your servant;
I am your servant and the child of your handmaid;
you have freed me from my bonds. ℟

I will offer you the sacrifice of thanksgiving
and call upon the name of the Lord.
I will fulfil my vows to the Lord
in the presence of all his people.
In the courts of the Lord's house,
in the midst of you, O Jerusalem. Alleluia! ℟

SECOND READING   1 Peter 1.17–23

A reading from the first letter of Peter.

If you invoke as Father the one who judges all people impartially according
to their deeds, live in reverent fear during the time of your exile. You know
that you were ransomed from the futile ways inherited from your ancestors,
not with perishable things like silver or gold, but with the precious blood of
Christ, like that of a lamb without defect or blemish. He was destined before
the foundation of the world, but was revealed at the end of the ages for your
sake. Through him you have come to trust in God, who raised him from the
dead and gave him glory, so that your faith and hope are set on God.

Now that you have purified your souls by your obedience to the truth so that
you have genuine mutual love, love one another deeply from the heart. You
have been born anew, not of perishable but of imperishable seed, through
the living and enduring word of God.

GOSPEL   Luke 24.13–35

Hear the gospel of our Lord Jesus Christ according to Luke.

On that same day, two of the disciples were going to a village called Emmaus,
about seven miles from Jerusalem, and talking with each other about all
these things that had happened. While they were talking and discussing,
Jesus himself came near and went with them, but their eyes were kept from
recognizing him. And he said to them, 'What are you discussing with each
other while you walk along?' They stood still, looking sad. Then one of them,
whose name was Cleopas, answered him, 'Are you the only stranger in

Jerusalem who does not know the things that have taken place there in these days?' Jesus asked them, 'What things?' They replied, 'The things about Jesus of Nazareth, who was a prophet mighty in deed and word before God and all the people, and how our chief priests and leaders handed him over to be condemned to death and crucified him. But we had hoped that he was the one to redeem Israel. Yes, and besides all this, it is now the third day since these things took place. Moreover, some women of our group astounded us. They were at the tomb early this morning, and when they did not find his body there, they came back and told us that they had indeed seen a vision of angels who said that he was alive. Some of those who were with us went to the tomb and found it just as the women had said; but they did not see Jesus.' Then he said to them, 'Oh, how foolish you are, and how slow of heart to believe all that the prophets have declared! Was it not necessary that the Messiah should suffer these things and then enter into his glory?' Then beginning with Moses and all the prophets, he interpreted to them the things about himself in all the scriptures.

As they came near the village to which they were going, he walked ahead as if he were going on. But they urged him strongly, saying, 'Stay with us, because it is almost evening and the day is now nearly over.' So he went in to stay with them. When he was at the table with them, he took bread, blessed and broke it, and gave it to them. Then their eyes were opened, and they recognized Jesus; and he vanished from their sight. They said to each other, 'Were not our hearts burning within us while he was talking to us on the road, while he was opening the scriptures to us?' That same hour they got up and returned to Jerusalem; and they found the eleven and their companions gathered together. They were saying, 'The Lord has risen indeed, and he has appeared to Simon!' Then they told what had happened on the road, and how he had been made known to them in the breaking of the bread.

EASTER 4   YEAR A

FIRST READING   Acts 2.42–47

A reading from the Acts of the Apostles.

Many were baptized and were added to the community. They devoted themselves to the apostles' teaching and fellowship, to the breaking of bread and the prayers.

Awe came upon everyone, because many wonders and signs were being done by the apostles. All who believed were together and had all things in common; they would sell their possessions and goods and distribute the proceeds to all, as any had need. Day by day, as they spent much time together in the temple, they broke bread at home and ate their food with glad and generous hearts, praising God and having the goodwill of all the people. And day by day the Lord added to their number those who were being saved.

PSALM   Psalm 23

℞ **The Lord is my shepherd;**
   I shall not be in want.

The Lord is my shepherd;
I shall not be in want.
He makes me lie down in green pastures
and leads me beside still waters. ℞

He revives my soul
and guides me along right pathways for his name's sake.
Though I walk through the valley of the shadow of death,
I shall fear no evil;
for you are with me;
your rod and your staff, they comfort me. ℞

You spread a table before me
in the presence of those who trouble me;
you have anointed my head with oil,
and my cup is running over.
Surely your goodness and mercy shall follow me
all the days of my life,
and I will dwell in the house of the Lord for ever. ℞

SECOND READING   1 Peter 2.19–25

A reading from the first letter of Peter.

Brothers and sisters: It is a credit to you if, being aware of God, you endure pain while suffering unjustly. If you endure when you are beaten for doing wrong, what credit is that? But if you endure when you do right and suffer for it, you have God's approval. For to this you have been called, because Christ also suffered for you, leaving you an example, so that you should follow in his steps. 'He committed no sin, and no deceit was found in his mouth.' When he was abused, he did not return abuse; when he suffered, he did not threaten; but he entrusted himself to the one who judges justly. He himself bore our sins in his body on the cross, so that, free from sins, we might live for righteousness; by his wounds you have been healed. For you were going astray like sheep, but now you have returned to the shepherd and guardian of your souls.

GOSPEL   John 10.1-10

Hear the gospel of our Lord Jesus Christ according to John.

Jesus said to the Pharisees: 'Very truly, I tell you, anyone who does not enter the sheepfold by the gate but climbs in by another way is a thief and a bandit. The one who enters by the gate is the shepherd of the sheep. The gatekeeper opens the gate for him, and the sheep hear his voice. He calls his own sheep by name and leads them out. When he has brought out all his own, he goes ahead of them, and the sheep follow him because they know his voice. They will not follow a stranger, but they will run from him because they do not know the voice of strangers.' Jesus used this figure of speech with them, but they did not understand what he was saying to them.

So again Jesus said to them, 'Very truly, I tell you, I am the gate for the sheep. All who came before me are thieves and bandits; but the sheep did not listen to them. I am the gate. Whoever enters by me will be saved, and will come in and go out and find pasture. The thief comes only to steal and kill and destroy. I came that they may have life, and have it abundantly.'

EASTER 5   YEAR A

FIRST READING   Acts 7.55-60

A reading from the Acts of the Apostles.

Standing before the high priest and the council, Stephen, filled with the Holy Spirit, gazed into heaven and saw the glory of God and Jesus standing at the right hand of God. 'Look,' he said, 'I see the heavens opened and the Son of Man standing at the right hand of God!' But they covered their ears, and with a loud shout all rushed together against him. Then they dragged him out of the city and began to stone him; and the witnesses laid their coats at the feet of a young man named Saul. While they were stoning Stephen, he prayed, 'Lord Jesus, receive my spirit.' Then he knelt down and cried out in a loud voice, 'Lord, do not hold this sin against them.' When he had said this, he died.

PSALM
Psalm 31.1–5, 15–16

℟ **Let your face shine on your servants**
  [and we shall be saved].

In you, O Lord, have I taken refuge;
let me never be put to shame;
deliver me in your righteousness.
Incline your ear to me;
make haste to deliver me. ℟

Be my strong rock, a castle to keep me safe,
for you are my crag and my stronghold;
for the sake of your name, lead me and guide me. ℟

Take me out of the net
that they have secretly set for me,
for you are my tower of strength.
Into your hands I commend my spirit,
for you have redeemed me,
O Lord, O God of truth. ℟

My times are in your hand;
rescue me from the hand of my enemies,
and from those who persecute me.
Make your face to shine upon your servant,
and in your loving-kindness save me. ℟

SECOND READING
1 Peter 2.2–10

A reading from the first letter of Peter.

Like newborn infants, long for the pure, spiritual milk, so that by it you may grow into salvation – if indeed you have tasted that the Lord is good.

Come to him, a living stone, though rejected by mortals yet chosen and precious in God's sight. Like living stones, let yourselves be built into a spiritual house, to be a holy priesthood, to offer spiritual sacrifices acceptable to God through Jesus Christ.

For it stands in scripture:
'See, I am laying in Zion a stone,
a cornerstone chosen and precious;
and whoever believes in him will not be put to shame.'
To you then who believe, he is precious; but for those who do not believe,
'The stone that the builders rejected has become the very head of the corner,'
and 'A stone that makes them stumble, and a rock that makes them fall.'
They stumble because they disobey the word, as they were destined to do.
But you are a chosen race, a royal priesthood, a holy nation, God's own
people, in order that you may proclaim the mighty acts of him who called
you out of darkness into his marvellous light. Once you were not a people,
but now you are God's people; once you had not received mercy, but now
you have received mercy.

GOSPEL   John 14.1–14

Hear the gospel of our Lord Jesus Christ according to John.

Jesus said to his disciples: 'Do not let your hearts be troubled. Believe in God,
believe also in me. In my Father's house there are many dwelling-places. If it
were not so, would I have told you that I go to prepare a place for you? And if
I go and prepare a place for you, I will come again and will take you to
myself, so that where I am, there you may be also. And you know the way to
the place where I am going.' Thomas said to him, 'Lord, we do not know
where you are going. How can we know the way?' Jesus said to him, 'I am the
way, and the truth, and the life. No one comes to the Father except through
me. If you know me, you will know my Father also. From now on you do
know him and have seen him.'

Philip said to him, 'Lord, show us the Father, and we will be satisfied.' Jesus
said to him, 'Have I been with you all this time, Philip, and you still do not
know me? Whoever has seen me has seen the Father. How can you say,
"Show us the Father"? Do you not believe that I am in the Father and the
Father is in me? The words that I say to you I do not speak on my own; but
the Father who dwells in me does his works. Believe me that I am in the
Father and the Father is in me; but if you do not, then believe me because of
the works themselves. Very truly, I tell you, the one who believes in me will
also do the works that I do and, in fact, will do greater works than these,
because I am going to the Father. I will do whatever you ask in my name, so
that the Father may be glorified in the Son. If in my name you ask me for
anything, I will do it.'

EASTER 6   YEAR A

FIRST READING   Acts 17.22–31

A reading from the Acts of the Apostles.

Then Paul stood in front of the Areopagus and said, 'Athenians, I see how extremely religious you are in every way. For as I went through the city and looked carefully at the objects of your worship, I found among them an altar with the inscription, "To an unknown god." What therefore you worship as unknown, this I proclaim to you. The God who made the world and everything in it, he who is Lord of heaven and earth, does not live in shrines made by human hands, nor is he served by human hands, as though he needed anything, since he himself gives to all mortals life and breath and all things. From one ancestor he made all nations to inhabit the whole earth, and he allotted the times of their existence and the boundaries of the places where they would live, so that they would search for God and perhaps grope for him and find him – though indeed he is not far from each one of us. For "In him we live and move and have our being"; as even some of your own poets have said, "For we too are his offspring."

Since we are God's offspring, we ought not to think that the deity is like gold, or silver, or stone, an image formed by the art and imagination of mortals. While God has overlooked the times of human ignorance, now he commands all people everywhere to repent, because he has fixed a day on which he will have the world judged in righteousness by a man whom he has appointed, and of this he has given assurance to all by raising him from the dead.'

PSALM   Psalm 66.7–18

℞ [Bless our God, you peoples;]
  let the sound of his praise be heard.

Bless our God, you peoples;
make the voice of his praise to be heard.
Who holds our souls in life,
and will not allow our feet to slip. ℞

For you, O God, have proved us;
you have tried us just as silver is tried.
You brought us into the snare;

you laid heavy burdens upon our backs.
You let enemies ride over our heads;
we went through fire and water;
but you brought us out into a place of refreshment. ℞

I will enter your house with burnt-offerings
and will pay you my vows,
which I promised with my lips
and spoke with my mouth when I was in trouble.
I will offer you sacrifices of fat beasts
with the smoke of rams;
I will give you oxen and goats. ℞

Come and listen, all you who fear God,
and I will tell you what he has done for me.
I called out to him with my mouth,
and his praise was on my tongue.
If I had found evil in my heart,
the Lord would not have heard me; ℞

But in truth God has heard me;
he has attended to the voice of my prayer.
Blessèd be God, who has not rejected my prayer,
nor withheld his love from me. ℞

SECOND READING   1 Peter 3.13–22

A reading from the first letter of Peter.

Who will harm you if you are eager to do what is good? But even if you do
suffer for doing what is right, you are blessed. Do not fear what they fear, and
do not be intimidated, but in your hearts sanctify Christ as Lord. Always be
ready to make your defence to anyone who demands from you an account of
the hope that is in you; yet do it with gentleness and reverence. Keep your
conscience clear, so that, when you are maligned, those who abuse you for
your good conduct in Christ may be put to shame. For it is better to suffer for
doing good, if suffering should be God's will, than to suffer for doing evil. For
Christ also suffered for sins once for all, the righteous for the unrighteous, in
order to bring you to God. He was put to death in the flesh, but made alive in
the spirit, in which also he went and made a proclamation to the spirits in
prison, who in former times did not obey, when God waited patiently in the
days of Noah, during the building of the ark, in which a few, that is, eight

persons, were saved through water. And baptism, which this prefigured, now saves you – not as a removal of dirt from the body, but as an appeal to God for a good conscience, through the resurrection of Jesus Christ, who has gone into heaven and is at the right hand of God, with angels, authorities, and powers made subject to him.

GOSPEL   John 14.15-21

Hear the gospel of our Lord Jesus Christ according to John.

Jesus said to his disciples: 'If you love me, you will keep my commandments. And I will ask the Father, and he will give you another Advocate, to be with you for ever. This is the Spirit of truth, whom the world cannot receive, because it neither sees him nor knows him. You know him, because he abides with you, and he will be in you.

I will not leave you orphaned; I am coming to you. In a little while the world will no longer see me, but you will see me; because I live, you also will live. On that day you will know that I am in my Father, and you in me, and I in you. They who have my commandments and keep them are those who love me; and those who love me will be loved by my Father, and I will love them and reveal myself to them.'

ASCENSION DAY   YEARS A B C

The reading from Acts must be used in the Revised Common Lectionary. Church of England provision allows Daniel 7.9-14 as an alternative First Reading, in which case Acts 1.1-11, rather than Ephesians 1.15-23, must be used as the Second Reading.

FIRST READING (Alternative readings)

Either   Acts 1.1-11

A reading from the Acts of the Apostles.

In the first book, Theophilus, I wrote about all that Jesus did and taught from the beginning until the day when he was taken up to heaven, after giving instructions through the Holy Spirit to the apostles whom he had chosen. After his suffering he presented himself alive to them by many convincing proofs, appearing to them during forty days and speaking about the kingdom of God. While staying with them, he ordered them not to leave Jerusalem, but to wait there for the promise of the Father. 'This,' he said, 'is what you have heard from me; for John baptized with water, but you will be baptized with the Holy Spirit not many days from now.'

So when they had come together, they asked him, 'Lord, is this the time when you will restore the kingdom to Israel?' He replied, 'It is not for you to know the times or periods that the Father has set by his own authority. But you will receive power when the Holy Spirit has come upon you; and you will be my witnesses in Jerusalem, in all Judea and Samaria, and to the ends of the earth.' When he had said this, as they were watching, he was lifted up, and a cloud took him out of their sight. While he was going and they were gazing up towards heaven, suddenly two men in white robes stood by them. They said, 'Men of Galilee, why do you stand looking up towards heaven? This Jesus, who has been taken up from you into heaven, will come in the same way as you saw him go into heaven.'

Or   **Daniel 7.9–14**

A reading from the book of Daniel.

As I watched, thrones were set in place,
and an Ancient One took his throne;
his clothing was white as snow,
and the hair of his head like pure wool;
his throne was fiery flames, and its wheels were burning fire.
A stream of fire issued and flowed out from his presence.
A thousand thousand served him,
and ten thousand times ten thousand stood attending him.
The court sat in judgement, and the books were opened.
I watched then because of the noise
of the arrogant words that the horn was speaking.
And as I watched, the beast was put to death,
and its body destroyed and given over to be burned with fire.
As for the rest of the beasts, their dominion was taken away,
but their lives were prolonged for a season and a time.
As I watched in the night visions,
I saw one like a human being coming with the clouds of heaven.
And he came to the Ancient One and was presented before him.
To him was given dominion and glory and kingship,
that all peoples, nations, and languages should serve him.
His dominion is an everlasting dominion that shall not pass away,
and his kingship is one that shall never be destroyed.

PSALM

Either

Psalm 47

℟ **God has gone up with a shout,**
   the Lord with the sound of the trumpet.

Clap your hands, all you peoples;
shout to God with a cry of joy.
For the Lord Most High is to be feared;
he is the great king over all the earth. ℟

He subdues the peoples under us,
and the nations under our feet.
He chooses our inheritance for us,
the pride of Jacob whom he loves. ℟

God has gone up with a shout,
the Lord with the sound of the ram's-horn.
Sing praises to God, sing praises;
sing praises to our king, sing praises. ℟

For God is king of all the earth;
sing praises with all your skill.
God reigns over the nations;
God sits upon his holy throne. ℟

The nobles of the peoples have gathered together
with the people of the God of Abraham.
The rulers of the earth belong to God,
and he is highly exalted. ℟

Or

Psalm 93

℟ **The Lord is king**
   and has girded himself with strength.

The Lord is king; he has put on splendid apparel;
the Lord has put on his apparel
and girded himself with strength.
He has made the whole world so sure
 that it cannot be moved; ℟

Ever since the world began,
your throne has been established;
you are from everlasting.
The waters have lifted up, O Lord,
the waters have lifted up their voice;
the waters have lifted up their pounding waves. ℟

Mightier than the sound of many waters,
mightier than the breakers of the sea,
mightier is the Lord who dwells on high.
Your testimonies are very sure,
and holiness adorns your house, O Lord,
for ever and for evermore. ℟

SECOND READING (Alternative readings)

Either
Ephesians 1.15–23

A reading from the letter of Paul to the Ephesians.

I have heard of your faith in the Lord Jesus and your love towards all the
saints, and for this reason I do not cease to give thanks for you as I remember
you in my prayers. I pray that the God of our Lord Jesus Christ, the Father of
glory, may give you a spirit of wisdom and revelation as you come to know
him, so that, with the eyes of your heart enlightened, you may know what is
the hope to which he has called you, what are the riches of his glorious
inheritance among the saints, and what is the immeasurable greatness of his
power for us who believe, according to the working of his great power. God
put this power to work in Christ when he raised him from the dead and
seated him at his right hand in the heavenly places, far above all rule and
authority and power and dominion, and above every name that is named,
not only in this age but also in the age to come. And he has put all things
under his feet and has made him the head over all things for the church,
which is his body, the fullness of him who fills all in all.

Or
Acts 1.1–11

A reading from the Acts of the Apostles.

For text see page 165.

GOSPEL   Luke 24.44–53

Hear the gospel of our Lord Jesus Christ according to Luke.

Jesus said to the disciples, 'These are my words that I spoke to you while I was still with you – that everything written about me in the law of Moses, the prophets, and the psalms must be fulfilled.' Then he opened their minds to understand the scriptures, and he said to them, 'Thus it is written, that the Messiah is to suffer and to rise from the dead on the third day, and that repentance and forgiveness of sins is to be proclaimed in his name to all nations, beginning from Jerusalem. You are witnesses of these things. And see, I am sending upon you what my Father promised; so stay here in the city until you have been clothed with power from on high.'

Then he led them out as far as Bethany, and, lifting up his hands, he blessed them. While he was blessing them, he withdrew from them and was carried up into heaven. And they worshipped him, and returned to Jerusalem with great joy; and they were continually in the temple blessing God.

EASTER 7   YEAR A

FIRST READING   Acts 1.6–14

A reading from the Acts of the Apostles.

When the apostles had come together, they asked him, 'Lord, is this the time when you will restore the kingdom to Israel?' He replied, 'It is not for you to know the times or periods that the Father has set by his own authority. But you will receive power when the Holy Spirit has come upon you; and you will be my witnesses in Jerusalem, in all Judea and Samaria, and to the ends of the earth.' When he had said this, as they were watching, he was lifted up, and a cloud took him out of their sight. While he was going and they were gazing up towards heaven, suddenly two men in white robes stood by them. They said, 'Men of Galilee, why do you stand looking up towards heaven? This Jesus, who has been taken up from you into heaven, will come in the same way as you saw him go into heaven.'

Then they returned to Jerusalem from the mount called Olivet, which is near Jerusalem, a sabbath day's journey away. When they had entered the city, they went to the room upstairs where they were staying, Peter, and John, and James, and Andrew, Philip and Thomas, Bartholomew and Matthew, James son of Alphaeus, and Simon the Zealot, and Judas son of James. All these were constantly devoting themselves to prayer, together with certain women, including Mary the mother of Jesus, as well as his brothers.

PSALM

℟ to God, O kingdoms of the earth;
[sing praises to the Lord].

Let God arise and let his enemies be scattered;
let those who hate him flee before him.
Let them vanish like smoke
when the wind drives it away;
as the wax melts at the fire,
so let the wicked perish at the presence of God. ℟

But let the righteous be glad and rejoice before God;
let them also be merry and joyful.
Sing to God, sing praises to his name;
exalt him who rides upon the heavens;
Yahweh is his name, rejoice before him! ℟

Father of orphans, defender of widows,
God in his holy habitation!
God gives the solitary a home
and brings forth prisoners into freedom;
but the rebels shall live in dry places. ℟

O God, when you went forth before your people,
when you marched through the wilderness,
The earth shook and the skies poured down rain,
at the presence of God, the God of Sinai,
at the presence of God, the God of Israel. ℟

You sent a gracious rain, O God, upon your inheritance;
you refreshed the land when it was weary.
Your people found their home in it;
in your goodness, O God,
you have made provision for the poor. ℟

Sing to God, O kingdoms of the earth;
sing praises to the Lord.
He rides in the heavens, the ancient heavens;
he sends forth his voice, his mighty voice. ℟

Ascribe power to God;
his majesty is over Israel;
his strength is in the skies.
How wonderful is God in his holy places!

the God of Israel giving strength and power to his people!
Blessèd be God! ℟

SECOND READING   1 Peter 4.12–14; 5.6–11

A reading from the first letter of Peter.

Beloved, do not be surprised at the fiery ordeal that is taking place among
you to test you, as though something strange were happening to you. But
rejoice in so far as you are sharing Christ's sufferings, so that you may also be
glad and shout for joy when his glory is revealed. If you are reviled for the
name of Christ, you are blessed, because the spirit of glory, which is the Spirit
of God, is resting on you.

Humble yourselves therefore under the mighty hand of God, so that he may
exalt you in due time. Cast all your anxiety on him, because he cares for you.
Discipline yourselves, keep alert. Like a roaring lion your adversary the devil
prowls around, looking for someone to devour. Resist him, steadfast in your
faith, for you know that your brothers and sisters throughout the world are
undergoing the same kinds of suffering. And after you have suffered for a
little while, the God of all grace, who has called you to his eternal glory in
Christ, will himself restore, support, strengthen, and establish you. To him be
the power for ever and ever. Amen.

GOSPEL   John 17.1–11

Hear the gospel of our Lord Jesus Christ according to John.

Jesus looked up to heaven and said, 'Father, the hour has come; glorify your
Son so that the Son may glorify you, since you have given him authority
over all people, to give eternal life to all whom you have given him. And this
is eternal life, that they may know you, the only true God, and Jesus Christ
whom you have sent. I glorified you on earth by finishing the work that you
gave me to do. So now, Father, glorify me in your own presence with the
glory that I had in your presence before the world existed.

I have made your name known to those whom you gave me from the world.
They were yours, and you gave them to me, and they have kept your word.
Now they know that everything you have given me is from you; for the
words that you gave to me I have given to them, and they have received
them and know in truth that I came from you; and they have believed that
you sent me. I am asking on their behalf; I am not asking on behalf of the
world, but on behalf of those whom you gave me, because they are yours. All

mine are yours, and yours are mine; and I have been glorified in them. And now I am no longer in the world, but they are in the world, and I am coming to you. Holy Father, protect them in your name that you have given me, so that they may be one, as we are one.'

PENTECOST (WHITSUNDAY)   YEAR A

The reading from Acts must be used as either the First or Second Reading.

FIRST READING (Alternative readings)

Either   Acts 2.1–21

A reading from the Acts of the Apostles.

When the day of Pentecost had come, they were all together in one place. And suddenly from heaven there came a sound like the rush of a violent wind, and it filled the entire house where they were sitting. Divided tongues, as of fire, appeared among them, and a tongue rested on each of them. All of them were filled with the Holy Spirit and began to speak in other languages, as the Spirit gave them ability.

Now there were devout Jews from every nation under heaven living in Jerusalem. And at this sound the crowd gathered and was bewildered, because each one heard them speaking in the native language of each. Amazed and astonished, they asked, 'Are not all these who are speaking Galileans? And how is it that we hear, each of us, in our own native language? Parthians, Medes, Elamites, and residents of Mesopotamia, Judea and Cappadocia, Pontus and Asia, Phrygia and Pamphylia, Egypt and the parts of Libya belonging to Cyrene, and visitors from Rome, both Jews and proselytes, Cretans and Arabs – in our own languages we hear them speaking about God's deeds of power.' All were amazed and perplexed, saying to one another, 'What does this mean?' But others sneered and said, 'They are filled with new wine.'

But Peter, standing with the eleven, raised his voice and addressed them, 'Men of Judea and all who live in Jerusalem, let this be known to you, and listen to what I say. Indeed, these are not drunk, as you suppose, for it is only nine o'clock in the morning. No, this is what was spoken through the prophet Joel:
"In the last days it will be, God declares,
that I will pour out my Spirit upon all flesh,

and your sons and your daughters shall prophesy,
and your young men shall see visions,
and your old men shall dream dreams.
Even upon my slaves, both men and women,
in those days I will pour out my Spirit;
and they shall prophesy.
And I will show portents in the heaven above
and signs on the earth below,
blood, and fire, and smoky mist.
The sun shall be turned to darkness and the moon to blood,
before the coming of the Lord's great and glorious day.
Then everyone who calls on the name of the Lord
shall be saved."'

Or   **Numbers 11.24–30**

A reading from the book of Numbers.

Moses went out and told the people the words of the LORD; and he gathered seventy elders of the people, and placed them all around the tent. Then the LORD came down in the cloud and spoke to him, and took some of the spirit that was on him and put it on the seventy elders; and when the spirit rested upon them, they prophesied. But they did not do so again.

Two men remained in the camp, one named Eldad, and the other named Medad, and the spirit rested on them; they were among those registered, but they had not gone out to the tent, and so they prophesied in the camp. And a young man ran and told Moses, 'Eldad and Medad are prophesying in the camp.' And Joshua son of Nun, the assistant of Moses, one of his chosen men, said, 'My lord Moses, stop them!' But Moses said to him, 'Are you jealous for my sake? Would that all the LORD's people were prophets, and that the LORD would put his spirit on them!' And Moses and the elders of Israel returned to the camp.

PSALM   **Psalm 104.25–35, 37**

℞ **Send forth your Spirit,**
  O Lord, and renew the face of the earth.

O Lord, how manifold are your works!
in wisdom you have made them all;
the earth is full of your creatures. ℞

Yonder is the great and wide sea
with its living things too many to number,
creatures both small and great.
There move the ships,
and there is that Leviathan,
which you have made for the sport of it. ℟

All of them look to you
to give them their food in due season.
You give it to them, they gather it;
you open your hand and they are filled with good things.
You hide your face and they are terrified;
you take away their breath
and they die and return to their dust. ℟

You send forth your Spirit and they are created;
and so you renew the face of the earth.
May the glory of the Lord endure for ever;
may the Lord rejoice in all his works.
He looks at the earth and it trembles;
he touches the mountains and they smoke. ℟

I will sing to the Lord as long as I live;
I will praise my God while I have my being.
May these words of mine please him;
I will rejoice in the Lord.
Bless the Lord, O my soul. Alleluia! ℟

SECOND READING (Alternative readings)

Either   **1 Corinthians 12.3b–13**

A reading from the first letter of Paul to the Corinthians.

No one can say 'Jesus is Lord' except by the Holy Spirit.

Now there are varieties of gifts, but the same Spirit; and there are varieties of
services, but the same Lord; and there are varieties of activities, but it is the
same God who activates all of them in everyone. To each is given the
manifestation of the Spirit for the common good. To one is given through
the Spirit the utterance of wisdom, and to another the utterance of
knowledge according to the same Spirit, to another faith by the same Spirit,

to another gifts of healing by the one Spirit, to another the working of miracles, to another prophecy, to another the discernment of spirits, to another various kinds of tongues, to another the interpretation of tongues. All these are activated by one and the same Spirit, who allots to each one individually just as the Spirit chooses.

For just as the body is one and has many members, and all the members of the body, though many, are one body, so it is with Christ. For in the one Spirit we were all baptized into one body – Jews or Greeks, slaves or free – and we were all made to drink of one Spirit.

Or   **Acts 2.1–21**

A reading from the Acts of the Apostles.

For text see page 172.

GOSPEL (Alternative readings)

Either   **John 20.19–23**

Hear the gospel of our Lord Jesus Christ according to John.

It was evening on the first day of the week, and the doors of the house where the disciples had met were locked for fear of the Jews. Jesus came and stood among them and said, 'Peace be with you.' After he said this, he showed them his hands and his side. Then the disciples rejoiced when they saw the Lord. Jesus said to them again, 'Peace be with you. As the Father has sent me, so I send you.' When he had said this, he breathed on them and said to them, 'Receive the Holy Spirit. If you forgive the sins of any, they are forgiven them; if you retain the sins of any, they are retained.'

Or   **John 7.37–39**

Hear the gospel of our Lord Jesus Christ according to John.

On the last day of the festival, the great day, while Jesus was standing in the temple, he cried out, 'Let anyone who is thirsty come to me, and let the one who believes in me drink. As the scripture has said, "Out of the believer's heart shall flow rivers of living water."' Now he said this about the Spirit, which believers in him were to receive; for as yet there was no Spirit, because Jesus was not yet glorified.

TRINITY SUNDAY   YEAR A

FIRST READING

The Revised Common Lectionary and the Church of England make alternative provision for the First Reading.

Either (Revised Common Lectionary)   Genesis 1.1 – 2.4a

A reading from the book of Genesis.

In the beginning when God created the heavens and the earth, the earth was a formless void and darkness covered the face of the deep, while a wind from God swept over the face of the waters. Then God said, 'Let there be light'; and there was light. And God saw that the light was good; and God separated the light from the darkness. God called the light Day, and the darkness he called Night. And there was evening and there was morning, the first day.

And God said, 'Let there be a dome in the midst of the waters, and let it separate the waters from the waters.' So God made the dome and separated the waters that were under the dome from the waters that were above the dome. And it was so. God called the dome Sky. And there was evening and there was morning, the second day.

And God said, 'Let the waters under the sky be gathered together into one place, and let the dry land appear.' And it was so. God called the dry land Earth, and the waters that were gathered together he called Seas. And God saw that it was good. Then God said, 'Let the earth put forth vegetation: plants yielding seed, and fruit trees of every kind on earth that bear fruit with the seed in it.' And it was so. The earth brought forth vegetation: plants yielding seed of every kind, and trees of every kind bearing fruit with the seed in it. And God saw that it was good. And there was evening and there was morning, the third day.

And God said, 'Let there be lights in the dome of the sky to separate the day from the night; and let them be for signs and for seasons and for days and years, and let them be lights in the dome of the sky to give light upon the earth.' And it was so. God made the two great lights – the greater light to rule the day and the lesser light to rule the night – and the stars. God set them in the dome of the sky to give light upon the earth, to rule over the day and over the night, and to separate the light from the darkness. And God saw that it was good. And there was evening and there was morning, the fourth day.

And God said, 'Let the waters bring forth swarms of living creatures, and let birds fly above the earth across the dome of the sky.' So God created the great sea monsters and every living creature that moves, of every kind, with which the waters swarm, and every winged bird of every kind. And God saw that it was good. God blessed them, saying, 'Be fruitful and multiply and fill the waters in the seas, and let birds multiply on the earth.' And there was evening and there was morning, the fifth day.

And God said, 'Let the earth bring forth living creatures of every kind: cattle and creeping things and wild animals of the earth of every kind.' And it was so. God made the wild animals of the earth of every kind, and the cattle of every kind, and everything that creeps upon the ground of every kind. And God saw that it was good.

Then God said, 'Let us make humankind in our image, according to our likeness; and let them have dominion over the fish of the sea, and over the birds of the air, and over the cattle, and over all the wild animals of the earth, and over every creeping thing that creeps upon the earth.' So God created humankind in his image, in the image of God he created them; male and female he created them. God blessed them, and God said to them, 'Be fruitful and multiply, and fill the earth and subdue it; and have dominion over the fish of the sea and over the birds of the air and over every living thing that moves upon the earth.' God said, 'See, I have given you every plant yielding seed that is upon the face of all the earth, and every tree with seed in its fruit; you shall have them for food. And to every beast of the earth, and to every bird of the air, and to everything that creeps on the earth, everything that has the breath of life, I have given every green plant for food.' And it was so. God saw everything that he had made, and indeed, it was very good. And there was evening and there was morning, the sixth day.

Thus the heavens and the earth were finished, and all their multitude. And on the seventh day God finished the work that he had done, and he rested on the seventh day from all the work that he had done. So God blessed the seventh day and hallowed it, because on it God rested from all the work that he had done in creation.

These are the generations of the heavens and the earth when they were created.

Or   **Isaiah 40.12–17, 27–31**

A reading from the book of the prophet Isaiah.

Who has measured the waters in the hollow of his hand
and marked off the heavens with a span,

enclosed the dust of the earth in a measure,
and weighed the mountains in scales and the hills in a balance?
Who has directed the spirit of the LORD,
or as his counsellor has instructed him?
Whom did he consult for his enlightenment,
and who taught him the path of justice?
Who taught him knowledge, and showed him the way of understanding?
Even the nations are like a drop from a bucket,
and are accounted as dust on the scales;
see, he takes up the isles like fine dust.
Lebanon would not provide fuel enough,
nor are its animals enough for a burnt-offering.
All the nations are as nothing before him;
they are accounted by him as less than nothing and emptiness.

Why do you say, O Jacob, and speak, O Israel,
'My way is hidden from the LORD,
and my right is disregarded by my God'?
Have you not known?
Have you not heard?
The LORD is the everlasting God,
the Creator of the ends of the earth.
He does not faint or grow weary; his understanding is unsearchable.
He gives power to the faint,
and strengthens the powerless.
Even youths will faint and be weary, and the young will fall exhausted;
but those who wait for the LORD shall renew their strength,
they shall mount up with wings like eagles,
they shall run and not be weary,
they shall walk and not faint.

PSALM   Psalm 8

℟ [O Lord our governor,]
    how exalted is your name in all the earth.

O Lord our governor,
how exalted is your name in all the world!
Out of the mouths of infants and children
your majesty is praised above the heavens.
You have set up a stronghold against your adversaries,
to quell the enemy and the avenger. ℟

When I consider your heavens, the work of your fingers,
the moon and the stars you have set in their courses,
What are mortals, that you should be mindful of them?
mere human beings, that you should seek them out?
You have made them little lower than the angels;
you adorn them with glory and honour. ℟

You give them mastery over the works of your hands;
and put all things under their feet,
All sheep and oxen,
even the wild beasts of the field,
The birds of the air, the fish of the sea,
and whatsoever walks in the paths of the sea. ℟

[O Lord our governor,
how exalted is your name in all the world!]

SECOND READING   2 Corinthians 13.11–13

A reading from the second letter of Paul to the Corinthians.

Brothers and sisters, put things in order, listen to my appeal, agree with one
another, live in peace; and the God of love and peace will be with you. Greet
one another with a holy kiss. All the saints greet you.

The grace of the Lord Jesus Christ, the love of God, and the communion of
the Holy Spirit be with all of you.

GOSPEL   Matthew 28.16–20

Hear the gospel of our Lord Jesus Christ according to Matthew.

The eleven disciples went to Galilee, to the mountain to which Jesus had
directed them. When they saw him, they worshipped him; but some
doubted. And Jesus came and said to them, 'All authority in heaven and on
earth has been given to me. Go therefore and make disciples of all nations,
baptizing them in the name of the Father and of the Son and of the Holy
Spirit, and teaching them to obey everything that I have commanded you.
And remember, I am with you always, to the end of the age.'

THANKSGIVING FOR HOLY COMMUNION   YEARS A B C (CORPUS CHRISTI)

Thursday after Trinity Sunday

FIRST READING   Genesis 14.18–20

A reading from the book of Genesis.

King Melchizedek of Salem brought out bread and wine; he was priest of God
Most High. He blessed him and said,
'Blessed be Abram by God Most High, maker of heaven and earth;
and blessed be God Most High,
who has delivered your enemies into your hand!'
And Abram gave him one-tenth of everything.

PSALM   Psalm 116.10–17

℟ **will walk in the presence of the Lord in the land of the living.**

How shall I repay the Lord
for all the good things he has done for me?
I will lift up the cup of salvation
and call upon the name of the Lord.
I will fulfil my vows to the Lord
in the presence of all his people. ℟

Precious in the sight of the Lord
is the death of his servants.
O Lord, I am your servant;
I am your servant and the child of your handmaid;
you have freed me from my bonds. ℟

I will offer you the sacrifice of thanksgiving
and call upon the name of the Lord.
I will fulfil my vows to the Lord
in the presence of all his people.
In the courts of the Lord's house,
in the midst of you, O Jerusalem.
Alleluia! ℟

SECOND READING   **1 Corinthians 11.23–26**

A reading from the first letter of Paul to the Corinthians.

For I received from the Lord what I also handed on to you, that the Lord
Jesus on the night when he was betrayed took a loaf of bread, and when he
had given thanks, he broke it and said, 'This is my body that is for you. Do
this in remembrance of me.' In the same way he took the cup also, after
supper, saying, 'This cup is the new covenant in my blood. Do this, as often
as you drink it, in remembrance of me.' For as often as you eat this bread and
drink the cup, you proclaim the Lord's death until he comes.

GOSPEL   **John 6.51–58**

Hear the gospel of our Lord Jesus Christ according to John.

Jesus said to the Jews: 'I am the living bread that came down from heaven.
Whoever eats of this bread will live for ever; and the bread that I will give for
the life of the world is my flesh.'

The Jews then disputed among themselves, saying, 'How can this man give
us his flesh to eat?' So Jesus said to them, 'Very truly, I tell you, unless you
eat the flesh of the Son of Man and drink his blood, you have no life in you.
Those who eat my flesh and drink my blood have eternal life, and I will raise
them up on the last day; for my flesh is true food and my blood is true drink.
Those who eat my flesh and drink my blood abide in me, and I in them. Just
as the living Father sent me, and I live because of the Father, so whoever eats
me will live because of me. This is the bread that came down from heaven,
not like that which your ancestors ate, and they died. But the one who eats
this bread will live for ever.'

† SUNDAY BETWEEN 24 AND 28 MAY   YEAR A
(if after Trinity Sunday)

PROPER 3

The Revised Common Lectionary provision for Epiphany 8 (above, pages 58–60) is used.

SUNDAYS AFTER TRINITY

*The Church of England names the Sundays after Trinity Sunday 'Sundays after Trinity'.
The readings are provided by calendar date. On most Sundays the First Reading and Psalm
follow two tracks. One track must be followed through the whole sequence.*

181

† SUNDAY BETWEEN 29 MAY AND 4 JUNE   YEAR A
(if after Trinity Sunday)
PROPER 4

TRACK 1

FIRST READING   **Genesis 6.9–22; 7.24; 8.14–19**

A reading from the book of Genesis.

These are the descendants of Noah. Noah was a righteous man, blameless in his generation; Noah walked with God. And Noah had three sons, Shem, Ham, and Japheth.

Now the earth was corrupt in God's sight, and the earth was filled with violence. And God saw that the earth was corrupt; for all flesh had corrupted its ways upon the earth. And God said to Noah, 'I have determined to make an end of all flesh, for the earth is filled with violence because of them; now I am going to destroy them along with the earth. Make yourself an ark of cypress wood; make rooms in the ark, and cover it inside and out with pitch. This is how you are to make it: the length of the ark three hundred cubits, its width fifty cubits, and its height thirty cubits. Make a roof for the ark, and finish it to a cubit above; and put the door of the ark in its side; make it with lower, second, and third decks. For my part, I am going to bring a flood of waters on the earth, to destroy from under heaven all flesh in which is the breath of life; everything that is on the earth shall die. But I will establish my covenant with you; and you shall come into the ark, you, your sons, your wife, and your sons' wives with you. And of every living thing, of all flesh, you shall bring two of every kind into the ark, to keep them alive with you; they shall be male and female. Of the birds according to their kinds, and of the animals according to their kinds, of every creeping thing of the ground according to its kind, two of every kind shall come in to you, to keep them alive. Also take with you every kind of food that is eaten, and store it up; and it shall serve as food for you and for them.' Noah did this; he did all that God commanded him.

And the waters swelled on the earth for one hundred and fifty days.

In the second month, on the twenty-seventh day of the month, the earth was dry. Then God said to Noah, 'Go out of the ark, you and your wife, and your sons and your sons' wives with you. Bring out with you every living thing that is with you of all flesh – birds and animals and every creeping thing that creeps on the earth – so that they may abound on the earth, and be fruitful and multiply on the earth.' So Noah went out with his sons and his wife and his sons' wives. And every animal, every creeping thing, and every bird, everything that moves on the earth, went out of the ark by families.

PSALM   Psalm 46

℟ **The Lord of hosts is with us,**
the God of Jacob is our stronghold.

God is our refuge and strength,
a very present help in trouble;
Therefore we will not fear, though the earth be moved,
and though the mountains be toppled
into the depths of the sea;
Though its waters rage and foam,
and though the mountains tremble at its tumult. ℟

[The Lord of hosts is with us;
the God of Jacob is our stronghold.]

There is a river whose streams
make glad the city of God,
the holy habitation of the Most High.
God is in the midst of her;
she shall not be overthrown;
God shall help her at the break of day.
The nations make much ado
and the kingdoms are shaken;
God has spoken and the earth shall melt away. ℟

[The Lord of hosts is with us; the God of Jacob is our stronghold.]

Come now and look upon the works of the Lord,
what awesome things he has done on earth.
It is he who makes war to cease in all the world;
he breaks the bow and shatters the spear
and burns the shields with fire.
'Be still, then, and know that I am God;
I will be exalted among the nations;
I will be exalted in the earth.' ℟

[The Lord of hosts is with us;
the God of Jacob is our stronghold.]

Or   TRACK 2

FIRST READING   Deuteronomy 11.18–21, 26–28

A reading from the book of Deuteronomy.

Thus says the Lord:
You shall put these words of mine in your heart and soul, and you shall bind
them as a sign on your hand, and fix them as an emblem on your forehead.
Teach them to your children, talking about them when you are at home and
when you are away, when you lie down and when you rise.
Write them on the doorposts of your house and on your gates,
so that your days and the days of your children may be multiplied in the
land that the LORD swore to your ancestors to give them, as long as the
heavens are above the earth.

See, I am setting before you today a blessing and a curse:
the blessing, if you obey the commandments of the LORD your God that I
am commanding you today;
and the curse, if you do not obey the commandments of the LORD your God,
but turn from the way that I am commanding you today, to follow other
gods that you have not known.

PSALM   Psalm 31.1–5, 19–24

℟ **Be my strong rock,**
   O Lord; a tower of strength.

In you, O Lord, have I taken refuge;
let me never be put to shame;
deliver me in your righteousness.
Incline your ear to me;
make haste to deliver me. ℟

Be my strong rock, a castle to keep me safe,
for you are my crag and my stronghold;
for the sake of your name, lead me and guide me. ℟

Take me out of the net
that they have secretly set for me,
for you are my tower of strength.
Into your hands I commend my spirit,
for you have redeemed me,
O Lord, O God of truth. ℟

How great is your goodness, O Lord,
which you have laid up for those who fear you;
which you have done in the sight of all
for those who put their trust in you.
You hide them in the covert of your presence
from those who slander them;
you keep them in your shelter from the strife of tongues. ℟

Blessèd be the Lord!
for he has shown me the wonders of his love
in a besieged city.
Yet I said in my alarm,
'I have been cut off from the sight of your eyes.'
Nevertheless, you heard the sound of my entreaty
when I cried out to you. ℟

Love the Lord, all you who worship him;
the Lord protects the faithful,
but repays to the full those who act haughtily.
Be strong and let your heart take courage,
all you who wait for the Lord. ℟

SECOND READING (Short or long reading)
Romans 1.16–17; 3.22b–28, (29–31)

A reading from the letter of Paul to the Romans.

I am not ashamed of the gospel; it is the power of God for salvation to everyone who has faith, to the Jew first and also to the Greek. For in it the righteousness of God is revealed through faith for faith; as it is written, 'The one who is righteous will live by faith.'

For there is no distinction, since all have sinned and fall short of the glory of God; they are now justified by his grace as a gift, through the redemption that is in Christ Jesus, whom God put forward as a sacrifice of atonement by his blood, effective through faith. He did this to show his righteousness, because in his divine forbearance he had passed over the sins previously committed; it was to prove at the present time that he himself is righteous and that he justifies the one who has faith in Jesus.

Then what becomes of boasting? It is excluded. By what law? By that of works? No, but by the law of faith. For we hold that a person is justified by faith apart from works prescribed by the law. [Or is God the God of Jews only? Is he not the God of Gentiles also? Yes, of Gentiles also, since God is one; and he will justify the circumcised on the ground of faith and the uncircumcised through that same faith. Do we then overthrow the law by this faith? By no means! On the contrary, we uphold the law.]

GOSPEL   **Matthew 7.21–29**

Hear the gospel of our Lord Jesus Christ according to Matthew.

Jesus went up the mountain with his disciples. He sat down and began to teach them: 'Not everyone who says to me, "Lord, Lord", will enter the kingdom of heaven, but only the one who does the will of my Father in heaven. On that day many will say to me, "Lord, Lord, did we not prophesy in your name, and cast out demons in your name, and do many deeds of power in your name?" Then I will declare to them, "I never knew you; go away from me, you evildoers."

Everyone then who hears these words of mine and acts on them will be like a wise man who built his house on rock. The rain fell, the floods came, and the winds blew and beat on that house, but it did not fall, because it had been founded on rock. And everyone who hears these words of mine and does not act on them will be like a foolish man who built his house on sand. The rain fell, and the floods came, and the winds blew and beat against that house, and it fell – and great was its fall!'

Now when Jesus had finished saying these things, the crowds were astounded at his teaching, for he taught them as one having authority, and not as their scribes.

† SUNDAY BETWEEN 5 AND 11 JUNE   YEAR A
(if after Trinity Sunday)
PROPER 5

TRACK 1

FIRST READING   **Genesis 12.1–9**

A reading from the book of Genesis.

The LORD said to Abram, 'Go from your country and your kindred and your father's house to the land that I will show you. I will make of you a great nation, and I will bless you, and make your name great, so that you will be a blessing. I will bless those who bless you, and the one who curses you I will curse; and in you all the families of the earth shall be blessed.'

So Abram went, as the LORD had told him; and Lot went with him. Abram was seventy-five years old when he departed from Haran. Abram took his wife Sarai and his brother's son Lot, and all the possessions that they had gathered, and the persons whom they had acquired in Haran; and they set forth to go to the land of Canaan. When they had come to the land of Canaan, Abram passed through the land to the place at Shechem, to the oak of Moreh. At that time the Canaanites were in the land. Then the LORD appeared to Abram, and said, 'To your offspring I will give this land.' So he built there an altar to the LORD, who had appeared to him. From there he moved on to the hill country on the east of Bethel, and pitched his tent, with Bethel on the west and Ai on the east; and there he built an altar to the LORD and invoked the name of the LORD. And Abram journeyed on by stages towards the Negeb.

PSALM   **Psalm 33.1–12**

℟ **Happy the people the Lord has chosen as his own!**

Rejoice in the Lord, you righteous;
it is good for the just to sing praises.
Praise the Lord with the harp;
play to him upon the psaltery and lyre.
Sing for him a new song;
sound a fanfare with all your skill upon the trumpet. ℟

For the word of the Lord is right,
and all his works are sure.
He loves righteousness and justice;
the loving-kindness of the Lord fills the whole earth.
By the word of the Lord were the heavens made,
by the breath of his mouth all the heavenly hosts. ℟

He gathers up the waters of the ocean
as in a water-skin and stores up the depths of the sea.
Let all the earth fear the Lord;
let all who dwell in the world stand in awe of him.
For he spoke and it came to pass;
he commanded and it stood fast. ℟

The Lord brings the will of the nations to naught;
he thwarts the designs of the peoples.
But the Lord's will stands fast for ever,
and the designs of his heart from age to age.
Happy is the nation whose God is the Lord!
happy the people he has chosen to be his own! ℟

Or   TRACK 2

FIRST READING   **Hosea 5.15 – 6.6**

A reading from the book of the prophet Hosea.

Hear the word of the LORD, O people of Israel:
I will return again to my place
until they acknowledge their guilt and seek my face.
In their distress they will beg my favour:
'Come, let us return to the LORD; for it is he who has torn, and he will heal
us; he has struck down, and he will bind us up.
After two days he will revive us; on the third day he will raise us up, that we
may live before him.
Let us know, let us press on to know the LORD;
his appearing is as sure as the dawn;
he will come to us like the showers,
like the spring rains that water the earth.'
What shall I do with you, O Ephraim? What shall I do with you, O Judah?
Your love is like a morning cloud, like the dew that goes away early.
Therefore I have hewn them by the prophets,

I have killed them by the words of my mouth,
and my judgement goes forth as the light.
For I desire steadfast love and not sacrifice,
the knowledge of God rather than burnt-offerings.

PSALM   **Psalm 50.7-15**

℟ **The Lord will show his salvation to the upright.**

Hear, O my people, and I will speak:
'O Israel, I will bear witness against you;
for I am God, your God.
I do not accuse you because of your sacrifices;
your offerings are always before me. ℟

I will take no bull-calf from your stalls,
nor he-goats out of your pens;
For the beasts of the forest are mine,
the herds in their thousands upon the hills.
I know every bird in the sky,
and the creatures of the fields are in my sight. ℟

If I were hungry, I would not tell you,
for the whole world is mine and all that is in it.
Do you think I eat the flesh of bulls,
or drink the blood of goats?
Offer to God a sacrifice of thanksgiving
and make good your vows to the Most High.
Call upon me in the day of trouble;
I will deliver you and you shall honour me.' ℟

SECOND READING   **ROMANS 4.13-25**

A reading from the letter of Paul to the Romans.

The promise that Abraham would inherit the world did not come to
Abraham or to his descendants through the law but through the
righteousness of faith. If it is the adherents of the law who are to be the heirs,
faith is null and the promise is void. For the law brings wrath; but where
there is no law, neither is there violation.

For this reason it depends on faith, in order that the promise may rest on
grace and be guaranteed to all his descendants, not only to the adherents of

the law but also to those who share the faith of Abraham (for he is the father of all of us, as it is written, 'I have made you the father of many nations') – Abraham believed in the presence of the God who gives life to the dead and calls into existence the things that do not exist. Hoping against hope, he believed that he would become 'the father of many nations,' according to what was said, 'So numerous shall your descendants be.' He did not weaken in faith when he considered his own body, which was already as good as dead (for he was about a hundred years old), or when he considered the barrenness of Sarah's womb. No distrust made him waver concerning the promise of God, but he grew strong in his faith as he gave glory to God, being fully convinced that God was able to do what he had promised.

Therefore his faith 'was reckoned to him as righteousness.' Now the words, 'it was reckoned to him,' were written not for his sake alone, but for ours also. It will be reckoned to us who believe in God who raised Jesus our Lord from the dead, who was handed over to death for our trespasses and was raised for our justification.

GOSPEL   Matthew 9.9–13, 18–26

Hear the gospel of our Lord Jesus Christ according to Matthew.

As Jesus was walking along, he saw a man called Matthew sitting at the tax booth; and he said to him, 'Follow me.' And he got up and followed him.

And as he sat at dinner in the house, many tax-collectors and sinners came and were sitting with him and his disciples. When the Pharisees saw this, they said to his disciples, 'Why does your teacher eat with tax-collectors and sinners?' But when he heard this, he said, 'Those who are well have no need of a physician, but those who are sick. Go and learn what this means, "I desire mercy, not sacrifice." For I have come to call not the righteous but sinners.'

While he was saying these things to them, suddenly a leader of the synagogue came in and knelt before him, saying, 'My daughter has just died; but come and lay your hand on her, and she will live.' And Jesus got up and followed him, with his disciples.

Then suddenly a woman who had been suffering from haemorrhages for twelve years came up behind him and touched the fringe of his cloak, for she said to herself, 'If I only touch his cloak, I will be made well.' Jesus turned, and seeing her he said, 'Take heart, daughter; your faith has made you well.' And instantly the woman was made well. When Jesus came to the leader's house and saw the flute-players and the crowd making a commotion, he said, 'Go away; for the girl is not dead but sleeping.'

And they laughed at him. But when the crowd had been put outside, he went in and took her by the hand, and the girl got up. And the report of this spread throughout that district.

† SUNDAY BETWEEN 12 AND 18 JUNE   YEAR A
(if after Trinity Sunday)
PROPER 6

TRACK 1

FIRST READING (Short or long reading)

Genesis 18.1–15; (21.1–7)

A reading from the book of Genesis.

The LORD appeared to Abraham by the oaks of Mamre, as he sat at the entrance of his tent in the heat of the day. He looked up and saw three men standing near him. When he saw them, he ran from the tent entrance to meet them, and bowed down to the ground. He said, 'My lord, if I find favour with you, do not pass by your servant. Let a little water be brought, and wash your feet, and rest yourselves under the tree. Let me bring a little bread, that you may refresh yourselves, and after that you may pass on – since you have come to your servant.' So they said, 'Do as you have said.' And Abraham hastened into the tent to Sarah, and said, 'Make ready quickly three measures of choice flour, knead it, and make cakes.' Abraham ran to the herd, and took a calf, tender and good, and gave it to the servant, who hastened to prepare it. Then he took curds and milk and the calf that he had prepared, and set it before them; and he stood by them under the tree while they ate.

They said to Abraham, 'Where is your wife Sarah?' And he said, 'There, in the tent.' Then one said, 'I will surely return to you in due season, and your wife Sarah shall have a son.' And Sarah was listening at the tent entrance behind him. Now Abraham and Sarah were old, advanced in age; it had ceased to be with Sarah after the manner of women. So Sarah laughed to herself, saying, 'After I have grown old, and my husband is old, shall I have pleasure?' The LORD said to Abraham, 'Why did Sarah laugh, and say, "Shall I indeed bear a child, now that I am old?" Is anything too wonderful for the LORD? At the set time I will return to you, in due season, and Sarah shall have a son.' But Sarah denied, saying, 'I did not laugh'; for she was afraid. He said, 'Oh yes, you did laugh.'

[The LORD dealt with Sarah as he had said, and the LORD did for Sarah as he had promised. Sarah conceived and bore Abraham a son in his old age, at the time of which God had spoken to him. Abraham gave the name Isaac to his son whom Sarah bore him. And Abraham circumcised his son Isaac when he was eight days old, as God had commanded him. Abraham was a hundred years old when his son Isaac was born to him. Now Sarah said, 'God has brought laughter for me; everyone who hears will laugh with me.' And she said, 'Who would ever have said to Abraham that Sarah would nurse children? Yet I have borne him a son in his old age.']

PSALM

Psalm 116.1, 10–17

℞ **I will walk in the presence of the Lord**
   in the land of the living.

I love the Lord,
because he has heard the voice of my supplication,
because he has inclined his ear to me
whenever I called upon him. ℞

How shall I repay the Lord
for all the good things he has done for me?
I will lift up the cup of salvation
and call upon the name of the Lord.
I will fulfil my vows to the Lord
in the presence of all his people. ℞

Precious in the sight of the Lord
is the death of his servants.
O Lord, I am your servant;
I am your servant and the child of your handmaid;
you have freed me from my bonds. ℞

I will offer you the sacrifice of thanksgiving
and call upon the name of the Lord.
I will fulfil my vows to the Lord
in the presence of all his people.
In the courts of the Lord's house,
in the midst of you, O Jerusalem. Alleluia! ℞

Or   TRACK 2

FIRST READING   **Exodus 19.2–8a**

A reading from the book of Exodus.

The Israelites had journeyed from Rephidim, entered the wilderness of Sinai, and camped in the wilderness; Israel camped there in front of the mountain. Then Moses went up to God; the LORD called to him from the mountain, saying, 'Thus you shall say to the house of Jacob, and tell the Israelites: You have seen what I did to the Egyptians, and how I bore you on eagles' wings and brought you to myself. Now therefore, if you obey my voice and keep my covenant, you shall be my treasured possession out of all the peoples. Indeed, the whole earth is mine, but you shall be for me a priestly kingdom and a holy nation. These are the words that you shall speak to the Israelites.'

So Moses came, summoned the elders of the people, and set before them all these words that the LORD had commanded him. The people all answered as one: 'Everything that the LORD has spoken we will do.'

PSALM   **Psalm 100**

℟ **We are the people and the sheep of his pasture.**

Be joyful in the Lord, all you lands;
serve the Lord with gladness
and come before his presence with a song.
Know this: The Lord himself is God;
he himself has made us and we are his;
we are his people and the sheep of his pasture. ℟

Enter his gates with thanksgiving;
go into his courts with praise;
give thanks to him and call upon his name.
For the Lord is good; his mercy is everlasting;
and his faithfulness endures from age to age. ℟

SECOND READING   **Romans 5.1–8**

A reading from the letter of Paul to the Romans.

Since we are justified by faith,
we have peace with God through our Lord Jesus Christ,
through whom we have obtained access to this grace in which we stand;

and we boast in our hope of sharing the glory of God.
And not only that,
but we also boast in our sufferings,
knowing that suffering produces endurance,
and endurance produces character,
and character produces hope,
and hope does not disappoint us,
because God's love has been poured into our hearts
through the Holy Spirit that has been given to us.

For while we were still weak,
at the right time Christ died for the ungodly.
Indeed, rarely will anyone die for a righteous person –
though perhaps for a good person
someone might actually dare to die.
But God proves his love for us
in that while we still were sinners Christ died for us.

GOSPEL (Short or long reading) Matthew 9.35 – 10.8, (9–23)

Hear the gospel of our Lord Jesus Christ according to Matthew.

Then Jesus went about all the cities and villages, teaching in their
synagogues, and proclaiming the good news of the kingdom, and curing
every disease and every sickness. When he saw the crowds, he had
compassion for them, because they were harassed and helpless, like sheep
without a shepherd. Then he said to his disciples, 'The harvest is plentiful,
but the labourers are few; therefore ask the Lord of the harvest to send out
labourers into his harvest.'

Then Jesus summoned his twelve disciples and gave them authority over
unclean spirits, to cast them out, and to cure every disease and every
sickness. These are the names of the twelve apostles: first, Simon, also known
as Peter, and his brother Andrew; James son of Zebedee, and his brother John;
Philip and Bartholomew; Thomas and Matthew the tax-collector; James son
of Alphaeus, and Thaddaeus; Simon the Cananaean, and Judas Iscariot, the
one who betrayed him.

These twelve Jesus sent out with the following instructions: 'Go nowhere
among the Gentiles, and enter no town of the Samaritans, but go rather to
the lost sheep of the house of Israel. As you go, proclaim the good news, "The
kingdom of heaven has come near." Cure the sick, raise the dead, cleanse the
lepers, cast out demons. You received without payment; give without

payment. [Take no gold, or silver, or copper in your belts, no bag for your journey, or two tunics, or sandals, or a staff; for labourers deserve their food. Whatever town or village you enter, find out who in it is worthy, and stay there until you leave. As you enter the house, greet it. If the house is worthy, let your peace come upon it; but if it is not worthy, let your peace return to you. If anyone will not welcome you or listen to your words, shake off the dust from your feet as you leave that house or town. Truly I tell you, it will be more tolerable for the land of Sodom and Gomorrah on the day of judgement than for that town.

See, I am sending you out like sheep into the midst of wolves; so be wise as serpents and innocent as doves. Beware of them, for they will hand you over to councils and flog you in their synagogues; and you will be dragged before governors and kings because of me, as a testimony to them and the Gentiles. When they hand you over, do not worry about how you are to speak or what you are to say; for what you are to say will be given to you at that time; for it is not you who speak, but the Spirit of your Father speaking through you. Brother will betray brother to death, and a father his child, and children will rise against parents and have them put to death; and you will be hated by all because of my name. But the one who endures to the end will be saved. When they persecute you in one town, flee to the next; for truly I tell you, you will not have gone through all the towns of Israel before the Son of Man comes.']

† SUNDAY BETWEEN 19 AND 25 JUNE YEAR A
(if after Trinity Sunday)
PROPER 7

TRACK 1

FIRST READING Genesis 21.8–21

A reading from the book of Genesis.

The child Isaac grew, and was weaned; and Abraham made a great feast on the day that Isaac was weaned. But Sarah saw the son of Hagar the Egyptian, whom she had borne to Abraham, playing with her son Isaac. So she said to Abraham, 'Cast out this slave woman with her son; for the son of this slave woman shall not inherit along with my son Isaac.' The matter was very distressing to Abraham on account of his son. But God said to Abraham, 'Do not be distressed because of the boy and because of your slave woman; whatever Sarah says to you, do as she tells you, for it is through Isaac that offspring shall be named after you. As for the son of the slave woman, I will make a nation of him also, because he is your offspring.' So Abraham rose early in the morning, and took bread and a skin of water, and gave it to Hagar, putting it on her shoulder, along with the child, and sent her away. And she departed, and wandered about in the wilderness of Beer-sheba.

When the water in the skin was gone, she cast the child under one of the bushes. Then she went and sat down opposite him a good way off, about the distance of a bowshot; for she said, 'Do not let me look on the death of the child.' And as she sat opposite him, she lifted up her voice and wept. And God heard the voice of the boy; and the angel of God called to Hagar from heaven, and said to her, 'What troubles you, Hagar? Do not be afraid; for God has heard the voice of the boy where he is. Come, lift up the boy and hold him fast with your hand, for I will make a great nation of him.' Then God opened her eyes and she saw a well of water. She went, and filled the skin with water, and gave the boy a drink.

God was with the boy, and he grew up; he lived in the wilderness, and became an expert with the bow. He lived in the wilderness of Paran; and his mother got a wife for him from the land of Egypt.

PSALM

Psalm 86.1–10, 16–17

℟ **You, O Lord, are gracious and full of compassion.**

Bow down your ear, O Lord, and answer me,
for I am poor and in misery.
Keep watch over my life, for I am faithful;
save your servant who trusts in you.
Be merciful to me, O Lord, for you are my God;
I call upon you all the day long. ℟

Gladden the soul of your servant,
for to you, O Lord, I lift up my soul.
For you, O Lord, are good and forgiving,
and great is your love towards all who call upon you. ℟

Give ear, O Lord, to my prayer,
and attend to the voice of my supplications.
In the time of my trouble I will call upon you,
for you will answer me.
Among the gods there is none like you, O Lord,
nor anything like your works. ℟

All nations you have made
will come and worship you, O Lord,
and glorify your name.
For you are great; you do wondrous things;
and you alone are God. ℟

Turn to me and have mercy upon me;
give your strength to your servant;
and save the child of your handmaid.
Show me a sign of your favour,
so that those who hate me may see it and be ashamed;
because you, O Lord, have helped me and comforted me. ℟

Or   TRACK 2

FIRST READING   **Jeremiah 20.7–13**

A reading from the book of the prophet Jeremiah.

Jeremiah cried out:

O LORD, you have enticed me,
and I was enticed; you have overpowered me,
and you have prevailed.
I have become a laughing-stock all day long;
everyone mocks me.
For whenever I speak, I must cry out,
I must shout, 'Violence and destruction!'
For the word of the LORD has become for me a reproach
and derision all day long.
If I say,
'I will not mention him, or speak any more in his name,'
then within me there is something like a burning fire shut up in my bones;
I am weary with holding it in, and I cannot.
For I hear many whispering:
'Terror is all around! Denounce him! Let us denounce him!'
All my close friends are watching for me to stumble.
'Perhaps he can be enticed, and we can prevail against him,
and take our revenge on him.'
But the LORD is with me like a dread warrior;
therefore my persecutors will stumble,
and they will not prevail.

They will be greatly shamed,
for they will not succeed.
Their eternal dishonour will never be forgotten.
O LORD of hosts, you test the righteous,
you see the heart and the mind;
let me see your retribution upon them,
for to you I have committed my cause.

Sing to the LORD; praise the LORD!
For he has delivered the life of the needy
from the hands of evildoers.

PSALM
Psalm 69.8–11, (12–17), 18–20

℞ In your great mercy, answer me, O God.

Surely, for your sake have I suffered reproach,
and shame has covered my face.
I have become a stranger to my own kindred,
an alien to my mother's children. ℞

Zeal for your house has eaten me up;
the scorn of those who scorn you has fallen upon me.
I humbled myself with fasting,
but that was turned to my reproach. ℞

[I put on sack-cloth also,
and became a byword among them.
Those who sit at the gate murmur against me,
and the drunkards make songs about me.
But as for me, this is my prayer to you,
at the time you have set, O Lord: ℞

'In your great mercy, O God,
answer me with your unfailing help.
Save me from the mire; do not let me sink;
let me be rescued from those who hate me
and out of the deep waters.
Let not the torrent of waters wash over me,
neither let the deep swallow me up;
do not let the Pit shut its mouth upon me. ℞]

Answer me, O Lord, for your love is kind;
in your great compassion, turn to me.
Hide not your face from your servant;
be swift and answer me, for I am in distress.
Draw near to me and redeem me;
because of my enemies deliver me.' ℟

SECOND READING — Romans 6.1b–11

A reading from the letter of Paul to the Romans.

Should we continue in sin in order that grace may abound? By no means!
How can we who died to sin go on living in it? Do you not know that all of
us who have been baptized into Christ Jesus were baptized into his death?
Therefore we have been buried with him by baptism into death, so that, just
as Christ was raised from the dead by the glory of the Father, so we too might
walk in newness of life.

For if we have been united with him in a death like his, we will certainly be
united with him in a resurrection like his. We know that our old self was
crucified with him so that the body of sin might be destroyed, and we might
no longer be enslaved to sin. For whoever has died is freed from sin. But if we
have died with Christ, we believe that we will also live with him. We know
that Christ, being raised from the dead, will never die again; death no longer
has dominion over him. The death he died, he died to sin, once for all; but
the life he lives, he lives to God. So you also must consider yourselves dead to
sin and alive to God in Christ Jesus.

GOSPEL — Matthew 10.24–39

Hear the gospel of our Lord Jesus Christ according to Matthew.

Jesus summoned the twelve and sent them out with the following
instruction: 'A disciple is not above the teacher, nor a slave above the master;
it is enough for the disciple to be like the teacher, and the slave like the
master. If they have called the master of the house Beelzebul, how much
more will they malign those of his household!

So have no fear of them; for nothing is covered up that will not be
uncovered, and nothing secret that will not become known. What I say to
you in the dark, tell in the light; and what you hear whispered, proclaim
from the housetops.

Do not fear those who kill the body but cannot kill the soul; rather fear him who can destroy both soul and body in hell.
Are not two sparrows sold for a penny? Yet not one of them will fall to the ground unperceived by your Father.
And even the hairs of your head are all counted.
So do not be afraid; you are of more value than many sparrows.

Everyone therefore who acknowledges me before others, I also will acknowledge before my Father in heaven;
but whoever denies me before others, I also will deny before my Father in heaven.

Do not think that I have come to bring peace to the earth; I have not come to bring peace, but a sword.
For I have come to set a man against his father,
and a daughter against her mother,
and a daughter-in-law against her mother-in-law;
and one's foes will be members of one's own household.
Whoever loves father or mother more than me is not worthy of me; and whoever loves son or daughter more than me is not worthy of me;
and whoever does not take up the cross and follow me is not worthy of me.
Those who find their life will lose it, and those who lose their life for my sake will find it.'

† SUNDAY BETWEEN 26 JUNE AND 2 JULY   YEAR A
PROPER 8

TRACK 1

FIRST READING   Genesis 22.1–14

A reading from the book of Genesis.

God tested Abraham. He said to him, 'Abraham!' And Abraham said, 'Here I am.' God said, 'Take your son, your only son Isaac, whom you love, and go to the land of Moriah, and offer him there as a burnt-offering on one of the mountains that I shall show you.' So Abraham rose early in the morning, saddled his donkey, and took two of his young men with him, and his son Isaac; he cut the wood for the burnt-offering, and set out and went to the place in the distance that God had shown him. On the third day Abraham looked up and saw the place far away. Then Abraham said to his young men,

'Stay here with the donkey; the boy and I will go over there; we will worship, and then we will come back to you.' Abraham took the wood of the burnt offering and laid it on his son Isaac, and he himself carried the fire and the knife. So the two of them walked on together. Isaac said to his father Abraham, 'Father!' And Abraham said, 'Here I am, my son.' Isaac said, 'The fire and the wood are here, but where is the lamb for a burnt-offering?' Abraham said, 'God himself will provide the lamb for a burnt-offering, my son.' So the two of them walked on together.

When they came to the place that God had shown him, Abraham built an altar there and laid the wood in order. He bound his son Isaac, and laid him on the altar, on top of the wood. Then Abraham reached out his hand and took the knife to kill his son. But the angel of the LORD called to him from heaven, and said, 'Abraham, Abraham!' And he said, 'Here I am.' The angel said, 'Do not lay your hand on the boy or do anything to him; for now I know that you fear God, since you have not withheld your son, your only son, from me.' And Abraham looked up and saw a ram, caught in a thicket by its horns. Abraham went and took the ram and offered it up as a burnt-offering instead of his son. So Abraham called that place 'The LORD will provide'; as it is said to this day, 'On the mount of the LORD it shall be provided.'

PSALM   Psalm 13

℞ **Look upon me and answer me, O Lord.**

How long, O Lord;
will you forget me for ever?
how long will you hide your face from me?
How long shall I have perplexity in my mind,
and grief in my heart, day after day?
how long shall my enemy triumph over me? ℞

Look upon me and answer me, O Lord my God;
give light to my eyes, lest I sleep in death;
Lest my enemy say, 'I have prevailed over him',
and my foes rejoice that I have fallen. ℞

But I put my trust in your mercy;
my heart is joyful because of your saving help.
I will sing to the Lord,
for he has dealt with me richly;
I will praise the name of the Lord Most High. ℞

Or   TRACK 2

FIRST READING   Jeremiah 28.5–9

A reading from the book of the prophet Jeremiah.

The prophet Jeremiah spoke to the prophet Hananiah in the presence of the priests and all the people who were standing in the house of the LORD; and the prophet Jeremiah said, 'Amen! May the LORD do so; may the LORD fulfil the words that you have prophesied, and bring back to this place from Babylon the vessels of the house of the LORD, and all the exiles. But listen now to this word that I speak in your hearing and in the hearing of all the people. The prophets who preceded you and me from ancient times prophesied war, famine, and pestilence against many countries and great kingdoms. As for the prophet who prophesies peace, when the word of that prophet comes true, then it will be known that the LORD has truly sent the prophet.'

PSALM   Psalm 89.1–4, 15–18

℟ **Your love, O Lord, for ever will I sing.**

Your love, O Lord, for ever will I sing;
from age to age my mouth will proclaim your faithfulness.
For I am persuaded that your love is established for ever;
you have set your faithfulness firmly in the heavens. ℟

'I have made a covenant with my chosen one;
I have sworn an oath to David my servant:
"I will establish your line for ever,
and preserve your throne for all generations."' ℟

Happy are the people who know the festal shout!
they walk, O Lord, in the light of your presence.
They rejoice daily in your name;
they are jubilant in your righteousness. ℟

For you are the glory of their strength,
and by your favour our might is exalted.
Truly, the Lord is our ruler;
the Holy One of Israel is our king. ℟

SECOND READING   Romans 6.12–23

A reading from the letter of Paul to the Romans.

Do not let sin exercise dominion in your mortal bodies, to make you obey their passions. No longer present your members to sin as instruments of wickedness, but present yourselves to God as those who have been brought from death to life, and present your members to God as instruments of righteousness. For sin will have no dominion over you, since you are not under law but under grace.

What then? Should we sin because we are not under law but under grace? By no means! Do you not know that if you present yourselves to anyone as obedient slaves, you are slaves of the one whom you obey, either of sin, which leads to death, or of obedience, which leads to righteousness? But thanks be to God that you, having once been slaves of sin, have become obedient from the heart to the form of teaching to which you were entrusted, and that you, having been set free from sin, have become slaves of righteousness.

I am speaking in human terms because of your natural limitations. For just as you once presented your members as slaves to impurity and to greater and greater iniquity, so now present your members as slaves to righteousness for sanctification. When you were slaves of sin, you were free in regard to righteousness. So what advantage did you then get from the things of which you now are ashamed? The end of those things is death. But now that you have been freed from sin and enslaved to God, the advantage you get is sanctification. The end is eternal life. For the wages of sin is death, but the free gift of God is eternal life in Christ Jesus our Lord.

GOSPEL   Matthew 10.40–42

Hear the gospel of our Lord Jesus Christ according to Matthew.

Jesus said to the twelve: 'Whoever welcomes you welcomes me, and whoever welcomes me welcomes the one who sent me. Whoever welcomes a prophet in the name of a prophet will receive a prophet's reward; and whoever welcomes a righteous person in the name of a righteous person will receive the reward of the righteous; and whoever gives even a cup of cold water to one of these little ones in the name of a disciple – truly I tell you, none of these will lose their reward.'

† SUNDAY BETWEEN 3 AND 9 JULY
PROPER 9

YEAR A

TRACK 1

FIRST READING   **Genesis 24.34–38, 42–49, 58–67**

A reading from the book of Genesis.

The servant whom Abraham had sent said to Laban: 'I am Abraham's servant. The LORD has greatly blessed my master, and he has become wealthy; he has given him flocks and herds, silver and gold, male and female slaves, camels and donkeys. And Sarah my master's wife bore a son to my master when she was old; and he has given him all that he has. My master made me swear, saying, "You shall not take a wife for my son from the daughters of the Canaanites, in whose land I live; but you shall go to my father's house, to my kindred, and get a wife for my son."

I came today to the spring, and said, "O LORD, the God of my master Abraham, if now you will only make successful the way I am going! I am standing here by the spring of water; let the young woman who comes out to draw, to whom I shall say, 'Please give me a little water from your jar to drink,' and who will say to me, 'Drink, and I will draw for your camels also' – let her be the woman whom the LORD has appointed for my master's son."

Before I had finished speaking in my heart, there was Rebekah coming out with her water jar on her shoulder; and she went down to the spring, and drew. I said to her, "Please let me drink." She quickly let down her jar from her shoulder, and said, "Drink, and I will also water your camels." So I drank, and she also watered the camels. Then I asked her, "Whose daughter are you?" She said, "The daughter of Bethuel, Nahor's son, whom Milcah bore to him." So I put the ring on her nose, and the bracelets on her arms. Then I bowed my head and worshipped the LORD, and blessed the LORD, the God of my master Abraham, who had led me by the right way to obtain the daughter of my master's kinsman for his son. Now then, if you will deal loyally and truly with my master, tell me; and if not, tell me, so that I may turn either to the right hand or to the left.'

And they called Rebekah, and said to her, 'Will you go with this man?' She said, 'I will.' So they sent away their sister Rebekah and her nurse along with Abraham's servant and his men. And they blessed Rebekah and said to her, 'May you, our sister, become thousands of myriads; may your offspring gain possession of the gates of their foes.' Then Rebekah and her maids rose up, mounted the camels, and followed the man; thus the servant took Rebekah, and went his way.

Now Isaac had come from Beer-lahai-roi, and was settled in the Negeb. Isaac went out in the evening to walk in the field; and looking up, he saw camels coming. And Rebekah looked up, and when she saw Isaac, she slipped quickly from the camel, and said to the servant, 'Who is the man over there, walking in the field to meet us?' The servant said, 'It is my master.' So she took her veil and covered herself. And the servant told Isaac all the things that he had done. Then Isaac brought her into his mother Sarah's tent. He took Rebekah, and she became his wife; and he loved her. So Isaac was comforted after his mother's death.

PSALM OR CANTICLE

Either   **Psalm 45.11–18**

℟ **Grace flows from your lips,**
  because God has blessed you for ever.

'Hear, O daughter; consider and listen closely;
forget your people and your family's house.
The king will have pleasure in your beauty;
he is your master; therefore do him honour. ℟

The people of Tyre are here with a gift;
the rich among the people seek your favour.'
All glorious is the princess as she enters;
her gown is cloth-of-gold. ℟

In embroidered apparel she is brought to the king;
after her the bridesmaids follow in procession.
With joy and gladness they are brought,
and enter into the palace of the king. ℟

'In place of fathers, O king, you shall have sons;
you shall make them princes over all the earth.
I will make your name to be remembered
from one generation to another;
therefore nations will praise you for ever and ever.' ℟

Or   **Song of Songs 2.8–13**

℟ **Arise, my love, my fair one,
and come away.**

The voice of my beloved!
Look, he comes,
leaping upon the mountains,
bounding over the hills.
My beloved is like a gazelle
or young stag.
Look, there he stands
behind our wall,
gazing in at the windows,
looking through the lattice. ℟

My beloved speaks and says to me:
'Arise, my love, my fair one,
and come away;
for now the winter is past,
the rain is over and gone.
The flowers appear on the earth;
the time of singing has come,
and the voice of the turtle dove
is heard in our land. ℟

The fig tree puts forth its figs,
and the vines are in blossom;
they give forth fragrance.
Arise, my love, my fair one,
and come away.' ℟

Or   TRACK 2

FIRST READING   **Zechariah 9.9–12**

A reading from the book of the prophet Zechariah.

Rejoice greatly, O daughter Zion!
Shout aloud, O daughter Jerusalem!
Lo, your king comes to you;
triumphant and victorious is he,

humble and riding on a donkey,
on a colt, the foal of a donkey.
He will cut off the chariot from Ephraim
and the war horse from Jerusalem;
and the battle-bow shall be cut off,
and he shall command peace to the nations;
his dominion shall be from sea to sea,
and from the River to the ends of the earth.

As for you also,
because of the blood of my covenant with you,
I will set your prisoners free from the waterless pit.
Return to your stronghold,
O prisoners of hope;
today I declare that I will restore to you double.

PSALM   Psalm 145.8–15

℟ **I will exalt you, O God my king,**
  [and bless your name for ever].

The Lord is gracious and full of compassion,
slow to anger and of great kindness.
The Lord is loving to everyone
and his compassion is over all his works.
All your works praise you, O Lord,
and your faithful servants bless you. ℟

They make known the glory of your kingdom
and speak of your power;
That the peoples may know of your power
and the glorious splendour of your kingdom.
Your kingdom is an everlasting kingdom;
your dominion endures throughout all ages. ℟

The Lord is faithful in all his words
and merciful in all his deeds.
The Lord upholds all those who fall;
he lifts up those who are bowed down. ℟

SECOND READING   Romans 7.15–25a

A reading from the letter of Paul to the Romans.

I do not understand my own actions. For I do not do what I want, but I do
the very thing I hate. Now if I do what I do not want, I agree that the law is
good. But in fact it is no longer I that do it, but sin that dwells within me. For
I know that nothing good dwells within me, that is, in my flesh. I can will
what is right, but I cannot do it. For I do not do the good I want, but the evil
I do not want is what I do. Now if I do what I do not want, it is no longer I
that do it, but sin that dwells within me.

So I find it to be a law that when I want to do what is good, evil lies close at
hand. For I delight in the law of God in my inmost self, but I see in my
members another law at war with the law of my mind, making me captive to
the law of sin that dwells in my members. Wretched man that I am! Who will
rescue me from this body of death? Thanks be to God through Jesus Christ
our Lord!

GOSPEL   Matthew 11.16–19, 25–30

Hear the gospel of our Lord Jesus Christ according to Matthew.

At that time Jesus said,'To what will I compare this generation? It is like
children sitting in the market-places and calling to one another, "We played
the flute for you, and you did not dance; we wailed, and you did not mourn."
For John came neither eating nor drinking, and they say, "He has a demon";
the Son of Man came eating and drinking, and they say, "Look, a glutton and
a drunkard, a friend of tax-collectors and sinners!" Yet wisdom is vindicated
by her deeds.

I thank you, Father, Lord of heaven and earth, because you have hidden
these things from the wise and the intelligent and have revealed them to
infants; yes, Father, for such was your gracious will. All things have been
handed over to me by my Father; and no one knows the Son except the
Father, and no one knows the Father except the Son and anyone to whom
the Son chooses to reveal him.

Come to me, all you that are weary and are carrying heavy burdens, and I
will give you rest. Take my yoke upon you, and learn from me; for I am
gentle and humble in heart, and you will find rest for your souls. For my
yoke is easy, and my burden is light.'

† SUNDAY BETWEEN 10 AND 16 JULY   YEAR A
PROPER 10

TRACK 1

FIRST READING   Genesis 25.19–34

A reading from the book of Genesis.

These are the descendants of Isaac, Abraham's son: Abraham was the father of
Isaac, and Isaac was forty years old when he married Rebekah, daughter of
Bethuel the Aramean of Paddan-aram, sister of Laban the Aramean. Isaac
prayed to the LORD for his wife, because she was barren; and the LORD
granted his prayer, and his wife Rebekah conceived. The children struggled
together within her; and she said, 'If it is to be this way, why do I live?' So she
went to inquire of the LORD. And the LORD said to her, 'Two nations are in
your womb, and two peoples born of you shall be divided; the one shall be
stronger than the other, the elder shall serve the younger.' When her time to
give birth was at hand, there were twins in her womb. The first came out red,
all his body like a hairy mantle; so they named him Esau. Afterwards his
brother came out, with his hand gripping Esau's heel; so he was named Jacob.
Isaac was sixty years old when she bore them.

When the boys grew up, Esau was a skilful hunter, a man of the field, while
Jacob was a quiet man, living in tents. Isaac loved Esau, because he was fond
of game; but Rebekah loved Jacob.

Once when Jacob was cooking a stew, Esau came in from the field, and he
was famished. Esau said to Jacob, 'Let me eat some of that red stuff, for I am
famished!' (Therefore he was called Edom.) Jacob said, 'First sell me your
birthright.' Esau said, 'I am about to die; of what use is a birthright to me?'
Jacob said, 'Swear to me first.' So he swore to him, and sold his birthright to
Jacob. Then Jacob gave Esau bread and lentil stew, and he ate and drank, and
rose and went his way. Thus Esau despised his birthright.

PSALM   Psalm 119.105–112

℟ O Lord, how I love your law.

Your word is a lantern to my feet
and a light upon my path.
I have sworn and am determined
to keep your righteous judgements. ℟

I am deeply troubled;
preserve my life, O Lord, according to your word.
Accept, O Lord, the willing tribute of my lips,
and teach me your judgements. ℟

My life is always in my hand,
yet I do not forget your law.
The wicked have set a trap for me,
but I have not strayed from your commandments. ℟

Your decrees are my inheritance for ever;
truly, they are the joy of my heart.
I have applied my heart to fulfil your statutes
for ever and to the end. ℟

Or   TRACK 2

FIRST READING   ·   **Isaiah 55.10–13**

A reading from the book of the prophet Isaiah.

Thus says the LORD:
As the rain and the snow come down from heaven,
and do not return there until they have watered the earth,
making it bring forth and sprout,
giving seed to the sower and bread to the eater,
so shall my word be that goes out from my mouth;
it shall not return to me empty,
but it shall accomplish that which I purpose,
and succeed in the thing for which I sent it.

For you shall go out in joy,
and be led back in peace;
the mountains and the hills before you shall burst into song,
and all the trees of the field shall clap their hands.
Instead of the thorn shall come up the cypress;
instead of the brier shall come up the myrtle;
and it shall be to the LORD for a memorial,
for an everlasting sign that shall not be cut off.

PSALM   **Psalm 65.(1–8), 9–13**

℟ **To you, O God, shall all flesh come,**
   [and you will blot out their sins].

[You are to be praised, O God, in Zion;
to you shall vows be performed in Jerusalem.
To you that hear prayer shall all flesh come,
because of their transgressions. ℟

Our sins are stronger than we are,
but you will blot them out.
Happy are they whom you choose
and draw to your courts to dwell there!
they will be satisfied by the beauty of your house,
by the holiness of your temple. ℟

Awesome things will you show us in your righteousness,
O God of our salvation,
O Hope of all the ends of the earth
and of the seas that are far away.
You make fast the mountains by your power;
they are girded about with might. ℟

You still the roaring of the seas,
the roaring of their waves,
and the clamour of the peoples.
Those who dwell at the ends of the earth
will tremble at your marvellous signs;
you make the dawn and the dusk to sing for joy. ℟]

You visit the earth and water it abundantly;
you make it very plenteous;
the river of God is full of water.
You prepare the grain,
for so you provide for the earth. ℟

You drench the furrows and smooth out the ridges;
with heavy rain you soften the ground
and bless its increase.
You crown the year with your goodness,
and your paths overflow with plenty.
May the fields of the wilderness be rich for grazing,
and the hills be clothed with joy. ℟

SECOND READING   **Romans 8.1–11**

A reading from the letter of Paul to the Romans.

There is now no condemnation for those who are in Christ Jesus.
For the law of the Spirit of life in Christ Jesus has set you free from the law of
sin and of death. For God has done what the law, weakened by the flesh,
could not do: by sending his own Son in the likeness of sinful flesh, and to
deal with sin, he condemned sin in the flesh, so that the just requirement of
the law might be fulfilled in us, who walk not according to the flesh but
according to the Spirit. For those who live according to the flesh set their
minds on the things of the flesh, but those who live according to the Spirit
set their minds on the things of the Spirit. To set the mind on the flesh is
death, but to set the mind on the Spirit is life and peace. For this reason the
mind that is set on the flesh is hostile to God; it does not submit to God's law
– indeed it cannot, and those who are in the flesh cannot please God.

But you are not in the flesh; you are in the Spirit, since the Spirit of God
dwells in you. Anyone who does not have the Spirit of Christ does not belong
to him. But if Christ is in you, though the body is dead because of sin, the
Spirit is life because of righteousness. If the Spirit of him who raised Jesus
from the dead dwells in you, he who raised Christ from the dead will give life
to your mortal bodies also through his Spirit that dwells in you.

GOSPEL   **Matthew 13.1–9, 18–23**

Hear the gospel of our Lord Jesus Christ according to Matthew.

Jesus went out of the house and sat beside the lake. Such great crowds
gathered around him that he got into a boat and sat there, while the whole
crowd stood on the beach. And he told them many things in parables,
saying: 'Listen! A sower went out to sow. And as he sowed, some seeds fell on
the path, and the birds came and ate them up. Other seeds fell on rocky
ground, where they did not have much soil, and they sprang up quickly,
since they had no depth of soil. But when the sun rose, they were scorched;
and since they had no root, they withered away. Other seeds fell among
thorns, and the thorns grew up and choked them. Other seeds fell on good
soil and brought forth grain, some a hundredfold, some sixty, some thirty.
Let anyone with ears listen!

Hear then the parable of the sower. When anyone hears the word of the
kingdom and does not understand it, the evil one comes and snatches away

what is sown in the heart; this is what was sown on the path. As for what was sown on rocky ground, this is the one who hears the word and immediately receives it with joy; yet such a person has no root, but endures only for a while, and when trouble or persecution arises on account of the word, that person immediately falls away. As for what was sown among thorns,this is the one who hears the word, but the cares of the world and the lure of wealth choke the word, and it yields nothing. But as for what was sown on good soil, this is the one who hears the word and understands it, who indeed bears fruit and yields, in one case a hundredfold, in another sixty, and in another thirty.'

† SUNDAY BETWEEN 17 AND 23 JULY   YEAR A
PROPER 11

TRACK 1

FIRST READING   **Genesis 28.10–19a**

A reading from the book of Genesis.

Jacob left Beer-sheba and went towards Haran. He came to a certain place and stayed there for the night, because the sun had set. Taking one of the stones of the place, he put it under his head and lay down in that place. And he dreamed that there was a ladder set up on the earth, the top of it reaching to heaven; and the angels of God were ascending and descending on it. And the LORD stood beside him and said, 'I am the LORD, the God of Abraham your father and the God of Isaac; the land on which you lie I will give to you and to your offspring; and your offspring shall be like the dust of the earth, and you shall spread abroad to the west and to the east and to the north and to the south; and all the families of the earth shall be blessed in you and in your offspring. Know that I am with you and will keep you wherever you go, and will bring you back to this land; for I will not leave you until I have done what I have promised you.' Then Jacob woke from his sleep and said, 'Surely the LORD is in this place – and I did not know it!' And he was afraid, and said, 'How awesome is this place! This is none other than the house of God, and this is the gate of heaven.' So Jacob rose early in the morning, and he took the stone that he had put under his head and set it up for a pillar and poured oil on the top of it. He called that place Bethel.

PSALM   Psalm 139.1–11, 22–23

℟ **You, O Lord, created my inward parts;**
   [you knit me together in my mother's womb].

Lord, you have searched me out and known me;
you know my sitting down and my rising up;
you discern my thoughts from afar.
You trace my journeys and my resting-places
and are acquainted with all my ways. ℟

Indeed, there is not a word on my lips,
but you, O Lord, know it altogether.
You press upon me behind and before
and lay your hand upon me.
Such knowledge is too wonderful for me;
it is so high that I cannot attain to it. ℟

Where can I go then from your Spirit?
where can I flee from your presence?
If I climb up to heaven, you are there;
if I make the grave my bed, you are there also.
If I take the wings of the morning
and dwell in the uttermost parts of the sea,
Even there your hand will lead me
and your right hand hold me fast. ℟

If I say, 'Surely the darkness will cover me,
and the light around me turn to night',
Darkness is not dark to you;
the night is as bright as the day;
darkness and light to you are both alike. ℟

Search me out, O God, and know my heart;
try me and know my restless thoughts.
Look well whether there be any wickedness in me
and lead me in the way that is everlasting. ℟

Or   TRACK 2

FIRST READING

Either   **Wisdom of Solomon 12.13, 16–19**

A reading from the book of Wisdom.

There is not any god besides you, Lord,
whose care is for all people,
to whom you should prove that you have not judged unjustly;
For your strength is the source of righteousness,
and your sovereignty over all causes you to spare all.
For you show your strength
when people doubt the completeness of your power,
and you rebuke any insolence among those who know it.
Although you are sovereign in strength,
you judge with mildness,
and with great forbearance you govern us;
for you have power to act whenever you choose.
Through such works you have taught your people
that the righteous must be kind,
and you have filled your children with good hope,
because you give repentance for sins.

Or   **Isaiah 44.6–8**

A reading from the book of the prophet Isaiah.

Thus says the LORD, the King of Israel,
and his Redeemer, the LORD of hosts:
I am the first and I am the last;
besides me there is no god.
Who is like me?
Let them proclaim it, let them declare and set it forth before me.
Who has announced from of old the things to come?
Let them tell us what is yet to be.
Do not fear, or be afraid;
have I not told you from of old and declared it?
You are my witnesses!
Is there any god besides me?
There is no other rock;
I know not one.

PSALM   Psalm 86.11–17

℟ **You, Lord, are gracious and full of compassion.**

Teach me your way, O Lord,
and I will walk in your truth;
knit my heart to you that I may fear your name.
I will thank you, O Lord my God, with all my heart,
and glorify your name for evermore.
For great is your love towards me;
you have delivered me from the nethermost Pit. ℟

The arrogant rise up against me, O God,
and a violent band seeks my life;
they have not set you before their eyes.
But you, O Lord, are gracious and full of compassion,
slow to anger and full of kindness and truth. ℟

Turn to me and have mercy upon me;
give your strength to your servant;
and save the child of your handmaid.
Show me a sign of your favour,
so that those who hate me may see it and be ashamed;
because you, O Lord, have helped me and comforted me. ℟

SECOND READING   Romans 8.12–25

A reading from the letter of Paul to the Romans.

Brothers and sisters, we are debtors, not to the flesh, to live according to the
flesh – for if you live according to the flesh, you will die; but if by the Spirit
you put to death the deeds of the body, you will live. For all who are led by
the Spirit of God are children of God. For you did not receive a spirit of
slavery to fall back into fear, but you have received a spirit of adoption.
When we cry, 'Abba! Father!' it is that very Spirit bearing witness with our
spirit that we are children of God, and if children, then heirs, heirs of God
and joint heirs with Christ – if, in fact, we suffer with him so that we may
also be glorified with him.

I consider that the sufferings of this present time are not worth comparing
with the glory about to be revealed to us. For the creation waits with eager
longing for the revealing of the children of God; for the creation was

subjected to futility, not of its own will but by the will of the one who subjected it, in hope that the creation itself will be set free from its bondage to decay and will obtain the freedom of the glory of the children of God. We know that the whole creation has been groaning in labour pains until now; and not only the creation, but we ourselves, who have the first fruits of the Spirit, groan inwardly while we wait for adoption, the redemption of our bodies. For in hope we were saved. Now hope that is seen is not hope. For who hopes for what is seen? But if we hope for what we do not see, we wait for it with patience.

GOSPEL   Matthew 13.24–30, 36–43

Hear the gospel of our Lord Jesus Christ according to Matthew.

Jesus put before the crowd another parable: 'The kingdom of heaven may be compared to someone who sowed good seed in his field; but while everybody was asleep, an enemy came and sowed weeds among the wheat, and then went away. So when the plants came up and bore grain then the weeds appeared as well. And the slaves of the householder came and said to him, "Master, did you not sow good seed in your field? Where, then, did these weeds come from?" He answered, "An enemy has done this." The slaves said to him, "Then do you want us to go and gather them?" But he replied, "No; for in gathering the weeds you would uproot the wheat along with them. Let both of them grow together until the harvest; and at harvest time I will tell the reapers, Collect the weeds first and bind them in bundles to be burned, but gather the wheat into my barn."'

Then Jesus left the crowds and went into the house. And his disciples approached him, saying, 'Explain to us the parable of the weeds of the field.' He answered, 'The one who sows the good seed is the Son of Man; the field is the world, and the good seed are the children of the kingdom; the weeds are the children of the evil one, and the enemy who sowed them is the devil; the harvest is the end of the age, and the reapers are angels. Just as the weeds are collected and burned up with fire, so will it be at the end of the age. The Son of Man will send his angels, and they will collect out of his kingdom all causes of sin and all evildoers, and they will throw them into the furnace of fire, where there will be weeping and gnashing of teeth. Then the righteous will shine like the sun in the kingdom of their Father. Let anyone with ears listen!'

† SUNDAY BETWEEN 24 AND 30 JULY
PROPER 12

YEAR A

TRACK 1

FIRST READING

Genesis 29.15–28

A reading from the book of Genesis.

Laban said to Jacob, 'Because you are my kinsman, should you therefore serve me for nothing? Tell me, what shall your wages be?' Now Laban had two daughters; the name of the elder was Leah, and the name of the younger was Rachel. Leah's eyes were lovely, and Rachel was graceful and beautiful. Jacob loved Rachel; so he said, 'I will serve you seven years for your younger daughter Rachel.' Laban said, 'It is better that I give her to you than that I should give her to any other man; stay with me.' So Jacob served seven years for Rachel, and they seemed to him but a few days because of the love he had for her.

Then Jacob said to Laban, 'Give me my wife that I may go in to her, for my time is completed.' So Laban gathered together all the people of the place, and made a feast. But in the evening he took his daughter Leah and brought her to Jacob; and he went in to her. (Laban gave his maid Zilpah to his daughter Leah to be her maid.) When morning came, it was Leah! And Jacob said to Laban, 'What is this you have done to me? Did I not serve with you for Rachel? Why then have you deceived me?' Laban said, 'This is not done in our country – giving the younger before the firstborn. Complete the week of this one, and we will give you the other also in return for serving me another seven years.' Jacob did so, and completed her week; then Laban gave him his daughter Rachel as a wife.

PSALM

Either

Psalm 105.1–11, 45b

℟ Sing to the Lord, sing praises to him.

Give thanks to the Lord and call upon his name;
make known his deeds among the peoples.
Sing to him, sing praises to him,
and speak of all his marvellous works.
Glory in his holy name;
let the hearts of those who seek the Lord rejoice. ℟

Search for the Lord and his strength;
continually seek his face.
Remember the marvels he has done,
his wonders and the judgements of his mouth,
O offspring of Abraham his servant,
O children of Jacob his chosen. ℟

He is the Lord our God;
his judgements prevail in all the world.
He has always been mindful of his covenant,
the promise he made for a thousand generations:
The covenant he made with Abraham,
the oath that he swore to Isaac, ℟

Which he established as a statute for Jacob,
an everlasting covenant for Israel,
Saying, 'To you will I give the land of Canaan
to be your allotted inheritance.'
Alleluia! ℟

Or   **Psalm 128**

℟ **Whoever fears the Lord**
  shall indeed be blessed.

Happy are they all who fear the Lord,
and who follow in his ways!
You shall eat the fruit of your labour;
happiness and prosperity shall be yours. ℟

Your wife shall be like a fruitful vine
within your house,
your children like olive shoots round about your table.
Whoever fears the Lord
shall thus indeed be blessed. ℟

The Lord bless you from Zion,
and may you see the prosperity of Jerusalem
all the days of your life.
May you live to see your children's children;
may peace be upon Israel. ℟

Or   TRACK 2

FIRST READING   1 Kings 3.5–12

A reading from the first book of Kings.

At Gibeon the LORD appeared to Solomon in a dream by night; and God said, 'Ask what I should give you.' And Solomon said, 'You have shown great and steadfast love to your servant my father David, because he walked before you in faithfulness, in righteousness, and in uprightness of heart towards you; and you have kept for him this great and steadfast love, and have given him a son to sit on his throne today. And now, O LORD my God, you have made your servant king in place of my father David, although I am only a little child; I do not know how to go out or come in. And your servant is in the midst of the people whom you have chosen, a great people, so numerous they cannot be numbered or counted. Give your servant therefore an understanding mind to govern your people, able to discern between good and evil; for who can govern this your great people?'

It pleased the Lord that Solomon had asked this. God said to him, 'Because you have asked this, and have not asked for yourself long life or riches, or for the life of your enemies, but have asked for yourself understanding to discern what is right, I now do according to your word. Indeed I give you a wise and discerning mind; no one like you has been before you and no one like you shall arise after you.'

PSALM   Psalm 119.129–136

℟ **Lord, how I love your law.**

Your decrees are wonderful;
therefore I obey them with all my heart.
When your word goes forth it gives light;
it gives understanding to the simple. ℟

I open my mouth and pant;
I long for your commandments.
Turn to me in mercy,
as you always do to those who love your name. ℟

Steady my footsteps in your word;
let no iniquity have dominion over me.

Rescue me from those who oppress me,
and I will keep your commandments. ℟

Let your countenance shine upon your servant
and teach me your statutes.
My eyes shed streams of tears,
because people do not keep your law. ℟

SECOND READING   Romans 8.26–39

A reading from the letter of Paul to the Romans.

The Spirit helps us in our weakness; for we do not know how to pray as we ought, but that very Spirit intercedes with sighs too deep for words. And God, who searches the heart, knows what is the mind of the Spirit, because the Spirit intercedes for the saints according to the will of God.

We know that all things work together for good for those who love God, who are called according to his purpose. For those whom he foreknew he also predestined to be conformed to the image of his Son, in order that he might be the firstborn within a large family. And those whom he predestined he also called; and those whom he called he also justified; and those whom he justified he also glorified.

What then are we to say about these things? If God is for us, who is against us? He who did not withhold his own Son, but gave him up for all of us, will he not with him also give us everything else? Who will bring any charge against God's elect? It is God who justifies. Who is to condemn? It is Christ Jesus, who died, yes, who was raised, who is at the right hand of God, who indeed intercedes for us. Who will separate us from the love of Christ? Will hardship, or distress, or persecution, or famine, or nakedness, or peril, or sword?
As it is written,
'For your sake we are being killed all day long;
we are accounted as sheep to be slaughtered.'
No, in all these things we are more than conquerors through him who loved us. For I am convinced that neither death, nor life, nor angels, nor rulers, nor things present, nor things to come, nor powers, nor height, nor depth, nor anything else in all creation, will be able to separate us from the love of God in Christ Jesus our Lord.

GOSPEL   **Matthew 13.31–33, 44–52**

Hear the gospel of our Lord Jesus Christ according to Matthew.

Jesus put before the crowd another parable: 'The kingdom of heaven is like a mustard seed that someone took and sowed in his field; it is the smallest of all the seeds, but when it has grown it is the greatest of shrubs and becomes a tree, so that the birds of the air come and make nests in its branches.'

He told them another parable: 'The kingdom of heaven is like yeast that a woman took and mixed in with three measures of flour until all of it was leavened.

The kingdom of heaven is like treasure hidden in a field, which someone found and hid; then in his joy he goes and sells all that he has and buys that field.

Again, the kingdom of heaven is like a merchant in search of fine pearls; on finding one pearl of great value, he went and sold all that he had and bought it.

Again, the kingdom of heaven is like a net that was thrown into the sea and caught fish of every kind; when it was full, they drew it ashore, sat down, and put the good into baskets but threw out the bad. So it will be at the end of the age. The angels will come out and separate the evil from the righteous and throw them into the furnace of fire, where there will be weeping and gnashing of teeth. Have you understood all this?' They answered, 'Yes.'

And he said to them, 'Therefore every scribe who has been trained for the kingdom of heaven is like the master of a household who brings out of his treasure what is new and what is old.'

† SUNDAY BETWEEN 31 JULY AND 6 AUGUST   YEAR A
PROPER 13

TRACK 1

FIRST READING   **Genesis 32.22–31**

A reading from the book of Genesis.

Jacob got up, took his two wives, his two maids, and his eleven children, and crossed the ford of the Jabbok. He took them and sent them across the stream, and likewise everything that he had. Jacob was left alone; and a man

wrestled with him until daybreak. When the man saw that he did not prevail
against Jacob, he struck him on the hip socket; and Jacob's hip was put out of
joint as he wrestled with him. Then he said, 'Let me go, for the day is
breaking.' But Jacob said, 'I will not let you go, unless you bless me.' So he
said to him, 'What is your name?' And he said, 'Jacob.' Then the man said,
'You shall no longer be called Jacob, but Israel, for you have striven with God
and with humans, and have prevailed.' Then Jacob asked him, 'Please tell me
your name.' But he said, 'Why is it that you ask my name?' And there he
blessed him. So Jacob called the place Peniel, saying, 'For I have seen God
face to face, and yet my life is preserved.' The sun rose upon him as he passed
Penuel, limping because of his hip.

PSALM   **Psalm 17.1–7, 16**

℞ **Show me, O Lord, your loving-kindness.**

Hear my plea of innocence, O Lord;
give heed to my cry;
listen to my prayer,
which does not come from lying lips.
Let my vindication come forth from your presence;
let your eyes be fixed on justice. ℞

Weigh my heart, summon me by night,
melt me down; you will find no impurity in me.
I give no offence with my mouth as others do;
I have heeded the words of your lips. ℞

My footsteps hold fast to the ways of your law;
in your paths my feet shall not stumble.
I call upon you, O God, for you will answer me;
incline your ear to me and hear my words. ℞

Show me your marvellous loving-kindness,
O Saviour of those who take refuge at your right hand
from those who rise up against them.
But at my vindication I shall see your face;
when I awake, I shall be satisfied, beholding your likeness. ℞

Or   TRACK 2

FIRST READING   Isaiah 55.1-5

A reading from the book of the prophet Isaiah.

The LORD says this:
Everyone who thirsts,
come to the waters;
and you that have no money,
come, buy and eat!
Come, buy wine and milk
without money and without price.
Why do you spend your money for that which is not bread,
and your labour for that which does not satisfy?
Listen carefully to me, and eat what is good,
and delight yourselves in rich food.
Incline your ear, and come to me;
listen, so that you may live.
I will make with you an everlasting covenant,
my steadfast, sure love for David.
See, I made him a witness to the peoples,
a leader and commander for the peoples.
See, you shall call nations that you do not know,
and nations that do not know you shall run to you,
because of the LORD your God, the Holy One of Israel,
for he has glorified you.

PSALM   Psalm 145.8-9, 15-22

℟ **You open wide your hand, O Lord,
[and satisfy the needs of every creature].**

The Lord is gracious and full of compassion,
slow to anger and of great kindness.
The Lord is loving to everyone
and his compassion is over all his works. ℟

The Lord upholds all those who fall;
he lifts up those who are bowed down.
The eyes of all wait upon you, O Lord,
and you give them their food in due season.

You open wide your hand
and satisfy the needs of every living creature. ℞

The Lord is righteous in all his ways
and loving in all his works.
The Lord is near to those who call upon him,
to all who call upon him faithfully.
He fulfils the desire of those who fear him,
he hears their cry and helps them. ℞

The Lord preserves all those who love him,
but he destroys all the wicked.
My mouth shall speak the praise of the Lord;
let all flesh bless his holy name for ever and ever. ℞

SECOND READING   Romans 9.1–5

A reading from the letter of Paul to the Romans.

I am speaking the truth in Christ. I am not lying; my conscience confirms it
by the Holy Spirit. I have great sorrow and unceasing anguish in my heart.
For I could wish that I myself were accursed and cut off from Christ for the
sake of my own people, my kindred according to the flesh. They are Israelites,
and to them belong the adoption, the glory, the covenants, the giving of the
law, the worship, and the promises; to them belong the patriarchs, and from
them, according to the flesh, comes the Messiah, who is over all, God blessed
for ever. Amen.

GOSPEL   Matthew 14.13–21

Hear the gospel of our Lord Jesus Christ according to Matthew.

When Jesus heard that Herod had beheaded John the Baptist, he withdrew in
a boat to a deserted place by himself. But when the crowds heard it, they
followed him on foot from the towns. When he went ashore, he saw a great
crowd; and he had compassion for them and cured their sick. When it was
evening, the disciples came to him and said, 'This is a deserted place, and the
hour is now late; send the crowds away so that they may go into the villages
and buy food for themselves.' Jesus said to them, 'They need not go away;
you give them something to eat.' They replied, 'We have nothing here but
five loaves and two fish.' And he said, 'Bring them here to me.' Then he
ordered the crowds to sit down on the grass. Taking the five loaves and the
two fish, he looked up to heaven, and blessed and broke the loaves, and gave

them to the disciples, and the disciples gave them to the crowds. And all ate and were filled; and they took up what was left over of the broken pieces, twelve baskets full. And those who ate were about five thousand men, besides women and children.

† SUNDAY BETWEEN 7 AND 13 AUGUST   YEAR A
PROPER 14

TRACK 1

FIRST READING   Genesis 37.1–4, 12–28

A reading from the book of Genesis.

Jacob settled in the land where his father had lived as an alien, the land of Canaan. This is the story of the family of Jacob.

Joseph, being seventeen years old, was shepherding the flock with his brothers; he was a helper to the sons of Bilhah and Zilpah, his father's wives; and Joseph brought a bad report of them to their father. Now Israel loved Joseph more than any other of his children, because he was the son of his old age; and he had made him a long robe with sleeves. But when his brothers saw that their father loved him more than all his brothers, they hated him, and could not speak peaceably to him.

Now his brothers went to pasture their father's flock near Shechem. And Israel said to Joseph, 'Are not your brothers pasturing the flock at Shechem? Come, I will send you to them.' He answered, 'Here I am.' So he said to him, 'Go now, see if it is well with your brothers and with the flock; and bring word back to me.' So he sent him from the valley of Hebron.

He came to Shechem, and a man found him wandering in the fields; the man asked him, 'What are you seeking?' 'I am seeking my brothers,' he said; 'tell me, please, where they are pasturing the flock.' The man said, 'They have gone away, for I heard them say, "Let us go to Dothan."' So Joseph went after his brothers, and found them at Dothan. They saw him from a distance, and before he came near to them, they conspired to kill him. They said to one another, 'Here comes this dreamer. Come now, let us kill him and throw him into one of the pits; then we shall say that a wild animal has devoured him, and we shall see what will become of his dreams.' But when Reuben heard it, he delivered him out of their hands, saying, 'Let us not take his life.' Reuben said to them, 'Shed no blood; throw him into this pit here in the wilderness, but lay no hand on him' – that he might rescue him out of their hand and restore him to his father. So when Joseph came to his brothers, they stripped him of his robe, the long robe with sleeves that he wore; and they took him and threw him into a pit. The pit was empty; there was no water in it.

Then they sat down to eat; and looking up they saw a caravan of Ishmaelites coming from Gilead, with their camels carrying gum, balm, and resin, on their way to carry it down to Egypt. Then Judah said to his brothers, 'What profit is it if we kill our brother and conceal his blood? Come, let us sell him to the Ishmaelites, and not lay our hands on him, for he is our brother, our own flesh.' And his brothers agreed. When some Midianite traders passed by, they drew Joseph up, lifting him out of the pit, and sold him to the Ishmaelites for twenty pieces of silver. And they took Joseph to Egypt.

PSALM   **Psalm 105.1–6, 16–22, 45b**

℞ **Sing to the Lord, sing praises to him.**

Give thanks to the Lord and call upon his name;
make known his deeds among the peoples.
Sing to him, sing praises to him,
and speak of all his marvellous works.
Glory in his holy name;
let the hearts of those who seek the Lord rejoice. ℞

Search for the Lord and his strength;
continually seek his face.
Remember the marvels he has done,
his wonders and the judgements of his mouth,
O offspring of Abraham his servant,
O children of Jacob his chosen. ℞

Then he called for a famine in the land
and destroyed the supply of bread.
He sent a man before them,
Joseph, who was sold as a slave.
They bruised his feet in fetters;
his neck they put in an iron collar.
Until his prediction came to pass,
the world of the Lord tested him. ℞

The king sent and released him;
the ruler of the peoples set him free.
He set him as master over his household,
as a ruler over all his possessions,
To instruct his princes according to his will
and to teach his elders wisdom.
Alleluia! ℟

Or   TRACK 2

FIRST READING   1 Kings 19.9–18

A reading from the first book of Kings.

When Elijah reached Horeb, the mountain of God, he came to a cave, and
spent the night there. Then the word of the LORD came to him, saying,
'What are you doing here, Elijah?' He answered, 'I have been very zealous for
the LORD, the God of hosts; for the Israelites have forsaken your covenant,
thrown down your altars, and killed your prophets with the sword. I alone
am left, and they are seeking my life, to take it away.'

He said, 'Go out and stand on the mountain before the LORD, for the LORD
is about to pass by.' Now there was a great wind, so strong that it was
splitting mountains and breaking rocks in pieces before the LORD, but the
LORD was not in the wind; and after the wind an earthquake, but the LORD
was not in the earthquake; and after the earthquake a fire, but the LORD was
not in the fire; and after the fire a sound of sheer silence. When Elijah heard
it, he wrapped his face in his mantle and went out and stood at the entrance
of the cave. Then there came a voice to him that said, 'What are you doing
here, Elijah?' He answered, 'I have been very zealous for the LORD, the God
of hosts; for the Israelites have forsaken your covenant, thrown down your
altars, and killed your prophets with the sword. I alone am left, and they are
seeking my life, to take it away.' Then the LORD said to him, 'Go, return on
your way to the wilderness of Damascus; when you arrive, you shall anoint
Hazael as king over Aram. Also you shall anoint Jehu son of Nimshi as king
over Israel; and you shall anoint Elisha son of Shaphat of Abel-meholah as
prophet in your place. Whoever escapes from the sword of Hazael, Jehu shall
kill; and whoever escapes from the sword of Jehu, Elisha shall kill. Yet I will
leave seven thousand in Israel, all the knees that have not bowed to Baal, and
every mouth that has not kissed him.'

PSALM   Psalm 85.8–13

℟ **Show us your mercy, O Lord,
and grant us your salvation**.

I will listen to what the Lord God is saying,
for he is speaking peace to his faithful people
and to those who turn their hearts to him.
Truly, his salvation is very near to those who fear him,
that his glory may dwell in our land. ℟

Mercy and truth have met together;
righteousness and peace have kissed each other.
Truth shall spring up from the earth,
and righteousness shall look down from heaven. ℟

The Lord will indeed grant prosperity,
and our land will yield its increase.
Righteousness shall go before him,
and peace shall be a pathway for his feet. ℟

SECOND READING   Romans 10.5–15

A reading from the letter of Paul to the Romans.

Moses writes concerning the righteousness that comes from the law, that 'the
person who does these things will live by them.' But the righteousness that
comes from faith says, 'Do not say in your heart, "Who will ascend into
heaven?"' (that is, to bring Christ down) 'or "Who will descend into the
abyss?"' (that is, to bring Christ up from the dead). But what does it say?
'The word is near you,
on your lips and in your heart'
(that is, the word of faith that we proclaim); because if you confess with your
lips that Jesus is Lord and believe in your heart that God raised him from the
dead, you will be saved. For one believes with the heart and so is justified,
and one confesses with the mouth and so is saved. The scripture says, 'No
one who believes in him will be put to shame.' For there is no distinction
between Jew and Greek; the same Lord is Lord of all and is generous to all
who call on him. For, 'Everyone who calls on the name of the Lord shall be
saved.'

But how are they to call on one in whom they have not believed? And how
are they to believe in one of whom they have never heard? And how are they

to hear without someone to proclaim him? And how are they to proclaim him unless they are sent? As it is written, 'How beautiful are the feet of those who bring good news!'

GOSPEL   Matthew 14.22–33

Hear the gospel of our Lord Jesus Christ according to Matthew.

Immediately after feeding the crowd with the five loaves and two fish, Jesus made the disciples get into the boat and go on ahead to the other side, while he dismissed the crowds. And after he had dismissed the crowds, he went up the mountain by himself to pray. When evening came, he was there alone, but by this time the boat, battered by the waves, was far from the land, for the wind was against them. And early in the morning he came walking towards them on the lake. But when the disciples saw him walking on the lake, they were terrified, saying, 'It is a ghost!' And they cried out in fear. But immediately Jesus spoke to them and said, 'Take heart, it is I; do not be afraid.'

Peter answered him, 'Lord, if it is you, command me to come to you on the water.' He said, 'Come.' So Peter got out of the boat, started walking on the water, and came towards Jesus. But when he noticed the strong wind, he became frightened, and beginning to sink, he cried out, 'Lord, save me!' Jesus immediately reached out his hand and caught him, saying to him, 'You of little faith, why did you doubt?' When they got into the boat, the wind ceased. And those in the boat worshipped him, saying, 'Truly you are the Son of God.'

† SUNDAY BETWEEN 14 AND 20 AUGUST   YEAR A
PROPER 15

TRACK 1

FIRST READING   Genesis 45.1–15

A reading from the book of Genesis.

Joseph could no longer control himself before all those who stood by him, and he cried out, 'Send everyone away from me.' So no one stayed with him when Joseph made himself known to his brothers. And he wept so loudly that the Egyptians heard it, and the household of Pharaoh heard it. Joseph said to his brothers, 'I am Joseph. Is my father still alive?' But his brothers could not answer him, so dismayed were they at his presence.

Then Joseph said to his brothers, 'Come closer to me.' And they came closer. He said, 'I am your brother, Joseph, whom you sold into Egypt. And now do not be distressed, or angry with yourselves, because you sold me here; for God sent me before you to preserve life. For the famine has been in the land these two years; and there are five more years in which there will be neither ploughing nor harvest. God sent me before you to preserve for you a remnant on earth, and to keep alive for you many survivors. So it was not you who sent me here, but God; he has made me a father to Pharaoh, and lord of all his house and ruler over all the land of Egypt. Hurry and go up to my father and say to him, "Thus says your son Joseph, God has made me lord of all Egypt; come down to me, do not delay. You shall settle in the land of Goshen, and you shall be near me, you and your children and your children's children, as well as your flocks, your herds, and all that you have. I will provide for you there – since there are five more years of famine to come – so that you and your household, and all that you have, will not come to poverty." And now your eyes and the eyes of my brother Benjamin see that it is my own mouth that speaks to you. You must tell my father how greatly I am honoured in Egypt, and all that you have seen. Hurry and bring my father down here.' Then he fell upon his brother Benjamin's neck and wept, while Benjamin wept upon his neck. And he kissed all his brothers and wept upon them; and after that his brothers talked with him.

PSALM   Psalm 133

℞ **How good and pleasant it is
    to live together in unity.**

O how good and pleasant it is,
when a family lives together in unity!
It is like fine oil upon the head
that runs down upon the beard,
Upon the beard of Aaron,
and runs down upon the collar of his robe. ℞

It is like the dew of Hermon
that falls upon the hills of Zion.
For there the Lord has ordained the blessing:
life for evermore. ℞

Or   TRACK 2

FIRST READING   Isaiah 56.1, 6–8

A reading from the book of the prophet Isaiah.

Thus says the LORD:
Maintain justice, and do what is right,
for soon my salvation will come,
and my deliverance be revealed.

And the foreigners who join themselves to the LORD,
to minister to him, to love the name of the LORD,
and to be his servants,
all who keep the sabbath, and do not profane it,
and hold fast my covenant –
these I will bring to my holy mountain,
and make them joyful in my house of prayer;
their burnt-offerings and their sacrifices
will be accepted on my altar;
for my house shall be called a house of prayer
for all peoples.
Thus says the Lord GOD,
who gathers the outcasts of Israel,
I will gather others to them besides those already gathered.

PSALM   Psalm 67

℟ **Let the peoples praise you, O God;**
  let all the peoples praise you.

May God be merciful to us and bless us,
show us the light of his countenance and come to us.
Let your ways be known upon earth,
your saving health among all nations. ℟

[Let the peoples praise you, O God;
let all the peoples praise you.]
Let the nations be glad and sing for joy,
for you judge the peoples with equity
and guide all the nations upon earth. ℟

[Let the peoples praise you, O God;
let all the peoples praise you.]
The earth has brought forth her increase;
may God, our own God, give us his blessing.
May God give us his blessing,
and may all the ends of the earth stand in awe of him. ℟

SECOND READING   Romans 11.1–2a, 29–32

A reading from the letter of Paul to the Romans.

I ask, then, has God rejected his people? By no means! I myself am an
Israelite, a descendant of Abraham, a member of the tribe of Benjamin. God
has not rejected his people whom he foreknew.

For the gifts and the calling of God are irrevocable. Just as you were once
disobedient to God but have now received mercy because of their
disobedience, so they have now been disobedient in order that, by the mercy
shown to you, they too may now receive mercy. For God has imprisoned all
in disobedience so that he may be merciful to all.

GOSPEL (Short or long reading)   Matthew 15.(10–20), 21–28

Hear the gospel of our Lord Jesus Christ according to Matthew.

[Then Jesus called the crowd to him and said to them, 'Listen and
understand: it is not what goes into the mouth that defiles a person, but it is
what comes out of the mouth that defiles.' Then the disciples approached
and said to him, 'Do you know that the Pharisees took offence when they
heard what you said?' He answered, 'Every plant that my heavenly Father has
not planted will be uprooted. Let them alone; they are blind guides of the
blind. And if one blind person guides another, both will fall into a pit.' But
Peter said to him, 'Explain this parable to us.' Then he said, 'Are you also still
without understanding? Do you not see that whatever goes into the mouth
enters the stomach, and goes out into the sewer? But what comes out of the
mouth proceeds from the heart, and this is what defiles. For out of the heart
come evil intentions, murder, adultery, fornication, theft, false witness,
slander. These are what defile a person, but to eat with unwashed hands does
not defile.']

Jesus went away to the district of Tyre and Sidon. A Canaanite woman from
that region came out and started shouting, 'Have mercy on me, Lord, Son of

David; my daughter is tormented by a demon.' But he did not answer her at all. And his disciples came and urged him, saying, 'Send her away, for she keeps shouting after us.' He answered, 'I was sent only to the lost sheep of the house of Israel.' But she came and knelt before him, saying, 'Lord, help me.' He answered, 'It is not fair to take the children's food and throw it to the dogs.' She said, 'Yes, Lord, yet even the dogs eat the crumbs that fall from their masters' table.' Then Jesus answered her, 'Woman, great is your faith! Let it be done for you as you wish.' And her daughter was healed instantly.

† SUNDAY BETWEEN 21 AND 27 AUGUST   YEAR A
PROPER 16

TRACK 1

FIRST READING   Exodus 1.8 – 2.10

A reading from the book of Exodus.

A new king arose over Egypt, who did not know Joseph. He said to his people, 'Look, the Israelite people are more numerous and more powerful than we. Come, let us deal shrewdly with them, or they will increase and, in the event of war, join our enemies and fight against us and escape from the land.' Therefore they set taskmasters over them to oppress them with forced labour. They built supply cities, Pithom and Rameses, for Pharaoh. But the more they were oppressed, the more they multiplied and spread, so that the Egyptians came to dread the Israelites. The Egyptians became ruthless in imposing tasks on the Israelites, and made their lives bitter with hard service in mortar and brick and in every kind of field labour. They were ruthless in all the tasks that they imposed on them.

The king of Egypt said to the Hebrew midwives, one of whom was named Shiphrah and the other Puah, 'When you act as midwives to the Hebrew women, and see them on the birthstool, if it is a boy, kill him; but if it is a girl, she shall live.' But the midwives feared God; they did not do as the king of Egypt commanded them, but they let the boys live. So the king of Egypt summoned the midwives and said to them, 'Why have you done this, and allowed the boys to live?' The midwives said to Pharaoh, 'Because the Hebrew women are not like the Egyptian women; for they are vigorous and give birth before the midwife comes to them.' So God dealt well with the midwives; and the people multiplied and became very strong. And because the midwives feared God, he gave them families.

Then Pharaoh commanded all his people, 'Every boy that is born to the Hebrews you shall throw into the Nile, but you shall let every girl live.'

Now a man from the house of Levi went and married a Levite woman. The woman conceived and bore a son; and when she saw that he was a fine baby, she hid him three months. When she could hide him no longer she got a papyrus basket for him, and plastered it with bitumen and pitch; she put the child in it and placed it among the reeds on the bank of the river. His sister stood at a distance, to see what would happen to him.

The daughter of Pharaoh came down to bathe at the river, while her attendants walked beside the river. She saw the basket among the reeds and sent her maid to bring it. When she opened it, she saw the child. He was crying, and she took pity on him, 'This must be one of the Hebrews' children,' she said. Then his sister said to Pharaoh's daughter, 'Shall I go and get you a nurse from the Hebrew women to nurse the child for you?' Pharaoh's daughter said to her, 'Yes.' So the girl went and called the child's mother. Pharaoh's daughter said to her, 'Take this child and nurse it for me, and I will give you your wages.' So the woman took the child and nursed it. When the child grew up, she brought him to Pharaoh's daughter, and she took him as her son. She named him Moses, 'because,' she said, 'I drew him out of the water.'

PSALM   Psalm 124

℟ **Our help is in the name of the Lord**
  [the maker of heaven and earth].

If the Lord had not been our side,
let Israel now say;
If the Lord had not been on our side,
when enemies rose up against us;
Then would they have swallowed us up alive
in their fierce anger towards us; ℟

Then would the waters have overwhelmed us
and the torrent gone over us;
Then would the raging waters
have gone right over us. ℟

Blessèd be the Lord!
he has not given us over to be a prey for their teeth.
We have escaped like a bird

235

from the snare of the fowler;
the snare is broken and we have escaped.
Our help is in the name of the Lord,
the maker of heaven and earth. ℟

Or   TRACK 2

FIRST READING   Isaiah 51.1–6

A reading from the book of the prophet Isaiah.

Listen to me, you that pursue righteousness,
you that seek the LORD.
Look to the rock from which you were hewn,
and to the quarry from which you were dug.
Look to Abraham your father
and to Sarah who bore you;
for he was but one when I called him,
but I blessed him and made him many.
For the LORD will comfort Zion;
he will comfort all her waste places,
and will make her wilderness like Eden,
her desert like the garden of the LORD;
joy and gladness will be found in her,
thanksgiving and the voice of song.

Listen to me, my people,
and give heed to me, my nation;
for a teaching will go out from me,
and my justice for a light to the peoples.
I will bring near my deliverance swiftly,
my salvation has gone out
and my arms will rule the peoples;
the coastlands wait for me,
and for my arm they hope.
Lift up your eyes to the heavens,
and look at the earth beneath;
for the heavens will vanish like smoke,
the earth will wear out like a garment,
and those who live on it will die like gnats;
but my salvation will be for ever,
and my deliverance will never be ended.

PSALM   **Psalm 138**

℟ **O Lord, your love endures for ever;**
 [do not abandon the works of your hands].

I will give thanks to you, O Lord, with my whole heart;
before the gods I will sing your praise.
I will bow down towards your holy temple
and praise your name,
because of your love and faithfulness;
For you have glorified your name
and your word above all things. ℟

When I called, you answered me;
you increased my strength within me.
All the kings of the earth will praise you, O Lord,
when they have heard the words of your mouth.
They will sing of the ways of the Lord,
that great is the glory of the Lord.
Though the Lord be high, he cares for the lowly;
he perceives the haughty from afar. ℟

Though I walk in the midst of trouble,
you keep me safe;
you stretch forth your hand
against the fury of my enemies;
your right hand shall save me.
The Lord will make good his purpose for me;
O Lord, your love endures for ever;
do not abandon the works of your hands. ℟

SECOND READING   **Romans 12.1-8**

A reading from the letter of Paul to the Romans.

I appeal to you therefore, brothers and sisters, by the mercies of God, to
present your bodies as a living sacrifice, holy and acceptable to God, which is
your spiritual worship. Do not be conformed to this world, but be
transformed by the renewing of your minds, so that you may discern what is
the will of God – what is good and acceptable and perfect.

For by the grace given to me I say to everyone among you not to think of
yourself more highly than you ought to think, but to think with sober

judgement, each according to the measure of faith that God has assigned. For as in one body we have many members, and not all the members have the same function, so we, who are many, are one body in Christ, and individually we are members one of another. We have gifts that differ according to the grace given to us: prophecy, in proportion to faith; ministry, in ministering; the teacher, in teaching; the exhorter, in exhortation; the giver, in generosity; the leader, in diligence; the compassionate, in cheerfulness.

GOSPEL   Matthew 16.13–20

Hear the gospel of our Lord Jesus Christ according to Matthew.

Now when Jesus came into the district of Caesarea Philippi, he asked his disciples, 'Who do people say that the Son of Man is?' And they said, 'Some say John the Baptist, but others Elijah, and still others Jeremiah or one of the prophets.' He said to them, 'But who do you say that I am?' Simon Peter answered, 'You are the Messiah, the Son of the living God.' And Jesus answered him, 'Blessed are you, Simon son of Jonah! For flesh and blood has not revealed this to you, but my Father in heaven. And I tell you, you are Peter, and on this rock I will build my church, and the gates of Hades will not prevail against it. I will give you the keys of the kingdom of heaven, and whatever you bind on earth will be bound in heaven, and whatever you loose on earth will be loosed in heaven.' Then he sternly ordered the disciples not to tell anyone that he was the Messiah.

† SUNDAY BETWEEN 28 AUGUST   YEAR A
AND 3 SEPTEMBER
PROPER 17

TRACK 1

FIRST READING   Exodus 3.1–15

A reading from the book of Exodus.

Moses was keeping the flock of his father-in-law Jethro, the priest of Midian; he led his flock beyond the wilderness, and came to Horeb, the mountain of God. There the angel of the LORD appeared to him in a flame of fire out of a bush; he looked, and the bush was blazing, yet it was not consumed. Then

Moses said, 'I must turn aside and look at this great sight, and see why the bush is not burned up.' When the LORD saw that he had turned aside to see, God called to him out of the bush, 'Moses, Moses!' And he said, 'Here I am.' Then he said, 'Come no closer! Remove the sandals from your feet, for the place on which you are standing is holy ground.'He said further, 'I am the God of your father, the God of Abraham, the God of Isaac, and the God of Jacob.' And Moses hid his face, for he was afraid to look at God.

Then the LORD said, 'I have observed the misery of my people who are in Egypt; I have heard their cry on account of their taskmasters. Indeed, I know their sufferings, and I have come down to deliver them from the Egyptians, and to bring them up out of that land to a good and broad land, a land flowing with milk and honey, to the country of the Canaanites, the Hittites, the Amorites, the Perizzites, the Hivites, and the Jebusites. The cry of the Israelites has now come to me; I have also seen how the Egyptians oppress them. So come, I will send you to Pharaoh to bring my people, the Israelites, out of Egypt.' But Moses said to God, 'Who am I that I should go to Pharaoh, and bring the Israelites out of Egypt?' He said, 'I will be with you; and this shall be the sign for you that it is I who sent you: when you have brought the people out of Egypt,
you shall worship God on this mountain.'

But Moses said to God, 'If I come to the Israelites and say to them, "The God of your ancestors has sent me to you," and they ask me, "What is his name?" what shall I say to them?' God said to Moses, 'I AM WHO I AM.' He said further, 'Thus you shall say to the Israelites, "I AM has sent me to you."'
God also said to Moses, 'Thus you shall say to the Israelites, "The LORD, the God of your ancestors, the God of Abraham, the God of Isaac, and the God of Jacob, has sent me to you": This is my name for ever, and this my title for all generations.'

PSALM   Psalm 105.1–6, 23–26, 45b

℟ **Sing to the Lord, sing praises to him.**

Give thanks to the Lord and call upon his name;
make known his deeds among the peoples.
Sing to him, sing praises to him,
and speak of all his marvellous works.
Glory in his holy name;
let the hearts of those who seek the Lord rejoice. ℟

Search for the Lord and his strength;
continually seek his face.
Remember the marvels he has done,
his wonders and the judgements of his mouth,
O offspring of Abraham his servant,
O children of Jacob his chosen. ℟

Israel came into Egypt,
and Jacob became a sojourner in the land of Ham.
The Lord made his people exceedingly fruitful;
he made them stronger than their enemies;
Whose heart he turned, so that they hated his people,
and dealt unjustly with his servants.
He sent Moses his servant,
and Aaron whom he had chosen.
Alleluia! ℟

Or   TRACK 2

FIRST READING   **Jeremiah 15.15–21**

A reading from the book of the prophet Jeremiah.

O LORD, you know;
remember me and visit me,
and bring down retribution for me on my persecutors.
In your forbearance do not take me away;
know that on your account I suffer insult.
Your words were found, and I ate them,
and your words became to me a joy
and the delight of my heart;
for I am called by your name,
O LORD, God of hosts.
I did not sit in the company of merrymakers,
nor did I rejoice;
under the weight of your hand I sat alone,
for you had filled me with indignation.
Why is my pain unceasing,
my wound incurable,
refusing to be healed?
Truly, you are to me like a deceitful brook,
like waters that fail.

Therefore thus says the LORD:
If you turn back, I will take you back,
and you shall stand before me.
If you utter what is precious, and not what is worthless,
you shall serve as my mouth.
It is they who will turn to you,
not you who will turn to them.
And I will make you to this people
a fortified wall of bronze;
they will fight against you,
but they shall not prevail over you,
for I am with you to save you
and deliver you, says the LORD.
I will deliver you out of the hand of the wicked,
and redeem you from the grasp of the ruthless.

PSALM

Psalm 26.1-8

℟ **Your love is before my eyes;**
 [I have walked faithfully with you].

Give judgement for me, O Lord,
for I have lived with integrity;
I have trusted in the Lord and have not faltered.
Test me, O Lord, and try me;
examine my heart and my mind. ℟

For your love is before my eyes;
I have walked faithfully with you.
I have not sat with the worthless,
nor do I consort with the deceitful.
I have hated the company of evildoers;
I will not sit down with the wicked. ℟

I will wash my hands in innocence, O Lord,
that I may go in procession round your altar,
Singing aloud a song of thanksgiving
and recounting all your wonderful deeds.
Lord, I love the house in which you dwell
and the place where your glory abides. ℟

SECOND READING **Romans 12.9–21**

A reading from the letter of Paul to the Romans.

Let love be genuine; hate what is evil, hold fast to what is good; love one another with mutual affection; outdo one another in showing honour. Do not lag in zeal, be ardent in spirit, serve the Lord. Rejoice in hope, be patient in suffering, persevere in prayer. Contribute to the needs of the saints; extend hospitality to strangers.

Bless those who persecute you; bless and do not curse them. Rejoice with those who rejoice, weep with those who weep. Live in harmony with one another; do not be haughty, but associate with the lowly; do not claim to be wiser than you are. Do not repay anyone evil for evil, but take thought for what is noble in the sight of all. If it is possible, so far as it depends on you, live peaceably with all. Beloved, never avenge yourselves, but leave room for the wrath of God; for it is written, 'Vengeance is mine, I will repay, says the Lord.' No, 'if your enemies are hungry, feed them; if they are thirsty, give them something to drink; for by doing this you will heap burning coals on their heads.' Do not be overcome by evil, but overcome evil with good.

GOSPEL **Matthew 16.21–28**

Hear the gospel of our Lord Jesus Christ according to Matthew.

From that time on, Jesus began to show his disciples that he must go to Jerusalem and undergo great suffering at the hands of the elders and chief priests and scribes, and be killed, and on the third day be raised. And Peter took him aside and began to rebuke him, saying, 'God forbid it, Lord! This must never happen to you.' But he turned and said to Peter, 'Get behind me, Satan! You are a stumbling-block to me; for you are setting your mind not on divine things but on human things.'

Then Jesus told his disciples, 'If any want to become my followers, let them deny themselves and take up their cross and follow me. For those who want to save their life will lose it, and those who lose their life for my sake will find it. For what will it profit them if they gain the whole world but forfeit their life? Or what will they give in return for their life?

For the Son of Man is to come with his angels in the glory of his Father, and then he will repay everyone for what has been done. Truly I tell you, there are some standing here who will not taste death before they see the Son of Man coming in his kingdom.'

† SUNDAY BETWEEN 4 AND 10 SEPTEMBER   YEAR A
PROPER 18

TRACK 1

FIRST READING   **Exodus 12.1–14**

A reading from the book of Exodus.

The LORD said to Moses and Aaron in the land of Egypt: This month shall mark for you the beginning of months; it shall be the first month of the year for you. Tell the whole congregation of Israel that on the tenth of this month they are to take a lamb for each family, a lamb for each household. If a household is too small for a whole lamb, it shall join its closest neighbour in obtaining one; the lamb shall be divided in proportion to the number of people who eat of it. Your lamb shall be without blemish, a year-old male; you may take it from the sheep or from the goats. You shall keep it until the fourteenth day of this month; then the whole assembled congregation of Israel shall slaughter it at twilight. They shall take some of the blood and put it on the two doorposts and the lintel of the houses in which they eat it. They shall eat the lamb that same night; they shall eat it roasted over the fire with unleavened bread and bitter herbs. Do not eat any of it raw or boiled in water, but roasted over the fire, with its head, legs, and inner organs. You shall let none of it remain until the morning; anything that remains until the morning you shall burn. This is how you shall eat it: your loins girded, your sandals on your feet, and your staff in your hand; and you shall eat it hurriedly. It is the passover of the LORD. For I will pass through the land of Egypt that night, and I will strike down every firstborn in the land of Egypt, both human beings and animals; on all the gods of Egypt I will execute judgements: I am the LORD. The blood shall be a sign for you on the houses where you live: when I see the blood, I will pass over you, and no plague shall destroy you when I strike the land of Egypt.

This day shall be a day of remembrance for you. You shall celebrate it as a festival to the LORD; throughout your generations you shall observe it as a perpetual ordinance.

PSALM   Psalm 149

℞ **Sing to the Lord**
   in the congregation of the faithful.

Alleluia!
Sing to the Lord a new song;
sing his praise in the congregation of the faithful.
Let Israel rejoice in his maker;
let the children of Zion be joyful in their king.
Let them praise his name in the dance;
let them sing praise to him with timbrel and harp. ℞

For the Lord takes pleasure in his people
and adorns the poor with victory.
Let the faithful rejoice in triumph;
let them be joyful on their beds. ℞

Let the praises of God be in their throat
and a two-edged sword in their hand;
To wreak vengeance on the nations
and punishment on the peoples; ℞

To bind their kings in chains
and their nobles with links of iron;
To inflict on them the judgement decreed;
this is glory for all his faithful people.
Alleluia! ℞

Or   TRACK 2

FIRST READING   Ezekiel 33.7–11

A reading from the book of the prophet Ezekiel.

The word of the Lord came to me: So you, mortal, I have made a sentinel for
the house of Israel; whenever you hear a word from my mouth, you shall
give them warning from me. If I say to the wicked, 'O wicked ones, you shall
surely die,' and you do not speak to warn the wicked to turn from their ways,
the wicked shall die in their iniquity, but their blood I will require at your
hand. But if you warn the wicked to turn from their ways, and they do not
turn from their ways, the wicked shall die in their iniquity, but you will have
saved your life.

Now you, mortal, say to the house of Israel, Thus you have said: 'Our transgressions and our sins weigh upon us, and we waste away because of them; how then can we live?' Say to them, As I live, says the Lord GOD, I have no pleasure in the death of the wicked, but that the wicked turn from their ways and live; turn back, turn back from your evil ways; for why will you die, O house of Israel?

PSALM   **Psalm 119.33–40**

℟ **Give me understanding and I shall keep your law.**

Teach me, O Lord, the way of your statutes,
and I shall keep it to the end.
Give me understanding and I shall keep your law;
I shall keep it with all my heart. ℟

Make me go in the path of your commandments,
for that is my desire.
Incline my heart to your decrees
and not to unjust gain. ℟

Turn my eyes from watching what is worthless;
give me life in your ways.
Fulfil your promise to your servant,
which you make to those who fear you. ℟

Turn away the reproach which I dread,
because your judgements are good.
Behold, I long for your commandments;
in your righteousness preserve my life. ℟

SECOND READING   **Romans 13.8–14**

A reading from the letter of Paul to the Romans.

Owe no one anything, except to love one another; for the one who loves another has fulfilled the law. The commandments, 'You shall not commit adultery; You shall not murder; You shall not steal; You shall not covet'; and any other commandment, are summed up in this word, 'Love your neighbour as yourself.' Love does no wrong to a neighbour; therefore, love is the fulfilling of the law.

Besides this, you know what time it is, how it is now the moment for you to wake from sleep. For salvation is nearer to us now than when we became believers; the night is far gone, the day is near. Let us then lay aside the works of darkness and put on the armour of light; let us live honourably as in the day, not in revelling and drunkenness, not in debauchery and licentiousness, not in quarrelling and jealousy. Instead, put on the Lord Jesus Christ, and make no provision for the flesh, to gratify its desires.

GOSPEL   Matthew 18.15–20

Hear the gospel of our Lord Jesus Christ according to Matthew.

Jesus spoke to his disciples. 'If another member of the church sins against you, go and point out the fault when the two of you are alone. If the member listens to you, you have regained that one. But if you are not listened to, take one or two others along with you, so that every word may be confirmed by the evidence of two or three witnesses. If the member refuses to listen to them, tell it to the church; and if the offender refuses to listen even to the church, let such a one be to you as a Gentile and a tax-collector. Truly I tell you, whatever you bind on earth will be bound in heaven, and whatever you loose on earth will be loosed in heaven. Again, truly I tell you, if two of you agree on earth about anything you ask, it will be done for you by my Father in heaven. For where two or three are gathered in my name, I am there among them.'

† SUNDAY BETWEEN 11 AND 17 SEPTEMBER   YEAR A
PROPER 19

TRACK 1

FIRST READING   Exodus 14.19–31

A reading from the book of Exodus.

The angel of God who was going before the Israelite army moved and went behind them; and the pillar of cloud moved from in front of them and took its place behind them. It came between the army of Egypt and the army of Israel. And so the cloud was there with the darkness, and it lit up the night; one did not come near the other all night.

Then Moses stretched out his hand over the sea. The LORD drove the sea back by a strong east wind all night, and turned the sea into dry land; and the waters were divided. The Israelites went into the sea on dry ground, the waters forming a wall for them on their right and on their left. The Egyptians pursued, and went into the sea after them, all of Pharaoh's horses, chariots, and chariot drivers. At the morning watch the LORD in the pillar of fire and cloud looked down upon the Egyptian army, and threw the Egyptian army into panic. He clogged their chariot wheels so that they turned with difficulty. The Egyptians said, 'Let us flee from the Israelites, for the LORD is fighting for them against Egypt.'

Then the LORD said to Moses, 'Stretch out your hand over the sea, so that the water may come back upon the Egyptians, upon their chariots and chariot drivers.' So Moses stretched out his hand over the sea, and at dawn the sea returned to its normal depth. As the Egyptians fled before it, the LORD tossed the Egyptians into the sea. The waters returned and covered the chariots and the chariot drivers, the entire army of Pharaoh that had followed them into the sea; not one of them remained. But the Israelites walked on dry ground through the sea, the waters forming a wall for them on their right and on their left.

Thus the LORD saved Israel that day from the Egyptians; and Israel saw the Egyptians dead on the seashore. Israel saw the great work that the LORD did against the Egyptians. So the people feared the LORD and believed in the LORD and in his servant Moses.

PSALM OR CANTICLE

Either   Psalm 114

℟ **Tremble, O earth, at the presence of the Lord.**

Alleluia!
When Israel came out of Egypt,
the house of Jacob from a people of strange speech,
Judah became God's sanctuary
and Israel his dominion. ℟

The sea beheld it and fled;
Jordan turned and went back.
The mountains skipped like rams,
and the little hills like young sheep. ℟

What ailed you, O sea, that you fled?
O Jordan, that you turned back?
You mountains, that you skipped like rams?
you little hills like young sheep? ℞

Tremble, O earth, at the presence of the Lord,
at the presence of the God of Jacob,
Who turned the hard rock into a pool of water
and flint-stone into a flowing spring. ℞

Or   **Exodus 15.1b–11, 21b**

℞ **The Lord is my strength and my might
[and he has become my salvation].**

I will sing to the LORD, for he has triumphed gloriously;
horse and rider he has thrown into the sea.
The LORD is my strength and my might,
and he has become my salvation;
this is my God, and I will praise him,
my father's God, and I will exalt him.
The LORD is a warrior;
the LORD is his name. ℞

Pharaoh's chariots and his army he cast into the sea;
his picked officers were sunk in the Red Sea.
The floods covered them;
they went down into the depths like a stone.
Your right hand, O LORD, glorious in power –
your right hand, O LORD, shattered the enemy. ℞

In the greatness of your majesty you overthrew your adversaries;
you sent out your fury,
it consumed them like stubble.
At the blast of your nostrils the waters piled up,
the floods stood up in a heap;
the deeps congealed in the heart of the sea. ℞

The enemy said, 'I will pursue, I will overtake,
I will divide the spoil, my desire shall have its fill of them.
I will draw my sword, my hand shall destroy them.'
You blew with your wind, the sea covered them;
they sank like lead in the mighty waters. ℞

Who is like you, O LORD, among the gods?
Who is like you, majestic in holiness,
awesome in splendour, doing wonders?
Sing to the LORD for he has triumphed gloriously;
horse and rider he has thrown into the sea. ℞

Or   TRACK 2

FIRST READING   **Genesis 50.15–21**

A reading from the book of Genesis.

Realizing that their father was dead, Joseph's brothers said, 'What if Joseph
still bears a grudge against us and pays us back in full for all the wrong that
we did to him?' So they approached Joseph, saying, 'Your father gave this
instruction before he died, "Say to Joseph: I beg you, forgive the crime of
your brothers and the wrong they did in harming you." Now therefore please
forgive the crime of the servants of the God of your father.' Joseph wept
when they spoke to him. Then his brothers also wept, fell down before him,
and said, 'We are here as your slaves.' But Joseph said to them, 'Do not be
afraid! Am I in the place of God? Even though you intended to do harm to
me, God intended it for good, in order to preserve a numerous people, as he
is doing today. So have no fear; I myself will provide for you and your little
ones.' In this way he reassured them, speaking kindly to them.

PSALM   **Psalm 103.(1–7), 8–13**

℞ **The Lord is full of compassion and mercy,**
   [slow to anger and of great kindness].

[Bless the Lord, O my soul,
and all that is within me, bless his holy name.
Bless the Lord, O my soul,
and forget not all his benefits. ℞

He forgives all your sins
and heals all your infirmities;
He redeems your life from the grave
and crowns you with mercy and loving-kindness; ℞

He satisfies you with good things,
and your youth is renewed like an eagle's.

The Lord executes righteousness
and judgement for all who are oppressed.
He made his ways known to Moses
and his works to the children of Israel. ℟]

The Lord is full of compassion and mercy,
slow to anger and of great kindness.
He will not always accuse us,
nor will he keep his anger for ever.
He has not dealt with us according to our sins,
nor rewarded us according to our wickedness. ℟

For as the heavens are high above the earth,
so is his mercy great upon those who fear him.
As far as the east is from the west,
so far has he removed our sins from us.
As a father cares for his children,
so does the Lord care for those who fear him. ℟

SECOND READING   **Romans 14.1–12**

A reading from the letter of Paul to the Romans.

Welcome those who are weak in faith, but not for the purpose of quarrelling over opinions. Some believe in eating anything, while the weak eat only vegetables. Those who eat must not despise those who abstain, and those who abstain must not pass judgement on those who eat; for God has welcomed them. Who are you to pass judgement on servants of another? It is before their own lord that they stand or fall. And they will be upheld, for the Lord is able to make them stand.

Some judge one day to be better than another, while others judge all days to be alike. Let all be fully convinced in their own minds. Those who observe the day, observe it in honour of the Lord. Also those who eat, eat in honour of the Lord, since they give thanks to God; while those who abstain, abstain in honour of the Lord and give thanks to God.

We do not live to ourselves, and we do not die to ourselves. If we live, we live to the Lord, and if we die, we die to the Lord; so then, whether we live or whether we die, we are the Lord's. For to this end Christ died and lived again, so that he might be Lord of both the dead and the living.

Why do you pass judgement on your brother or sister? Or you, why do you despise your brother or sister? For we will all stand before the judgement seat of God.
For it is written,
'As I live, says the Lord, every knee shall bow to me,
and every tongue shall give praise to God.'
So then, each of us will be accountable to God.

GOSPEL   Matthew 18.21–35

Hear the gospel of our Lord Jesus Christ according to Matthew.

Peter came and said to Jesus, 'Lord, if another member of the church sins against me, how often should I forgive? As many as seven times?' Jesus said to him, 'Not seven times, but, I tell you, seventy-seven times.

For this reason the kingdom of heaven may be compared to a king who wished to settle accounts with his slaves. When he began the reckoning, one who owed him ten thousand talents was brought to him; and, as he could not pay, his lord ordered him to be sold, together with his wife and children and all his possessions, and payment to be made. So the slave fell on his knees before him, saying, "Have patience with me, and I will pay you everything." And out of pity for him, the lord of that slave released him and forgave him the debt. But that same slave, as he went out, came upon one of his fellow-slaves who owed him a hundred denarii; and seizing him by the throat, he said, "Pay what you owe." Then his fellow-slave fell down and pleaded with him, "Have patience with me, and I will pay you." But he refused; then he went and threw him into prison until he would pay the debt. When his fellow-slaves saw what had happened, they were greatly distressed, and they went and reported to their lord all that had taken place. Then his lord summoned him and said to him, "You wicked slave! I forgave you all that debt because you pleaded with me. Should you not have had mercy on your fellow-slave, as I had mercy on you?" And in anger his lord handed him over to be tortured until he would pay his entire debt. So my heavenly Father will also do to every one of you, if you do not forgive your brother or sister from your heart.'

† SUNDAY BETWEEN 18 AND 24 SEPTEMBER   YEAR A
PROPER 20

TRACK 1

FIRST READING   Exodus 16.2–15

A reading from the book of Exodus.

The whole congregation of the Israelites complained against Moses and
Aaron in the wilderness. The Israelites said to them, 'If only we had died by
the hand of the LORD in the land of Egypt, when we sat by the fleshpots and
ate our fill of bread; for you have brought us out into this wilderness to kill
this whole assembly with hunger.'

Then the LORD said to Moses, 'I am going to rain bread from heaven for you,
and each day the people shall go out and gather enough for that day. In that
way I will test them, whether they will follow my instruction or not. On the
sixth day, when they prepare what they bring in, it will be twice as much as
they gather on other days.' So Moses and Aaron said to all the Israelites, 'In
the evening you shall know that it was the LORD who brought you out of
the land of Egypt, and in the morning you shall see the glory of the LORD,
because he has heard your complaining against the LORD. For what are we,
that you complain against us?' And Moses said, 'When the LORD gives you
meat to eat in the evening and your fill of bread in the morning, because the
LORD has heard the complaining that you utter against him – what are we?
Your complaining is not against us but against the LORD.'

Then Moses said to Aaron, 'Say to the whole congregation of the Israelites,
"Draw near to the LORD, for he has heard your complaining."' And as Aaron
spoke to the whole congregation of the Israelites, they looked towards the
wilderness, and the glory of the LORD appeared in the cloud. The LORD
spoke to Moses and said, 'I have heard the complaining of the Israelites; say
to them, "At twilight you shall eat meat, and in the morning you shall have
your fill of bread; then you shall know that I am the LORD your God."'

In the evening quails came up and covered the camp; and in the morning
there was a layer of dew around the camp. When the layer of dew lifted,
there on the surface of the wilderness was a fine flaky substance, as fine as
frost on the ground. When the Israelites saw it, they said to one another,
'What is it?' For they did not know what it was. Moses said to them, 'It is the
bread that the LORD has given you to eat.'

PSALM   Psalm 105.1-6, 37-45

℟ Sing to the Lord, sing praises to him.

Give thanks to the Lord and call upon his name;
make known his deeds among the peoples.
Sing to him, sing praises to him,
and speak of all his marvellous works.
Glory in his holy name;
let the hearts of those who seek the Lord rejoice. ℟

Search for the Lord and his strength;
continually seek his face.
Remember the marvels he has done,
his wonders and the judgements of his mouth,
O offspring of Abraham his servant,
O children of Jacob his chosen. ℟

He led out his people with silver and gold;
in all their tribes there was not one that stumbled.
Egypt was glad of their going,
because they were afraid of them.
He spread out a cloud for a covering
and a fire to give light in the night season. ℟

They asked and quails appeared,
and he satisfied them with bread from heaven.
He opened the rock and water flowed,
so the river ran in the dry places.
For God remembered his holy word
and Abraham his servant. ℟

So he led forth his people with gladness,
his chosen with shouts of joy.
He gave his people the lands of the nations,
and they took the fruit of others' toil,
That they might keep his statutes
and observe his laws.
Alleluia! ℟

Or   TRACK 2

FIRST READING   **Jonah 3.10 – 4.11**

A reading from the book of Jonah.

When God saw what the people of Nineveh did, how they turned from their evil ways, God changed his mind about the calamity that he had said he would bring upon them; and he did not do it. But this was very displeasing to Jonah, and he became angry. He prayed to the LORD and said, 'O LORD! Is not this what I said while I was still in my own country? That is why I fled to Tarshish at the beginning; for I knew that you are a gracious God and merciful, slow to anger, and abounding in steadfast love, and ready to relent from punishing. And now, O LORD, please take my life from me, for it is better for me to die than to live.' And the LORD said, 'Is it right for you to be angry?' Then Jonah went out of the city and sat down east of the city, and made a booth for himself there. He sat under it in the shade, waiting to see what would become of the city.

The LORD God appointed a bush, and made it come up over Jonah, to give shade over his head, to save him from his discomfort; so Jonah was very happy about the bush. But when dawn came up the next day, God appointed a worm that attacked the bush, so that it withered. When the sun rose, God prepared a sultry east wind, and the sun beat down on the head of Jonah so that he was faint and asked that he might die. He said, 'It is better for me to die than to live.'

But God said to Jonah, 'Is it right for you to be angry about the bush?' And he said, 'Yes, angry enough to die.'Then the LORD said, 'You are concerned about the bush, for which you did not labour and which you did not grow; it came into being in a night and perished in a night. And should I not be concerned about Nineveh, that great city, in which there are more than a hundred and twenty thousand people who do not know their right hand from their left, and also many animals?'

PSALM   **Psalm 145.1–8**

℟ **The Lord is near to those who call upon him.**

I will exalt you, O God my King,
and bless your name for ever and ever.
Every day will I bless you
and praise your name for ever and ever. ℟

Great is the Lord and greatly to be praised;
there is no end to his greatness.
One generation shall praise your works to another
and shall declare your power. ℟

I will ponder the glorious splendour of your majesty
and all your marvellous works.
They shall speak of the might of your wondrous acts,
and I will tell of your greatness. ℟

They shall publish the remembrance
of your great goodness;
they shall sing of your righteous deeds.
The Lord is gracious and full of compassion,
slow to anger and of great kindness. ℟

SECOND READING   Philippians 1.21–30

A reading from the letter of Paul to the Philippians.

For to me, living is Christ and dying is gain. If I am to live in the flesh, that
means fruitful labour for me; and I do not know which I prefer. I am hard
pressed between the two: my desire is to depart and be with Christ, for that is
far better; but to remain in the flesh is more necessary for you. Since I am
convinced of this, I know that I will remain and continue with all of you for
your progress and joy in faith, so that I may share abundantly in your
boasting in Christ Jesus when I come to you again.

Only, live your life in a manner worthy of the gospel of Christ, so that,
whether I come and see you or am absent and hear about you, I will know
that you are standing firm in one spirit, striving side by side with one mind
for the faith of the gospel, and are in no way intimidated by your opponents.
For them this is evidence of their destruction, but of your salvation. And this
is God's doing. For he has graciously granted you the privilege not only of
believing in Christ, but of suffering for him as well – since you are having the
same struggle that you saw I had and now hear that I still have.

GOSPEL   **Matthew 20.1–16**

Hear the gospel of our Lord Jesus Christ according to Matthew.

Jesus said to his disciples: 'The kingdom of heaven is like a landowner who went out early in the morning to hire labourers for his vineyard. After agreeing with the labourers for the usual daily wage, he sent them into his vineyard. When he went out about nine o'clock, he saw others standing idle in the market-place; and he said to them, "You also go into the vineyard, and I will pay you whatever is right." So they went. When he went out again about noon and about three o'clock, he did the same. And about five o'clock he went out and found others standing around; and he said to them, "Why are you standing here idle all day?" They said to him, "Because no one has hired us." He said to them, "You also go into the vineyard." When evening came, the owner of the vineyard said to his manager, "Call the labourers and give them their pay, beginning with the last and then going to the first." When those hired about five o'clock came, each of them received the usual daily wage. Now when the first came, they thought they would receive more; but each of them also received the usual daily wage. And when they received it, they grumbled against the landowner, saying, "These last worked only one hour, and you have made them equal to us who have borne the burden of the day and the scorching heat." But he replied to one of them, "Friend, I am doing you no wrong; did you not agree with me for the usual daily wage? Take what belongs to you and go; I choose to give to this last the same as I give to you. Am I not allowed to do what I choose with what belongs to me? Or are you envious because I am generous?"
So the last will be first, and the first will be last.'

† SUNDAY BETWEEN 25 SEPTEMBER   YEAR A
AND 1 OCTOBER
PROPER 21

TRACK 1

FIRST READING   **Exodus 17.1–7**

A reading from the book of Exodus.

From the wilderness of Sin the whole congregation of the Israelites journeyed by stages, as the LORD commanded. They camped at Rephidim, but there was no water for the people to drink. The people quarrelled with Moses, and said, 'Give us water to drink.' Moses said to them, 'Why do you quarrel with me? Why do you test the LORD?' But the people thirsted there for water; and the people complained against Moses and said, 'Why did you bring us out of Egypt, to kill us and our children and livestock with thirst?' So Moses cried out to the LORD, 'What shall I do with this people? They are almost ready to stone me.' The LORD said to Moses, 'Go on ahead of the people, and take some of the elders of Israel with you; take in your hand the staff with which you struck the Nile, and go. I will be standing there in front of you on the rock at Horeb. Strike the rock, and water will come out of it, so that the people may drink.' Moses did so, in the sight of the elders of Israel. He called the place Massah and Meribah, because the Israelites quarrelled and tested the LORD, saying, 'Is the LORD among us or not?'

PSALM   Psalm 78.1–4, 12–16

℟ We will recount the wonderful works of the Lord.

Hear my teaching, O my people;
incline your ears to the words of my mouth.
I will open my mouth in a parable;
I will declare the mysteries of ancient times. ℟

That which we have heard and known,
and what our forebears have told us,
we will not hide from their children.
We will recount to generations to come
the praiseworthy deeds and the power of the Lord,
and the wonderful works he has done. ℟

He worked marvels in the sight of their forebears,
in the land of Egypt, in the field of Zoan.
He split open the sea and let them pass through;
he made the waters stand up like walls. ℟

He led them with a cloud by day,
and all the night through with a glow of fire.
He split the hard rocks in the wilderness
and gave them drink as from the great deep.
He brought streams out of the cliff,
and the waters gushed out like rivers. ℟

Or TRACK 2

FIRST READING Ezekiel 18.1–4, 25–32

A reading from the book of the prophet Ezekiel.

The word of the LORD came to me: What do you mean by repeating this proverb concerning the land of Israel, 'The parents have eaten sour grapes, and the children's teeth are set on edge'? As I live, says the Lord GOD, this proverb shall no more be used by you in Israel. Know that all lives are mine; the life of the parent as well as the life of the child is mine: it is only the person who sins that shall die.

Yet you say, 'The way of the Lord is unfair.' Hear now, O house of Israel: Is my way unfair? Is it not your ways that are unfair? When the righteous turn away from their righteousness and commit iniquity, they shall die for it; for the iniquity that they have committed they shall die. Again, when the wicked turn away from the wickedness they have committed and do what is lawful and right, they shall save their life. Because they considered and turned away from all the transgressions that they had committed, they shall surely live; they shall not die. Yet the house of Israel says, 'The way of the Lord is unfair.' O house of Israel, are my ways unfair? Is it not your ways that are unfair? Therefore I will judge you, O house of Israel, all of you according to your ways, says the Lord GOD. Repent and turn from all your transgressions; otherwise iniquity will be your ruin. Cast away from you all the transgressions that you have committed against me, and get yourselves a new heart and a new spirit! Why will you die, O house of Israel? For I have no pleasure in the death of anyone, says the Lord GOD. Turn, then, and live.

PSALM Psalm 25.1–9

℟ **Remember, O Lord, your compassion and love.**

To you, O Lord, I lift up my soul;
my God, I put my trust in you;
let me not be humiliated,
nor let my enemies triumph over me.
Let none who look to you be put to shame;
let the treacherous be disappointed in their schemes. ℟

Show me your ways, O Lord,
and teach me your paths.
Lead me in your truth and teach me,
for you are the God of my salvation;
in you have I trusted all the day long. ℟

Remember, O Lord, your compassion and love,
for they are from everlasting.
Remember not the sins of my youth
and my transgressions;
remember me according to your love
and for the sake of your goodness, O Lord. ℟

Gracious and upright is the Lord;
therefore he teaches sinners in his way.
He guides the humble in doing right
and teaches his way to the lowly.
All the paths of the Lord are love and faithfulness
to those who keep his covenant and his testimonies. ℟

SECOND READING   Philippians 2.1–13

A reading from the letter of Paul to the Philippians.

If then there is any encouragement in Christ, any consolation from love, any
sharing in the Spirit, any compassion and sympathy, make my joy complete:
be of the same mind, having the same love, being in full accord and of one
mind. Do nothing from selfish ambition or conceit, but in humility regard
others as better than yourselves. Let each of you look not to your own
interests, but to the interests of others. Let the same mind be in you that was
in Christ Jesus,

who, though he was in the form of God, did not regard equality with God as
something to be exploited, but emptied himself, taking the form of a slave,
being born in human likeness. And being found in human form, he humbled
himself and became obedient to the point of death – even death on a cross.

Therefore God also highly exalted him and gave him the name that is above
every name, so that at the name of Jesus every knee should bend, in heaven
and on earth and under the earth, and every tongue should confess that Jesus
Christ is Lord, to the glory of God the Father.

Therefore, my beloved, just as you have always obeyed me, not only in my presence, but much more now in my absence, work out your own salvation with fear and trembling; for it is God who is at work in you, enabling you both to will and to work for his good pleasure.

GOSPEL   Matthew 21.23–32

Hear the gospel of our Lord Jesus Christ according to Matthew.

When Jesus entered the temple, the chief priests and the elders of the people came to him as he was teaching, and said, 'By what authority are you doing these things, and who gave you this authority?' Jesus said to them, 'I will also ask you one question; if you tell me the answer, then I will also tell you by what authority I do these things. Did the baptism of John come from heaven, or was it of human origin?' And they argued with one another, 'If we say, "From heaven," he will say to us, "Why then did you not believe him?" But if we say, "Of human origin," we are afraid of the crowd; for all regard John as a prophet.' So they answered Jesus, 'We do not know.' And he said to them, 'Neither will I tell you by what authority I am doing these things.

What do you think? A man had two sons; he went to the first and said, "Son, go and work in the vineyard today." He answered, "I will not"; but later he changed his mind and went. The father went to the second and said the same; and he answered, "I go, sir"; but he did not go. Which of the two did the will of his father?' They said, 'The first.' Jesus said to them, 'Truly I tell you, the tax-collectors and the prostitutes are going into the kingdom of God ahead of you. For John came to you in the way of righteousness and you did not believe him, but the tax-collectors and the prostitutes believed him; and even after you saw it, you did not change your minds and believe him.'

† SUNDAY BETWEEN 2 AND 8 OCTOBER   YEAR A
PROPER 22

TRACK 1

FIRST READING   Exodus 20.1–4, 7–9, 12–20

A reading from the book of Exodus.

Then God spoke all these words: I am the LORD your God, who brought you out of the land of Egypt, out of the house of slavery; you shall have no other gods before me. You shall not make for yourself an idol, whether in the form of anything that is in heaven above, or that is on the earth beneath, or that is in the water under the earth. You shall not make wrongful use of the name of the LORD your God, for the LORD will not acquit anyone who misuses his name. Remember the sabbath day, and keep it holy. Six days you shall labour and do all your work. Honour your father and your mother, so that your days may be long in the land that the LORD your God is giving you. You shall not murder. You shall not commit adultery. You shall not steal. You shall not bear false witness against your neighbour. You shall not covet your neighbour's house; you shall not covet your neighbour's wife, or male or female slave, or ox, or donkey, or anything that belongs to your neighbour.

When all the people witnessed the thunder and lightning, the sound of the trumpet, and the mountain smoking, they were afraid and trembled and stood at a distance, and said to Moses, 'You speak to us, and we will listen; but do not let God speak to us, or we will die.' Moses said to the people, 'Do not be afraid; for God has come only to test you and to put the fear of him upon you so that you do not sin.'

PSALM   Psalm 19

℞ **The commandment of the Lord is clear**
   and gives light to the eyes.

The heavens declare the glory of God,
and the firmament shows his handiwork.
One day tells its tale to another,
and one night imparts knowledge to another.
Although they have no words or language,
and their voices are not heard,
Their sound has gone out into all lands,
and their message to the ends of the world. ℞

In the deep has he set a pavilion for the sun;
it comes forth like a bridegroom out of his chamber;
it rejoices like a champion to run its course.
It goes forth from the uttermost edge of the heavens
and runs about to the end of it again;
nothing is hidden from its burning heat. ℞

The law of the Lord is perfect
and revives the soul;
the testimony of the Lord is sure
and gives wisdom to the innocent.
The statutes of the Lord are just

and rejoice the heart;
the commandment of the Lord is clear
and gives light to the eyes. ℟

The fear of the Lord is clean
and endures for ever;
the judgements of the Lord are true
and righteous altogether.
More to be desired are they than gold,
more than much fine gold,
sweeter far than honey,
than honey in the comb. ℟

By them also is your servant enlightened,
and in keeping them there is great reward.
Who can tell how often he offends?
Cleanse me from my secret faults. ℟

Above all, keep your servant from presumptuous sins;
let them not get dominion over me;
then shall I be whole and sound,
and innocent of a great offence.
Let the words of my mouth and the meditation of my heart
be acceptable in your sight,
O Lord, my strength and my redeemer. ℟

Or   TRACK 2

FIRST READING   Isaiah 5.1–7

A reading from the book of the prophet Isaiah.

Let me sing for my beloved
my love-song concerning his vineyard:
My beloved had a vineyard on a very fertile hill.
He dug it and cleared it of stones,
and planted it with choice vines;
he built a watch-tower in the midst of it,
and hewed out a wine vat in it;
he expected it to yield grapes,
but it yielded wild grapes.

And now, inhabitants of Jerusalem and people of Judah,
judge between me and my vineyard.

What more was there to do for my vineyard
that I have not done in it?
When I expected it to yield grapes,
why did it yield wild grapes?

And now I will tell you what I will do to my vineyard.
I will remove its hedge, and it shall be devoured;
I will break down its wall, and it shall be trampled down.
I will make it a waste;
it shall not be pruned or hoed,
and it shall be overgrown with briers and thorns;
I will also command the clouds
that they rain no rain upon it.
For the vineyard of the Lord of hosts is the house of Israel,
and the people of Judah are his pleasant planting:
he expected justice, but saw bloodshed;
righteousness, but heard a cry!

PSALM   **Psalm 80.7–14**

℟ **For the vineyard of the Lord of hosts
   is the house of Israel.**

Restore us, O God of hosts;
show the light of your countenance
and we shall be saved.
You have brought a vine out of Egypt;
you cast out the nations and planted it.
You prepared the ground for it;
it took root and filled the land. ℟

The mountains were covered by its shadow
and the towering cedar trees by its boughs.
You stretched out its tendrils to the Sea
and its branches to the River. ℟

Why have you broken down its wall,
so that all who pass by pluck off its grapes?
The wild boar of the forest has ravaged it,
and the beasts of the field have grazed upon it.
Turn now, O God of hosts, look down from heaven;
behold and tend this vine;
preserve what your right hand has planted. ℟

SECOND READING **Philippians 3.4b-14**

A reading from the letter of Paul to the Philippians.

If anyone else has reason to be confident in the flesh, I have more: circumcised on the eighth day, a member of the people of Israel, of the tribe of Benjamin, a Hebrew born of Hebrews; as to the law, a Pharisee; as to zeal, a persecutor of the church; as to righteousness under the law, blameless. Yet whatever gains I had, these I have come to regard as loss because of Christ. More than that, I regard everything as loss because of the surpassing value of knowing Christ Jesus my Lord. For his sake I have suffered the loss of all things, and I regard them as rubbish, in order that I may gain Christ and be found in him, not having a righteousness of my own that comes from the law, but one that comes through faith in Christ, the righteousness from God based on faith. I want to know Christ and the power of his resurrection and the sharing of his sufferings by becoming like him in his death, if somehow I may attain the resurrection from the dead.

Not that I have already obtained this or have already reached the goal; but I press on to make it my own, because Christ Jesus has made me his own. Beloved, I do not consider that I have made it my own; but this one thing I do: forgetting what lies behind and straining forward to what lies ahead, I press on towards the goal for the prize of the heavenly call of God in Christ Jesus.

GOSPEL **Matthew 21.33-46**

Hear the gospel of our Lord Jesus Christ according to Matthew.

Jesus said to the chief priests and the elders of the people: 'Listen to another parable. There was a landowner who planted a vineyard, put a fence around it, dug a wine press in it, and built a watch-tower. Then he leased it to tenants and went to another country. When the harvest time had come, he sent his slaves to the tenants to collect his produce. But the tenants seized his slaves and beat one, killed another, and stoned another. Again he sent other slaves, more than the first; and they treated them in the same way. Finally he sent his son to them, saying, "They will respect my son." But when the tenants saw the son, they said to themselves, "This is the heir; come, let us kill him and get his inheritance." So they seized him, threw him out of the vineyard, and killed him. Now when the owner of the vineyard comes, what will he do to those tenants?' They said to him, 'He will put those wretches to a miserable death, and lease the vineyard to other tenants who will give him the produce at the harvest time.'

Jesus said to them, 'Have you never read in the scriptures: "The stone that the builders rejected has become the cornerstone; this was the Lord's doing, and it is amazing in our eyes"?

Therefore I tell you, the kingdom of God will be taken away from you and given to a people that produces the fruits of the kingdom. The one who falls on this stone will be broken to pieces; and it will crush anyone on whom it falls.' When the chief priests and the Pharisees heard his parables, they realized that he was speaking about them. They wanted to arrest him, but they feared the crowds, because they regarded him as a prophet.

† SUNDAY BETWEEN 9 AND 15 OCTOBER YEAR A
PROPER 23

TRACK 1

FIRST READING   **Exodus 32.1–14**

A reading from the book of Exodus.

When the people of Israel saw that Moses delayed to come down from the mountain, the people gathered around Aaron, and said to him, 'Come, make gods for us, who shall go before us; as for this Moses, the man who brought us up out of the land of Egypt, we do not know what has become of him.' Aaron said to them, 'Take off the gold rings that are on the ears of your wives, your sons, and your daughters, and bring them to me.' So all the people took off the gold rings from their ears, and brought them to Aaron. He took the gold from them, formed it in a mould, and cast an image of a calf; and they said, 'These are your gods, O Israel, who brought you up out of the land of Egypt!' When Aaron saw this, he built an altar before it; and Aaron made proclamation and said, 'Tomorrow shall be a festival to the LORD.' They rose early the next day, and offered burnt-offerings and brought sacrifices of well–being; and the people sat down to eat and drink, and rose up to revel.

The LORD said to Moses, 'Go down at once! Your people, whom you brought up out of the land of Egypt, have acted perversely; they have been quick to turn aside from the way that I commanded them; they have cast for themselves an image of a calf, and have worshipped it and sacrificed to it, and said, "These are your gods, O Israel, who brought you up out of the land of Egypt!"' The LORD said to Moses, 'I have seen this people, how stiff-necked they are. Now let me alone, so that my wrath may burn hot against them and I may consume them; and of you I will make a great nation.'

But Moses implored the LORD his God, and said, 'O LORD, why does your wrath burn hot against your people, whom you brought out of the land of Egypt with great power and with a mighty hand? Why should the Egyptians say, "It was with evil intent that he brought them out to kill them in the mountains, and to consume them from the face of the earth"? Turn from your fierce wrath; change your mind and do not bring disaster on your people. Remember Abraham, Isaac, and Israel, your servants, how you swore to them by your own self, saying to them, "I will multiply your descendants like the stars of heaven, and all this land that I have promised I will give to your descendants, and they shall inherit it for ever."' And the LORD changed his mind about the disaster that he planned to bring on his people.

PSALM   **Psalm 106.1–6, 19–23**

℟ **Who can declare the mighty acts of the Lord?**

Alleluia!
Give thanks to the Lord, for he is good,
for his mercy endures for ever.
Who can declare the mighty acts of the Lord
or show forth all his praise? ℟

Happy are those who act with justice
and always do what is right!
Remember me, O Lord,
with the favour you have for your people,
and visit me with your saving help;
That I may see the prosperity of your elect
and be glad with the gladness of your people,
that I may glory with your inheritance.
We have sinned as our forebears did;
we have done wrong and dealt wickedly. ℟

Israel made a bull-calf at Horeb
and worshipped a molten image;
And so they exchanged their Glory
for the image of an ox that feeds on grass.
They forgot God their saviour,
who had done great things in Egypt,
Wonderful deeds in the land of Ham,
and fearful things at the Red Sea. ℟

So he would have destroyed them,
had not Moses his chosen
stood before him in the breach,
to turn away his wrath from consuming them. ℟

Or   TRACK 2

FIRST READING   **Isaiah 25.1–9**

A reading from the book of the prophet Isaiah.

O LORD, you are my God;
I will exalt you, I will praise your name;
for you have done wonderful things,
plans formed of old, faithful and sure.
For you have made the city a heap,
the fortified city a ruin;
the palace of aliens is a city no more,
it will never be rebuilt.
Therefore strong peoples will glorify you;
cities of ruthless nations will fear you.
For you have been a refuge to the poor,
a refuge to the needy in their distress,
a shelter from the rainstorm and a shade from the heat.
When the blast of the ruthless was like a winter rainstorm,
the noise of aliens like heat in a dry place,
you subdued the heat with the shade of clouds;
the song of the ruthless was stilled.
On this mountain the LORD of hosts will make for all peoples
a feast of rich food, a feast of well-matured wines,
of rich food filled with marrow,
of well-matured wines strained clear.
And he will destroy on this mountain
the shroud that is cast over all peoples,
the sheet that is spread over all nations;
he will swallow up death for ever.
Then the Lord GOD will wipe away the tears from all faces,
and the disgrace of his people
he will take away from all the earth,
for the LORD has spoken.
It will be said on that day,

Lo, this is our God;
we have waited for him,
so that he might save us.
This is the LORD for whom we have waited;
let us be glad and rejoice in his salvation.

PSALM   Psalm 23

℞ **I will dwell in the house of the Lord for ever**.

The Lord is my shepherd;
I shall not be in want.
He makes me lie down in green pastures
and leads me beside still waters. ℞

He revives my soul
and guides me along right pathways for his name's sake.
Though I walk through the valley of the shadow of death,
I shall fear no evil;
for you are with me;
your rod and your staff, they comfort me. ℞

You spread a table before me
in the presence of those who trouble me;
you have anointed my head with oil,
and my cup is running over.
Surely your goodness and mercy shall follow me
all the days of my life,
and I will dwell in the house of the Lord for ever. ℞

SECOND READING   Philippians 4.1-9

A reading from the letter of Paul to the Philippians.

My brothers and sisters, whom I love and long for, my joy and crown, stand firm in the Lord in this way, my beloved.

I urge Euodia and I urge Syntyche to be of the same mind in the Lord. Yes, and I ask you also, my loyal companion, help these women, for they have struggled beside me in the work of the gospel, together with Clement and the rest of my co-workers, whose names are in the book of life.

Rejoice in the Lord always; again I will say, Rejoice. Let your gentleness be known to everyone. The Lord is near. Do not worry about anything, but in everything by prayer and supplication with thanksgiving let your requests be made known to God. And the peace of God, which surpasses all understanding, will guard your hearts and your minds in Christ Jesus.

Finally, beloved, whatever is true, whatever is honourable, whatever is just, whatever is pure, whatever is pleasing, whatever is commendable, if there is any excellence and if there is anything worthy of praise, think about these things. Keep on doing the things that you have learned and received and heard and seen in me, and the God of peace will be with you.

GOSPEL   Matthew 22.1–14

Hear the gospel of our Lord Jesus Christ according to Matthew.

Once more Jesus spoke to the chief priests and Pharisees in parables, saying: 'The kingdom of heaven may be compared to a king who gave a wedding banquet for his son. He sent his slaves to call those who had been invited to the wedding banquet, but they would not come. Again he sent other slaves, saying, "Tell those who have been invited: Look, I have prepared my dinner, my oxen and my fat calves have been slaughtered, and everything is ready; come to the wedding banquet." But they made light of it and went away, one to his farm, another to his business, while the rest seized his slaves, maltreated them, and killed them. The king was enraged. He sent his troops, destroyed those murderers, and burned their city. Then he said to his slaves, "The wedding is ready, but those invited were not worthy. Go therefore into the main streets, and invite everyone you find to the wedding banquet." Those slaves went out into the streets and gathered all whom they found, both good and bad; so the wedding hall was filled with guests.

But when the king came in to see the guests, he noticed a man there who was not wearing a wedding robe, and he said to him, "Friend, how did you get in here without a wedding robe?" And he was speechless. Then the king said to the attendants, "Bind him hand and foot, and throw him into the outer darkness, where there will be weeping and gnashing of teeth." For many are called, but few are chosen.'

† SUNDAY BETWEEN 16 AND 22 OCTOBER   YEAR A
PROPER 24

TRACK 1

FIRST READING   Exodus 33.12–23

A reading from the book of Exodus.

Moses said to the LORD, 'See, you have said to me, "Bring up this people"; but you have not let me know whom you will send with me. Yet you have said, "I know you by name, and you have also found favour in my sight." Now if I have found favour in your sight, show me your ways, so that I may know you and find favour in your sight. Consider too that this nation is your people.' He said, 'My presence will go with you, and I will give you rest.' And he said to him, 'If your presence will not go, do not carry us up from here. For how shall it be known that I have found favour in your sight, I and your people, unless you go with us? In this way, we shall be distinct, I and your people, from every people on the face of the earth.'

The LORD said to Moses, 'I will do the very thing that you have asked; for you have found favour in my sight, and I know you by name.' Moses said, 'Show me your glory, I pray.' And he said, 'I will make all my goodness pass before you, and will proclaim before you the name, "The LORD"; and I will be gracious to whom I will be gracious, and will show mercy on whom I will show mercy. But,' he said, 'you cannot see my face; for no one shall see me and live.' And the LORD continued, 'See, there is a place by me where you shall stand on the rock; and while my glory passes by I will put you in a cleft of the rock, and I will cover you with my hand until I have passed by; then I will take away my hand, and you shall see my back; but my face shall not be seen.'

PSALM   Psalm 99

℟ He spoke to them out of the pillar of cloud.

The Lord is king; let the people tremble;
he is enthroned upon the cherubim; let the earth shake.
The Lord is great in Zion;
he is high above all peoples.
Let them confess his name, which is great and awesome;
he is the Holy One. ℟

'O mighty King, lover of justice,
you have established equity;
you have executed justice and righteousness in Jacob.'
Proclaim the greatness of the Lord our God
and fall down before his footstool;
he is the Holy One. ℞

Moses and Aaron among his priests,
and Samuel among those who call upon his name,
they called upon the Lord and he answered them.
He spoke to them out of the pillar of cloud;
they kept his testimonies
and the decree that he gave them. ℞

'O Lord our God, you answered them indeed;
you were a God who forgave them,
yet punished them for their evil deeds.'
Proclaim the greatness of the Lord our God
and worship him upon his holy hill;
for the Lord our God is the Holy One. ℞

Or   TRACK 2

FIRST READING   **Isaiah 45.1–7**

A reading from the book of the prophet Isaiah.

Thus says the LORD to his anointed, to Cyrus,
whose right hand I have grasped to subdue nations before him
and strip kings of their robes, to open doors before him –
and the gates shall not be closed:
I will go before you and level the mountains,
I will break in pieces the doors of bronze and cut through the bars of iron,
I will give you the treasures of darkness
and riches hidden in secret places,
so that you may know that it is I,
the LORD, the God of Israel,
who call you by your name.
For the sake of my servant Jacob,
and Israel my chosen,
I call you by your name, I surname you,
though you do not know me.

I am the LORD, and there is no other;
besides me there is no god.
I arm you,though you do not know me,
so that they may know,
from the rising of the sun and from the west,
that there is no one besides me;
I am the LORD, and there is no other.
I form light and create darkness,
I make weal and create woe;
I the LORD do all these things.

PSALM

Psalm 96.1–9, (10–13)

℞ Ascribe to the Lord honour and power.

Sing to the Lord a new song;
sing to the Lord, all the whole earth.
Sing to the Lord and bless his name;
proclaim the good news of his salvation from day to day.
Declare his glory among the nations
and his wonders among all peoples. ℞

For great is the Lord and greatly to be praised;
he is more to be feared than all gods.
As for all the gods of the nations, they are but idols;
but it is the Lord who made the heavens.
O the majesty and magnificence of his presence!
O the power and the splendour of his sanctuary! ℞

Ascribe to the Lord, you families of the peoples;
ascribe to the Lord honour and power.
Ascribe to the Lord the honour due to his name;
bring offerings and come into his courts.
Worship the Lord in the beauty of holiness;
let the whole earth tremble before him. ℞

[Tell it out among the nations: 'The Lord is king!
he has made the world so firm that it cannot be moved;
he will judge the peoples with equity.'
Let the heavens rejoice and let the earth be glad;
let the sea thunder and all that is in it;
let the field be joyful and all that is therein. ℞

Then shall all the trees of the wood shout for joy
before the Lord when he comes,
when he comes to judge the earth.
He will judge the world with righteousness
and the peoples with his truth. ℟]

SECOND READING   1 Thessalonians 1.1–10

A reading from the first letter of Paul to the Thessalonians.

From Paul, Silvanus, and Timothy, To the church of the Thessalonians in God
the Father and the Lord Jesus Christ: Grace to you and peace.

We always give thanks to God for all of you and mention you in our prayers,
constantly remembering before our God and Father your work of faith and
labour of love and steadfastness of hope in our Lord Jesus Christ. For we
know, brothers and sisters beloved by God, that he has chosen you, because
our message of the gospel came to you not in word only, but also in power
and in the Holy Spirit and with full conviction; just as you know what kind
of persons we proved to be among you for your sake. And you became
imitators of us and of the Lord, for in spite of persecution you received the
word with joy inspired by the Holy Spirit, so that you became an example to
all the believers in Macedonia and in Achaia. For the word of the Lord has
sounded forth from you not only in Macedonia and Achaia, but in every
place your faith in God has become known, so that we have no need to speak
about it. For the people of those regions report about us what kind of
welcome we had among you, and how you turned to God from idols, to serve
a living and true God, and to wait for his Son from heaven, whom he raised
from the dead – Jesus, who rescues us from the wrath that is coming.

GOSPEL   Matthew 22.15–22

Hear the gospel of our Lord Jesus Christ according to Matthew.

When the chief priests and Pharisees had heard the parables, they realized
that Jesus was speaking about them. Then the Pharisees went and plotted to
entrap him in what he said. So they sent their disciples to him, along with
the Herodians, saying, 'Teacher, we know that you are sincere, and teach the
way of God in accordance with truth, and show deference to no one; for you
do not regard people with partiality. Tell us, then, what you think. Is it lawful
to pay taxes to the emperor, or not?' But Jesus, aware of their malice, said,

'Why are you putting me to the test, you hypocrites? Show me the coin used for the tax.' And they brought him a denarius. Then he said to them, 'Whose head is this, and whose title?' They answered, 'The emperor's.' Then he said to them, 'Give therefore to the emperor the things that are the emperor's, and to God the things that are God's.' When they heard this, they were amazed; and they left him and went away.

† SUNDAY BETWEEN 23 AND 29 OCTOBER   YEAR A
PROPER 25

Provision for Proper 25 is identical in the Revised Common Lectionary and the Church of England provision, but the Church of England adds alternative readings for Bible Sunday (see pages 277–279).

TRACK 1

FIRST READING   **Deuteronomy 34.1–12**

A reading from the book of Deuteronomy.

Moses went up from the plains of Moab to Mount Nebo, to the top of Pisgah, which is opposite Jericho, and the LORD showed him the whole land: Gilead as far as Dan, all Naphtali, the land of Ephraim and Manasseh, all the land of Judah as far as the Western Sea, the Negeb, and the Plain – that is, the valley of Jericho, the city of palm trees – as far as Zoar. The LORD said to him, 'This is the land of which I swore to Abraham, to Isaac, and to Jacob, saying, "I will give it to your descendants"; I have let you see it with your eyes, but you shall not cross over there. Then Moses, the servant of the LORD, died there in the land of Moab, at the Lord's command. He was buried in a valley in the land of Moab, opposite Beth-peor, but no one knows his burial place to this day. Moses was one hundred and twenty years old when he died; his sight was unimpaired and his vigour had not abated. The Israelites wept for Moses in the plains of Moab thirty days; then the period of mourning for Moses was ended. Joshua son of Nun was full of the spirit of wisdom, because Moses had laid his hands on him; and the Israelites obeyed him, doing as the LORD had commanded Moses.

Never since has there arisen a prophet in Israel like Moses, whom the LORD knew face to face. He was unequalled for all the signs and wonders that the LORD sent him to perform in the land of Egypt, against Pharaoh and all his servants and his entire land, and for all the mighty deeds and all the terrifying displays of power that Moses performed in the sight of all Israel.

PSALM   Psalm 90.1–6, 13–17

℟ **Satisfy us by your loving-kindness:**
  so shall we rejoice and be glad.

Lord, you have been our refuge
from one generation to another.
Before the mountains were brought forth,
or the land and the earth were born,
from age to age you are God.
You turn us back to the dust and say,
'Go back, O child of earth.' ℟

For a thousand years in your sight
are like yesterday when it is past
and like a watch in the night.
You sweep us away like a dream;
we fade away suddenly like the grass.
In the morning it is green and flourishes;
in the evening it is dried up and withered. ℟

Return, O Lord; how long will you tarry?
be gracious to your servants.
Satisfy us by your loving-kindness in the morning;
so shall we rejoice and be glad all the days of our life.
Make us glad by the measure of the days
that you afflicted us
and the years in which we suffered adversity. ℟

Show your servants your works
and your splendour to their children.
May the graciousness of the Lord our God be upon us;
prosper the work of our hands;
prosper our handiwork. ℟

Or   TRACK 2

FIRST READING   Leviticus 19.1–2, 15–18

A reading from the book of Leviticus.

The LORD spoke to Moses, saying: 'Speak to all the congregation of the
people of Israel and say to them: You shall be holy, for I the LORD your God
am holy.

You shall not render an unjust judgement; you shall not be partial to the poor or defer to the great: with justice you shall judge your neighbour.

You shall not go around as a slanderer among your people, and you shall not profit by the blood of your neighbour: I am the LORD.

You shall not hate in your heart anyone of your kin; you shall reprove your neighbour, or you will incur guilt yourself. You shall not take vengeance or bear a grudge against any of your people, but you shall love your neighbour as yourself: I am the LORD.'

PSALM   Psalm 1

℞ **Happy are they who trust in the Lord!**

Happy are they who have not walked
in the counsel of the wicked,
nor lingered in the way of sinners,
nor sat in the seats of the scornful!
Their delight is in the law of the Lord,
and they meditate on his law day and night. ℞

They are like trees planted by streams of water,
bearing fruit in due season,
with leaves that do not wither;
everything they do shall prosper. ℞

It is not so with the wicked:
they are like chaff which the wind blows away;
Therefore the wicked shall not stand upright
when judgement comes,
nor the sinner in the council of the righteous.
For the Lord knows the way of the righteous,
but the way of the wicked is doomed. ℞

SECOND READING   1 Thessalonians 2.1–8

A reading from the first letter of Paul to the Thessalonians.

You yourselves know, brothers and sisters, that our coming to you was not in vain, but though we had already suffered and been shamefully mistreated at Philippi, as you know, we had courage in our God to declare to you the gospel of God in spite of great opposition. For our appeal does not spring from deceit or impure motives or trickery, but just as we have been approved by God to be entrusted with the message of the gospel, even so we speak, not to please mortals, but to please God who tests our hearts. As you know and as God is our witness, we never came with words of flattery or with a pretext for greed; nor did we seek praise from mortals, whether from you or from others, though we might have made demands as apostles of Christ. But we were gentle among you, like a nurse tenderly caring for her own children. So deeply do we care for you that we are determined to share with you not only the gospel of God but also our own selves, because you have become very dear to us.

GOSPEL   Matthew 22.34–46

Hear the gospel of our Lord Jesus Christ according to Matthew.

When the Pharisees heard that he had silenced the Sadducees, they gathered together, and one of them, a lawyer, asked him a question to test him. 'Teacher, which commandment in the law is the greatest?' He said to him, '"You shall love the Lord your God with all your heart, and with all your soul, and with all your mind." This is the greatest and first commandment. And a second is like it: "You shall love your neighbour as yourself." On these two commandments hang all the law and the prophets.'

Now while the Pharisees were gathered together, Jesus asked them this question: 'What do you think of the Messiah? Whose son is he?' They said to him, 'The son of David.' He said to them, 'How is it then that David by the Spirit calls him Lord, saying, "The Lord said to my Lord, 'Sit at my right hand, until I put your enemies under your feet'"? If David thus calls him Lord, how can he be his son?' No one was able to give him an answer, nor from that day did anyone dare to ask him any more questions.

Or

† BIBLE SUNDAY   YEAR A

FIRST READING (Short or long reading)
Nehemiah 8.1–4a, (5–6), 8–12

A reading from the book of Nehemiah.

All the people gathered together into the square before the Water Gate. They told the scribe Ezra to bring the book of the law of Moses, which the LORD had given to Israel. Accordingly, the priest Ezra brought the law before the assembly, both men and women and all who could hear with understanding. This was on the first day of the seventh month. He read from it facing the square before the Water Gate from early morning until midday, in the presence of the men and the women and those who could understand; and the ears of all the people were attentive to the book of the law. The scribe Ezra stood on a wooden platform that had been made for the purpose;

[And Ezra opened the book in the sight of all the people, for he was standing above all the people; and when he opened it, all the people stood up. Then Ezra blessed the LORD, the great God, and all the people answered, 'Amen, Amen,' lifting up their hands. Then they bowed their heads and worshipped the LORD with their faces to the ground.]

So they read from the book, from the law of God, with interpretation. They gave the sense, so that the people understood the reading. And Nehemiah, who was the governor, and Ezra the priest and scribe, and the Levites who taught the people said to all the people, 'This day is holy to the LORD your God; do not mourn or weep.' For all the people wept when they heard the words of the law. Then he said to them, 'Go your way, eat the fat and drink sweet wine and send portions of them to those for whom nothing is prepared, for this day is holy to our LORD; and do not be grieved, for the joy of the LORD is your strength.' So the Levites stilled all the people, saying, 'Be quiet, for this day is holy; do not be grieved.' And all the people went their way to eat and drink and to send portions and to make great rejoicing, because they had understood the words that were declared to them.

PSALM   Psalm 119.9–16

℟ **Happy are they who walk in the law of the Lord.**

How shall the young cleanse their way?
By keeping to your words.
With my whole heart I seek you;
let me not stray from your commandments. ℟

I treasure your promise in my heart,
that I may not sin against you.
Blessèd are you, O Lord;
instruct me in your statutes. ℟

With my lips will I recite
all the judgements of your mouth.
I have taken greater delight in the way of your decrees
than in all manner of riches. ℟

I will meditate on your commandments
and give attention to your ways.
My delight is in your statutes;
I will not forget your word. ℟

SECOND READING   Colossians 3.12–17

A reading from the letter of Paul to the Colossians.

As God's chosen ones, holy and beloved, clothe yourselves with compassion,
kindness, humility, meekness, and patience. Bear with one another and, if
anyone has a complaint against another, forgive each other; just as the Lord
has forgiven you, so you also must forgive. Above all, clothe yourselves with
love, which binds everything together in perfect harmony. And let the peace
of Christ rule in your hearts, to which indeed you were called in the one
body. And be thankful. Let the word of Christ dwell in you richly; teach and
admonish one another in all wisdom; and with gratitude in your hearts sing
psalms, hymns, and spiritual songs to God. And whatever you do, in word or
deed, do everything in the name of the Lord Jesus, giving thanks to God the
Father through him.

GOSPEL   Matthew 24.30–35

Hear the gospel of our Lord Jesus Christ according to Matthew.

Jesus said to his disciples: 'The sign of the Son of Man will appear in heaven,
and then all the tribes of the earth will mourn, and they will see "the Son of
Man coming on the clouds of heaven" with power and great glory. And he
will send out his angels with a loud trumpet call, and they will gather his
elect from the four winds, from one end of heaven to the other.

From the fig tree learn its lesson: as soon as its branch becomes tender and
puts forth its leaves, you know that summer is near. So also, when you see all
these things, you know that he is near, at the very gates. Truly I tell you, this
generation will not pass away until all these things have taken place. Heaven
and earth will pass away, but my words will not pass away.'

† DEDICATION FESTIVAL   YEAR A

First Sunday in October or Last Sunday after Trinity

FIRST READING (Alternative readings)

Either   **1 Kings 8.22–30**

A reading from the first book of Kings.

Solomon stood before the altar of the LORD in the presence of all the assembly of Israel, and spread out his hands to heaven. He said, 'O LORD, God of Israel, there is no God like you in heaven above or on earth beneath, keeping covenant and steadfast love for your servants who walk before you with all their heart, the covenant that you kept for your servant my father David as you declared to him; you promised with your mouth and have this day fulfilled with your hand. Therefore, O LORD, God of Israel, keep for your servant my father David that which you promised him, saying, "There shall never fail you a successor before me to sit on the throne of Israel, if only your children look to their way, to walk before me as you have walked before me." Therefore, O God of Israel, let your word be confirmed, which you promised to your servant my father David.

But will God indeed dwell on the earth? Even heaven and the highest heaven cannot contain you, much less this house that I have built! Have regard to your servant's prayer and his plea, O LORD my God, heeding the cry and the prayer that your servant prays to you today; that your eyes may be open night and day towards this house, the place of which you said, "My name shall be there," that you may heed the prayer that your servant prays towards this place. Hear the plea of your servant and of your people Israel when they pray towards this place; O hear in heaven your dwelling-place; heed and forgive.'

Or   **Revelation 21.9–14**

A reading from the book of Revelation.

One of the seven angels who had the seven bowls full of the seven last plagues came and said to me, 'Come, I will show you the bride, the wife of the Lamb.' And in the spirit he carried me away to a great, high mountain and showed me the holy city Jerusalem coming down out of heaven from God. It has the glory of God and a radiance like a very rare jewel, like jasper, clear as crystal. It has a great, high wall with twelve gates, and at the gates twelve angels, and on the gates are inscribed the names of the twelve tribes of the Israelites; on the east three gates, on the north three gates, on the south three gates, and on the west three gates. And the wall of the city has twelve foundations, and on them are the twelve names of the twelve apostles of the Lamb.

PSALM   **Psalm 122**

℟ **I was glad when they said to me,**
   let us go to the house of the Lord.

I was glad when they said to me,
'Let us go to the house of the Lord.'
Now our feet are standing
within your gates, O Jerusalem. ℟

Jerusalem is built as a city
that is at unity with itself.
To which the tribes go up, the tribes of the Lord,
the assembly of Israel, to praise the name of the Lord.
For there are the thrones of judgement,
the thrones of the house of David. ℟

Pray for the peace of Jerusalem:
'May they prosper who love you.
Peace be within your walls
and quietness within your towers. ℟

For my family and companions' sake,
I pray for your prosperity.
Because of the house of the Lord our God,
I will seek to do you good.' ℟

SECOND READING   **Hebrews 12.18–24**

A reading from the letter to the Hebrews.

You have not come to something that can be touched, a blazing fire, and darkness, and gloom, and a tempest, and the sound of a trumpet, and a voice whose words made the hearers beg that not another word be spoken to them.

(For they could not endure the order that was given, 'If even an animal touches the mountain, it shall be stoned to death.' Indeed, so terrifying was the sight that Moses said, 'I tremble with fear.') But you have come to Mount Zion and to the city of the living God, the heavenly Jerusalem, and to innumerable angels in festal gathering, and to the assembly of the firstborn who are enrolled in heaven, and to God the judge of all, and to the spirits of the righteous made perfect, and to Jesus, the mediator of a new covenant, and to the sprinkled blood that speaks a better word than the blood of Abel.

GOSPEL   Matthew 21.12–16

Hear the gospel of our Lord Jesus Christ according to Matthew.

Jesus entered the temple and drove out all who were selling and buying in the temple, and he overturned the tables of the money-changers and the seats of those who sold doves. He said to them, 'It is written,
"My house shall be called a house of prayer";
but you are making it a den of robbers.'
The blind and the lame came to him in the temple, and he cured them. But when the chief priests and the scribes saw the amazing things that he did, and heard the children crying out in the temple, 'Hosanna to the Son of David,' they became angry and said to him, 'Do you hear what these are saying?' Jesus said to them, 'Yes; have you never read,
"Out of the mouths of infants and nursing babies
you have prepared praise for yourself"?'

SUNDAYS BEFORE ADVENT

In the weeks after All Saints' Day the Church of England provision designates Sundays 'Sundays before Advent', while the Revised Common Lectionary continues with 'Propers' designated by calendar dates.

† 4 BEFORE ADVENT
PROPER 26

YEAR A

*In Church of England provision this Sunday may be kept as All Saints' Sunday
(see pages 287–289) or else the provision below is used. The Revised Common Lectionary
continues to provide two tracks for the First Reading and Psalms. Church of England provision
allows only Track 2. The Church of England Gospel is different from the Revised Common
Lectionary provision.*

TRACK 1

Revised Common Lectionary only

FIRST READING　　　　　　　　　　　　　　　　**Joshua 3.7–17**

A reading from the book of Joshua.

The LORD said to Joshua, 'This day I will begin to exalt you in the sight of all
Israel, so that they may know that I will be with you as I was with Moses. You
are the one who shall command the priests who bear the ark of the covenant,
"When you come to the edge of the waters of the Jordan, you shall stand still
in the Jordan."' Joshua then said to the Israelites, 'Draw near and hear the
words of the LORD your God.' Joshua said, 'By this you shall know that
among you is the living God who without fail will drive out from before you
the Canaanites, Hittites, Hivites, Perizzites, Girgashites, Amorites, and
Jebusites: the ark of the covenant of the Lord of all the earth is going to pass
before you into the Jordan. So now select twelve men from the tribes of
Israel, one from each tribe. When the soles of the feet of the priests who bear
the ark of the LORD, the Lord of all the earth, rest in the waters of the
Jordan, the waters of the Jordan flowing from above shall be cut off; they
shall stand in a single heap.'

When the people set out from their tents to cross over the Jordan, the priests
bearing the ark of the covenant were in front of the people. Now the Jordan
overflows all its banks throughout the time of harvest. So when those who
bore the ark had come to the Jordan, and the feet of the priests bearing the
ark were dipped in the edge of the water, the waters flowing from above
stood still, rising up in a single heap far off at Adam, the city that is beside
Zarethan, while those flowing towards the sea of the Arabah, the Dead Sea,
were wholly cut off. Then the people crossed over opposite Jericho. While all
Israel were crossing over on dry ground, the priests who bore the ark of the
covenant of the LORD stood on dry ground in the middle of the Jordan, until
the entire nation finished crossing over the Jordan.

PSALM   Psalm 107.1–7, 33–37

℞ **Give thanks to the Lord for his mercy**
   [and the wonders he does for his children].

Give thanks to the Lord, for he is good,
and his mercy endures for ever.
Let all those whom the Lord has redeemed proclaim
that he redeemed them from the hand of the foe.
He gathered them out of the lands;
from the east and from the west,
from the north and from the south. ℞

Some wandered in desert wastes;
they found no way to a city where they might dwell.
They were hungry and thirsty;
their spirits languished within them.
Then they cried to the Lord in their trouble,
and he delivered them from their distress. ℞

He put their feet on a straight path
to go to a city where they might dwell.
The Lord changed rivers into deserts,
and water-springs into thirsty ground,
A fruitful land into salt flats,
because of the wickedness of those who dwell there. ℞

He changed deserts into pools of water
and dry land into water-springs.
He settled the hungry there,
and they founded a city to dwell in.
They sowed fields and planted vineyards,
and brought in a fruitful harvest. ℞

Or   TRACK 2

FIRST READING   Micah 3.5–12

A reading from the book of the prophet Micah.

Thus says the LORD concerning the prophets who lead my people astray,
who cry 'Peace' when they have something to eat, but declare war against
those who put nothing into their mouths.

Therefore it shall be night to you, without vision, and darkness to you, without revelation. The sun shall go down upon the prophets, and the day shall be black over them; the seers shall be disgraced, and the diviners put to shame; they shall all cover their lips, for there is no answer from God. But as for me, I am filled with power, with the spirit of the LORD, and with justice and might, to declare to Jacob his transgression and to Israel his sin.

Hear this, you rulers of the house of Jacob and chiefs of the house of Israel, who abhor justice and pervert all equity, who build Zion with blood and Jerusalem with wrong! Its rulers give judgement for a bribe, its priests teach for a price, its prophets give oracles for money; yet they lean upon the LORD and say, 'Surely the LORD is with us! No harm shall come upon us.' Therefore because of you Zion shall be ploughed as a field; Jerusalem shall become a heap of ruins, and the mountain of the house a wooded height.

PSALM   Psalm 43

℟ **Give judgement for me, O God,**
   and defend my cause.

Give judgement for me, O God,
and defend my cause against an ungodly people;
deliver me from the deceitful and the wicked.
For you are the God of my strength;
why have you put me from you?
and why do I go so heavily
while the enemy oppresses me? ℟

Send out your light and your truth,
that they may lead me,
and bring me to your holy hill
and to your dwelling;
That I may go to the altar of God,
to the God of my joy and gladness;
and on the harp I will give thanks to you,
O God my God. ℟

Why are you so full of heaviness, O my soul?
and why are you so disquieted within me?
Put your trust in God;
for I will yet give thanks to him,
who is the help of my countenance, and my God. ℟

SECOND READING   1 Thessalonians 2.9-13

A reading from the first letter of Paul to the Thessalonians.

You remember our labour and toil, brothers and sisters; we worked night and day, so that we might not burden any of you while we proclaimed to you the gospel of God. You are witnesses, and God also, how pure, upright, and blameless our conduct was towards you believers. As you know, we dealt with each one of you like a father with his children, urging and encouraging you and pleading that you lead a life worthy of God, who calls you into his own kingdom and glory.

We also constantly give thanks to God for this, that when you received the word of God that you heard from us, you accepted it not as a human word but as what it really is, God's word, which is also at work in you believers.

GOSPEL

Either (Revised Common Lectionary)   Matthew 23.1-12

Hear the gospel of our Lord Jesus Christ according to Matthew.

Jesus said to the crowds and to his disciples, 'The scribes and the Pharisees sit on Moses' seat; therefore, do whatever they teach you and follow it; but do not do as they do, for they do not practise what they teach. They tie up heavy burdens, hard to bear, and lay them on the shoulders of others; but they themselves are unwilling to lift a finger to move them. They do all their deeds to be seen by others; for they make their phylacteries broad and their fringes long. They love to have the place of honour at banquets and the best seats in the synagogues, and to be greeted with respect in the market-places, and to have people call them rabbi. But you are not to be called rabbi, for you have one teacher, and you are all students. And call no one your father on earth, for you have one Father – the one in heaven. Nor are you to be called instructors, for you have one instructor, the Messiah. The greatest among you will be your servant. All who exalt themselves will be humbled, and all who humble themselves will be exalted.'

Or   **Matthew 24.1–14**

Hear the gospel of our Lord Jesus Christ according to Matthew.

As Jesus came out of the temple and was going away, his disciples came to point out to him the buildings of the temple. Then he asked them, 'You see all these, do you not? Truly I tell you, not one stone will be left here upon another; all will be thrown down.' When he was sitting on the Mount of Olives, the disciples came to him privately, saying, 'Tell us, when will this be, and what will be the sign of your coming and of the end of the age?' Jesus answered them, 'Beware that no one leads you astray. For many will come in my name, saying, "I am the Messiah!" and they will lead many astray. And you will hear of wars and rumours of wars; see that you are not alarmed; for this must take place, but the end is not yet. For nation will rise against nation, and kingdom against kingdom, and there will be famines and earthquakes in various places: all this is but the beginning of the birth pangs. Then they will hand you over to be tortured and will put you to death, and you will be hated by all nations because of my name.

Then many will fall away, and they will betray one another and hate one another. And many false prophets will arise and lead many astray. And because of the increase of lawlessness, the love of many will grow cold. But the one who endures to the end will be saved. And this good news of the kingdom will be proclaimed throughout the world, as a testimony to all the nations; and then the end will come.'

† ALL SAINTS' SUNDAY   YEAR A

Sunday between 30 October and 5 November (or, if this is not kept as All Saints' Sunday, 1 November itself)

FIRST READING   Revelation 7.9–17

A reading from the book of Revelation.

After this I looked, and there was a great multitude that no one could count, from every nation, from all tribes and peoples and languages, standing before the throne and before the Lamb, robed in white, with palm branches in their hands. They cried out in a loud voice, saying 'Salvation belongs to our God who is seated on the throne, and to the Lamb!' And all the angels stood around the throne and around the elders and the four living creatures, and they fell on their faces before the throne and worshipped God, singing, 'Amen! Blessing and glory and wisdom and thanksgiving and honour and power and might be to our God for ever and ever! Amen.' Then one of the elders addressed me, saying, 'Who are these, robed in white, and where have they come from?' I said to him, 'Sir, you are the one that knows.' Then he said to me, 'These are they who have come out of the great ordeal; they have washed their robes and made them white in the blood of the Lamb. For this reason they are before the throne of God, and worship him day and night within his temple, and the one who is seated on the throne will shelter them. They will hunger no more, and thirst no more; the sun will not strike them, nor any scorching heat; for the Lamb at the centre of the throne will be their shepherd, and he will guide them to springs of the water of life, and God will wipe away every tear from their eyes.'

PSALM   Psalm 34.1–10

℟ **Those who trust in him will understand truth
[and the faithful will abide with him in love].**

I will bless the Lord at all times;
his praise shall ever be in my mouth.
I will glory in the Lord;
let the humble hear and rejoice.
Proclaim with me the greatness of the Lord;
let us exalt his name together. ℟

I sought the Lord and he answered me
and delivered me out of all my terror.
Look upon him and be radiant,
and let not your faces be ashamed.
I called in my affliction and the Lord heard me
and saved me from all my troubles. ℟

The angel of the Lord
encompasses those who fear him,
and he will deliver them.
Taste and see that the Lord is good;
happy are they who trust in him! ℟

Fear the Lord, you that are his saints,
for those who fear him lack nothing.
The young lions lack and suffer hunger,
but those who seek the Lord
lack nothing that is good. ℞

SECOND READING   1 John 3.1–3

A reading from the first letter of John.

See what love the Father has given us, that we should be called children of
God; and that is what we are. The reason the world does not know us is that
it did not know him. Beloved, we are God's children now; what we will be
has not yet been revealed. What we do know is this: when he is revealed, we
will be like him, for we will see him as he is. And all who have this hope in
him purify themselves, just as he is pure.

GOSPEL   Matthew 5.1–12

Hear the gospel of our Lord Jesus Christ according to Matthew.

When Jesus saw the crowds, he went up the mountain; and after he sat
down, his disciples came to him. Then he began to speak, and taught them,
saying:

'Blessed are the poor in spirit, for theirs is the kingdom of heaven. Blessed are
those who mourn, for they will be comforted. Blessed are the meek, for they
will inherit the earth. Blessed are those who hunger and thirst for
righteousness, for they will be filled. Blessed are the merciful, for they will
receive mercy. Blessed are the pure in heart, for they will see God. Blessed are
the peacemakers, for they will be called children of God. Blessed are those
who are persecuted for righteousness' sake, for theirs is the kingdom of
heaven. Blessed are you when people revile you and persecute you and utter
all kinds of evil against you falsely on my account.

Rejoice and be glad, for your reward is great in heaven, for in the same way
they persecuted the prophets who were before you.'

† ALL SAINTS' DAY   YEARS A B C

For use on 1 November if the material for All Saints' Sunday is used on the Sunday.

FIRST READING (Alternative readings)

Either   Isaiah 56.3–8

A reading from the book of the prophet Isaiah.

Do not let the foreigner joined to the LORD say,
'The LORD will surely separate me from his people';
and do not let the eunuch say, 'I am just a dry tree.'
For thus says the LORD:
To the eunuchs who keep my sabbaths,
who choose the things that please me and hold fast my covenant,

I will give, in my house and within my walls,
a monument and a name better than sons and daughters;
I will give them an everlasting name that shall not be cut off.
And the foreigners who join themselves to the LORD,
to minister to him, to love the name of the LORD, and to be his servants,
all who keep the sabbath, and do not profane it,
and hold fast my covenant –
these I will bring to my holy mountain,
and make them joyful in my house of prayer;
their burnt-offerings and their sacrifices will be accepted on my altar;
for my house shall be called a house of prayer for all peoples.
Thus says the Lord GOD, who gathers the outcasts of Israel,
I will gather others to them besides those already gathered.

Or   2 Esdras 2.42–48

A reading from the second book of Esdras.

I, Ezra, saw on Mount Zion a great multitude that I could not number, and
they all were praising the Lord with songs. In their midst was a young man of
great stature, taller than any of the others, and on the head of each of them
he placed a crown, but he was more exalted than they. And I was held
spellbound. Then I asked an angel, 'Who are these, my lord?' He answered
and said to me, 'These are they who have put off mortal clothing and have
put on the immortal, and have confessed the name of God. Now they are

being crowned, and receive palms.' Then I said to the angel, 'Who is that young man who is placing crowns on them and putting palms in their hands?'He answered and said to me, 'He is the Son of God, whom they confessed in the world.' So I began to praise those who had stood valiantly for the name of the Lord. Then the angel said to me, 'Go, tell my people how great and many are the wonders of the Lord God that you have seen.'

PSALM   Psalm 33.1–5

℟ **The Lord spoke to him face to face**
  [as one speaks to a friend].

Rejoice in the Lord, you righteous;
it is good for the just to sing praises.
Praise the Lord with the harp;
play to him upon the psaltery and lyre.
Sing for him a new song;
sound a fanfare with all your skill upon the trumpet. ℟

For the word of the Lord is right,
and all his works are sure.
He loves righteousness and justice;
the loving-kindness of the Lord fills the whole earth. ℟

SECOND READING   Hebrews 12.18–24

A reading from the letter to the Hebrews.

You have not come to something that can be touched, a blazing fire, and darkness, and gloom, and a tempest, and the sound of a trumpet, and a voice whose words made the hearers beg that not another word be spoken to them. (For they could not endure the order that was given, 'If even an animal touches the mountain, it shall be stoned to death.' Indeed, so terrifying was the sight that Moses said, 'I tremble with fear.') But you have come to Mount Zion and to the city of the living God, the heavenly Jerusalem, and to innumerable angels in festal gathering, and to the assembly of the firstborn who are enrolled in heaven, and to God the judge of all, and to the spirits of the righteous made perfect, and to Jesus, the mediator of a new covenant, and to the sprinkled blood that speaks a better word than the blood of Abel.

GOSPEL   Matthew 5.1–12

Hear the gospel of our Lord Jesus Christ according to Matthew.

When Jesus saw the crowds, he went up the mountain; and after he sat down, his disciples came to him. Then he began to speak, and taught them, saying:

'Blessed are the poor in spirit, for theirs is the kingdom of heaven. Blessed are those who mourn, for they will be comforted. Blessed are the meek, for they will inherit the earth. Blessed are those who hunger and thirst for righteousness, for they will be filled. Blessed are the merciful, for they will receive mercy. Blessed are the pure in heart, for they will see God. Blessed are the peacemakers, for they will be called children of God. Blessed are those who are persecuted for righteousness' sake, for theirs is the kingdom of heaven. Blessed are you when people revile you and persecute you and utter all kinds of evil against you falsely on my account. Rejoice and be glad, for your reward is great in heaven, for in the same way they persecuted the prophets who were before you.'

† 3 BEFORE ADVENT   YEAR A
PROPER 27

The Revised Common Lectionary continues to provide two tracks. Church of England allows only Track 2 (which this week has alternative readings).

TRACK 1

Revised Common Lectionary only

FIRST READING   Joshua 24.1–3a, 14–25

A reading from the book of Joshua.

Joshua gathered all the tribes of Israel to Shechem, and summoned the elders, the heads, the judges, and the officers of Israel; and they presented themselves before God. And Joshua said to all the people, 'Thus says the LORD, the God of Israel: Long ago your ancestors – Terah and his sons Abraham and Nahor – lived beyond the Euphrates and served other gods. Then I took your father Abraham from beyond the River and led him through all the land of Canaan and made his offspring many.

Now therefore revere the LORD, and serve him in sincerity and in faithfulness; put away the gods that your ancestors served beyond the River and in Egypt, and serve the LORD. Now if you are unwilling to serve the LORD, choose this day whom you will serve, whether the gods your ancestors served in the region beyond the River or the gods of the Amorites in whose land you are living; but as for me and my household, we will serve the LORD.'

Then the people answered, 'Far be it from us that we should forsake the LORD to serve other gods; for it is the LORD our God who brought us and our ancestors up from the land of Egypt, out of the house of slavery, and who did those great signs in our sight. He protected us along all the way that we went, and among all the peoples through whom we passed; and the LORD drove out before us all the peoples, the Amorites who lived in the land. Therefore we also will serve the LORD, for he is our God.'

But Joshua said to the people, 'You cannot serve the LORD, for he is a holy God. He is a jealous God; he will not forgive your transgressions or your sins. If you forsake the LORD and serve foreign gods, then he will turn and do you harm, and consume you, after having done you good.' And the people said to Joshua, 'No, we will serve the LORD!' Then Joshua said to the people, 'You are witnesses against yourselves that you have chosen the LORD, to serve him.' And they said, 'We are witnesses.' He said, 'Then put away the foreign gods that are among you, and incline your hearts to the LORD, the God of Israel.' The people said to Joshua, 'The LORD our God we will serve, and him we will obey.' So Joshua made a covenant with the people that day, and made statutes and ordinances for them at Shechem.

PSALM   Psalm 78.1–7

℟ **We will recount the wonderful works of the Lord.**

Hear my teaching, O my people;
incline your ears to the words of my mouth.
I will open my mouth in a parable;
I will declare the mysteries of ancient times. ℟

That which we have heard and known,
and what our forebears have told us,
we will not hide from their children.
We will recount to generations to come
the praiseworthy deeds and the power of the Lord,
and the wonderful works he has done. ℟

He gave his decrees to Jacob
and established a law for Israel,
which he commanded them to teach their children;
That the generations to come might know,
and the children yet unborn;
that they in their turn might tell it to their children;
So that they might put their trust in God,
and not forget the deeds of God,
but keep his commandments. ℟

Or   TRACK 2

FIRST READING (Alternative readings)

Either   **Wisdom of Solomon 6.12–16**

A reading from the book of Wisdom.

Wisdom is radiant and unfading,
and she is easily discerned by those who love her,
and is found by those who seek her.
She hastens to make herself known to those who desire her.
One who rises early to seek her will have no difficulty,
for she will be found sitting at the gate.
To fix one's thought on her is perfect understanding,
and one who is vigilant on her account will soon be free from care,
because she goes about seeking those worthy of her,
and she graciously appears to them in their paths,
and meets them in every thought.

CANTICLE   **Wisdom of Solomon 6.17–20**

℟ **Glory to the One who gives me wisdom.**

The beginning of wisdom is the most sincere desire for instruction,
and concern for instruction is love of her,
and love of her is the keeping of her laws,
and giving heed to her laws is assurance of immortality,
and immortality brings one near to God;

so the desire for wisdom leads to a kingdom. ℟

Or   **Amos 5.18–24**

A reading from the book of the prophet Amos.

Alas for you who desire the day of the LORD!
Why do you want the day of the LORD?
It is darkness, not light;
as if someone fled from a lion, and was met by a bear;
or went into the house and rested a hand against the wall,
and was bitten by a snake.
Is not the day of the LORD darkness, not light,
and gloom with no brightness in it?

I hate, I despise your festivals,
and I take no delight in your solemn assemblies.
Even though you offer me your burnt-offerings and grain-offerings,
I will not accept them;
and the offerings of well-being of your fatted animals
I will not look upon.
Take away from me the noise of your songs;
I will not listen to the melody of your harps.
But let justice roll down like waters,
and righteousness like an ever-flowing stream.

PSALM   Psalm 70

℟ **You are my helper and deliverer.**
   [O Lord, make haste to help me.]

Be pleased, O God, to deliver me;
O Lord, make haste to help me.
Let those who seek my life
be ashamed and altogether dismayed;
let those who take pleasure in my misfortune
draw back and be disgraced. ℟

Let those who say to me 'Aha!'
and gloat over me turn back,
because they are ashamed.
Let all who seek you rejoice and be glad in you;
let those who love your salvation say for ever,
'Great is the Lord!' ℟

But as for me, I am poor and needy;
come to me speedily, O God.
You are my helper and my deliverer;
O Lord, do not tarry. ℟

SECOND READING   1 Thessalonians 4.13–18

A reading from the first letter of Paul to the Thessalonians.

We do not want you to be uninformed, brothers and sisters, about those who
have died, so that you may not grieve as others do who have no hope. For
since we believe that Jesus died and rose again, even so, through Jesus, God
will bring with him those who have died. For this we declare to you by the
word of the Lord, that we who are alive, who are left until the coming of the
Lord, will by no means precede those who have died. For the Lord himself,
with a cry of command, with the archangel's call and with the sound of
God's trumpet, will descend from heaven, and the dead in Christ will rise
first. Then we who are alive, who are left, will be caught up in the clouds
together with them to meet the Lord in the air; and so we will be with the
Lord for ever. Therefore encourage one another with these words.

GOSPEL   Matthew 25.1–13

Hear the gospel of our Lord Jesus Christ according to Matthew.

Jesus spoke this parable to the disciples: 'The kingdom of heaven will be like
this. Ten bridesmaids took their lamps and went to meet the bridegroom.
Five of them were foolish, and five were wise. When the foolish took their
lamps, they took no oil with them; but the wise took flasks of oil with their
lamps. As the bridegroom was delayed, all of them became drowsy and slept.
But at midnight there was a shout, "Look! Here is the bridegroom! Come out
to meet him." Then all those bridesmaids got up and trimmed their lamps.
The foolish said to the wise, "Give us some of your oil, for our lamps are
going out." But the wise replied, "No! there will not be enough for you and
for us; you had better go to the dealers and buy some for yourselves." And
while they went to buy it, the bridegroom came, and those who were ready
went with him into the wedding banquet; and the door was shut. Later the
other bridesmaids came also, saying, "Lord, lord, open to us." But he replied,
"Truly I tell you, I do not know you." Keep awake therefore, for you know
neither the day nor the hour.'

† 2 BEFORE ADVENT
PROPER 28

YEAR A

The Revised Common Lectionary continues to provide two tracks. Church of England provision allows only Track 2.

TRACK 1

Revised Common Lectionary only

FIRST READING

Judges 4.1–7

A reading from the book of Judges.

The Israelites again did what was evil in the sight of the LORD, after Ehud died. So the LORD sold them into the hand of King Jabin of Canaan, who reigned in Hazor; the commander of his army was Sisera, who lived in Harosheth-ha-goiim. Then the Israelites cried out to the LORD for help; for he had nine hundred chariots of iron, and had oppressed the Israelites cruelly for twenty years.

At that time Deborah, a prophetess, wife of Lappidoth, was judging Israel. She used to sit under the palm of Deborah between Ramah and Bethel in the hill country of Ephraim; and the Israelites came up to her for judgement. She sent and summoned Barak son of Abinoam from Kedesh in Naphtali, and said to him, 'The LORD, the God of Israel, commands you, "Go, take position at Mount Tabor, bringing ten thousand from the tribe of Naphtali and the tribe of Zebulun. I will draw out Sisera, the general of Jabin's army, to meet you by the Wadi Kishon with his chariots and his troops; and I will give him into your hand."'

PSALM

Psalm 123

℟ **Our eyes look to the Lord our God,
until he shows us his mercy.**

To you I lift up my eyes,
to you enthroned in the heavens.
As the eyes of servants look to the hand of their masters,
and the eyes of a maid to the hand of her mistress,
So our eyes look to the Lord our God,
until he show us his mercy. ℟

Have mercy upon us, O Lord, have mercy,
for we have had more than enough of contempt,
Too much of the scorn of the indolent rich,
and of the derision of the proud. ℟

Or   TRACK 2

FIRST READING   **Zephaniah 1.7, 12–18**

A reading from the book of the prophet Zephaniah.

Be silent before the Lord GOD!
For the day of the LORD is at hand;
the LORD has prepared a sacrifice,
he has consecrated his guests.

At that time I will search Jerusalem with lamps,
and I will punish the people who rest complacently on their dregs,
those who say in their hearts,
'The LORD will not do good,
nor will he do harm.'
Their wealth shall be plundered,
and their houses laid waste.
Though they build houses,
they shall not inhabit them;
though they plant vineyards,
they shall not drink wine from them.

The great day of the LORD is near,
near and hastening fast;
the sound of the day of the LORD is bitter,
the warrior cries aloud there.
That day will be a day of wrath,
a day of distress and anguish,
a day of ruin and devastation,
a day of darkness and gloom,
a day of clouds and thick darkness,
a day of trumpet blast
and battle cry against the fortified cities
and against the lofty battlements.
I will bring such distress upon people
that they shall walk like the blind;
because they have sinned against the LORD,

their blood shall be poured out like dust,
and their flesh like dung.
Neither their silver nor their gold will be able to save them
on the day of the Lord's wrath;
in the fire of his passion the whole earth shall be consumed;
for a full, a terrible end he will make of all the inhabitants of the earth.

PSALM   **Psalm 90.1–8, (9–11), 12**

℟ **Satisfy us by your loving-kindness;**
  so shall we rejoice and be glad.

Lord, you have been our refuge
from one generation to another.
Before the mountains were brought forth,
or the land and the earth were born,
from age to age you are God.
You turn us back to the dust and say,
'Go back, O child of earth.' ℟

For a thousand years in your sight
are like yesterday when it is past
and like a watch in the night.
You sweep us away like a dream;
we fade away suddenly like the grass.
In the morning it is green and flourishes;
in the evening it is dried up and withered. ℟

For we consume away in your displeasure;
we are afraid because of your wrathful indignation.
Our iniquities you have set before you,
and our secret sins in the light of your countenance. ℟

[When you are angry, all our days are gone;
we bring our years to an end like a sigh.
The span of our life is seventy years,
perhaps in strength even eighty;
yet the sum of them is but labour and sorrow,
for they pass away quickly and we are gone.
Who regards the power of your wrath?
who rightly fears your indignation? ℟]

So teach us to number our days
that we may apply our hearts to wisdom. ℟

SECOND READING 1 Thessalonians 5.1–11

A reading from the first letter of Paul to the Thessalonians.

Concerning the times and the seasons, brothers and sisters, you do not need to have anything written to you. For you yourselves know very well that the day of the Lord will come like a thief in the night. When they say, 'There is peace and security,' then sudden destruction will come upon them, as labour pains come upon a pregnant woman, and there will be no escape! But you, beloved, are not in darkness, for that day to surprise you like a thief; for you are all children of light and children of the day; we are not of the night or of darkness. So then let us not fall asleep as others do, but let us keep awake and be sober; for those who sleep sleep at night, and those who are drunk get drunk at night. But since we belong to the day, let us be sober, and put on the breastplate of faith and love, and for a helmet the hope of salvation. For God has destined us not for wrath but for obtaining salvation through our Lord Jesus Christ, who died for us, so that whether we are awake or asleep we may live with him. Therefore encourage one another and build up each other, as indeed you are doing.

GOSPEL Matthew 25.14–30

Hear the gospel of our Lord Jesus Christ according to Matthew.

Jesus said to his disciples, 'The kingdom of heaven is as if a man, going on a journey, summoned his slaves and entrusted his property to them; to one he gave five talents, to another two, to another one, to each according to his ability. Then he went away. The one who had received the five talents went off at once and traded with them, and made five more talents. In the same way, the one who had the two talents made two more talents. But the one who had received the one talent went off and dug a hole in the ground and hid his master's money. After a long time the master of those slaves came and settled accounts with them. Then the one who had received the five talents came forward, bringing five more talents, saying, "Master, you handed over to me five talents; see, I have made five more talents." His master said to him, "Well done, good and trustworthy slave; you have been trustworthy in a few things, I will put you in charge of many things; enter into the joy of your master." And the one with the two talents also came forward, saying, "Master, you handed over to me two talents; see, I have made two more talents." His master said to him, "Well done, good and trustworthy slave; you have been trustworthy in a few things, I will put you in charge of many things; enter into the joy of your master." Then the one who had received the one talent also came forward, saying, "Master, I knew that you were a harsh man, reaping where you did not sow, and gathering where you did not scatter seed; so I was afraid, and I went and hid your talent in the ground. Here you have what is yours." But his master replied, "You wicked and lazy slave! You knew, did you, that I reap where I did not sow, and gather where I did not scatter? Then you ought to have invested my money with the bankers, and on my return I would have received what was my own with interest. So take the talent from him, and give it to the one with the ten talents. For to all those who have, more will be given, and they will have an abundance; but from those who have nothing, even what they have will be taken away. As for this worthless slave, throw him into the outer darkness, where there will be weeping and gnashing of teeth."'

CHRIST THE KING YEAR A

FIRST READING Ezekiel 34.11-16, 20-24

A reading from the book of the prophet Ezekiel.

Thus says the Lord GOD: I myself will search for my sheep, and will seek them out. As shepherds seek out their flocks when they are among their scattered sheep, so I will seek out my sheep. I will rescue them from all the places to which they have been scattered on a day of clouds and thick darkness. I will bring them out from the peoples and gather them from the countries, and will bring them into their own land; and I will feed them on the mountains of Israel, by the watercourses, and in all the inhabited parts of the land. I will feed them with good pasture, and the mountain heights of Israel shall be their pasture; there they shall lie down in good grazing land, and they shall feed on rich pasture on the mountains of Israel. I myself will be the shepherd of my sheep, and I will make them lie down, says the Lord GOD. I will seek the lost, and I will bring back the strayed, and I will bind up the injured, and I will strengthen the weak, but the fat and the strong I will destroy. I will feed them with justice.

Therefore, thus says the Lord GOD to them: I myself will judge between the fat sheep and the lean sheep. Because you pushed with flank and shoulder, and butted at all the weak animals with your horns until you scattered them far and wide, I will save my flock, and they shall no longer be ravaged; and I will judge between sheep and sheep. I will set up over them one shepherd, my servant David, and he shall feed them: he shall feed them and be their shepherd. And I, the LORD, will be their God, and my servant David shall be prince among them; I, the LORD, have spoken.

PSALM

Either

Psalm 100

℟ **We are his people and the sheep of his pasture.**

Be joyful in the Lord, all you lands;
serve the Lord with gladness
and come before his presence with a song.
Know this: The Lord himself is God;
he himself has made us and we are his;
we are his people and the sheep of his pasture. ℟

Enter his gates with thanksgiving;
go into his courts with praise;
give thanks to him and call upon his name.
For the Lord is good; his mercy is everlasting;
and his faithfulness endures from age to age. ℟

Or

Psalm 95.1–7a

℟ **The Lord is a great God,**
and a great king above all gods.

Come, let us sing to the Lord;
let us shout for joy to the rock of our salvation.
Let us come before his presence with thanksgiving
and raise a loud shout to him with psalms.
For the Lord is a great God,
and a great king above all gods. ℟

In his hand are the depths of the earth,
and the heights of the hills are his also.
The sea is his, for he made it,
and his hands have moulded the dry land. ℟

Come, let us bow down and bend the knee,
and kneel before the Lord our Maker.
For he is our God,
and we are the people of his pasture
and the sheep of his hand. ℟

SECOND READING   Ephesians 1.15–23

A reading from the letter of Paul to the Ephesians.

I have heard of your faith in the Lord Jesus and your love towards all the saints, and for this reason I do not cease to give thanks for you as I remember you in my prayers. I pray that the God of our Lord Jesus Christ, the Father of glory, may give you a spirit of wisdom and revelation as you come to know him, so that, with the eyes of your heart enlightened, you may know what is the hope to which he has called you, what are the riches of his glorious inheritance among the saints, and what is the immeasurable greatness of his power for us who believe, according to the working of his great power. God put this power to work in Christ when he raised him from the dead and seated him at his right hand in the heavenly places, far above all rule and authority and power and dominion, and above every name that is named, not only in this age but also in the age to come. And he has put all things under his feet and has made him the head over all things for the church, which is his body, the fullness of him who fills all in all.

GOSPEL   Matthew 25.31–46

Hear the gospel of our Lord Jesus Christ according to Matthew.

Jesus said to his disciples: 'When the Son of Man comes in his glory, and all the angels with him, then he will sit on the throne of his glory. All the nations will be gathered before him, and he will separate people one from another as a shepherd separates the sheep from the goats, and he will put the sheep at his right hand and the goats at the left. Then the king will say to those at his right hand, "Come, you that are blessed by my Father, inherit the kingdom prepared for you from the foundation of the world; for I was hungry and you gave me food, I was thirsty and you gave me something to drink, I was a stranger and you welcomed me, I was naked and you gave me clothing, I was sick and you took care of me, I was in prison and you visited me." Then the righteous will answer him, "Lord, when was it that we saw you hungry and gave you food, or thirsty and gave you something to drink? And when was it that we saw you a stranger and welcomed you, or naked and gave you clothing? And when was it that we saw you sick or in prison and visited you?" And the king will answer them, "Truly I tell you, just as you did it to one of the least of these who are members of my family, you did it to me." Then he will say to those at his left hand, "You that are accursed, depart from me into the eternal fire prepared for the devil and his angels; for I was hungry and you gave me no food, I was thirsty and you gave me nothing to drink, I was a stranger and you did not welcome me, naked and you did not give me clothing, sick and in prison and you did not visit me." Then they also will answer, "Lord, when was it that we saw you hungry or thirsty or a stranger or naked or sick or in prison, and did not take care of you?" Then he will answer them, "Truly I tell you, just as you did not do it to one of the least of these, you did not do it to me." And these will go away into eternal punishment, but the righteous into eternal life.'

PRINCIPAL SERVICE YEAR B

FIRST READING   **Isaiah 64.1–9**

A reading from the book of the prophet Isaiah.

O that you would tear open the heavens and come down,
so that the mountains would quake at your presence –
as when fire kindles brushwood
and the fire causes water to boil –
to make your name known to your adversaries,
so that the nations might tremble at your presence!
When you did awesome deeds that we did not expect,
you came down, the mountains quaked at your presence.
From ages past no one has heard,
no ear has perceived,
no eye has seen any God besides you,
who works for those who wait for him.
You meet those who gladly do right,
those who remember you in your ways.
But you were angry, and we sinned;
because you hid yourself we transgressed.
We have all become like one who is unclean,
and all our righteous deeds are like a filthy cloth.
We all fade like a leaf,
and our iniquities, like the wind, take us away.
There is no one who calls on your name,
or attempts to take hold of you;
for you have hidden your face from us,
and have delivered us into the hand of our iniquity.
Yet, O LORD, you are our Father;
we are the clay, and you are our potter;
we are all the work of your hand.
Do not be exceedingly angry, O LORD,
and do not remember iniquity for ever.
Now consider, we are all your people.

PSALM   Psalm 80.1–7, 16–18

℟ [Restore us, O God of hosts;]
Show the light of your countenance and we shall be saved.

Hear, O Shepherd of Israel, leading Joseph like a flock;
shine forth, you that are enthroned upon the cherubim.
In the presence of Ephraim, Benjamin and Manasseh,
stir up your strength and come to help us. ℟

[Restore us, O God of hosts;
show the light of your countenance and we shall be saved.]

O Lord God of hosts,
how long will you be angered
despite the prayers of your people? ℟

You have fed them with the bread of tears;
you have given them bowls of tears to drink.
You have made us the derision of our neighbours,
and our enemies laugh us to scorn. ℟

[Restore us, O God of hosts;
show the light of your countenance and we shall be saved.]

Let your hand be upon the man of your right hand,
the son of man you have made so strong for yourself.
And so will we never turn away from you;
give us life, that we may call upon your name. ℟

[Restore us, O Lord God of hosts;
show the light of your countenance and we shall be saved.]

SECOND READING   1 Corinthians 1.3–9

A reading from the first letter of Paul to the Corinthians.

My brothers and sisters: Grace to you and peace from God our Father and the
Lord Jesus Christ.

I give thanks to my God always for you because of the grace of God that has
been given you in Christ Jesus, for in every way you have been enriched in
him, in speech and knowledge of every kind – just as the testimony of Christ
has been strengthened among you – so that you are not lacking in any
spiritual gift as you wait for the revealing of our Lord Jesus Christ. He will
also strengthen you to the end, so that you may be blameless on the day of

our Lord Jesus Christ. God is faithful; by him you were called into the fellowship of his Son, Jesus Christ our Lord.

GOSPEL   Mark 13.24–37

Hear the gospel of our Lord Jesus Christ according to Mark.

Jesus said to his disciples: 'In those days, after that suffering, the sun will be darkened, and the moon will not give its light, and the stars will be falling from heaven, and the powers in the heavens will be shaken. Then they will see "the Son of Man coming in clouds" with great power and glory. Then he will send out the angels, and gather his elect from the four winds, from the ends of the earth to the ends of heaven.

From the fig tree learn its lesson: as soon as its branch becomes tender and puts forth its leaves, you know that summer is near. So also, when you see these things taking place, you know that he is near, at the very gates. Truly I tell you, this generation will not pass away until all these things have taken place. Heaven and earth will pass away, but my words will not pass away.

But about that day or hour no one knows, neither the angels in heaven, nor the Son, but only the Father. Beware, keep alert; for you do not know when the time will come. It is like a man going on a journey, when he leaves home and puts his slaves in charge, each with his work and commands the doorkeeper to be on the watch. Therefore, keep awake – for you do not know when the master of the house will come, in the evening, or at midnight, or at cockcrow, or at dawn, or else he may find you asleep when he comes suddenly. And what I say to you I say to all: Keep awake.'

ADVENT 2   YEAR B

FIRST READING   Isaiah 40.1–11

A reading from the book of the prophet Isaiah.

Comfort, O comfort my people, says your God.
Speak tenderly to Jerusalem,
and cry to her
that she has served her term,
that her penalty is paid,
that she has received from the Lord's hand
double for all her sins.

A voice cries out:
'In the wilderness prepare the way of the LORD,
make straight in the desert a highway for our God.
Every valley shall be lifted up,
and every mountain and hill be made low;
the uneven ground shall become level,
and the rough places a plain.
Then the glory of the LORD shall be revealed,
and all people shall see it together,
for the mouth of the LORD has spoken.'
A voice says, 'Cry out!'
And I said, 'What shall I cry?'
All people are grass,
their constancy is like the flower of the field.
The grass withers, the flower fades,
when the breath of the LORD blows upon it;
surely the people are grass.
The grass withers, the flower fades;
but the word of our God will stand for ever.
Get you up to a high mountain,
O Zion, herald of good tidings;
lift up your voice with strength,
O Jerusalem, herald of good tidings, lift it up, do not fear;
say to the cities of Judah, 'Here is your God!'
See, the Lord GOD comes with might,
and his arm rules for him;
his reward is with him, and his recompense before him.
He will feed his flock like a shepherd;
he will gather the lambs in his arms,
and carry them in his bosom,
and gently lead the mother sheep.

PSALM   Psalm 85.1-2, 8-13

℟ **Show us your mercy, O Lord,
and grant us your salvation.**

You have been gracious to your land, O Lord,
you have restored the good fortune of Jacob.
You have forgiven the iniquity of your people
and blotted out all their sins. ℟

I will listen to what the Lord God is saying,
for he is speaking peace to his faithful people
and to those who turn their hearts to him.
Truly, his salvation is very near to those who fear him,
 that his glory may dwell in our land. ℟

Mercy and truth have met together;
 righteousness and peace have kissed each other.
Truth shall spring up from the earth,
 and righteousness shall look down from heaven. ℟

The Lord will indeed grant prosperity,
and our land will yield its increase.
Righteousness shall go before him,
and peace shall be a pathway for his feet. ℟

SECOND READING   2 Peter 3.8–15a

A reading from the second letter of Peter.

Do not ignore this one fact, beloved, that with the Lord one day is like a thousand years, and a thousand years are like one day. The Lord is not slow about his promise, as some think of slowness, but is patient with you, not wanting any to perish, but all to come to repentance. But the day of the Lord will come like a thief, and then the heavens will pass away with a loud noise, and the elements will be dissolved with fire, and the earth and everything that is done on it will be disclosed.

Since all these things are to be dissolved in this way, what sort of persons ought you to be in leading lives of holiness and godliness, waiting for and hastening the coming of the day of God, because of which the heavens will be set ablaze and dissolved, and the elements will melt with fire? But, in accordance with his promise, we wait for new heavens and a new earth, where righteousness is at home. Therefore, beloved, while you are waiting for these things, strive to be found by him at peace, without spot or blemish; and regard the patience of our Lord as salvation.

GOSPEL   Mark 1.1–8

Hear the gospel of our Lord Jesus Christ according to Mark.

The beginning of the good news of Jesus Christ, the Son of God.
As it is written in the prophet Isaiah,

309

'See, I am sending my messenger ahead of you,
who will prepare your way;
the voice of one crying out in the wilderness:
"Prepare the way of the Lord,
make his paths straight,"'
John the baptizer appeared in the wilderness, proclaiming a baptism of
repentance for the forgiveness of sins. And people from the whole Judean
countryside and all the people of Jerusalem were going out to him, and were
baptized by him in the river Jordan, confessing their sins. Now John was
clothed with camel's hair, with a leather belt around his waist, and he ate
locusts and wild honey. He proclaimed, 'The one who is more powerful than
I is coming after me; I am not worthy to stoop down and untie the thong of
his sandals. I have baptized you with water; but he will baptize you with the
Holy Spirit.'

ADVENT 3   YEAR B

FIRST READING   Isaiah 61.1–4, 8–11

A reading from the book of the prophet Isaiah.

The servant of the LORD said:

The spirit of the Lord GOD is upon me,
because the LORD has anointed me;
he has sent me to bring good news to the oppressed,
to bind up the broken-hearted,
to proclaim liberty to the captives,
and release to the prisoners;
to proclaim the year of the Lord's favour,
and the day of vengeance of our God;
to comfort all who mourn;
to provide for those who mourn in Zion –
to give them a garland instead of ashes,
the oil of gladness instead of mourning,
the mantle of praise instead of a faint spirit.
They will be called oaks of righteousness,
the planting of the LORD, to display his glory.
They shall build up the ancient ruins,
they shall raise up the former devastations;
they shall repair the ruined cities,
the devastations of many generations.

For I the LORD love justice,
I hate robbery and wrongdoing;
I will faithfully give them their recompense,
and I will make an everlasting covenant with them.
Their descendants shall be known among the nations,
and their offspring among the peoples;
all who see them
shall acknowledge that they are a people
whom the LORD has blessed.
I will greatly rejoice in the LORD,
my whole being shall exult in my God;
for he has clothed me with the garments of salvation,
he has covered me with the robe of righteousness,
as a bridegroom decks himself with a garland,
and as a bride adorns herself with her jewels.
For as the earth brings forth its shoots,
and as a garden causes what is sown in it to spring up,
so the Lord GOD will cause righteousness and praise
to spring up before all the nations.

PSALM OR CANTICLE

Either   Psalm 126

℟ **The Lord has done great things for us
   [and we are glad indeed].**

When the Lord restored the fortunes of Zion,
then were we like those who dream.
Then was our mouth filled with laughter,
and our tongue with shouts of joy. ℟

Then they said among the nations,
'The Lord has done great things for them.'
The Lord has done great things for us,
and we are glad indeed. ℟

Restore our fortunes, O Lord
like the watercourses of the Negev.
Those who sowed with tears
will reap with songs of joy.
Those who go out weeping, carrying the seed,
will come again with joy, shouldering their sheaves. ℟

Or Luke 1.46b–55

℟ **My spirit rejoices in God my Saviour.**

My soul proclaims the greatness of the Lord;
My spirit rejoices in God my Saviour.
For he has looked with favour on his lowly servant;
from this day all generations will call me blessèd.
The Almighty has done great things for me,
and holy is his name. ℟

He has mercy on those who fear him
in every generation.
He has shown the strength of his arm;
he has scattered the proud in their conceit. ℟

He has cast down the mighty from their thrones
and has lifted up the lowly.
He has filled the hungry with good things
and the rich he has sent away empty. ℟

He has come to the help of his servant, Israel,
for he has remembered his promise of mercy.
The promise he made to our forebears:
to Abraham and his children for ever. ℟

SECOND READING 1 Thessalonians 5.16–24

A reading from the first letter of Paul to the Thessalonians.

My brothers and sisters, Rejoice always, pray without ceasing, give thanks in all circumstances; for this is the will of God in Christ Jesus for you. Do not quench the Spirit. Do not despise the words of prophets, but test everything; hold fast to what is good; abstain from every form of evil.

May the God of peace himself sanctify you entirely; and may your spirit and soul and body be kept sound and blameless at the coming of our Lord Jesus Christ. The one who calls you is faithful, and he will do this.

GOSPEL   **John 1.6–8, 19–28**

Hear the gospel of our Lord Jesus Christ according to John.

There was a man sent from God, whose name was John. He came as a witness to testify to the light, so that all might believe through him. He himself was not the light, but he came to testify to the light.

This is the testimony given by John when the Jews sent priests and Levites from Jerusalem to ask him, 'Who are you?' He confessed and did not deny it, but confessed, 'I am not the Messiah.' And they asked him, 'What then? Are you Elijah?' He said, 'I am not.' 'Are you the prophet?' He answered, 'No.' Then they said to him, 'Who are you? Let us have an answer for those who sent us. What do you say about yourself?' He said, 'I am the voice of one crying out in the wilderness, "Make straight the way of the Lord,"' as the prophet Isaiah said. Now they had been sent from the Pharisees. They asked him, 'Why then are you baptizing if you are neither the Messiah, nor Elijah, nor the prophet?' John answered them, 'I baptize with water. Among you stands one whom you do not know, the one who is coming after me; I am not worthy to untie the thong of his sandal.' This took place in Bethany across the Jordan where John was baptizing.

ADVENT 4   YEAR B

FIRST READING   **2 Samuel 7.1–11, 16**

A reading from the second book of Samuel.

Now when David, the king was settled in his house, and the LORD had given him rest from all his enemies around him, the king said to the prophet Nathan, 'See now, I am living in a house of cedar, but the ark of God stays in a tent.' Nathan said to the king, 'Go, do all that you have in mind; for the LORD is with you.'

But that same night the word of the LORD came to Nathan: Go and tell my servant David: Thus says the LORD: Are you the one to build me a house to live in? I have not lived in a house since the day I brought up the people of Israel from Egypt to this day, but I have been moving about in a tent and a tabernacle. Wherever I have moved about among all the people of Israel, did I ever speak a word with any of the tribal leaders of Israel, whom I commanded to shepherd my people Israel, saying, 'Why have you not built me a house of cedar?' Now therefore you shall say to my servant David: Thus says the LORD of hosts: I took you from the pasture, from following the sheep to be prince over my people Israel; and I have been with you wherever you went, and have cut off all your enemies from before you; and I will make for you a great name, like the name of the great ones of the earth. And I will appoint a place for my people Israel and will plant them, so that they may live in their own place, and be disturbed no more; and evildoers shall afflict them no more, as formerly, from the time that I appointed judges over my people Israel; and I will give you rest from all your enemies. Moreover the Lord declares to you, David, that the Lord will make you a house.

Your house and your kingdom shall be made sure for ever before me; your throne shall be established for ever.

CANTICLE OR PSALM

Either   Luke 1.46b–55

℞ **My spirit rejoices in God my Saviour.**

My soul proclaims the greatness of the Lord;
My spirit rejoices in God my Saviour.
For he has looked with favour on his lowly servant,
from this day all generations will call me blessèd.
The Almighty has done great things for me,
and holy is his name. ℞

He has mercy on those who fear him
in every generation.
He has shown the strength of his arm,
he has scattered the proud in their conceit. ℞

He has cast down the mighty from their thrones
and has lifted up the lowly.
He has filled the hungry with good things
and the rich he has sent away empty. ℞

He has come to the help of his servant, Israel,
for he has remembered his promise of mercy.
The promise he made to our forebears:
to Abraham and his children for ever. ℞

Or   **Psalm 89.1–4, 19–26**

℞ **Your love, O Lord, for ever will I sing.**

Your love, O Lord, for ever will I sing;
from age to age my mouth will proclaim your faithfulness.
For I am persuaded that your love is established for ever;
you have set your faithfulness firmly in the heavens. ℞

'I have made a covenant with my chosen one;
I have sworn an oath to David my servant:
"I will establish your line for ever,
and preserve your throne for all generations."' ℞

You spoke once in a vision
and said to your faithful people:
'I have set the crown upon a warrior
and have exalted one chosen out of the people.
I have found David my servant;
with my holy oil have I anointed him. ℞

My hand will hold him fast
and my arm will make him strong.
No enemy shall deceive him,
nor the wicked bring him down.
I will crush his foes before him
and strike down those who hate him. ℞

My faithfulness and love shall be with him,
and he shall be victorious through my name.
I shall make his dominion extend
from the Great Sea to the River.
He will say to me, "You are my Father,
my God and the rock of my salvation."' ℞

SECOND READING   **Romans 16.25–27**

A reading from the letter of Paul to the Romans.

To God who is able to strengthen you according to my gospel and the
proclamation of Jesus Christ, according to the revelation of the mystery that
was kept secret for long ages but is now disclosed, and through the prophetic

writings is made known to all the Gentiles, according to the command of the
eternal God, to bring about the obedience of faith – to the only wise God,
through Jesus Christ, to whom be the glory for ever! Amen.

GOSPEL Luke 1.26–38

Hear the gospel of our Lord Jesus Christ according to Luke.

In the sixth month the angel Gabriel was sent by God to a town in Galilee
called Nazareth, to a virgin engaged to a man whose name was Joseph, of the
house of David. The virgin's name was Mary. And he came to her and said,
'Greetings, favoured one! The Lord is with you.' But she was much perplexed
by his words and pondered what sort of greeting this might be. The angel
said to her, 'Do not be afraid, Mary, for you have found favour with God. And
now, you will conceive in your womb and bear a son, and you will name him
Jesus. He will be great, and will be called the Son of the Most High, and the
Lord God will give to him the throne of his ancestor David. He will reign
over the house of Jacob for ever, and of his kingdom there will be no end.'
Mary said to the angel, 'How can this be, since I am a virgin?' The angel said
to her, 'The Holy Spirit will come upon you, and the power of the Most High
will overshadow you; therefore the child to be born will be holy; he will be
called Son of God. And now, your relative Elizabeth in her old age has also
conceived a son; and this is the sixth month for her who was said to be
barren. For nothing will be impossible with God.' Then Mary said, 'Here am I,
the servant of the Lord; let it be with me according to your word.' Then the
angel departed from her.

CHRISTMAS DAY

25 December

Any of the sets of readings on pages 11–20 may be used on the evening of Christmas Eve and on Christmas Day. Set III should be used at some service during the celebration.

CHRISTMAS, SETS I, II, III   YEARS A B C

For texts see Year A, pages 11–14, 14–17, 17–20.

CHRISTMAS 1   YEAR B

The Church of England provides a different Gospel from the Revised Common Lectionary.

FIRST READING   ISAIAH 61.10 – 62.3

A reading from the book of the prophet Isaiah.

I will greatly rejoice in the LORD,
my whole being shall exult in my God;
for he has clothed me with the garments of salvation,
he has covered me with the robe of righteousness,
as a bridegroom decks himself with a garland,
and as a bride adorns herself with her jewels.
For as the earth brings forth its shoots,
and as a garden causes what is sown in it to spring up,
so the Lord GOD will cause righteousness and praise
to spring up before all the nations.

For Zion's sake I will not keep silent,
and for Jerusalem's sake I will not rest,
until her vindication shines out like the dawn,
and her salvation like a burning torch.
The nations shall see your vindication,
and all the kings your glory;
and you shall be called by a new name
that the mouth of the LORD will give.
You shall be a crown of beauty in the hand of the LORD,
and a royal diadem in the hand of your God.

PSALM

℟ **Praise, O praise the name of the Lord.**

Alleluia!
Praise the Lord from the heavens;
praise him in the heights.
Praise him, all you angels of his;
praise him, all his host.
Praise him, sun and moon;
praise him, all you shining stars. ℟

Praise him, heaven of heavens,
and you waters above the heavens.
Let them praise the name of the Lord;
for he commanded and they were created.
He made them stand fast for ever and ever;
he gave them a law which shall not pass away. ℟

Praise the Lord from the earth,
you sea-monsters and all deeps;
Fire and hail, snow and fog,
tempestuous wind, doing his will;
Mountains and all hills,
fruit trees and all cedars; ℟

Wild beasts and all cattle,
creeping things and winged birds;
Kings of the earth and all peoples,
princes and all rulers of the world;
Young men and maidens,
old and young together. ℟

Let them praise the name of the Lord,
for his name only is exalted,
his splendour is over earth and heaven.
He has raised up strength for his people
and praise for all his loyal servants,
the children of Israel, a people who are near him.
Alleluia! ℟

SECOND READING   Galatians 4.4–7

A reading from the letter of Paul to the Galatians.

When the fullness of time had come, God sent his Son, born of a woman, born under the law, in order to redeem those who were under the law, so that we might receive adoption as children.

And because you are children, God has sent the Spirit of his Son into our hearts, crying, 'Abba! Father!' So you are no longer a slave but a child, and if a child then also an heir, through God.

GOSPEL

Either (Revised Common Lectionary)   Luke 2.22–40

Hear the gospel of our Lord Jesus Christ according to Luke.

When the time came for their purification according to the law of Moses, Mary and Joseph brought Jesus up to Jerusalem to present him to the Lord (as it is written in the law of the Lord, 'Every firstborn male shall be designated as holy to the Lord'), and they offered a sacrifice according to what is stated in the law of the Lord, 'a pair of turtle-doves or two young pigeons.'

Now there was a man in Jerusalem whose name was Simeon; this man was righteous and devout, looking forward to the consolation of Israel, and the Holy Spirit rested on him. It had been revealed to him by the Holy Spirit that he would not see death before he had seen the Lord's Messiah. Guided by the Spirit, Simeon came into the temple; and when the parents brought in the child Jesus, to do for him what was customary under the law, Simeon took him in his arms and praised God, saying,
'Master, now you are dismissing your servant in peace,
according to your word;
for my eyes have seen your salvation,
which you have prepared in the presence of all peoples,
a light for revelation to the Gentiles
and for glory to your people Israel.'

And the child's father and mother were amazed at what was being said about him. Then Simeon blessed them and said to his mother Mary, 'This child is destined for the falling and the rising of many in Israel, and to be a sign that will be opposed so that the inner thoughts of many will be revealed – and a sword will pierce your own soul too.'

There was also a prophet, Anna the daughter of Phanuel, of the tribe of Asher. She was of a great age, having lived with her husband seven years after her marriage, then as a widow to the age of eighty-four. She never left the temple but worshipped there with fasting and prayer night and day. At that moment she came, and began to praise God and to speak about the child to all who were looking for the redemption of Jerusalem.

When they had finished everything required by the law of the Lord, they returned to Galilee, to their own town of Nazareth. The child grew and became strong, filled with wisdom; and the favour of God was upon him.

† Or   **Luke 2.15–21**

Hear the gospel of our Lord Jesus Christ according to Luke.

When the angels had left them and gone into heaven, the shepherds said to one another, 'Let us go now to Bethlehem and see this thing that has taken place, which the Lord has made known to us.' So they went with haste and found Mary and Joseph, and the child lying in the manger. When they saw this, they made known what had been told them about this child; and all who heard it were amazed at what the shepherds told them. But Mary treasured all these words and pondered them in her heart. The shepherds returned, glorifying and praising God for all they had heard and seen, as it had been told them.

After eight days had passed, it was time to circumcise the child; and he was called Jesus, the name given by the angel before he was conceived in the womb.

CHRISTMAS 2   YEARS A B C

For text see Year A, pages 23–27.

EPIPHANY OF THE LORD   YEARS A B C

6 January

For text see Year A, pages 28–30.

BAPTISM OF CHRIST   YEAR B

FIRST READING   Genesis 1.1–5

A reading from the book of Genesis.

In the beginning when God created the heavens and the earth, the earth was a formless void and darkness covered the face of the deep, while a wind from God swept over the face of the waters. Then God said, 'Let there be light'; and there was light. And God saw that the light was good; and God separated the light from the darkness. God called the light Day, and the darkness he called Night. And there was evening and there was morning, the first day.

PSALM   Psalm 29

℟ **The voice of the Lord is upon the waters;**
  [the God of glory thunders].

Ascribe to the Lord, you gods,
ascribe to the Lord glory and strength.
Ascribe to the Lord the glory due to his name;
worship the Lord in the beauty of holiness. ℟

The voice of the Lord is upon the waters;
the God of glory thunders;
the Lord is upon the mighty waters.
The voice of the Lord is a powerful voice;
the voice of the Lord is a voice of splendour. ℟

The voice of the Lord breaks the cedar trees;
the Lord breaks the cedars of Lebanon;
He makes Lebanon skip like a calf,
and Mount Hermon like a young wild ox. ℟

The voice of the Lord splits the flames of fire;
the voice of the Lord shakes the wilderness;
the Lord shakes the wilderness of Kadesh.
The voice of the Lord makes the oak trees writhe
and strips the forests bare.
And in the temple of the Lord
all are crying, 'Glory!' ℟

The Lord sits enthroned above the flood;
the Lord sits enthroned as king for evermore.
The Lord shall give strength to his people;
the Lord shall give his people the blessing of peace. ℟

SECOND READING   Acts 19.1–7

A reading from the Acts of the Apostles.

While Apollos was in Corinth, Paul passed through the in land regions and came to Ephesus, where he found some disciples. He said to them, 'Did you receive the Holy Spirit when you became believers?' They replied, 'No, we have not even heard that there is a Holy Spirit.' Then he said, 'Into what then were you baptized?' They answered, 'Into John's baptism.' Paul said, 'John baptized with the baptism of repentance, telling the people to believe in the one who was to come after him, that is, in Jesus.' On hearing this, they were baptized in the name of the Lord Jesus. When Paul had laid his hands on them, the Holy Spirit came upon them, and they spoke in tongues and prophesied – altogether there were about twelve of them.

GOSPEL   Mark 1.4–11

Hear the gospel of our Lord Jesus Christ according to Mark.

John the baptizer appeared in the wilderness, proclaiming a baptism of repentance for the forgiveness of sins. And people from the whole Judean countryside and all the people of Jerusalem were going out to him, and were baptized by him in the river Jordan, confessing their sins. Now John was clothed with camel's hair, with a leather belt around his waist, and he ate locusts and wild honey. He proclaimed, 'The one who is more powerful than I is coming after me; I am not worthy to stoop down and untie the thong of his sandals. I have baptized you with water; but he will baptize you with the Holy Spirit.'

In those days Jesus came from Nazareth of Galilee and was baptized by John in the Jordan. And just as he was coming up out of the water, he saw the heavens torn apart and the Spirit descending like a dove on him. And a voice came from heaven, 'You are my Son, the Beloved; with you I am well pleased.'

EPIPHANY 2   YEAR B

The Church of England provides a different Second Reading from the Revised Common Lectionary.

FIRST READING (Short or long reading)

1 Samuel 3.1-10, (11-20)

A reading from the first book of Samuel.

The boy Samuel was ministering to the LORD under Eli. The word of the LORD was rare in those days; visions were not widespread. At that time Eli, whose eyesight had begun to grow dim so that he could not see, was lying down in his room; the lamp of God had not yet gone out, and Samuel was lying down in the temple of the LORD, where the ark of God was. Then the LORD called, 'Samuel! Samuel!' and he said, 'Here I am!' and ran to Eli, and said, 'Here I am, for you called me.' But he said, 'I did not call; lie down again.' So he went and lay down. The LORD called again, 'Samuel!' Samuel got up and went to Eli, and said, 'Here I am, for you called me.' But he said, 'I did not call, my son; lie down again.' Now Samuel did not yet know the LORD, and the word of the LORD had not yet been revealed to him. The LORD called Samuel again, a third time. And he got up and went to Eli, and said, 'Here I am, for you called me.' Then Eli perceived that the LORD was calling the boy. Therefore Eli said to Samuel, 'Go, lie down; and if he calls you, you shall say, "Speak, LORD, for your servant is listening."' So Samuel went and lay down in his place.

Now the LORD came and stood there, calling as before, 'Samuel! Samuel!' And Samuel said, 'Speak, for your servant is listening.' [Then the LORD said to Samuel, 'See, I am about to do something in Israel that will make both ears of anyone who hears of it tingle. On that day I will fulfil against Eli all that I have spoken concerning his house, from beginning to end. For I have told him that I am about to punish his house for ever, for the iniquity that he knew, because his sons were blaspheming God, and he did not restrain them. Therefore I swear to the house of Eli that the iniquity of Eli's house shall not be expiated by sacrifice or offering for ever.'

Samuel lay there until morning; then he opened the doors of the house of the LORD. Samuel was afraid to tell the vision to Eli. But Eli called Samuel and said, 'Samuel, my son.' He said, 'Here I am.' Eli said, 'What was it that he told you? Do not hide it from me. May God do so to you and more also, if you hide anything from me of all that he told you.' So Samuel told him everything and hid nothing from him. Then he said, 'It is the LORD; let him do what seems good to him.'

As Samuel grew up, the LORD was with him and let none of his words fall to the ground. And all Israel from Dan to Beer-sheba knew that Samuel was a trustworthy prophet of the LORD.]

PSALM   Psalm 139.1–5, 12–17

℟ **I will thank you
because I am marvellously made.**

Lord, you have searched me out and known me;
you know my sitting down and my rising up;
you discern my thoughts from afar.
You trace my journeys and my resting-places
and are acquainted with all my ways. ℟

Indeed, there is not a word on my lips,
but you, O Lord, know it altogether.
You press upon me behind and before
and lay your hand upon me.
Such knowledge is too wonderful for me;
it is so high that I cannot attain to it. ℟

For you yourself created my inmost parts;
you knit me together in my mother's womb.
I will thank you because I am marvellously made;
your works are wonderful and I know it well. ℟

My body was not hidden from you,
while I was being made in secret
and woven in the depths of the earth.
Your eyes beheld my limbs, yet unfinished in the womb;
all of them were written in your book;
they were fashioned day by day,
when as yet there was none of them. ℟

How deep I find your thoughts, O God!
how great is the sum of them!
If I were to count them,
they would be more in number than the sand;
to count them all,
my life span would need to be like yours. ℞

SECOND READING

Either (Revised Common Lectionary)   1 Corinthians 6.12–20

A reading from the first letter of Paul to the Corinthians.

Brothers and sisters,'All things are lawful for me,' but not all things are beneficial. 'All things are lawful for me,' but I will not be dominated by anything. 'Food is meant for the stomach and the stomach for food,' and God will destroy both one and the other. The body is meant not for fornication but for the Lord, and the Lord for the body. And God raised the Lord and will also raise us by his power. Do you not know that your bodies are members of Christ? Should I therefore take the members of Christ and make them members of a prostitute? Never! Do you not know that whoever is united to a prostitute becomes one body with her? For it is said, 'The two shall be one flesh.' But anyone united to the Lord becomes one spirit with him. Shun fornication! Every sin that a person commits is outside the body; but the fornicator sins against the body itself. Or do you not know that your body is a temple of the Holy Spirit within you, which you have from God, and that you are not your own? For you were bought with a price; therefore glorify God in your body.

† Or   Revelation 5.1–10

I saw in the right hand of the one seated on the throne a scroll written on the inside and on the back, sealed with seven seals; and I saw a mighty angel proclaiming with a loud voice, 'Who is worthy to open the scroll and break its seals?' And no one in heaven or on earth or under the earth was able to open the scroll or to look into it. And I began to weep bitterly because no one was found worthy to open the scroll or to look into it. Then one of the elders said to me, 'Do not weep. See, the Lion of the tribe of Judah, the Root of David, has conquered, so that he can open the scroll and its seven seals.'

Then I saw between the throne and the four living creatures and among the elders a Lamb standing as if it had been slaughtered, having seven horns and seven eyes, which are the seven spirits of God sent out into all the earth. He went and took the scroll from the right hand of the one who was seated on the throne. When he had taken the scroll, the four living creatures and the twenty-four elders fell before the Lamb, each holding a harp and golden bowls full of incense, which are the prayers of the saints. They sing a new song: 'You are worthy to take the scroll and to open its seals, for you were slaughtered and by your blood you ransomed for God saints from every tribe and language and people and nation; you have made them to be a kingdom and priests serving our God, and they will reign on earth.'

GOSPEL   John 1.43–51

Hear the gospel of our Lord Jesus Christ according to John.

The next day Jesus decided to go to Galilee. He found Philip and said to him, 'Follow me.' Now Philip was from Bethsaida, the city of Andrew and Peter. Philip found Nathanael and said to him, 'We have found him about whom Moses in the law and also the prophets wrote, Jesus son of Joseph from Nazareth.' Nathanael said to him, 'Can anything good come out of Nazareth?' Philip said to him, 'Come and see.' When Jesus saw Nathanael coming toward him, he said of him, 'Here is truly an Israelite in whom there is no deceit!' Nathanael asked him, 'Where did you come to know me?' Jesus answered, 'I saw you under the fig tree before Philip called you.' Nathanael replied, 'Rabbi, you are the Son of God! You are the King of Israel!' Jesus answered, 'Do you believe because I told you that I saw you under the fig tree? You will see greater things than these.' And he said to him, 'Very truly, I tell you, you will see heaven opened and the angels of God ascending and descending upon the Son of Man.'

EPIPHANY 3   YEAR B

The Revised Common Lectionary and the Church of England make different provision for today. For Church of England provision see page 328–330.

REVISED COMMON LECTIONARY

FIRST READING   Jonah 3.1–5, 10

A reading from the book of Jonah.

The word of the LORD came to Jonah, saying, 'Get up, go to Nineveh, that great city, and proclaim to it the message that I tell you.' So Jonah set out and went to Nineveh, according to the word of the LORD. Now Nineveh was an exceedingly large city, a three days' walk across. Jonah began to go into the city, going a day's walk. And he cried out, 'Forty days more, and Nineveh shall be overthrown!' And the people of Nineveh believed God; they proclaimed a fast, and everyone, great and small, put on sackcloth.

When God saw what they did, how they turned from their evil ways, God changed his mind about the calamity that he had said he would bring upon them; and he did not do it.

PSALM   Psalm 62.6–14

℞ **God alone is my rock and my salvation.**

For God alone my soul in silence waits;
truly, my hope is in him.
He alone is my rock and my salvation,
my stronghold, so that I shall not be shaken. ℞

In God is my safety and my honour;
God is my strong rock and my refuge.
Put your trust in him always, O people,
pour out your hearts before him, for God is our refuge. ℞

Those of high degree are but a fleeting breath,
even those of low estate cannot be trusted.
On the scales they are lighter than a breath,
all of them together.
Put no trust in extortion;
in robbery take no empty pride;
though wealth increase, set not your heart upon it. ℞

God has spoken once, twice have I heard it,
that power belongs to God.
Steadfast love is yours, O Lord,
for you repay everyone according to his deeds. ℞

SECOND READING   1 Corinthians 7.29–31

A reading from the first letter of Paul to the Corinthians.

Brothers and sisters, the appointed time has grown short; from now on, let even those who have wives be as though they had none, and those who mourn as though they were not mourning, and those who rejoice as though they were not rejoicing, and those who buy as though they had no possessions, and those who deal with the world as though they had no dealings with it. For the present form of this world is passing away.

GOSPEL   Mark 1.14–20

Hear the gospel of our Lord Jesus Christ according to Mark.

After John was arrested, Jesus came to Galilee, proclaiming the good news of God, and saying, 'The time is fulfilled, and the kingdom of God has come near; repent, and believe in the good news.'

As Jesus passed along the Sea of Galilee, he saw Simon and his brother Andrew casting a net into the lake – for they were fishermen. And Jesus said to them, 'Follow me and I will make you fish for people.' And immediately they left their nets and followed him. As he went a little farther, he saw James son of Zebedee and his brother John, who were in their boat mending the nets. Immediately he called them; and they left their father Zebedee in the boat with the hired men, and followed him.

Or

† CHURCH OF ENGLAND

FIRST READING   Genesis 14.17–20

A reading from the book of Genesis.

After Abram's return from the defeat of Chedorlaomer and the kings who were with him, the king of Sodom went out to meet him at the Valley of

Shaveh (that is, the King's Valley). And King Melchizedek of Salem brought out bread and wine; he was priest of God Most High.
He blessed him and said,
'Blessed be Abram by God Most High, maker of heaven and earth;
and blessed be God Most High,
who has delivered your enemies into your hand!'
And Abram gave him one-tenth of everything.

PSALM   Psalm 128

℞ **Whoever fears the Lord**
    shall indeed be blessed.

Happy are they all who fear the Lord,
and who follow in his ways!
You shall eat the fruit of your labour;
happiness and prosperity shall be yours. ℞

Your wife shall be like a fruitful vine
within your house,
your children like olive shoots round about your table.
Whoever fears the Lord
shall thus indeed be blessed. ℞

The Lord bless you from Zion,
and may you see the prosperity of Jersualem
all the days of our life.
May you live to see your children's children;
may peace be upon Israel. ℞

SECOND READING   Revelation 19.6–10

A reading from the book of Revelation.

I heard what seemed to be the voice of a great multitude, like the sound of many waters and like the sound of mighty thunder-peals, crying out,
'Hallelujah! For the Lord our God the Almighty reigns.
Let us rejoice and exult and give him the glory,
for the marriage of the Lamb has come,
and his bride has made herself ready;
to her it has been granted to be clothed with fine linen, bright and pure' –
for the fine linen is the righteous deeds of the saints.

And the angel said to me, 'Write this: Blessed are those who are invited to the marriage supper of the Lamb.' And he said to me, 'These are true words of God.' Then I fell down at his feet to worship him, but he said to me, 'You must not do that! I am a fellow-servant with you and your comrades who hold the testimony of Jesus. Worship God! For the testimony of Jesus is the spirit of prophecy.'

GOSPEL   John 2.1–11

Hear the gospel of our Lord Jesus Christ according to John.

There was a wedding in Cana of Galilee, and the mother of Jesus was there. Jesus and his disciples had also been invited to the wedding. When the wine gave out, the mother of Jesus said to him, 'They have no wine.' And Jesus said to her, 'Woman, what concern is that to you and to me? My hour has not yet come.' His mother said to the servants, 'Do whatever he tells you.' Now standing there were six stone water-jars for the Jewish rites of purification, each holding twenty or thirty gallons. Jesus said to them, 'Fill the jars with water.' And they filled them up to the brim. He said to them, 'Now draw some out, and take it to the chief steward.' So they took it. When the steward tasted the water that had become wine, and did not know where it came from (though the servants who had drawn the water knew), the steward called the bridegroom and said to him, 'Everyone serves the good wine first, and then the inferior wine after the guests have become drunk. But you have kept the good wine until now.' Jesus did this, the first of his signs, in Cana of Galilee, and revealed his glory; and his disciples believed in him.

EPIPHANY 4   YEAR B

The Church of England provides a different Second Reading from the Revised Common Lectionary.

FIRST READING   Deuteronomy 18.15–20

A reading from the book of Deuteronomy.

Moses spoke to the people; he said: The LORD your God will raise up for you a prophet like me from among your own people; you shall heed such a prophet. This is what you requested of the LORD your God at Horeb on the day of the assembly when you said: 'If I hear the voice of the LORD my God any more, or ever again see this great fire, I will die.' Then the LORD replied to me: 'They are right in what they have said. I will raise up for them a prophet like you from among their own people; I will put my words in the mouth of the prophet, who shall speak to them everything that I command. Anyone who does not heed the words that the prophet shall speak in my name, I myself will hold accountable. But any prophet who speaks in the name of other gods, or who presumes to speak in my name a word that I have not commanded the prophet to speak – that prophet shall die.'

PSALM **Psalm 111**

℟ **Great are the deeds of the Lord!**
   [They are studied by all who delight in them.]

Alleluia!
I will give thanks to the Lord with my whole heart,
in the assembly of the upright, in the congregation.
Great are the deeds of the Lord!
they are studied by all who delight in them.
His work is full of majesty and splendour,
and his righteousness endures for ever. ℟

He makes his marvellous works to be remembered;
the Lord is gracious and full of compassion.
He gives food to those who fear him;
he is ever mindful of his covenant.
He has shown his people the power of his works
in giving them the lands of the nations. ℟

The works of his hands are faithfulness and justice;
all his commandments are sure.
They stand fast for ever and ever,
because they are done in truth and equity. ℟

He sent redemption to his people;
he commanded his covenant for ever;
holy and awesome is his name.
The fear of the Lord is the beginning of wisdom;
those who act accordingly have a good understanding;
his praise endures for ever. ℟

SECOND READING

Either (Revised Common Lectionary)   1 Corinthians 8.1–13

A reading from the first letter of Paul to the Corinthians.

Concerning food sacrificed to idols: we know that 'all of us possess knowledge.' Knowledge puffs up, but love builds up. Anyone who claims to know something does not yet have the necessary knowledge; but anyone who loves God is known by him.

Hence, as to the eating of food offered to idols, we know that 'no idol in the world really exists,' and that 'there is no God but one.' Indeed, even though there may be so-called gods in heaven or on earth – as in fact there are many gods and many lords – yet for us there is one God, the Father, from whom are all things and for whom we exist, and one Lord, Jesus Christ, through whom are all things and through whom we exist.

It is not everyone, however, who has this knowledge. Since some have become so accustomed to idols until now, they still think of the food they eat as food offered to an idol; and their conscience, being weak, is defiled. 'Food will not bring us close to God.' We are no worse off if we do not eat, and no better off if we do. But take care that this liberty of yours does not somehow become a stumbling-block to the weak. For if others see you, who possess knowledge, eating in the temple of an idol, might they not, since their conscience is weak, be encouraged to the point of eating food sacrificed to idols? So by your knowledge those weak believers for whom Christ died are destroyed. But when you thus sin against members of your family, and wound their conscience when it is weak, you sin against Christ. Therefore, if food is a cause of their falling, I will never eat meat, so that I may not cause one of them to fall.

† Or   **Revelation 12.1–5a**

A reading from the book of Revelation.

A great portent appeared in heaven: a woman clothed with the sun, with the moon under her feet, and on her head a crown of twelve stars. She was pregnant and was crying out in birth pangs, in the agony of giving birth. Then another portent appeared in heaven: a great red dragon, with seven heads and ten horns, and seven diadems on his heads. His tail swept down a third of the stars of heaven and threw them to the earth. Then the dragon stood before the woman who was about to bear a child, so that he might devour her child as soon as it was born. And she gave birth to a son, a male child, who is to rule all the nations with a rod of iron.

GOSPEL   **Mark 1.21–28**

Hear the gospel of our Lord Jesus Christ according to Mark.

The disciples went to Capernaum; and when the sabbath came, ~~John~~ Jesus entered the synagogue and taught. They were astounded at his teaching, for he taught them as one having authority, and not as the scribes. Just then there was in their synagogue a man with an unclean spirit, and he cried out, 'What have you to do with us, Jesus of Nazareth? Have you come to destroy us? I know who you are, the Holy One of God.' But Jesus rebuked him, saying, 'Be silent, and come out of him!' And the unclean spirit, throwing him into convulsions and crying with a loud voice, came out of him. They were all amazed, and they kept on asking one another, 'What is this? A new teaching – with authority! He commands even the unclean spirits, and they obey him.' At once his fame began to spread throughout the surrounding region of Galilee.

THE PRESENTATION OF CHRIST YEARS A B C

2 February

For text see Year A, pages 44–48.

ORDINARY TIME

*In the weeks between now and Lent the Revised Common Lectionary designates Sundays
'Sundays after Epiphany', The Church of England provision designates them
'Sundays before Lent' with readings according to calendar date.*

EPIPHANY 5 YEAR B
SUNDAY BETWEEN 3 AND 9 FEBRUARY
(if earlier than 2 before Lent)

FIRST READING Isaiah 40.21–31

A reading from the book of the prophet Isaiah.

Have you not known?
Have you not heard?
Has it not been told you from the beginning?
Have you not understood from the foundations of the earth?
It is he who sits above the circle of the earth,
and its inhabitants are like grasshoppers;
who stretches out the heavens like a curtain,
and spreads them like a tent to live in;
who brings princes to naught,
and makes the rulers of the earth as nothing.

Scarcely are they planted, scarcely sown,
scarcely has their stem taken root in the earth,
when he blows upon them,
and they wither, and the tempest carries them off like stubble.

To whom then will you compare me,
or who is my equal? says the Holy One.
Lift up your eyes on high and see:
Who created these?
He who brings out their host and numbers them,
calling them all by name;

because he is great in strength, mighty in power,
not one is missing.

Why do you say,
O Jacob, and speak,
O Israel, 'My way is hidden from the LORD,
and my right is disregarded by my God'?
Have you not known?
Have you not heard?
The LORD is the everlasting God,
the Creator of the ends of the earth.
He does not faint or grow weary;
his understanding is unsearchable.
He gives power to the faint,
and strengthens the powerless.
Even youths will faint and be weary,
and the young will fall exhausted;
but those who wait for the LORD shall renew their strength,
they shall mount up with wings like eagles,
they shall run and not be weary,
they shall walk and not faint.

PSALM   **Psalm 147.1–12, 20c**

℞ **Sing praises to our God,**
    who heals the brokenhearted.
Alleluia!
How good it is to sing praises to our God!
how pleasant it is to honour him with praise!
The Lord rebuilds Jerusalem;
he gathers the exiles of Israel.
He heals the brokenhearted
and binds up their wounds.
He counts the number of the stars
and calls them all by their names. ℞

Great is our Lord and mighty in power;
there is no limit to his wisdom.
The Lord lifts up the lowly,
but casts the wicked to the ground.
Sing to the Lord with thanksgiving;
make music to our God upon the harp. ℞

He covers the heavens with clouds
and prepares rain for the earth;
He makes grass to grow upon the mountains
and green plants to serve us all.
He provides food for flocks and herds
and for the young ravens when they cry. ℞

He is not impressed by the might of a horse,
he has no pleasure in human strength;
But the Lord has pleasure in those who fear him,
in those who await his gracious favour. Alleluia! ℞

SECOND READING   1 Corinthians 9.16–23

A reading from the first letter of Paul to the Corinthians.

If I proclaim the gospel, this gives me no ground for boasting, for an obligation is laid on me, and woe to me if I do not proclaim the gospel! For if I do this of my own will, I have a reward; but if not of my own will, I am entrusted with a commission. What then is my reward? Just this: that in my proclamation I may make the gospel free of charge, so as not to make full use of my rights in the gospel. For though I am free with respect to all, I have made myself a slave to all, so that I might win more of them.

To the Jews I became as a Jew, in order to win Jews. To those under the law I became as one under the law (though I myself am not under the law) so that I might win those under the law. To those outside the law I became as one outside the law (though I am not free from God's law but am under Christ's law) so that I might win those outside the law. To the weak I became weak, so that I might win the weak. I have become all things to all people, that I might by all means save some. I do it all for the sake of the gospel, so that I may share in its blessings.

GOSPEL   Mark 1.29–39

Hear the gospel of our Lord Jesus Christ according to Mark.

As soon as Jesus and his disciples left the synagogue, they entered the house of Simon and Andrew, with James and John. Now Simon's mother-in-law was in bed with a fever, and they told him about her at once. He came and took her by the hand and lifted her up. Then the fever left her, and she began to serve them.

That evening, at sundown, they brought to him all who were sick or possessed with demons. And the whole city was gathered around the door. And he cured many who were sick with various diseases, and cast out many demons; and he would not permit the demons to speak, because they knew him.

In the morning, while it was still very dark, he got up and went out to a deserted place, and there he prayed. And Simon and his companions hunted for him. When they found him, they said to him, 'Everyone is searching for you.' He answered, 'Let us go on to the neighbouring towns, so that I may proclaim the message there also; for that is what I came out to do.' And he went throughout Galilee, proclaiming the message in their synagogues and casting out demons.

EPIPHANY 6   YEAR B
SUNDAY BETWEEN 10 AND 16 FEBRUARY
(if earlier than 2 before Lent)

FIRST READING   2 Kings 5.1-14

A reading from the second book of Kings.

Naaman, commander of the army of the king of Aram, was a great man and in high favour with his master, because by him the LORD had given victory to Aram. The man, though a mighty warrior, suffered from leprosy. Now the Arameans on one of their raids had taken a young girl captive from the land of Israel, and she served Naaman's wife. She said to her mistress, 'If only my lord were with the prophet who is in Samaria! He would cure him of his leprosy.' So Naaman went in and told his lord just what the girl from the land of Israel had said. And the king of Aram said, 'Go then, and I will send along a letter to the king of Israel.' He went, taking with him ten talents of silver, six thousand shekels of gold, and ten sets of garments. He brought the letter to the king of Israel, which read, 'When this letter reaches you, know that I have sent to you my servant Naaman, that you may cure him of his leprosy.' When the king of Israel read the letter, he tore his clothes and said, 'Am I God, to give death or life, that this man sends word to me to cure a man of his leprosy? Just look and see how he is trying to pick a quarrel with me.'

But when Elisha the man of God heard that the king of Israel had torn his clothes, he sent a message to the king, 'Why have you torn your clothes? Let him come to me, that he may learn that there is a prophet in Israel.' So Naaman came with his horses and chariots, and halted at the entrance of

Elisha's house. Elisha sent a messenger to him, saying, 'Go, wash in the Jordan seven times, and your flesh shall be restored and you shall be clean.' But Naaman became angry and went away, saying, 'I thought that for me he would surely come out, and stand and call on the name of the LORD his God, and would wave his hand over the spot, and cure the leprosy! Are not Abana and Pharpar, the rivers of Damascus, better than all the waters of Israel? Could I not wash in them, and be clean?' He turned and went away in a rage. But his servants approached and said to him, 'Father, if the prophet had commanded you to do something difficult, would you not have done it? How much more, when all he said to you was, "Wash, and be clean"?' So he went down and immersed himself seven times in the Jordan, according to the word of the man of God; his flesh was restored like the flesh of a young boy, and he was clean.

PSALM   Psalm 30

℟   **O Lord my God, I cried out to you,**
    and you restored me to health.
    or
℟   **You have made us, Lord, as strong as the mountains.**

I will exalt you, O Lord,
because you have lifted me up
and have not let my enemies triumph over me.
O Lord my God, I cried out to you,
and you restored me to health.
You brought me up, O Lord, from the dead;
you restored my life as I was going down to the grave. ℟

Sing to the Lord, you servants of his;
give thanks for the remembrance of his holiness.
For his wrath endures but the twinkling of an eye,
his favour for a lifetime.
Weeping may spend the night,
but joy comes in the morning. ℟

While I felt secure, I said,
'I shall never be disturbed.
You, Lord, with your favour,
made me as strong as the mountains.'
Then you hid your face,
and I was filled with fear. ℟

I cried to you, O Lord;
I pleaded with the Lord, saying,
'What profit is there in my blood,
if I go down to the Pit?
will the dust praise you or declare your faithfulness?
Hear, O Lord, and have mercy upon me;
O Lord, be my helper.' ℟

You have turned my wailing into dancing;
you have put off my sack-cloth and clothed me with joy;
Therefore my heart sings to you without ceasing;
O Lord my God, I will give you thanks for ever. ℟

SECOND READING   1 Corinthians 9.24–27

A reading from the first letter of Paul to the Corinthians.

Do you not know that in a race the runners all compete, but only one
receives the prize? Run in such a way that you may win it. Athletes exercise
self-control in all things; they do it to receive a perishable garland, but we an
imperishable one. So I do not run aimlessly, nor do I box as though beating
the air; but I punish my body and enslave it, so that after proclaiming to
others I myself should not be disqualified.

GOSPEL   Mark 1.40–45

Hear the gospel of our Lord Jesus Christ according to Mark.

A leper came to Jesus begging him, and kneeling he said to him, 'If you
choose, you can make me clean.' Moved with pity, Jesus stretched out his
hand and touched him, and said to him, 'I do choose. Be made clean!'
Immediately the leprosy left him, and he was made clean. After sternly
warning him he sent him away at once, saying to him, 'See that you say
nothing to anyone; but go, show yourself to the priest, and offer for your
cleansing what Moses commanded, as a testimony to them.' But he went out
and began to proclaim it freely, and to spread the word, so that Jesus could
no longer go into a town openly, but stayed out in the country; and people
came to him from every quarter.

EPIPHANY 7
SUNDAY BETWEEN 17 AND 23 FEBRUARY
(if earlier than 2 before Lent)

YEAR B

FIRST READING

Isaiah 43.18–25

A reading from the book of the prophet Isaiah.

The Lord said:
Do not remember the former things,
or consider the things of old.
I am about to do a new thing;
now it springs forth, do you not perceive it?
I will make a way in the wilderness
and rivers in the desert.
The wild animals will honour me,
the jackals and the ostriches;
for I give water in the wilderness, rivers in the desert,
to give drink to my chosen people,
the people whom I formed for myself
so that they might declare my praise.

Yet you did not call upon me, O Jacob;
but you have been weary of me, O Israel!
You have not brought me your sheep for burnt-offerings,
or honoured me with your sacrifices.
I have not burdened you with offerings,
or wearied you with frankincense.
You have not bought me sweet cane with money,
or satisfied me with the fat of your sacrifices.
But you have burdened me with your sins;
you have wearied me with your iniquities.
I, I am He
who blots out your transgressions for my own sake,
and I will not remember your sins.

PSALM

℟ **Lord, be merciful to me:**
heal me, for I have sinned against you.

Happy are they who consider the poor and needy!
the Lord will deliver them in the time of trouble.
The Lord preserves them and keeps them alive,
so that they may be happy in the land;
he does not hand them over to the will of their enemies. ℟

The Lord sustains them on their sick-bed
and ministers to them in their illness.
I said, 'Lord, be merciful to me;
heal me, for I have sinned against you.' ℟

My enemies are saying wicked things about me:
'When will he die and his name perish?'
Even if they come to see me, they speak empty words;
their heart collects false rumours;
they go outside and spread them. ℟

All my enemies whisper together about me
and devise evil against me.
'A deadly thing', they say, 'has fastened on him;
he has taken to his bed and will never get up again.'
Even my best friend, whom I trusted,
who broke bread with me,
has lifted up his heel and turned against me. ℟

But you, O Lord, be merciful to me and raise me up,
and I shall repay them.
By this I know you are pleased with me,
that my enemy does not triumph over me.
In my integrity you hold me fast,
and shall set me before your face for ever.
Blessèd be the Lord God of Israel,
from age to age. Amen. Amen. ℟

SECOND READING   2 Corinthians 1.18–22

A reading from the second letter of Paul to the Corinthians.

As surely as God is faithful, our word to you has not been 'Yes and No.' For the Son of God, Jesus Christ, whom we proclaimed among you, Silvanus and Timothy and I, was not 'Yes and No'; but in him it is always 'Yes.' For in him every one of God's promises is a 'Yes.' For this reason it is through him that we say the 'Amen,' to the glory of God. But it is God who establishes us with you in Christ and has anointed us, by putting his seal on us and giving us his Spirit in our hearts as a first instalment.

GOSPEL   Mark 2.1–12

Hear the gospel of our Lord Jesus Christ according to Mark.

When Jesus returned to Capernaum, it was reported that he was at home. So many gathered around that there was no longer room for them, not even in front of the door; and he was speaking the word to them. Then some people came, bringing to him a paralysed man, carried by four of them. And when they could not bring him to Jesus because of the crowd, they removed the roof above him; and after having dug through it, they let down the mat on which the paralytic lay. When Jesus saw their faith, he said to the paralytic, 'Son, your sins are forgiven.' Now some of the scribes were sitting there, questioning in their hearts, 'Why does this fellow speak in this way? It is blasphemy! Who can forgive sins but God alone?' At once Jesus perceived in his spirit that they were discussing these questions among themselves; and he said to them, 'Why do you raise such questions in your hearts? Which is easier, to say to the paralytic, "Your sins are forgiven," or to say, "Stand up and take your mat and walk"? But so that you may know that the Son of Man has authority on earth to forgive sins' – he said to the paralytic – 'I say to you, stand up, take your mat and go to your home.' And he stood up, and immediately took the mat and went out before all of them; so that they were all amazed and glorified God, saying, 'We have never seen anything like this!'

EPIPHANY 8
SECOND SUNDAY BEFORE LENT

YEAR B

The Revised Common Lectionary and the Church of England make different provision for today.
For Church of England provision see pages 345–348.

REVISED COMMON LECTIONARY

FIRST READING

Hosea 2.14–20

A reading from the book of the prophet Hosea.

The LORD says this concerning Israel, his people:
I will now persuade her, and bring her into the wilderness,
and speak tenderly to her.
From there I will give her her vineyards,
and make the Valley of Achor a door of hope.
There she shall respond as in the days of her youth,
as at the time when she came out of the land of Egypt.
On that day, says the LORD, you will call me, 'My husband,' and no longer
will you call me, 'My Baal.' For I will remove the names of the Baals from her
mouth, and they shall be mentioned by name no more. I will make for you a
covenant on that day with the wild animals, the birds of the air, and the
creeping things of the ground; and I will abolish the bow, the sword, and war
from the land; and I will make you lie down in safety. And I will take you for
my wife for ever; I will take you for my wife in righteousness and in justice,
in steadfast love, and in mercy. I will take you for my wife in faithfulness;
and you shall know the LORD.

PSALM

Psalm 103.1–13, 22

℟ **Bless the Lord, O my soul!**

Bless the Lord, O my soul,
and all that is within me, bless his holy name.
Bless the Lord, O my soul,
and forget not all his benefits. ℟

He forgives all your sins
and heals all your infirmities;
He redeems your life from the grave
and crowns you with mercy and loving-kindness;
He satisfies you with good things,
and your youth is renewed like an eagle's. ℟

The Lord executes righteousness
and judgement for all who are oppressed.
He made his ways known to Moses
and his works to the children of Israel. ℟

The Lord is full of compassion and mercy,
slow to anger and of great kindness.
He will not always accuse us,
nor will he keep his anger for ever.
He has not dealt with us according to our sins,
nor rewarded us according to our wickedness. ℟

For as the heavens are high above the earth,
so is his mercy great upon those who fear him.
As far as the east is from the west,
so far has he removed our sins from us. ℟

As a father cares for his children,
so does the Lord care for those who fear him.
Bless the Lord, all you works of his,
in all places of his dominion;
bless the Lord, O my soul. ℟

SECOND READING   2 Corinthians 3.1b–6

A reading from the second letter of Paul to the Corinthians.

We do not need, as some do, letters of recommendation to you or from you,
do we? You yourselves are our letter, written on our hearts, to be known and
read by all; and you show that you are a letter of Christ, prepared by us,
written not with ink but with the Spirit of the living God, not on tablets of
stone but on tablets of human hearts.

Such is the confidence that we have through Christ towards God. Not that
we are competent of ourselves to claim anything as coming from us; our
competence is from God, who has made us competent to be ministers of a
new covenant, not of letter but of spirit; for the letter kills, but the Spirit
gives life.

GOSPEL   Mark 2.13–22

Hear the gospel of our Lord Jesus Christ according to Mark.

Jesus went out again beside the lake; the whole crowd gathered around him, and he taught them. As he was walking along, he saw Levi son of Alphaeus sitting at the tax booth, and he said to him, 'Follow me.' And he got up and followed him. And as he sat at dinner in Levi's house, many tax-collectors and sinners were also sitting with Jesus and his disciples – for there were many who followed him. When the scribes of the Pharisees saw that he was eating with sinners and tax-collectors, they said to his disciples, 'Why does he eat with tax-collectors and sinners?'

When Jesus heard this, he said to them, 'Those who are well have no need of a physician, but those who are sick; I have come to call not the righteous but sinners.'

Now John's disciples and the Pharisees were fasting; and people came and said to him, 'Why do John's disciples and the disciples of the Pharisees fast, but your disciples do not fast?' Jesus said to them, 'The wedding-guests cannot fast while the bridegroom is with them, can they? As long as they have the bridegroom with them, they cannot fast. The days will come when the bridegroom is taken away from them, and then they will fast on that day.

No one sews a piece of unshrunk cloth on an old cloak; otherwise, the patch pulls away from it, the new from the old, and a worse tear is made. And no one puts new wine into old wineskins; otherwise, the wine will burst the skins, and the wine is lost, and so are the skins; but one puts new wine into fresh wineskins.'

Or

† CHURCH OF ENGLAND

FIRST READING   Proverbs 8.1, 22–31

A reading from the book of Proverbs.

Does not wisdom call,
and does not understanding raise her voice?

The LORD created me at the beginning of his work,
the first of his acts of long ago.
Ages ago I was set up,
at the first, before the beginning of the earth.

When there were no depths I was brought forth,
when there were no springs abounding with water.
Before the mountains had been shaped,
before the hills, I was brought forth –
when he had not yet made earth and fields,
or the world's first bits of soil.
When he established the heavens, I was there,
when he drew a circle on the face of the deep,
when he made firm the skies above,
when he established the fountains of the deep,
when he assigned to the sea its limit,
so that the waters might not transgress his command,
when he marked out the foundations of the earth,
then I was beside him, like a master worker;
and I was daily his delight,
rejoicing before him always,
rejoicing in his inhabited world
and delighting in the human race.

PSALM   Psalm 104.25–37

℟ **Send forth your Spirit, O Lord,**
  and renew the face of the earth.

O Lord, how manifold are your works!
in wisdom you have made them all;
the earth is full of your creatures. ℟

Yonder is the great and wide sea
with its living things too many to number,
creatures both small and great.
There move the ships,
and there is that Leviathan,
which you have made for the sport of it. ℟

All of them look to you
to give them their food in due season.
You give it to them, they gather it;
you open your hand and they are filled with good things.
You hide your face and they are terrified;
you take away their breath
and they die and return to their dust. ℟

You send forth your Spirit and they are created;
and so you renew the face of the earth.
May the glory of the Lord endure for ever;
may the Lord rejoice in all his works.
He looks at the earth and it trembles;
he touches the mountains and they smoke. ℟

I will sing to the Lord as long as I live;
I will praise my God while I have my being.
May these words of mine please him;
I will rejoice in the Lord.
Let sinners be consumed out the earth,
and the wicked be no more.
Bless the Lord, O my soul. Alleluia! ℟

SECOND READING   Colossians 1.15–20

A reading from the letter of Paul to the Colossians.

Christ is the image of the invisible God, the firstborn of all creation; for in
him all things in heaven and on earth were created, things visible and
invisible, whether thrones or dominions or rulers or powers – all things have
been created through him and for him. He himself is before all things, and in
him all things hold together. He is the head of the body, the church; he is the
beginning, the firstborn from the dead, so that he might come to have first
place in everything. For in him all the fullness of God was pleased to dwell,
and through him God was pleased to reconcile to himself all things, whether
on earth or in heaven, by making peace through the blood of his cross.

GOSPEL   John 1.1–14

Hear the gospel of our Lord Jesus Christ according to John.

In the beginning was the Word, and the Word was with God, and the Word
was God. He was in the beginning with God. All things came into being
through him, and without him not one thing came into being. What has
come into being in him was life, and the life was the light of all people. The
light shines in the darkness, and the darkness did not overcome it.

There was a man sent from God, whose name was John. He came as a witness
to testify to the light, so that all might believe through him. He himself was
not the light, but he came to testify to the light. The true light, which
enlightens everyone, was coming into the world.

He was in the world, and the world came into being through him; yet the world did not know him. He came to what was his own, and his own people did not accept him. But to all who received him, who believed in his name, he gave power to become children of God, who were born, not of blood or of the will of the flesh or of the will of man, but of God.

And the Word became flesh and lived among us, and we have seen his glory, the glory as of a father's only son, full of grace and truth.

EPIPHANY 9   YEAR B
SUNDAY NEXT BEFORE LENT

On this Sunday the Church of England allows only one of the two options in the Revised Common Lectionary. Both provisions are given below. The Church of England provision is the first set.

FIRST READING   2 Kings 2.1–12

A reading from the second book of Kings.

When the LORD was about to take Elijah up to heaven by a whirlwind, Elijah and Elisha were on their way from Gilgal. Elijah said to Elisha, 'Stay here; for the LORD has sent me as far as Bethel.' But Elisha said, 'As the LORD lives, and as you yourself live, I will not leave you.' So they went down to Bethel. The company of prophets who were in Bethel came out to Elisha, and said to him, 'Do you know that today the LORD will take your master away from you?' And he said, 'Yes, I know; keep silent.' Elijah said to him, 'Elisha, stay here; for the LORD has sent me to Jericho.' But he said, 'As the LORD lives, and as you yourself live, I will not leave you.' So they came to Jericho.

The company of prophets who were at Jericho drew near to Elisha, and said to him, 'Do you know that today the LORD will take your master away from you?' And he answered, 'Yes, I know; be silent.' Then Elijah said to him, 'Stay here; for the LORD has sent me to the Jordan.' But he said, 'As the LORD lives, and as you yourself live, I will not leave you.' So the two of them went on. Fifty men of the company of prophets also went, and stood at some distance from them, as they both were standing by the Jordan. Then Elijah took his mantle and rolled it up, and struck the water; the water was parted to the one side and to the other, until the two of them crossed on dry ground. When they had crossed, Elijah said to Elisha, 'Tell me what I may do for you, before I am taken from you.' Elisha said, 'Please let me inherit a double share of your spirit.'

He responded, 'You have asked a hard thing; yet, if you see me as I am being taken from you, it will be granted you; if not, it will not.' As they continued walking and talking, a chariot of fire and horses of fire separated the two of them, and Elijah ascended in a whirlwind into heaven. Elisha kept watching and crying out, 'Father, father! The chariots of Israel and its horsemen!' But when he could no longer see him, he grasped his own clothes and tore them in two pieces.

PSALM   Psalm 50.1–6

℟ **Our God will come and will not keep silence.**

The Lord, the God of gods, has spoken;
he has called the earth
from the rising of the sun to its setting.
Out of Zion, perfect in its beauty,
God reveals himself in glory. ℟

Our God will come and will not keep silence;
before him there is a consuming flame,
and round about him a raging storm.
He calls the heavens and the earth from above
to witness the judgement of his people. ℟

'Gather before me my loyal followers,
those who have made a covenant with me
and sealed it with sacrifice.'
Let the heavens declare the rightness of his cause;
for God himself is judge. ℟

SECOND READING   2 Corinthians 4.3–6

A reading from the second letter of Paul to the Corinthians.

Even if our gospel is veiled, it is veiled to those who are perishing. In their case the god of this world has blinded the minds of the unbelievers, to keep them from seeing the light of the gospel of the glory of Christ, who is the image of God. For we do not proclaim ourselves; we proclaim Jesus Christ as Lord and ourselves as your slaves for Jesus' sake. For it is the God who said, 'Let light shine out of darkness,' who has shone in our hearts to give the light of the knowledge of the glory of God in the face of Jesus Christ.

GOSPEL   Mark 9.2-9

Hear the gospel of our Lord Jesus Christ according to Mark.

Jesus took with him Peter and James and John, and led them up a high mountain apart, by themselves. And he was transfigured before them, and his clothes became dazzling white, such as no one on earth could bleach them. And there appeared to them Elijah with Moses, who were talking with Jesus. Then Peter said to Jesus, 'Rabbi, it is good for us to be here; let us make three dwellings, one for you, one for Moses, and one for Elijah.' He did not know what to say, for they were terrified. Then a cloud overshadowed them, and from the cloud there came a voice, 'This is my Son, the Beloved; listen to him!' Suddenly when they looked around, they saw no one with them any more, but only Jesus.

As they were coming down the mountain, he ordered them to tell no one about what they had seen, until after the Son of Man had risen from the dead.

Or

REVISED COMMON LECTIONARY ONLY

FIRST READING   Deuteronomy 5.12-15

A reading from the book of Deuteronomy.

The LORD says this: Observe the sabbath day and keep it holy, as the LORD your God commanded you. Six days you shall labour and do all your work. But the seventh day is a sabbath to the LORD your God; you shall not do any work – you, or your son or your daughter, or your male or female slave, or your ox or your donkey, or any of your livestock, or the resident alien in your towns, so that your male and female slave may rest as well as you. Remember that you were a slave in the land of Egypt, and the LORD your God brought you out from there with a mighty hand and an outstretched arm; therefore the LORD your God commanded you to keep the sabbath day.

PSALM   Psalm 81.1-10

℟ **Sing with joy to God our strength.**

Sing with joy to God our strength
and raise a loud shout to the God of Jacob.

Raise a song and sound the timbrel,
the merry harp and the lyre.
Blow the ram's-horn at the new moon,
and at the full moon, the day of our feast. ℟

For this is a statute for Israel,
a law of the God of Jacob.
He laid it as a solemn charge upon Joseph,
when he came out of the land of Egypt. ℟

I heard an unfamiliar voice saying,
'I eased his shoulder from the burden;
his hands were set free from bearing the load.'
You called on me in trouble and I saved you;
I answered you from the secret place of thunder
and tested you at the waters of Meribah. ℟

Hear, O my people, and I will admonish you:
O Israel, if you would but listen to me!
There shall be no strange god among you;
you shall not worship a foreign god.
I am the Lord your God,
who brought you out of the land of Egypt and said,
'Open your mouth wide and I will fill it.' ℟

SECOND READING   2 Corinthians 4.5–12

A reading from the second letter of Paul to the Corinthians.

We do not proclaim ourselves; we proclaim Jesus Christ as Lord and ourselves
as your slaves for Jesus' sake. For it is the God who said, 'Let light shine out of
darkness,' who has shone in our hearts to give the light of the knowledge of
the glory of God in the face of Jesus Christ.

But we have this treasure in clay jars, so that it may be made clear that this
extraordinary power belongs to God and does not come from us. We
are afflicted in every way, but not crushed; perplexed, but not driven to despair;
persecuted, but not forsaken; struck down, but not destroyed; always carrying
in the body the death of Jesus, so that the life of Jesus may also be made
visible in our bodies. For while we live, we are always being given up to death
for Jesus' sake, so that the life of Jesus may be made visible in our mortal
flesh. So death is at work in us, but life in you.

351

GOSPEL **Mark 2.23 – 3.6**

Hear the gospel of our Lord Jesus Christ according to Mark.

One sabbath Jesus was going through the cornfields; and as they made their way his disciples began to pluck heads of grain. The Pharisees said to him, 'Look, why are they doing what is not lawful on the sabbath?' And he said to them, 'Have you never read what David did when he and his companions were hungry and in need of food? He entered the house of God, when Abiathar was high priest, and ate the bread of the Presence, which it is not lawful for any but the priests to eat, and he gave some to his companions.' Then he said to them, 'The sabbath was made for humankind, and not humankind for the sabbath; so the Son of Man is lord even of the sabbath.' Again he entered the synagogue, and a man was there who had a withered hand. They watched him to see whether he would cure him on the sabbath, so that they might accuse him. And he said to the man who had the withered hand, 'Come forward.' Then he said to them, 'Is it lawful to do good or to do harm on the sabbath, to save life or to kill?' But they were silent. He looked around at them with anger; he was grieved at their hardness of heart and said to the man, 'Stretch out your hand.' He stretched it out, and his hand was restored. The Pharisees went out and immediately conspired with the Herodians against him, how to destroy him.

ASH WEDNESDAY YEARS A B C

For text see Year A, pages 70–76.

LENT 1 YEAR B

FIRST READING Genesis 9.8–17

A reading from the book of Genesis.

God said to Noah and to his sons with him, 'As for me, I am establishing my covenant with you and your descendants after you, and with every living creature that is with you, the birds, the domestic animals, and every animal of the earth with you, as many as came out of the ark. I establish my covenant with you, that never again shall all flesh be cut off by the waters of a flood, and never again shall there be a flood to destroy the earth.' God said, 'This is the sign of the covenant that I make between me and you and every living creature that is with you, for all future generations: I have set my bow in the clouds, and it shall be a sign of the covenant between me and the earth. When I bring clouds over the earth and the bow is seen in the clouds, I will remember my covenant that is between me and you and every living creature of all flesh; and the waters shall never again become a flood to destroy all flesh. When the bow is in the clouds, I will see it and remember the everlasting covenant between God and every living creature of all flesh that is on the earth.' God said to Noah, 'This is the sign of the covenant that I have established between me and all flesh that is on the earth.'

PSALM   **Psalm 25.1–10**

℟ **Your paths, O Lord, are love and faithfulness
    [to those who keep your covenant].**

To you, O Lord, I lift up my soul;
my God, I put my trust in you;
let me not be humiliated,
nor let my enemies triumph over me.
Let none who look to you be put to shame;
let the treacherous be disappointed in their schemes. ℟

✝ Show me your ways, O Lord,
and teach me your paths.
Lead me in your truth and teach me,
for you are the God of my salvation;
in you have I trusted all the day long. ℟

Remember, O Lord, your compassion and love,
for they are from everlasting.
Remember not the sins of my youth
and my transgressions;
remember me according to your love
and for the sake of your goodness, O Lord. ℟

Gracious and upright is the Lord;
therefore he teaches sinners in his way.
He guides the humble in doing right
and teaches his way to the lowly.
All the paths of the Lord are love and faithfulness
to those who keep his covenant and his testimonies.
For your name's sake, O Lord,
forgive my sin, for it is great. ℟

SECOND READING   1 Peter 3.18–22

A reading from the first letter of Peter.

Christ also suffered for sins once for all, the righteous for the unrighteous, in order to bring you to God. He was put to death in the flesh, but made alive in the spirit, in which also he went and made a proclamation to the spirits in prison, who in former times did not obey, when God waited patiently in the days of Noah, during the building of the ark, in which a few, that is, eight persons, were saved through water. And baptism, which this prefigured, now saves you – not as a removal of dirt from the body, but as an appeal to God for a good conscience, through the resurrection of Jesus Christ, who has gone into heaven and is at the right hand of God, with angels, authorities, and powers made subject to him.

GOSPEL   Mark 1.9–15

Hear the gospel of our Lord Jesus Christ according to Mark.

In those days Jesus came from Nazareth of Galilee and was baptized by John in the Jordan. And just as he was coming up out of the water, he saw the heavens torn apart and the Spirit descending like a dove on him. And a voice came from heaven, 'You are my Son, the Beloved; with you I am well pleased.'

And the Spirit immediately drove him out into the wilderness. He was in the wilderness forty days, tempted by Satan; and he was with the wild beasts; and the angels waited on him.

Now after John was arrested, Jesus came to Galilee, proclaiming the good news of God, and saying, 'The time is fulfilled, and the kingdom of God has come near; repent, and believe in the good news.'

LENT 2   YEAR B

FIRST READING   Genesis 17.1–7, 15–16

A reading from the book of Genesis.

When Abram was ninety-nine years old, the LORD appeared to Abram, and said to him, 'I am God Almighty; walk before me, and be blameless. And I will make my covenant between me and you, and will make you exceedingly numerous.' Then Abram fell on his face; and God said to him, 'As for me, this is my covenant with you: You shall be the ancestor of a multitude of nations. No longer shall your name be Abram, but your name shall be Abraham; for I have made you the ancestor of a multitude of nations. I will make you exceedingly fruitful; and I will make nations of you, and kings shall come from you. I will establish my covenant between me and you, and your offspring after you throughout their generations, for an everlasting covenant, to be God to you and to your offspring after you.'

God said to Abraham, 'As for Sarai your wife, you shall not call her Sarai, but Sarah shall be her name. I will bless her, and moreover I will give you a son by her. I will bless her, and she shall give rise to nations; kings of peoples shall come from her.'

PSALM   Psalm 22.22–30

℟ **All the ends of the earth shall turn to you, O Lord.**

Praise the Lord, you that fear him;
stand in awe of him, O offspring of Israel;
all you of Jacob's line, give glory.
For he does not despise nor abhor
the poor in their poverty;
neither does he hide his face from them;
but when they cry to him he hears them. ℟

My praise is of him in the great assembly;
I will perform my vows
in the presence of those who worship him.
The poor shall eat and be satisfied,
and those who seek the Lord shall praise him:
'May your heart live for ever!' ℟

All the ends of the earth
shall remember and turn to the Lord,
and all the families of the nations
shall bow before him.
For kingship belongs to the Lord;
he rules over the nations. ℟

To him alone all who sleep in the earth
bow down in worship;
all who go down to the dust fall before him.
My soul shall live for him;
my descendants shall serve him;
they shall be known as the Lord's for ever.
They shall come and make known to a people yet unborn
the saving deeds that he has done. ℟

SECOND READING   Romans 4.13–25

A reading from the letter of Paul to the Romans.

The promise that he would inherit the world did not come to Abraham or to
his descendants through the law but through the righteousness of faith. If it
is the adherents of the law who are to be the heirs, faith is null and the
promise is void. For the law brings wrath; but where there is no law, neither
is there violation.

For this reason it depends on faith, in order that the promise may rest on
grace and be guaranteed to all his descendants, not only to the adherents of
the law but also to those who share the faith of Abraham (for he is the father
of all of us, as it is written, 'I have made you the father of many nations') –
Abraham believed in the presence of the God who gives life to the dead and
calls into existence the things that do not exist. Hoping against hope, he
believed that he would become 'the father of many nations,' according to
what was said, 'So numerous shall your descendants be.' He did not weaken
in faith when he considered his own body, which was already as good as
dead (for he was about a hundred years old), or when he considered the
barrenness of Sarah's womb. No distrust made him waver concerning the
promise of God, but he grew strong in his faith as he gave glory to God,
being fully convinced that God was able to do what he had promised.
Therefore his faith 'was reckoned to him as righteousness.' Now the words, 'it
was reckoned to him,' were written not for his sake alone, but for ours also. It
will be reckoned to us who believe in him who raised Jesus our Lord from the

dead, who was handed over to death for our trespasses and was raised for our justification.

GOSPEL

The Revised Common Lectionary provides alternative Gospels.
Church of England provision allows only the first of these (Mark 8.31–38).

Either   Mark 8.31–38

Hear the gospel of our Lord Jesus Christ according to Mark.

Jesus began to teach his disciples that the Son of Man must undergo great suffering, and be rejected by the elders, the chief priests, and the scribes, and be killed, and after three days rise again. He said all this quite openly. And Peter took him aside and began to rebuke him. But turning and looking at his disciples, he rebuked Peter and said, 'Get behind me, Satan! For you are setting your mind not on divine things but on human things.'

He called the crowd with his disciples, and said to them, 'If any want to become my followers, let them deny themselves and take up their cross and follow me. For those who want to save their life will lose it, and those who lose their life for my sake, and for the sake of the gospel, will save it. For what will it profit them to gain the whole world and forfeit their life? Indeed, what can they give in return for their life? Those who are ashamed of me and of my words in this adulterous and sinful generation, of them the Son of Man will also be ashamed when he comes in the glory of his Father with the holy angels.'

Or (Revised Common Lectionary only)   Mark 9.2–9

Hear the gospel of our Lord Jesus Christ according to Mark.

Jesus took with him Peter and James and John,
and led them up a high mountain apart, by themselves.
And he was transfigured before them,
and his clothes became dazzling white,
such as no one on earth could bleach them.
And there appeared to them Elijah with Moses,
who were talking with Jesus.
Then Peter said to Jesus, 'Rabbi, it is good for us to be here;
let us make three dwellings,

one for you, one for Moses, and one for Elijah.'
He did not know what to say,
for they were terrified.
Then a cloud overshadowed them,
and from the cloud there came a voice,
'This is my Son, the Beloved; listen to him!'
Suddenly when they looked around,
they saw no one with them any more, but only Jesus.

As they were coming down the mountain,
he ordered them to tell no one about what they had seen,
until after the Son of Man had risen from the dead.

LENT 3   YEAR B

FIRST READING   Exodus 20.1–17

A reading from the book of Exodus.

Then God spoke all these words: I am the LORD your God, who brought you out of the land of Egypt, out of the house of slavery; you shall have no other gods before me.

You shall not make for yourself an idol, whether in the form of anything that is in heaven above, or that is on the earth beneath, or that is in the water under the earth.
You shall not bow down to them or worship them;
for I the LORD your God am a jealous God,
punishing children for the iniquity of parents,
to the third and the fourth generation of those who reject me,
but showing steadfast love to the thousandth generation
of those who love me and keep my commandments.

You shall not make wrongful use of the name of the LORD your God,
for the LORD will not acquit anyone who misuses his name.

Remember the sabbath day, and keep it holy. Six days you shall labour and do all your work. But the seventh day is a sabbath to the LORD your God; you shall not do any work – you, your son or your daughter, your male or female slave, your livestock, or the alien resident in your towns. For in six days the LORD made heaven and earth, the sea, and all that is in them, but rested the seventh day; therefore the LORD blessed the sabbath day and consecrated it.

Honour your father and your mother, so that your days may be long in the land that the LORD your God is giving you.

You shall not murder.

You shall not commit adultery.

You shall not steal.

You shall not bear false witness against your neighbour.

You shall not covet your neighbour's house; you shall not covet your neighbour's wife, or male or female slave, or ox, or donkey, or anything that belongs to your neighbour.

PSALM   Psalm 19

℟ **You, Lord, have the words of eternal life.**
   or
℟ **The statutes of the Lord are just
   and rejoice the heart.**

The heavens declare the glory of God,
and the firmament shows his handiwork.
One day tells its tale to another,
and one night imparts knowledge to another.
Although they have no words or language,
and their voices are not heard,
Their sound has gone out into all lands,
and their message to the ends of the world. ℟

In the deep has he set a pavilion for the sun;
it comes forth like a bridegroom out of his chamber;
it rejoices like a champion to run its course.
It goes forth from the uttermost edge of the heavens
and runs about to the end of it again;
nothing is hidden from its burning heat. ℟

The law of the Lord is perfect
and revives the soul;
the testimony of the Lord is sure
and gives wisdom to the innocent.
The statutes of the Lord are just
and rejoice the heart;
the commandment of the Lord is clear
and gives light to the eyes. ℟

The fear of the Lord is clean
and endures for ever;
the judgements of the Lord are true
and righteous altogether.
More to be desired are they than gold,
more than much fine gold,
sweeter far than honey,
than honey in the comb. ℞

By them also is your servant enlightened,
and in keeping them there is great reward.
Who can tell how often he offends?
Cleanse me from my secret faults.
Above all, keep your servant from presumptuous sins;
let them not get dominion over me;
then shall I be whole and sound,
and innocent of a great offence. ℞

Let the words of my mouth and the meditation of my heart
be acceptable in your sight,
O Lord, my strength and my redeemer. ℞

SECOND READING   1 Corinthians 1.18–25

A reading from the first letter of Paul to the Corinthians.

The message about the cross is foolishness to those who are perishing, but to
us who are being saved it is the power of God.
For it is written,
'I will destroy the wisdom of the wise,
and the discernment of the discerning I will thwart.'
Where is the one who is wise? Where is the scribe? Where is the debater of
this age? Has not God made foolish the wisdom of the world? For since, in
the wisdom of God, the world did not know God through wisdom, God
decided, through the foolishness of our proclamation, to save those who
believe. For Jews demand signs and Greeks desire wisdom, but we proclaim
Christ crucified, a stumbling-block to Jews and foolishness to Gentiles, but to
those who are the called, both Jews and Greeks, Christ the power of God and
the wisdom of God. For God's foolishness is wiser than human wisdom, and
God's weakness is stronger than human strength.

GOSPEL   John 2.13–22

Hear the gospel of our Lord Jesus Christ according to John.

The Passover of the Jews was near, and Jesus went up to Jerusalem. In the temple he found people selling cattle, sheep, and doves, and the money-changers seated at their tables. Making a whip of cords, he drove all of them out of the temple, both the sheep and the cattle. He also poured out the coins of the money-changers and overturned their tables. He told those who were selling the doves, 'Take these things out of here! Stop making my Father's house a market-place!' His disciples remembered that it was written, 'Zeal for your house will consume me.' The Jews then said to him, 'What sign can you show us for doing this?' Jesus answered them, 'Destroy this temple, and in three days I will raise it up.' They then said, 'This temple has been under construction for forty-six years, and will you raise it up in three days?' But he was speaking of the temple of his body. After he was raised from the dead, his disciples remembered that he had said this; and they believed the scripture and the word that Jesus had spoken.

LENT 4   YEAR B

Provision for Lent 4 is included in the Revised Common Lectionary and the Church of England provision, but the Church of England adds alternative readings for Mothering Sunday. For text see Year A, pages 88–92.

FIRST READING   Numbers 21.4–9

A reading from the book of Numbers.

The Israelites set out by the way to the Red Sea, to go around the land of Edom; but the people became impatient on the way. The people spoke against God and against Moses, 'Why have you brought us up out of Egypt to die in the wilderness? For there is no food and no water, and we detest this miserable food.' Then the LORD sent poisonous serpents among the people, and they bit the people, so that many Israelites died. The people came to Moses and said, 'We have sinned by speaking against the LORD and against you; pray to the LORD to take away the serpents from us.' So Moses prayed for the people. And the LORD said to Moses, 'Make a poisonous serpent, and set it on a pole; and everyone who is bitten shall look at it and live.' So Moses made a serpent of bronze, and put it upon a pole; and whenever a serpent bit someone, that person would look at the serpent of bronze and live.

PSALM

Psalm 107.1–3, 17–22

℟ Give thanks to the Lord, for he is good,
     and his mercy endures for ever.

or

℟ Give thanks to the Lord for his mercy.

Give thanks to the Lord, for he is good,
and his mercy endures for ever. ℟

Let all those whom the Lord has redeemed proclaim
that he redeemed them from the hand of the foe.
He gathered them out of the lands;
from the east and from the west,
from the north and from the south. ℟

Some were fools and took to rebellious ways;
they were afflicted because of their sins.
They abhorred all manner of food
and drew near to death's door.
Then they cried to the Lord in their trouble,
and he delivered them from their distress. ℟

He sent forth his word and healed them
and saved them from the grave.
Let them give thanks to the Lord for his mercy
and the wonders he does for his children.
Let them offer a sacrifice of thanksgiving
and tell of his acts with shouts of joy. ℟

SECOND READING

Ephesians 2.1–10

A reading from the letter of Paul to the Ephesians.

You were dead through the trespasses and sins in which you once lived,
following the course of this world, following the ruler of the power of the air,
the spirit that is now at work among those who are disobedient. All of us
once lived among them in the passions of our flesh, following the desires of
flesh and senses, and we were by nature children of wrath, like everyone else.
But God, who is rich in mercy, out of the great love with which he loved us
even when we were dead through our trespasses, made us alive together with
Christ – by grace you have been saved – and raised us up with him and seated
us with him in the heavenly places in Christ Jesus, so that in the ages to
come he might show the immeasurable riches of his grace in kindness toward

us in Christ Jesus. For by grace you have been saved through faith, and this is not your own doing; it is the gift of God – not the result of works, so that no one may boast. For we are what he has made us, created in Christ Jesus for good works, which God prepared beforehand to be our way of life.

GOSPEL   John 3.14–21

Hear the gospel of our Lord Jesus Christ according to John.

Jesus said to Nicodemus: 'Just as Moses lifted up the serpent in the wilderness, so must the Son of Man be lifted up, that whoever believes in him may have eternal life.

For God so loved the world that he gave his only Son, so that everyone who believes in him may not perish but may have eternal life.

Indeed, God did not send the Son into the world to condemn the world, but in order that the world might be saved through him. Those who believe in him are not condemned; but those who do not believe are condemned already, because they have not believed in the name of the only Son of God. And this is the judgement, that the light has come into the world, and people loved darkness rather than light because their deeds were evil. For all who do evil hate the light and do not come to the light, so that their deeds may not be exposed. But those who do what is true come to the light, so that it may be clearly seen that their deeds have been done in God.'

Or

† MOTHERING SUNDAY   YEARS A B C

For text see Year A, pages 88–92.

LENT 5   YEAR B

FIRST READING   Jeremiah 31.31–34

A reading from the book of the prophet Jeremiah.

The days are surely coming, says the LORD,
when I will make a new covenant with the house of Israel and the house of Judah. It will not be like the covenant that I made with their ancestors when I took them by the hand to bring them out of the land of Egypt – a covenant that they broke, though I was their husband, says the LORD. But this is the

covenant that I will make with the house of Israel after those days, says the LORD: I will put my law within them, and I will write it on their hearts; and I will be their God, and they shall be my people. No longer shall they teach one another, or say to each other, 'Know the LORD,' for they shall all know me, from the least of them to the greatest, says the LORD; for I will forgive their iniquity, and remember their sin no more.

PSALM

Either   Psalm 51.1–12

℟ **A clean heart create in me, O God.**

Have mercy on me, O God,
according to your loving-kindness;
in your great compassion blot out my offences.
Wash me through and through from my wickedness
and cleanse me from my sin. ℟

For I know my transgressions,
and my sin is ever before me.
Against you only have I sinned
and done what is evil in your sight.
And so you are justified when you speak
and upright in your judgement. ℟

Indeed, I have been wicked from my birth,
a sinner from my mother's womb.
For behold, you look for truth deep within me,
and will make me understand wisdom secretly. ℟

Purge me from my sin and I shall be pure;
wash me and I shall be clean indeed.
Make me hear of joy and gladness,
that the body you have broken may rejoice. ℟

Hide your face from my sins
and blot out all my iniquities.
Create in me a clean heart, O God,
and renew a right spirit within me.
Cast me not away from your presence
and take not your holy Spirit from me. ℟

Or   **Psalm 119.9–16**

℟   **O Lord, how I love your law.**

How shall the young cleanse their way?
By keeping to your words.
With my whole heart I seek you;
let me not stray from your commandments. ℟

I treasure your promise in my heart,
that I may not sin against you.
Blessèd are you, O Lord;
instruct me in your statutes. ℟

With my lips will I recite
all the judgements of your mouth.
I have taken greater delight in the way of your decrees
than in all manner of riches. ℟

I will meditate on your commandments
and give attention to your ways.
My delight is in your statutes;
I will not forget your word. ℟

SECOND READING   **Hebrews 5.5–10**

A reading from the letter to the Hebrews.

Christ did not glorify himself in becoming a high priest,
but was appointed by the one who said to him,
'You are my Son, today I have begotten you';
as he says also in another place,
'You are a priest for ever,
according to the order of Melchizedek.'
In the days of his flesh, Jesus offered up prayers and supplications, with loud
cries and tears, to the one who was able to save him from death, and he was
heard because of his reverent submission. Although he was a Son, he learned
obedience through what he suffered; and having been made perfect, he
became the source of eternal salvation for all who obey him, having been
designated by God a high priest according to the order of Melchizedek.

GOSPEL   John 12.20–33

Hear the gospel of our Lord Jesus Christ according to John.

Among those who went up to worship at the festival were some Greeks. They came to Philip, who was from Bethsaida in Galilee, and said to him, 'Sir, we wish to see Jesus.' Philip went and told Andrew; then Andrew and Philip went and told Jesus. Jesus answered them, 'The hour has come for the Son of Man to be glorified. Very truly, I tell you, unless a grain of wheat falls into the earth and dies, it remains just a single grain; but if it dies, it bears much fruit. Those who love their life lose it, and those who hate their life in this world will keep it for eternal life. Whoever serves me must follow me, and where I am, there will my servant be also. Whoever serves me, the Father will honour.

'Now my soul is troubled. And what should I say – "Father, save me from this hour"? No, it is for this reason that I have come to this hour. Father, glorify your name.' Then a voice came from heaven, 'I have glorified it, and I will glorify it again.' The crowd standing there heard it and said that it was thunder. Others said, 'An angel has spoken to him.' Jesus answered, 'This voice has come for your sake, not for mine. Now is the judgement of this world; now the ruler of this world will be driven out. And I, when I am lifted up from the earth, will draw all people to myself.' He said this to indicate the kind of death he was to die.

PALM SUNDAY (LENT 6)   YEAR B

LITURGY OF PALMS

GOSPEL

Either   Mark 11.1–11

Hear the gospel of our Lord Jesus Christ according to Mark.

When Jesus and his disciples were approaching Jerusalem, at Bethphage and Bethany, near the Mount of Olives, Jesus sent two of his disciples and said to them, 'Go into the village ahead of you, and immediately as you enter it, you will find tied there a colt that has never been ridden; untie it and bring it. If anyone says to you, "Why are you doing this?" just say this, "The Lord needs it and will send it back here immediately."' They went away and found a colt tied near a door, outside in the street. As they were untying it, some of the bystanders said to them, 'What are you doing, untying the colt?' They told them what Jesus had said; and they allowed them to take it. Then they brought the colt to Jesus and threw their cloaks on it; and he sat on it. Many people spread their cloaks on the road, and others spread leafy branches that they had cut in the fields.

Then those who went ahead and those who followed were shouting, 'Hosanna!

Blessed is the one who comes in the name of the Lord!

Blessed is the coming kingdom of our ancestor David!

Hosanna in the highest heaven!'

Then he entered Jerusalem and went into the temple; and when he had looked around at everything, as it was already late, he went out to Bethany with the twelve.

Or   **John 12.12–16**

Hear the gospel of our Lord Jesus Christ according to John.

The great crowd that had come to the festival heard that Jesus was coming to Jerusalem.

So they took branches of palm trees and went out to meet him, shouting, 'Hosanna!

Blessed is the one who comes in the name of the Lord –

the King of Israel!'

Jesus found a young donkey and sat on it; as it is written:

'Do not be afraid, daughter of Zion.

Look, your king is coming,

sitting on a donkey's colt!'

His disciples did not understand these things at first; but when Jesus was glorified, then they remembered that these things had been written of him and had been done to him.

PSALM   **Psalm 118.1–2, 19–29**

℟ **This is the day that the Lord has made;
we will rejoice and be glad in it.**

Give thanks to the Lord, for he is good;
his mercy endures for ever.
Let Israel now proclaim,
'His mercy endures for ever.' ℟

Open for me the gates of righteousness;
I will enter them; I will offer thanks to the Lord.
'This is the gate of the Lord;
whoever is righteous may enter.' ℟

I will give thanks to you, for you answered me
and have become my salvation.
The same stone which the builders rejected
has become the chief corner-stone. ℟

This is the Lord's doing,
and it is marvellous in our eyes.
On this day the Lord has acted;
we will rejoice and be glad in it. ℟

Hosanna, Lord, hosanna!
Lord, send us now success.
Blessèd is he who comes in the name of the Lord;
we bless you from the house of the Lord. ℟

God is the Lord; he has shined upon us;
form a procession with branches
up to the horns of the altar.
'You are my God and I will thank you;
you are my God and I will exalt you.'
Give thanks to the Lord, for he is good;
his mercy endures for ever. ℟

LITURGY OF THE PASSION

FIRST READING   Isaiah 50.4–9a

A reading from the book of the prophet Isaiah.

The servant of the LORD said:
The Lord GOD has given me the tongue of a teacher,
that I may know how to sustain the weary with a word.
Morning by morning he wakens –
wakens my ear to listen as those who are taught.
The Lord GOD has opened my ear,
and I was not rebellious,
I did not turn backwards.
I gave my back to those who struck me,

and my cheeks to those who pulled out the beard;
I did not hide my face
from insult and spitting.

The Lord GOD helps me;
therefore I have not been disgraced;
therefore I have set my face like flint,
and I know that I shall not be put to shame;
he who vindicates me is near.
Who will contend with me?
Let us stand up together.
Who are my adversaries?
Let them confront me.
It is the Lord GOD who helps me;
who will declare me guilty?

PSALM   Psalm 31.9–16

℟ **I have trusted in you, O Lord.**
   [I have said, 'You are my God.']
   or
℟ **My God, my God, why have you forsaken me?**

Have mercy on me, O Lord, for I am in trouble;
my eye is consumed with sorrow,
and also my throat and my belly.
For my life is wasted with grief,
and my years with sighing;
my strength fails me because of affliction,
and my bones are consumed. ℟

I have become a reproach to all my enemies
and even to my neighbours,
a dismay to those of my acquaintance;
when they see me in the street they avoid me.
I am forgotten like the dead, out of mind;
I am as useless as a broken pot. ℟

For I have heard the whispering of the crowd;
fear is all around;
they put their heads together against me;
they plot to take my life.
But as for me, I have trusted in you, O Lord.
I have said, 'You are my God. ℟

My times are in your hand;
rescue me from the hand of my enemies,
and from those who persecute me.
Make your face to shine upon your servant,
and in your loving-kindness save me.' ℟

SECOND READING   Philippians 2.5–11

A reading from the letter of Paul to the Philippians.

Let the same mind be in you that was in Christ Jesus,
who, though he was in the form of God,
did not regard equality with God
as something to be exploited,
but emptied himself,
taking the form of a slave,
being born in human likeness.
And being found in human form,
he humbled himself
and became obedient to the point of death –
even death on a cross.

Therefore God also highly exalted him
and gave him the name that is above every name,
so that at the name of Jesus every knee should bend,
in heaven and on earth and under the earth,
and every tongue should confess that Jesus Christ is Lord,
to the glory of God the Father.

PASSION (Long or short reading)
Mark 14.1 – 15.47 or Mark 15.1–39, (40–47)

Hear the passion of our Lord Jesus Christ according to Mark.

[It was two days before the Passover and the festival of Unleavened Bread.
The chief priests and the scribes were looking for a way to arrest Jesus by
stealth and kill him; for they said, 'Not during the festival, or there may be a
riot among the people.'

While he was at Bethany in the house of Simon the leper, as he sat at the
table, a woman came with an alabaster jar of very costly ointment of nard,
and she broke open the jar and poured the ointment on his head. But some

were there who said to one another in anger, 'Why was the ointment wasted in this way? For this ointment could have been sold for more than three hundred denarii, and the money given to the poor.' And they scolded her. But Jesus said, 'Let her alone; why do you trouble her? She has performed a good service for me. For you always have the poor with you, and you can show kindness to them whenever you wish; but you will not always have me. She has done what she could; she has anointed my body beforehand for its burial. Truly I tell you, wherever the good news is proclaimed in the whole world, what she has done will be told in remembrance of her.'

Then Judas Iscariot, who was one of the twelve, went to the chief priests in order to betray him to them. When they heard it, they were greatly pleased, and promised to give him money. So he began to look for an opportunity to betray him.

On the first day of Unleavened Bread, when the Passover lamb is sacrificed, his disciples said to him, 'Where do you want us to go and make the preparations for you to eat the Passover?' So he sent two of his disciples, saying to them, 'Go into the city, and a man carrying a jar of water will meet you; follow him, and wherever he enters, say to the owner of the house, "The Teacher asks, Where is my guest room where I may eat the Passover with my disciples?" He will show you a large room upstairs, furnished and ready. Make preparations for us there.' So the disciples set out and went to the city, and found everything as he had told them; and they prepared the Passover meal.

When it was evening, he came with the twelve. And when they had taken their places and were eating, Jesus said, 'Truly I tell you, one of you will betray me, one who is eating with me.' They began to be distressed and to say to him one after another, 'Surely, not I?' He said to them, 'It is one of the twelve, one who is dipping bread into the bowl with me. For the Son of Man goes as it is written of him, but woe to that one by whom the Son of Man is betrayed! It would have been better for that one not to have been born.'

While they were eating, he took a loaf of bread, and after blessing it he broke it, gave it to them, and said, 'Take; this is my body.' Then he took a cup, and after giving thanks he gave it to them, and all of them drank from it. He said to them, 'This is my blood of the covenant, which is poured out for many. Truly I tell you, I will never again drink of the fruit of the vine until that day when I drink it new in the kingdom of God.'

When they had sung the hymn, they went out to the Mount of Olives. And Jesus said to them,
'You will all become deserters; for it is written,
"I will strike the shepherd, and the sheep will be scattered."

But after I am raised up, I will go before you to Galilee.' Peter said to him, 'Even though all become deserters, I will not.' Jesus said to him, 'Truly I tell you, this day, this very night, before the cock crows twice, you will deny me three times.' But he said vehemently, 'Even though I must die with you, I will not deny you.' And all of them said the same.

They went to a place called Gethsemane; and he said to his disciples, 'Sit here while I pray.' He took with him Peter and James and John, and began to be distressed and agitated. And said to them, 'I am deeply grieved, even to death; remain here, and keep awake.' And going a little farther, he threw himself on the ground and prayed that, if it were possible, the hour might pass from him. He said, 'Abba, Father, for you all things are possible; remove this cup from me; yet, not what I want, but what you want.' He came and found them sleeping; and he said to Peter, 'Simon, are you asleep? Could you not keep awake one hour? Keep awake and pray that you may not come into the time of trial; the spirit indeed is willing, but the flesh is weak.' And again he went away and prayed, saying the same words. And once more he came and found them sleeping, for their eyes were very heavy; and they did not know what to say to him. He came a third time and said to them, 'Are you still sleeping and taking your rest? Enough! The hour has come; the Son of Man is betrayed into the hands of sinners. Get up, let us be going. See, my betrayer is at hand.'

Immediately, while he was still speaking, Judas, one of the twelve, arrived; and with him there was a crowd with swords and clubs, from the chief priests, the scribes, and the elders. Now the betrayer had given them a sign, saying, 'The one I will kiss is the man; arrest him and lead him away under guard.' So when he came, he went up to him at once and said, 'Rabbi!' and kissed him. Then they laid hands on him and arrested him. But one of those who stood near drew his sword and struck the slave of the high priest, cutting off his ear. Then Jesus said to them, 'Have you come out with swords and clubs to arrest me as though I were a bandit? Day after day I was with you in the temple teaching, and you did not arrest me. But let the scriptures be fulfilled.' All of them deserted him and fled.

A certain young man was following Jesus, wearing nothing but a linen cloth. They caught hold of him, but he left the linen cloth and ran off naked.

They took Jesus to the high priest; and all the chief priests, the elders, and the scribes were assembled. Peter had followed him at a distance, right into the courtyard of the high priest; and he was sitting with the guards, warming himself at the fire. Now the chief priests and the whole council were looking for testimony against Jesus to put him to death; but they found none. For many gave false testimony against him, and their testimony did not agree. Some stood up and gave false testimony against him, saying, 'We heard him say, "I will destroy this temple that is made with hands, and in three days I will build another, not made with hands."' But even on this point their testimony did not agree. Then the high priest stood up before them and asked Jesus, 'Have you no answer? What is it that they testify against you?' But he was silent and did not answer. Again the high priest asked him, 'Are you the Messiah, the Son of the Blessed One?' Jesus said, 'I am; and "you will see the Son of Man seated at the right hand of the Power," and "coming with the clouds of heaven."' Then the high priest tore his clothes and said, 'Why do we still need witnesses? You have heard his blasphemy! What is your decision?' All of them condemned him as deserving death. Some began to spit on him, to blindfold him, and to strike him, saying to him, 'Prophesy!' The guards also took him over and beat him.

While Peter was below in the courtyard, one of the servant-girls of the high priest came by. When she saw Peter warming himself, she stared at him and said, 'You also were with Jesus, the man from Nazareth.' But he denied it, saying, 'I do not know or understand what you are talking about.' And he went out into the forecourt. Then the cock crowed. And the servant-girl, on seeing him, began again to say to the bystanders, 'This man is one of them.' But again he denied it. Then after a little while the bystanders again said to Peter, 'Certainly you are one of them; for you are a Galilean.' But he began to curse, and he swore an oath, 'I do not know this man you are talking about.' At that moment the cock crowed for the second time. Then Peter remembered that Jesus had said to him, 'Before the cock crows twice, you will deny me three times.' And he broke down and wept.]

As soon as it was morning, the chief priests held a consultation with the elders and scribes and the whole council. They bound Jesus, led him away, and handed him over to Pilate. Pilate asked him, 'Are you the King of the Jews?' He answered him, 'You say so.' Then the chief priests accused him of many things. Pilate asked him again, 'Have you no answer? See how many charges they bring against you.' But Jesus made no further reply, so that Pilate was amazed.

Now at the festival he used to release a prisoner for them, anyone for whom they asked. Now a man called Barabbas was in prison with the rebels who had committed murder during the insurrection. So the crowd came and began to ask Pilate to do for them according to his custom. Then he answered them, 'Do you want me to release for you the King of the Jews?' For he realized that it was out of jealousy that the chief priests had handed him over. But the chief priests stirred up the crowd to have him release Barabbas for them instead. Pilate spoke to them again, 'Then what do you wish me to do with the man you call the King of the Jews?' They shouted back, 'Crucify him!' Pilate asked them, 'Why, what evil has he done?' But they shouted all the more, 'Crucify him!' So Pilate, wishing to satisfy the crowd, released Barabbas for them; and after flogging Jesus, he handed him over to be crucified.

Then the soldiers led him into the courtyard of the palace (that is, the governor's headquarters); and they called together the whole cohort. And they clothed him in a purple cloak; and after twisting some thorns into a crown, they put it on him. And they began saluting him, 'Hail, King of the Jews!' They struck his head with a reed, spat upon him, and knelt down in homage to him. After mocking him, they stripped him of the purple cloak and put his own clothes on him. Then they led him out to crucify him.

They compelled a passer-by, who was coming in from the country, to carry his cross; it was Simon of Cyrene, the father of Alexander and Rufus. Then they brought Jesus to the place called Golgotha (which means the place of a skull). And they offered him wine mixed with myrrh; but he did not take it. And they crucified him, and divided his clothes among them, casting lots to decide what each should take.

It was nine o'clock in the morning when they crucified him. The inscription of the charge against him read, 'The King of the Jews.' And with him they crucified two bandits, one on his right and one on his left. Those who passed by derided him, shaking their heads and saying, 'Aha! You who would destroy the temple and build it in three days, save yourself, and come down from the cross!' In the same way the chief priests, along with the scribes, were also mocking him among themselves and saying, 'He saved others; he cannot save himself. Let the Messiah, the King of Israel, come down from the cross now, so that we may see and believe.' Those who were crucified with him also taunted him.

When it was noon, darkness came over the whole land until three in the afternoon. At three o'clock Jesus cried out with a loud voice, 'Eloi, Eloi, lema sabachthani?' which means, 'My God, my God, why have you forsaken me?' When some of the bystanders heard it, they said, 'Listen, he is calling for Elijah.' And someone ran, filled a sponge with sour wine, put it on a stick, and gave it to him to drink, saying, 'Wait, let us see whether Elijah will come to take him down.' Then Jesus gave a loud cry and breathed his last. And the curtain of the temple was torn in two, from top to bottom. Now when the centurion, who stood facing him, saw that in this way he breathed his last, he said, 'Truly this man was God's Son!'

[There were also women looking on from a distance; among them were Mary Magdalene, and Mary the mother of James the younger and of Joses, and Salome. These used to follow him and provided for him when he was in Galilee; and there were many other women who had come up with him to Jerusalem.

When evening had come, and since it was the day of Preparation, that is, the day before the sabbath, Joseph of Arimathea, a respected member of the council, who was also himself waiting expectantly for the kingdom of God, went boldly to Pilate and asked for the body of Jesus. Then Pilate wondered if he were already dead; and summoning the centurion, he asked him whether he had been dead for some time. When he learned from the centurion that he was dead, he granted the body to Joseph. Then Joseph bought a linen cloth, and taking down the body, wrapped it in the linen cloth, and laid it in a tomb that had been hewn out of the rock. He then rolled a stone against the door of the tomb. Mary Magdalene and Mary the mother of Joses saw where the body was laid.]

MONDAY, TUESDAY AND WEDNESDAY   YEARS A B C
IN HOLY WEEK, MAUNDY THURSDAY, GOOD FRIDAY
AND EASTER EVE

For texts see Year A, pages 104–127.

EASTER VIGIL   YEARS A B C

For Old Testament readings and New Testament reading see Year A, pages 128–148.
Year B has its own Gospel.

GOSPEL   **YEAR B**   **Mark 16.1–8**

Hear the gospel of our Lord Jesus Christ according to Mark.

When the sabbath was over, Mary Magdalene, and Mary the mother of James, and Salome bought spices, so that they might go and anoint him. And very early on the first day of the week, when the sun had risen, they went to the tomb. They had been saying to one another, 'Who will roll away the stone for us from the entrance to the tomb?' When they looked up, they saw that the stone, which was very large, had already been rolled back. As they entered the tomb, they saw a young man, dressed in a white robe, sitting on the right side; and they were alarmed. But he said to them, 'Do not be alarmed; you are looking for Jesus of Nazareth, who was crucified. He has been raised; he is not here. Look, there is the place they laid him. But go, tell his disciples and Peter that he is going ahead of you to Galilee; there you will see him, just as he told you.' So they went out and fled from the tomb, for terror and amazement had seized them; and they said nothing to anyone, for they were afraid.

EASTER DAY   YEAR B

The following readings and psalms are provided for use at the principal Easter Day Service. Acts 10.34–43 should be read as either the First or Second Reading.

FIRST READING (Alternative readings)

Either   **Acts 10.34–43**

A reading from the Acts of the Apostles.

Peter began to speak to those assembled in the house of Cornelius: 'I truly understand that God shows no partiality, but in every nation anyone who fears him and does what is right is acceptable to him. You know the message he sent to the people of Israel, preaching peace by Jesus Christ – he is Lord of all. That message spread throughout Judea, beginning in Galilee after the baptism that John announced: how God anointed Jesus of Nazareth with the Holy Spirit and with power; how he went about doing good and healing all who were oppressed by the devil, for God was with him. We are witnesses to all that he did both in Judea and in Jerusalem. They put him to death by hanging him on a tree; but God raised him on the third day and allowed him to appear, not to all the people but to us who were chosen by God as witnesses, and who ate and drank with him after he rose from the dead. He commanded us to preach to the people and to testify that he is the one ordained by God as judge of the living and the dead. All the prophets testify about him that everyone who believes in him receives forgiveness of sins through his name.'

Or   Isaiah 25.6–9

A reading from the book of the prophet Isaiah.

On this mountain
the LORD of hosts will make for all peoples a feast of rich food,
a feast of well-matured wines, of rich food filled with marrow,
of well-matured wines strained clear.
And he will destroy on this mountain
the shroud that is cast over all peoples,
the sheet that is spread over all nations;
he will swallow up death for ever.
Then the Lord GOD will wipe away the tears from all faces,
and the disgrace of his people he will take away from all the earth,
for the LORD has spoken.
It will be said on that day,
Lo, this is our God;
we have waited for him,
so that he might save us.
This is the LORD for whom we have waited;
let us be glad and rejoice in his salvation.

PSALM   Psalm 118.1–2, 14–24

℟ **This is the day that the Lord has made;
we will rejoice and be glad in it.**

Give thanks to the Lord, for he is good;
his mercy endures for ever.
Let Israel now proclaim,
'His mercy endures for ever.' ℟

The Lord is my strength and my song,
and he has become my salvation.
There is a sound of exultation and victory
in the tents of the righteous:
'The right hand of the Lord has triumphed!
the right hand of the Lord is exalted!
the right hand of the Lord has triumphed!' ℟

I shall not die, but live,
and declare the works of the Lord.
The Lord has punished me sorely,
but he did not hand me over to death.
Open for me the gates of righteousness;
I will enter them; I will offer thanks to the Lord. ℟

'This is the gate of the Lord;
whoever is righteous may enter.'
I will give thanks to you, for you answered me
and have become my salvation.
The same stone which the builders rejected
has become the chief corner-stone. ℟

This is the Lord's doing,
and it is marvellous in our eyes.
On this day the Lord has acted;
we will rejoice and be glad in it. ℟

SECOND READING (Alternative readings)

Either   **1 Corinthians 15.1–11**

A reading from the first letter of Paul to the Corinthians.

I would remind you, brothers and sisters, of the good news that I proclaimed
to you, which you in turn received, in which also you stand, through which
also you are being saved, if you hold firmly to the message that I proclaimed
to you – unless you have come to believe in vain. For I handed on to you as
of first importance what I in turn had received: that Christ died for our sins
in accordance with the scriptures,

and that he was buried, and that he was raised on the third day in
accordance with the scriptures, and that he appeared to Cephas, then to the
twelve. Then he appeared to more than five hundred brothers and sisters at
one time, most of whom are still alive, though some have died. Then he
appeared to James, then to all the apostles. Last of all, as to one untimely
born, he appeared also to me. For I am the least of the apostles, unfit to be
called an apostle, because I persecuted the church of God. But by the grace of
God I am what I am, and his grace towards me has not been in vain. On the
contrary, I worked harder than any of them – though it was not I, but the
grace of God that is with me. Whether then it was I or they, so we proclaim
and so you have come to believe.

Or   **Acts 10.34–43**

A reading from the Acts of the Apostles.

For text see page 376.

GOSPEL (Alternative readings)

Either   **John 20.1–18**

Hear the gospel of our Lord Jesus Christ according to John.

Early on the first day of the week, while it was still dark, Mary Magdalene came to the tomb and saw that the stone had been removed from the tomb. So she ran and went to Simon Peter and the other disciple, the one whom Jesus loved, and said to them, 'They have taken the Lord out of the tomb, and we do not know where they have laid him.' Then Peter and the other disciple set out and went towards the tomb. The two were running together, but the other disciple outran Peter and reached the tomb first. He bent down to look in and saw the linen wrappings lying there, but he did not go in. Then Simon Peter came, following him, and went into the tomb. He saw the linen wrappings lying there, and the cloth that had been on Jesus' head, not lying with the linen wrappings but rolled up in a place by itself. Then the other disciple, who reached the tomb first, also went in, and he saw and believed; for as yet they did not understand the scripture, that he must rise from the dead. Then the disciples returned to their homes. But Mary stood weeping outside the tomb. As she wept, she bent over to look into the tomb; and she saw two angels in white, sitting where the body of Jesus had been lying, one at the head and the other at the feet. They said to her, 'Woman, why are you weeping?' She said to them, 'They have taken away my Lord, and I do not know where they have laid him.' When she had said this, she turned around and saw Jesus standing there, but she did not know that it was Jesus. Jesus said to her, 'Woman, why are you weeping? For whom are you looking?' Supposing him to be the gardener, she said to him, 'Sir, if you have carried him away, tell me where you have laid him, and I will take him away.' Jesus said to her, 'Mary!' She turned and said to him in Hebrew, 'Rabbouni!' (which means Teacher). Jesus said to her, 'Do not hold on to me, because I have not yet ascended to the Father. But go to my brothers and say to them, "I am ascending to my Father and your Father, to my God and your God."' Mary Magdalene went and announced to the disciples, 'I have seen the Lord'; and she told them that he had said these things to her.

Or   **Mark 16.1–8**

Hear the gospel of our Lord Jesus Christ according to Mark.

When the sabbath was over, Mary Magdalene, and Mary the mother of James, and Salome bought spices, so that they might go and anoint him. And very early on the first day of the week, when the sun had risen, they went to the tomb. They had been saying to one another, 'Who will roll away the stone for us from the entrance to the tomb?' When they looked up, they saw that the stone, which was very large, had already been rolled back. As they entered the tomb, they saw a young man, dressed in a white robe, sitting on the right side; and they were alarmed. But he said to them, 'Do not be alarmed; you are looking for Jesus of Nazareth, who was crucified. He has been raised; he is not here. Look, there is the place they laid him. But go, tell his disciples and Peter that he is going ahead of you to Galilee; there you will see him, just as he told you.' So they went out and fled from the tomb, for terror and amazement had seized them; and they said nothing to anyone, for they were afraid.

OLD TESTAMENT READINGS FOR SUNDAYS IN EASTERTIDE

For those who require an Old Testament reading on the Sundays in Eastertide, provision is made in the Supplement, pages 831–844 (Church of England) or 844–857 (Church of Ireland/Church in Wales). If these are used, the reading from Acts must be used as the Second Reading.

EASTER 2   YEAR B

FIRST READING   Acts 4.32–35

A reading from the Acts of the Apostles.

The whole group of those who believed were of one heart and soul, and no one claimed private ownership of any possessions, but everything they owned was held in common. With great power the apostles gave their testimony to the resurrection of the Lord Jesus, and great grace was upon them all. There was not a needy person among them, for as many as owned lands or houses sold them and brought the proceeds of what was sold. They laid it at the apostles' feet, and it was distributed to each as any had need.

PSALM

Psalm 133

℟ **How good and pleasant it is
to live together in unity.**

O how good and pleasant it is,
when a family lives together in unity!
It is like fine oil upon the head
that runs down upon the beard,
Upon the beard of Aaron,
and runs down upon the collar of his robe. ℟

It is like the dew of Hermon
that falls upon the hills of Zion.
For there the Lord has ordained the blessing:
life for evermore. ℟

SECOND READING

1 John 1.1 – 2.2

A reading from the first letter of John.

We declare to you what was from the beginning, what we have heard, what
we have seen with our eyes, what we have looked at and touched with our
hands, concerning the word of life – this life was revealed, and we have seen
it and testify to it, and declare to you the eternal life that was with the Father
and was revealed to us – we declare to you what we have seen and heard so
that you also may have fellowship with us; and truly our fellowship is with
the Father and with his Son Jesus Christ. We are writing these things so that
our joy may be complete.

This is the message we have heard from him and proclaim to you, that God is
light and in him there is no darkness at all. If we say that we have fellowship
with him while we are walking in darkness, we lie and do not do what is true;
but if we walk in the light as he himself is in the light, we have fellowship
with one another, and the blood of Jesus his Son cleanses us from all sin. If
we say that we have no sin, we deceive ourselves, and the truth is not in us. If
we confess our sins, he who is faithful and just will forgive us our sins and
cleanse us from all unrighteousness. If we say that we have not sinned, we
make him a liar, and his word is not in us.

My little children, I am writing these things to you so that you may not sin.
But if anyone does sin, we have an advocate with the Father, Jesus Christ the
righteous; and he is the atoning sacrifice for our sins, and not for ours only
but also for the sins of the whole world.

GOSPEL John 20.19–31

Hear the gospel of our Lord Jesus Christ according to John.

It was evening on the first day of the week, and the doors of the house where the disciples had met were locked for fear of the Jews. Jesus came and stood among them and said, 'Peace be with you.' After he said this, he showed them his hands and his side. Then the disciples rejoiced when they saw the Lord. Jesus said to them again, 'Peace be with you. As the Father has sent me, so I send you.' When he had said this, he breathed on them and said to them, 'Receive the Holy Spirit. If you forgive the sins of any, they are forgiven them; if you retain the sins of any, they are retained.'

But Thomas (who was called the Twin), one of the twelve, was not with them when Jesus came. So the other disciples told him, 'We have seen the Lord.' But he said to them, 'Unless I see the mark of the nails in his hands, and put my finger in the mark of the nails and my hand in his side, I will not believe.' A week later his disciples were again in the house, and Thomas was with them. Although the doors were shut, Jesus came and stood among them and said, 'Peace be with you.' Then he said to Thomas, 'Put your finger here and see my hands. Reach out your hand and put it in my side. Do not doubt but believe.' Thomas answered him, 'My Lord and my God!' Jesus said to him, 'Have you believed because you have seen me? Blessed are those who have not seen and yet have come to believe.'

Now Jesus did many other signs in the presence of his disciples, which are not written in this book. But these are written so that you may come to believe that Jesus is the Messiah, the Son of God, and that through believing you may have life in his name.

EASTER 3 YEAR B

FIRST READING Acts 3.12–19

A reading from the Acts of the Apostles.

Peter addressed the people, 'You Israelites, why do you wonder at this, or why do you stare at us, as though by our own power or piety we had made him walk? The God of Abraham, the God of Isaac, and the God of Jacob, the God of our ancestors has glorified his servant Jesus, whom you handed over and rejected in the presence of Pilate, though he had decided to release him. But you rejected the Holy and Righteous One and asked to have a murderer given to you, and you killed the Author of life, whom God raised from the dead. To this we are witnesses. And by faith in his name, his name itself has made this man strong, whom you see and know; and the faith that is through Jesus has given him this perfect health in the presence of all of you.

And now, friends, I know that you acted in ignorance, as did also your rulers. In this way God fulfilled what he had foretold through all the prophets, that his Messiah would suffer. Repent therefore, and turn to God so that your sins may be wiped out.'

PSALM   Psalm 4

℟ **Lift up the light of your countenance
   upon us, O Lord.**

Answer me when I call, O God, defender of my cause;
you set me free when I am hard-pressed;
have mercy on me and hear my prayer.
'You mortals, how long will you dishonour my glory;
how long will you worship dumb idols
and run after false gods?' ℟

Know that the Lord does wonders for the faithful;
when I call upon the Lord, he will hear me.
Tremble, then, and do not sin;
speak to your heart in silence upon your bed. ℟

Offer the appointed sacrifices
and put your trust in the Lord.
Many are saying,
'O that we might see better times!'
Lift up the light of your countenance upon us, O Lord. ℟

You have put gladness in my heart,
more than when grain and wine and oil increase.
I lie down in peace; at once I fall asleep;
for only you, Lord, make me dwell in safety. ℟

SECOND READING   1 John 3.1–7

A reading from the first letter of John.

See what love the Father has given us, that we should be called children of God; and that is what we are. The reason the world does not know us is that it did not know him. Beloved, we are God's children now; what we will be has not yet been revealed. What we do know is this: when he is revealed, we will be like him, for we will see him as he is. And all who have this hope in him purify themselves, just as he is pure.

Everyone who commits sin is guilty of lawlessness; sin is lawlessness. You know that he was revealed to take away sins, and in him there is no sin. No one who abides in him sins; no one who sins has either seen him or known him. Little children, let no one deceive you. Everyone who does what is right is righteous, just as he is righteous.

GOSPEL   Luke 24.36–48

Hear the gospel of our Lord Jesus Christ according to Luke.

While the eleven and their companions were talking about what they had heard, Jesus himself stood among them and said to them, 'Peace be with you.' They were startled and terrified, and thought that they were seeing a ghost. He said to them, 'Why are you frightened, and why do doubts arise in your hearts? Look at my hands and my feet; see that it is I myself. Touch me and see; for a ghost does not have flesh and bones as you see that I have.' And when he had said this, he showed them his hands and his feet. While in their joy they were disbelieving and still wondering, he said to them, 'Have you anything here to eat?' They gave him a piece of broiled fish, and he took it and ate in their presence.

Then he said to them, 'These are my words that I spoke to you while I was still with you – that everything written about me in the law of Moses, the prophets, and the psalms must be fulfilled.' Then he opened their minds to understand the scriptures, and he said to them, 'Thus it is written, that the Messiah is to suffer and to rise from the dead on the third day, and that repentance and forgiveness of sins is to be proclaimed in his name to all nations, beginning from Jerusalem. You are witnesses of these things.'

EASTER 4   YEAR B

FIRST READING   Acts 4.5–12

A reading from the Acts of the Apostles.

The Jewish rulers, elders, and scribes assembled in Jerusalem, with Annas the high priest, Caiaphas, John, and Alexander, and all who were of the high-priestly family. When they had made the prisoners stand in their midst, they inquired, 'By what power or by what name did you do this?' Then Peter, filled with the Holy Spirit, said to them, 'Rulers of the people and elders, if we are questioned today because of a good deed done to someone who was sick and are asked how this man has been healed, let it be known to all of you, and to all the people of Israel, that this man is standing before you in good health by the name of Jesus Christ of Nazareth, whom you crucified, whom God raised from the dead. This Jesus is "the stone that was rejected by you, the builders; it has become the cornerstone." There is salvation in no one else, for there is no other name under heaven given among mortals by which we must be saved.'

PSALM   Psalm 23

℞ **The Lord is my shepherd;**
   I shall not be in want.

The Lord is my shepherd;
I shall not be in want.
He makes me lie down in green pastures
and leads me beside still waters. ℞

He revives my soul
and guides me along right pathways for his name's sake.
Though I walk through the valley of the shadow of death,
I shall fear no evil;
for you are with me;
your rod and your staff, they comfort me. ℞

You spread a table before me
in the presence of those who trouble me;
you have anointed my head with oil,
and my cup is running over.
Surely your goodness and mercy shall follow me
all the days of my life,
and I will dwell in the house of the Lord for ever. ℞

SECOND READING   **1 John 3.16–24**

A reading from the first letter of John.

We know love by this, that the Son of God laid down his life for us – and we
ought to lay down our lives for one another. How does God's love abide in
anyone who has the world's goods and sees a brother or sister in need and yet
refuses help?

Little children, let us love, not in word or speech, but in truth and action.
And by this we will know that we are from the truth and will reassure our
hearts before him whenever our hearts condemn us; for God is greater than
our hearts, and he knows everything. Beloved, if our hearts do not condemn
us, we have boldness before God; and we receive from him whatever we ask,
because we obey his commandments and do what pleases God. And this is
his commandment, that we should believe in the name of his Son Jesus
Christ and love one another, just as he has commanded us.

All who obey his commandments abide in him, and he abides in them. And
by this we know that he abides in us, by the Spirit that he has given us.

GOSPEL   **John 10.11–18**

Hear the gospel of our Lord Jesus Christ according to John.

Jesus said to the Pharisees: I am the good shepherd. The good shepherd lays
down his life for the sheep. The hired hand, who is not the shepherd and
does not own the sheep, sees the wolf coming and leaves the sheep and runs
away – and the wolf snatches them and scatters them. The hired hand runs
away because a hired hand does not care for the sheep. I am the good
shepherd. I know my own and my own know me, just as the Father knows
me and I know the Father. And I lay down my life for the sheep. I have other
sheep that do not belong to this fold. I must bring them also, and they will
listen to my voice. So there will be one flock, one shepherd. For this reason
the Father loves me, because I lay down my life in order to take it up again.
No one takes it from me, but I lay it down of my own accord. I have power to
lay it down, and I have power to take it up again. I have received this
command from my Father.'

EASTER 5 YEAR B

FIRST READING Acts 8.26–40

A reading from the Acts of the Apostles.

An angel of the Lord said to Philip, 'Get up and go toward the south to the road that goes down from Jerusalem to Gaza.' (This is a wilderness road.) So he got up and went. Now there was an Ethiopian eunuch, a court official of the Candace, queen of the Ethiopians, in charge of her entire treasury. He had come to Jerusalem to worship and was returning home; seated in his chariot, he was reading the prophet Isaiah. Then the Spirit said to Philip, 'Go over to this chariot and join it.' So Philip ran up to it and heard him reading the prophet Isaiah. He asked, 'Do you understand what you are reading?' He replied, 'How can I, unless someone guides me?' And he invited Philip to get in and sit beside him. Now the passage of the scripture that he was reading was this:
'Like a sheep he was led to the slaughter,
and like a lamb silent before its shearer,
so he does not open his mouth.
In his humiliation justice was denied him.
Who can describe his generation?
For his life is taken away from the earth.'
The eunuch asked Philip, 'About whom, may I ask you, does the prophet say this, about himself or about someone else?' Then Philip began to speak, and starting with this scripture, he proclaimed to him the good news about Jesus. As they were going along the road, they came to some water; and the eunuch said, 'Look, here is water! What is to prevent me from being baptized?' He commanded the chariot to stop, and both of them, Philip and the eunuch, went down into the water, and Philip baptized him. When they came up out of the water, the Spirit of the Lord snatched Philip away; the eunuch saw him no more, and went on his way rejoicing. But Philip found himself at Azotus, and as he was passing through the region, he proclaimed the good news to all the towns until he came to Caesarea.

PSALM   Psalm 22.24–30

℟ **All the ends of the earth shall turn to you, O Lord.**

My praise is of him in the great assembly,
I will perform my vows
in the presence of those who worship him.
The poor shall eat and be satisfied,
and those who seek the Lord shall praise him:
'May your heart live for ever!' ℟

All the ends of the earth
shall remember and turn to the Lord,
and all the families of the nations
shall bow before him.
For kingship belongs to the Lord;
he rules over the nations. ℟

To him alone all who sleep in the earth
bow down in worship;
all who go down to the dust fall before him.
My soul shall live for him;
my descendants shall serve him;
they shall be known as the Lord's for ever.
They shall come and make known to a people yet unborn
the saving deeds that he has done. ℟

SECOND READING   1 John 4.7–21

A reading from the first letter of John.

Beloved, let us love one another, because love is from God; everyone who
loves is born of God and knows God. Whoever does not love does not know
God, for God is love. God's love was revealed among us in this way: God sent
his only Son into the world so that we might live through him.In this is love,
not that we loved God but that he loved us and sent his Son to be the
atoning sacrifice for our sins. Beloved, since God loved us so much, we also
ought to love one another. No one has ever seen God; if we love one another,
God lives in us, and his love is perfected in us.

By this we know that we abide in him and he in us, because he has given us
of his Spirit. And we have seen and do testify that the Father has sent his Son
as the Saviour of the world. God abides in those who confess that Jesus is the
Son of God, and they abide in God. So we have known and believe the love

that God has for us. God is love, and those who abide in love abide in God, and God abides in them. Love has been perfected among us in this: that we may have boldness on the day of judgement, because as he is, so are we in this world. There is no fear in love, but perfect love casts out fear; for fear has to do with punishment, and whoever fears has not reached perfection in love. We love because he first loved us.Those who say, 'I love God,' and hate their brothers or sisters, are liars; for those who do not love a brother or sister whom they have seen, cannot love God whom they have not seen. The commandment we have from him is this: those who love God must love their brothers and sisters also.

GOSPEL   John 15.1–8

Hear the gospel of our Lord Jesus Christ according to John.

Jesus said to his disciples: 'I am the true vine, and my Father is the vine-grower. He removes every branch in me that bears no fruit. Every branch that bears fruit he prunes to make it bear more fruit. You have already been cleansedby the word that I have spoken to you. Abide in me as I abide in you. Just as the branch cannot bear fruit by itself unless it abides in the vine, neither can you unless you abide in me. I am the vine, you are the branches. Those who abide in me and I in them bear much fruit, because apart from me you can do nothing. Whoever does not abide in me is thrown away like a branch and withers; such branches are gathered, thrown into the fire, and burned. If you abide in me, and my words abide in you,ask for whatever you wish, and it will be done for you. My Father is glorified by this, that you bear much fruit and become my disciples.'

EASTER 6   YEAR B

FIRST READING   Acts 10.44–48

A reading from the Acts of the Apostles.

While Peter was speaking, the Holy Spirit fell upon all who heard the word. The circumcised believers who had come with Peter were astounded that the gift of the Holy Spirit had been poured out even on the Gentiles, for they heard them speaking in tongues and extolling God. Then Peter said, 'Can anyone withhold the water for baptizing these people who have received the Holy Spirit just as we have?' So he ordered them to be baptized in the name of Jesus Christ. Then they invited him to stay for several days.

PSALM

Psalm 98

℟ **The Lord has made known his victory**
in the sight of the nations.

Sing to the Lord a new song,
for he has done marvellous things.
With his right hand and his holy arm
has he won for himself the victory. ℟

The Lord has made known his victory;
his righteousness has he openly shown
in the sight of the nations.
He remembers his mercy and faithfulness
to the house of Israel,
and all the ends of the earth have seen
the victory of our God. ℟

Shout with joy to the Lord, all you lands;
lift up your voice, rejoice and sing.
Sing to the Lord with the harp,
with the harp and the voice of song.
With trumpets and the sound of the horn
shout with joy before the King, the Lord. ℟

Let the sea make a noise and all that is in it,
the lands and those who dwell therein.
Let the rivers clap their hands,
and let the hills ring out with joy before the Lord,
when he comes to judge the earth.
In righteousness shall he judge the world,
and the peoples with equity. ℟

SECOND READING

1 John 5.1–6

A reading from the first letter of John.

Everyone who believes that Jesus is the Christ has been born of God, and
everyone who loves the parent loves the child. By this we know that we love
the children of God, when we love God and obey his commandments. For
the love of God is this, that we obey his commandments. And his
commandments are not burdensome, for whatever is born of God conquers
the world. And this is the victory that conquers the world, our faith. Who is it
that conquers the world but the one who believes that Jesus is the Son of God?

This is the one who came by water and blood, Jesus Christ, not with the water only but with the water and the blood. And the Spirit is the one that testifies, for the Spirit is the truth.

GOSPEL   John 15.9–17

Hear the gospel of our Lord Jesus Christ according to John.

Jesus said to his disciples: 'As the Father has loved me, so I have loved you; abide in my love. If you keep my commandments, you will abide in my love, just as I have kept my Father's commandments and abide in his love. I have said these things to you so that my joy may be in you, and that your joy may be complete.

This is my commandment, that you love one another as I have loved you. No one has greater love than this, to lay down one's life for one's friends. You are my friends if you do what I command you. I do not call you servants any longer, because the servant does not know what the master is doing; but I have called you friends, because I have made known to you everything that I have heard from my Father. You did not choose me but I chose you. And I appointed you to go and bear fruit, fruit that will last, so that the Father will give you whatever you ask him in my name. I am giving you these commands so that you may love one another.'

ASCENSION DAY   YEARS A B C

For text see Year A, pages 165–169.

EASTER 7   YEAR B

FIRST READING   Acts 1.15–17, 21–26

A reading from the Acts of the Apostles.

In those days Peter stood up among the believers (together the crowd numbered about one hundred and twenty people). He said, 'Friends, the scripture had to be fulfilled, which the Holy Spirit through David foretold concerning Judas, who became a guide for those who arrested Jesus – for he was numbered among us and was allotted his share in this ministry.

So one of the men who have accompanied us throughout the time that the Lord Jesus went in and out among us, beginning from the baptism of John until the day when he was taken up from us – one of these must become a witness with us to his resurrection.' So they proposed two, Joseph called Barsabbas, who was also known as Justus, and Matthias. Then they prayed and said, 'Lord, you know everyone's heart. Show us which one of these two you have chosen to take the place in this ministry and apostleship from which Judas turned aside to go to his own place.' And they cast lots for them, and the lot fell on Matthias; and he was added to the eleven apostles.

PSALM   Psalm 1

℟ **Happy are they who trust in the Lord.**
   or
℟ **The Lord knows the way of the righteous.**

Happy are they who have not walked
in the counsel of the wicked,
nor lingered in the way of sinners,
nor sat in the seats of the scornful!
Their delight is in the law of the Lord,
and they meditate on his law day and night. ℟

They are like trees planted by streams of water,
bearing fruit in due season,
with leaves that do not wither;
everything they do shall prosper. ℟

It is not so with the wicked:
they are like chaff which the wind blows away;
Therefore the wicked shall not stand upright
when judgement comes,
nor the sinner in the council of the righteous.
For the Lord knows the way of the righteous,
but the way of the wicked is doomed. ℟

SECOND READING   1 John 5.9–13

A reading from the first letter of John.

If we receive human testimony, the testimony of God is greater; for this is the testimony of God that he has testified to his Son. Those who believe in the Son of God have the testimony in their hearts. Those who do not believe in

God have made him a liar by not believing in the testimony that God has given concerning his Son. And this is the testimony: God gave us eternal life, and this life is in his Son. Whoever has the Son has life; whoever does not have the Son of God does not have life.

I write these things to you who believe in the name of the Son of God, so that you may know that you have eternal life.

GOSPEL   John 17.6–19

Hear the gospel of our Lord Jesus Christ according to John.

Jesus looked up to heaven and prayed: 'Father, I have made your name known to those whom you gave me from the world. They were yours, and you gave them to me, and they have kept your word. Now they know that everything you have given me is from you; for the words that you gave to me I have given to them, and they have received them and know in truth that I came from you; and they have believed that you sent me. I am asking on their behalf; I am not asking on behalf of the world, but on behalf of those whom you gave me, because they are yours. All mine are yours, and yours are mine; and I have been glorified in them. And now I am no longer in the world, but they are in the world, and I am coming to you. Holy Father, protect them in your name that you have given me, so that they may be one, as we are one. While I was with them, I protected them in your name that you have given me. I guarded them, and not one of them was lost except the one destined to be lost, so that the scripture might be fulfilled. But now I am coming to you, and I speak these things in the world so that they may have my joy made complete in themselves. I have given them your word, and the world has hated them because they do not belong to the world, just as I do not belong to the world. I am not asking you to take them out of the world, but I ask you to protect them from the evil one. They do not belong to the world, just as I do not belong to the world. Sanctify them in the truth; your word is truth. As you have sent me into the world, so I have sent them into the world. And for their sakes I sanctify myself, so that they also may be sanctified in truth.'

PENTECOST (WHITSUNDAY) YEAR B

The reading from Acts must be used, as either the First or Second Reading.

FIRST READING (Alternative readings)

Either Acts 2.1–21

A reading from the Acts of the Apostles.

When the day of Pentecost had come, they were all together in one place. And suddenly from heaven there came a sound like the rush of a violent wind, and it filled the entire house where they were sitting. Divided tongues, as of fire, appeared among them, and a tongue rested on each of them. All of them were filled with the Holy Spirit and began to speak in other languages, as the Spirit gave them ability.

Now there were devout Jews from every nation under heaven living in Jerusalem. And at this sound the crowd gathered and was bewildered, because each one heard them speaking in their native language. Amazed and astonished, they asked, 'Are not all these who are speaking Galileans? And how is it that we hear, each of us, in our own native language? Parthians, Medes, Elamites, and residents of Mesopotamia, Judea and Cappadocia, Pontus and Asia, Phrygia and Pamphylia, Egypt and the parts of Libya belonging to Cyrene, and visitors from Rome, both Jews and proselytes, Cretans and Arabs – in our own languages we hear them speaking about God's deeds of power.' All were amazed and perplexed, saying to one another, 'What does this mean?' But others sneered and said, 'They are filled with new wine.'

But Peter, standing with the eleven, raised his voice and addressed them, 'Men of Judea and all who live in Jerusalem, let this be known to you, and listen to what I say. Indeed, these are not drunk, as you suppose, for it is only nine o'clock in the morning. No, this is what was spoken through the prophet Joel:
"In the last days it will be, God declares,
that I will pour out my Spirit upon all flesh,
and your sons and your daughters shall prophesy,
and your young men shall see visions,
and your old men shall dream dreams.
Even upon my slaves, both men and women,
in those days I will pour out my Spirit;

and they shall prophesy.
And I will show portents in the heaven above
and signs on the earth below,
blood, and fire, and smoky mist.
The sun shall be turned to darkness and the moon to blood,
before the coming of the Lord's great and glorious day.
Then everyone who calls on the name of the Lord
shall be saved."'

Or   **Ezekiel 37.1–14**

A reading from the book of the prophet Ezekiel.

The hand of the LORD came upon me, and he brought me out by the spirit of the LORD and set me down in the middle of a valley; it was full of bones. He led me all around them; there were very many lying in the valley, and they were very dry. He said to me, 'Mortal, can these bones live?' I answered, 'O Lord GOD, you know.' Then he said to me, 'Prophesy to these bones, and say to them: O dry bones, hear the word of the LORD. Thus says the Lord GOD to these bones: I will cause breath to enter you, and you shall live. I will lay sinews on you, and will cause flesh to come upon you, and cover you with skin, and put breath in you, and you shall live; and you shall know that I am the LORD.'

So I prophesied as I had been commanded; and as I prophesied, suddenly there was a noise, a rattling, and the bones came together, bone to its bone. I looked, and there were sinews on them, and flesh had come upon them, and skin had covered them; but there was no breath in them. Then he said to me, 'Prophesy to the breath, prophesy, mortal, and say to the breath: Thus says the Lord GOD: Come from the four winds, O breath, and breathe upon these slain, that they may live.' I prophesied as he commanded me, and the breath came into them, and they lived, and stood on their feet, a vast multitude.

Then he said to me, 'Mortal, these bones are the whole house of Israel. They say, "Our bones are dried up, and our hope is lost; we are cut off completely." Therefore prophesy, and say to them, Thus says the Lord GOD: I am going to open your graves, and bring you up from your graves, O my people; and I will bring you back to the land of Israel. And you shall know that I am the LORD, when I open your graves, and bring you up from your graves, O my people. I will put my spirit within you, and you shall live, and I will place you on your own soil; then you shall know that I, the LORD, have spoken and will act, says the LORD.'

PSALM

Psalm 104.25–35, 37

℟ **Send forth your Spirit, O Lord,**
and renew the face of the earth.

O Lord, how manifold are your works!
in wisdom you have made them all;
the earth is full of your creatures. ℟

Yonder is the great and wide sea
with its living things too many to number,
creatures both small and great.
There move the ships,
and there is that Leviathan,
which you have made for the sport of it. ℟

All of them look to you
to give them their food in due season.
You give it to them, they gather it;
you open your hand and they are filled with good things.
You hide your face and they are terrified;
you take away their breath
and they die and return to their dust. ℟

You send forth your Spirit and they are created;
and so you renew the face of the earth.
May the glory of the Lord endure for ever;
may the Lord rejoice in all his works.
He looks at the earth and it trembles;
he touches the mountains and they smoke. ℟

I will sing to the Lord as long as I live;
I will praise my God while I have my being.
May these words of mine please him;
I will rejoice in the Lord.
Bless the Lord, O my soul,
Alleluia! ℟

SECOND READING (Alternative readings)

Either   Romans 8.22–27

A reading from the letter of Paul to the Romans.

We know that the whole creation has been groaning in labour pains until now; and not only the creation, but we ourselves, who have the first fruits of the Spirit, groan inwardly while we wait for adoption, the redemption of our bodies. For in hope we were saved. Now hope that is seen is not hope. For who hopes for what is seen? But if we hope for what we do not see, we wait for it with patience. Likewise the Spirit helps us in our weakness; for we do not know how to pray as we ought, but that very Spirit intercedes with sighs too deep for words. And God, who searches the heart, knows what is the mind of the Spirit, because the Spirit intercedes for the saints according to the will of God.

Or   Acts 2.1–21

A reading from the Acts of the Apostles.

For text see above, page 394.

GOSPEL   John 15.26–27, 16.4b–15

Hear the gospel of our Lord Jesus Christ according to John.

Jesus spoke to his disciples: 'When the Advocate comes, whom I will send to you from the Father, the Spirit of truth who comes from the Father, he will testify on my behalf. You also are to testify because you have been with me from the beginning.

I have said these things to you so that when their hour comes you may remember that I told you about them. I did not say these things to you from the beginning, because I was with you. But now I am going to him who sent me; yet none of you asks me, "Where are you going?" But because I have said these things to you, sorrow has filled your hearts. Nevertheless I tell you the truth: it is to your advantage that I go away, for if I do not go away, the Advocate will not come to you; but if I go, I will send him to you. And when he comes, he will prove the world wrong about sin and righteousness and judgement: about sin, because they do not believe in me; about righteousness, because I am going to the Father and you will see me no longer; about judgement, because the ruler of this world has been condemned. I still have many things to say to you, but you cannot bear them now.

When the Spirit of truth comes, he will guide you into all the truth; for he will not speak on his own, but will speak whatever he hears, and he will declare to you the things that are to come. He will glorify me, because he will take what is mine and declare it to you. All that the Father has is mine. For this reason I said that he will take what is mine and declare it to you.'

TRINITY SUNDAY   YEAR B

FIRST READING   Isaiah 6.1-8

A reading from the book of the prophet Isaiah.

In the year that King Uzziah died, I saw the Lord sitting on a throne, high and lofty; and the hem of his robe filled the temple. Seraphs were in attendance above him; each had six wings: with two they covered their faces, and with two they covered their feet, and with two they flew.
And one called to another and said:
'Holy, holy, holy is the LORD of hosts;
the whole earth is full of his glory.'
The pivots on the thresholds shook at the voices of those who called, and the house filled with smoke. And I said: 'Woe is me! I am lost, for I am a man of unclean lips, and I live among a people of unclean lips; yet my eyes have seen the King, the LORD of hosts!'

Then one of the seraphs flew to me, holding a live coal that had been taken from the altar with a pair of tongs. The seraph touched my mouth with it and said: 'Now that this has touched your lips, your guilt has departed and your sin is blotted out. ' Then I heard the voice of the Lord saying, 'Whom shall I send, and who will go for us?' And I said, 'Here am I; send me!'

PSALM   Psalm 29

℟ **The Lord shall give his people**
   the blessing of peace.
   or
℟ **In God's temple all cry 'Glory!'**

Ascribe to the Lord, you gods,
ascribe to the Lord glory and strength.
Ascribe to the Lord the glory due to his name;
worship the Lord in the beauty of holiness. ℟

The voice of the Lord is upon the waters;
the God of glory thunders;
the Lord is upon the mighty waters.
The voice of the Lord is a powerful voice;
the voice of the Lord is a voice of splendour. ℟

The voice of the Lord breaks the cedar trees;
the Lord breaks the cedars of Lebanon;
He makes Lebanon skip like a calf,
and Mount Hermon like a young wild ox. ℟

The voice of the Lord splits the flames of fire;
the voice of the Lord shakes the wilderness;
the Lord shakes the wilderness of Kadesh.
The voice of the Lord makes the oak trees writhe
and strips the forests bare.
And in the temple of the Lord
all are crying, 'Glory!'
The Lord sits enthroned above the flood;
the Lord sits enthroned as king for evermore.
The Lord shall give strength to his people;
the Lord shall give his people the blessing of peace. ℟

SECOND READING   Romans 8.12–17

A reading from the letter of Paul to the Romans.

Brothers and sisters, we are debtors, not to the flesh, to live according to the flesh – for if you live according to the flesh, you will die; but if by the Spirit you put to death the deeds of the body, you will live. For all who are led by the Spirit of God are children of God. For you did not receive a spirit of slavery to fall back into fear, but you have received a spirit of adoption. When we cry, 'Abba! Father!' it is that very Spirit bearing witness with our spirit that we are children of God, and if children, then heirs, heirs of God and joint heirs with Christ – if, in fact, we suffer with him so that we may also be glorified with him.

GOSPEL John 3.1–17

Hear the gospel of our Lord Jesus Christ according to John.

There was a Pharisee named Nicodemus, a leader of the Jews. He came to Jesus by night and said to him, 'Rabbi, we know that you are a teacher who has come from God; for no one can do these signs that you do apart from the presence of God.' Jesus answered him, 'Very truly, I tell you, no one can see the kingdom of God without being born from above.' Nicodemus said to him, 'How can anyone be born after having grown old? Can one enter a second time into the mother's womb and be born?' Jesus answered, 'Very truly, I tell you, no one can enter the kingdom of God without being born of water and Spirit. What is born of the flesh is flesh, and what is born of the Spirit is spirit. Do not be astonished that I said to you, "You must be born from above." The wind blows where it chooses, and you hear the sound of it, but you do not know where it comes from or where it goes. So it is with everyone who is born of the Spirit.' Nicodemus said to him, 'How can these things be?' Jesus answered him, 'Are you a teacher of Israel, and yet you do not understand these things?

Very truly, I tell you, we speak of what we know and testify to what we have seen; yet you do not receive our testimony. If I have told you about earthly things and you do not believe, how can you believe if I tell you about heavenly things? No one has ascended into heaven except the one who descended from heaven, the Son of Man. And just as Moses lifted up the serpent in the wilderness, so must the Son of Man be lifted up, that whoever believes in him may have eternal life.

For God so loved the world that he gave his only Son, so that everyone who believes in him may not perish but may have eternal life.

Indeed, God did not send the Son into the world to condemn the world, but in order that the world might be saved through him.'

THANKSGIVING FOR HOLY COMMUNION (CORPUS CHRISTI)

YEARS A B C

For text see Year A, pages 180–181.

† SUNDAY BETWEEN 24 AND 28 MAY
(if after Trinity Sunday)
PROPER 3

YEAR B

The Revised Common Lectionary provision for Epiphany 8 (above, pages 343–345) is used.

SUNDAYS AFTER TRINITY

The Church of England names the Sundays after Trinity Sunday 'Sundays after Trinity'. The readings are provided by calendar date.

On most Sundays the First Reading and Psalm follow two tracks. One track must be followed through the whole sequence.

† SUNDAY BETWEEN 29 MAY AND 4 JUNE
(if after Trinity Sunday)
PROPER 4

YEAR B

TRACK 1

FIRST READING (Short or long reading)

1 Samuel 3.1-10, (11-20)

A reading from the first book of Samuel.

The boy Samuel was ministering to the LORD under Eli. The word of the LORD was rare in those days; visions were not widespread.

At that time Eli, whose eyesight had begun to grow dim so that he could not see, was lying down in his room; the lamp of God had not yet gone out, and Samuel was lying down in the temple of the LORD, where the ark of God was. Then the LORD called, 'Samuel! Samuel!' and he said, 'Here I am!' and ran to Eli, and said, 'Here I am, for you called me.' But he said, 'I did not call; lie down again.' So he went and lay down. The LORD called again, 'Samuel!' Samuel got up and went to Eli, and said, 'Here I am, for you called me.' But he said, 'I did not call, my son; lie down again.' Now Samuel did not yet know the LORD, and the word of the LORD had not yet been revealed to him. The LORD called Samuel again, a third time. And he got up and went to Eli, and said, 'Here I am, for you called me.' Then Eli perceived that the LORD was calling the boy. Therefore Eli said to Samuel, 'Go, lie down; and if he calls you, you shall say, "Speak, LORD, for your servant is listening." So Samuel went and lay down in his place.

Now the LORD came and stood there, calling as before, 'Samuel! Samuel!' And Samuel said, 'Speak, for your servant is listening.' [Then the LORD said to Samuel, 'See, I am about to do something in Israel that will make both ears of anyone who hears of it tingle. On that day I will fulfil against Eli all that I have spoken concerning his house, from beginning to end. For I have told him that I am about to punish his house for ever, for the iniquity that he knew, because his sons were blaspheming God, and he did not restrain them. Therefore I swear to the house of Eli that the iniquity of Eli's house shall not be expiated by sacrifice or offering for ever.'

Samuel lay there until morning; then he opened the doors of the house of the LORD. Samuel was afraid to tell the vision to Eli. But Eli called Samuel and said, 'Samuel, my son.' He said, 'Here I am.'

Eli said, 'What was it that he told you? Do not hide it from me. May God do so to you and more also, if you hide anything from me of all that he told you.' So Samuel told him everything and hid nothing from him. Then he said, 'It is the LORD; let him do what seems good to him.'

As Samuel grew up, the LORD was with him and let none of his words fall to the ground. And all Israel from Dan to Beer-sheba knew that Samuel was a trustworthy prophet of the LORD.]

PSALM Psalm 139.1–5, 12–17

℟ **Where, Lord, can I flee from your presence?**

Lord, you have searched me out and known me;
you know my sitting down and my rising up;
you discern my thoughts from afar.
You trace my journeys and my resting-places
and are acquainted with all my ways. ℟

Indeed, there is not a word on my lips,
but you, O Lord, know it altogether.
You press upon me behind and before

and lay your hand upon me.
Such knowledge is too wonderful for me;
it is so high that I cannot attain to it. ℟

For you yourself created my inmost parts;
you knit me together in my mother's womb.
I will thank you because I am marvellously made;
your works are wonderful and I know it well. ℟

My body was not hidden from you,
while I was being made in secret
and woven in the depths of the earth.
Your eyes beheld my limbs, yet unfinished in the womb;
all of them were written in your book;
they were fashioned day by day,
when as yet there was none of them. ℟

How deep I find your thoughts, O God!
how great is the sum of them!
If I were to count them,
they would be more in number than the sand;
to count them all,
my life span would need to be like yours. ℟

Or   TRACK 2

FIRST READING   **Deuteronomy 5.12–15**

A reading from the book of Deuteronomy.

The LORD says this: Observe the sabbath day and keep it holy, as the LORD
your God commanded you. For six days you shall labour and do all your
work. But the seventh day is a sabbath to the LORD your God; you shall not
do any work – you, or your son or your daughter, or your male or female
slave, or your ox or your donkey, or any of your livestock, or the resident
alien in your towns, so that your male and female slave may rest as well as
you. Remember that you were a slave in the land of Egypt, and the LORD
your God brought you out from there with a mighty hand and an
outstretched arm; therefore the LORD your God commanded you to keep the
sabbath day.

PSALM

℟ **Sing with joy to God our strength.**

Sing with joy to God our strength
and raise a loud shout to the God of Jacob.
Raise a song and sound the timbrel,
the merry harp and the lyre.
Blow the ram's-horn at the new moon,
and at the full moon, the day of our feast. ℟

For this is a statute for Israel,
a law of the God of Jacob.
He laid it as a solemn charge upon Joseph,
when he came out of the land of Egypt. ℟

I heard an unfamiliar voice saying,
'I eased his shoulder from the burden;
his hands were set free from bearing the load.'
You called on me in trouble and I saved you;
I answered you from the secret place of thunder
and tested you at the waters of Meribah. ℟

Hear, O my people, and I will admonish you:
O Israel, if you would but listen to me!
There shall be no strange god among you;
you shall not worship a foreign god.
I am the Lord your God,
who brought you out of the land of Egypt and said,
'Open your mouth wide and I will fill it.' ℟

SECOND READING

A reading from the second letter of Paul to the Corinthians.

We do not proclaim ourselves; we proclaim Jesus Christ as Lord and ourselves as your slaves for Jesus' sake. For it is the God who said, 'Let light shine out of darkness,' who has shone in our hearts to give the light of the knowledge of the glory of God in the face of Jesus Christ.

But we have this treasure in clay jars, so that it may be made clear that this extraordinary power belongs to God and does not come from us. We are afflicted in every way, but not crushed; perplexed, but not driven to despair; persecuted, but not forsaken; struck down, but not destroyed; always carrying in the body the death of Jesus, so that the life of Jesus may also be made visible in our bodies. For while we live, we are always being given up to death for Jesus' sake, so that the life of Jesus may be made visible in our mortal flesh. So death is at work in us, but life in you.

GOSPEL   **Mark 2.23 – 3.6**

Hear the gospel of our Lord Jesus Christ according to Mark.

One sabbath Jesus was going through the cornfields; and as they made their way his disciples began to pluck heads of grain. The Pharisees said to him, 'Look, why are they doing what is not lawful on the sabbath?' And he said to them, 'Have you never read what David did when he and his companions were hungry and in need of food? He entered the house of God, when Abiathar was high priest, and ate the bread of the Presence, which it is not lawful for any but the priests to eat, and he gave some to his companions.' Then he said to them, 'The sabbath was made for humankind and not humankind for the sabbath; so the Son of Man is lord even of the sabbath.'

Again he entered the synagogue, and a man was there who had a withered hand. They watched him to see whether he would cure him on the sabbath, so that they might accuse him. And he said to the man who had the withered hand, 'Come forward.' Then he said to the Pharisees, 'Is it lawful to do good or to do harm on the sabbath, to save life or to kill?' But they were silent. He looked around at them with anger; he was grieved at their hardness of heart and said to the man, 'Stretch out your hand.' He stretched it out, and his hand was restored. The Pharisees went out and immediately conspired with the Herodians against Jesus, how to destroy him.

† SUNDAY BETWEEN 5 AND 11 JUNE   **YEAR B**
(if after Trinity Sunday)
PROPER 5

TRACK 1

FIRST READING (Short or long reading)
1 Samuel 8.4–11, (12–15), 16–20; (11.14–15)

A reading from the first book of Samuel.

All the elders of Israel gathered together and came to Samuel at Ramah. They said to him, 'You are old and your sons do not follow in your ways; appoint for us, then, a king to govern us, like other nations.' But the thing displeased

Samuel when they said, 'Give us a king to govern us.' Samuel prayed to the LORD, and the LORD said to Samuel, 'Listen to the voice of the people in all that they say to you; for they have not rejected you, but they have rejected me from being king over them. Just as they have done to me, from the day I brought them up out of Egypt to this day, forsaking me and serving other gods, so also they are doing to you. Now then, listen to their voice; only – you shall solemnly warn them, and show them the ways of the king who shall reign over them.'

So Samuel reported all the words of the LORD to the people who were asking him for a king. He said, 'These will be the ways of the king who will reign over you: he will take your sons and appoint them to his chariots and to be his horsemen, and to run before his chariots; [He will appoint for himself commanders of thousands and commanders of fifties, and some to plough his ground and to reap his harvest, and to make his implements of war and the equipment of his chariots. He will take your daughters to be perfumers and cooks and bakers. He will take the best of your fields and vineyards and olive orchards and give them to his courtiers. He will take one-tenth of your grain and of your vineyards and give it to his officers and his courtiers.]

He will take your male and female slaves, and the best of your cattle and donkeys, and put them to his work. He will take one-tenth of your flocks, and you shall be his slaves. And in that day you will cry out because of your king, whom you have chosen for yourselves; but the LORD will not answer you in that day.'

But the people refused to listen to the voice of Samuel; they said, 'No! but we are determined to have a king over us, so that we also may be like other nations, and that our king may govern us and go out before us and fight our battles.' [Samuel said to the people, 'Come, let us go to Gilgal and there renew the kingship.' So all the people went to Gilgal, and there they made Saul king before the LORD in Gilgal. There they sacrificed offerings of well-being before the LORD, and there Saul and all the Israelites rejoiced greatly.]

PSALM   Psalm 138

℞ When I called, O Lord, you answered me.

I will give thanks to you, O Lord, with my whole heart;
before the gods I will sing your praise.
I will bow down towards your holy temple
and praise your name,

because of your love and faithfulness;
For you have glorified your name
and your word above all things. ℟

When I called, you answered me;
you increased my strength within me.
All the kings of the earth will praise you, O Lord,
when they have heard the words of your mouth. ℟

They will sing of the ways of the Lord,
that great is the glory of the Lord.
Though the Lord be high, he cares for the lowly;
he perceives the haughty from afar. ℟

Though I walk in the midst of trouble,
you keep me safe;
you stretch forth your hand
against the fury of my enemies;
your right hand shall save me.
The Lord will make good his purpose for me;
O Lord, your love endures for ever;
do not abandon the works of your hands. ℟

Or TRACK 2

FIRST READING **Genesis 3.8–15**

A reading from the book of Genesis.

The man and the woman heard the sound of the LORD God walking in the garden at the time of the evening breeze, and the man and his wife hid themselves from the presence of the LORD God among the trees of the garden. But the LORD God called to the man, and said to him, 'Where are you?' He said, 'I heard the sound of you in the garden, and I was afraid, because I was naked; and I hid myself.' He said, 'Who told you that you were naked? Have you eaten from the tree of which I commanded you not to eat?' The man said, 'The woman whom you gave to be with me, she gave me fruit from the tree, and I ate.' Then the LORD God said to the woman, 'What is this that you have done?' The woman said, 'The serpent tricked me, and I ate.'
The LORD God said to the serpent,
'Because you have done this,

cursed are you among all animals
and among all wild creatures;
upon your belly you shall go,
and dust you shall eat
all the days of your life.
I will put enmity between you and the woman,
and between your offspring and hers;
he will strike your head,
and you will strike his heel.'

PSALM   Psalm 130

℞ **With the Lord there is mercy
and plenteous redemption.**

Out of the depths have I called to you, O Lord;
Lord, hear my voice;
let your ears consider well the voice of my supplication.
If you, Lord, were to note what is done amiss,
O Lord, who could stand?
For there is forgiveness with you;
therefore you shall be feared. ℞

I wait for the Lord; my soul waits for him;
in his word is my hope.
My soul waits for the Lord,
more than the night-watch for the morning,
more than the night-watch for the morning. ℞

O Israel, wait for the Lord,
for with the Lord there is mercy;
With him there is plenteous redemption,
and he shall redeem Israel from all their sins. ℞

SECOND READING   2 Corinthians 4.13 – 5.1

A reading from the second letter of Paul to the Corinthians.

Just as we have the same spirit of faith that is in accordance with scripture – 'I believed, and so I spoke' – we also believe, and so we speak, because we know that the one who raised the Lord Jesus will raise us also with Jesus, and will bring us with you into his presence. Yes, everything is for your sake, so that grace, as it extends to more and more people, may increase thanksgiving, to the glory of God.

So we do not lose heart. Even though our outer nature is wasting away, our inner nature is being renewed day by day. For this slight momentary affliction is preparing us for an eternal weight of glory beyond all measure, because we look not at what can be seen but at what cannot be seen; for what can be seen is temporary, but what cannot be seen is eternal.

For we know that if the earthly tent we live in is destroyed, we have a building from God, a house not made with hands, eternal in the heavens.

GOSPEL   Mark 3.20–35

Hear the gospel of our Lord Jesus Christ according to Mark.

The crowd came together again, so that Jesus and his companions could not even eat. When his family heard it, they went out to restrain him, for people were saying, 'He has gone out of his mind.' And the scribes who came down from Jerusalem said, 'He has Beelzebul, and by the ruler of the demons he casts out demons.' And he called them to him, and spoke to them in parables, 'How can Satan cast out Satan? If a kingdom is divided against itself, that kingdom cannot stand. And if a house is divided against itself, that house will not be able to stand. And if Satan has risen up against himself and is divided, he cannot stand, but his end has come. But no one can enter a strong man's house and plunder his property without first tying up the strong man; then indeed the house can be plundered.

Truly I tell you, people will be forgiven for their sins and whatever blasphemies they utter; but whoever blasphemes against the Holy Spirit can never have forgiveness, but is guilty of an eternal sin' – for they had said, 'He has an unclean spirit.'

Then his mother and his brothers came; and standing outside, they sent to him and called him. A crowd was sitting around him; and they said to him, 'Your mother and your brothers and sisters are outside, asking for you.' And he replied, 'Who are my mother and my brothers?' And looking at those who sat around him, he said, 'Here are my mother and my brothers! Whoever does the will of God is my brother and sister and mother.'

† SUNDAY BETWEEN 12 AND 18 JUNE   YEAR B
(if after Trinity Sunday)
PROPER 6

TRACK 1

FIRST READING   **1 Samuel 15.34 – 16.13**

A reading from the first book of Samuel.

Samuel went to Ramah; and Saul went up to his house in Gibeah of Saul. Samuel did not see Saul again until the day of his death, but Samuel grieved over Saul. And the LORD was sorry that he had made Saul king over Israel.

The LORD said to Samuel, 'How long will you grieve over Saul? I have rejected him from being king over Israel. Fill your horn with oil and set out; I will send you to Jesse the Bethlehemite, for I have provided for myself a king among his sons.' Samuel said, 'How can I go? If Saul hears of it, he will kill me. ' And the LORD said, 'Take a heifer with you, and say, "I have come to sacrifice to the LORD." Invite Jesse to the sacrifice, and I will show you what you shall do; and you shall anoint for me the one whom I name to you.' Samuel did what the LORD commanded, and came to Bethlehem. The elders of the city came to meet him trembling, and said, 'Do you come peaceably?' He said, 'Peaceably; I have come to sacrifice to the LORD; sanctify yourselves and come with me to the sacrifice.' And he sanctified Jesse and his sons and invited them to the sacrifice.

When they came, he looked on Eliab and thought, 'Surely the Lord's anointed is now before the LORD.' But the LORD said to Samuel, 'Do not look on his appearance or on the height of his stature, because I have rejected him; for the LORD does not see as mortals see; they look on the outward appearance, but the LORD looks on the heart.' Then Jesse called Abinadab, and made him pass before Samuel. He said, 'Neither has the LORD chosen this one.' Then Jesse made Shammah pass by. And he said, 'Neither has the LORD chosen this one.' Jesse made seven of his sons pass before Samuel, and Samuel said to Jesse, 'The LORD has not chosen any of these.' Samuel said to Jesse, 'Are all your sons here?' And he said, 'There remains yet the youngest, but he is keeping the sheep.' And Samuel said to Jesse, 'Send and bring him; for we will not sit down until he comes here.' He sent and brought him in. Now he was ruddy, and had beautiful eyes, and was handsome. The LORD said, 'Rise and anoint him; for this is the one.' Then Samuel took the horn of

oil, and anointed him in the presence of his brothers; and the spirit of the
LORD came mightily upon David from that day forward. Samuel then set out
and went to Ramah.

PSALM

Psalm 20

℟ **We will call upon the name of the Lord our God.**

May the Lord answer you in the day of trouble,
the name of the God of Jacob defend you;
Send you help from his holy place
and strengthen you out of Zion; ℟

Remember all your offerings
and accept your burnt sacrifice;
Grant you your heart's desire
and prosper all your plans. ℟

We will shout for joy at your victory
and triumph in the name of our God;
may the Lord grant all your requests.
Now I know that the Lord gives victory
to his anointed;
he will answer him out of his holy heaven,
with the victorious strength of his right hand. ℟

Some put their trust in chariots and some in horses,
but we will call upon the name of the Lord our God.
They collapse and fall down,
but we will arise and stand upright.
O Lord, give victory to the king
and answer us when we call. ℟

Or   TRACK 2

FIRST READING

Ezekiel 17.22–24

A reading from the book of the prophet Ezekiel.

Thus says the Lord GOD:
I myself will take a sprig
from the lofty top of a cedar;

I will set it out.
I will break off a tender one
from the topmost of its young twigs;
I myself will plant it on a high and lofty mountain.
On the mountain height of Israel
I will plant it,
in order that it may produce boughs and bear fruit,
and become a noble cedar.
Under it every kind of bird will live;
in the shade of its branches will nest
winged creatures of every kind.
All the trees of the field shall know
that I am the LORD.
I bring low the high tree,
I make high the low tree;
I dry up the green tree
and make the dry tree flourish.
I the LORD have spoken;
I will accomplish it.

PSALM   Psalm 92.1–4, 11–14

℟ **It is a good thing to give thanks to the Lord.**

It is a good thing to give thanks to the Lord,
and to sing praises to your name, O Most High;
To tell of your loving-kindness early in the morning
and of your faithfulness in the night season; ℟

On the psaltery and on the lyre
and to the melody of the harp.
For you have made me glad by your acts, O Lord;
and I shout for joy because of the works of your hands. ℟

The righteous shall flourish like a palm tree,
and shall spread abroad like a cedar of Lebanon.
Those who are planted in the house of the Lord
shall flourish in the courts of our God; ℟

They shall still bear fruit in old age;
they shall be green and succulent;
That they may show how upright the Lord is,
my rock, in whom there is no fault. ℟

SECOND READING (Short or long reading)
Corinthians 5.6–10, (11–13), 14–17

A reading from the second letter of Paul to the Corinthians.

Brothers and sisters, we are always confident; even though we know that while we are at home in the body we are away from the Lord – for we walk by faith, not by sight. Yes, we do have confidence, and we would rather be away from the body and at home with the Lord. So whether we are at home or away, we make it our aim to please him. For all of us must appear before the judgement seat of Christ, so that each may receive recompense for what has been done in the body, whether good or evil.

[Therefore, knowing the fear of the Lord, we try to persuade others; but we ourselves are well known to God, and I hope that we are also well known to your consciences. We are not commending ourselves to you again, but giving you an opportunity to boast about us, so that you may be able to answer those who boast in outward appearance and not in the heart. For if we are beside ourselves, it is for God; if we are in our right mind, it is for you.]

The love of Christ urges us on, because we are convinced that one has died for all; therefore all have died. And he died for all, so that those who live might live no longer for themselves, but for him who died and was raised for them.

From now on, therefore, we regard no one from a human point of view; even though we once knew Christ from a human point of view, we know him no longer in that way. So if anyone is in Christ, there is a new creation: everything old has passed away; see, everything has become new!

GOSPEL   Mark 4.26–34

Hear the gospel of our Lord Jesus Christ according to Mark.

Such a large crowd gathered around Jesus that he got into a boat and began to teach them using many parables. Jesus said, 'The kingdom of God is as if someone would scatter seed on the ground, and would sleep and rise night and day, and the seed would sprout and grow, he does not know how. The earth produces of itself, first the stalk, then the head, then the full grain in the head. But when the grain is ripe, at once he goes in with his sickle, because the harvest has come.'

Jesus also said, 'With what can we compare the kingdom of God, or what parable will we use for it? It is like a mustard seed, which, when sown upon the ground, is the smallest of all the seeds on earth; yet when it is sown it grows up and becomes the greatest of all shrubs, and puts forth large branches, so that the birds of the air can make nests in its shade.'

With many such parables he spoke the word to them, as they were able to hear it; he did not speak to them except in parables, but he explained everything in private to his disciples.

† SUNDAY BETWEEN 19 AND 25 JUNE   YEAR B
(if after Trinity Sunday)
PROPER 7

On this Sunday Track 1 has alternative First Readings and Psalms.

TRACK 1

FIRST READING (Alternative readings)

Either (Short or long reading)
1 Samuel 17.(1a, 4–11, 19–23), 32–49

A reading from the first book of Samuel.

[The Philistines gathered their armies for battle; they were gathered at Socoh, which belongs to Judah, and encamped between Socoh and Azekah, in Ephes-dammim.

And there came out from the camp of the Philistines a champion named Goliath, of Gath, whose height was six cubits and a span. He had a helmet of bronze on his head, and he was armed with a coat of mail; the weight of the coat was five thousand shekels of bronze. He had greaves of bronze on his legs and a javelin of bronze slung between his shoulders. The shaft of his spear was like a weaver's beam, and his spear's head weighed six hundred shekels of iron; and his shield-bearer went before him. He stood and shouted to the ranks of Israel, 'Why have you come out to draw up for battle? Am I not a Philistine, and are you not servants of Saul? Choose a man for yourselves, and let him come down to me. If he is able to fight with me and kill me, then we will be your servants; but if I prevail against him and kill him, then you shall be our servants and serve us.' And the Philistine said, 'Today I defy the ranks of Israel! Give me a man, that we may fight together.' When Saul and all Israel heard these words of the Philistine, they were dismayed and greatly afraid.

Now Saul, and all the men of Israel, were in the valley of Elah, fighting with the Philistines. David rose early in the morning, left someone in charge of the sheep, took the provisions, and went as Jesse had commanded him. He came to the encampment as the army was going forth to the battle line, shouting the war cry. Israel and the Philistines drew up for battle, army against army. David left the things in charge of the keeper of the baggage, ran to the ranks, and went and greeted his brothers. As he talked with them, the champion, the Philistine of Gath, Goliath by name, came up out of the ranks of the Philistines, and spoke the same words as before. And David heard him.]

David said to Saul, 'Let no one's heart fail because of him; your servant will go and fight with this Philistine.' Saul said to David, 'You are not able to go against this Philistine to fight with him; for you are just a boy, and he has been a warrior from his youth.' But David said to Saul, 'Your servant used to keep sheep for his father; and whenever a lion or a bear came, and took a lamb from the flock, I went after it and struck it down, rescuing the lamb from its mouth; and if it turned against me, I would catch it by the jaw, strike it down, and kill it. Your servant has killed both lions and bears; and this uncircumcised Philistine shall be like one of them, since he has defied the armies of the living God.' David said, 'The LORD, who saved me from the paw of the lion and from the paw of the bear, will save me from the hand of this Philistine.' So Saul said to David, 'Go, and may the LORD be with you!'

Saul clothed David with his armour; he put a bronze helmet on his head and clothed him with a coat of mail. David strapped Saul's sword over the armour, and he tried in vain to walk, for he was not used to them. Then David said to Saul, 'I cannot walk with these; for I am not used to them.' So David removed them. Then he took his staff in his hand, and chose five smooth stones from the wadi, and put them in his shepherd's bag, in the pouch; his sling was in his hand, and he drew near to the Philistine.

The Philistine came on and drew near to David, with his shield-bearer in front of him. When the Philistine looked and saw David, he disdained him, for he was only a youth, ruddy and handsome in appearance. The Philistine said to David, 'Am I a dog, that you come to me with sticks?' And the Philistine cursed David by his gods. The Philistine said to David, 'Come to me, and I will give your flesh to the birds of the air and to the wild animals of the field.' But David said to the Philistine, 'You come to me with sword and spear and javelin; but I come to you in the name of the LORD of hosts, the God of the armies of Israel, whom you have defied. This very day the LORD will deliver you into my hand, and I will strike you down and cut off your head; and I will give the dead bodies of the Philistine army this very day to the birds of the air and to the wild animals of the earth, so that all the earth may know that there is a God in Israel, and that all this assembly may know that the LORD does not save by sword and spear; for the battle is the Lord's and he will give you into our hand.'

When the Philistine drew nearer to meet David, David ran quickly toward the battle line to meet the Philistine. David put his hand in his bag, took out a stone, slung it, and struck the Philistine on his forehead; the stone sank into his forehead, and he fell face down on the ground.

PSALM   Psalm 9.9–20

℟ **Let the ungodly know they are but mortal.**

The Lord will be a refuge for the oppressed,
a refuge in time of trouble.
Those who know your name will put their trust in you,
for you never forsake those who seek you, O Lord.
Sing praise to the Lord who dwells in Zion;
proclaim to the peoples the things he has done. ℟

The avenger of blood will remember them;
he will not forget the cry of the afflicted.
Have pity on me, O Lord;
see the misery I suffer from those who hate me,
O you who lift me up from the gate of death;
So that I may tell of all your praises
and rejoice in your salvation
in the gates of the city of Zion. ℟

The ungodly have fallen into the pit they dug,
and in the snare they set is their own foot caught.
The Lord is known by his acts of justice;
the wicked are trapped in the works of their own hands.
The wicked shall be given over to the grave,
and also all the peoples that forget God. ℟

For the needy shall not always be forgotten,
and the hope of the poor shall not perish for ever.
Rise up, O Lord,
let not the ungodly have the upper hand;
let them be judged before you.
Put fear upon them, O Lord;
let the ungodly know they are but mortal. ℟

Or

FIRST READING   1 Samuel 17.57 – 18.5, 10–16

A reading from the first book of Samuel.

On David's return from killing the Philistine, Abner took him and brought him before Saul, with the head of the Philistine in his hand. Saul said to him, 'Whose son are you, young man?' And David answered, 'I am the son of your servant Jesse the Bethlehemite.'

David went out and was successful wherever Saul sent him; as a result, Saul set him over the army. And all the people, even the servants of Saul, approved.

The next day an evil spirit from God rushed upon Saul, and he raved within his house, while David was playing the lyre, as he did day by day. Saul had his spear in his hand; and Saul threw the spear, for he thought, 'I will pin David to the wall.' But David eluded him twice.

Saul was afraid of David, because the LORD was with him but had departed from Saul. So Saul removed him from his presence, and made him a commander of a thousand; and David marched out and came in, leading the army. David had success in all his undertakings; for the LORD was with him. When Saul saw that he had great success, he stood in awe of him. But all Israel and Judah loved David; for it was he who marched out and came in leading them.

PSALM   Psalm 133

℟ **The Lord has ordained the blessing:**
   life for evermore.

O how good and pleasant it is,
when a family lives together in unity!
It is like fine oil upon the head
that runs down upon the beard,
Upon the beard of Aaron,
and runs down upon the collar of his robe. ℟

It is like the dew of Hermon
that falls upon the hills of Zion.
For there the Lord has ordained the blessing:
life for evermore. ℟

Or   TRACK 2

FIRST READING   Job 38.1–11

A reading from the book of Job.

The LORD answered Job out of the whirlwind:
'Who is this that darkens counsel by words without knowledge?
Gird up your loins like a man,
I will question you, and you shall declare to me.

Where were you when I laid the foundation of the earth?
Tell me, if you have understanding.
Who determined its measurements –
surely you know!
Or who stretched the line upon it?
On what were its bases sunk,
or who laid its cornerstone
when the morning stars sang together
and all the heavenly beings shouted for joy?

Or who shut in the sea with doors
when it burst out from the womb? –
when I made the clouds its garment,
and thick darkness its swaddling band,
and prescribed bounds for it,
and set bars and doors,
and said, "Thus far shall you come, and no farther,
and here shall your proud waves be stopped"?'

PSALM   Psalm 107.1–3, 23–32

℟ **Give thanks to the Lord for he is good,**
   and his mercy endures for ever.

Give thanks to the Lord, for he is good,
and his mercy endures for ever.
Let all those whom the Lord has redeemed proclaim
that he redeemed them from the hand of the foe.
He gathered them out of the lands;
from the east and from the west,
from the north and from the south. ℟

Some went down to the sea in ships
and plied their trade in deep waters;
They beheld the works of the Lord
and his wonders in the deep.
Then he spoke and a stormy wind arose,
which tossed high the waves of the sea. ℟

They mounted up to the heavens
and fell back to the depths;
their hearts melted because of their peril.
They reeled and staggered like drunkards
and were at their wits' end.
Then they cried to the Lord in their trouble,
and he delivered them from their distress. ℟

He stilled the storm to a whisper
and quieted the waves of the sea.
Then were they glad because of the calm,
and he brought them
to the harbour they were bound for. ℟

Let them give thanks to the Lord for his mercy
and the wonders he does for his children.
Let them exalt him in the congregation of the people
and praise him in the council of the elders. ℟

SECOND READING   2 Corinthians 6.1–13

A reading from the second letter of Paul to the Corinthians.

As we work together with Christ, we urge you also not to accept the grace of
God in vain.
For he says,
'At an acceptable time I have listened to you,
and on a day of salvation I have helped you.'
See, now is the acceptable time;
see, now is the day of salvation!
We are putting no obstacle in anyone's way, so that no fault may be found
with our ministry, but as servants of God we have commended ourselves in
every way: through great endurance, in afflictions, hardships, calamities,
beatings, imprisonments, riots, labours, sleepless nights, hunger; by purity,
knowledge, patience, kindness, holiness of spirit, genuine love, truthful

speech, and the power of God; with the weapons of righteousness for the right hand and for the left; in honour and dishonour, in ill repute and good repute. We are treated as impostors, and yet are true; as unknown, and yet are well known; as dying, and see – we are alive; as punished, and yet not killed; as sorrowful, yet always rejoicing; as poor, yet making many rich; as having nothing, and yet possessing everything.

We have spoken frankly to you Corinthians; our heart is wide open to you. There is no restriction in our affections, but only in yours. In return – I speak as to children – open wide your hearts also.

GOSPEL
Mark 4.35–41

Hear the gospel of our Lord Jesus Christ according to Mark.

When evening had come, Jesus said to his disciples, 'Let us go across to the other side.' And leaving the crowd behind, they took him with them in the boat, just as he was. Other boats were with him. A great gale arose, and the waves beat into the boat, so that the boat was already being swamped. But he was in the stern, asleep on the cushion; and they woke him up and said to him, 'Teacher, do you not care that we are perishing?' He woke up and rebuked the wind, and said to the sea, 'Peace! Be still!' Then the wind ceased, and there was a dead calm. He said to them, 'Why are you afraid? Have you still no faith?' And they were filled with great awe and said to one another, 'Who then is this, that even the wind and the sea obey him?'

† SUNDAY BETWEEN 26 JUNE AND 2 JULY   YEAR B
PROPER 8

TRACK 1

FIRST READING
2 Samuel 1.1, 17–27

A reading from the second book of Samuel.

After the death of Saul, when David had returned from defeating the Amalekites, David remained two days in Ziklag.

David intoned this lamentation over Saul and his son Jonathan.

(He ordered that The Song of the Bow be taught to the people of Judah; it is written in the Book of Jashar.) He said:

Your glory, O Israel,
lies slain upon your high places!
How the mighty have fallen!
Tell it not in Gath,
proclaim it not in the streets of Ashkelon;
or the daughters of the Philistines will rejoice,
the daughters of the uncircumcised will exult.

You mountains of Gilboa,
let there be no dew or rain upon you,
nor bounteous fields!
For there the shield of the mighty was defiled,
the shield of Saul, anointed with oil no more.

From the blood of the slain, from the fat of the mighty,
the bow of Jonathan did not turn back,
nor the sword of Saul return empty.

Saul and Jonathan, beloved and lovely!
In life and in death they were not divided;
they were swifter than eagles,
they were stronger than lions.

O daughters of Israel, weep over Saul,
who clothed you with crimson, in luxury,
who put ornaments of gold on your apparel.

How the mighty have fallen in the midst of the battle!
Jonathan lies slain upon your high places.

I am distressed for you, my brother Jonathan;
greatly beloved were you to me;
your love to me was wonderful,
passing the love of women.

How the mighty have fallen,
and the weapons of war perished!

PSALM   Psalm 130

℟ **Out of the depths have I called you, O Lord.**
or
℟ **O daughters of Israel, weep over Saul.**

Out of the depths have I called to you, O Lord;
Lord, hear my voice;
let your ears consider well the voice of my supplication.
If you, Lord, were to note what is done amiss,
O Lord, who could stand? ℟

For there is forgiveness with you;
therefore you shall be feared.
I wait for the Lord; my soul waits for him;
in his word is my hope.
My soul waits for the Lord,
more than the night-watch for the morning,
more than the night-watch for the morning. ℟

O Israel, wait for the Lord,
for with the Lord there is mercy;
With him there is plenteous redemption,
and he shall redeem Israel from all their sins. ℟

Or   TRACK 2

FIRST READING   Wisdom of Solomon 1.13–15; 2.23–24

A reading from the book of Wisdom.

God did not make death,
and he does not delight in the death of the living.
For he created all things so that they might exist;
the generative forces of the world are wholesome,
and there is no destructive poison in them,
and the dominion of Hades is not on earth.
For righteousness is immortal.

for God created us for incorruption,
and made us in the image of his own eternity,
but through the devil's envy death entered the world,
and those who belong to his company experience it.

The Canticle Lamentations 3.22–33 may be used in place of Wisdom 1.13–15;
2.23–24 as the First Reading.

CANTICLE OR PSALM

Either   **Lamentations 3.22–33**

℟ **The Lord is good to those who wait for him.**

The steadfast love of the LORD never ceases,
his mercies never come to an end.
They are new every morning;
great is your faithfulness. ℟

'The LORD is my portion,' says my soul,
'therefore I will hope in him.'
The LORD is good to those who wait for him,
to the soul that seeks him.
It is good that one should wait quietly for the salvation of the LORD. ℟

It is good for one to bear the yoke in youth,
to sit alone in silence when the Lord has imposed it,
to put one's mouth to the dust (there may yet be hope),
to give one's cheek to the smiter,
and be filled with insults. ℟

For the Lord will not reject for ever.
Although he causes grief,
he will have compassion according to the abundance of his steadfast love;
for he does not willingly afflict or grieve anyone. ℟

Or   **Psalm 30**

℟ **To you, O Lord, my heart shall sing without ceasing.**

I will exalt you, O Lord,
because you have lifted me up
and have not let my enemies triumph over me.
O Lord my God, I cried out to you,
and you restored me to health.
You brought me up, O Lord, from the dead;
you restored my life as I was going down to the grave. ℟

Sing to the Lord, you servants of his;
give thanks for the remembrance of his holiness.
For his wrath endures but the twinkling of an eye,
his favour for a lifetime.
Weeping may spend the night,
but joy comes in the morning. ℟

While I felt secure, I said,
'I shall never be disturbed.
You, Lord, with your favour,
made me as strong as the mountains.'
Then you hid your face,
and I was filled with fear. ℟

I cried to you, O Lord;
I pleaded with the Lord, saying,
'What profit is there in my blood,
if I go down to the Pit?
will the dust praise you or declare your faithfulness?
Hear, O Lord, and have mercy upon me;
O Lord, be my helper.' ℟

You have turned my wailing into dancing;
you have put off my sack-cloth and clothed me with joy;
Therefore my heart sings to you without ceasing;
O Lord my God, I will give you thanks for ever. ℟

SECOND READING   2 Corinthians 8.7–15

A reading from the second letter of Paul to the Corinthians.

You excel in everything – in faith, in speech, in knowledge, in utmost eagerness, and in our love for you – so we want you to excel also in this generous undertaking.

I do not say this as a command, but I am testing the genuineness of your love against the earnestness of others. For you know the generous act of our Lord Jesus Christ, that though he was rich, yet for your sakes he became poor, so that by his poverty you might become rich. And in this matter I am giving my advice: it is appropriate for you who began last year not only to do something but even to desire to do something – now finish doing it, so that your eagerness may be matched by completing it according to your means. For if the eagerness is there, the gift is acceptable according to what one has –

not according to what one does not have. I do not mean that there should be relief for others and pressure on you, but it is a question of a fair balance between your present abundance and their need, so that their abundance may be for your need, in order that there may be a fair balance.
As it is written,
'The one who had much did not have too much,
and the one who had little did not have too little.'

GOSPEL   Mark 5.21–43

Hear the gospel of our Lord Jesus Christ according to Mark.

When Jesus had crossed again in the boat to the other side, a great crowd gathered around him; and he was by the lake. Then one of the leaders of the synagogue named Jairus came and, when he saw him, fell at his feet and begged him repeatedly, 'My little daughter is at the point of death. Come and lay your hands on her, so that she may be made well, and live.' So he went with him.

And a large crowd followed him and pressed in on him. Now there was a woman who had been suffering from haemorrhages for twelve years. She had endured much under many physicians, and had spent all that she had; and she was no better, but rather grew worse. She had heard about Jesus, and came up behind him in the crowd and touched his cloak, for she said, 'If I but touch his clothes, I will be made well.' Immediately her haemorrhage stopped; and she felt in her body that she was healed of her disease. Immediately aware that power had gone forth from him, Jesus turned about in the crowd and said, 'Who touched my clothes?' And his disciples said to him, 'You see the crowd pressing in on you; how can you say, "Who touched me?"' He looked all around to see who had done it. But the woman, knowing what had happened to her, came in fear and trembling, fell down before him, and told him the whole truth. He said to her, 'Daughter, your faith has made you well; go in peace, and be healed of your disease.'

While he was still speaking, some people came from the leader's house to say, 'Your daughter is dead. Why trouble the teacher any further?' But overhearing what they said, Jesus said to the leader of the synagogue, 'Do not fear, only believe.' He allowed no one to follow him except Peter, James, and John, the brother of James. When they came to the house of the leader of the synagogue, he saw a commotion, people weeping and wailing loudly. When he had entered, he said to them, 'Why do you make a commotion and weep? The child is not dead but sleeping.' And they laughed at him. Then he put them all outside, and took the child's father and mother and those who were with him, and went in where the child was. He took her by the hand and said to her, 'Talitha cum,' which means, 'Little girl, get up!' And immediately the girl got up and began to walk about (she was twelve years of age). At this they were overcome with amazement. He strictly ordered them that no one should know this, and told them to give her something to eat.

† SUNDAY BETWEEN 3 AND 9 JULY   YEAR B
PROPER 9

TRACK 1

FIRST READING   2 Samuel 5.1–5, 9–10

A reading from the second book of Samuel.

All the tribes of Israel came to David at Hebron, and said, 'Look, we are your bone and flesh. For some time, while Saul was king over us, it was you who led out Israel and brought it in. The LORD said to you: It is you who shall be shepherd of my people Israel, you who shall be ruler over Israel.' So all the elders of Israel came to the king at Hebron; and King David made a covenant with them at Hebron before the LORD, and they anointed David king over Israel. David was thirty years old when he began to reign, and he reigned forty years. At Hebron he reigned over Judah seven years and six months; and at Jerusalem he reigned over all Israel and Judah thirty-three years.

David occupied the stronghold, and named it the city of David. David built the city all around from the Millo inward. And David became greater and greater, for the LORD, the God of hosts, was with him.

PSALM   Psalm 48

℟ In the city of our God is his holy hill.

Great is the Lord and highly to be praised;
in the city of our God is his holy hill.
Beautiful and lofty, the joy of all the earth,
is the hill of Zion,
the very centre of the world
and the city of the great king.
God is in her citadels;
he is known to be her sure refuge. ℟

Behold, the kings of the earth assembled
and marched forward together.
They looked and were astounded;
they retreated and fled in terror.
Trembling seized them there;
they writhed like a woman in childbirth,
like ships of the sea when the east wind shatters them. ℟

As we have heard, so have we seen,
in the city of the Lord of hosts, in the city of our God;
God has established her for ever.
We have waited in silence
on your loving-kindness, O God,
in the midst of your temple. ℟

Your praise, like your name, O God,
reaches to the world's end;
your right hand is full of justice.
Let Mount Zion be glad
and the cities of Judah rejoice,
because of your judgements. ℟

Make the circuit of Zion; walk round about her;
count the number of her towers.
Consider well her bulwarks; examine her strongholds;
that you may tell those who come after.
This God is our God for ever and ever;
he shall be our guide for evermore. ℟

Or TRACK 2

FIRST READING   Ezekiel 2.1–5

A reading from the book of the prophet Ezekiel.

The heavens were opened, and I saw visions of God. When I saw this, I fell
on my face, and I heard the voice of someone speaking. He said to me: O
mortal, stand up on your feet, and I will speak with you. And when he spoke
to me, a spirit entered into me and set me on my feet; and I heard him
speaking to me. He said to me, Mortal, I am sending you to the people of
Israel, to a nation of rebels who have rebelled against me; they and their
ancestors have transgressed against me to this very day. The descendants are

impudent and stubborn. I am sending you to them, and you shall say to them, 'Thus says the Lord GOD.' Whether they hear or refuse to hear (for they are a rebellious house), they shall know that there has been a prophet among them.

PSALM

℟ **Our eyes look to the Lord our God,**
  until he shows us his mercy.

To you I lift up my eyes,
to you enthroned in the heavens.
As the eyes of servants look to the hand of their masters,
and the eyes of a maid to the hand of her mistress,
So our eyes look to the Lord our God,
until he show us his mercy. ℟

Have mercy upon us, O Lord, have mercy,
for we have had more than enough of contempt,
Too much of the scorn of the indolent rich,
and of the derision of the proud. ℟

SECOND READING

2 Corinthians 12.2–10

A reading from the second letter of Paul to the Corinthians.

I know a person in Christ who fourteen years ago was caught up to the third heaven – whether in the body or out of the body I do not know; God knows. And I know that such a person – whether in the body or out of the body I do not know; God knows – was caught up into Paradise and heard things that are not to be told, that no mortal is permitted to repeat. On behalf of such a one I will boast, but on my own behalf I will not boast, except of my weaknesses. But if I wish to boast, I will not be a fool, for I will be speaking the truth. But I refrain from it, so that no one may think better of me than what is seen in me or heard from me,

even considering the exceptional character of the revelations. Therefore, to keep me from being too elated, a thorn was given me in the flesh, a messenger of Satan to torment me, to keep me from being too elated. Three times I appealed to the Lord about this, that it would leave me, but he said to me, 'My grace is sufficient for you, for power is made perfect in weakness.' So, I will boast all the more gladly of my weaknesses, so that the power of Christ may dwell in me. Therefore I am content with weaknesses, insults, hardships, persecutions, and calamities for the sake of Christ; for whenever I am weak, then I am strong.

GOSPEL   MARK 6.1–13

Hear the gospel of our Lord Jesus Christ according to Mark.

Jesus came to his home town, and his disciples followed him. On the sabbath he began to teach in the synagogue, and many who heard him were astounded. They said, 'Where did this man get all this? What is this wisdom that has been given to him? What deeds of power are being done by his hands! Is not this the carpenter, the son of Mary and brother of James and Joses and Judas and Simon, and are not his sisters here with us?' And they took offence at him. Then Jesus said to them, 'Prophets are not without honour, except in their home town, and among their own kin, and in their own house.' And he could do no deed of power there, except that he laid his hands on a few sick people and cured them. And he was amazed at their unbelief. Then he went about among the villages teaching. He called the twelve and began to send them out two by two, and gave them authority over the unclean spirits. He ordered them to take nothing for their journey except a staff; no bread, no bag, no money in their belts; but to wear sandals and not to put on two tunics. He said to them, 'Wherever you enter a house, stay there until you leave the place. If any place will not welcome you and they refuse to hear you, as you leave, shake off the dust that is on your feet as a testimony against them.' So they went out and proclaimed that all should repent. They cast out many demons, and anointed with oil many who were sick and cured them.

† SUNDAY BETWEEN 10 AND 16 JULY   YEAR B
PROPER 10

TRACK 1

FIRST READING   2 Samuel 6.1–5, 12b–19

A reading from the second book of Samuel.

David again gathered all the chosen men of Israel, thirty thousand. David and all the people with him set out and went from Baale-judah, to bring up from there the ark of God, which is called by the name of the LORD of hosts who is enthroned on the cherubim. They carried the ark of God on a new cart, and brought it out of the house of Abinadab, which was on the hill. Uzzah and Ahio, the sons of Abinadab, were driving the new cart with the ark of God; and Ahio went in front of the ark. David and all the house of Israel were dancing before the LORD with all their might, with songs and lyres and harps and tambourines and castanets and cymbals.

So David went and brought up the ark of God from the house of Obed-edom to the city of David with rejoicing; and when those who bore the ark of the LORD had gone six paces, he sacrificed an ox and a fatling. David danced before the LORD with all his might; David was girded with a linen ephod. So David and all the house of Israel brought up the ark of the LORD with shouting, and with the sound of the trumpet. As the ark of the LORD came into the city of David. Michal daughter of Saul looked out of the window, and saw King David leaping and dancing before the LORD; and she despised him in her heart.

They brought in the ark of the LORD, and set it in its place, inside the tent that David had pitched for it; and David offered burnt offerings and offerings of well-being before the LORD. When David had finished offering the burnt offerings and the offerings of well-being, he blessed the people in the name of the LORD of hosts, and distributed food among all the people, the whole multitude of Israel, both men and women, to each a cake of bread, a portion of meat, and a cake of raisins. Then all the people went back to their homes.

PSALM   Psalm 24

℞ **The King of glory shall come in.**

The earth is the Lord's and all that is in it,
the world and all who dwell therein.
For it is he who founded it upon the seas
and made it firm upon the rivers of the deep. ℞

'Who can ascend the hill of the Lord?
and who can stand in his holy place?'
'Those who have clean hands and a pure heart,
who have not pledged themselves to falsehood,
nor sworn by what is a fraud. ℞

They shall receive a blessing from the Lord
and a just reward from the God of their salvation.'

Such is the generation of those who seek him,
of those who seek your face, O God of Jacob. ℟

Lift up your heads, O gates;
lift them high, O everlasting doors;
and the King of glory shall come in.
'Who is this King of glory?'
'The Lord, strong and mighty,
the Lord, mighty in battle.' ℟

Lift up your heads, O gates;
lift them high, O everlasting doors;
and the King of glory shall come in.
'Who is he, this King of glory?'
'The Lord of hosts,
he is the King of glory.' ℟

Or   TRACK 2

FIRST READING   **Amos 7.7–15**

A reading from the book of the prophet Amos.

This is what the Lord God showed me: the Lord was standing beside a wall
built with a plumb line, with a plumb line in his hand.
 And the LORD said to me,
'Amos, what do you see?' And I said,
'A plumb line.' Then the Lord said,
'See, I am setting a plumb line in the midst of my people Israel;
I will never again pass them by;
the high places of Isaac shall be made desolate,
and the sanctuaries of Israel shall be laid waste,
and I will rise against the house of Jeroboam with the sword.'
Then Amaziah, the priest of Bethel, sent to King Jeroboam of Israel, saying,
'Amos has conspired against you in the very centre of the house of Israel; the
land is not able to bear all his words.
For thus Amos has said,
"Jeroboam shall die by the sword,
and Israel must go into exile away from his land."'
And Amaziah said to Amos, 'O seer, go, flee away to the land of Judah, earn
your bread there, and prophesy there; but never again prophesy at Bethel, for
it is the king's sanctuary, and it is a temple of the kingdom.' Then Amos

answered Amaziah, 'I am no prophet, nor a prophet's son; but I am a herdsman, and a dresser of sycamore trees, and the LORD took me from following the flock, and the LORD said to me, "Go, prophesy to my people Israel."'

PSALM   Psalm 85.8–13

℟ Show us your mercy, O Lord,
   and grant us your salvation.

I will listen to what the Lord God is saying,
for he is speaking peace to his faithful people
and to those who turn their hearts to him.
Truly, his salvation is very near to those who fear him,
that his glory may dwell in our land. ℟

Mercy and truth have met together;
righteousness and peace have kissed each other.
Truth shall spring up from the earth,
and righteousness shall look down from heaven. ℟

The Lord will indeed grant prosperity,
and our land will yield its increase.
Righteousness shall go before him,
and peace shall be a pathway for his feet. ℟

SECOND READING   Ephesians 1.3–14

A reading from the letter of Paul to the Ephesians.

Blessed be the God and Father of our Lord Jesus Christ, who has blessed us in Christ with every spiritual blessing in the heavenly places, just as he chose us in Christ before the foundation of the world to be holy and blameless before him in love. He destined us for adoption as his children through Jesus Christ, according to the good pleasure of his will, to the praise of his glorious grace that he freely bestowed on us in the Beloved. In him we have redemption through his blood, the forgiveness of our trespasses, according to the riches of his grace that he lavished on us. With all wisdom and insight he has made known to us the mystery of his will, according to his good pleasure that he set forth in Christ, as a plan for the fullness of time, to gather up all things in Christ, things in heaven and things on earth.

In Christ we have also obtained an inheritance, having been destined according to the purpose of him who accomplishes all things according to his counsel and will, so that we, who were the first to set our hope on Christ, might live for the praise of his glory. In him you also, when you had heard the word of truth, the gospel of your salvation, and had believed in him, were marked with the seal of the promised Holy Spirit; this is the pledge of our inheritance towards redemption as God's own people, to the praise of his glory.

GOSPEL   MARK 6.14–29

Hear the gospel of our Lord Jesus Christ according to Mark.

King Herod heard of the healings and other miracles, for Jesus' name had become known. Some were saying, 'John the baptizer has been raised from the dead; and for this reason these powers are at work in him.' But others said, 'It is Elijah.' And others said, 'It is a prophet, like one of the prophets of old.' But when Herod heard of it, he said, 'John, whom I beheaded, has been raised.'

For Herod himself had sent men who arrested John, bound him, and put him in prison on account of Herodias, his brother Philip's wife, because Herod had married her. For John had been telling Herod, 'It is not lawful for you to have your brother's wife.' And Herodias had a grudge against him, and wanted to kill him. But she could not, for Herod feared John, knowing that he was a righteous and holy man, and he protected him. When he heard him, he was greatly perplexed; and yet he liked to listen to him. But an opportunity came when Herod on his birthday gave a banquet for his courtiers and officers and for the leaders of Galilee.

When his daughter Herodias came in and danced, she pleased Herod and his guests; and the king said to the girl, 'Ask me for whatever you wish, and I will give it.' And he solemnly swore to her, 'Whatever you ask me, I will give you, even half of my kingdom.' She went out and said to her mother, 'What should I ask for?' She replied, 'The head of John the Baptist.' Immediately she rushed back to the king and requested, 'I want you to give me at once the head of John the Baptizer on a platter.' The king was deeply grieved; yet out of regard for his oaths and for the guests, he did not want to refuse her. Immediately the king sent a soldier of the guard with orders to bring John's head. He went and beheaded him in the prison, brought his head on a platter, and gave it to the girl. Then the girl gave it to her mother. When his disciples heard about it, they came and took his body, and laid it in a tomb.

† SUNDAY BETWEEN 17 AND 23 JULY   YEAR B
PROPER 11

TRACK 1

FIRST READING   **2 Samuel 7.1–14a**

A reading from the second book of Samuel.

When David was settled in his house, and the LORD had given him rest from all his enemies around him, the king said to the prophet Nathan, 'See now, I am living in a house of cedar, but the ark of God stays in a tent.' Nathan said to the king, 'Go, do all that you have in mind; for the LORD is with you.'

But that same night the word of the LORD came to Nathan: Go and tell my servant David: Thus says the LORD: Are you the one to build me a house to live in? I have not lived in a house since the day I brought up the people of Israel from Egypt to this day, but I have been moving about in a tent and a tabernacle. Wherever I have moved about among all the people of Israel, did I ever speak a word with any of the tribal leaders of Israel, whom I commanded to shepherd my people Israel, saying, 'Why have you not built me a house of cedar?' Now therefore thus you shall say to my servant David: Thus says the LORD of hosts: I took you from the pasture, from following the sheep to be prince over my people Israel; and I have been with you wherever you went, and have cut off all your enemies from before you; and I will make for you a great name, like the name of the great ones of the earth. And I will appoint a place for my people Israel and will plant them, so that they may live in their own place, and be disturbed no more; and evildoers shall afflict them no more, as formerly, from the time that I appointed judges over my people Israel; and I will give you rest from all your enemies. Moreover the LORD declares to you, David, that the LORD will make you a house. When your days are fulfilled and you lie down with your ancestors, I will raise up your offspring after you, who shall come forth from your body, and I will establish his kingdom. He shall build a house for my name, and I will establish the throne of his kingdom for ever. I will be a father to him, and he shall be a son to me.

PSALM **Psalm 89.20–37**

℞ **I will make David my firstborn
[and higher than the kings of the earth].**

'I have found David my servant;
with my holy oil have I anointed him.
My hand will hold him fast
and my arm will make him strong.
No enemy shall deceive him,
nor the wicked bring him down. ℞

I will crush his foes before him
and strike down those who hate him.
My faithfulness and love shall be with him,
and he shall be victorious through my name.
I shall make his dominion extend
from the Great Sea to the River. ℞

He will say to me, "You are my Father,
my God and the rock of my salvation."
I will make him my first-born
and higher than the kings of the earth.
I will keep my love for him for ever,
and my covenant will stand firm for him. ℞

I will establish his line for ever
and his throne as the days of heaven.
If his children forsake my law
and do not walk according to my judgements; ℞

If they break my statutes
and do not keep my commandments;
I will punish their transgressions with a rod
and their iniquities with the lash;
But I will not take my love from him,
nor let my faithfulness prove false. ℞

I will not break my covenant,
nor change what has gone out of my lips.
Once for all I have sworn by my holiness:
"I will not lie to David. ℞

His line shall endure for ever
and his throne as the sun before me;
It shall stand fast for evermore like the moon,
the abiding witness in the sky."' ℟

Or   TRACK 2

FIRST READING   Jeremiah 23.1–6

A reading from the book of the prophet Jeremiah.

Woe to the shepherds who destroy and scatter the sheep of my pasture! says
the LORD. Therefore thus says the LORD, the God of Israel, concerning the
shepherds who shepherd my people: It is you who have scattered my flock,
and have driven them away, and you have not attended to them. So I will
attend to you for your evil doings, says the LORD. Then I myself will gather
the remnant of my flock out of all the lands where I have driven them, and I
will bring them back to their fold, and they shall be fruitful and multiply. I
will raise up shepherds over them who will shepherd them, and they shall
not fear any longer, or be dismayed, nor shall any be missing, says the LORD.
The days are surely coming, says the LORD, when I will raise up for David a
righteous Branch, and he shall reign as king and deal wisely, and shall
execute justice and righteousness in the land. In his days Judah will be saved
and Israel will live in safety. And this is the name by which he will be called:
'The LORD is our righteousness.'

PSALM   Psalm 23

**℟ The Lord is my shepherd;
I shall not be in want.**

The Lord is my shepherd;
I shall not be in want.
He makes me lie down in green pastures
and leads me beside still waters. ℟

He revives my soul
and guides me along right pathways for his name's sake.
Though I walk through the valley of the shadow of death,
I shall fear no evil;
for you are with me;
your rod and your staff, they comfort me. ℟

You spread a table before me
in the presence of those who trouble me;
you have anointed my head with oil,
and my cup is running over.
Surely your goodness and mercy shall follow me
all the days of my life,
and I will dwell in the house of the Lord for ever. ℞

SECOND READING   Ephesians 2.11–22

A reading from the letter of Paul to the Ephesians.

Remember that at one time you Gentiles by birth, called 'the uncircumcision'
by those who are called 'the circumcision' – a physical circumcision made in
the flesh by human hands – remember that you were at that time without
Christ, being aliens from the commonwealth of Israel, and strangers to the
covenants of promise, having no hope and without God in the world. But
now in Christ Jesus you who once were far off have been brought near by the
blood of Christ. For he is our peace; in his flesh he has made both groups
into one and has broken down the dividing wall, that is, the hostility
between us. He has abolished the law with its commandments and
ordinances, that he might create in himself one new humanity in place of
the two, thus making peace, and might reconcile both groups to God in one
body through the cross, thus putting to death that hostility through it. So he
came and proclaimed peace to you who were far off and peace to those who
were near; for through him both of us have access in one Spirit to the Father.
So then you are no longer strangers and aliens, but you are citizens with the
saints and also members of the household of God, built upon the foundation
of the apostles and prophets, with Christ Jesus himself as the cornerstone. In
him the whole structure is joined together and grows into a holy temple in
the Lord; in whom you also are built together spiritually into a dwelling-
place for God.

GOSPEL   Mark 6.30–34, 53–56

Hear the gospel of our Lord Jesus Christ according to Mark.

The apostles returned from their mission. They gathered around Jesus, and
told him all that they had done and taught. He said to them, 'Come away to
a deserted place all by yourselves and rest a while.' For many were coming
and going, and they had no leisure even to eat. And they went away in the

boat to a deserted place by themselves. Now many saw them going and recognized them, and they hurried there on foot from all the towns and arrived ahead of them. As he went ashore, he saw a great crowd; and he had compassion for them, because they were like sheep without a shepherd; and he began to teach them many things. When they had crossed over, they came to land at Gennesaret and moored the boat. When they got out of the boat, people at once recognized him, and rushed about that whole region and began to bring the sick on mats to wherever they heard he was. And wherever he went, into villages or cities or farms, they laid the sick in the market-places, and begged him that they might touch even the fringe of his cloak; and all who touched it were healed.

† SUNDAY BETWEEN 24 AND 30 JULY   YEAR B
PROPER 12

TRACK 1

FIRST READING   **2 Samuel 11.1–15**

A reading from the second book of Samuel.

In the spring of the year, the time when kings go out to battle, David sent Joab with his officers and all Israel with him; they ravaged the Ammonites, and besieged Rabbah. But David remained at Jerusalem. It happened, late one afternoon, when David rose from his couch and was walking about on the roof of the king's house, that he saw from the roof a woman bathing; the woman was very beautiful.

David sent someone to inquire about the woman. It was reported, 'This is Bathsheba daughter of Eliam, the wife of Uriah the Hittite.' So David sent messengers to get her, and she came to him, and he lay with her. (Now she was purifying herself after her period.) Then she returned to her house. The woman conceived; and she sent and told David, 'I am pregnant.' So David sent word to Joab, 'Send me Uriah the Hittite.' And Joab sent Uriah to David. When Uriah came to him, David asked how Joab and the people fared, and how the war was going. Then David said to Uriah, 'Go down to your house, and wash your feet.' Uriah went out of the king's house, and there followed him a present from the king. But Uriah slept at the entrance of the king's house with all the servants of his lord, and did not go down to his house. When they told David, 'Uriah did not go down to his house,' David said to

Uriah, 'You have just come from a journey. Why did you not go down to your house?' Uriah said to David, 'The ark and Israel and Judah remain in booths; and my lord Joab and the servants of my lord are camping in the open field; shall I then go to my house, to eat and to drink, and to lie with my wife? As you live, and as your soul lives, I will not do such a thing.' Then David said to Uriah, 'Remain here today also, and tomorrow I will send you back.' So Uriah remained in Jerusalem that day. On the next day, David invited him to eat and drink in his presence and made him drunk; and in the evening he went out to lie on his couch with the servants of his lord, but he did not go down to his house.

In the morning David wrote a letter to Joab, and sent it by the hand of Uriah. In the letter he wrote, 'Set Uriah in the forefront of the hardest fighting, and then draw back from him, so that he may be struck down and die.'

PSALM   Psalm 14

℟ Have they no knowledge, all those evildoers
  [who eat up my people like bread]?

The fool has said in his heart, 'There is no God.'
All are corrupt and commit abominable acts;
there is none who does any good.
The Lord looks down from heaven upon us all,
to see if there is any who is wise,
if there is one who seeks after God. ℟

Everyone has proved faithless;
all alike have turned bad;
there is none who does good; no, not one.
Have they no knowledge, all those evildoers
who eat up my people like bread
and do not call upon the Lord? ℟

See how they tremble with fear,
because God is in the company of the righteous.
Their aim is to confound the plans of the afflicted,
but the Lord is their refuge.
O that Israel's deliverance would come out of Zion!
when the Lord restores the fortunes of his people,
Jacob will rejoice and Israel be glad. ℟

Or   TRACK 2

FIRST READING   **2 Kings 4.42–44**

A reading from the second book of Kings.

A man came bringing food from the first fruits to Elisha, the man of God: twenty loaves of barley and fresh ears of grain in his sack. Elisha said, 'Give it to the people and let them eat.' But his servant said, 'How can I set this before a hundred people?' So he repeated, 'Give it to the people and let them eat, for thus says the LORD, "They shall eat and have some left."' He set it before them, they ate, and had some left, according to the word of the LORD.

PSALM   **Psalm 145.10–19**

℞ **You open wide your hand, O Lord,
and satisfy our needs.**

All your works praise you, O Lord,
and your faithful servants bless you. ℞

They make known the glory of your kingdom
and speak of your power;
That the peoples may know of your power
and the glorious splendour of your kingdom. ℞

Your kingdom is an everlasting kingdom;
your dominion endures throughout all ages.
The Lord is faithful in all his words
and merciful in all his deeds.
The Lord upholds all those who fall;
he lifts up those who are bowed down. ℞

The eyes of all wait upon you, O Lord,
and you give them their food in due season.
You open wide your hand
and satisfy the needs of every living creature. ℞

The Lord is righteous in all his ways
and loving in all his works.
The Lord is near to those who call upon him,
to all who call upon him faithfully. ℞

SECOND READING   Ephesians 3.14–21

A reading from the letter of Paul to the Ephesians.

I bow my knees before the Father, from whom every family in heaven and on earth takes its name. I pray that, according to the riches of his glory, he may grant that you may be strengthened in your inner being with power through his Spirit, and that Christ may dwell in your hearts through faith, as you are being rooted and grounded in love. I pray that you may have the power to comprehend, with all the saints, what is the breadth and length and height and depth, and to know the love of Christ that surpasses knowledge, so that you may be filled with all the fullness of God.

Now to him who by the power at work within us is able to accomplish abundantly far more than all we can ask or imagine, to him be glory in the church and in Christ Jesus to all generations, for ever and ever. Amen.

GOSPEL   John 6.1–21

Hear the gospel of our Lord Jesus Christ according to John.

Jesus went to the other side of the Sea of Galilee, also called the Sea of Tiberias. A large crowd kept following him, because they saw the signs that he was doing for the sick. Jesus went up the mountain and sat down there with his disciples. Now the Passover, the festival of the Jews, was near. When he looked up and saw a large crowd coming towards him, Jesus said to Philip, 'Where are we to buy bread for these people to eat?' He said this to test him, for he himself knew what he was going to do. Philip answered him, 'Six months' wages would not buy enough bread for each of them to get a little.' One of his disciples, Andrew, Simon Peter's brother, said to Jesus, 'There is a boy here who has five barley loaves and two fish. But what are they among so many people?' Jesus said, 'Make the people sit down.' Now there was a great deal of grass in the place; so they sat down, about five thousand in all. Then Jesus took the loaves, and when he had given thanks, he distributed them to those who were seated; so also the fish, as much as they wanted. When they were satisfied, he told his disciples, 'Gather up the fragments left over, so that nothing may be lost.' So they gathered them up, and from the fragments of the five barley loaves, left by those who had eaten, they filled twelve baskets. When the people saw the sign that he had done, they began to say, 'This is indeed the prophet who is to come into the world.' When Jesus realized that they were about to come and take him by force to make him king, he withdrew again to the mountain by himself. When evening came, his disciples went down to the lake, got into a boat, and started across the lake to Capernaum. It was now dark, and Jesus had not yet come to them. The lake became rough because a strong wind was blowing. When they had rowed about three or four miles, they saw Jesus walking on the lake and coming near the boat, and they were terrified. But he said to them, 'It is I; do not be afraid.' Then they wanted to take him into the boat, and immediately the boat reached the land towards which they were going.

† SUNDAY BETWEEN 31 JULY AND 6 AUGUST   YEAR B
PROPER 13

TRACK 1

FIRST READING   **2 Samuel 11.26 – 12.13a**

A reading from the second book of Samuel.

When the wife of Uriah heard that her husband was dead, she made lamentation for him. When the mourning was over, David sent and brought her to his house, and she became his wife, and bore him a son.

But the thing that David had done displeased the LORD, The LORD sent Nathan to David. He came to him, and said to him, 'There were two men in a certain city, the one rich and the other poor. The rich man had very many flocks and herds; but the poor man had nothing but one little ewe lamb, which he had bought. He brought it up, and it grew up with him and with his children; it used to eat of his meagre fare, and drink from his cup, and lie in his bosom, and it was like a daughter to him. Now there came a traveller to the rich man, and he was loath to take one of his own flock or herd to prepare for the wayfarer who had come to him, but he took the poor man's lamb, and prepared that for the guest who had come to him.' Then David's anger was greatly kindled against the man. He said to Nathan, 'As the LORD lives, the man who has done this deserves to die; he shall restore the lamb fourfold, because he did this thing, and because he had no pity.' Nathan said to David, 'You are the man! Thus says the LORD, the God of Israel: I anointed you king over Israel, and I rescued you from the hand of Saul; I gave you your master's house, and your master's wives into your bosom, and gave you the house of Israel and of Judah; and if that had been too little, I would have added as much more. Why have you despised the word of the LORD, to do what is evil in his sight? You have struck down Uriah the Hittite with the sword, and have taken his wife to be your wife, and have killed him with the sword of the Ammonites. Now therefore the sword shall never depart from your house, for you have despised me, and have taken the wife of Uriah the Hittite to be your wife. Thus says the LORD: I will raise up trouble against you from within your own house; and I will take your wives before your eyes, and give them to your neighbour, and he shall lie with your wives in the sight of this very sun. For you did it secretly; but I will do this thing before all Israel, and before the sun.' David said to Nathan, 'I have sinned against the LORD.' Nathan said to David, 'Now the LORD has put away your sin; you shall not die.'

PSALM

Psalm 51.1–12

℟ **I know my transgressions, O God**
  [and my sin is ever before me].

Have mercy on me, O God,
according to your loving-kindness;
in your great compassion blot out my offences.
Wash me through and through from my wickedness
and cleanse me from my sin. ℟

For I know my transgressions,
and my sin is ever before me.
Against you only have I sinned
and done what is evil in your sight.
And so you are justified when you speak
and upright in your judgement. ℟

Indeed, I have been wicked from my birth,
a sinner from my mother's womb.
For behold, you look for truth deep within me,
and will make me understand wisdom secretly. ℟

Purge me from my sin and I shall be pure;
wash me and I shall be clean indeed.
Make me hear of joy and gladness,
that the body you have broken may rejoice.
Hide your face from my sins
and blot out all my iniquities. ℟

Create in me a clean heart, O God,
and renew a right spirit within me.
Cast me not away from your presence
and take not your holy Spirit from me. ℟

Or   TRACK 2

FIRST READING   **Exodus 16.2–4, 9–15**

A reading from the book of Exodus.

The whole congregation of the Israelites complained against Moses and
Aaron in the wilderness. The Israelites said to them, 'If only we had died by
the hand of the LORD in the land of Egypt, when we sat by the fleshpots and
ate our fill of bread; for you have brought us out into this wilderness to kill
this whole assembly with hunger.'

Then the LORD said to Moses, 'I am going to rain bread from heaven for you,
and each day the people shall go out and gather enough for that day. In that
way I will test them, whether they will follow my instruction or not.'

Then Moses said to Aaron, 'Say to the whole congregation of the Israelites,
"Draw near to the LORD, for he has heard your complaining."' And as Aaron
spoke to the whole congregation of the Israelites, they looked toward the
wilderness, and the glory of the LORD appeared in the cloud. The LORD
spoke to Moses and said, 'I have heard the complaining of the Israelites; say
to them, "At twilight you shall eat meat, and in the morning you shall have
your fill of bread; then you shall know that I am the LORD your God."'

In the evening quails came up and covered the camp; and in the morning
there was a layer of dew around the camp. When the layer of dew lifted,
there on the surface of the wilderness was a fine flaky substance, as fine as
frost on the ground. When the Israelites saw it, they said to one another,
'What is it?' For they did not know what it was. Moses said to them, 'It is the
bread that the LORD has given you to eat.'

PSALM   Psalm 78.23–29

℟ **The Lord gave them grain from heaven.**

The Lord commanded the clouds above
and opened the doors of heaven.
He rained down manna upon them to eat
and gave them grain from heaven.
So mortals ate the bread of angels;
he provided for them food enough. ℟

He caused the east wind to blow in the heavens
And led out the south wind by his might.
He rained down flesh upon them like dust
and winged birds like the sand of the sea. ℟

He let it fall in the midst of their camp
and round about their dwellings.
So they ate and were well filled,
for he gave them what they craved. ℟

SECOND READING   Ephesians 4.1–16

A reading from the letter of Paul to the Ephesians.

I, the prisoner in the Lord, beg you to lead a life worthy of the calling to
which you have been called, with all humility and gentleness, with patience,
bearing with one another in love, making every effort to maintain the unity
of the Spirit in the bond of peace. There is one body and one Spirit, just as
you were called to the one hope of your calling, one Lord, one faith, one
baptism, one God and Father of all, who is above all and through all and
in all
But each of us was given grace
according to the measure of Christ's gift.
Therefore it is said,
'When he ascended on high he made captivity itself a captive;
he gave gifts to his people.'
(When it says, 'He ascended,' what does it mean but that he had also
descended into the lower parts of the earth? He who descended is the same
one who ascended far above all the heavens, so that he might fill all things.)
The gifts he gave were that some would be apostles, some prophets, some
evangelists, some pastors and teachers, to equip the saints for the work of

ministry, for building up the body of Christ, until all of us come to the unity of the faith and of the knowledge of the Son of God, to maturity, to the measure of the full stature of Christ. We must no longer be children, tossed to and fro and blown about by every wind of doctrine, by people's trickery, by their craftiness in deceitful scheming. But speaking the truth in love, we must grow up in every way into him who is the head, into Christ, from whom the whole body, joined and knit together by every ligament with which it is equipped, as each part is working properly, promotes the body's growth in building itself up in love.

GOSPEL   John 6.24–35

Hear the gospel of our Lord Jesus Christ according to John.

When the crowd saw that neither Jesus nor his disciples were at the place where Jesus had given the bread, they themselves got into the boats and went to Capernaum looking for Jesus.

When they found him on the other side of the lake, they said to him, 'Rabbi, when did you come here?' Jesus answered them, 'Very truly, I tell you, you are looking for me, not because you saw signs, but because you ate your fill of the loaves. Do not work for the food that perishes, but for the food that endures for eternal life, which the Son of Man will give you. For it is on him that God the Father has set his seal.' Then they said to him, 'What must we do to perform the works of God?' Jesus answered them, 'This is the work of God, that you believe in him whom he has sent.' So they said to him, 'What sign are you going to give us then, so that we may see it and believe you? What work are you performing? Our ancestors ate the manna in the wilderness; as it is written, "He gave them bread from heaven to eat."' Then Jesus said to them, 'Very truly, I tell you, it was not Moses who gave you the bread from heaven, but it is my Father who gives you the true bread from heaven. For the bread of God is that which comes down from heaven and gives life to the world.' They said to him, 'Sir, give us this bread always.'

Jesus said to them, 'I am the bread of life. Whoever comes to me will never be hungry, and whoever believes in me will never be thirsty.'

† SUNDAY BETWEEN 7 AND 13 AUGUST   YEAR B
PROPER 14

TRACK 1

FIRST READING   **2 Samuel 18.5–9, 15, 31–33**

A reading from the second book of Samuel.

The king ordered Joab and Abishai and Ittai, saying, 'Deal gently for my sake with the young man Absalom.' And all the people heard when the king gave orders to all the commanders concerning Absalom.

So the army went out into the field against Israel; and the battle was fought in the forest of Ephraim. The men of Israel were defeated there by the servants of David, and the slaughter there was great on that day, twenty thousand men. The battle spread over the face of all the country; and the forest claimed more victims that day than the sword.

Absalom happened to meet the servants of David. Absalom was riding on his mule, and the mule went under the thick branches of a great oak. His head caught fast in the oak, and he was left hanging between heaven and earth, while the mule that was under him went on.

And ten young men, Joab's armour-bearers, surrounded Absalom and struck him, and killed him.

Then the Cushite came; and the Cushite said, 'Good tidings for my lord the king! For the LORD has vindicated you this day, delivering you from the power of all who rose up against you.' The king said to the Cushite, 'Is it well with the young man Absalom?' The Cushite answered, 'May the enemies of my lord the king, and all who rise up to do you harm, be like that young man.' The king was deeply moved, and went up to the chamber over the gate, and wept; and as he went, he said, 'O my son Absalom, my son, my son Absalom! Would I had died instead of you, O Absalom, my son, my son!'

PSALM Psalm 130

℟ **Out of the depths have I called you, O Lord**
 [Lord, hear my voice].

Out of the depths have I called to you, O Lord;
Lord, hear my voice;
let your ears consider well the voice of my supplication.
If you, Lord, were to note what is done amiss,
O Lord, who could stand?
For there is forgiveness with you;
therefore you shall be feared. ℟

I wait for the Lord; my soul waits for him;
in his word is my hope.
My soul waits for the Lord,
more than the night-watch for the morning,
more than the night-watch for the morning. ℟

O Israel, wait for the Lord,
for with the Lord there is mercy;
With him there is plenteous redemption,
and he shall redeem Israel from all their sins. ℟

Or TRACK 2

FIRST READING 1 Kings 19.4–8

A reading from the first book of Kings.

Elijah went a day's journey into the wilderness, and came and sat down
under a solitary broom tree. He asked that he might die: 'It is enough; now, O
LORD, take away my life, for I am no better than my ancestors.' Then he lay
down under the broom tree and fell asleep. Suddenly an angel touched him
and said to him, 'Get up and eat.' He looked, and there at his head was a cake
baked on hot stones, and a jar of water. He ate and drank, and lay down
again. The angel of the LORD came a second time, touched him, and said,
'Get up and eat, otherwise the journey will be too much for you.' He got up,
and ate and drank; then he went in the strength of that food forty days and
forty nights to Horeb the mount of God.

PSALM   **Psalm 34.1–8**

℞ **Turn from evil and do good.**

I will bless the Lord at all times;
his praise shall ever be in my mouth.
 I will glory in the Lord;
let the humble hear and rejoice. ℞

Proclaim with me the greatness of the Lord;
let us exalt his name together.
I sought the Lord and he answered me
and delivered me out of all my terror. ℞

Look upon him and be radiant,
and let not your faces be ashamed.
I called in my affliction and the Lord heard me
and saved me from all my troubles. ℞

The angel of the Lord
encompasses those who fear him,
and he will deliver them.
Taste and see that the Lord is good;
happy are they who trust in him! ℞

SECOND READING   **Ephesians 4.25 – 5.2**

A reading from the letter of Paul to the Ephesians.

Putting away falsehood, let all of us speak the truth to our neighbours, for we
are members of one another. Be angry but do not sin; do not let the sun go
down on your anger, and do not make room for the devil. Thieves must give
up stealing; rather let them labour and work honestly with their own hands,
so as to have something to share with the needy. Let no evil talk come out of
your mouths, but only what is useful for building up, as there is need, so that
your words may give grace to those who hear. And do not grieve the Holy
Spirit of God, with which you were marked with a seal for the day of
redemption. Put away from you all bitterness and wrath and anger and
wrangling and slander, together with all malice, and be kind to one another,
tender-hearted, forgiving one another, as God in Christ has forgiven you.
Therefore be imitators of God, as beloved children, and live in love, as Christ
loved us and gave himself up for us, a fragrant offering and sacrifice to God.

GOSPEL   **John 6.35, 41–51**

Hear the gospel of our Lord Jesus Christ according to John.

Jesus said to the crowd, 'I am the bread of life. Whoever comes to me will never be hungry, and whoever believes in me will never be thirsty.'

Then the Jews began to complain about him because he said, 'I am the bread that came down from heaven.' They were saying, 'Is not this Jesus, the son of Joseph, whose father and mother we know? How can he now say, "I have come down from heaven"?' Jesus answered them, 'Do not complain among yourselves. No one can come to me unless drawn by the Father who sent me; and I will raise that person up on the last day. It is written in the prophets, "And they shall all be taught by God." Everyone who has heard and learned from the Father comes to me. Not that anyone has seen the Father except the one who is from God; he has seen the Father. Very truly, I tell you, whoever believes has eternal life. I am the bread of life. Your ancestors ate the manna in the wilderness, and they died. This is the bread that comes down from heaven, so that one may eat of it and not die. I am the living bread that came down from heaven. Whoever eats of this bread will live for ever; and the bread that I will give for the life of the world is my flesh.'

† SUNDAY BETWEEN 14 AND 20 AUGUST   YEAR B
PROPER 15

TRACK 1

FIRST READING   **1 Kings 2.10–12; 3.3–14**

A reading from the first book of Kings.

David slept with his ancestors, and was buried in the city of David. The time that David reigned over Israel was forty years; he reigned seven years in Hebron, and thirty-three years in Jerusalem. So Solomon sat on the throne of his father David; and his kingdom was firmly established.

Solomon loved the LORD, walking in the statutes of his father David; only, he sacrificed and offered incense at the high places. The king went to Gibeon to sacrifice there, for that was the principal high place; Solomon used to offer a thousand burnt-offerings on that altar. At Gibeon the LORD appeared to Solomon in a dream by night; and God said, 'Ask what I should give you.'

And Solomon said, 'You have shown great and steadfast love to your servant my father David, because he walked before you in faithfulness, in righteousness, and in uprightness of heart towards you; and you have kept for him this great and steadfast love, and have given him a son to sit on his throne today. And now, O LORD my God, you have made your servant king in place of my father David, although I am only a little child; I do not know how to go out or come in. And your servant is in the midst of the people whom you have chosen, a great people, so numerous they cannot be numbered or counted. Give your servant therefore an understanding mind to govern your people, able to discern between good and evil; for who can govern this your great people?'

It pleased the Lord that Solomon had asked this. God said to him, 'Because you have asked this, and have not asked for yourself long life or riches, or for the life of your enemies, but have asked for yourself understanding to discern what is right, I now do according to your word. Indeed I give you a wise and discerning mind; no one like you has been before you and no one like you shall arise after you. I give you also what you have not asked, both riches and honour all your life; no other king shall compare with you. If you will walk in my ways, keeping my statutes and my commandments, as your father David walked, then I will lengthen your life.'

PSALM   Psalm 111

℟ **The fear of the Lord is the beginning of wisdom.**

Alleluia!
I will give thanks to the Lord with my whole heart,
in the assembly of the upright, in the congregation.
Great are the deeds of the Lord!
they are studied by all who delight in them.
His work is full of majesty and splendour,
and his righteousness endures for ever. ℟

He makes his marvellous works to be remembered;
the Lord is gracious and full of compassion.
He gives food to those who fear him;
he is ever mindful of his covenant. ℟

He has shown his people the power of his works
in giving them the lands of the nations.
The works of his hands are faithfulness and justice;
all his commandments are sure.
They stand fast for ever and ever,
because they are done in truth and equity. ℟

He sent redemption to his people;
he commanded his covenant for ever;
holy and awesome is his name.
The fear of the Lord is the beginning of wisdom;
those who act accordingly have a good understanding;
his praise endures for ever. ℟

Or   TRACK 2

FIRST READING   **Proverbs 9.1–6**

A reading from the book of Proverbs.

Wisdom has built her house,
she has hewn her seven pillars.
She has slaughtered her animals,
she has mixed her wine,
she has also set her table.
She has sent out her servant-girls,
she calls from the highest places in the town,
'You that are simple, turn in here!'
To those without sense she says,
'Come, eat of my bread
and drink of the wine I have mixed.
Lay aside immaturity, and live,
and walk in the way of insight.'

PSALM   **Psalm 34.9–14**

℟ **The Lord is near to the brokenhearted.**
   or
℟ **The Lord ransoms the life of his servants.**

Fear the Lord, you that are his saints,
for those who fear him lack nothing.

The young lions lack and suffer hunger,
but those who seek the Lord
lack nothing that is good. ℟

Come, children, and listen to me;
I will teach you the fear of the Lord.
Who among you loves life
and desires long life to enjoy prosperity? ℟

Keep your tongue from evil-speaking
and your lips from lying words.
Turn from evil and do good;
seek peace and pursue it. ℟

SECOND READING   Ephesians 5.15–20

A reading from the letter of Paul to the Ephesians.

Brothers and sisters, be careful then how you live, not as unwise people but
as wise, making the most of the time, because the days are evil. So do not be
foolish, but understand what the will of the Lord is. Do not get drunk with
wine, for that is debauchery; but be filled with the Spirit, as you sing psalms
and hymns and spiritual songs among yourselves, singing and making
melody to the Lord in your hearts, giving thanks to God the Father at all
times and for everything in the name of our Lord Jesus Christ.

GOSPEL   John 6.51–58

Hear the gospel of our Lord Jesus Christ according to John.

Jesus said to the crowd: 'I am the living bread that came down from heaven.
Whoever eats of this bread will live for ever; and the bread that I will give for
the life of the world is my flesh.'

The Jews then disputed among themselves, saying, 'How can this man give us
his flesh to eat?' So Jesus said to them, 'Very truly, I tell you, unless you eat
the flesh of the Son of Man and drink his blood, you have no life in you.
Those who eat my flesh and drink my blood have eternal life, and I will raise
them up on the last day; for my flesh is true food and my blood is true drink.
Those who eat my flesh and drink my blood abide in me, and I in them. Just
as the living Father sent me, and I live because of the Father, so whoever eats
me will live because of me. This is the bread that came down from heaven,
not like that which your ancestors ate, and they died. But the one who eats
this bread will live for ever.'

† SUNDAY BETWEEN 21 AND 27 AUGUST   YEAR B
PROPER 16

TRACK 1

FIRST READING (Short or long reading)
1 Kings 8.(1, 6, 10–11), 22–30, 41–43

A reading from the first book of Kings.

[Then Solomon assembled the elders of Israel and all the heads of the tribes, the leaders of the ancestral houses of the Israelites, before King Solomon in Jerusalem, to bring up the ark of the covenant of the LORD out of the city of David, which is Zion. Then the priests brought the ark of the covenant of the LORD to its place, in the inner sanctuary of the house, in the most holy place, underneath the wings of the cherubim. And when the priests came out of the holy place, a cloud filled the house of the LORD, so that the priests could not stand to minister because of the cloud; for the glory of the LORD filled the house of the LORD.]

Then Solomon stood before the altar of the LORD in the presence of all the assembly of Israel, and spread out his hands to heaven. He said, 'O LORD, God of Israel, there is no God like you in heaven above or on earth beneath, keeping covenant and steadfast love for your servants who walk before you with all their heart, the covenant that you kept for your servant my father David as you declared to him; you promised with your mouth and have this day fulfilled with your hand. Therefore, O LORD, God of Israel, keep for your servant my father David that which you promised him, saying, "There shall never fail you a successor before me to sit on the throne of Israel, if only your children look to their way, to walk before me as you have walked before me." Therefore, O God of Israel, let your word be confirmed, which you promised to your servant my father David.

But will God indeed dwell on the earth? Even heaven and the highest heaven cannot contain you, much less this house that I have built! Have regard to your servant's prayer and his plea, O LORD my God, heeding the cry and the prayer that your servant prays to you today; that your eyes may be open night and day towards this house, the place of which you said, "My name shall be there," that you may heed the prayer that your servant prays toward this place. Hear the plea of your servant and of your people Israel when they pray towards this place; O hear in heaven your dwelling-place; heed and forgive.

Likewise when a foreigner, who is not of your people Israel, comes from a distant land because of your name – for they shall hear of your great name, your mighty hand, and your outstretched arm – when a foreigner comes and prays toward this house, then hear in heaven your dwelling place, and do according to all that the foreigner calls to you, so that all the peoples of the earth may know your name and fear you, as do your people Israel, and so that they may know that your name has been invoked on this house that I have built.'

PSALM   Psalm 84

℞ **Happy are they who dwell in your house!**
   or
℞ **Lord God of hosts, hear my prayer**
   [hearken, O God of Jacob].

How dear to me is your dwelling, O Lord of hosts!
My soul has a desire and longing
   for the courts of the Lord;
my heart and my flesh rejoice in the living God. ℞

The sparrow has found her a house
and the swallow a nest
   where she may lay her young;
by the side of your altars, O Lord of hosts,
   my King and my God. ℞

Happy are they who dwell in your house!
they will always be praising you.
Happy are the people whose strength is in you!
   whose hearts are set on the pilgrims' way. ℞

Those who go through the desolate valley
will find it a place of springs,
   for the early rains have covered it with pools of water.
They will climb from height to height,
   and the God of gods will reveal himself in Zion.
Lord God of hosts, hear my prayer;
   hearken, O God of Jacob. ℞

Behold our defender, O God;
and look upon the face of your anointed.
For one day in your courts
is better than a thousand in my own room,
and to stand at the threshold of the house of my God
than to dwell in the tents of the wicked. ℟

For the Lord God is both sun and shield;
he will give grace and glory;
No good thing will the Lord withhold
from those who walk with integrity.
O Lord of hosts,
happy are they who put their trust in you! ℟

Or   TRACK 2

FIRST READING   Joshua 24.1–2a, 14–18

A reading from the book of Joshua.

Joshua gathered all the tribes of Israel to Shechem, and summoned the elders, the heads, the judges, and the officers of Israel; and they presented themselves before God. And Joshua said to all the people, 'Now therefore revere the LORD, and serve him in sincerity and in faithfulness; put away the gods that your ancestors served beyond the River and in Egypt, and serve the LORD. Now if you are unwilling to serve the LORD, choose this day whom you will serve, whether the gods your ancestors served in the region beyond the River or the gods of the Amorites in whose land you are living; but as for me and my household, we will serve the LORD.'

Then the people answered, 'Far be it from us that we should forsake the LORD to serve other gods; for it is the LORD our God who brought us and our ancestors up from the land of Egypt, out of the house of slavery, and who did those great signs in our sight. He protected us along all the way that we went, and among all the peoples through whom we passed; and the LORD drove out before us all the peoples, the Amorites who lived in the land. Therefore we also will serve the LORD, for he is our God.'

PSALM   **Psalm 34.15–22**

℞ **I sought the Lord, and he answered me**
  [and delivered me out of all my terror].

The eyes of the Lord are upon the righteous,
and his ears are open to their cry.
The face of the Lord is against those who do evil,
to root out the remembrance of them from the earth. ℞

The righteous cry and the Lord hears them
and delivers them from all their troubles.
The Lord is near to the brokenhearted
and will save those whose spirits are crushed. ℞

Many are the troubles of the righteous,
but the Lord will deliver him out of them all.
He will keep safe all his bones;
not one of them shall be broken. ℞

Evil shall slay the wicked,
and those who hate the righteous will be punished.
The Lord ransoms the life of his servants,
and none will be punished who trust in him. ℞

SECOND READING   **Ephesians 6.10–20**

A reading from the letter of Paul to the Ephesians.

Be strong in the Lord and in the strength of his power. Put on the whole
armour of God, so that you may be able to stand against the wiles of the
devil. For our struggle is not against enemies of blood and flesh, but against
the rulers, against the authorities, against the cosmic powers of this present
darkness, against the spiritual forces of evil in the heavenly places. Therefore
take up the whole armour of God, so that you may be able to withstand on
that evil day, and having done everything, to stand firm. Stand therefore, and
fasten the belt of truth around your waist, and put on the breastplate of
righteousness. As shoes for your feet put on whatever will make you ready to
proclaim the gospel of peace. With all of these, take the shield of faith, with
which you will be able to quench all the flaming arrows of the evil one.
Take the helmet of salvation, and the sword of the Spirit, which is the word
of God.

Pray in the Spirit at all times in every prayer and supplication. To that end keep alert and always persevere in supplication for all the saints. Pray also for me, so that when I speak, a message may be given to me to make known with boldness the mystery of the gospel, for which I am an ambassador in chains. Pray that I may declare it boldly, as I must speak.

GOSPEL   John 6.56–69

Hear the gospel of our Lord Jesus Christ according to John.

Jesus said to the crowd: 'Those who eat my flesh and drink my blood abide in me, and I in them. Just as the living Father sent me, and I live because of the Father, so whoever eats me will live because of me. This is the bread that came down from heaven, not like that which your ancestors ate, and they died. But the one who eats this bread will live for ever.' He said these things while he was teaching in the synagogue at Capernaum.

When many of his disciples heard it, they said, 'This teaching is difficult; who can accept it?' But Jesus, being aware that his disciples were complaining about it, said to them, 'Does this offend you? Then what if you were to see the Son of Man ascending to where he was before? It is the spirit that gives life; the flesh is useless. The words that I have spoken to you are spirit and life. But among you there are some who do not believe.' For Jesus knew from the first who were the ones that did not believe, and who was the one that would betray him. And he said, 'For this reason I have told you that no one can come to me unless it is granted by the Father.'

Because of this many of his disciples turned back and no longer went about with him. So Jesus asked the twelve, 'Do you also wish to go away?' Simon Peter answered him, 'Lord, to whom can we go? You have the words of eternal life. We have come to believe and know that you are the Holy One of God.'

† SUNDAY BETWEEN 28 AUGUST AND 3 SEPTEMBER

YEAR B

PROPER 17

TRACK 1

FIRST READING   **Song of Solomon 2.8–13**

A reading from the book of the Song of Solomon.

The voice of my beloved!
Look, he comes, leaping upon the mountains, bounding over the hills.
My beloved is like a gazelle or a young stag.
Look, there he stands behind our wall,
gazing in at the windows, looking through the lattice.
My beloved speaks and says to me:
'Arise, my love, my fair one, and come away;
for now the winter is past, the rain is over and gone.
The flowers appear on the earth;
the time of singing has come,
and the voice of the turtle-dove is heard in our land.
The fig tree puts forth its figs, and the vines are in blossom;
they give forth fragrance.
Arise, my love, my fair one, and come away.'

PSALM   **Psalm 45.1–2, 7–10**

℟ **Grace flows from your lips,
because God has blessed you for ever.**

My heart is stirring with a noble song;
let me recite what I have fashioned for the king;
my tongue shall be the pen of a skilled writer.
You are the fairest of men;
grace flows from your lips,
because God has blessed you for ever. ℟

Your throne, O God, endures for ever and ever,
a sceptre of righteousness is the sceptre of your kingdom;
you love righteousness and hate iniquity;
Therefore God, your God, has anointed you
with the oil of gladness above your fellows. ℟

All your garments are fragrant with myrrh, aloes and cassia,
and the music of strings from ivory palaces makes you glad.
Kings' daughters stand among the ladies of the court;
on your right is the queen,
adorned with the gold of Ophir. ℟

Or   TRACK 2

FIRST READING   Deuteronomy 4.1-2, 6-9

A reading from the book of Deuteronomy.

Moses spoke to the people; he said: So now, Israel, give heed to the statutes
and ordinances that I am teaching you to observe, so that you may live to
enter and occupy the land that the LORD, the God of your ancestors, is
giving you. You must neither add anything to what I command you nor take
away anything from it, but keep the commandments of the LORD your God
with which I am charging you.

You must observe them diligently, for this will show your wisdom and
discernment to the peoples, who, when they hear all these statutes, will say,
'Surely this great nation is a wise and discerning people!' For what other great
nation has a god so near to it as the LORD our God is whenever we call to
him? And what other great nation has statutes and ordinances as just as this
entire law that I am setting before you today?

But take care and watch yourselves closely, so as neither to forget the things
that your eyes have seen nor to let them slip from your mind all the days of
your life; make them known to your children and your children's children.

PSALM   Psalm 15

℟ **Those who do what is right
will dwell in the presence of the Lord.**

Lord, who may dwell in your tabernacle?
who may abide upon your holy hill?
Whoever leads a blameless life and does what is right,
who speaks the truth from his heart. ℟

There is no guile upon his tongue;
he does no evil to his friend;
he does not heap contempt upon his neighbour.

In his sight the wicked are rejected,
but he honours those who fear the Lord. ℟

He has sworn to do no wrong
and does not take back his word.
He does not give his money in hope of gain,
nor does he take a bribe against the innocent.
Whoever does these things
shall never be overthrown. ℟

SECOND READING   James 1.17–27

A reading from the letter of James.

Every generous act of giving, with every perfect gift, is from above, coming
down from the Father of lights, with whom there is no variation or shadow
due to change. In fulfilment of his own purpose he gave us birth by the word
of truth, so that we would become a kind of first fruits of his creatures.

You must understand this, my beloved: let everyone be quick to listen, slow
to speak, slow to anger; for your anger does not produce God's righteousness.
Therefore rid yourselves of all sordidness and rank growth of wickedness,
and welcome with meekness the implanted word that has the power to save
your souls.

But be doers of the word, and not merely hearers who deceive themselves.
For if any are hearers of the word and not doers, they are like those who look
at themselves in a mirror; for they look at themselves and, on going away,
immediately forget what they were like. But those who look into the perfect
law, the law of liberty, and persevere, being not hearers who forget but doers
who act – they will be blessed in their doing. If any think they are religious,
and do not bridle their tongues but deceive their hearts, their religion is
worthless.

Religion that is pure and undefiled before God, the Father, is this: to care
for orphans and widows in their distress, and to keep oneself unstained by
the world.

GOSPEL   Mark 7.1–8, 14–15, 21–23

Hear the gospel of our Lord Jesus Christ according to Mark.

When the Pharisees and some of the scribes who had come from Jerusalem
gathered around Jesus, they noticed that some of his disciples were eating

with defiled hands, that is, without washing them. (For the Pharisees, and all the Jews, do not eat unless they thoroughly wash their hands, thus observing the tradition of the elders; and they do not eat anything from the market unless they wash it; and there are also many other traditions that they observe, the washing of cups, pots, and bronze kettles.) So the Pharisees and the scribes asked him, 'Why do your disciples not live according to the tradition of the elders, but eat with defiled hands?'

Jesus said to them,

'Isaiah prophesied rightly about you hypocrites,
as it is written,
"This people honours me with their lips,
but their hearts are far from me;
in vain do they worship me,
teaching human precepts as doctrines."
You abandon the commandment of God and hold to human tradition.'

Then he called the crowd again and said to them, 'Listen to me, all of you, and understand: there is nothing outside a person that by going in can defile, but the things that come out are what defile. For it is from within, from the human heart, that evil intentions come: fornication, theft, murder, adultery, avarice, wickedness, deceit, licentiousness, envy, slander, pride, folly. All these evil things come from within, and they defile a person.'

† SUNDAY BETWEEN 4 AND 10 SEPTEMBER   YEAR B PROPER 18

TRACK 1

FIRST READING   **Proverbs 22.1–2, 8–9, 22–23**

A reading from the book of Proverbs.

A good name is to be chosen rather than great riches,
and favour is better than silver or gold.
The rich and the poor have this in common:
the LORD is the maker of them all.

Whoever sows injustice will reap calamity,
and the rod of anger will fail.
Those who are generous are blessed,
for they share their bread with the poor.

Do not rob the poor because they are poor,
or crush the afflicted at the gate;
for the LORD pleads their cause
and despoils of life those who despoil them.

PSALM

℟ **Show your goodness, O Lord,**
   to those who are good.

Those who trust in the Lord are like Mount Zion,
which cannot be moved, but stands fast for ever.
The hills stand about Jerusalem;
so does the Lord stand round about his people,
from this time forth for evermore. ℟

The sceptre of the wicked shall not hold sway
over the land allotted to the just,
so that the just shall not put their hands to evil.
Show your goodness, O Lord, to those who are good
and to those who are true of heart. ℟

As for those who turn aside to crooked ways,
the Lord will lead them away with the evildoers;
but peace be upon Israel. ℟

Or TRACK 2

FIRST READING

Isaiah 35.4–7a

A reading from the book of the prophet Isaiah.

Say to those who are of a fearful heart,
'Be strong, do not fear!
Here is your God.
He will come with vengeance, with terrible recompense.
He will come and save you.'

Then the eyes of the blind shall be opened,
and the ears of the deaf unstopped;
then the lame shall leap like a deer,
and the tongue of the speechless sing for joy.

For waters shall break forth in the wilderness,
and streams in the desert;
the burning sand shall become a pool,
and the thirsty ground springs of water.

PSALM

℟ **You open wide your hand, O Lord,**
   and satisfy our needs.

Alleluia!
Praise the Lord, O my soul!
I will praise the Lord as long as I live;
I will sing praises to my God while I have my being. ℟

Put not your trust in rulers,
nor in any child of earth,
for there is no help in them.
When they breathe their last, they return to earth,
and in that day their thoughts perish. ℟

Happy are they who have the God of Jacob
for their help!
whose hope is in the Lord their God;
Who made heaven and earth, the seas,
and all that is in them;
who keeps his promise for ever;
Who gives justice to those who are oppressed,
and food to those who hunger. ℟

The Lord sets the prisoners free;
the Lord opens the eyes of the blind;
the Lord lifts up those who are bowed down;
The Lord loves the righteous;
the Lord cares for the stranger;
he sustains the orphan and widow,
but frustrates the way of the wicked. ℟

The Lord shall reign for ever,
your God, O Zion, throughout all generations.
Alleluia! ℟

SECOND READING   **James 2.1–10, (11–13), 14–17**

A reading from the letter of James.

My brothers and sisters, do you with your acts of favouritism really believe in
our glorious Lord Jesus Christ? For if a person with gold rings and in fine
clothes comes into your assembly, and if a poor person in dirty clothes also
comes in, and if you take notice of the one wearing the fine clothes and say,
'Have a seat here, please,' while to the one who is poor you say, 'Stand there,'
or, 'Sit at my feet,' have you not made distinctions among yourselves, and
become judges with evil thoughts? Listen, my beloved brothers and sisters.
Has not God chosen the poor in the world to be rich in faith and to be heirs
of the kingdom that he has promised to those who love him? But you have
dishonoured the poor. Is it not the rich who oppress you? Is it not they who
drag you into court? Is it not they who blaspheme the excellent name that
was invoked over you?

You do well if you really fulfil the royal law according to the scripture, 'You
shall love your neighbour as yourself.' But if you show partiality, you commit
sin and are convicted by the law as transgressors. For whoever keeps the
whole law but fails in one point has become accountable for all of it. [For the
one who said, 'You shall not commit adultery,' also said, 'You shall not
murder.' Now if you do not commit adultery but if you murder, you have
become a transgressor of the law. So speak and so act as those who are to be
judged by the law of liberty. For judgement will be without mercy to anyone
who has shown no mercy; mercy triumphs over judgement.]

What good is it, my brothers and sisters, if you say you have faith but do not
have works? Can faith save you? If a brother or sister is naked and lacks daily
food, and one of you says to them, 'Go in peace; keep warm and eat your fill,'
and yet you do not supply their bodily needs, what is the good of that? So
faith by itself, if it has no works, is dead.

GOSPEL   **Mark 7.24–37**

Hear the gospel of our Lord Jesus Christ according to Mark.

Jesus set out and went away to the region of Tyre. He entered a house and did
not want anyone to know he was there. Yet he could not escape notice, but a
woman whose little daughter had an unclean spirit immediately heard about
him, and she came and bowed down at his feet. Now the woman was a
Gentile, of Syrophoenician origin. She begged him to cast the demon out of

her daughter. He said to her, 'Let the children be fed first, for it is not fair to take the children's food and throw it to the dogs.' But she answered him, 'Sir, even the dogs under the table eat the children's crumbs.' Then he said to her, 'For saying that, you may go – the demon has left your daughter.' So she went home, found the child lying on the bed, and the demon gone.

Then he returned from the region of Tyre, and went by way of Sidon towards the Sea of Galilee, in the region of the Decapolis. They brought to him a deaf man who had an impediment in his speech; and they begged him to lay his hand on him. He took him aside in private, away from the crowd, and put his fingers into his ears, and he spat and touched his tongue. Then looking up to heaven, he sighed and said to him, 'Ephphatha,' that is, 'Be opened.' And immediately his ears were opened, his tongue was released, and he spoke plainly. Then Jesus ordered them to tell no one; but the more he ordered them, the more zealously they proclaimed it. They were astounded beyond measure, saying, 'He has done everything well; he even makes the deaf to hear and the mute to speak.'

SUNDAY BETWEEN 11 AND 17 SEPTEMBER   YEAR B
PROPER 19

TRACK 1

FIRST READING   **Proverbs 1.20–33**

A reading from the book of Proverbs.

Wisdom cries out in the street;
in the squares she raises her voice.
At the busiest corner she cries out;
at the entrance of the city gates she speaks:
'How long, O simple ones,
will you love being simple?
How long will scoffers delight in their scoffing
and fools hate knowledge?
Give heed to my reproof;
I will pour out my thoughts to you;
I will make my words known to you.
Because I have called and you refused,
have stretched out my hand and no one heeded,
and because you have ignored all my counsel

and would have none of my reproof,
I also will laugh at your calamity;
I will mock when panic strikes you,
when panic strikes you like a storm,
and your calamity comes like a whirlwind,
when distress and anguish come upon you.
Then they will call upon me,
but I will not answer;
they will seek me diligently, but will not find me.
Because they hated knowledge
and did not choose the fear of the LORD,
would have none of my counsel,
and despised all my reproof,
therefore they shall eat the fruit of their way
and be sated with their own devices.
For waywardness kills the simple,
and the complacency of fools destroys them;
but those who listen to me will be secure
and will live at ease, without dread of disaster.'

PSALM OR CANTICLE

Either   **Psalm 19**

℞ **The commandment of the Lord is clear
    and gives light to the eyes.**

The heavens declare the glory of God,
and the firmament shows his handiwork.
One day tells its tale to another,
and one night imparts knowledge to another.
Although they have no words or language,
and their voices are not heard,
Their sound has gone out into all lands,
and their message to the ends of the world. ℞

In the deep has he set a pavilion for the sun;
it comes forth like a bridegroom out of his chamber;
it rejoices like a champion to run its course.
It goes forth from the uttermost edge of the heavens
and runs about to the end of it again;
nothing is hidden from its burning heat. ℞

The law of the Lord is perfect
and revives the soul;
the testimony of the Lord is sure
and gives wisdom to the innocent.
The statutes of the Lord are just
and rejoice the heart;
the commandment of the Lord is clear
and gives light to the eyes. ℟

The fear of the Lord is clean
and endures for ever;
the judgements of the Lord are true
and righteous altogether.
More to be desired are they than gold,
more than much fine gold,
sweeter far than honey,
than honey in the comb. ℟

By them also is your servant enlightened,
and in keeping them there is great reward.
Who can tell how often he offends?
Cleanse me from my secret faults.
Above all, keep your servant from presumptuous sins;
let them not get dominion over me;
then shall I be whole and sound,
and innocent of a great offence. ℟

Let the words of my mouth and the meditation of my heart
be acceptable in your sight,
O Lord, my strength and my redeemer. ℟

Or   **Wisdom of Solomon 7.26 – 8.1**

℟ God loves the person who lives with wisdom.

Wisdom is a reflection of eternal light,
a spotless mirror of the working of God,
and an image of his goodness. ℟

Although she is but one, she can do all things,
and while remaining in herself, she renews all things;
in every generation she passes into holy souls

and makes them friends of God, and prophets;
for God loves nothing so much
as the person who lives with wisdom. ℟

She is more beautiful than the sun,
and excels every constellation of the stars.
Compared with the light she is found to be superior,
for it is succeeded by the night,
but against wisdom evil does not prevail.
She reaches mightily from one end of the earth to the other,
and she orders all things well. ℟

Or   TRACK 2

FIRST READING   **Isaiah 50.4–9a**

A reading from the book of the prophet Isaiah.

The servant of the Lord said:
The Lord GOD has given me the tongue of a teacher,
that I may know how to sustain the weary with a word.
Morning by morning he wakens –
wakens my ear to listen as those who are taught.
The Lord GOD has opened my ear,
and I was not rebellious,
I did not turn backward.
I gave my back to those who struck me,
and my cheeks to those who pulled out the beard;
I did not hide my face from insult and spitting.
The Lord GOD helps me;
therefore I have not been disgraced;
therefore I have set my face like flint,
and I know that I shall not be put to shame;
he who vindicates me is near.
Who will contend with me?
Let us stand up together.
Who are my adversaries?
Let them confront me.
It is the Lord GOD who helps me;
who will declare me guilty?

PSALM   Psalm 116.1–8

℞ **I will walk in the presence of the Lord
in the land of the living.**

I love the Lord,
because he has heard the voice of my supplication,
because he has inclined his ear to me
whenever I called upon him.
The cords of death entangled me;
the grip of the grave took hold of me;
I came to grief and sorrow. ℞

Then I called upon the name of the Lord:
'O Lord, I pray you, save my life.'
Gracious is the Lord and righteous;
our God is full of compassion. ℞

The Lord watches over the innocent;
I was brought very low and he helped me.
Turn again to your rest, O my soul,
for the Lord has treated you well. ℞

For you have rescued my life from death,
my eyes from tears and my feet from stumbling.
I will walk in the presence of the Lord
in the land of the living. ℞

SECOND READING   James 3.1–12

A reading from the letter of James.

Not many of you should become teachers, my brothers and sisters, for you
know that we who teach will be judged with greater strictness. For all of us
make many mistakes. Anyone who makes no mistakes in speaking is
perfect, able to keep the whole body in check with a bridle. If we put bits
into the mouths of horses to make them obey us, we guide their whole
bodies. Or look at ships: though they are so large that it takes strong winds to
drive them, yet they are guided by a very small rudder wherever the will of
the pilot directs. So also the tongue is a small member, yet it boasts of
great exploits.

How great a forest is set ablaze by a small fire! And the tongue is a fire. The tongue is placed among our members as a world of iniquity; it stains the whole body, sets on fire the cycle of nature, and is itself set on fire by hell. For every species of beast and bird, of reptile and sea creature, can be tamed and has been tamed by the human species, but no one can tame the tongue – a restless evil, full of deadly poison. With it we bless the Lord and Father, and with it we curse those who are made in the likeness of God. From the same mouth come blessing and cursing. My brothers and sisters, this ought not to be so. Does a spring pour forth from the same opening both fresh and brackish water? Can a fig tree, my brothers and sisters, yield olives, or a grapevine figs? No more can salt water yield fresh.

GOSPEL   Mark 8.27–38

Hear the gospel of our Lord Jesus Christ according to Mark.

Jesus went on with his disciples to the villages of Caesarea Philippi; and on the way he asked his disciples, 'Who do people say that I am?' And they answered him, 'John the Baptist; and others, Elijah; and still others, one of the prophets.' Jesus asked them, 'But who do you say that I am?' Peter answered him, 'You are the Messiah.' And he sternly ordered them not to tell anyone about him.

Then he began to teach them that the Son of Man must undergo great suffering, and be rejected by the elders, the chief priests, and the scribes, and be killed, and after three days rise again. He said all this quite openly. And Peter took him aside and began to rebuke him. But turning and looking at his disciples, he rebuked Peter and said, 'Get behind me, Satan! For you are setting your mind not on divine things but on human things.'

He called the crowd with his disciples, and said to them, 'If any want to become my followers, let them deny themselves and take up their cross and follow me. For those who want to save their life will lose it, and those who lose their life for my sake, and for the sake of the gospel, will save it. For what will it profit them to gain the whole world and forfeit their life? Indeed, what can they give in return for their life? Those who are ashamed of me and of my words in this adulterous and sinful generation, of them the Son of Man will also be ashamed when he comes in the glory of his Father with the holy angels.'

† SUNDAY BETWEEN 18 AND 24 SEPTEMBER   YEAR B
PROPER 20

TRACK 1

FIRST READING   Proverbs 31.10–31

A reading from the book of Proverbs.

A capable wife who can find?
She is far more precious than jewels.
The heart of her husband trusts in her,
and he will have no lack of gain.
She does him good, and not harm,
all the days of her life.
She seeks wool and flax,
and works with willing hands.
She is like the ships of the merchant,
she brings her food from far away.
She rises while it is still night
and provides food for her household
and tasks for her servant-girls.
She considers a field and buys it;
with the fruit of her hands she plants a vineyard.
She girds herself with strength,
and makes her arms strong.
She perceives that her merchandise is profitable.
Her lamp does not go out at night.
She puts her hands to the distaff,
and her hands hold the spindle.
She opens her hand to the poor,
and reaches out her hands to the needy.
She is not afraid for her household when it snows,
for all her household are clothed in crimson.
She makes herself coverings;
her clothing is fine linen and purple.
Her husband is known in the city gates,
taking his seat among the elders of the land.
She makes linen garments and sells them;
she supplies the merchant with sashes.

Strength and dignity are her clothing,
and she laughs at the time to come.
She opens her mouth with wisdom,
and the teaching of kindness is on her tongue.
She looks well to the ways of her household,
and does not eat the bread of idleness.
Her children rise up and call her happy;
her husband too, and he praises her:
'Many women have done excellently,
but you surpass them all.'
Charm is deceitful,
and beauty is vain,
but a woman who fears the LORD is to be praised.
Give her a share in the fruit of her hands,
and let her works praise her in the city gates.

PSALM   Psalm 1

℟ **Happy are they who delight in the law of the Lord.**

Happy are they who have not walked
in the counsel of the wicked,
nor lingered in the way of sinners,
nor sat in the seats of the scornful!
Their delight is in the law of the Lord,
and they meditate on his law day and night. ℟

They are like trees planted by streams of water,
bearing fruit in due season,
with leaves that do not wither;
everything they do shall prosper. ℟

It is not so with the wicked:
they are like chaff which the wind blows away;
Therefore the wicked shall not stand upright
when judgement comes,
nor the sinner in the council of the righteous.
For the Lord knows the way of the righteous,
but the way of the wicked is doomed. ℟

Or   TRACK 2

FIRST READING (Alternative readings)

Either   **Wisdom of Solomon 1.16 – 2.1, 12–22**

A reading from the book of Wisdom.

The ungodly by their words and deeds summoned death;
considering him a friend,
they pined away and made a covenant with him,
because they are fit to belong to his company.
For they reasoned unsoundly, saying to themselves,
'Short and sorrowful is our life,
and there is no remedy when a life comes to its end,
and no one has been known to return from Hades.

Let us lie in wait for the righteous man,
because he is inconvenient to us and opposes our actions;
he reproaches us for sins against the law,
and accuses us of sins against our training.
He professes to have knowledge of God,
and calls himself a child of the Lord.
He became to us a reproof of our thoughts;
the very sight of him is a burden to us,
because his manner of life is unlike that of others,
and his ways are strange.
We are considered by him as something base,
and he avoids our ways as unclean;
he calls the last end of the righteous happy,
and boasts that God is his father.
Let us see if his words are true,
and let us test what will happen at the end of his life;
for if the righteous man is God's child, he will help him,
and will deliver him from the hand of his adversaries.
Let us test him with insult and torture,
so that we may find out how gentle he is,
and make trial of his forbearance.
Let us condemn him to a shameful death,
for, according to what he says, he will be protected.'
Thus they reasoned, but they were led astray,
for their wickedness blinded them,

and they did not know the secret purposes of God,
nor hoped for the wages of holiness,
nor discerned the prize for blameless souls;

Or   **Jeremiah 11.18–20**

A reading from the book of the prophet Jeremiah.

It was the LORD who made it known to me,
and I knew; then you showed me their evil deeds.
But I was like a gentle lamb led to the slaughter.
And I did not know it was against me that they devised schemes, saying,
'Let us destroy the tree with its fruit,
let us cut him off from the land of the living,
so that his name will no longer be remembered!'
But you, O LORD of hosts,
who judge righteously,
who try the heart and the mind,
let me see your retribution upon them,
for to you I have committed my cause.

PSALM   **Psalm 54**

℟ **The Lord sustains my life.**

Save me, O God, by your name;
in your might, defend my cause.
Hear my prayer, O God;
give ear to the words of my mouth. ℟

For the arrogant have risen up against me,
and the ruthless have sought my life,
those who have no regard for God.
Behold, God is my helper;
it is the Lord who sustains my life. ℟

Render evil to those who spy on me;
in your faithfulness, destroy them.
I will offer you a freewill sacrifice
and praise your name, O Lord, for it is good.
For you have rescued me from every trouble,
and my eye has seen the ruin of my foes. ℟

SECOND READING   James 3.13 – 4.3, 7–8a

A reading from the letter of James.

Who is wise and understanding among you? Show by your good life that your works are done with gentleness born of wisdom. But if you have bitter envy and selfish ambition in your hearts, do not be boastful and false to the truth. Such wisdom does not come down from above, but is earthly, unspiritual, devilish. For where there is envy and selfish ambition, there will also be disorder and wickedness of every kind. But the wisdom from above is first pure, then peaceable, gentle, willing to yield, full of mercy and good fruits, without a trace of partiality or hypocrisy. And a harvest of righteousness is sown in peace for those who make peace.

Those conflicts and disputes among you, where do they come from? Do they not come from your cravings that are at war within you? You want something and do not have it; so you commit murder. And you covet something and cannot obtain it; so you engage in disputes and conflicts. You do not have, because you do not ask. You ask and do not receive, because you ask wrongly, in order to spend what you get on your pleasures.

Submit yourselves therefore to God. Resist the devil, and he will flee from you. Draw near to God, and he will draw near to you.

GOSPEL   Mark 9.30–37

Hear the gospel of our Lord Jesus Christ according to Mark.

After leaving the mountain Jesus and his disciples went on from there and passed through Galilee. He did not want anyone to know it; for he was teaching his disciples, saying to them, 'The Son of Man is to be betrayed into human hands, and they will kill him, and three days after being killed, he will rise again.' But they did not understand what he was saying and were afraid to ask him.

Then they came to Capernaum; and when he was in the house he asked them, 'What were you arguing about on the way?' But they were silent, for on the way they had argued with one another who was the greatest. He sat down, called the twelve, and said to them, 'Whoever wants to be first must be last of all and servant of all.' Then he took a little child and put it among them; and taking it in his arms, he said to them, 'Whoever welcomes one such child in my name welcomes me, and whoever welcomes me welcomes not me but the one who sent me.'

† SUNDAY BETWEEN 25 SEPTEMBER AND 1 OCTOBER PROPER 21

YEAR B

TRACK 1

FIRST READING   Esther 7.1–6, 9–10; 9.20–22

A reading from the book of Esther.

The king and Haman went in to feast with Queen Esther. On the second day, as they were drinking wine, the king again said to Esther, 'What is your petition, Queen Esther? It shall be granted you. And what is your request? Even to the half of my kingdom, it shall be fulfilled.' Then Queen Esther answered, 'If I have won your favour, O king, and if it pleases the king, let my life be given me – that is my petition – and the lives of my people – that is my request. For we have been sold, I and my people, to be destroyed, to be killed, and to be annihilated. If we had been sold merely as slaves, men and women, I would have held my peace; but no enemy can compensate for this damage to the king.' Then King Ahasuerus said to Queen Esther, 'Who is he, and where is he, who presumed to do this?' Esther said, 'A foe and enemy, this wicked Haman!' Then Haman was terrified before the king and queen. Then Harbona, one of the eunuchs in attendance on the king, said, 'Look, the very gallows that Haman has prepared for Mordecai, whose word saved the king, stands at Haman's house, fifty cubits high.' And the king said, 'Hang him on that.' So they hanged Haman on the gallows that he had prepared for Mordecai. Then the anger of the king abated.

Mordecai recorded these things, and sent letters to all the Jews who were in all the provinces of King Ahasuerus, both near and far, enjoining them that they should keep the fourteenth day of the month Adar and also the fifteenth day of the same month, year by year, as the days on which the Jews gained relief from their enemies, and as the month that had been turned for them from sorrow into gladness and from mourning into a holiday; that they should make them days of feasting and gladness, days for sending gifts of food to one another and presents to the poor.

PSALM

℞ **Our help is in the name of the Lord**
[the maker of heaven and earth].

If the Lord had not been on our side,
let Israel now say;
If the Lord had not been on our side,
when enemies rose up against us;
Then would they have swallowed us up alive
in their fierce anger towards us; ℞

Then would the waters have overwhelmed us
and the torrent gone over us;
Then would the raging waters
have gone right over us.
Blessèd be the Lord!
he has not given us over to be a prey for their teeth. ℞

We have escaped like a bird
from the snare of the fowler;
the snare is broken and we have escaped.
Our help is in the name of the Lord,
the maker of heaven and earth. ℞

Or   TRACK 2

FIRST READING   **Numbers 11.4–6, 10–16, 24–29**

A reading from the book of Numbers.

The rabble among the people had a strong craving; and the Israelites also
wept again, and said, 'If only we had meat to eat! We remember the fish we
used to eat in Egypt for nothing, the cucumbers, the melons, the leeks, the
onions, and the garlic; but now our strength is dried up, and there is nothing
at all but this manna to look at.'

Moses heard the people weeping throughout their families, all at the
entrances of their tents. Then the LORD became very angry, and Moses was
displeased. So Moses said to the LORD, 'Why have you treated your servant
so badly? Why have I not found favour in your sight, that you lay the burden
of all this people on me? Did I conceive all this people? Did I give birth to

them, that you should say to me, "Carry them in your bosom, as a nurse carries a sucking child," to the land that you promised on oath to their ancestors? Where am I to get meat to give to all this people? For they come weeping to me and say, "Give us meat to eat!" I am not able to carry all this people alone, for they are too heavy for me. If this is the way you are going to treat me, put me to death at once – if I have found favour in your sight – and do not let me see my misery.'

So the LORD said to Moses, 'Gather for me seventy of the elders of Israel, whom you know to be the elders of the people and officers over them; bring them to the tent of meeting, and have them take their place there with you.'

So Moses went out and told the people the words of the LORD; and he gathered seventy elders of the people, and placed them all around the tent. Then the LORD came down in the cloud and spoke to him, and took some of the spirit that was on him and put it on the seventy elders; and when the spirit rested upon them, they prophesied. But they did not do so again. Two men remained in the camp, one named Eldad, and the other named Medad, and the spirit rested on them; they were among those registered, but they had not gone out to the tent, and so they prophesied in the camp. And a young man ran and told Moses, 'Eldad and Medad are prophesying in the camp.' And Joshua son of Nun, the assistant of Moses, one of his chosen men, said, 'My lord Moses, stop them!' But Moses said to him, 'Are you jealous for my sake? Would that all the Lord's people were prophets, and that the LORD would put his spirit on them!'

PSALM   Psalm 19.7–14

℟ **The law of the Lord is perfect and revives the soul.**

The law of the Lord is perfect
and revives the soul;
the testimony of the Lord is sure
and gives wisdom to the innocent.
The statutes of the Lord are just
and rejoice the heart;
the commandment of the Lord is clear
and gives light to the eyes. ℟

The fear of the Lord is clean
and endures for ever;
the judgements of the Lord are true
and righteous altogether.
More to be desired are they than gold,
more than much fine gold,
sweeter far than honey,
than honey in the comb. ℟

By them also is your servant enlightened,
and in keeping them there is great reward.
Who can tell how often he offends?
Cleanse me from my secret faults.
Above all, keep your servant from presumptuous sins;
let them not get dominion over me;
then shall I be whole and sound,
and innocent of a great offence. ℟

Let the words of my mouth and the meditation of my heart
be acceptable in your sight,
O Lord, my strength and my redeemer. ℟

SECOND READING   James 5.13–20

A reading from the letter of James.

Are any among you suffering? They should pray. Are any cheerful? They should sing songs of praise. Are any among you sick? They should call for the elders of the church and have them pray over them, anointing them with oil in the name of the Lord. The prayer of faith will save the sick, and the Lord will raise them up; and anyone who has committed sins will be forgiven. Therefore confess your sins to one another, and pray for one another, so that you may be healed. The prayer of the righteous is powerful and effective. Elijah was a human being like us, and he prayed fervently that it might not rain, and for three years and six months it did not rain on the earth. Then he prayed again, and the heaven gave rain and the earth yielded its harvest.

My brothers and sisters, if anyone among you wanders from the truth and is brought back by another, you should know that whoever brings back a sinner from wandering will save the sinner's soul from death and will cover a multitude of sins.

GOSPEL   Mark 9.38–50

Hear the gospel of our Lord Jesus Christ according to Mark.

After Jesus had finished teaching the disciples, John said to him, 'Teacher, we saw someone casting out demons in your name, and we tried to stop him, because he was not following us.' But Jesus said, 'Do not stop him; for no one who does a deed of power in my name will be able soon afterwards to speak evil of me. Whoever is not against us is for us. For truly I tell you, whoever gives you a cup of water to drink because you bear the name of Christ will by no means lose the reward.

If any of you put a stumbling-block before one of these little ones who believe in me, it would be better for you if a great millstone were hung around your neck and you were thrown into the sea. If your hand causes you to stumble, cut it off; it is better for you to enter life maimed than to have two hands and to go to hell, to the unquenchable fire. And if your foot causes you to stumble, cut it off; it is better for you to enter life lame than to have two feet and to be thrown into hell. And if your eye causes you to stumble, tear it out; it is better for you to enter the kingdom of God with one eye than to have two eyes and to be thrown into hell, where their worm never dies, and the fire is never quenched. For everyone will be salted with fire. Salt is good; but if salt has lost its saltiness, how can you season it? Have salt in yourselves, and be at peace with one another.'

† SUNDAY BETWEEN 2 AND 8 OCTOBER   YEAR B
PROPER 22

TRACK 1

FIRST READING   Job 1.1; 2.1–10

A reading from the book of Job.

There was once a man in the land of Uz whose name was Job. That man was blameless and upright, one who feared God and turned away from evil.

One day the heavenly beings came to present themselves before the LORD, and Satan also came among them to present himself before the LORD. The LORD said to Satan, 'Where have you come from?' Satan answered the LORD, 'From going to and fro on the earth, and from walking up and down on it.'

The LORD said to Satan, 'Have you considered my servant Job? There is no one like him on the earth, a blameless and upright man who fears God and turns away from evil. He still persists in his integrity, although you incited me against him, to destroy him for no reason.' Then Satan answered the LORD, 'Skin for skin! All that people have they will give to save their lives. But stretch out your hand now and touch his bone and his flesh, and he will curse you to your face.' The LORD said to Satan, 'Very well, he is in your power; only spare his life.'

So Satan went out from the presence of the LORD, and inflicted loathsome sores on Job from the sole of his foot to the crown of his head. Job took a potsherd with which to scrape himself, and sat among the ashes.

Then his wife said to him, 'Do you still persist in your integrity? Curse God, and die.' But he said to her, 'You speak as any foolish woman would speak. Shall we receive the good at the hand of God, and not receive the bad?' In all this Job did not sin with his lips.

PSALM

Psalm 26

℟ **I will live with integrity, O Lord;**
[redeem me and have pity on me].

Give judgement for me, O Lord,
for I have lived with integrity;
I have trusted in the Lord and have not faltered.
Test me, O Lord, and try me;
examine my heart and my mind. ℟

For your love is before my eyes;
I have walked faithfully with you.
I have not sat with the worthless,
nor do I consort with the deceitful.
I have hated the company of evildoers;
I will not sit down with the wicked. ℟

I will wash my hands in innocence, O Lord,
that I may go in procession round your altar,
Singing aloud a song of thanksgiving
and recounting all your wonderful deeds. ℟

Lord, I love the house in which you dwell
and the place where your glory abides.
Do not sweep me away with sinners,

nor my life with those who thirst for blood,
Whose hands are full of evil plots,
and their right hand full of bribes. ℟

As for me, I will live with integrity;
redeem me, O Lord, and have pity on me.
My foot stands on level ground;
in the full assembly I will bless the Lord. ℟

Or   TRACK 2

FIRST READING   **Genesis 2.18–24**

A reading from the book of Genesis.

The LORD God said, 'It is not good that the man should be alone; I will make him a helper as his partner.' So out of the ground the LORD God formed every animal of the field and every bird of the air, and brought them to the man to see what he would call them; and whatever the man called every living creature, that was its name. The man gave names to all cattle, and to the birds of the air, and to every animal of the field; but for the man there was not found a helper as his partner. So the LORD God caused a deep sleep to fall upon the man, and he slept; then he took one of his ribs and closed up its place with flesh. And the rib that the LORD God had taken from the man he made into a woman and brought her to the man.
Then the man said,
'This at last is bone of my bones
and flesh of my flesh;
this one shall be called Woman,
for out of Man this one was taken.'
Therefore a man leaves his father and his mother and clings to his wife, and they become one flesh.

PSALM   **Psalm 8**

℟ **How exalted is your name in all the world!**

O Lord our governor,
how exalted is your name in all the world!
Out of the mouths of infants and children
your majesty is praised above the heavens.
You have set up a stronghold against your adversaries,
to quell the enemy and the avenger. ℟

When I consider your heavens, the work of your fingers,
the moon and the stars you have set in their courses,
What are mortals, that you should be mindful of them?
mere human beings, that you should seek them out? ℟

You have made them little lower than the angels;
you adorn them with glory and honour.
You give them mastery over the works of your hands;
and put all things under their feet, ℟

All sheep and oxen,
even the wild beasts of the field,
The birds of the air, the fish of the sea,
and whatsoever walks in the paths of the sea.
O Lord our governor,
how exalted is your name in all the world! ℟

SECOND READING
Hebrews 1.1–4; 2.5–12

A reading from the letter to the Hebrews.

Long ago God spoke to our ancestors in many and various ways by the
prophets, but in these last days he has spoken to us by a Son, whom he
appointed heir of all things, through whom he also created the worlds. He is
the reflection of God's glory and the exact imprint of God's very being, and
he sustains all things by his powerful word. When he had made purification
for sins, he sat down at the right hand of the Majesty on high, having
become as much superior to angels as the name he has inherited is more
excellent than theirs.

Now God did not subject the coming world, about which we are speaking, to
angels. But someone has testified somewhere,
'What are human beings that you are mindful of them,
or mortals, that you care for them?
You have made them for a little while lower than the angels;
you have crowned them with glory and honour,
subjecting all things under their feet.'
Now in subjecting all things to them, God left nothing outside their control.
As it is, we do not yet see everything in subjection to them, but we do see
Jesus, who for a little while was made lower than the angels, now crowned
with glory and honour because of the suffering of death, so that by the grace
of God he might taste death for everyone.

It was fitting that God, for whom and through whom all things exist, in bringing many children to glory, should make the pioneer of their salvation perfect through sufferings. For the one who sanctifies and those who are sanctified all have one Father. For this reason Jesus is not ashamed to call them brothers and sisters, saying,
'I will proclaim your name to my brothers and sisters,
in the midst of the congregation I will praise you.'

GOSPEL   Mark 10.2–16

Hear the gospel of our Lord Jesus Christ according to Mark.

Some Pharisees came, and to test Jesus they asked, 'Is it lawful for a man to divorce his wife?' He answered them, 'What did Moses command you?' They said, 'Moses allowed a man to write a certificate of dismissal and to divorce her.' But Jesus said to them, 'Because of your hardness of heart he wrote this commandment for you. But from the beginning of creation, "God made them male and female." "For this reason a man shall leave his father and mother and be joined to his wife, and the two shall become one flesh." So they are no longer two, but one flesh. Therefore what God has joined together, let no one separate.'

Then in the house the disciples asked him again about this matter. Jesus said to them, 'Whoever divorces his wife and marries another commits adultery against her; and if she divorces her husband and marries another, she commits adultery.'

People were bringing little children to him in order that he might touch them; and the disciples spoke sternly to them. But when Jesus saw this, he was indignant and said to them, 'Let the little children come to me; do not stop them; for it is to such as these that the kingdom of God belongs. Truly I tell you, whoever does not receive the kingdom of God as a little child will never enter it.' And he took them up in his arms, laid his hands on them, and blessed them.

† SUNDAY BETWEEN 9 AND 15 OCTOBER   YEAR B
PROPER 23

TRACK 1

FIRST READING   Job 23.1–9, 16–17

A reading from the book of Job.

Job answered his companions:
'Today also my complaint is bitter;
his hand is heavy despite my groaning.
Oh, that I knew where I might find him,
that I might come even to his dwelling!
I would lay my case before him,
and fill my mouth with arguments.
I would learn what he would answer me,
and understand what he would say to me.
Would he contend with me in the greatness of his power? No;
but he would give heed to me.
There an upright person could reason with him,
and I should be acquitted for ever by my judge.

If I go forward, he is not there;
or backward, I cannot perceive him;
on the left he hides,
and I cannot behold him;
I turn to the right,
but I cannot see him.
God has made my heart faint;
the Almighty has terrified me;
If only I could vanish in darkness,
and thick darkness would cover my face!'

PSALM   Psalm 22.1–15

℟ Why are you so far from the words of my distress?

My God, my God, why have you forsaken me?
and are so far from my cry
and from the words of my distress?

O my God, I cry in the daytime,
but you do not answer;
by night as well, but I find no rest.
Yet you are the Holy One,
enthroned upon the praises of Israel. ℟

Our forebears put their trust in you;
they trusted and you delivered them.
They cried out to you and were delivered;
they trusted in you and were not put to shame. ℟

But as for me, I am a worm and no man,
scorned by all and despised by the people.
All who see me laugh me to scorn;
they curl their lips and wag their heads, saying,
'He trusted in the Lord; let him deliver him;
let him rescue him, if he delights in him.' ℟

Yet you are he who took me out of the womb,
and kept me safe upon my mother's breast.
I have been entrusted to you ever since I was born;
you were my God
when I was still in my mother's womb. ℟

Be not far from me, for trouble is near,
and there is none to help.
Many young bulls encircle me;
strong bulls of Bashan surround me.
They open wide their jaws at me,
like a ravening and a roaring lion. ℟

I am poured out like water;
all my bones are out of joint;
my heart within my breast is melting wax.
My mouth is dried out like a pot-sherd;
my tongue sticks to the roof of my mouth;
and you have laid me in the dust of the grave. ℟

Or   TRACK 2

FIRST READING   Amos 5.6–7, 10–15

A reading from the book of the prophet Amos.

Seek the LORD and live,
or he will break out against the house of Joseph like fire,
and it will devour Bethel, with no one to quench it.
Ah, you that turn justice to wormwood,
and bring righteousness to the ground!

They hate the one who reproves in the gate,
and they abhor the one who speaks the truth.
Therefore because you trample on the poor
and take from them levies of grain,
you have built houses of hewn stone,
but you shall not live in them;
you have planted pleasant vineyards,
but you shall not drink their wine.
For I know how many are your transgressions,
and how great are your sins –
you who afflict the righteous,
who take a bribe, and push aside the needy in the gate.
Therefore the prudent will keep silent in such a time;
for it is an evil time.

Seek good and not evil, that you may live;
and so the LORD, the God of hosts,
will be with you, just as you have said.
Hate evil and love good,
and establish justice in the gate;
it may be that the LORD, the God of hosts,
will be gracious to the remnant of Joseph.

PSALM   Psalm 90.13–17

℟ **We shall rejoice and be glad**
  all the days of our life.
  or
℟ **O Lord, be gracious to your servants.**

Return, O Lord; how long will you tarry?
be gracious to your servants.
Satisfy us by your loving-kindness in the morning;
so shall we rejoice and be glad all the days of our life. ℟

Make us glad by the measure of the days
that you afflicted us
and the years in which we suffered adversity.
Show your servants your works
and your splendour to their children. ℟

May the graciousness of the Lord our God be upon us;
prosper the work of our hands;
prosper our handiwork. ℟

SECOND READING   Hebrews 4.12–16

A reading from the letter to the Hebrews.

The word of God is living and active, sharper than any two-edged sword,
piercing until it divides soul from spirit, joints from marrow; it is able to
judge the thoughts and intentions of the heart. And before him no creature is
hidden, but all are naked and laid bare to the eyes of the one to whom we
must render an account.

Since, then, we have a great high priest who has passed through the heavens,
Jesus, the Son of God, let us hold fast to our confession. For we do not have a
high priest who is unable to sympathize with our weaknesses, but we have
one who in every respect has been tested as we are, yet without sin. Let us
therefore approach the throne of grace with boldness, so that we may receive
mercy and find grace to help in time of need.

GOSPEL   **Mark 10.17–31**

Hear the gospel of our Lord Jesus Christ according to Mark.

As Jesus was setting out on a journey, a man ran up and knelt before him, and asked him, 'Good Teacher, what must I do to inherit eternal life?' Jesus said to him, 'Why do you call me good? No one is good but God alone. You know the commandments: "You shall not murder; You shall not commit adultery; You shall not steal; You shall not bear false witness; You shall not defraud; Honour your father and mother."' He said to Jesus, 'Teacher, I have kept all these since my youth.' Jesus, looking at him, loved him and said, 'You lack one thing; go, sell what you own, and give the money to the poor, and you will have treasure in heaven; then come, follow me.' When he heard this, he was shocked and went away grieving, for he had many possessions.

Then Jesus looked around and said to his disciples, 'How hard it will be for those who have wealth to enter the kingdom of God!' And the disciples were perplexed at these words. But Jesus said to them again, 'Children, how hard it is to enter the kingdom of God! It is easier for a camel to go through the eye of a needle than for someone who is rich to enter the kingdom of God.' They were greatly astounded and said to one another, 'Then who can be saved?' Jesus looked at them and said, 'For mortals it is impossible, but not for God; for God all things are possible.'

Peter began to say to him, 'Look, we have left everything and followed you.' Jesus said, 'Truly I tell you there is no one who has left house or brothers or sisters or mother or father or children or fields, for my sake and for the sake of the good news, who will not receive a hundredfold now in this age – houses, brothers and sisters, mothers and children, and fields – but with persecutions – and in the age to come eternal life. But many who are first will be last, and the last will be first.'

† SUNDAY BETWEEN 16 AND 22 OCTOBER   YEAR B
PROPER 24

TRACK 1

FIRST READING (Short or long reading)   Job 38.1–7, (34–41)

A reading from the book of Job.

The LORD answered Job out of the whirlwind:
'Who is this that darkens counsel
by words without knowledge?
Gird up your loins like a man,
I will question you, and you shall declare to me.
Where were you when I laid the foundation of the earth?
Tell me, if you have understanding.
Who determined its measurements –
surely you know!
Or who stretched the line upon it?
On what were its bases sunk,
or who laid its cornerstone
when the morning stars sang together
and all the heavenly beings shouted for joy?

[Can you lift up your voice to the clouds,
so that a flood of waters may cover you?
Can you send forth lightnings,
so that they may go and say to you,
"Here we are"?
Who has put wisdom in the inward parts,
or given understanding to the mind?
Who has the wisdom to number the clouds?
Or who can tilt the waterskins of the heavens,
when the dust runs into a mass and the clods cling together?

Can you hunt the prey for the lion,
or satisfy the appetite of the young lions,
when they crouch in their dens,
or lie in wait in their covert?
Who provides for the raven its prey,
when its young ones cry to God,
and wander about for lack of food?']

491

PSALM   **Psalm 104.1–9, 25, 37b**

℞ **At your rebuke, O Lord, the waters fled.**
  [They shall not again cover the earth.]

Bless the Lord, O my soul;
O Lord my God, how excellent is your greatness!
you are clothed with majesty and splendour.
You wrap yourself with light as with a cloak
and spread out the heavens like a curtain. ℞

You lay the beams of your chambers
in the waters above;
you make the clouds your chariot;
you ride on the wings of the wind.
You make the winds your messengers
and flames of fire your servants. ℞

You have set the earth upon its foundations,
so that it never shall move at any time.
You covered it with the deep as with a mantle;
the waters stood higher than the mountains. ℞

At your rebuke they fled;
at the voice of your thunder they hastened away.
They went up into the hills
and down to the valleys beneath,
to the places you had appointed for them. ℞

You set the limits that they should not pass;
they shall not again cover the earth.
O Lord, how manifold are your works!
in wisdom you have made them all;
the earth is full of your creatures.
Alleluia! ℞

Or   TRACK 2

FIRST READING   **Isaiah 53.4–12**

A reading from the book of the prophet Isaiah.

Surely he has borne our infirmities
and carried our diseases;

yet we accounted him stricken,
struck down by God, and afflicted.
But he was wounded for our transgressions,
crushed for our iniquities;
upon him was the punishment that made us whole,
and by his bruises we are healed.
All we like sheep have gone astray;
we have all turned to our own way,
and the LORD has laid on him the iniquity of us all.

He was oppressed, and he was afflicted,
yet he did not open his mouth;
like a lamb that is led to the slaughter,
and like a sheep that before its shearers is silent,
so he did not open his mouth.
By a perversion of justice he was taken away.
Who could have imagined his future?
For he was cut off from the land of the living,
stricken for the transgression of my people.
They made his grave with the wicked
and his tomb with the rich,
although he had done no violence,
and there was no deceit in his mouth.

Yet it was the will of the LORD to crush him with pain.
When you make his life an offering for sin,
he shall see his offspring, and shall prolong his days;
through him the will of the LORD shall prosper.
Out of his anguish he shall see light;
he shall find satisfaction through his knowledge.
The righteous one, my servant, shall make many righteous,
and he shall bear their iniquities.
Therefore I will allot him a portion with the great,
and he shall divide the spoil with the strong;
because he poured out himself to death,
and was numbered with the transgressors;
yet he bore the sin of many,
and made intercession for the transgressors.

PSALM   Psalm 91.9–16

℟ **The Lord shall give his angels charge over you**
   [to keep you in all your ways].

Because you have made the Lord your refuge,
and the Most High your habitation;
No evil shall happen to you,
neither shall any plague come near your dwelling. ℟

For he shall give his angels charge over you,
to keep you in all your ways.
They shall bear you in their hands,
lest you dash your foot against a stone. ℟

You shall tread upon the lion and adder;
you shall trample the young lion and the serpent under your feet.
Because he is bound to me in love,
therefore will I deliver him;
I will protect him, because he knows my name. ℟

He shall call upon me and I will answer him;
I am with him in trouble,
I will rescue him and bring him to honour.
With long life will I satisfy him,
and show him my salvation. ℟

SECOND READING   Hebrews 5.1–10

A reading from the letter to the Hebrews.

Every high priest chosen from among mortals is put in charge of things
pertaining to God on their behalf, to offer gifts and sacrifices for sins. He is
able to deal gently with the ignorant and wayward, since he himself is subject
to weakness; and because of this he must offer sacrifice for his own sins as
well as for those of the people. And one does not presume to take this
honour, but takes it only when called by God, just as Aaron was.
So also Christ did not glorify himself in becoming a high priest,
but was appointed by the one who said to him,
'You are my Son,
today I have begotten you'; as he says also in another place,
'You are a priest for ever,
according to the order of Melchizedek.'

In the days of his flesh, Jesus offered up prayers and supplications, with loud cries and tears, to the one who was able to save him from death, and he was heard because of his reverent submission. Although he was a Son, he learned obedience through what he suffered; and having been made perfect, he became the source of eternal salvation for all who obey him, having been designated by God a high priest according to the order of Melchizedek.

GOSPEL   Mark 10.35–45

Hear the gospel of our Lord Jesus Christ according to Mark.

James and John, the sons of Zebedee, came forward to Jesus and said to him, 'Teacher, we want you to do for us whatever we ask of you.' And he said to them, 'What is it you want me to do for you?' And they said to him, 'Grant us to sit, one at your right hand and one at your left, in your glory.' But Jesus said to them, 'You do not know what you are asking. Are you able to drink the cup that I drink, or be baptized with the baptism that I am baptized with?' They replied, 'We are able.' Then Jesus said to them, 'The cup that I drink you will drink; and with the baptism with which I am baptized, you will be baptized; but to sit at my right hand or at my left is not mine to grant, but it is for those for whom it has been prepared.'

When the ten heard this, they began to be angry with James and John. So Jesus called them and said to them, 'You know that among the Gentiles those whom they recognize as their rulers lord it over them, and their great ones are tyrants over them. But it is not so among you; but whoever wishes to become great among you must be your servant, and whoever wishes to be first among you must be slave of all. For the Son of Man came not to be served but to serve, and to give his life a ransom for many.'

† SUNDAY BETWEEN 23 AND 29 OCTOBER   YEAR B
PROPER 25

Pvision for Proper 25 is identical in the Revised Common Lectionary and the Church of England provision, but the Church of England adds alternative readings for Bible Sunday (below, pages 500–502).

TRACK 1

FIRST READING   **Job 42.1–6, 10–17**

A reading from the book of Job.

Job answered the LORD:
'I know that you can do all things,
and that no purpose of yours can be thwarted.
"Who is this that hides counsel without knowledge?"
Therefore I have uttered what I did not understand,
things too wonderful for me,
which I did not know.
"Hear, and I will speak;
I will question you, and you declare to me."
I had heard of you by the hearing of the ear,
but now my eye sees you;
therefore I despise myself,
and repent in dust and ashes.'

And the LORD restored the fortunes of Job when he had prayed for his friends; and the LORD gave Job twice as much as he had before. Then there came to him all his brothers and sisters and all who had known him before, and they ate bread with him in his house; they showed him sympathy and comforted him for all the evil that the LORD had brought upon him; and each of them gave him a piece of money and a gold ring. The LORD blessed the latter days of Job more than his beginning; and he had fourteen thousand sheep, six thousand camels, a thousand yoke of oxen, and a thousand donkeys. He also had seven sons and three daughters. He named the first Jemimah, the second Keziah, and the third Keren-happuch. In all the land there were no women so beautiful as Job's daughters; and their father gave them an inheritance along with their brothers. After this Job lived one hundred and forty years, and saw his children, and his children's children, four generations. And Job died, old and full of days.

PSALM   **Psalm 34.1–8, 19–22**

℟ **I sought the Lord, and he answered me**
  [and delivered me out of all my terror].

I will bless the Lord at all times;
his praise shall ever be in my mouth.
I will glory in the Lord;
let the humble hear and rejoice.
Proclaim with me the greatness of the Lord;
let us exalt his name together. ℟

I sought the Lord and he answered me
and delivered me out of all my terror.
Look upon him and be radiant,
and let not your faces be ashamed. ℟

I called in my affliction and the Lord heard me
and saved me from all my troubles.
The angel of the Lord
encompasses those who fear him,
and he will deliver them. ℟

Taste and see that the Lord is good;
happy are they who trust in him!
Many are the troubles of the righteous,
but the Lord will deliver him out of them all. ℟

He will keep safe all his bones;
not one of them shall be broken.
Evil shall slay the wicked,
and those who hate the righteous will be punished.
The Lord ransoms the life of his servants,
and none will be punished who trust in him. ℟

Or   TRACK 2

FIRST READING   **Jeremiah 31.7–9**

A reading from the book of the prophet Jeremiah.

Thus says the LORD:
Sing aloud with gladness for Jacob,
and raise shouts for the chief of the nations;

proclaim, give praise, and say,
'Save, O LORD, your people,
the remnant of Israel.'
See, I am going to bring them from the land of the north,
and gather them from the farthest parts of the earth,
among them the blind and the lame,
those with child and those in labour, together;
a great company, they shall return here.
With weeping they shall come,
and with consolations I will lead them back,
I will let them walk by brooks of water,
in a straight path in which they shall not stumble;
for I have become a father to Israel,
and Ephraim is my firstborn.

PSALM   Psalm 126

℟ **The Lord has done great things for us
[and we are glad].**

When the Lord restored the fortunes of Zion,
then were we like those who dream.
Then was our mouth filled with laughter,
and our tongue with shouts of joy. ℟

Then they said among the nations,
'The Lord has done great things for them.'
The Lord has done great things for us,
and we are glad indeed. ℟

Restore our fortunes, O Lord,
like the watercourses of the Negev.
Those who sowed with tears
will reap with songs of joy.
Those who go out weeping, carrying the seed,
will come again with joy, shouldering their sheaves. ℟

SECOND READING   Hebrews 7.23–28

A reading from the letter to the Hebrews.

The former priests were many in number, because they were prevented by
death from continuing in office; but he holds his priesthood permanently,
because he continues for ever. Consequently he is able for all time to save
those who approach God through him, since he always lives to make
intercession for them. For it was fitting that we should have such a high
priest, holy, blameless, undefiled, separated from sinners, and exalted above
the heavens. Unlike the other high priests, he has no need to offer sacrifices
day after day, first for his own sins, and then for those of the people; this he
did once for all when he offered himself. For the law appoints as high priests
those who are subject to weakness, but the word of the oath, which came
later than the law, appoints a Son who has been made perfect for ever.

GOSPEL   Mark 10.46B–52

Hear the gospel of our Lord Jesus Christ according to Mark.

As Jesus and his disciples and a large crowd were leaving Jericho, Bartimaeus
son of Timaeus, a blind beggar, was sitting by the roadside. When he heard
that it was Jesus of Nazareth, he began to shout out and say, 'Jesus, Son of
David, have mercy on me!' Many sternly ordered him to be quiet, but he
cried out even more loudly, 'Son of David, have mercy on me!' Jesus stood
still and said, 'Call him here.' And they called the blind man, saying to him,
'Take heart; get up, he is calling you.' So throwing off his cloak, he sprang up
and came to Jesus. Then Jesus said to him, 'What do you want me to do for
you?' The blind man said to him, 'My teacher, let me see again.' Jesus said to
him, 'Go; your faith has made you well.' Immediately he regained his sight
and followed him on the way.

Or

† BIBLE SUNDAY YEAR B

FIRST READING Isaiah 55.1–11

A reading from the book of the prophet Isaiah.

The LORD says this:
Everyone who thirsts,
come to the waters;
and you that have no money,
come, buy and eat!
Come, buy wine and milk
without money and without price.
Why do you spend your money for that which is not bread,
and your labour for that which does not satisfy?
Listen carefully to me, and eat what is good,
and delight yourselves in rich food.
Incline your ear, and come to me;
listen, so that you may live.
I will make with you an everlasting covenant,
my steadfast, sure love for David.
See, I made him a witness to the peoples,
a leader and commander for the peoples.
See, you shall call nations that you do not know,
and nations that do not know you shall run to you,
because of the LORD your God, the Holy One of Israel,
for he has glorified you.

Seek the LORD while he may be found,
call upon him while he is near;
let the wicked forsake their way,
and the unrighteous their thoughts;
let them return to the LORD, that he may have mercy on them,
and to our God, for he will abundantly pardon.
For my thoughts are not your thoughts,
nor are your ways my ways, says the LORD.
For as the heavens are higher than the earth,
so are my ways higher than your ways
and my thoughts than your thoughts.
For as the rain and the snow come down from heaven,

and do not return there until they have watered the earth,
making it bring forth and sprout,
giving seed to the sower and bread to the eater,
so shall my word be that goes out from my mouth;
it shall not return to me empty,
but it shall accomplish that which I purpose,
and succeed in the thing for which I sent it.

PSALM   **Psalm 19.7–14**

℟ **The law of the Lord is perfect and revives the soul.**

The law of the Lord is perfect
and revives the soul;
the testimony of the Lord is sure
and gives wisdom to the innocent.
The statutes of the Lord are just
and rejoice the heart;
the commandment of the Lord is clear
and gives light to the eyes. ℟

The fear of the Lord is clean
and endures for ever;
the judgements of the Lord are true
and righteous altogether.
More to be desired are they than gold,
more than much fine gold,
sweeter far than honey,
than honey in the comb. ℟

By them also is your servant enlightened,
and in keeping them there is great reward.
Who can tell how often he offends?
Cleanse me from my secret faults.
Above all, keep your servant from presumptuous sins;
let them not get dominion over me;
then shall I be whole and sound,
and innocent of a great offence. ℟

Let the words of my mouth and the meditation of my heart
be acceptable in your sight,
O Lord, my strength and my redeemer. ℟

SECOND READING   2 Timothy 3.14 – 4.5

A reading from the second letter of Paul to Timothy.

Continue in what you have learned and firmly believed, knowing from whom you learned it, and how from childhood you have known the sacred writings that are able to instruct you for salvation through faith in Christ Jesus. All scripture is inspired by God and is useful for teaching, for reproof, for correction, and for training in righteousness, so that everyone who belongs to God may be proficient, equipped for every good work.

In the presence of God and of Christ Jesus, who is to judge the living and the dead, and in view of his appearing and his kingdom, I solemnly urge you: proclaim the message; be persistent whether the time is favourable or unfavourable; convince, rebuke, and encourage, with the utmost patience in teaching. For the time is coming when people will not put up with sound doctrine, but having itching ears, they will accumulate for themselves teachers to suit their own desires, and will turn away from listening to the truth and wander away to myths. As for you, always be sober, endure suffering, do the work of an evangelist, carry out your ministry fully.

GOSPEL   John 5.36–47

Hear the gospel of our Lord Jesus Christ according to John.

Jesus said to the Jews: 'I have a testimony greater than John's. The works that the Father has given me to complete, the very works that I am doing, testify on my behalf that the Father has sent me. And the Father who sent me has himself testified on my behalf. You have never heard his voice or seen his form, and you do not have his word abiding in you, because you do not believe him whom he has sent.

You search the scriptures because you think that in them you have eternal life; and it is they that testify on my behalf. Yet you refuse to come to me to have life. I do not accept glory from human beings. But I know that you do not have the love of God in you. I have come in my Father's name, and you do not accept me; if another comes in his own name, you will accept him. How can you believe when you accept glory from one another and do not seek the glory that comes from the one who alone is God? Do not think that I will accuse you before the Father; your accuser is Moses, on whom you have set your hope. If you believed Moses, you would believe me, for he wrote about me. But if you do not believe what he wrote, how will you believe what I say?'

† DEDICATION FESTIVAL   YEAR B

First Sunday in October or Last Sunday after Trinity

FIRST READING (Alternative readings)

Either   Genesis 28.11–18

A reading from the book of Genesis.

Jacob came to a certain place and stayed there for the night, because the sun had set. Taking one of the stones of the place, he put it under his head and lay down in that place. And he dreamed that there was a ladder set up on the earth, the top of it reaching to heaven; and the angels of God were ascending and descending on it. And the LORD stood beside him and said, 'I am the LORD, the God of Abraham your father and the God of Isaac; the land on which you lie I will give to you and to your offspring; and your offspring shall be like the dust of the earth, and you shall spread abroad to the west and to the east and to the north and to the south; and all the families of the earth shall be blessed in you and in your offspring. Know that I am with you and will keep you wherever you go, and will bring you back to this land; for I will not leave you until I have done what I have promised you.' Then Jacob woke from his sleep and said, 'Surely the LORD is in this place – and I did not know it!' And he was afraid, and said, 'How awesome is this place! This is none other than the house of God, and this is the gate of heaven.'

So Jacob rose early in the morning, and he took the stone that he had put under his head and set it up for a pillar and poured oil on the top of it.

Or   Revelation 21.9–14

A reading from the book of Revelation.

One of the seven angels who had the seven bowls full of the seven last plagues came and said to me, 'Come, I will show you the bride, the wife of the Lamb.' And in the spirit he carried me away to a great, high mountain and showed me the holy city Jerusalem coming down out of heaven from God. It has the glory of God and a radiance like a very rare jewel, like jasper, clear as crystal. It has a great, high wall with twelve gates, and at the gates twelve angels, and on the gates are inscribed the names of the twelve tribes of the Israelites; on the east three gates, on the north three gates, on the south three gates, and on the west three gates. And the wall of the city has twelve foundations, and on them are the twelve names of the twelve apostles of the Lamb.

PSALM

Psalm 122

℞ I was glad when they said to me,
   'Let us go to the house of the Lord'.

I was glad when they said to me,
'Let us go to the house of the Lord.'
Now our feet are standing
within your gates, O Jerusalem. ℞

Jerusalem is built as a city
that is at unity with itself.
To which the tribes go up, the tribes of the Lord,
the assembly of Israel, to praise the name of the Lord.
For there are the thrones of judgement,
the thrones of the house of David. ℞

Pray for the peace of Jerusalem:
 'May they prosper who love you.
Peace be within your walls
and quietness within your towers. ℞

For my family and companions' sake,
I pray for your prosperity.
Because of the house of the Lord our God,
I will seek to do you good.' ℞

SECOND READING

1 Peter 2.1–10

A reading from the first letter of Peter.

Rid yourselves, therefore, of all malice, and all guile, insincerity, envy, and all slander. Like newborn infants, long for the pure, spiritual milk, so that by it you may grow into salvation – if indeed you have tasted that the Lord is good.

Come to him, a living stone, though rejected by mortals yet chosen and precious in God's sight, Like living stones, let yourselves be built into a spiritual house, to be a holy priesthood, to offer spiritual sacrifices acceptable to God through Jesus Christ. For it stands in scripture:
'See, I am laying in Zion a stone,
a cornerstone chosen and precious;
and whoever believes in him will not be put to shame.'

To you then who believe, he is precious; but for those who do not believe,
'The stone that the builders rejected
has become the very head of the corner,'
and 'A stone that makes them stumble,
and a rock that makes them fall.'
They stumble because they disobey the word, as they were destined to do.

But you are a chosen race, a royal priesthood, a holy nation, God's own
people, in order that you may proclaim the mighty acts of him who called
you out of darkness into his marvellous light.
Once you were not a people,
but now you are God's people;
once you had not received mercy,
but now you have received mercy.

GOSPEL   John 10.22–29

Hear the gospel of our Lord Jesus Christ according to John.

At that time the festival of the Dedication took place in Jerusalem. It was
winter, and Jesus was walking in the temple, in the portico of Solomon. So
the Jews gathered around him and said to him, 'How long will you keep us in
suspense? If you are the Messiah, tell us plainly.' Jesus answered, 'I have told
you, and you do not believe. The works that I do in my Father's name testify
to me; but you do not believe, because you do not belong to my sheep. My
sheep hear my voice. I know them, and they follow me. I give them eternal
life, and they will never perish. No one will snatch them out of my hand.
What my Father has given me is greater than all else, and no one can snatch
it out of the Father's hand.'

SUNDAYS BEFORE ADVENT

*In the weeks after All Saints' Day the Church of England provision designates Sundays
'Sundays before Advent', while the Revised Common Lectionary continues with
'Propers' designated by calendar dates.*

† 4 BEFORE ADVENT   YEAR B
PROPER 26

In Church of England provision this Sunday may be kept as All Saints' Sunday (see pages 510–513) or else the provision below is used. The Revised Common Lectionary continues to provide two tracks for the First Reading and Psalms. Church of England provision allows only Track 2.

TRACK 1

Revised Common Lectionary only

FIRST READING   Ruth 1.1–18

A reading from the book of Ruth.

In the days when the judges ruled, there was a famine in the land, and a certain man of Bethlehem in Judah went to live in the country of Moab, he and his wife and two sons. The name of the man was Elimelech and the name of his wife Naomi, and the names of his two sons were Mahlon and Chilion; they were Ephrathites from Bethlehem in Judah. They went into the country of Moab and remained there. But Elimelech, the husband of Naomi, died, and she was left with her two sons. These took Moabite wives; the name of the one was Orpah and the name of the other Ruth. When they had lived there about ten years, both Mahlon and Chilion also died, so that the woman was left without her two sons and her husband.

Then she started to return with her daughters-in-law from the country of Moab, for she had heard in the country of Moab that the LORD had had consideration for his people and given them food. So she set out from the place where she had been living, she and her two daughters-in-law, and they went on their way to go back to the land of Judah. But Naomi said to her two daughters-in-law, 'Go back each of you to your mother's house.

May the LORD deal kindly with you, as you have dealt with the dead and with me. The LORD grant that you may find security, each of you in the house of your husband.' Then she kissed them, and they wept aloud. They said to her, 'No, we will return with you to your people.' But Naomi said, 'Turn back, my daughters, why will you go with me? Do I still have sons in my womb that they may become your husbands? Turn back, my daughters, go your way, for I am too old to have a husband. Even if I thought there was hope for me, even if I should have a husband tonight and bear sons, would you then wait until they were grown? Would you then refrain from marrying? No, my daughters, it has been far more bitter for me than for you, because the hand of the LORD has turned against me.' Then they wept aloud again. Orpah kissed her mother-in-law, but Ruth clung to her. So she said, 'See, your sister-in-law has gone back to her people and to her gods; return after your sister-in-law.' But Ruth said,

'Do not press me to leave you or to turn back from following you!
Where you go, I will go;
Where you lodge, I will lodge;
your people shall be my people,
and your God my God.
Where you die, I will die –
there will I be buried.
May the LORD do thus and so to me,
and more as well, if even death parts me from you!'
When Naomi saw that she was determined to go with her, she said no more to her.

PSALM   Psalm 146

℟ **The Lord has done great things for us
    [and we are glad].**

Alleluia!
Praise the Lord, O my soul!
I will praise the Lord as long as I live;
I will sing praises to my God while I have my being. ℟

Put not your trust in rulers,
nor in any child of earth,
for there is no help in them.
When they breathe their last, they return to earth,
and in that day their thoughts perish. ℟

Happy are they who have the God of Jacob
for their help!
whose hope is in the Lord their God;
Who made heaven and earth, the seas,
and all that is in them;
who keeps his promise for ever;
Who gives justice to those who are oppressed,
and food to those who hunger. ℟

507

The Lord sets the prisoners free;
the Lord opens the eyes of the blind;
the Lord lifts up those who are bowed down;
The Lord loves the righteous;
the Lord cares for the stranger;
he sustains the orphan and widow,
but frustrates the way of the wicked. ℟

The Lord shall reign for ever,
your God, O Zion, throughout all generations.
Alleluia! ℟

Or   TRACK 2

FIRST READING   **Deuteronomy 6.1–9**

A reading from the book of Deuteronomy.

This is the commandment – the statutes and the ordinances – that the LORD
your God charged me to teach you to observe in the land that you are about
to cross into and occupy, so that you and your children and your children's
children may fear the LORD your God all the days of your life, and keep all
his decrees and his commandments that I am commanding you, so that your
days may be long. Hear therefore, O Israel, and observe them diligently, so
that it may go well with you, and so that you may multiply greatly in a land
flowing with milk and honey, as the LORD, the God of your ancestors, has
promised you.

Hear, O Israel: The LORD is our God, the LORD alone. You shall love the
LORD your God with all your heart, and with all your soul, and with all your
might. Keep these words that I am commanding you today in your heart.
Recite them to your children and talk about them when you are at home and
when you are away, when you lie down and when you rise. Bind them as a
sign on your hand, fix them as an emblem on your forehead, and write them
on the doorposts of your house and on your gates.

PSALM   **Psalm 119.1–8**

℟ **Lord, may I keep your statutes.**

Happy are they whose way is blameless,
who walk in the law of the Lord!

Happy are they who observe his decrees
and seek him with all their hearts! ℞

Who never do any wrong,
but always walk in his ways.
You laid down your commandments,
that we should fully keep them. ℞

O that my ways were made so direct
that I might keep your statutes!
Then I should not be put to shame,
when I regard all your commandments. ℞

I will thank you with an unfeigned heart,
when I have learned your righteous judgements.
I will keep your statutes;
do not utterly forsake me. ℞

SECOND READING   Hebrews 9.11–14

A reading from the letter to the Hebrews.

Christ came as a high priest of the good things that have come, then through
the greater and perfect tent (not made with hands, that is, not of this
creation), he entered once for all into the Holy Place, not with the blood of
goats and calves, but with his own blood, thus obtaining eternal redemption.
For if the blood of goats and bulls, with the sprinkling of the ashes of a heifer,
sanctifies those who have been defiled so that their flesh is purified, how
much more will the blood of Christ, who through the eternal Spirit offered
himself without blemish to God, purify our conscience from dead works to
worship the living God!

GOSPEL   Mark 12.28–34

Hear the gospel of our Lord Jesus Christ according to Mark.

One of the scribes came near and heard the religious authorities disputing
with one another, and seeing that Jesus answered them well, he asked him,
'Which commandment is the first of all?' Jesus answered, 'The first is, "Hear,
O Israel: the Lord our God, the Lord is one; you shall love the Lord your God
with all your heart, and with all your soul, and with all your mind, and with
all your strength."

The second is this, "You shall love your neighbour as yourself." There is no other commandment greater than these.' Then the scribe said to him, 'You are right, Teacher; you have truly said that "he is one, and besides him there is no other"; and "to love him with all the heart, and with all the understanding, and with all the strength," and "to love one's neighbour as oneself" – this is much more important than all whole burnt-offerings and sacrifices.' When Jesus saw that he answered wisely, he said to him, 'You are not far from the kingdom of God.' After that no one dared to ask him any question.

† ALL SAINTS' SUNDAY   YEAR B

Sunday between 30 October and 5 November (or, if this is not kept as All Saints' Sunday, 1 November itself)

FIRST READING (Alternative readings)

Either   **Wisdom of Solomon 3.1–9**

A reading from the book of Wisdom.

The souls of the righteous are in the hand of God,
and no torment will ever touch them.

In the eyes of the foolish they seemed to have died,
and their departure was thought to be a disaster,

and their going from us to be their destruction;
but they are at peace.

For though in the sight of others they were punished,
their hope is full of immortality.

Having been disciplined a little,
they will receive great good,
because God tested them and found them worthy of himself;

like gold in the furnace he tried them,
and like a sacrificial burnt-offering he accepted them.

In the time of their visitation they will shine forth,
and will run like sparks through the stubble.

They will govern nations and rule over peoples,
and the Lord will reign over them for ever.

Those who trust in him will understand truth,
and the faithful will abide with him in love,
because grace and mercy are upon his holy ones,
and he watches over his elect.

Or   **Isaiah 25.6–9**

A reading from the book of the prophet Isaiah.

On this mountain the LORD of hosts will make for all peoples
a feast of rich food, a feast of well-matured wines,
of rich food filled with marrow,
of well-matured wines strained clear.
And he will destroy on this mountain
the shroud that is cast over all peoples,
the sheet that is spread over all nations;
he will swallow up death for ever.
Then the Lord GOD will wipe away the tears from all faces,
and the disgrace of his people
he will take away from all the earth,
for the LORD has spoken.
It will be said on that day,
Lo, this is our God;
we have waited for him,
so that he might save us.
This is the LORD for whom we have waited;
let us be glad and rejoice in his salvation.

PSALM   **Psalm 24.1–6**

℟ **The souls of the righteous are in the hand of God**
   [no torment will ever touch them].

The earth is the Lord's and all that is in it,
the world and all who dwell therein.
For it is he who founded it upon the seas
and made it firm upon the rivers of the deep. ℟

'Who can ascend the hill of the Lord?
and who can stand in his holy place?'
'Those who have clean hands and a pure heart,
who have not pledged themselves to falsehood,
nor sworn by what is a fraud. ℟

They shall receive a blessing from the Lord
and a just reward from the God of their salvation.'
Such is the generation of those who seek him,
of those who seek your face, O God of Jacob. ℞

SECOND READING   Revelation 21.1-6a

A reading from the book of Revelation.

I, John, saw a new heaven and a new earth; for the first heaven and the first
earth had passed away, and the sea was no more. And I saw the holy city, the
new Jerusalem, coming down out of heaven from God, prepared as a bride
adorned for her husband. And I heard a loud voice from the throne saying,
'See, the home of God is among mortals.
He will dwell with them;
they will be his peoples,
and God himself will be with them;
he will wipe every tear from their eyes.
Death will be no more;
mourning and crying and pain will be no more,
for the first things have passed away.'
And the one who was seated on the throne said, 'See, I am making all things
new.' Also he said, 'Write this, for these words are trustworthy and true.'
Then he said to me, 'It is done! I am the Alpha and the Omega, the
beginning and the end.'

GOSPEL   John 11.32-44

Hear the gospel of our Lord Jesus Christ according to John.

When Mary came where Jesus was and saw him, she knelt at his feet and said
to him, 'Lord, if you had been here, my brother would not have died.' When
Jesus saw her weeping, and the Jews who came with her also weeping, he was
greatly disturbed in spirit and deeply moved. He said, 'Where have you laid
him?' They said to him, 'Lord, come and see.' Jesus began to weep. So the
Jews said, 'See how he loved him!' But some of them said, 'Could not he who
opened the eyes of the blind man have kept this man from dying?'

Then Jesus, again greatly disturbed, came to the tomb. It was a cave, and a
stone was lying against it. Jesus said, 'Take away the stone.' Martha, the sister
of the dead man, said to him, 'Lord, already there is a stench because he has

been dead four days.' Jesus said to her, 'Did I not tell you that if you believed, you would see the glory of God?' So they took away the stone. And Jesus looked upward and said, 'Father, I thank you for having heard me. I knew that you always hear me, but I have said this for the sake of the crowd standing here, so that they may believe that you sent me.' When he had said this, he cried with a loud voice, 'Lazarus, come out!' The dead man came out, his hands and feet bound with strips of cloth, and his face wrapped in a cloth. Jesus said to them, 'Unbind him, and let him go.'

ALL SAINTS' DAY   YEARS A B C

For use on 1 November if the material for All Saints' Sunday is used on the Sunday. See Year A, pages 290–292.

† 3 BEFORE ADVENT   YEAR B
PROPER 27

The Revised Common Lectionary and the Church of England make different provision for today. For the Church of England provision see pages 517–518 below.

REVISED COMMON LECTIONARY

TRACK 1

FIRST READING   **Ruth 3.1–5; 4.13–17**

A reading from the book of Ruth.

Naomi, Ruth's mother-in-law, said to her, 'My daughter, I need to seek some security for you, so that it may be well with you. Now here is our kinsman Boaz, with whose young women you have been working. See, he is winnowing barley tonight at the threshing-floor. Now wash and anoint yourself, and put on your best clothes and go down to the threshing-floor; but do not make yourself known to the man until he has finished eating and drinking. When he lies down, observe the place where he lies; then, go and uncover his feet and lie down; and he will tell you what to do.' She said to her, 'All that you tell me I will do.'

So Boaz took Ruth and she became his wife. When they came together, the LORD made her conceive, and she bore a son. Then the women said to Naomi, 'Blessed be the LORD, who has not left you this day without next-of-kin; and may his name be renowned in Israel! He shall be to you a restorer of life and a nourisher of your old age; for your daughter-in-law who loves you, who is more to you than seven sons, has borne him.' Then Naomi took the child and laid him in her bosom, and became his nurse. The women of the neighbourhood gave him a name, saying, 'A son has been born to Naomi.' They named him Obed; he became the father of Jesse, the father of David.

PSALM   Psalm 127

℟ **The fruit of the womb is a gift.**

Unless the Lord builds the house,
their labour is in vain who build it.
Unless the Lord watches over the city,
in vain the guard keeps vigil. ℟

It is in vain that you rise so early
and go to bed so late;
vain, too, to eat the bread of toil,
for he gives to his belovèd sleep.
Children are a heritage from the Lord,
and the fruit of the womb is a gift. ℟

Like arrows in the hand of a warrior
are the children of one's youth.
Happy are they who have their quiver full of them!
they shall not be put to shame
when they contend with their enemies in the gate. ℟

Or   TRACK 2

FIRST READING   1 Kings 17.8–16

A reading from the first book of Kings.

The word of the LORD came to Elijah, saying, 'Go now to Zarephath, which belongs to Sidon, and live there; for I have commanded a widow there to feed you.' So he set out and went to Zarephath. When he came to the gate of the town, a widow was there gathering sticks; he called to her and said, 'Bring me a little water in a vessel, so that I may drink.' As she was going to bring it, he called to her and said, 'Bring me a morsel of bread in your hand.' But she said, 'As the LORD your God lives, I have nothing baked, only a handful of meal in a jar, and a little oil in a jug; I am now gathering a couple of sticks, so that I may go home and prepare it for myself and my son, that we may eat it, and die.' Elijah said to her, 'Do not be afraid; go and do as you have said; but first make me a little cake of it and bring it to me, and afterwards make something for yourself and your son. For thus says the LORD the God of Israel: The jar of meal will not be emptied and the jug of oil will not fail until the day that the LORD sends rain on the earth.' She went and did as Elijah said, so that she as well as he and her household ate for many days. The jar of meal was not emptied, neither did the jug of oil fail, according to the word of the LORD that he spoke by Elijah.

PSALM   Psalm 146

℟ **I will praise the Lord as long as I live.**

Alleluia!
Praise the Lord, O my soul!
I will praise the Lord as long as I live;
I will sing praises to my God while I have my being. ℟

Put not your trust in rulers,
nor in any child of earth,
for there is no help in them.
When they breathe their last, they return to earth,
and in that day their thoughts perish. ℟

Happy are they who have the God of Jacob
for their help!
whose hope is in the Lord their God;
Who made heaven and earth, the seas,
and all that is in them;
who keeps his promise for ever;
Who gives justice to those who are oppressed,
and food to those who hunger. ℟

The Lord sets the prisoners free;
the Lord opens the eyes of the blind;
the Lord lifts up those who are bowed down;
The Lord loves the righteous;
the Lord cares for the stranger;
he sustains the orphan and widow,
but frustrates the way of the wicked. ℟

The Lord shall reign for ever,
your God, O Zion, throughout all generations.
Alleluia! ℟

SECOND READING   Hebrews 9.24–28

A reading from the letter to the Hebrews.

Christ did not enter a sanctuary made by human hands, a mere copy of the
true one, but he entered into heaven itself, now to appear in the presence of
God on our behalf. Nor was it to offer himself again and again, as the high
priest enters the Holy Place year after year with blood that is not his own; for
then he would have had to suffer again and again since the foundation of the
world. But as it is, he has appeared once for all at the end of the age to
remove sin by the sacrifice of himself. And just as it is appointed for mortals
to die once, and after that the judgement, so Christ, having been offered
once to bear the sins of many, will appear a second time, not to deal with sin,
but to save those who are eagerly waiting for him.

GOSPEL   Mark 12.38–44

Hear the gospel of our Lord Jesus Christ according to Mark.

Jesus was teaching in the temple, and a large crowd was listening to him. He
said, 'Beware of the scribes, who like to walk around in long robes, and to be
greeted with respect in the marketplaces, and to have the best seats in the
synagogues and places of honour at banquets! They devour widows' houses
and for the sake of appearance say long prayers. They will receive the greater
condemnation.'

He sat down opposite the treasury, and watched the crowd putting money
into the treasury. Many rich people put in large sums. A poor widow came
and put in two small copper coins, which are worth a penny. Then he called
his disciples and said to them, 'Truly I tell you, this poor widow has put in
more than all those who are contributing to the treasury. For all of them have
contributed out of their abundance; but she out of her poverty has put in
everything she had, all she had to live on.'

Or

† CHURCH OF ENGLAND

FIRST READING   Jonah 3.1–5, 10

A reading from the book of Jonah.

The word of the LORD came to Jonah, saying, 'Get up, go to Nineveh, that great city, and proclaim to it the message that I tell you.' So Jonah set out and went to Nineveh, according to the word of the LORD. Now Nineveh was an exceedingly large city, a three days' walk across. Jonah began to go into the city, going a day's walk. And he cried out, 'Forty days more, and Nineveh shall be overthrown!' And the people of Nineveh believed God; they proclaimed a fast, and everyone, great and small, put on sackcloth.

When God saw what they did, how they turned from their evil ways, God changed his mind about the calamity that he had said he would bring upon them; and he did not do it.

PSALM   Psalm 62.6–14

℟ **God alone is my rock and my salvation.**

For God alone my soul in silence waits;
truly, my hope is in him.
He alone is my rock and my salvation,
my stronghold, so that I shall not be shaken.
In God is my safety and my honour;
God is my strong rock and my refuge. ℟

Put your trust in him always, O people,
pour out your hearts before him, for God is our refuge.
Those of high degree are but a fleeting breath,
even those of low estate cannot be trusted.
On the scales they are lighter than a breath,
all of them together. ℟

Put no trust in extortion;
in robbery take no empty pride;
though wealth increase, set not your heart upon it.
God has spoken once, twice have I heard it,
that power belongs to God.
Steadfast love is yours, O Lord,
for you repay everyone according to his deeds. ℟

SECOND READING   Hebrews 9.24–28

A reading from the letter to the Hebrews.

Christ did not enter a sanctuary made by human hands, a mere copy of the
true one, but he entered into heaven itself, now to appear in the presence of
God on our behalf. Nor was it to offer himself again and again, as the high
priest enters the Holy Place year after year with blood that is not his own; for
then he would have had to suffer again and again since the foundation of the
world. But as it is, he has appeared once for all at the end of the age to
remove sin by the sacrifice of himself. And just as it is appointed for mortals
to die once, and after that the judgement, so Christ, having been offered
once to bear the sins of many, will appear a second time, not to deal with sin,
but to save those who are eagerly waiting for him.

GOSPEL   Mark 1.14–20

Hear the gospel of our Lord Jesus Christ according to Mark.

After John was arrested, Jesus came to Galilee, proclaiming the good news of
God, and saying, 'The time is fulfilled, and the kingdom of God has come
near; repent, and believe in the good news.'

As Jesus passed along the Sea of Galilee, he saw Simon and his brother
Andrew casting a net into the lake – for they were fishermen. And Jesus said
to them, 'Follow me and I will make you fish for people.' And immediately
they left their nets and followed him. As he went a little farther, he saw James
son of Zebedee and his brother John, who were in their boat mending the
nets. Immediately he called them; and they left their father Zebedee in the
boat with the hired men, and followed him.

† 2 BEFORE ADVENT
PROPER 28

YEAR B

The Revised Common Lectionary continues to provide two tracks. Church of England provision allows only Track 2.

TRACK 1

Revised Common Lectionary only

FIRST READING
1 Samuel 1.4–20

A reading from the first book of Samuel.

On the day when Elkanah the husband of Hannah and Peninnah sacrificed, he would give portions to his wife Peninnah and to all her sons and daughters; but to Hannah he gave a double portion, because he loved her, though the LORD had closed her womb. Her rival used to provoke her severely, to irritate her, because the LORD had closed her womb. So it went on year by year; as often as she went up to the house of the LORD, she used to provoke her. Therefore Hannah wept and would not eat. Her husband Elkanah said to her, 'Hannah, why do you weep? Why do you not eat? Why is your heart sad? Am I not more to you than ten sons?'

After they had eaten and drunk at Shiloh, Hannah rose and presented herself before the LORD. Now Eli the priest was sitting on the seat beside the doorpost of the temple of the LORD. She was deeply distressed and prayed to the LORD, and wept bitterly. She made this vow: 'O LORD of hosts, if only you will look on the misery of your servant, and remember me, and not forget your servant, but will give to your servant a male child, then I will set him before you as a nazirite until the day of his death. He shall drink neither wine nor intoxicants, and no razor shall touch his head.'

As she continued praying before the LORD, Eli observed her mouth. Hannah was praying silently; only her lips moved, but her voice was not heard; therefore Eli thought she was drunk. So Eli said to her, 'How long will you make a drunken spectacle of yourself? Put away your wine.' But Hannah answered, 'No, my lord, I am a woman deeply troubled; I have drunk neither wine nor strong drink, but I have been pouring out my soul before the LORD. Do not regard your servant as a worthless woman, for I have been speaking out of my great anxiety and vexation all this time.' Then Eli answered, 'Go in peace; the God of Israel grant the petition you have made to him.' And she said, 'Let your servant find favour in your sight.' Then the woman went to her quarters, ate and drank with her husband, and her countenance was sad no longer.

They rose early in the morning and worshipped before the LORD; then they went back to their house at Ramah. Elkanah knew his wife Hannah, and the LORD remembered her. In due time Hannah conceived and bore a son. She named him Samuel, for she said, 'I have asked him of the LORD.'

CANTICLE   1 Samuel 2.1–10

℞ **My heart exults in the Lord;**
   [my strength is exalted in my God].

My heart exults in the LORD;
my strength is exalted in my God.
My mouth derides my enemies,
because I rejoice in my victory.
There is no Holy One like the LORD,
no one besides you;
there is no Rock like our God. ℞

Talk no more so very proudly,
let not arrogance come from your mouth;
for the LORD is a God of knowledge,
and by him actions are weighed.
The bows of the mighty are broken,
but the feeble gird on strength. ℞

Those who were full have hired themselves out for bread,
but those who were hungry are fat with spoil.
The barren has borne seven,
but she who has many children is forlorn.
The LORD kills and brings to life;
he brings down to Sheol and raises up. ℞

The LORD makes poor and makes rich;
he brings low, he also exalts.
He raises up the poor from the dust;
he lifts the needy from the ash heap,
to make them sit with princes and inherit a seat of honour.
For the pillars of the earth are the Lord's,
and on them he has set the world. ℞

He will guard the feet of his faithful ones,
but the wicked shall be cut off in darkness;

for not by might does one prevail.
The LORD! His adversaries shall be shattered;
the Most High will thunder in heaven.
The LORD will judge the ends of the earth;
he will give strength to his king,
and exalt the power of his anointed. ℟

Or   TRACK 2

FIRST READING   **Daniel 12.1–3**

A reading from the book of Daniel.

In the third year of King Cyrus a word was revealed to Daniel. 'At that time
Michael, the great prince, the protector of your people, shall arise. There shall
be a time of anguish, such as has never occurred since nations first came into
existence. But at that time your people shall be delivered, everyone who is
found written in the book. Many of those who sleep in the dust of the earth
shall awake, some to everlasting life, and some to shame and everlasting
contempt. Those who are wise shall shine like the brightness of the sky, and
those who lead many to righteousness, like the stars for ever and ever.'

PSALM   **Psalm 16**

℟ **You, Lord, are my portion and my cup.**
    or
℟ **My body shall rest in hope.**

Protect me, O God, for I take refuge in you;
I have said to the Lord, 'You are my Lord,
my good above all other.'
All my delight is upon the godly that are in the land,
upon those who are noble among the people. ℟

But those who run after other gods
shall have their troubles multiplied.
Their libations of blood I will not offer,
nor take the names of their gods upon my lips.
O Lord, you are my portion and my cup;
it is you who uphold my lot. ℟

My boundaries enclose a pleasant land;
indeed, I have a goodly heritage.
I will bless the Lord who gives me counsel;
my heart teaches me, night after night.
I have set the Lord always before me;
because he is at my right hand I shall not fall. ℟

My heart, therefore, is glad and my spirit rejoices;
my body also shall rest in hope.
For you will not abandon me to the grave,
nor let your holy one see the Pit.
You will show me the path of life;
in your presence there is fullness of joy,
and in your right hand are pleasures for evermore. ℟

SECOND READING   Hebrews 10.11–14, (15–18), 19–25

A reading from the letter to the Hebrews.

Every priest stands day after day at his service, offering again and again the
same sacrifices that can never take away sins. But when Christ had offered for
all time a single sacrifice for sins, 'he sat down at the right hand of God,' and
since then has been waiting 'until his enemies would be made a footstool for
his feet.' For by a single offering he has perfected for all time those who are
sanctified. [And the Holy Spirit also testifies to us, for after saying,
'This is the covenant that I will make with them after those days,
says the Lord:
I will put my laws in their hearts,
and I will write them on their minds,'
he also adds,
'I will remember their sins and their lawless deeds no more.'
Where there is forgiveness of these, there is no longer any offering for sin.]

Therefore, my friends, since we have confidence to enter the sanctuary by the
blood of Jesus, by the new and living way that he opened for us through the
curtain (that is, through his flesh), and since we have a great priest over the
house of God, let us approach with a true heart in full assurance of faith,
with our hearts sprinkled clean from an evil conscience and our bodies
washed with pure water. Let us hold fast to the confession of our hope
without wavering, for he who has promised is faithful. And let us consider
how to provoke one another to love and good deeds, not neglecting to meet
together, as is the habit of some, but encouraging one another, and all the
more as you see the Day approaching.

GOSPEL **Mark 13.1–8**

Hear the gospel of our Lord Jesus Christ according to Mark.

As Jesus came out of the temple, one of his disciples said to him, 'Look, Teacher, what large stones and what large buildings!' Then Jesus asked him, 'Do you see these great buildings? Not one stone will be left here upon another; all will be thrown down.'

When he was sitting on the Mount of Olives opposite the temple, Peter, James, John, and Andrew asked him privately, 'Tell us, when will this be, and what will be the sign that all these things are about to be accomplished?' Then Jesus began to say to them, 'Beware that no one leads you astray. Many will come in my name and say, "I am he!" and they will lead many astray. When you hear of wars and rumours of wars, do not be alarmed; this must take place, but the end is still to come. For nation will rise against nation, and kingdom against kingdom; there will be earthquakes in various places; there will be famines. This is but the beginning of the birth pangs.'

CHRIST THE KING YEAR B

The Revised Common Lectionary continues to provide two tracks. Church of England provision allows only Track 2.

TRACK 1

Revised Common Lectionary only

FIRST READING **2 Samuel 23.1–7**

A reading from the second book of Samuel.

These are the last words of David:
The oracle of David, son of Jesse,
the oracle of the man whom God exalted,
the anointed of the God of Jacob,
the favourite of the Strong One of Israel:
The spirit of the LORD speaks through me,
his word is upon my tongue.
The God of Israel has spoken, the Rock of Israel has said to me:
One who rules over people justly, ruling in the fear of God,
is like the light of morning, like the sun rising on a cloudless morning,
gleaming from the rain on the grassy land.

Is not my house like this with God?
For he has made with me an everlasting covenant,
ordered in all things and secure.
Will he not cause to prosper all my help and my desire?
But the godless are all like thorns that are thrown away;
for they cannot be picked up with the hand;
to touch them one uses an iron bar or the shaft of a spear.
And they are entirely consumed in fire on the spot.

PSALM   Psalm 132.1–13, (14–19)

℟ **The Lord will set his son upon his throne.**

Lord, remember David
and all the hardships he endured;
How he swore an oath to the Lord
and vowed a vow to the Mighty One of Jacob: ℟

'I will not come under the roof of my house,
nor climb up into my bed;
I will not allow my eyes to sleep,
nor let my eyelids slumber;
Until I find a place for the Lord,
a dwelling for the Mighty One of Jacob.' ℟

'The Ark! We heard it was in Ephratha;
we found it in the fields of Jearim.
Let us go to God's dwelling place;
let us fall upon our knees before his footstool.' ℟

Arise, O Lord, into your resting-place,
you and the ark of your strength.
Let your priests be clothed with righteousness;
let your faithful people sing with joy.
For your servant David's sake,
do not turn away the face of your anointed. ℟

The Lord has sworn an oath to David;
in truth, he will not break it:
'A son, the fruit of your body
will I set upon your throne.
If your children keep my covenant
and my testimonies that I shall teach them,
their children will sit upon your throne for evermore.' ℟

[For the Lord has chosen Zion,
he has desired her for his habitation:
'This shall be my resting-place for ever;
here will I dwell, for I delight in her. ℞

I will surely bless her provisions,
and satisfy her poor with bread.
I will clothe her priests with salvation,
and her faithful people will rejoice and sing. ℞

There will I make the horn of David flourish;
I have prepared a lamp for my anointed.
As for his enemies, I will clothe them with shame;
but as for him, his crown will shine.' ℞]

Or   TRACK 2

FIRST READING   **Daniel 7.9–10, 13–14**

A reading from the book of Daniel.

As I watched,
thrones were set in place,
and an Ancient One took his throne,
his clothing was white as snow,
and the hair of his head like pure wool;
his throne was fiery flames,
and its wheels were burning fire.
A stream of fire issued
and flowed out from his presence.
A thousand thousand served him,
and ten thousand times ten thousand stood attending him.
The court sat in judgement, and the books were opened.

As I watched in the night visions,
I saw one like a human being coming with the clouds of heaven.
And he came to the Ancient One
and was presented before him.
To him was given dominion and glory and kingship,
that all peoples, nations, and languages should serve him.
His dominion is an everlasting dominion
that shall not pass away,
and his kingship is one that shall never be destroyed.

PSALM

Psalm 93

℟ **The Lord has girded himself with strength.**

The Lord is king; he has put on splendid apparel;
the Lord has put on his apparel
and girded himself with strength.
He has made the whole world so sure
that it cannot be moved;
Ever since the world began,
your throne has been established;
you are from everlasting. ℟

The waters have lifted up, O Lord,
the waters have lifted up their voice;
the waters have lifted up their pounding waves.
Mightier than the sound of many waters,
mightier than the breakers of the sea,
mightier is the Lord who dwells on high. ℟

Your testimonies are very sure,
and holiness adorns your house, O Lord,
for ever and for evermore. ℟

SECOND READING

Revelation 1.4b–8

A reading from the book of Revelation.

Grace to you and peace from God who is and who was and who is to come,
and from the seven spirits who are before his throne, and from Jesus Christ,
the faithful witness, the firstborn of the dead, and the ruler of the kings of
the earth. To him who loves us and freed us from our sins by his blood, and
made us to be a kingdom, priests serving his God and Father, to him be glory
and dominion for ever and ever. Amen.
Look! He is coming with the clouds;
every eye will see him even those who pierced him;
and on his account all the tribes of the earth will wail.
So it is to be. Amen.
'I am the Alpha and the Omega,' says the Lord God, who is and who was and
who is to come, the Almighty.

GOSPEL   **John 18.33b–37**

Hear the gospel of our Lord Jesus Christ according to John.

Pilate asked Jesus, 'Are you the King of the Jews?' Jesus answered, 'Do you ask this on your own, or did others tell you about me?' Pilate replied, 'I am not a Jew, am I? Your own nation and the chief priests have handed you over to me. What have you done?' Jesus answered, 'My kingdom is not from this world. If my kingdom were from this world, my followers would be fighting to keep me from being handed over to the Jews. But as it is, my kingdom is not from here.' Pilate asked him, 'So you are a king?' Jesus answered, 'You say that I am a king. For this I was born, and for this I came into the world, to testify to the truth. Everyone who belongs to the truth listens to my voice.

PRINCIPAL SERVICE, YEAR C

ADVENT 1

FIRST READING Jeremiah 33.14–16

A reading from the book of the prophet Jeremiah.

The days are surely coming, says the LORD, when I will fulfil the promise I made to the house of Israel and the house of Judah. In those days and at that time I will cause a righteous Branch to spring up for David; and he shall execute justice and righteousness in the land. In those days Judah will be saved and Jerusalem will live in safety. And this is the name by which it will be called: 'The LORD is our righteousness.'

PSALM Psalm 25.1–10

℟ **To you, O Lord, I lift up my soul.**

To you, O Lord, I lift up my soul;
 my God, I put my trust in you;
 let me not be humiliated,
 nor let my enemies triumph over me.
Let none who look to you be put to shame;
 let the treacherous be disappointed in their schemes. ℟

Show me your ways, O Lord,
 and teach me your paths.
Lead me in your truth and teach me,
 for you are the God of my salvation;
 in you have I trusted all the day long. ℟

Remember, O Lord, your compassion and love,
 for they are from everlasting.
Remember not the sins of my youth
 and my transgressions;
 remember me according to your love
 and for the sake of your goodness, O Lord. ℟

Gracious and upright is the Lord;
 therefore he teaches sinners in his way.
He guides the humble in doing right
 and teaches his way to the lowly. ℟

All the paths of the Lord are love and faithfulness
to those who keep his covenant and his testimonies.
For your name's sake, O Lord,
forgive my sin, for it is great. ℟

SECOND READING   1 Thessalonians 3.9–13

A reading from the first letter of Paul to the Thessalonians.

How can we thank God enough for you in return for all the joy that we feel
before our God because of you? Night and day we pray most earnestly that
we may see you face to face and restore whatever is lacking in your faith.

Now may our God and Father himself and our Lord Jesus direct our way to
you. And may the Lord make you increase and abound in love for one
another and for all, just as we abound in love for you. And may he so
strengthen your hearts in holiness that you may be blameless before our God
and Father at the coming of our Lord Jesus with all his saints.

GOSPEL   Luke 21.25–36

Hear the gospel of our Lord Jesus Christ according to Luke.

Jesus said to his disciples: 'There will be signs in the sun, the moon, and the
stars, and on the earth distress among nations confused by the roaring of the
sea and the waves. People will faint from fear and foreboding of what is
coming upon the world, for the powers of the heavens will be shaken. Then
they will see "the Son of Man coming in a cloud" with power and great glory.
Now when these things begin to take place, stand up and raise your heads,
because your redemption is drawing near.'

Then he told them a parable: 'Look at the fig tree and all the trees; as soon as
they sprout leaves you can see for yourselves and know that summer is
already near. So also, when you see these things taking place, you know that
the kingdom of God is near. Truly I tell you, this generation will not pass
away until all things have taken place. Heaven and earth will pass away, but
my words will not pass away.

Be on guard so that your hearts are not weighed down with dissipation and
drunkenness and the worries of this life, and that day catch you
unexpectedly, like a trap. For it will come upon all who live on the face of
the whole earth. Be alert at all times, praying that you may have the
strength to escape all these things that will take place, and to stand before
the Son of Man.'

ADVENT 2   YEAR C

FIRST READING (Alternative readings)

Either   Baruch 5.1–9

A reading from the book of the prophet Baruch.

Take off the garment of your sorrow and affliction, O Jerusalem,
and put on for ever the beauty of the glory from God.
Put on the robe of the righteousness that comes from God;
put on your head the diadem of the glory of the Everlasting;
for God will show your splendour everywhere under heaven.
For God will give you evermore the name,
'Righteous Peace, Godly Glory.'
Arise, O Jerusalem, stand upon the height;
look toward the east,
and see your children gathered from west and east
at the word of the Holy One,
rejoicing that God has remembered them.
For they went out from you on foot,
led away by their enemies;
but God will bring them back to you,
carried in glory, as on a royal throne.
For God has ordered that every high mountain
and the everlasting hills be made low
and the valleys filled up, to make level ground,
so that Israel may walk safely in the glory of God.
The woods and every fragrant tree
have shaded Israel at God's command.
For God will lead Israel with joy,
in the light of his glory,
with the mercy and righteousness that come from him.

Or   Malachi 3.1–4

A reading from the book of the prophet Malachi.

Thus says the LORD God:

See, I am sending my messenger to prepare the way before me, and the Lord whom you seek will suddenly come to his temple. The messenger of the covenant in whom you delight – indeed, he is coming, says the LORD of hosts. But who can endure the day of his coming, and who can stand when he appears?

For he is like a refiner's fire and like fullers' soap; he will sit as a refiner and purifier of silver, and he will purify the descendants of Levi and refine them like gold and silver, until they present offerings to the LORD in righteousness. Then the offering of Judah and Jerusalem will be pleasing to the LORD as in the days of old and as in former years.

CANTICLE   Luke 1.68–79

℟ **Blessed be the Lord, who sets his people free.**

Blessèd be the Lord, the God of Israel,
for he has come to his people and set them free.
He has raised up for us a mighty Saviour,
born of the house of his servant, David. ℟

Through his holy prophets he promised of old,
that he would save us from our enemies,
from the hands of all that hate us.
He promised to show mercy to our forebears
and to remember his holy covenant. ℟

This was the oath he swore to our father Abraham:
to set us free from the hands of our enemies,
free to worship him without fear,
holy and righteous in his sight,
all the days of our life. ℟

You, my child,
shall be called the prophet of the Most High,
for you will go before the Lord to prepare his way,
To give his people knowledge of salvation,
by the forgiveness of their sins. ℟

In the tender compassion of our God,
the dawn from on high shall break upon us,
To shine on those who dwell in darkness
and the shadow of death,
and to guide our feet into the way of peace. ℟

SECOND READING   **Philippians 1.3-11**

A reading from the letter of Paul to the Philippians.

My brothers and sisters,
I thank my God every time I remember you, constantly praying with joy in every one of my prayers for all of you, because of your sharing in the gospel from the first day until now. I am confident of this, that the one who began a good work among you will bring it to completion by the day of Jesus Christ. It is right for me to think this way about all of you, because you hold me in your heart, for all of you share in God's grace with me, both in my imprisonment and in the defence and confirmation of the gospel. For God is my witness, how I long for all of you with the compassion of Christ Jesus. And this is my prayer, that your love may overflow more and more with knowledge and full insight to help you to determine what is best, so that in the day of Christ you may be pure and blameless, having produced the harvest of righteousness that comes through Jesus Christ for the glory and praise of God.

GOSPEL   **Luke 3.1-6**

Hear the gospel of our Lord Jesus Christ according to Luke.

In the fifteenth year of the reign of Emperor Tiberius, when Pontius Pilate was governor of Judea, and Herod was ruler of Galilee, and his brother Philip ruler of the region of Ituraea and Trachonitis, and Lysanias ruler of Abilene, during the high-priesthood of Annas and Caiaphas, the word of God came to John son of Zechariah in the wilderness. He went into all the region around the Jordan, proclaiming a baptism of repentance for the forgiveness of sins, as it is written in the book of the words of the prophet Isaiah,
'The voice of one crying out in the wilderness:
"Prepare the way of the Lord, make his paths straight.
Every valley shall be filled,
and every mountain and hill shall be made low,
and the crooked shall be made straight,
and the rough ways made smooth;
and all flesh shall see the salvation of God."'

ADVENT 3 YEAR C

FIRST READING Zephaniah 3.14–20

A reading from the book of the prophet Zephaniah.

Sing aloud, O daughter Zion; shout, O Israel!
Rejoice and exult with all your heart,
O daughter Jerusalem!
The LORD has taken away the judgements against you,
he has turned away your enemies.
The king of Israel, the LORD, is in your midst;
you shall fear disaster no more.
On that day it shall be said to Jerusalem:
Do not fear, O Zion;
do not let your hands grow weak.
The LORD, your God, is in your midst,
a warrior who gives victory;
he will rejoice over you with gladness,
he will renew you in his love;
he will exult over you with loud singing
as on a day of festival.
I will remove disaster from you,
so that you will not bear reproach for it.
I will deal with all your oppressors at that time.
And I will save the lame and gather the outcast,
and I will change their shame into praise and renown in all the earth.
At that time I will bring you home,
at the time when I gather you;
for I will make you renowned
and praised among all the peoples of the earth,
when I restore your fortunes before your eyes, says the LORD.

CANTICLE Isaiah 12.2–6

℞ **Shout aloud and sing for joy,**
for great in your midst is the Holy One of Israel.

Surely God is my salvation;
I will trust, and will not be afraid,
for the LORD GOD is my strength and my might;

he has become my salvation.
With joy you will draw water
from the wells of salvation. ℟

And you will say on that day:
Give thanks to the LORD,
call on his name;
make known his deeds among the nations;
proclaim that his name is exalted.
Sing praises to the LORD,
for he has done gloriously;
let this be known in all the earth. ℟

[Shout aloud and sing for joy, O royal Zion,
for great in your midst is the Holy One of Israel.]

SECOND READING   Philippians 4.4–7

A reading from the letter of Paul to the Philippians.

Rejoice in the Lord always; again I will say, Rejoice. Let your gentleness be
known to everyone. The Lord is near. Do not worry about anything, but in
everything by prayer and supplication with thanksgiving let your requests be
made known to God. And the peace of God, which surpasses all
understanding, will guard your hearts and your minds in Christ Jesus.

GOSPEL   Luke 3.7–18

Hear the gospel of our Lord Jesus Christ according to Luke.

John said to the crowds that came out to be baptized by him, 'You brood of
vipers! Who warned you to flee from the wrath to come?
Bear fruits worthy of repentance. Do not begin to say to yourselves, "We have
Abraham as our ancestor"; for I tell you, God is able from these stones to raise
up children to Abraham. Even now the axe is lying at the root of the trees;
every tree therefore that does not bear good fruit is cut down and thrown
into the fire.' And the crowds asked him, 'What then should we do?' In reply
he said to them, 'Whoever has two coats must share with anyone who has
none; and whoever has food must do likewise.' Even tax-collectors came to
be baptized, and they asked him, 'Teacher, what should we do?' He said to
them, 'Collect no more than the amount prescribed for you.' Soldiers also
asked him, 'And we, what should we do?' He said to them, 'Do not extort

money from anyone by threats or false accusation, and be satisfied with your wages.' As the people were filled with expectation, and all were questioning in their hearts concerning John, whether he might be the Messiah, John answered all of them by saying, 'I baptize you with water; but one who is more powerful than I is coming; I am not worthy to untie the thong of his sandals. He will baptize you with the Holy Spirit and fire. His winnowing-fork is in his hand, to clear his threshing-floor and to gather the wheat into his granary; but the chaff he will burn with unquenchable fire.'

So, with many other exhortations, he proclaimed the good news to the people.

ADVENT 4   YEAR C

FIRST READING   Micah 5.2–5a

A reading from the book of the prophet Micah.

The LORD says to his people:
But you, O Bethlehem of Ephrathah,
who are one of the little clans of Judah,
 from you shall come forth for me
one who is to rule in Israel,
whose origin is from of old, from ancient days.
Therefore he shall give them up until the time
when she who is in labour has brought forth;
then the rest of his kindred
shall return to the people of Israel.
And he shall stand and feed his flock
in the strength of the LORD,
in the majesty of the name of the LORD his God.
And they shall live secure,
for now he shall be great to the ends of the earth;
and he shall be the one of peace.

CANTICLE OR PSALM

Either   Luke 1.46b–55

℟ **My spirit rejoices in God my Saviour.**

My soul proclaims the greatness of the Lord;
My spirit rejoices in God my Saviour.
For he has looked with favour on his lowly servant,
from this day all generations will call me blessèd.
The Almighty has done great things for me,
and holy is his name. ℟

He has mercy on those who fear him
in every generation.
He has shown the strength of his arm;
he has scattered the proud in their conceit. ℟

He has cast down the mighty from their thrones
and he has lifted up the lowly.
He has filled the hungry with good things,
and the rich he has sent away empty. ℟

He has come to the help of his servant, Israel,
for he has remembered his promise of mercy.
The promise he made to our forebears;
to Abraham and his children for ever. ℟

Or   Psalm 80.1–7

℟ **Restore us, O God of hosts;**
    show the light of your countenance
    and we shall be saved.

Hear, O Shepherd of Israel, leading Joseph like a flock;
shine forth, you that are enthroned upon the cherubim.
In the presence of Ephraim, Benjamin and Manasseh,
stir up your strength and come to help us. ℟

[Restore us, O God of hosts;
show the light of your countenance
and we shall be saved.]

O Lord God of hosts,
how long will you be angered
despite the prayers of your people?
You have fed them with the bread of tears;
you have given them bowls of tears to drink.
You have made us the derision of our neighbours,
and our enemies laugh us to scorn. ℟

[Restore us, O God of hosts;
show the light of your countenance
and we shall be saved.]

SECOND READING   Hebrews 10.5–10

A reading from the letter to the Hebrews.

When Christ came into the world, he said,
'Sacrifices and offerings you have not desired,
but a body you have prepared for me;
in burnt-offerings and sin-offerings
you have taken no pleasure.
Then I said,
"See, God, I have come to do your will, O God"
(in the scroll of the book, it is written of me).'
When Christ said, 'You have neither desired nor taken pleasure in sacrifices
and offerings and burnt offerings and sin offerings' (these are offered
according to the law), then he added, 'See, I have come to do your will.' He
abolishes the first in order to establish the second. And it is by God's will
that we have been sanctified through the offering of the body of Jesus Christ
once for all.

GOSPEL (Short or long reading) Luke 1.39–45, (46–55)

Hear the gospel of our Lord Jesus Christ according to Luke.

Mary set out and went with haste to a Judean town in the hill country, where she entered the house of Zechariah and greeted Elizabeth. When Elizabeth heard Mary's greeting, the child leapt in her womb. And Elizabeth was filled with the Holy Spirit and exclaimed with a loud cry, 'Blessed are you among women, and blessed is the fruit of your womb. And why has this happened to me, that the mother of my Lord comes to me? For as soon as I heard the sound of your greeting, the child in my womb leapt for joy. And blessed is she who believed that there would be a fulfilment of what was spoken to her by the Lord.'

[And Mary said,
'My soul magnifies the Lord,
and my spirit rejoices in God my Saviour,
for he has looked with favour on the lowliness of his servant.
Surely, from now on all generations will call me blessed;
for the Mighty One has done great things for me,
and holy is his name.
His mercy is for those who fear him
from generation to generation.
He has shown strength with his arm;
he has scattered the proud in the thoughts of their hearts.
He has brought down the powerful from their thrones,
and lifted up the lowly;
he has filled the hungry with good things,
and sent the rich away empty.
He has helped his servant Israel,
in remembrance of his mercy,
according to the promise he made to our ancestors,
to Abraham and to his descendants for ever.']

CHRISTMAS DAY

25 December

Any of the sets of readings on pages 11–20 may be used on the evening of Christmas Eve and on Christmas Day. Set III should be used at some service during the celebration.

CHRISTMAS, SETS I, II, III   YEARS A B C

For text see Year A, pages 11–14, 14–17, 17–20.

CHRISTMAS 1   YEAR C

FIRST READING   1 Samuel 2.18–20, 26

A reading from the first book of Samuel.

Samuel was ministering before the LORD, a boy wearing a linen ephod. His mother used to make for him a little robe and take it to him each year, when she went up with her husband to offer the yearly sacrifice. Then Eli would bless Elkanah and his wife, and say, 'May the LORD repay you with children by this woman for the gift that she made to the LORD'; and then they would return to their home.

Now the boy Samuel continued to grow both in stature and in favour with the LORD and with the people.

PSALM   Psalm 148

℟ **Praise, O praise the name of the Lord.**

Alleluia!
Praise the Lord from the heavens;
praise him in the heights.
Praise him, all you angels of his;
praise him, all his host.
Praise him, sun and moon;
praise him, all you shining stars. ℟

Praise him, heaven of heavens,
and you waters above the heavens.
Let them praise the name of the Lord;
for he commanded and they were created.
He made them stand fast for ever and ever;
he gave them a law which shall not pass away. ℟

Praise the Lord from the earth,
you sea-monsters and all deeps;
Fire and hail, snow and fog,

tempestuous wind, doing his will;
Mountains and all hills,
fruit trees and all cedars; ℟

Wild beasts and all cattle,
creeping things and winged birds;
Kings of the earth and all peoples,
princes and all rulers of the world;
Young men and maidens,
old and young together. ℟

Let them praise the name of the Lord,
for his name only is exalted,
his splendour is over earth and heaven.
He has raised up strength for his people
and praise for all his loyal servants,
the children of Israel, a people who are near him. Alleluia! ℟

SECOND READING   Colossians 3.12–17

A reading from the letter of Paul to the Colossians.

As God's chosen ones, holy and beloved, clothe yourselves with compassion, kindness, humility, meekness, and patience. Bear with one another and, if anyone has a complaint against another, forgive each other; just as the Lord has forgiven you, so you also must forgive. Above all, clothe yourselves with love, which binds everything together in perfect harmony. And let the peace of Christ rule in your hearts, to which indeed you were called in the one body. And be thankful.

Let the word of Christ dwell in you richly; teach and admonish one another in all wisdom; and with gratitude in your hearts sing psalms, hymns, and spiritual songs to God. And whatever you do, in word or deed, do everything in the name of the Lord Jesus, giving thanks to God the Father through him.

GOSPEL   Luke 2.41–52

Hear the gospel of our Lord Jesus Christ according to Luke.

Every year the parents of Jesus went to Jerusalem for the festival of the Passover. And when he was twelve years old, they went up as usual for the festival. When the festival was ended and they started to return, the boy Jesus stayed behind in Jerusalem, but his parents did not know it. Assuming that he was in the group of travellers, they went a day's journey. Then they started to look for him among their relatives and friends. When they did not find him, they returned to Jerusalem to search for him. After three days they found him in the temple, sitting among the teachers, listening to them and asking them questions. And all who heard him were amazed at his understanding and his answers. When his parents saw him they were astonished; and his mother said to him, 'Child, why have you treated us like this? Look, your father and I have been searching for you in great anxiety.' He said to them, 'Why were you searching for me? Did you not know that I must be in my Father's house?' But they did not understand what he said to them. Then he went down with them and came to Nazareth, and was obedient to them. His mother treasured all these things in her heart.

And Jesus increased in wisdom and in years, and in divine and human favour.

CHRISTMAS 2   YEARS A B C

For text see Year A, pages 23–27.

EPIPHANY OF THE LORD   YEARS A B C

6 January   *For text see Year A, pages 28–30.*

BAPTISM OF CHRIST   YEAR C

FIRST READING   Isaiah 43.1–7

A reading from the prophet Isaiah.

Thus says the LORD,
he who created you, O Jacob, he who formed you, O Israel:
Do not fear, for I have redeemed you;
I have called you by name, you are mine.
When you pass through the waters, I will be with you;
and through the rivers, they shall not overwhelm you;
when you walk through fire you shall not be burned,
and the flame shall not consume you.

For I am the LORD your God,
the Holy One of Israel, your Saviour.
I give Egypt as your ransom,
Ethiopia and Seba in exchange for you.
Because you are precious in my sight, and honoured, and I love you,
I give people in return for you,
nations in exchange for your life.
Do not fear, for I am with you;
I will bring your offspring from the east,
and from the west I will gather you;
I will say to the north, 'Give them up,'
and to the south, 'Do not withhold;
bring my sons from far away
and my daughters from the end of the earth –
everyone who is called by my name,
whom I created for my glory, whom I formed and made.'

PSALM   Psalm 29

℟ **The voice of the Lord is upon the waters
[the God of glory thunders].**
or
℟ **The Lord shall give his people
the blessing of peace.**

Ascribe to the Lord, you gods,
ascribe to the Lord glory and strength.
Ascribe to the Lord the glory due to his name;
worship the Lord in the beauty of holiness. ℟

The voice of the Lord is upon the waters;
the God of glory thunders;
the Lord is upon the mighty waters.
The voice of the Lord is a powerful voice;
the voice of the Lord is a voice of splendour. ℟

The voice of the Lord breaks the cedar trees;
the Lord breaks the cedars of Lebanon;
He makes Lebanon skip like a calf,
and Mount Hermon like a young wild ox. ℟

The voice of the Lord splits the flames of fire;
the voice of the Lord shakes the wilderness;
the Lord shakes the wilderness of Kadesh.
The voice of the Lord makes the oak trees writhe
and strips the forests bare.
And in the temple of the Lord
all are crying, 'Glory!' ℟

The Lord sits enthroned above the flood;
the Lord sits enthroned as king for evermore.
The Lord shall give strength to his people;
the Lord shall give his people the blessing of peace. ℟

SECOND READING   Acts 8.14–17

A reading from the Acts of the Apostles.

When the apostles at Jerusalem heard that Samaria had accepted the word of God, they sent Peter and John to them. The two went down and prayed for them that they might receive the Holy Spirit (for as yet the Spirit had not come upon any of them; they had only been baptized in the name of the Lord Jesus). Then Peter and John laid their hands on them, and they received the Holy Spirit.

GOSPEL   Luke 3.15–17, 21–22

Hear the gospel of our Lord Jesus Christ according to Luke.

In the wilderness John proclaimed a baptism of repentance.
As the people were filled with expectation, and all were questioning in their hearts concerning John, whether he might be the Messiah, John answered all of them by saying, 'I baptize you with water; but one who is more powerful than I is coming; I am not worthy to untie the thong of his sandals. He will baptize you with the Holy Spirit and fire. His winnowing-fork is in his hand, to clear his threshing-floor and to gather the wheat into his granary; but the chaff he will burn with unquenchable fire.'

Now when all the people were baptized, and when Jesus also had been baptized and was praying, the heaven was opened, and the Holy Spirit descended upon him in bodily form like a dove. And a voice came from heaven, 'You are my Son, the Beloved; with you I am well pleased.'

EPIPHANY 2   YEAR C

FIRST READING   Isaiah 62.1-5

A reading from the book of the prophet Isaiah.

The LORD says this:

For Zion's sake I will not keep silent,
and for Jerusalem's sake I will not rest,
until her vindication shines out like the dawn,
and her salvation like a burning torch.
The nations shall see your vindication,
and all the kings your glory;
and you shall be called by a new name
that the mouth of the LORD will give.
You shall be a crown of beauty in the hand of the LORD,
and a royal diadem in the hand of your God.
You shall no more be termed Forsaken,
and your land shall no more be termed Desolate;
but you shall be called My Delight Is in Her,
and your land Married;
for the LORD delights in you,
and your land shall be married.
For as a young man marries a young woman,
so shall your builder marry you,
and as the bridegroom rejoices over the bride,
so shall your God rejoice over you.

PSALM   Psalm 36.5-10

℟ With you is the well of life
   [and in your light we see light].

Your love, O Lord, reaches to the heavens,
and your faithfulness to the clouds.
Your righteousness is like the strong mountains,
your justice like the great deep;
you save both human and beast, O Lord. ℟

How priceless is your love, O God!
your people take refuge under the shadow of your wings.
They feast upon the abundance of your house;
you give them drink from the river of your delights. ℟

For with you is the well of life,
and in your light we see light.
Continue your loving-kindness to those who know you,
and your favour to those who are true of heart. ℟

SECOND READING   1 Corinthians 12.1–11

A reading from the first letter of Paul to the Corinthians.

Concerning spiritual gifts, brothers and sisters, I do not want you to be uninformed. You know that when you were pagans, you were enticed and led astray to idols that could not speak. Therefore I want you to understand that no one speaking by the Spirit of God ever says 'Let Jesus be cursed!' and no one can say 'Jesus is Lord' except by the Holy Spirit.

Now there are varieties of gifts, but the same Spirit; and there are varieties of services, but the same Lord; and there are varieties of activities, but it is the same God who activates all of them in everyone. To each is given the manifestation of the Spirit for the common good. To one is given through the Spirit the utterance of wisdom, and to another the utterance of knowledge according to the same Spirit, to another faith by the same Spirit, to another gifts of healing by the one Spirit, to another the working of miracles, to another prophecy, to another the discernment of spirits, to another various kinds of tongues, to another the interpretation of tongues. All these are activated by one and the same Spirit, who allots to each one individually just as the Spirit chooses.

GOSPEL   John 2.1–11

Hear the gospel of our Lord Jesus Christ according to John.

There was a wedding in Cana of Galilee, and the mother of Jesus was there. Jesus and his disciples had also been invited to the wedding. When the wine gave out, the mother of Jesus said to him, 'They have no wine.' And Jesus said to her, 'Woman, what concern is that to you and to me? My hour has not yet come.' His mother said to the servants, 'Do whatever he tells you.' Now standing there were six stone water-jars for the Jewish rites of purification, each holding twenty or thirty gallons. Jesus said to them, 'Fill the jars with water.' And they filled them up to the brim. He said to them, 'Now draw some out, and take it to the chief steward.' So they took it. When the steward tasted the water that had become wine, and did not know where it came from (though the servants who had drawn the water knew), the steward called the bridegroom and said to him, 'Everyone serves the good wine first, and then the inferior wine after the guests have become drunk. But you have kept the good wine until now.' Jesus did this, the first of his signs, in Cana of Galilee, and revealed his glory; and his disciples believed in him.

EPIPHANY 3   YEAR C

FIRST READING   **Nehemiah 8.1–3, 5–6, 8–10**

A reading from the book of Nehemiah.

All the people gathered together into the square before the Water Gate. They told the scribe Ezra to bring the book of the law of Moses, which the LORD had given to Israel. Accordingly, the priest Ezra brought the law before the assembly, both men and women and all who could hear with understanding. This was on the first day of the seventh month.
He read from it facing the square before the Water Gate from early morning until midday, in the presence of the men and the women and those who could understand; and the ears of all the people were attentive to the book of the law.

And Ezra opened the book in the sight of all the people, for he was standing above all the people; and when he opened it, all the people stood up. Then Ezra blessed the LORD, the great God and all the people answered, 'Amen, Amen,' lifting up their hands. Then they bowed their heads and worshipped the LORD with their faces to the ground. So they read from the book, from the law of God, with interpretation. They gave the sense, so that the people understood the reading.

And Nehemiah, who was the governor, and Ezra the priest and scribe, and the Levites who taught the people said to all the people, 'This day is holy to the LORD your God; do not mourn or weep.' For all the people wept when they heard the words of the law. Then he said to them, 'Go your way, eat the fat and drink sweet wine and send portions of them to those for whom nothing is prepared, for this day is holy to our LORD; and do not be grieved, for the joy of the LORD is your strength.'

PSALM

℟ **Your words are spirit, Lord, and they are life.**
  or
℟ **The statutes of the Lord are just and rejoice the heart.**

The heavens declare the glory of God,
and the firmament shows his handiwork.
One day tells its tale to another,
and one night imparts knowledge to another.
Although they have no words or language,
and their voices are not heard,
Their sound has gone out into all lands,
and their message to the ends of the world. ℟

In the deep has he set a pavilion for the sun;
it comes forth like a bridegroom out of his chamber;
it rejoices like a champion to run its course.
It goes forth from the uttermost edge of the heavens
and runs about to the end of it again;
nothing is hidden from its burning heat. ℟

The law of the Lord is perfect
and revives the soul;
the testimony of the Lord is sure
and gives wisdom to the innocent.
The statutes of the Lord are just
and rejoice the heart;
the commandment of the Lord is clear
and gives light to the eyes. ℟

The fear of the Lord is clean
and endures for ever;
the judgements of the Lord are true
and righteous altogether.
More to be desired are they than gold,
more than much fine gold,
sweeter far than honey,
than honey in the comb. ℟

By them also is your servant enlightened,
and in keeping them there is great reward.
Who can tell how often he offends?
Cleanse me from my secret faults.

Above all, keep your servant from presumptuous sins;
let them not get dominion over me;
then shall I be whole and sound,
and innocent of a great offence. ℞

Let the words of my mouth and the meditation of my heart
be acceptable in your sight,
O Lord, my strength and my redeemer. ℞

SECOND READING   **1 Corinthians 12.12–31a**

A reading from the first letter of Paul to the Corinthians.

Just as the body is one and has many members, and all the members of the body, though many, are one body, so it is with Christ. For in the one Spirit we were all baptized into one body – Jews or Greeks, slaves or free – and we were all made to drink of one Spirit.

Indeed, the body does not consist of one member but of many. If the foot would say, 'Because I am not a hand, I do not belong to the body,' that would not make it any less a part of the body. And if the ear would say, 'Because I am not an eye, I do not belong to the body,' that would not make it any less a part of the body. If the whole body were an eye, where would the hearing be? If the whole body were hearing, where would the sense of smell be? But as it is, God arranged the members in the body, each one of them, as he chose. If all were a single member, where would the body be? As it is, there are many members, yet one body. The eye cannot say to the hand, 'I have no need of you,' nor again the head to the feet, 'I have no need of you.' On the contrary, the members of the body that seem to be weaker are indispensable, and those members of the body that we think less honourable we clothe with greater honour, and our less respectable members are treated with greater respect; whereas our more respectable members do not need this. But God has so arranged the body, giving the greater honour to the inferior member, that there may be no dissension within the body, but the members may have the same care for one another. If one member suffers, all suffer together with it; if one member is honoured, all rejoice together with it.

Now you are the body of Christ and individually members of it. And God has appointed in the church first apostles, second prophets, third teachers; then deeds of power, then gifts of healing, forms of assistance, forms of leadership various kinds of tongues. Are all apostles? Are all prophets? Are all teachers? Do all work miracles? Do all possess gifts of healing? Do all speak in tongues? Do all interpret? But strive for the greater gifts.

GOSPEL   Luke 4.14-21

Hear the gospel of our Lord Jesus Christ according to Luke.

Jesus, filled with the power of the Spirit, returned to Galilee, and a report about him spread through all the surrounding country. He began to teach in their synagogues and was praised by everyone.

When he came to Nazareth, where he had been brought up, he went to the synagogue on the sabbath day, as was his custom. He stood up to read, and the scroll of the prophet Isaiah was given to him. He unrolled the scroll and found the place where it was written:
'The Spirit of the Lord is upon me,
because he has anointed me to bring good news to the poor.
He has sent me to proclaim release to the captives
and recovery of sight to the blind,
to let the oppressed go free,
to proclaim the year of the Lord's favour.'
And he rolled up the scroll, gave it back to the attendant, and sat down. The eyes of all in the synagogue were fixed on him. Then he began to say to them, 'Today this scripture has been fulfilled in your hearing.'

EPIPHANY 4   YEAR C

The Revised Common Lectionary and the Church of England make different provision for today.
For Church of England provision see pages 553–555 below.

REVISED COMMON LECTIONARY

FIRST READING   Jeremiah 1.4-10

A reading from the book of the prophet Jeremiah.

The word of the LORD came to me saying,
'Before I formed you in the womb I knew you,
and before you were born I consecrated you;
I appointed you a prophet to the nations.'
Then I said, 'Ah, Lord GOD!
Truly I do not know how to speak, for I am only a boy.'
But the LORD said to me,
'Do not say, "I am only a boy";
for you shall go to all to whom I send you,

and you shall speak whatever I command you,
Do not be afraid of them,
for I am with you to deliver you, says the LORD.'
Then the LORD put out his hand and touched my mouth;
and the LORD said to me,
'Now I have put my words in your mouth.
See, today I appoint you over nations and over kingdoms,
to pluck up and to pull down, to destroy
and to overthrow, to build and to plant.'

PSALM   Psalm 71.1–6

℟ **You are my hope, O Lord God,**
  [my confidence since I was young].

In you, O Lord, have I taken refuge;
let me never be ashamed.
In your righteousness, deliver me and set me free;
incline your ear to me and save me. ℟

Be my strong rock, a castle to keep me safe;
you are my crag and my stronghold.
Deliver me, my God, from the hand of the wicked,
from the clutches of the evildoer and the oppressor. ℟

For you are my hope, O Lord God,
my confidence since I was young.
I have been sustained by you ever since I was born;
from my mother's womb you have been my strength;
my praise shall be always of you. ℟

SECOND READING   1 Corinthians 13.1–13

A reading from the first letter of Paul to the Corinthians.

If I speak in the tongues of mortals and of angels, but do not have love, I am
a noisy gong or a clanging cymbal. And if I have prophetic powers, and
understand all mysteries and all knowledge, and if I have all faith, so as to
remove mountains, but do not have love, I am nothing. If I give away all my
possessions, and if I hand over my body so that I may boast, but do not have
love, I gain nothing.

Love is patient; love is kind; love is not envious or boastful or arrogant or rude. It does not insist on its own way; it is not irritable or resentful; it does not rejoice in wrongdoing, but rejoices in the truth. It bears all things, believes all things, hopes all things, endures all things.

Love never ends. But as for prophecies, they will come to an end; as for tongues, they will cease; as for knowledge, it will come to an end. For we know only in part, and we prophesy only in part; but when the complete comes, the partial will come to an end. When I was a child, I spoke like a child, I thought like a child, I reasoned like a child; when I became an adult, I put an end to childish ways. For now we see in a mirror, dimly, but then we will see face to face. Now I know only in part; then I will know fully, even as I have been fully known. And now faith, hope, and love abide, these three; and the greatest of these is love.

GOSPEL   Luke 4.21–30

Hear the gospel of our Lord Jesus Christ according to Luke.

Jesus read from the prophet Isaiah. Then he began to say to those in the synagogue, 'Today this scripture has been fulfilled in your hearing.' All spoke well of him and were amazed at the gracious words that came from his mouth. They said, 'Is not this Joseph's son?' Jesus said to them, 'Doubtless you will quote to me this proverb, "Doctor, cure yourself!" And you will say, "Do here also in your home town the things that we have heard you did at Capernaum."' And he said, 'Truly I tell you, no prophet is accepted in the prophet's home town. But the truth is, there were many widows in Israel in the time of Elijah, when the heaven was shut up three years and six months, and there was a severe famine over all the land; yet Elijah was sent to none of them except to a widow at Zarephath in Sidon. There were also many lepers in Israel in the time of the prophet Elisha, and none of them was cleansed except Naaman the Syrian.' When they heard this, all in the synagogue were filled with rage. They got up, drove him out of the town, and led him to the brow of the hill on which their town was built, so that they might hurl him off the cliff. But he passed through the midst of them and went on his way.

Or

† CHURCH OF ENGLAND

FIRST READING   Ezekiel 43.27 – 44.4

A reading from the book of the prophet Ezekiel.

The LORD said to Ezekiel: 'When these days are over, then from the eighth day onward the priests shall offer upon the altar your burnt offerings and your offerings of well–being; and I will accept you, says the Lord GOD.'

Then he brought me back to the outer gate of the sanctuary, which faces east: and it was shut. The LORD said to me: This gate shall remain shut: it shall not be opened, and no one shall enter by it; for the LORD, the God of Israel, has entered by it; therefore it shall remain shut. Only the prince, because he is a prince, may sit in it to eat food before the LORD: he shall enter by way of the vestibule of the gate and shall go out by the same way.

Then he brought me by way of the north gate to the front of the temple; and I looked, and lo! the glory of the LORD filled the temple of the LORD: and I fell upon my face.

PSALM   Psalm 48

℟ **We have waited on your loving-kindness, O God,**
   in the midst of your temple.

Great is the Lord and highly to be praised;
in the city of our God is his holy hill.
Beautiful and lofty, the joy of all the earth,
is the hill of Zion,
the very centre of the world
and the city of the great king.
God is in her citadels;
he is known to be her sure refuge. ℟

Behold, the kings of the earth assembled
and marched forward together.
They looked and were astounded;
they retreated and fled in terror.
Trembling seized them there;
they writhed like a woman in childbirth,
like ships of the sea when the east wind shatters them. ℟

As we have heard, so have we seen,
in the city of the Lord of hosts, in the city of our God;
God has established her for ever.
We have waited in silence
on your loving-kindness, O God,
in the midst of your temple. ℟

Your praise, like your name, O God,
reaches to the world's end;
your right hand is full of justice.
Let Mount Zion be glad
and the cities of Judah rejoice,
because of your judgements. ℟

Make the circuit of Zion; walk round about her;
count the number of her towers.
Consider well her bulwarks; examine her strongholds;
that you may tell those who come after.
This God is our God for ever and ever;
he shall be our guide for evermore. ℟

SECOND READING   1 Corinthians 13.1–13

A reading from the first letter of Paul to the Corinthians.

If I speak in the tongues of mortals and of angels, but do not have love, I am a noisy gong or a clanging cymbal. And if I have prophetic powers, and understand all mysteries and all knowledge, and if I have all faith, so as to remove mountains, but do not have love, I am nothing. If I give away all my possessions, and if I hand over my body so that I may boast, but do not have love, I gain nothing.

Love is patient; love is kind; love is not envious or boastful or arrogant or rude. It does not insist on its own way; it is not irritable or resentful; it does not rejoice in wrongdoing, but rejoices in the truth. It bears all things, believes all things, hopes all things, endures all things.

Love never ends. But as for prophecies, they will come to an end; as for tongues, they will cease; as for knowledge, it will come to an end. For we know only in part, and we prophesy only in part;

but when the complete comes, the partial will come to an end. When I was a child, I spoke like a child, I thought like a child, I reasoned like a child; when I became an adult, I put an end to childish ways. For now we see in a mirror, dimly, but then we will see face to face. Now I know only in part; then I will know fully, even as I have been fully known. And now faith, hope, and love abide, these three; and the greatest of these is love.

GOSPEL   Luke 2.22–40

Hear the gospel of our Lord Jesus Christ according to Luke.

When the time came for their purification according to the law of Moses, Mary and Joseph brought Jesus up to Jerusalem to present him to the Lord (as it is written in the law of the Lord, 'Every firstborn male shall be designated as holy to the Lord'), and they offered a sacrifice according to what is stated in the law of the Lord, 'a pair of turtle-doves or two young pigeons.'

Now there was a man in Jerusalem whose name was Simeon; this man was righteous and devout, looking forward to the consolation of Israel, and the Holy Spirit rested on him. It had been revealed to him by the Holy Spirit that he would not see death before he had seen the Lord's Messiah. Guided by the Spirit, Simeon came into the temple; and when the parents brought in the child Jesus, to do for him what was customary under the law, Simeon took him in his arms and praised God, saying,

'Master, now you are dismissing your servant in peace,
according to your word;
for my eyes have seen your salvation,
which you have prepared in the presence of all peoples,
a light for revelation to the Gentiles
and for glory to your people Israel.'

And the child's father and mother were amazed at what was being said about him. Then Simeon blessed them and said to his mother Mary, 'This child is destined for the falling and the rising of many in Israel, and to be a sign that will be opposed so that the inner thoughts of many will be revealed – and a sword will pierce your own soul too.'

There was also a prophet, Anna the daughter of Phanuel, of the tribe of Asher. She was of a great age, having lived with her husband seven years after her marriage, then as a widow to the age of eighty-four. She never left the temple but worshipped there with fasting and prayer night and day. At that moment she came, and began to praise God and to speak about the child to all who were looking for the redemption of Jerusalem.

When they had finished everything required by the law of the Lord, they returned to Galilee, to their own town of Nazareth. The child grew and became strong, filled with wisdom; and the favour of God was upon him.

THE PRESENTATION OF CHRIST   YEARS A B C

2 February   *For text see Year A, pages 44–48.*

ORDINARY TIME

*In the weeks between now and Lent the Revised Common Lectionary designates Sundays
'Sundays after Epiphany'. The Church of England provision designates them 'Sundays before
Lent' with readings according to calendar date.*

EPIPHANY 5   YEAR C
† SUNDAY BETWEEN 3 AND 9 FEBRUARY
(if earlier than 2 before Lent)

FIRST READING (Short or long reading)   Isaiah 6.1–8, (9–13)

A reading from the book of the prophet Isaiah.

In the year that King Uzziah died, I saw the Lord sitting on a throne, high
and lofty; and the hem of his robe filled the temple. Seraphs were in
attendance above him; each had six wings: with two they covered their faces,
and with two they covered their feet, and with two they flew. And one called
to another and said:
'Holy, holy, holy is the LORD of hosts;
the whole earth is full of his glory.'
The pivots on the thresholds shook at the voices of those who called, and the
house filled with smoke. And I said: 'Woe is me! I am lost, for I am a man of
unclean lips, and I live among a people of unclean lips; yet my eyes have
seen the King, the LORD of hosts!'

Then one of the seraphs flew to me, holding a live coal that had been taken
from the altar with a pair of tongs. The seraph touched my mouth with it
and said: 'Now that this has touched your lips, your guilt has departed and
your sin is blotted out.' Then I heard the voice of the Lord saying, 'Whom
shall I send, and who will go for us?' And I said, 'Here am I; send me!' [And
he said, 'Go and say to this people:
"Keep listening, but do not comprehend;
keep looking, but do not understand."
Make the mind of this people dull,
and stop their ears, and shut their eyes,
so that they may not look with their eyes, and listen with their ears,
and comprehend with their minds,

and turn and be healed.'
Then I said, 'How long, O Lord?'
And he said: 'Until cities lie waste without inhabitant,
and houses without people, and the land is utterly desolate;
until the LORD sends everyone far away,
and vast is the emptiness in the midst of the land.
Even if a tenth part remain in it,
it will be burned again,
like a terebinth or an oak whose stump remains standing when it is felled.
The holy seed is its stump.']

PSALM   Psalm 138

℟ **Before the gods I will sing your praise, O Lord.**
   or
℟ **Great is the glory of the Lord!**

I will give thanks to you, O Lord, with my whole heart;
before the gods I will sing your praise.
I will bow down towards your holy temple
and praise your name,
because of your love and faithfulness;
For you have glorified your name
and your word above all things. ℟

When I called, you answered me;
you increased my strength within me.
All the kings of the earth will praise you, O Lord,
when they have heard the words of your mouth.
They will sing of the ways of the Lord,
that great is the glory of the Lord.
Though the Lord be high, he cares for the lowly;
he perceives the haughty from afar. ℟

Though I walk in the midst of trouble,
you keep me safe;
you stretch forth your hand
against the fury of my enemies;
your right hand shall save me.
The Lord will make good his purpose for me;
O Lord, your love endures for ever;
do not abandon the works of your hands. ℟

SECOND READING   1 Corinthians 15.1–11

A reading from the first letter of Paul to the Corinthians.

I would remind you, brothers and sisters, of the good news that I proclaimed to you, which you in turn received, in which also you stand, through which also you are being saved, if you hold firmly to the message that I proclaimed to you – unless you have come to believe in vain.

For I handed on to you as of first importance what I in turn had received: that Christ died for our sins in accordance with the scriptures, and that he was buried, and that he was raised on the third day in accordance with the scriptures, and that he appeared to Cephas, then to the twelve. Then he appeared to more than five hundred brothers and sisters at one time, most of whom are still alive, though some have died. Then he appeared to James, then to all the apostles. Last of all, as to someone untimely born, he appeared also to me. For I am the least of the apostles, unfit to be called an apostle, because I persecuted the church of God. But by the grace of God I am what I am, and his grace towards me has not been in vain. On the contrary, I worked harder than any of them – though it was not I, but the grace of God that is with me. Whether then it was I or they, so we proclaim and so you have come to believe.

GOSPEL   Luke 5.1–11

Hear the gospel of our Lord Jesus Christ according to Luke.

While Jesus was standing beside the lake of Gennesaret, and the crowd was pressing in on him to hear the word of God, he saw two boats there at the shore of the lake; the fishermen had gone out of them and were washing their nets. He got into one of the boats, the one belonging to Simon, and asked him to put out a little way from the shore. Then he sat down and taught the crowds from the boat. When he had finished speaking, he said to Simon, 'Put out into the deep water and let down your nets for a catch.' Simon answered, 'Master, we have worked all night long but have caught nothing. Yet if you say so, I will let down the nets.' When they had done this, they caught so many fish that their nets were beginning to break. So they signalled their partners in the other boat to come and help them. And they came and filled both boats, so that they began to sink. But when Simon Peter saw it, he fell down at Jesus' knees, saying, 'Go away from me, Lord, for I am a sinful man!' For he and all who were with him were amazed at the catch of fish that they had taken; and so also were James and John, sons of Zebedee, who were partners with Simon. Then Jesus said to Simon, 'Do not be afraid; from now on you will be catching people.' When they had brought their boats to shore, they left everything and followed Jesus.

EPIPHANY 6   YEAR C
† SUNDAY BETWEEN 10 AND 16 FEBRUARY
(if earlier than 2 before Lent)

FIRST READING   Jeremiah 17.5–10

A reading from the book of the prophet Jeremiah.

Thus says the LORD:
Cursed are those who trust in mere mortals
and make mere flesh their strength,
whose hearts turn away from the LORD.
They shall be like a shrub in the desert,
and shall not see when relief comes.
They shall live in the parched places of the wilderness,
in an uninhabited salt land.

Blessed are those who trust in the LORD,
whose trust is the LORD.
They shall be like a tree planted by water,
sending out its roots by the stream.
It shall not fear when heat comes,
and its leaves shall stay green;
in the year of drought it is not anxious,
and it does not cease to bear fruit.

The heart is devious above all else;
it is perverse – who can understand it?
I the LORD test the mind and search the heart,
to give to all according to their ways,
according to the fruit of their doings.

PSALM

℟ **Happy are they who walk in the law of the Lord.**

Happy are they who have not walked
in the counsel of the wicked,
nor lingered in the way of sinners,
nor sat in the seats of the scornful!
Their delight is in the law of the Lord,
and they meditate on his law day and night. ℟

They are like trees planted by streams of water,
bearing fruit in due season,
with leaves that do not wither;
everything they do shall prosper.
It is not so with the wicked:
they are like chaff which the wind blows away; ℟

Therefore the wicked shall not stand upright
when judgement comes,
nor the sinner in the council of the righteous.
For the Lord knows the way of the righteous,
but the way of the wicked is doomed. ℟

SECOND READING

1 Corinthians 15.12–20

A reading from the first letter of Paul to the Corinthians.

If Christ is proclaimed as raised from the dead, how can some of you say
there is no resurrection of the dead? If there is no resurrection of the dead,
then Christ has not been raised; and if Christ has not been raised, then our
proclamation has been in vain and your faith has been in vain. We are even
found to be misrepresenting God, because we testified of God that he raised
Christ – whom he did not raise if it is true that the dead are not raised. For if
the dead are not raised, then Christ has not been raised. If Christ has not
been raised, your faith is futile and you are still in your sins. Then those also
who have died in Christ have perished. If for this life only we have hoped in
Christ, we are of all people most to be pitied. But in fact Christ has been
raised from the dead, the first fruits of those who have died.

GOSPEL   **Luke 6.17-26**

Hear the gospel of our Lord Jesus Christ according to Luke.

He came down with them and stood on a level place, with a great crowd of his disciples and a great multitude of people from all Judea, Jerusalem, and the coast of Tyre and Sidon. They had come to hear him and to be healed of their diseases; and those who were troubled with unclean spirits were cured. And all in the crowd were trying to touch him, for power came out from him and healed all of them.

Then he looked up at his disciples and said:
'Blessed are you who are poor,
for yours is the kingdom of God.
Blessed are you who are hungry now,
for you will be filled.
Blessed are you who weep now,
for you will laugh.
Blessed are you when people hate you, and when they exclude you, revile you, and defame you on account of the Son of Man. Rejoice on that day and leap for joy, for surely your reward is great in heaven; for that is what their ancestors did to the prophets.
But woe to you who are rich,
for you have received your consolation.
Woe to you who are full now,
for you will be hungry.
Woe to you who are laughing now,
for you will mourn and weep.
Woe to you when all speak well of you, for that is what their ancestors did to the false prophets.'

EPIPHANY 7   YEAR C
† SUNDAY BETWEEN 17 AND 23 FEBRUARY
(if earlier than 2 before Lent)

FIRST READING   **Genesis 45.3-11, 15**

A reading from the book of Genesis.

Joseph said to his brothers, 'I am Joseph. Is my father still alive?' But his brothers could not answer him, so dismayed were they at his presence.

Then Joseph said to his brothers, 'Come closer to me.' And they came closer. He said, 'I am your brother, Joseph, whom you sold into Egypt. And now do not be distressed, or angry with yourselves, because you sold me here; for God sent me before you to preserve life. For the famine has been in the land these two years; and there are five more years in which there will be neither ploughing nor harvest. God sent me before you to preserve for you a remnant on earth, and to keep alive for you many survivors. So it was not you who sent me here, but God; he has made me a father to Pharaoh, and lord of all his house and ruler over all the land of Egypt. Hurry and go up to my father and say to him, "Thus says your son Joseph, God has made me lord of all Egypt; come down to me, do not delay. You shall settle in the land of Goshen, and you shall be near me, you and your children and your children's children, as well as your flocks, your herds, and all that you have. I will provide for you there – since there are five more years of famine to come – so that you and your household, and all that you have, will not come to poverty."'

And he kissed all his brothers and wept upon them; and after that his brothers talked with him.

PSALM   **Psalm 37.1–12, 41–42**

℞ **Commit your way to the Lord and trust in him.**
   or
℞ **Dwell in the land and feed on its riches.**

Do not fret yourself because of evildoers;
do not be jealous of those who do wrong.
For they shall soon wither like the grass,
and like the green grass fade away.
Put your trust in the Lord and do good;
dwell in the land and feed on its riches. ℞

Take delight in the Lord,
and he shall give you your heart's desire.
Commit your way to the Lord
and put your trust in him,
and he will bring it to pass.
He will make your righteousness as clear as the light
and your just dealing as the noonday. ℞

Be still before the Lord
and wait patiently for him.

Do not fret yourself over the one who prospers,
the one who succeeds in evil schemes.
Refrain from anger, leave rage alone;
do not fret yourself; it leads only to evil. ℟

For evildoers shall be cut off,
but those who wait upon the Lord
shall possess the land.
In a little while the wicked shall be no more;
you shall search out their place,
but they will not be there.
But the lowly shall possess the land;
they will delight in abundance of peace. ℟

But the deliverance of the righteous comes from the Lord;
he is their stronghold in time of trouble.
The Lord will help them and rescue them;
he will rescue them from the wicked and deliver them,
because they seek refuge in him. ℟

SECOND READING   1 Corinthians 15.35–38, 42–50

A reading from the first letter of Paul to the Corinthians.

Someone will ask, 'How are the dead raised? With what kind of body do they come?' Fool! What you sow does not come to life unless it dies. And as for what you sow, you do not sow the body that is to be, but a bare seed, perhaps of wheat or of some other grain. But God gives it a body as he has chosen, and to each kind of seed its own body.

So it is with the resurrection of the dead. What is sown is perishable, what is raised is imperishable. It is sown in dishonour, it is raised in glory. It is sown in weakness, it is raised in power. It is sown a physical body, it is raised a spiritual body. If there is a physical body, there is also a spiritual body. Thus it is written, 'The first man, Adam, became a living being'; the last Adam became a life-giving spirit. But it is not the spiritual that is first, but the physical, and then the spiritual. The first man was from the earth, a man of dust; the second man is from heaven. As was the man of dust, so are those who are of the dust; and as is the man of heaven, so are those who are of heaven. Just as we have borne the image of the man of dust, we will also bear the image of the man of heaven.

What I am saying, brothers and sisters, is this: flesh and blood cannot inherit the kingdom of God, nor does the perishable inherit the imperishable.

GOSPEL   Luke 6.27–38

Hear the gospel of our Lord Jesus Christ according to Luke.

Jesus said to his disciples, 'I say to you that listen, Love your enemies, do good to those who hate you, bless those who curse you, pray for those who abuse you. If anyone strikes you on the cheek, offer the other also; and from anyone who takes away your coat do not withhold even your shirt. Give to everyone who begs from you; and if anyone takes away your goods, do not ask for them again. Do to others as you would have them do to you.

If you love those who love you, what credit is that to you? For even sinners love those who love them. If you do good to those who do good to you, what credit is that to you? For even sinners do the same. If you lend to those from whom you hope to receive, what credit is that to you? Even sinners lend to sinners, to receive as much again. But love your enemies, do good, and lend, expecting nothing in return. Your reward will be great, and you will be children of the Most High; for he is kind to the ungrateful and the wicked. Be merciful, just as your Father is merciful.

Do not judge, and you will not be judged; do not condemn, and you will not be condemned. Forgive, and you will be forgiven; give, and it will be given to you. A good measure, pressed down, shaken together, running over, will be put into your lap; for the measure you give will be the measure you get back.'

EPIPHANY 8   YEAR C
† SECOND SUNDAY BEFORE LENT

The Revised Common Lectionary and the Church of England make different provision for today.
For Church of England provision see pages 567–570 below.

REVISED COMMON LECTIONARY

FIRST READING

Either   Ecclesiasticus 27.4–7

A reading from the book of Ecclesiasticus.

When a sieve is shaken, the refuse appears;
so do a person's faults when he speaks.
The kiln tests the potter's vessels;

so the test of a person is in his conversation.
Its fruit discloses the cultivation of a tree;
so a person's speech discloses the cultivation of his mind.
Do not praise anyone before he speaks,
for this is the way people are tested.

Or   **Isaiah 55.10–13**

A reading from the book of the prophet Isaiah.

Thus says the LORD:
As the rain and the snow come down from heaven,
and do not return there until they have watered the earth,
making it bring forth and sprout,
giving seed to the sower and bread to the eater,
so shall my word be that goes out from my mouth;
it shall not return to me empty,
but it shall accomplish that which I purpose,
and succeed in the thing for which I sent it.

For you shall go out in joy,
and be led back in peace;
the mountains and the hills before you shall burst into song,
and all the trees of the field shall clap their hands.
Instead of the thorn shall come up the cypress;
instead of the brier shall come up the myrtle;
and it shall be to the LORD for a memorial,
for an everlasting sign that shall not be cut off.

PSALM   **Psalm 92.1–4, 11–14**

℟ **It is a good thing to give thanks to the Lord.**

It is a good thing to give thanks to the Lord,
and to sing praises to your name, O Most High;
To tell of your loving-kindness early in the morning
and of your faithfulness in the night season;
On the psaltery and on the lyre
and to the melody of the harp.
For you have made me glad by your acts, O Lord;
and I shout for joy because of the works of your hands. ℟

The righteous shall flourish like a palm tree,
and shall spread abroad like a cedar of Lebanon.
Those who are planted in the house of the Lord
shall flourish in the courts of our God; ℟

They shall still bear fruit in old age;
they shall be green and succulent;
That they may show how upright the Lord is,
my rock, in whom there is no fault. ℟

SECOND READING   1 Corinthians 15.51-58

A reading from the first letter of Paul to the Corinthians.

Listen, I will tell you a mystery! We will not all die, but we will all be
changed, in a moment, in the twinkling of an eye, at the last trumpet. For
the trumpet will sound, and the dead will be raised imperishable, and we will
be changed. For this perishable body must put on imperishability, and this
mortal body must put on immortality. When this perishable body puts on
imperishability, and this mortal body puts on immortality, then the saying
that is written will be fulfilled:
'Death has been swallowed up in victory.'
'Where, O death, is your victory?
Where, O death, is your sting?'
The sting of death is sin, and the power of sin is the law. But thanks be to
God, who gives us the victory through our Lord Jesus Christ.

Therefore, my beloved, be steadfast, immovable, always excelling in the work
of the Lord, because you know that in the Lord your labour is not in vain.

GOSPEL   Luke 6.39-49

Hear the gospel of our Lord Jesus Christ according to Luke.

Jesus told the disciples a parable: 'Can a blind person guide a blind person?
Will not both fall into a pit? A disciple is not above the teacher, but everyone
who is fully qualified will be like the teacher. Why do you see the speck in
your neighbour's eye, but do not notice the log in your own eye? Or how can
you say to your neighbour, "Friend, let me take out the speck in your eye,"
when you yourself do not see the log in your own eye? You hypocrite, first
take the log out of your own eye, and then you will see clearly to take the
speck out of your neighbour's eye.

No good tree bears bad fruit, nor again does a bad tree bear good fruit; for each tree is known by its own fruit. Figs are not gathered from thorns, nor are grapes picked from a bramble bush. The good person out of the good treasure of the heart produces good, and the evil person out of the evil treasure produces evil;

Why do you call me "Lord, Lord," and do not do what I tell you? I will show you what someone is like who comes to me, hears my words, and acts on them. That one is like a man building a house, who dug deeply and laid the foundation on rock; when a flood arose, the river burst against that house but could not shake it, because it had been well built. But the one who hears and does not act is like a man who built a house on the ground without a foundation. When the river burst against it, immediately it fell, and great was the ruin of that house.'

Or

† SECOND SUNDAY BEFORE LENT

FIRST READING   Genesis 2.4b–9, 15–25

A reading from the book of Genesis.

In the day that the LORD God made the earth and the heavens, when no plant of the field was yet in the earth and no herb of the field had yet sprung up – for the LORD God had not caused it to rain upon the earth, and there was no one to till the ground; but a stream would rise from the earth, and water the whole face of the ground – then the LORD God formed man from the dust of the ground, and breathed into his nostrils the breath of life; and the man became a living being. And the LORD God planted a garden in Eden, in the east; and there he put the man whom he had formed. Out of the ground the LORD God made to grow every tree that is pleasant to the sight and good for food, the tree of life also in the midst of the garden, and the tree of the knowledge of good and evil.

The LORD God took the man and put him in the garden of Eden to till it and keep it. And the LORD God commanded the man, 'You may freely eat of every tree of the garden; but of the tree of the knowledge of good and evil you shall not eat, for in the day that you eat of it you shall die.'

Then the LORD God said, 'It is not good that the man should be alone; I will make him a helper as his partner.' So out of the ground the LORD God formed every animal of the field and every bird of the air, and brought them

to the man to see what he would call them; and whatever the man called
every living creature, that was its name. The man gave names to all cattle,
and to the birds of the air, and to every animal of the field; but for the man
there was not found a helper as his partner. So the LORD God caused a deep
sleep to fall upon the man, and he slept; then he took one of his ribs and
closed up its place with flesh. And the rib that the LORD God had taken from
the man he made into a woman and brought her to the man.
Then the man said,
'This at last is bone of my bones
and flesh of my flesh;
this one shall be called Woman,
for out of Man this one was taken.'
Therefore a man leaves his father and his mother and clings to his wife, and
they become one flesh. And the man and his wife were both naked, and were
not ashamed.

PSALM   Psalm 65

℟ **You visit the earth and water it,**
[you make it very plenteous].

You are to be praised, O God, in Zion;
to you shall vows be performed in Jerusalem.
To you that hear prayer shall all flesh come,
because of their transgressions.
Our sins are stronger than we are,
but you will blot them out. ℟

Happy are they whom you choose
and draw to your courts to dwell there!
they will be satisfied by the beauty of your house,
by the holiness of your temple.
Awesome things will you show us in your righteousness,
O God of our salvation,
O Hope of all the ends of the earth
and of the seas that are far away. ℟

You make fast the mountains by your power;
they are girded about with might.
You still the roaring of the seas,
the roaring of their waves,
and the clamour of the peoples.

Those who dwell at the ends of the earth
will tremble at your marvellous signs;
you make the dawn and the dusk to sing for joy. ℟

You visit the earth and water it abundantly;
you make it very plenteous;
the river of God is full of water.
You prepare the grain,
for so you provide for the earth.
You drench the furrows and smooth out the ridges;
with heavy rain you soften the ground
and bless its increase. ℟

You crown the year with your goodness,
and your paths overflow with plenty.
May the fields of the wilderness be rich for grazing,
and the hills be clothed with joy.
May the meadows cover themselves with flocks
and the valleys cloak themselves with grain;
let them shout for joy and sing. ℟

SECOND READING   Revelation 4

A reading from the book of Revelation.

After this I looked, and there in heaven a door stood open! And the first
voice, which I had heard speaking to me like a trumpet, said, 'Come up here,
and I will show you what must take place after this.' At once I was in the
spirit, and there in heaven stood a throne, with one seated on the throne!
And the one seated there looks like jasper and carnelian, and around the
throne is a rainbow that looks like an emerald. Around the throne are
twenty-four thrones, and seated on the thrones are twenty-four elders,
dressed in white robes, with golden crowns on their heads. Coming from the
throne are flashes of lightning, and rumblings and peals of thunder, and in
front of the throne burn seven flaming torches, which are the seven spirits of
God; and in front of the throne there is something like a sea of glass, like
crystal.

Around the throne, and on each side of the throne, are four living creatures,
full of eyes in front and behind: the first living creature like a lion, the
second living creature like an ox, the third living creature with a face like a
human face, and the fourth living creature like a flying eagle. And the four
living creatures, each of them with six wings, are full of eyes all around and

inside. Day and night without ceasing they sing,
'Holy, holy, holy, the Lord God the Almighty,
who was and is and is to come.'
And whenever the living creatures give glory and honour and thanks to the
one who is seated on the throne, who lives for ever and ever, the twenty-four
elders fall before the one who is seated on the throne and worship the one
who lives for ever and ever; they cast their crowns before the throne, singing,
'You are worthy, our Lord and God,
to receive glory and honour and power,
for you created all things,
and by your will they existed and were created.'

GOSPEL   Luke 8.22–25

Hear the gospel of our Lord Jesus Christ according to Luke.

One day Jesus got into a boat with his disciples, and he said to them, 'Let us
go across to the other side of the lake.' So they put out, and while they were
sailing he fell asleep. A gale swept down on the lake, and the boat was filling
with water, and they were in danger. They went to him and woke him up,
shouting, 'Master, Master, we are perishing!' And he woke up and rebuked the
wind and the raging waves; they ceased, and there was a calm. He said to
them, 'Where is your faith?' They were afraid and amazed, and said to one
another, 'Who then is this, that he commands even the winds and the water,
and they obey him?'

EPIPHANY 9   YEAR C
† SUNDAY NEXT BEFORE LENT

*On this Sunday the Church of England allows only one of the two options in the Revised
Common Lectionary. Both provisions are given below.
The Church of England provision is the first set.*

FIRST READING   Exodus 34.29–35

A reading from the book of Exodus.

Moses came down from Mount Sinai. As he came down from the mountain
with the two tablets of the covenant in his hand, Moses did not know that
the skin of his face shone because he had been talking with God. When
Aaron and all the Israelites saw Moses, the skin of his face was shining, and

they were afraid to come near him. But Moses called to them; and Aaron and all the leaders of the congregation returned to him, and Moses spoke with them. Afterwards all the Israelites came near, and he gave them in commandment all that the LORD had spoken with him on Mount Sinai. When Moses had finished speaking with them, he put a veil on his face; but whenever Moses went in before the LORD to speak with him, he would take the veil off, until he came out; and when he came out, and told the Israelites what he had been commanded, the Israelites would see the face of Moses, that the skin of his face was shining; and Moses would put the veil on his face again, until he went in to speak with him.

PSALM   Psalm 99

℟ **Proclaim the greatness of the Lord our God.**

The Lord is king; let the people tremble;
he is enthroned upon the cherubim; let the earth shake.
The Lord is great in Zion;
he is high above all peoples.
Let them confess his name, which is great and awesome;
he is the Holy One. ℟

'O mighty King, lover of justice,
you have established equity;
you have executed justice and righteousness in Jacob.'
Proclaim the greatness of the Lord our God
and fall down before his footstool;
he is the Holy One. ℟

Moses and Aaron among his priests,
and Samuel among those who call upon his name,
they called upon the Lord and he answered them.
He spoke to them out of the pillar of cloud;
they kept his testimonies
and the decree that he gave them. ℟

'O Lord our God, you answered them indeed;
you were a God who forgave them,
yet punished them for their evil deeds.'
Proclaim the greatness of the Lord our God
and worship him upon his holy hill;
for the Lord our God is the Holy One. ℟

SECOND READING   2 Corinthians 3.12 – 4.2

A reading from the second letter of Paul to the Corinthians.

Since we have such a hope, we act with great boldness, not like Moses, who put a veil over his face to keep the people of Israel from gazing at the end of the glory that was being set aside. But their minds were hardened. Indeed, to this very day, when they hear the reading of the old covenant, that same veil is still there, since only in Christ is it set aside. Indeed, to this very day whenever Moses is read, a veil lies over their minds; but when one turns to the Lord, the veil is removed. Now the Lord is the Spirit, and where the Spirit of the Lord is, there is freedom. And all of us, with unveiled faces, seeing the glory of the Lord as though reflected in a mirror, are being transformed into the same image from one degree of glory to another; for this comes from the Lord, the Spirit.

Therefore, since it is by God's mercy that we are engaged in this ministry, we do not lose heart. We have renounced the shameful things that one hides; we refuse to practise cunning or to falsify God's word; but by the open statement of the truth we commend ourselves to the conscience of everyone in the sight of God.

GOSPEL (Short or long reading)   Luke 9.28b–36, (37–43)

Hear the gospel of our Lord Jesus Christ according to Luke.

Jesus took with him Peter and John and James, and went up on the mountain to pray. And while he was praying, the appearance of his face changed, and his clothes became dazzling white. Suddenly they saw two men, Moses and Elijah, talking to him. They appeared in glory and were speaking of his departure, which he was about to accomplish at Jerusalem.

Now Peter and his companions were weighed down with sleep; but since they had stayed awake, they saw his glory and the two men who stood with him. Just as they were leaving him, Peter said to Jesus, 'Master, it is good for us to be here; let us make three dwellings, one for you, one for Moses, and one for Elijah.' Peter did not know what he said.

While he was saying this, a cloud came and overshadowed them; and they were terrified as they entered the cloud. Then from the cloud came a voice that said, 'This is my Son, my Chosen; listen to him!' When the voice had spoken, Jesus was found alone. And the disciples kept silent and in those days told no one any of the things they had seen. [On the next day, when they had come down from the mountain, a great crowd met him. Just then a man from the crowd shouted, 'Teacher, I beg you to look at my son; he is my only child. Suddenly a spirit seizes him, and all at once he shrieks. It throws him into convulsions until he foams at the mouth; it mauls him and will scarcely leave him.

I begged your disciples to cast it out, but they could not.' Jesus answered, 'You faithless and perverse generation, how much longer must I be with you and bear with you? Bring your son here.' While he was coming, the demon dashed him to the ground in convulsions. But Jesus rebuked the unclean spirit, healed the boy, and gave him back to his father. And all were astounded at the greatness of God. Everyone was amazed at all that he was doing.]

Or

REVISED COMMON LECTIONARY ONLY

FIRST READING   **1 Kings 8.22–23, 41–43**

A reading from the first book of Kings.

Solomon stood before the altar of the LORD in the presence of all the assembly of Israel, and spread out his hands to heaven. He said, 'O LORD, God of Israel, there is no God like you in heaven above or on earth beneath, keeping covenant and steadfast love for your servants who walk before you with all their heart.

When a foreigner, who is not of your people Israel, comes from a distant land because of your name – for they shall hear of your great name, your mighty hand, and your outstretched arm – when a foreigner comes and prays towards this house, then hear in heaven your dwelling-place, and do according to all that the foreigner calls to you, so that all the peoples of the earth may know your name and fear you, as do your people Israel, and so that they may know that your name has been invoked on this house that I have built.'

PSALM Psalm 96.1–9

℟ **Ascribe to the Lord honour and power.**

Sing to the Lord a new song;
sing to the Lord, all the whole earth.
Sing to the Lord and bless his name;
proclaim the good news of his salvation from day to day.
Declare his glory among the nations
and his wonders among all peoples. ℟

For great is the Lord and greatly to be praised;
he is more to be feared than all gods.
As for all the gods of the nations, they are but idols;
but it is the Lord who made the heavens.
O the majesty and magnificence of his presence!
O the power and the splendour of his sanctuary! ℟

Ascribe to the Lord, you families of the peoples;
ascribe to the Lord honour and power.
Ascribe to the Lord the honour due to his name;
bring offerings and come into his courts.
Worship the Lord in the beauty of holiness;
let the whole earth tremble before him. ℟

SECOND READING   Galatians 1.1–12

A reading from the letter of Paul to the Galatians.

Paul an apostle – sent neither by human commission nor from human authorities, but through Jesus Christ and God the Father, who raised him from the dead – and all the members of God's family who are with me, To the churches of Galatia:

Grace to you and peace from God our Father and the Lord Jesus Christ, who gave himself for our sins to set us free from the present evil age, according to the will of our God and Father, to whom be the glory for ever and ever. Amen.

I am astonished that you are so quickly deserting the one who called you in the grace of Christ and are turning to a different gospel – not that there is another gospel, but there are some who are confusing you and want to pervert the gospel of Christ. But even if we or an angel from heaven should proclaim to you a gospel contrary to what we proclaimed to you, let that one be accursed! As we have said before, so now I repeat, if anyone proclaims to you a gospel contrary to what you received, let that one be accursed!

Am I now seeking human approval, or God's approval? Or am I trying to please people? If I were still pleasing people, I would not be a servant of Christ.

For I want you to know, brothers and sisters, that the gospel that was proclaimed by me is not of human origin; for I did not receive it from a human source, nor was I taught it, but I received it through a revelation of Jesus Christ.

GOSPEL   Luke 7.1b–10

Hear the gospel of our Lord Jesus Christ according to Luke.

Jesus entered the town of Capernaum. A centurion there had a slave whom he valued highly, and who was ill and close to death. When he heard about Jesus, he sent some Jewish elders to him, asking him to come and heal his slave. When they came to Jesus, they appealed to him earnestly, saying, 'He is worthy of having you do this for him, for he loves our people, and it is he who built our synagogue for us.' And Jesus went with them, but when he was not far from the house, the centurion sent friends to say to him, 'Lord, do not trouble yourself, for I am not worthy to have you come under my roof; therefore I did not presume to come to you. But only speak the word, and let my servant be healed. For I also am a man set under authority, with soldiers under me; and I say to one, "Go," and he goes, and to another, "Come," and he comes, and to my slave, "Do this," and the slave does it.' When Jesus heard this he was amazed at him, and turning to the crowd that followed him, he said, 'I tell you, not even in Israel have I found such faith.' When those who had been sent returned to the house, they found the slave in good health.

ASH WEDNESDAY

YEARS A B C

For text see Year A, pages 70–76.

LENT 1

YEAR C

FIRST READING   **Deuteronomy 26.1–11**

A reading from the book of Deuteronomy.

Moses spoke to the people, saying: When you have come into the land that the LORD your God is giving you as an inheritance to possess, and you possess it, and settle in it, you shall take some of the first of all the fruit of the ground, which you harvest from the land that the LORD your God is giving you, and you shall put it in a basket and go to the place that the LORD your God will choose as a dwelling for his name. You shall go to the priest who is in office at that time, and say to him, 'Today I declare to the LORD your God that I have come into the land that the LORD swore to our ancestors to give us.' When the priest takes the basket from your hand and sets it down before the altar of the LORD your God, you shall make this response before the LORD your God: 'A wandering Aramean was my ancestor; he went down into Egypt and lived there as an alien, few in number, and there he became a great nation, mighty and populous. When the Egyptians treated us harshly and afflicted us, by imposing hard labour on us, we cried to the LORD, the God of our ancestors; the LORD heard our voice and saw our affliction, our toil, and our oppression. The LORD brought us out of Egypt with a mighty hand and an outstretched arm, with a terrifying display of power, and with signs and wonders; and he brought us into this place and gave us this land, a land flowing with milk and honey. So now I bring the first of the fruit of the ground that you, O LORD, have given me.' You shall set it down before the LORD your God and bow down before the LORD your God. Then you, together with the Levites and the aliens who reside among you, shall celebrate with all the bounty that the LORD your God has given to you and to your house.

PSALM   **Psalm 91.1-2, 9-16**

℞ **Be with me, O Lord, in trouble.**
  or
℞ **You, O Lord, are my refuge**
  [my God in whom I put my trust].

He who dwells in the shelter of the Most High,
abides under the shadow of the Almighty.
He shall say to the Lord,
'You are my refuge and my stronghold,
my God in whom I put my trust.' ℞

Because you have made the Lord your refuge,
and the Most High your habitation,
There shall no evil happen to you,
neither shall any plague come near your dwelling. ℞

For he shall give his angels charge over you,
to keep you in all your ways.
They shall bear you in their hands,
lest you dash your foot against a stone. ℞

You shall tread upon the lion and adder;
you shall trample the young lion and the serpent
under your feet.
Because he is bound to me in love,
therefore will I deliver him;
I will protect him, because he knows my name. ℞

He shall call upon me and I will answer him;
I am with him in trouble,
I will rescue him and bring him to honour.
With long life will I satisfy him,
and show him my salvation. ℞

SECOND READING   **Romans 10.8b-13**

A reading from the letter of Paul to the Romans.

What does scripture say?
'The word is near you,
on your lips and in your heart'

(that is, the word of faith that we proclaim); because if you confess with your lips that Jesus is Lord and believe in your heart that God raised him from the dead, you will be saved. For one believes with the heart and so is justified, and one confesses with the mouth and so is saved. The scripture says, 'No one who believes in him will be put to shame.' For there is no distinction between Jew and Greek; the same Lord is Lord of all and is generous to all who call on him. For, 'Everyone who calls on the name of the Lord shall be saved.'

GOSPEL   Luke 4.1–13

Hear the gospel of our Lord Jesus Christ according to Luke.

Jesus, full of the Holy Spirit, returned from the Jordan and was led by the Spirit in the wilderness, where for forty days he was tempted by the devil. He ate nothing at all during those days, and when they were over, he was famished. The devil said to him, 'If you are the Son of God, command this stone to become a loaf of bread.' Jesus answered him, 'It is written, "One does not live by bread alone."'

Then the devil led him up and showed him in an instant all the kingdoms of the world. And the devil said to him, 'To you I will give their glory and all this authority; for it has been given over to me, and I give it to anyone I please. If you, then, will worship me, it will all be yours.' Jesus answered him, 'It is written, "Worship the Lord your God, and serve only him."'

Then the devil took him to Jerusalem, and placed him on the pinnacle of the temple, saying to him, 'If you are the Son of God, throw yourself down from here, for it is written,
"He will command his angels concerning you, to protect you,"
and "On their hands they will bear you up,
so that you will not dash your foot against a stone."'
Jesus answered him, 'It is said, "Do not put the Lord your God to the test."'
When the devil had finished every test, he departed from him until an opportune time.

LENT 2   YEAR C

FIRST READING   **Genesis 15.1–12, 17–18**

A reading from the book of Genesis.

The word of the LORD came to Abram in a vision, 'Do not be afraid, Abram, I am your shield; your reward shall be very great.' But Abram said, 'O Lord GOD, what will you give me, for I continue childless, and the heir of my house is Eliezer of Damascus?' And Abram said, 'You have given me no offspring, and so a slave born in my house is to be my heir.' But the word of the LORD came to him, 'This man shall not be your heir; no one but your very own issue shall be your heir.' He brought him outside and said, 'Look towards heaven and count the stars, if you are able to count them.' Then he said to him, 'So shall your descendants be.' And he believed the LORD; and the LORD reckoned it to him as righteousness.

Then he said to him, 'I am the LORD who brought you from Ur of the Chaldeans, to give you this land to possess.' But he said, 'O Lord GOD, how am I to know that I shall possess it?' He said to him, 'Bring me a heifer three years old, a female goat three years old, a ram three years old, a turtle-dove, and a young pigeon.' He brought him all these and cut them in two, laying each half over against the other; but he did not cut the birds in two. And when birds of prey came down on the carcasses, Abram drove them away.

As the sun was going down, a deep sleep fell upon Abram, and a deep and terrifying darkness descended upon him.

When the sun had gone down and it was dark, a smoking fire-pot and a flaming torch passed between these pieces. On that day the LORD made a covenant with Abram, saying, 'To your descendants I give this land, from the river of Egypt to the great river, the river Euphrates.'

PSALM   **Psalm 27**

℟ **The Lord is my light and my salvation.**

The Lord is my light and my salvation;
whom then shall I fear?
the Lord is the strength of my life;
of whom then shall I be afraid?
When evildoers came upon me to eat up my flesh,
it was they, my foes and my adversaries,
who stumbled and fell. ℟

Though an army should encamp against me,
yet my heart shall not be afraid;
And though war should rise up against me,
yet will I put my trust in him. ℟

One thing have I asked of the Lord;
one thing I seek;
that I may dwell in the house of the Lord
all the days of my life;
To behold the fair beauty of the Lord
and to seek him in his temple. ℟

For in the day of trouble
he shall keep me safe in his shelter;
he shall hide me in the secrecy of his dwelling
and set me high upon a rock. ℟

Even now he lifts up my head
above my enemies round about me;
Therefore I will offer in his dwelling an oblation
with sounds of great gladness;
I will sing and make music to the Lord. ℟

Hearken to my voice, O Lord, when I call;
have mercy on me and answer me.
You speak in my heart and say, 'Seek my face.'
Your face, Lord, will I seek.
Hide not your face from me,
nor turn away your servant in displeasure. ℟

You have been my helper;
cast me not away;
do not forsake me, O God of my salvation.
Though my father and my mother forsake me,
the Lord will sustain me. ℟

Show me your way, O Lord;
lead me on a level path, because of my enemies.
Deliver me not into the hand of my adversaries,
for false witnesses have risen up against me,
and also those who speak malice. ℟

What if I had not believed
that I should see the goodness of the Lord

in the land of the living!
O tarry and await the Lord's pleasure;
be strong and he shall comfort your heart;
wait patiently for the Lord. ℟

SECOND READING   Philippians 3.17 – 4.1

A reading from the letter of Paul to the Philippians.

Brothers and sisters, join in imitating me, and observe those who live according to the example you have in us. For many live as enemies of the cross of Christ; I have often told you of them, and now I tell you even with tears. Their end is destruction; their god is the belly; and their glory is in their shame; their minds are set on earthly things. But our citizenship is in heaven, and it is from there that we are expecting a Saviour, the Lord Jesus Christ. He will transform the body of our humiliation that it may be conformed to the body of his glory, by the power that also enables him to make all things subject to himself. Therefore, my brothers and sisters, whom I love and long for, my joy and crown, stand firm in the Lord in this way, my beloved.

GOSPEL

The Revised Common Lectionary provides alternative Gospels. Church of England
provision allows only the first of these (Luke 13.31–35).

Either   Luke 13.31–35

Hear the gospel of our Lord Jesus Christ according to Luke.

At that very hour some Pharisees came and said to him, 'Get away from here, for Herod wants to kill you.' He said to them, 'Go and tell that fox for me, "Listen, I am casting out demons and performing cures today and tomorrow, and on the third day I finish my work. Yet today, tomorrow, and the next day I must be on my way, because it is impossible for a prophet to be killed away from Jerusalem." Jerusalem, Jerusalem, the city that kills the prophets and stones those who are sent to it! How often have I desired to gather your children together as a hen gathers her brood under her wings, and you were not willing! See, your house is left to you. And I tell you, you will not see me until the time comes when you say, "Blessed is the one who comes in the name of the Lord."'

Or (Revised Common Lectionary only)   **Luke 9.28b–36**

Hear the gospel of our Lord Jesus Christ according to Luke.

Jesus took with him Peter and John and James, and went up on the mountain to pray. And while he was praying, the appearance of his face changed, and his clothes became dazzling white. Suddenly they saw two men, Moses and Elijah, talking to him. They appeared in glory and were speaking of his departure, which he was about to accomplish at Jerusalem. Now Peter and his companions were weighed down with sleep; but since they had stayed awake, they saw his glory and the two men who stood with him. Just as they were leaving him, Peter said to Jesus, 'Master, it is good for us to be here; let us make three dwellings, one for you, one for Moses, and one for Elijah.' Peter did not know what he said. While he was saying this, a cloud came and overshadowed them; and they were terrified as they entered the cloud. Then from the cloud came a voice that said, 'This is my Son, my Chosen; listen to him!' When the voice had spoken, Jesus was found alone. And the disciples kept silent and in those days told no one any of the things they had seen.

LENT 3   YEAR C

FIRST READING   **Isaiah 55.1–9**

A reading from the book of the prophet Isaiah.

The LORD says this:

Everyone who thirsts,
come to the waters;
and you that have no money,
come, buy and eat!
Come, buy wine and milk
without money and without price.
Why do you spend your money for that which is not bread,
and your labour for that which does not satisfy?
Listen carefully to me, and eat what is good,
and delight yourselves in rich food.
Incline your ear, and come to me;
listen, so that you may live.
I will make with you an everlasting covenant,
my steadfast, sure love for David.
See, I made him a witness to the peoples,

a leader and commander for the peoples.
See, you shall call nations that you do not know,
and nations that do not know you shall run to you,
because of the LORD your God, the Holy One of Israel,
for he has glorified you.
Seek the LORD while he may be found,
call upon him while he is near;
let the wicked forsake their way,
and the unrighteous their thoughts;
let them return to the LORD, that he may have mercy on them,
and to our God, for he will abundantly pardon.
For my thoughts are not your thoughts,
nor are your ways my ways, says the LORD.
For as the heavens are higher than the earth,
so are my ways higher than your ways
and my thoughts than your thoughts.

PSALM   **Psalm 63.1–8**

℟ **My soul thirsts for you, O my God.**

O God, you are my God; eagerly I seek you;
my soul thirsts for you, my flesh faints for you,
as in a barren and dry land where there is no water;
Therefore I have gazed upon you in your holy place,
that I might behold your power and your glory. ℟

For your loving-kindness is better than life itself;
my lips shall give you praise.
So will I bless you as long as I live
and lift up my hands in your name. ℟

My soul is content, as with marrow and fatness,
and my mouth praises you with joyful lips,
When I remember you upon my bed,
and meditate on you in the night watches. ℟

For you have been my helper,
and under the shadow of your wings I will rejoice.
My soul clings to you;
your right hand holds me fast. ℟

SECOND READING 1 Corinthians 10.1–13

A reading from the first letter of Paul to the Corinthians.

I do not want you to be unaware, brothers and sisters, that our ancestors were all under the cloud, and all passed through the sea, and all were baptized into Moses in the cloud and in the sea, and all ate the same spiritual food, and all drank the same spiritual drink. For they drank from the spiritual rock that followed them, and the rock was Christ. Nevertheless, God was not pleased with most of them, and they were struck down in the wilderness.

Now these things occurred as examples for us, so that we might not desire evil as they did. Do not become idolaters as some of them did; as it is written, 'The people sat down to eat and drink, and they rose up to play.' We must not indulge in sexual immorality as some of them did, and twenty-three thousand fell in a single day. We must not put Christ to the test, as some of them did, and were destroyed by serpents. And do not complain as some of them did, and were destroyed by the destroyer. These things happened to them to serve as an example, and they were written down to instruct us, on whom the ends of the ages have come. So if you think you are standing, watch out that you do not fall. No testing has overtaken you that is not common to everyone. God is faithful, and he will not let you be tested beyond your strength, but with the testing he will also provide the way out so that you may be able to endure it.

GOSPEL Luke 13.1–9

Hear the gospel of our Lord Jesus Christ according to Luke.

There were some present who told Jesus about the Galileans whose blood Pilate had mingled with their sacrifices. He asked them 'Do you think that because these Galileans suffered in this way they were worse sinners than all other Galileans? No, I tell you; but unless you repent, you will all perish as they did. Or those eighteen who were killed when the tower of Siloam fell on them – do you think that they were worse offenders than all the others living in Jerusalem? No, I tell you; but unless you repent, you will all perish just as they did.'

Then he told this parable: 'A man had a fig tree planted in his vineyard; and he came looking for fruit on it and found none. So he said to the gardener, "See here! For three years I have come looking for fruit on this fig tree, and still I find none. Cut it down! Why should it be wasting the soil?" He replied,

"Sir, let it alone for one more year, until I dig around it and put manure on it. If it bears fruit next year, well and good; but if not, you can cut it down."'

LENT 4   YEAR C

Provision for Lent 4 is included in the Revised Common Lectionary and the Church of England provision, but the Church of England adds alternative readings for Mothering Sunday. For text see Year A, pages 88–92.

FIRST READING   Joshua 5.9–12

A reading from the book of Joshua.

After the Israelites had crossed over the Jordan river,

The LORD said to Joshua, 'Today I have rolled away from you the disgrace of Egypt.' And so that place is called Gilgal to this day.

While the Israelites were camped in Gilgal they kept the passover in the evening on the fourteenth day of the month in the plains of Jericho. On the day after the passover, on that very day, they ate the produce of the land, unleavened cakes and parched grain. The manna ceased on the day they ate the produce of the land, and the Israelites no longer had manna; they ate the crops of the land of Canaan that year.

PSALM   Psalm 32

℟ **You, O Lord, are my hiding-place,**
   [you preserve me from trouble].

Happy are they whose transgressions are forgiven,
and whose sin is put away!
Happy are they to whom the Lord imputes no guilt,
and in whose spirit there is no guile! ℟

While I held my tongue, my bones withered away,
because of my groaning all day long.
For your hand was heavy upon me day and night;
my moisture was dried up as in the heat of summer. ℟

Then I acknowledged my sin to you,
and did not conceal my guilt.
I said, 'I will confess my transgressions to the Lord';
then you forgave me the guilt of my sin. ℟

Therefore all the faithful will make their prayers to you
in time of trouble;
when the great waters overflow, they shall not reach them.
You are my hiding-place;
you preserve me from trouble;
you surround me with shouts of deliverance. ℟

'I will instruct you and teach you
in the way that you should go;
I will guide you with my eye.
Do not be like horse or mule,
which have no understanding;
who must be fitted with bit and bridle,
or else they will not stay near you.' ℟

Great are the tribulations of the wicked;
but mercy embraces those who trust in the Lord.
Be glad, you righteous, and rejoice in the Lord;
shout for joy, all who are true of heart. ℟

SECOND READING   2 Corinthians 5.16–21

A reading from the second letter of Paul to the Corinthians.

From now on, we regard no one from a human point of view; even though
we once knew Christ from a human point of view, we know him no longer in
that way. So if anyone is in Christ, there is a new creation: everything old has
passed away; see, everything has become new! All this is from God, who
reconciled us to himself through Christ, and has given us the ministry of
reconciliation; that is, in Christ God was reconciling the world to himself,
not counting their trespasses against them, and entrusting the message of
reconciliation to us. So we are ambassadors for Christ, since God is making
his appeal through us; we entreat you on behalf of Christ, be reconciled to
God. For our sake he made him to be sin who knew no sin, so that in him we
might become the righteousness of God.

GOSPEL   Luke 15.1–3, 11b–32

Hear the gospel of our Lord Jesus Christ according to Luke.

All the tax collectors and sinners were coming near to listen to Jesus. And the
Pharisees and the scribes were grumbling and saying, 'This fellow welcomes
sinners and eats with them.'

So he told them this parable:

'There was a man who had two sons. The younger of them said to his father, "Father, give me the share of the property that will belong to me." So he divided his property between them. A few days later the younger son gathered all he had and travelled to a distant country, and there he squandered his property in dissolute living. When he had spent everything, a severe famine took place throughout that country, and he began to be in need. So he went and hired himself out to one of the citizens of that country, who sent him to his fields to feed the pigs. He would gladly have filled himself with the pods that the pigs were eating; and no one gave him anything. But when he came to himself he said, "How many of my father's hired hands have bread enough and to spare, but here I am dying of hunger! I will get up and go to my father, and I will say to him, 'Father, I have sinned against heaven and before you; I am no longer worthy to be called your son; treat me like one of your hired hands.'" So he set off and went to his father. But while he was still far off, his father saw him and was filled with compassion; he ran and put his arms around him and kissed him. Then the son said to him, "Father, I have sinned against heaven and before you; I am no longer worthy to be called your son." But the father said to his slaves, "Quickly, bring out a robe – the best one – and put it on him; put a ring on his finger and sandals on his feet. And get the fatted calf and kill it, and let us eat and celebrate; for this son of mine was dead and is alive again; he was lost and is found!" And they began to celebrate.

Now his elder son was in the field; and when he came and approached the house, he heard music and dancing. He called one of the slaves and asked what was going on. He replied, "Your brother has come, and your father has killed the fatted calf, because he has got him back safe and sound."
Then he became angry and refused to go in. His father came out and began to plead with him. But he answered his father, "Listen! For all these years I have been working like a slave for you, and I have never disobeyed your command; yet you have never given me even a young goat so that I might celebrate with my friends. But when this son of yours came back, who has devoured your property with prostitutes, you killed the fatted calf for him!" Then the father said to him, "Son, you are always with me, and all that is mine is yours. But we had to celebrate and rejoice, because this brother of yours was dead and has come to life; he was lost and has been found."'

Or

† MOTHERING SUNDAY

YEARS A B C

For text see Year A, pages 88–92.

LENT 5

YEAR C

FIRST READING

Isaiah 43.16–21

A reading from the book of the prophet Isaiah.

Thus says the LORD, who makes a way in the sea, a path in the mighty waters, who brings out chariot and horse, army and warrior; they lie down, they cannot rise, they are extinguished, quenched like a wick: Do not remember the former things, or consider the things of old. I am about to do a new thing; now it springs forth, do you not perceive it? I will make a way in the wilderness and rivers in the desert. The wild animals will honour me, the jackals and the ostriches; for I give water in the wilderness, rivers in the desert, to give drink to my chosen people, the people whom I formed for myself so that they might declare my praise.

PSALM

Psalm 126

℟ **The Lord has done great things for us
[and we are glad indeed].**

When the Lord restored the fortunes of Zion,
then were we like those who dream.
Then was our mouth filled with laughter,
and our tongue with shouts of joy. ℟

Then they said among the nations,
'The Lord has done great things for them.'
The Lord has done great things for us,
and we are glad indeed. ℟

Restore our fortunes, O Lord,
like the watercourses of the Negev.
Those who sowed with tears
will reap with songs of joy.
Those who go out weeping, carrying the seed,
will come again with joy, shouldering their sheaves. ℟

SECOND READING   **Philippians 3.4b–14**

A reading from the letter of Paul to the Philippians.

If anyone else has reason to be confident in the flesh, I have more: circumcised on the eighth day, a member of the people of Israel, of the tribe of Benjamin, a Hebrew born of Hebrews; as to the law, a Pharisee; as to zeal, a persecutor of the church; as to righteousness under the law, blameless.

Yet whatever gains I had, these I have come to regard as loss because of Christ. More than that, I regard everything as loss because of the surpassing value of knowing Christ Jesus my Lord. For his sake I have suffered the loss of all things, and I regard them as rubbish, in order that I may gain Christ and be found in him, not having a righteousness of my own that comes from the law, but one that comes through faith in Christ, the righteousness from God based on faith. I want to know Christ and the power of his resurrection and the sharing of his sufferings by becoming like him in his death, if somehow I may attain the resurrection from the dead.

Not that I have already obtained this or have already reached the goal; but I press on to make it my own, because Christ Jesus has made me his own. Beloved, I do not consider that I have made it my own; but this one thing I do: forgetting what lies behind and straining forward to what lies ahead, I press on towards the goal for the prize of the heavenly call of God in Christ Jesus.

GOSPEL   **John 12.1–8**

Hear the gospel of our Lord Jesus Christ according to John.

Six days before the Passover Jesus came to Bethany, the home of Lazarus, whom he had raised from the dead. There they gave a dinner for him. Martha served, and Lazarus was one of those at the table with him. Mary took a pound of costly perfume made of pure nard, anointed Jesus' feet, and wiped them with her hair. The house was filled with the fragrance of the perfume. But Judas Iscariot, one of his disciples (the one who was about to betray him), said, 'Why was this perfume not sold for three hundred denarii and the money given to the poor?' (He said this not because he cared about the poor, but because he was a thief; he kept the common purse and used to steal what was put into it.) Jesus said, 'Leave her alone. She bought it so that she might keep it for the day of my burial. You always have the poor with you, but you do not always have me.'

PALM SUNDAY (LENT 6)   YEAR C

LITURGY OF PALMS

GOSPEL   Luke 19.28–40

Hear the gospel of our Lord Jesus Christ according to Luke.

Jesus went on ahead, going up to Jerusalem.

When he had come near Bethphage and Bethany, at the place called the
Mount of Olives, he sent two of the disciples, saying,
'Go into the village ahead of you, and as you enter it you will find tied there
a colt that has never been ridden. Untie it and bring it here. If anyone asks
you, "Why are you untying it?" just say this, "The Lord needs it."'
So those who were sent departed and found it as he had told them. As they
were untying the colt, its owners asked them, 'Why are you untying the
colt?' They said, 'The Lord needs it.' Then they brought it to Jesus; and after
throwing their cloaks on the colt, they set Jesus on it. As he rode along,
people kept spreading their cloaks on the road. As he was now approaching
the path down from the Mount of Olives, the whole multitude of the
disciples began to praise God joyfully with a loud voice for all the deeds of
power that they had seen, saying,

'Blessed is the king who comes in the name of the Lord!
Peace in heaven,
and glory in the highest heaven!'
Some of the Pharisees in the crowd said to him, 'Teacher, order your disciples
to stop.' He answered, 'I tell you, if these were silent, the stones would shout
out.'

PSALM   Psalm 118.1–2, 19–29

℟ **This is the day that the Lord has made;
we will rejoice and be glad in it.**

Give thanks to the Lord, for he is good;
his mercy endures for ever.
Let Israel now proclaim,
'His mercy endures for ever.' ℟

Open for me the gates of righteousness;
I will enter them; I will offer thanks to the Lord.

'This is the gate of the Lord;
whoever is righteous may enter.' ℞

I will give thanks to you, for you answered me
and have become my salvation.
The same stone which the builders rejected
has become the chief corner-stone. ℞

This is the Lord's doing,
and it is marvellous in our eyes.
On this day the Lord has acted;
we will rejoice and be glad in it. ℞

Hosanna, Lord, hosanna!
Lord, send us now success.
Blessèd is he who comes in the name of the Lord;
we bless you from the house of the Lord. ℞

God is the Lord; he has shined upon us;
form a procession with branches
up to the horns of the altar.
'You are my God and I will thank you;
you are my God and I will exalt you.'
Give thanks to the Lord, for he is good;
his mercy endures for ever. ℞

LITURGY OF THE PASSION

FIRST READING   **Isaiah 50.4–9a**

A reading from the book of the prophet Isaiah.

The servant of the LORD said:
The Lord GOD has given me the tongue of a teacher,
that I may know how to sustain the weary with a word.
Morning by morning he wakens –
wakens my ear to listen as those who are taught.
The Lord GOD has opened my ear,
and I was not rebellious,
I did not turn backwards.
I gave my back to those who struck me,
and my cheeks to those who pulled out the beard;
I did not hide may face

from insult and spitting.
The Lord GOD helps me;
therefore I have not been disgraced;
therefore I have set my face like flint,
and I know that I shall not be be put to shame;
he who vindicates me is near.
Who will contend with me?
Let us stand up together.
Who are my adversaries?
Let them confront me.
It is the Lord GOD who helps me;
who will declare me guilty?

PSALM

Psalm 31.9–16

℞ **My God, my God, why have you forsaken me?**
  or
℞ **I have trusted in you.**
  You are my God.

Have mercy on me, O Lord, for I am in trouble;
my eye is consumed with sorrow,
and also my throat and my belly.
For my life is wasted with grief,
and my years with sighing;
my strength fails me because of affliction,
and my bones are consumed. ℞

I have become a reproach to all my enemies
and even to my neighbours,
a dismay to those of my acquaintance;
when they see me in the street they avoid me. ℞

I am forgotten like the dead, out of mind;
I am as useless as a broken pot.
For I have heard the whispering of the crowd;
fear is all around;
they put their heads together against me
they plot to take away my life ℞

But as for me, I have trusted in you, O Lord.
I have said, 'You are my God.
My times are in your hand;

rescue me from the hand of my enemies,
and from those who persecute me.
Make your face to shine upon your servant,
and in your loving-kindness save me.' ℟

SECOND READING   Philippians 2.5–11

A reading from the letter of Paul to the Philippians.

Let the same mind be in you that was in Christ Jesus,
who, though he was in the form of God,
did not regard equality with God
as something to be exploited,
but emptied himself,
taking the form of a slave,
being born in human likeness.
And being found in human form,
he humbled himself
and became obedient to the point of death –
even death on a cross.

Therefore God also highly exalted him
and gave him the name that is above every name,
so that at the name of Jesus every knee should bend,
in heaven and on earth and under the earth,
and every tongue should confess that Jesus Christ is Lord,
to the glory of God the Father.

PASSION (Long or short reading)
Luke 22.14 – 23.56 or Luke 23.1–49

Hear the passion of our Lord Jesus Christ according to Luke.

[Jesus took his place at the table, and the apostles with him. He said to them,
'I have eagerly desired to eat this Passover with you before I suffer; for I tell
you, I will not eat it until it is fulfilled in the kingdom of God.' Then he took
a cup, and after giving thanks he said, 'Take this and divide it among
yourselves; for I tell you that from now on I will not drink of the fruit of the
vine until the kingdom of God comes.' Then he took a loaf of bread, and
when he had given thanks, he broke it and gave it to them, saying, 'This is
my body, which is given for you. Do this in remembrance of me.' And he did

the same with the cup after supper, saying, 'This cup that is poured out for you is the new covenant in my blood. But see, the one who betrays me is with me, and his hand is on the table. For the Son of Man is going as it has been determined, but woe to that one by whom he is betrayed!' Then they began to ask one another, which one of them it could be who would do this.

A dispute also arose among them as to which one of them was to be regarded as the greatest. But he said to them, 'The kings of the Gentiles lord it over them; and those in authority over them are called benefactors. But not so with you; rather the greatest among you must become like the youngest, and the leader like one who serves. For who is greater, the one who is at the table or the one who serves? Is it not the one at the table? But I am among you as one who serves.

You are those who have stood by me in my trials; and I confer on you, just as my Father has conferred on me, a kingdom, so that you may eat and drink at my table in my kingdom, and you will sit on thrones judging the twelve tribes of Israel.

Simon, Simon, listen! Satan has demanded to sift all of you like wheat, but I have prayed for you that your own faith may not fail; and you, when once you have turned back, strengthen your brothers.' And he said to him, 'Lord, I am ready to go with you to prison and to death!' Jesus said, 'I tell you, Peter, the cock will not crow this day, until you have denied three times that you know me.'

He said to them, 'When I sent you out without a purse, bag, or sandals, did you lack anything?' They said, 'No, not a thing.' He said to them, 'But now, the one who has a purse must take it, and likewise a bag. And the one who has no sword must sell his cloak and buy one. For I tell you, this scripture must be fulfilled in me, "And he was counted among the lawless"; and indeed what is written about me is being fulfilled.' They said, 'Lord, look, here are two swords.' He replied, 'It is enough.'

He came out and went, as was his custom, to the Mount of Olives; and the disciples followed him. When he reached the place, he said to them, 'Pray that you may not come into the time of trial.' Then he withdrew from them about a stone's throw, knelt down, and prayed, 'Father, if you are willing, remove this cup from me; yet, not my will but yours be done.' Then an angel from heaven appeared to him and gave him strength. In his anguish he prayed more earnestly, and his sweat became like great drops of blood falling down on the ground. When he got up from prayer, he came to the disciples and found them sleeping because of grief, and he said to them, 'Why are you sleeping? Get up and pray that you may not come into the time of trial.'

While he was still speaking, suddenly a crowd came, and the one called Judas, one of the twelve, was leading them. He approached Jesus to kiss him; but Jesus said to him, 'Judas, is it with a kiss that you are betraying the Son of Man?' When those who were around him saw what was coming, they asked, 'Lord, should we strike with the sword?' Then one of them struck the slave of the high priest and cut off his right ear. But Jesus said, 'No more of this!' And he touched his ear and healed him. Then Jesus said to the chief priests, the officers of the temple police, and the elders who had come for him, 'Have you come out with swords and clubs as if I were a bandit? When I was with you day after day in the temple, you did not lay hands on me. But this is your hour, and the power of darkness!'

Then they seized him and led him away, bringing him into the high priest's house. But Peter was following at a distance. When they had kindled a fire in the middle of the courtyard and sat down together, Peter sat among them. Then a servant-girl, seeing him in the firelight, stared at him and said, 'This man also was with him.' But he denied it, saying, 'Woman, I do not know him.' A little later someone else, on seeing him, said, 'You also are one of them.' But Peter said, 'Man, I am not!' Then about an hour later still another kept insisting, 'Surely this man also was with him; for he is a Galilean.' But Peter said, 'Man, I do not know what you are talking about!' At that moment, while he was still speaking, the cock crowed. The Lord turned and looked at Peter. Then Peter remembered the word of the Lord, how he had said to him, 'Before the cock crows today, you will deny me three times.' And he went out and wept bitterly.

Now the men who were holding Jesus began to mock him and beat him; they also blindfolded him and kept asking him, 'Prophesy! Who is it that struck you?' They kept heaping many other insults on him.

When day came, the assembly of the elders of the people, both chief priests and scribes, gathered together, and they brought him to their council. They said, 'If you are the Messiah, tell us.' He replied, 'If I tell you, you will not believe; and if I question you, you will not answer. But from now on the Son of Man will be seated at the right hand of the power of God.' All of them asked, 'Are you, then, the Son of God?' He said to them, 'You say that I am.' Then they said, 'What further testimony do we need? We have heard it ourselves from his own lips!']

Then the assembly rose as a body and brought Jesus before Pilate. They began to accuse him, saying, 'We found this man perverting our nation, forbidding us to pay taxes to the emperor, and saying that he himself is the Messiah, a king.' Then Pilate asked him, 'Are you the king of the Jews?' He answered,

'You say so.' Then Pilate said to the chief priests and the crowds, 'I find no basis for an accusation against this man.' But they were insistent and said, 'He stirs up the people by teaching throughout all Judea, from Galilee where he began even to this place.'

When Pilate heard this, he asked whether the man was a Galilean. And when he learned that he was under Herod's jurisdiction, he sent him off to Herod, who was himself in Jerusalem at that time. When Herod saw Jesus, he was very glad, for he had been wanting to see him for a long time, because he had heard about him and was hoping to see him perform some sign. He questioned him at some length, but Jesus gave him no answer. The chief priests and the scribes stood by, vehemently accusing him. Even Herod with his soldiers treated him with contempt and mocked him; then he put an elegant robe on him, and sent him back to Pilate. That same day Herod and Pilate became friends with each other; before this they had been enemies.

Pilate then called together the chief priests, the leaders, and the people, and said to them, 'You brought me this man as one who was perverting the people; and here I have examined him in your presence and have not found this man guilty of any of your charges against him. Neither has Herod, for he sent him back to us. Indeed, he has done nothing to deserve death. I will therefore have him flogged and release him.' Now he was obliged to release someone for them at the festival.

Then they all shouted out together, 'Away with this fellow! Release Barabbas for us!' (This was a man who had been put in prison for an insurrection that had taken place in the city, and for murder.) Pilate, wanting to release Jesus, addressed them again; but they kept shouting, 'Crucify, crucify him!' A third time he said to them, 'Why, what evil has he done? I have found in him no ground for the sentence of death; I will therefore have him flogged and then release him.' But they kept urgently demanding with loud shouts that he should be crucified; and their voices prevailed. So Pilate gave his verdict that their demand should be granted. He released the man they asked for, the one who had been put in prison for insurrection and murder, and he handed Jesus over as they wished.

As they led him away, they seized a man, Simon of Cyrene, who was coming from the country, and they laid the cross on him, and made him carry it behind Jesus. A great number of the people followed him, and among them were women who were beating their breasts and wailing for him. But Jesus turned to them and said, 'Daughters of Jerusalem, do not weep for me, but weep for yourselves and for your children. For the days are surely coming when they will say, "Blessed are the barren, and the wombs that never bore, and the breasts that never nursed." Then they will begin to say to the mountains, "Fall on us"; and to the hills, "Cover us." For if they do this when the wood is green, what will happen when it is dry?'

Two others also, who were criminals, were led away to be put to death with him. When they came to the place that is called The Skull, they crucified Jesus there with the criminals, one on his right and one on his left. Then Jesus said, 'Father, forgive them; for they do not know what they are doing.' And they cast lots to divide his clothing. And the people stood by, watching; but the leaders scoffed at him, saying, 'He saved others; let him save himself if he is the Messiah of God, his chosen one!' The soldiers also mocked him, coming up and offering him sour wine, and saying, 'If you are the King of the Jews, save yourself!' There was also an inscription over him, 'This is the King of the Jews.'

One of the criminals who were hanged there kept deriding him and saying, 'Are you not the Messiah? Save yourself and us!' But the other rebuked him, saying, 'Do you not fear God, since you are under the same sentence of condemnation? And we indeed have been condemned justly, for we are getting what we deserve for our deeds, but this man has done nothing wrong.' Then he said, 'Jesus, remember me when you come into your kingdom.' Jesus replied, 'Truly I tell you, today you will be with me in Paradise.'

It was now about noon, and darkness came over the whole land until three in the afternoon, while the sun's light failed; and the curtain of the temple was torn in two. Then Jesus, crying with a loud voice, said, 'Father, into your hands I commend my spirit.' Having said this, he breathed his last. When the centurion saw what had taken place, he praised God and said, 'Certainly this man was innocent.' And when all the crowds who had gathered there for this spectacle saw what had taken place, they returned home, beating their breasts. But all his acquaintances, including the women who had followed him from Galilee, stood at a distance, watching these things.

[Now there was a good and righteous man named Joseph, who, though a member of the council, had not agreed to their plan and action. He came from the Jewish town of Arimathea, and he was waiting expectantly for the kingdom of God.

This man went to Pilate and asked for the body of Jesus. Then he took it down, wrapped it in a linen cloth, and laid it in a rock-hewn tomb where no one had ever been laid. It was the day of Preparation, and the sabbath was beginning. The women who had come with him from Galilee followed, and they saw the tomb and how his body was laid. Then they returned, and prepared spices and ointments. On the sabbath they rested according to the commandment.]

MONDAY, TUESDAY AND WEDNESDAY   YEARS A B C
IN HOLY WEEK, MAUNDY THURSDAY,
GOOD FRIDAY AND EASTER EVE

For texts see Year A, pages 104–106, 107–110, 110–112, 112–115, 115–124, 124–127.

EASTER VIGIL   YEARS A B C

For Old Testament readings and New Testament reading see Year A, pages 128–149.
Year C has its own Gospel.

GOSPEL   **YEAR C**   **Luke 24.1–12**

Hear the gospel of our Lord Jesus Christ according to Luke.

On the first day of the week, at early dawn, the women who had accompanied Jesus came to the tomb, taking the spices that they had prepared. They found the stone rolled away from the tomb, but when they went in they did not find the body. While they were perplexed about this, suddenly two men in dazzling clothes stood beside them. the women were terrified and bowed their faces to the ground but the men said to them, 'Why do you look for the living among the dead? He is not here, but has risen. Remember how he told you while he was still in Galilee, that the Son of Man must be handed over to sinners, and be crucified, and on the third day rise again.' Then they rememberd Jesus' words, and returning from the tomb, they told all this to the eleven and to all the rest. Now it was Mary Magdalene, Joanna, Mary the mother of James, and the other women with them who told this to the apostles. But these words seemed to them an idle tale, and they did not believe them. But Peter got up and ran to the tomb; stooping and looking in he saw the linen cloths by themselves; then he went home, amazed at what had happened.

EASTER DAY   YEAR C

The following readings and psalms are provided for use at the principal Easter Day Service.
Acts 10.34–43 should be read as either the First or Second Reading.

FIRST READING (Alternative readings)

Either   Acts 10.34–43

A reading from the Acts of the Apostles.

Peter began to speak to those assembled in the house of Cornelius 'I truly understand that God shows no partiality, but in every nation anyone who fears him and does what is right is acceptable to him. You know the message he sent to the people of Israel, preaching peace by Jesus Christ – he is Lord of all.

That message spread throughout Judea, beginning in Galilee after the baptism that John announced: how God anointed Jesus of Nazareth with the Holy Spirit and with power; how he went about doing good and healing all who were oppressed by the devil, for God was with him. We are witnesses to all that he did both in Judea and in Jerusalem. They put him to death by hanging him on a tree; but God raised him on the third day and allowed him to appear, not to all the people but to us who were chosen by God as witnesses, and who ate and drank with him after he rose from the dead. He commanded us to preach to the people and to testify that he is the one ordained by God as judge of the living and the dead. All the prophets testify about him that everyone who believes in him receives forgiveness of sins through his name.'

Or   Isaiah 65.17–25

A reading from the book of the prophet Isaiah

I am about to create new heavens and a new earth;
the former things shall not be remembered or come to mind.
But be glad and rejoice for ever in what I am creating;
for I am about to create Jerusalem as a joy,
and its people as a delight.
I will rejoice in Jerusalem, and delight in my people;
no more shall the sound of weeping be heard in it,
or the cry of distress.

No more shall there be in it an infant that lives but a few days,
or an old person who does not live out a lifetime;
for one who dies at a hundred years will be considered a youth,
and one who falls short of a hundred will be considered accursed.
They shall build houses and inhabit them;
they shall plant vineyards and eat their fruit.
They shall not build and another inhabit;
they shall not plant and another eat;
for like the days of a tree shall the days of my people be,
and my chosen shall long enjoy the work of their hands.
They shall not labour in vain,
or bear children for calamity;
for they shall be offspring blessed by the LORD –
and their descendants as well.
Before they call I will answer,
while they are yet speaking I will hear.
The wolf and the lamb shall feed together,
the lion shall eat straw like the ox;
but the serpent –
its food shall be dust!
They shall not hurt or destroy on all my holy mountain,
says the LORD.

PSALM   Psalm 118.1–2, 14–24

℟ **This is the day that the Lord has made;**
  we will rejoice and be glad in it.
  or
℟ **Give thanks to the Lord, for he is good;**
  his mercy endures for ever.

Give thanks to the Lord, for he is good;
his mercy endures for ever.
Let Israel now proclaim,
'His mercy endures for ever.' ℟

The Lord is my strength and my song,
and he has become my salvation.
There is a sound of exultation and victory
in the tents of the righteous:

'The right hand of the Lord has triumphed!
the right hand of the Lord is exalted!
the right hand of the Lord has triumphed!' ℞

I shall not die, but live,
and declare the works of the Lord.
The Lord has punished me sorely,
but he did not hand me over to death.
Open for me the gates of righteousness;
I will enter them; I will offer thanks to the Lord. ℞

'This is the gate of the Lord;
whoever is righteous may enter.'
I will give thanks to you, for you answered me
and have become my salvation.
The same stone which the builders rejected
has become the chief corner-stone. ℞

This is the Lord's doing,
and it is marvellous in our eyes.
On this day the Lord has acted;
we will rejoice and be glad in it. ℞

SECOND READING (Alternative readings)

Either   **1 Corinthians 15.19–26**

A reading from the first letter of Paul to the Corinthians.

If for this life only we have hoped in Christ, we are of all people most to be pitied.

But in fact Christ has been raised from the dead, the first fruits of those who have died. For since death came through a human being, the resurrection of the dead has also come through a human being; for as all die in Adam, so all will be made alive in Christ. But each in his own order: Christ the first fruits, then at his coming those who belong to Christ. Then comes the end, when he hands over the kingdom to God the Father, after he has destroyed every ruler and every authority and power. For he must reign until he has put all his enemies under his feet. The last enemy to be destroyed is death.

Or   **Acts 10.34–43**

A reading from the Acts of the Apostles.

For text see above, page 599.

GOSPEL (Alternative readings)

Either   **John 20.1–18**

Hear the gospel of our Lord Jesus Christ according to John.

Early on the first day of the week, while it was still dark, Mary Magdalene came to the tomb and saw that the stone had been removed from the tomb. So she ran and went to Simon Peter and the other disciple, the one whom Jesus loved, and said to them, 'They have taken the Lord out of the tomb, and we do not know where they have laid him.' Then Peter and the other disciple set out and went towards the tomb. The two were running together, but the other disciple outran Peter and reached the tomb first. He bent down to look in and saw the linen wrappings lying there, but he did not go in. Then Simon Peter came, following him, and went into the tomb. He saw the linen wrappings lying there, and the cloth that had been on Jesus' head, not lying with the linen wrappings but rolled up in a place by itself. Then the other disciple, who reached the tomb first, also went in, and he saw and believed; for as yet they did not understand the scripture, that he must rise from the dead. Then the disciples returned to their homes.

But Mary stood weeping outside the tomb. As she wept, she bent over to look into the tomb; and she saw two angels in white, sitting where the body of Jesus had been lying, one at the head and the other at the feet. They said to her, 'Woman, why are you weeping?' She said to them, 'They have taken away my Lord, and I do not know where they have laid him.' When she had said this, she turned around and saw Jesus standing there, but she did not know that it was Jesus. Jesus said to her, 'Woman, why are you weeping? For whom are you looking?' Supposing him to be the gardener, she said to him, 'Sir, if you have carried him away, tell me where you have laid him, and I will take him away.' Jesus said to her, 'Mary!' She turned and said to him in Hebrew, 'Rabbouni!' (which means Teacher). Jesus said to her, 'Do not hold on to me, because I have not yet ascended to the Father. But go to my brothers and say to them, "I am ascending to my Father and your Father, to my God and your God."' Mary Magdalene went and announced to the disciples, 'I have seen the Lord'; and she told them that he had said these things to her.

Or   **Luke 24.1–12**

Hear the gospel of our Lord Jesus Christ according to Luke.

On the first day of the week, at early dawn, the women who had
accompanied Jesus came to the tomb, taking the spices that they had
prepared. They found the stone rolled away from the tomb, but when they
went in, they did not find the body. While they were perplexed about this,
suddenly two men in dazzling clothes stood beside them. The women were
terrified and bowed their faces to the ground, but the men said to them,
'Why do you look for the living among the dead? He is not here, but has
risen. Remember how he told you, while he was still in Galilee, that the Son
of Man must be handed over to sinners, and be crucified, and on the third
day rise again.' Then they remembered Jesus' words, and returning from the
tomb, they told all this to the eleven and to all the rest. Now it was Mary
Magdalene, Joanna, Mary the mother of James, and the other women with
them who told this to the apostles. But these words seemed to them an idle
tale, and they did not believe them. But Peter got up and ran to the tomb;
stooping and looking in, he saw the linen cloths by themselves; then he went
home, amazed at what had happened.

OLD TESTAMENT READINGS FOR SUNDAYS IN EASTERTIDE

*For those who require an Old Testament reading on the Sundays in Eastertide, provision is
made in the Supplement, pages 831–844 (Church of England) or 844–857
(Church of Ireland/Church in Wales). If these are used, the reading from Acts must be used as
the Second Reading.*

EASTER 2   YEAR C

FIRST READING   Acts 5.27–32

A reading from the Acts of the Apostles.

When the temple police had brought the apostles, they made them stand
before the council. The high priest questioned them, saying, 'We gave you
strict orders not to teach in this name, yet here you have filled Jerusalem
with your teaching and you are determined to bring this man's blood on us.'
But Peter and the apostles answered, 'We must obey God rather than any
human authority. The God of our ancestors raised up Jesus, whom you had
killed by hanging him on a tree. God exalted him at his right hand as Leader

and Saviour that he might give repentance to Israel and forgiveness of sins.
And we are witnesses to these things, and so is the Holy Spirit whom God has
given to those who obey him.'

PSALM

Either   Psalm 118.14–29

℟ **This is the day that the Lord has made;**
  we will rejoice and be glad in it.
  or
℟ **Give thanks to the Lord, for he is good;**
  his mercy endures for ever.

The Lord is my strength and my song,
and he has become my salvation.
There is a sound of exultation and victory
in the tents of the righteous:
'The right hand of the Lord has triumphed!
the right hand of the Lord is exalted!
the right hand of the Lord has triumphed!' ℟

I shall not die, but live,
and declare the works of the Lord.
The Lord has punished me sorely,
but he did not hand me over to death.
Open for me the gates of righteousness;
I will enter them; I will offer thanks to the Lord. ℟

'This is the gate of the Lord;
whoever is righteous may enter.'
I will give thanks to you, for you answered me
and have become my salvation.
The same stone which the builders rejected
has become the chief corner-stone.
This is the Lord's doing,
and it is marvellous in our eyes. ℟

On this day the Lord has acted;
we will rejoice and be glad in it.
Hosanna, Lord, hosanna!
Lord, send us now success.

Blessèd is he who comes in the name of the Lord;
we bless you from the house of the Lord. ℟

God is the Lord; he has shined upon us;
form a procession with branches
up to the horns of the altar.
'You are my God and I will thank you;
you are my God and I will exalt you.'
Give thanks to the Lord, for he is good;
his mercy endures for ever. ℟

Or   **Psalm 150**

℟ **Praise God in his holy temple.**

Alleluia!
Praise God in his holy temple;
Praise him in the firmament of his power.
Praise him for his mighty acts;
praise him for his excellent greatness. ℟

Praise him with the blast of the ram's-horn;
praise him with lyre and harp.
Praise him with timbrel and dance;
praise him with strings and pipe. ℟

Praise him with resounding cymbals;
praise him with loud-clanging cymbals.
Let everything that has breath
praise the Lord. Alleluia! ℟

SECOND READING   **Revelation 1.4–8**

A reading from the book of Revelation.

John to the seven churches that are in Asia: Grace to you and peace from him
who is and who was and who is to come, and from the seven spirits who are
before his throne, and from Jesus Christ, the faithful witness, the firstborn of
the dead, and the ruler of the kings of the earth. To him who loves us and
freed us from our sins by his blood, and made us to be a kingdom, priests
serving his God and Father, to him be glory and dominion for ever and ever.
Amen.

Look! He is coming with the clouds;
every eye will see him,
even those who pierced him;
and on his account all the tribes of the earth will wail.
So it is to be. Amen.
'I am the Alpha and the Omega,' says the Lord God, who is and who was and
who is to come, the Almighty.

GOSPEL   John 20.19-31

Hear the gospel of our Lord Jesus Christ according to John.

It was evening on the first day of the week, and the doors of the house where
the disciples had met were locked for fear of the Jews. Jesus came and stood
among them and said, 'Peace be with you.' After he said this, he showed
them his hands and his side. Then the disciples rejoiced when they saw the
Lord. Jesus said to them again, 'Peace be with you. As the Father has sent me,
so I send you.' When he had said this, he breathed on them and said to
them, 'Receive the Holy Spirit. If you forgive the sins of any, they are forgiven
them; if you retain the sins of any, they are retained.'

But Thomas (who was called the Twin), one of the twelve, was not with them
when Jesus came. So the other disciples told him, 'We have seen the Lord.'
But he said to them, 'Unless I see the mark of the nails in his hands, and put
my finger in the mark of the nails and my hand in his side, I will not
believe.'

A week later his disciples were again in the house, and Thomas was with
them. Although the doors were shut, Jesus came and stood among them and
said, 'Peace be with you.' Then he said to Thomas, 'Put your finger here and
see my hands. Reach out your hand and put it in my side. Do not doubt but
believe.' Thomas answered him, 'My Lord and my God!' Jesus said to him,
'Have you believed because you have seen me? Blessed are those who have
not seen and yet have come to believe.'

Now Jesus did many other signs in the presence of his disciples, which are
not written in this book. But these are written so that you may come to
believe that Jesus is the Messiah, the Son of God, and that through believing
you may have life in his name.

EASTER 3 {: .left} YEAR C {: .right}

EASTER 3   **YEAR C**

FIRST READING (Short or long reading)   **Acts 9.1–6, (7–20)**

A reading from the Acts of the Apostles.

Saul, still breathing threats and murder against the disciples of the Lord, went to the high priest and asked him for letters to the synagogues at Damascus, so that if he found any who belonged to the Way, men or women, he might bring them bound to Jerusalem. Now as he was going along and approaching Damascus, suddenly a light from heaven flashed around him. He fell to the ground and heard a voice saying to him, 'Saul, Saul, why do you persecute me?' He asked, 'Who are you, Lord?' The reply came, 'I am Jesus, whom you are persecuting. But get up and enter the city, and you will be told what you are to do.' [The men who were travelling with him stood speechless because they heard the voice but saw no one. Saul got up from the ground, and though his eyes were open, he could see nothing; so they led him by the hand and brought him into Damascus. For three days he was without sight, and neither ate nor drank.

Now there was a disciple in Damascus named Ananias. The Lord said to him in a vision, 'Ananias.' He answered, 'Here I am, Lord.' The Lord said to him, 'Get up and go to the street called Straight, and at the house of Judas look for a man of Tarsus named Saul. At this moment he is praying, and he has seen in a vision a man named Ananias come in and lay his hands on him so that he might regain his sight.' But Ananias answered, 'Lord, I have heard from many about this man, how much evil he has done to your saints in Jerusalem; and here he has authority from the chief priests to bind all who invoke your name.' But the Lord said to him, 'Go, for he is an instrument whom I have chosen to bring my name before Gentiles and kings and before the people of Israel; I myself will show him how much he must suffer for the sake of my name.' So Ananias went and entered the house. He laid his hands on Saul and said, 'Brother Saul, the Lord Jesus, who appeared to you on your way here, has sent me so that you may regain your sight and be filled with the Holy Spirit.' And immediately something like scales fell from his eyes, and his sight was restored. Then he got up and was baptized, and after taking some food, he regained his strength.

For several days he was with the disciples in Damascus, and immediately he began to proclaim Jesus in the synagogues, saying, 'He is the Son of God.']

PSALM   **Psalm 30**

℟ **I will exalt you, O Lord,**
   because you have lifted me up.
   or
℟ **You have made me, Lord, as strong as the mountains.**

I will exalt you, O Lord,
because you have lifted me up
and have not let my enemies triumph over me.
O Lord my God, I cried out to you,
and you restored me to health.
You brought me up, O Lord, from the dead;
you restored my life as I was going down to the grave. ℟

Sing to the Lord, you servants of his;
give thanks for the remembrance of his holiness.
For his wrath endures but the twinkling of an eye,
his favour for a lifetime.
Weeping may spend the night,
but joy comes in the morning. ℟

While I felt secure, I said,
'I shall never be disturbed.
You, Lord, with your favour,
made me as strong as the mountains.'
Then you hid your face,
and I was filled with fear. ℟

I cried to you, O Lord;
I pleaded with the Lord, saying,
'What profit is there in my blood,
if I go down to the Pit?
will the dust praise you or declare your faithfulness?
Hear, O Lord, and have mercy upon me;
O Lord, be my helper.' ℟

You have turned my wailing into dancing;
you have put off my sack-cloth and clothed me with joy;
Therefore my heart sings to you without ceasing;
O Lord my God, I will give you thanks for ever. ℟

SECOND READING   **Revelation 5.11–14**

A reading from the book of Revelation.

I, John, looked, and I heard the voice of many angels surrounding the throne
and the living creatures and the elders; they numbered myriads of myriads
and thousands of thousands,
singing with full voice,
'Worthy is the Lamb that was slaughtered
to receive power and wealth and wisdom and might
and honour and glory and blessing!'
Then I heard every creature in heaven and on earth
and under the earth and in the sea,
and all that is in them, singing,
'To the one seated on the throne and to the Lamb
be blessing and honour and glory and might
for ever and ever!' And the four living creatures said, 'Amen!'
And the elders fell down and worshipped.

GOSPEL   **John 21.1–19**

Hear the gospel of our Lord Jesus Christ according to John.

Jesus showed himself again to the disciples by the Sea of Tiberias; and he
showed himself in this way. Gathered there together were Simon Peter,
Thomas called the Twin, Nathanael of Cana in Galilee, the sons of Zebedee,
and two others of his disciples. Simon Peter said to them, 'I am going
fishing.' They said to him, 'We will go with you.' They went out and got into
the boat, but that night they caught nothing.

Just after daybreak, Jesus stood on the beach; but the disciples did not know
that it was Jesus. Jesus said to them, 'Children, you have no fish, have you?'
They answered him, 'No.' He said to them, 'Cast the net to the right side of
the boat, and you will find some.' So they cast it, and now they were not able
to haul it in because there were so many fish. That disciple whom Jesus loved
said to Peter, 'It is the Lord!' When Simon Peter heard that it was the Lord, he
put on some clothes, for he was naked, and jumped into the lake. But the
other disciples came in the boat, dragging the net full of fish, for they were
not far from the land, only about a hundred yards off.

When they had gone ashore, they saw a charcoal fire there, with fish on it,
and bread. Jesus said to them, 'Bring some of the fish that you have just
caught.' So Simon Peter went aboard and hauled the net ashore, full of large

fish, a hundred and fifty-three of them; and though there were so many, the net was not torn. Jesus said to them, 'Come and have breakfast.' Now none of the disciples dared to ask him, 'Who are you?' because they knew it was the Lord. Jesus came and took the bread and gave it to them, and did the same with the fish. This was now the third time that Jesus appeared to the disciples after he was raised from the dead.

When they had finished breakfast, Jesus said to Simon Peter, 'Simon son of John, do you love me more than these?' He said to him, 'Yes, Lord; you know that I love you.' Jesus said to him, 'Feed my lambs.' A second time he said to him, 'Simon son of John, do you love me?' He said to him, 'Yes, Lord; you know that I love you.' Jesus said to him, 'Tend my sheep.' He said to him the third time, 'Simon son of John, do you love me?' Peter felt hurt because he said to him the third time, 'Do you love me?' And he said to him, 'Lord, you know everything; you know that I love you.' Jesus said to him, 'Feed my sheep. Very truly, I tell you, when you were younger, you used to fasten your own belt and go wherever you wished. But when you grow old, you will stretch out your hands, and someone else will fasten a belt around you and take you where you do not wish to go.' He said this to indicate the kind of death by which he would glorify God. After this he said to him, 'Follow me.'

EASTER 4   YEAR C

FIRST READING   Acts 9.36–43

A reading from the Acts of the Apostles.

In Joppa there was a disciple whose name was Tabitha, which in Greek is Dorcas. She was devoted to good works and acts of charity. At that time she became ill and died. When they had washed her, they laid her in a room upstairs. Since Lydda was near Joppa, the disciples, who heard that Peter was there, sent two men to him with the request, 'Please come to us without delay.' So Peter got up and went with them; and when he arrived, they took him to the room upstairs. All the widows stood beside him, weeping and showing tunics and other clothing that Dorcas had made while she was with them. Peter put all of them outside, and then he knelt down and prayed. He turned to the body and said, 'Tabitha, get up.' Then she opened her eyes, and seeing Peter, she sat up. He gave her his hand and helped her up. Then calling the saints and widows, he showed her to be alive. This became known throughout Joppa, and many believed in the Lord. Meanwhile he stayed in Joppa for some time with a certain Simon, a tanner.

PSALM   Psalm 23

℟ **The Lord is my shepherd;**
I shall not be in want.

The Lord is my shepherd;
I shall not be in want.
He makes me lie down in green pastures
and leads me beside still waters. ℟

He revives my soul
and guides me along right pathways for his name's sake.
Though I walk through the valley of the shadow of death,
I shall fear no evil;
for you are with me;
your rod and your staff, they comfort me. ℟

You spread a table before me
in the presence of those who trouble me;
you have anointed my head with oil,
and my cup is running over.
Surely your goodness and mercy shall follow me
all the days of my life,
and I will dwell in the house of the Lord for ever. ℟

SECOND READING   Revelation 7.9–17

A reading from the book of Revelation.

After this I looked, and there was a great multitude that no one could count,
from every nation, from all tribes and peoples and languages, standing before
the throne and before the Lamb, robed in white, with palm branches in their
hands. They cried out in a loud voice, saying
'Salvation belongs to our God who is seated on the throne,
and to the Lamb!'
And all the angels stood around the throne and around the elders and the
four living creatures, and they fell on their faces before the throne and
worshipped God,
singing, 'Amen! Blessing and glory and wisdom and thanksgiving
and honour and power and might be to our God for ever and ever! Amen.'
Then one of the elders addressed me, saying, 'Who are these, robed in white,
and where have they come from?' I said to him, 'Sir, you are the one that

knows.' Then he said to me, 'These are they who have come out of the great ordeal; they have washed their robes and made them white in the blood of the Lamb.
For this reason they are before the throne of God,
and worship him day and night within his temple,
and the one who is seated on the throne will shelter them.
They will hunger no more, and thirst no more;
the sun will not strike them, nor any scorching heat;
for the Lamb at the centre of the throne will be their shepherd,
and he will guide them to springs of the water of life,
and God will wipe away every tear from their eyes.'

GOSPEL   John 10.22–30

Hear the gospel of our Lord Jesus Christ according to John.

At that time the festival of the Dedication took place in Jerusalem.
It was winter,

and Jesus was walking in the temple, in the portico of Solomon. So the Jews gathered around him and said to him, 'How long will you keep us in suspense? If you are the Messiah, tell us plainly.' Jesus answered, 'I have told you, and you do not believe. The works that I do in my Father's name testify to me; but you do not believe, because you do not belong to my sheep. My sheep hear my voice. I know them, and they follow me. I give them eternal life, and they will never perish. No one will snatch them out of my hand. What my Father has given me is greater than all else, and no one can snatch it out of the Father's hand. The Father and I are one.'

EASTER 5   YEAR C

FIRST READING   Acts 11.1–18

A reading from the Acts of the Apostles.

The apostles and the believers who were in Judea heard that the Gentiles had also accepted the word of God. So when Peter went up to Jerusalem, the circumcised believers criticized him, saying, 'Why did you go to uncircumcised men and eat with them?' Then Peter began to explain it to them, step by step, saying, 'I was in the city of Joppa praying, and in a trance

I saw a vision. There was something like a large sheet coming down from heaven, being lowered by its four corners; and it came close to me. As I looked at it closely I saw four-footed animals, beasts of prey, reptiles, and birds of the air. I also heard a voice saying to me, "Get up, Peter; kill and eat." But I replied, "By no means, Lord; for nothing profane or unclean has ever entered my mouth." But a second time the voice answered from heaven, "What God has made clean, you must not call profane." This happened three times; then everything was pulled up again to heaven. At that very moment three men, sent to me from Caesarea, arrived at the house where we were. The Spirit told me to go with them and not to make a distinction between them and us. These six brothers also accompanied me, and we entered the man's house. He told us how he had seen the angel standing in his house and saying, "Send to Joppa and bring Simon, who is called Peter; he will give you a message by which you and your entire household will be saved." And as I began to speak, the Holy Spirit fell upon them just as it had upon us at the beginning. And I remembered the word of the Lord, how he had said, "John baptized with water, but you will be baptized with the Holy Spirit." If then God gave them the same gift that he gave us when we believed in the Lord Jesus Christ, who was I that I could hinder God?' When they heard this, they were silenced. And they praised God, saying, 'Then God has given even to the Gentiles the repentance that leads to life.'

PSALM   Psalm 148

℟ **Praise, O praise the name of the Lord.**

Alleluia!
Praise the Lord from the heavens;
praise him in the heights.
Praise him, all you angels of his;
praise him, all his host.
Praise him, sun and moon;
praise him, all you shining stars. ℟

Praise him, heaven of heavens,
and you waters above the heavens.
Let them praise the name of the Lord;
 for he commanded and they were created.
He made them stand fast for ever and ever;
he gave them a law which shall not pass away. ℟

Praise the Lord from the earth,
you sea-monsters and all deeps;
Fire and hail, snow and fog,
tempestuous wind, doing his will;
Mountains and all hills,
fruit trees and all cedars;
Wild beasts and all cattle,
creeping things and winged birds; ℟

Kings of the earth and all peoples,
princes and all rulers of the world;
Young men and maidens,
old and young together.
Let them praise the name of the Lord,
for his name only is exalted,
his splendour is over earth and heaven. ℟

He has raised up strength for his people
and praise for all his loyal servants,
the children of Israel, a people who are near him.
Alleluia! ℟

SECOND READING   Revelation 21.1–6

A reading from the book of Revelation.

I, John, saw a new heaven and a new earth; for the first heaven and the first
earth had passed away, and the sea was no more. And I saw the holy city, the
new Jerusalem, coming down out of heaven from God, prepared as a bride
adorned for her husband. And I heard a loud voice from the throne saying,
'See, the home of God is among mortals.
He will dwell with them;
they will be his peoples,
and God himself will be with them;
he will wipe every tear from their eyes.
Death will be no more;
mourning and crying and pain will be no more,
for the first things have passed away.'
And the one who was seated on the throne said, 'See, I am making all things
new.' Also he said, 'Write this, for these words are trustworthy and true.'
Then he said to me, 'It is done! I am the Alpha and the Omega, the

beginning and the end. To the thirsty I will give water as a gift from the spring of the water of life.'

GOSPEL   John 13.31–35

Hear the gospel of our Lord Jesus Christ according to John.

During the supper, when Judas had gone out, Jesus said, 'Now the Son of Man has been glorified, and God has been glorified in him. If God has been glorified in him, God will also glorify him in himself and will glorify him at once. Little children, I am with you only a little longer. You will look for me; and as I said to the Jews so now I say to you, "Where I am going, you cannot come." I give you a new commandment, that you love one another. Just as I have loved you, you also should love one another. By this everyone will know that you are my disciples, if you have love for one another.'

EASTER 6   YEAR C

FIRST READING   Acts 16.9–15

A reading from the Acts of the Apostles.

During the night Paul had a vision: there stood a man of Macedonia pleading with him and saying, 'Come over to Macedonia and help us.' When he had seen the vision, we immediately tried to cross over to Macedonia, being convinced that God had called us to proclaim the good news to them.

We set sail from Troas and took a straight course to Samothrace, the following day to Neapolis, and from there to Philippi, which is a leading city of the district of Macedonia and a Roman colony. We remained in this city for some days. On the sabbath day we went outside the gate by the river, where we supposed there was a place of prayer; and we sat down and spoke to the women who had gathered there. A certain woman named Lydia, a worshipper of God, was listening to us; she was from the city of Thyatira and a dealer in purple cloth. The Lord opened her heart to listen eagerly to what was said by Paul. When she and her household were baptized, she urged us, saying, 'If you have judged me to be faithful to the Lord, come and stay at my home.' And she prevailed upon us.

PSALM   Psalm 67

℟ **Let the peoples praise you, O God,**
  let all the peoples praise you.

May God be merciful to us and bless us,
show us the light of his countenance and come to us.
Let your ways be known upon earth,
your saving health among all nations. ℟

[Let the peoples praise you, O God;
let all the peoples praise you.]

Let the nations be glad and sing for joy,
for you judge the peoples with equity
and guide all the nations upon earth. ℟

[Let the peoples praise you, O God;
let all the peoples praise you.]

The earth has brought forth her increase;
may God, our own God, give us his blessing.
May God give us his blessing,
and may all the ends of the earth stand in awe of him. ℟

SECOND READING   Revelation 21.10, 22 – 22.5

A reading from the book of Revelation.

In the spirit the angel carried me away to a great, high mountain and showed
me the holy city Jerusalem coming down out of heaven from God.

I saw no temple in the city, for its temple is the Lord God the Almighty and
the Lamb. And the city has no need of sun or moon to shine on it, for the
glory of God is its light, and its lamp is the Lamb. The nations will walk by its
light, and the kings of the earth will bring their glory into it. Its gates will
never be shut by day – and there will be no night there. People will bring into
it the glory and the honour of the nations. But nothing unclean will enter it,
nor anyone who practices abomination or falsehood, but only those who are
written in the Lamb's book of life.

Then the angel showed me the river of the water of life, bright as crystal,
flowing from the throne of God and of the Lamb through the middle of the
street of the city. On either side of the river is the tree of life with its twelve
kinds of fruit, producing its fruit each month; and the leaves of the tree are

for the healing of the nations. Nothing accursed will be found there any more. But the throne of God and of the Lamb will be in it, and his servants will worship him; they will see his face, and his name will be on their foreheads. And there will be no more night; they need no light of lamp or sun, for the Lord God will be their light, and they will reign for ever and ever.

GOSPEL (Alternative readings)

Either   John 14.23–29

Hear the gospel of our Lord Jesus Christ according to John.

Jesus said to his disciples: 'Those who love me will keep my word, and my Father will love them, and we will come to them and make our home with them. Whoever does not love me does not keep my words; and the word that you hear is not mine, but is from the Father who sent me.

I have said these things to you while I am still with you. But the Advocate, the Holy Spirit, whom the Father will send in my name, will teach you everything, and remind you of all that I have said to you. Peace I leave with you; my peace I give to you. I do not give to you as the world gives. Do not let your hearts be troubled, and do not let them be afraid. You heard me say to you, "I am going away, and I am coming to you." If you loved me, you would rejoice that I am going to the Father, because the Father is greater than I. And now I have told you this before it occurs, so that when it does occur, you may believe.'

Or   John 5.1–9

Hear the gospel of our Lord Jesus Christ according to John.

After this there was a festival of the Jews, and Jesus went up to Jerusalem.

Now in Jerusalem by the Sheep Gate there is a pool, called in Hebrew Beth-zatha, which has five porticoes. In these lay many invalids – blind, lame, and paralysed. One man was there who had been ill for thirty-eight years. When Jesus saw him lying there and knew that he had been there a long time, he said to him, 'Do you want to be made well?' The sick man answered him, 'Sir, I have no one to put me into the pool when the water is stirred up; and while I am making my way, someone else steps down ahead of me.' Jesus said to him, 'Stand up, take your mat and walk.' At once the man was made well, and he took up his mat and began to walk. Now that day was a sabbath.

ASCENSION DAY   YEARS A B C

For text see Year A, pages 165–169.

EASTER 7   YEAR C

FIRST READING   Acts 16.16–34

A reading from the Acts of the Apostles.

One day, as we were going to the place of prayer, we met a slave-girl who had
a spirit of divination and brought her owners a great deal of money by
fortune-telling. While she followed Paul and us, she would cry out, 'These
men are slaves of the Most High God, who proclaim to you a way of
salvation.' She kept doing this for many days. But Paul, very much annoyed,
turned and said to the spirit, 'I order you in the name of Jesus Christ to come
out of her.' And it came out that very hour. But when her owners saw that
their hope of making money was gone, they seized Paul and Silas and
dragged them into the market-place before the authorities. When they had
brought them before the magistrates, they said, 'These men are disturbing
our city; they are Jews and are advocating customs that are not lawful for us
as Romans to adopt or observe.' The crowd joined in attacking them, and the
magistrates had them stripped of their clothing and ordered them to be
beaten with rods. After they had given them a severe flogging, they threw
them into prison and ordered the jailer to keep them securely. Following
these instructions, he put them in the innermost cell and fastened their feet
in the stocks.

About midnight Paul and Silas were praying and singing hymns to God, and
the prisoners were listening to them. Suddenly there was an earthquake, so
violent that the foundations of the prison were shaken; and immediately all
the doors were opened and everyone's chains were unfastened. When the
jailer woke up and saw the prison doors wide open, he drew his sword and
was about to kill himself, since he supposed that the prisoners had escaped.
But Paul shouted in a loud voice, 'Do not harm yourself, for we are all here.'
The jailer called for lights, and rushing in, he fell down trembling before Paul
and Silas. Then he brought them outside and said, 'Sirs, what must I do to be
saved?' They answered, 'Believe on the Lord Jesus, and you will be saved, you
and your household.' They spoke the word of the Lord to him and to all who
were in his house. At the same hour of the night he took them and washed

their wounds; then he and his entire family were baptized without delay. He brought them up into the house and set food before them; and he and his entire household rejoiced that he had become a believer in God.

PSALM   **Psalm 97**

℟ **The Lord is king,**
   most high over all the earth.

The Lord is king; let the earth rejoice;
let the multitude of the isles be glad.
Clouds and darkness are round about him,
righteousness and justice
are the foundations of his throne.
A fire goes before him
and burns up his enemies on every side. ℟

His lightnings light up the world;
the earth sees it and is afraid.
The mountains melt like wax
at the presence of the Lord,
at the presence of the Lord of the whole earth.
The heavens declare his righteousness,
and all the peoples see his glory. ℟

Confounded be all who worship carved images
and delight in false gods!
Bow down before him, all you gods.
Zion hears and is glad and the cities of Judah rejoice,
because of your judgements, O Lord.
For you are the Lord: most high over all the earth;
you are exalted far above all gods. ℟

The Lord loves those who hate evil;
he preserves the lives of his saints
and delivers them from the hand of the wicked.

Light has sprung up for the righteous,
and joyful gladness for those who are true-hearted.
Rejoice in the Lord, you righteous,
and give thanks to his holy name. ℟

SECOND READING   Revelation 22.12–14, 16–17, 20–21

A reading from the book of Revelation.

I, John, heard a voice saying to me: 'See, I am coming soon; my reward is with me, to repay according to everyone's work. I am the Alpha and the Omega, the first and the last, the beginning and the end.'

Blessed are those who wash their robes, so that they will have the right to the tree of life and may enter the city by the gates.

'It is I, Jesus, who sent my angel to you with this testimony for the churches. I am the root and the descendant of David, the bright morning star.'
The Spirit and the bride say, 'Come.'
And let everyone who hears say, 'Come.'
And let everyone who is thirsty come.
Let anyone who wishes take the water of life as a gift.

The one who testifies to these things says,
'Surely I am coming soon.'
Amen. Come, Lord Jesus!

The grace of the Lord Jesus be with all the saints. Amen.

GOSPEL   John 17.20–26

Hear the gospel of our Lord Jesus Christ according to John.

Jesus looked up to heaven and prayed: 'Holy Father,
I ask not only on behalf of these, but also on behalf of those who will believe in me through their word, that they may all be one. As you, Father, are in me and I am in you, may they also be in us, so that the world may believe that you have sent me. The glory that you have given me I have given them, so that they may be one, as we are one, I in them and you in me, that they may become completely one, so that the world may know that you have sent me and have loved them even as you have loved me. Father, I desire that those also, whom you have given me, may be with me where I am, to see my glory, which you have given me because you loved me before the foundation of the world.

Righteous Father, the world does not know you, but I know you; and these know that you have sent me. I made your name known to them, and I will make it known, so that the love with which you have loved me may be in them, and I in them.'

PENTECOST (WHITSUNDAY)   YEAR C

The reading from Acts must be used as either the First or Second Reading.

FIRST READING (Alternative readings)

Either   **Acts 2.1–21**

A reading from the Acts of the Apostles.

When the day of Pentecost had come, they were all together in one place. And suddenly from heaven there came a sound like the rush of a violent wind, and it filled the entire house where they were sitting. Divided tongues, as of fire, appeared among them, and a tongue rested on each of them. All of them were filled with the Holy Spirit and began to speak in other languages, as the Spirit gave them ability.

Now there were devout Jews from every nation under heaven living in Jerusalem. And at this sound the crowd gathered and was bewildered, because each one heard them speaking in their native language. Amazed and astonished, they asked, 'Are not all these who are speaking Galileans? And how is it that we hear, each of us, in our own native language? Parthians, Medes, Elamites, and residents of Mesopotamia, Judea and Cappadocia, Pontus and Asia, Phrygia and Pamphylia, Egypt and the parts of Libya belonging to Cyrene, and visitors from Rome, both Jews and proselytes, Cretans and Arabs – in our own languages we hear them speaking about God's deeds of power.' All were amazed and perplexed, saying to one another, 'What does this mean?' But others sneered and said, 'They are filled with new wine.'

But Peter, standing with the eleven, raised his voice and addressed them, 'Men of Judea and all who live in Jerusalem, let this be known to you, and listen to what I say. Indeed, these are not drunk, as you suppose, for it is only nine o'clock in the morning. No, this is what was spoken through the prophet Joel: "In the last days it will be, God declares, that I will pour out my Spirit upon all flesh, and your sons and your daughters shall prophesy, and your young men shall see visions, and your old men shall dream dreams. Even upon my slaves, both men and women, in those days I will pour out my Spirit; and they shall prophesy. And I will show portents in the heaven above and signs on the earth below, blood, and fire, and smoky mist. The sun shall be turned to darkness and the moon to blood, before the coming of the Lord's great and glorious day. Then everyone who calls on the name of the Lord shall be saved."'

Or   **Genesis 11.1–9**

A reading from the book of Genesis.

Now the whole earth had one language and the same words. And as they migrated from the east, they came upon a plain in the land of Shinar and settled there. And they said to one another, 'Come, let us make bricks, and burn them thoroughly.' And they had brick for stone, and bitumen for mortar. Then they said, 'Come, let us build ourselves a city, and a tower with its top in the heavens, and let us make a name for ourselves; otherwise we shall be scattered abroad upon the face of the whole earth.' The LORD came down to see the city and the tower, which mortals had built. And the LORD said, 'Look, they are one people, and they have all one language; and this is only the beginning of what they will do; nothing that they propose to do will now be impossible for them. Come, let us go down, and confuse their language there, so that they will not understand one another's speech.' So the LORD scattered them abroad from there over the face of all the earth, and they left off building the city. Therefore it was called Babel, because there the LORD confused the language of all the earth; and from there the LORD scattered them abroad over the face of all the earth.

PSALM   **Psalm 104.25–35, 37**

℟ **Send forth your Spirit, O Lord,**
   and renew the face of the earth.

O Lord, how manifold are your works!
in wisdom you have made them all;
the earth is full of your creatures. ℟

Yonder is the great and wide sea
with its living things too many to number,
creatures both small and great.
There move the ships,
and there is that Leviathan,
which you have made for the sport of it. ℟

All of them look to you
to give them their food in due season.
You give it to them, they gather it;
you open your hand and they are filled with good things.
You hide your face and they are terrified;
you take away their breath
and they die and return to their dust. ℟

You send forth your Spirit and they are created;
and so you renew the face of the earth.
May the glory of the Lord endure for ever;
may the Lord rejoice in all his works.
He looks at the earth and it trembles;
he touches the mountains and they smoke. ℟

I will sing to the Lord as long as I live;
I will praise my God while I have my being.
May these words of mine please him;
I will rejoice in the Lord.
Bless the Lord, O my soul,
Alleluia! ℟

SECOND READING (Alternative readings)

Either   Romans 8.14–17

A reading from the letter of Paul to the Romans.

All who are led by the Spirit of God are children of God. For you did not
receive a spirit of slavery to fall back into fear, but you have received a spirit
of adoption. When we cry, 'Abba! Father!' it is that very Spirit bearing witness
with our spirit that we are children of God, and if children, then heirs, heirs
of God and joint heirs with Christ – if, in fact, we suffer with him so that we
may also be glorified with him.

Or   Acts 2.1–21

A reading from the Acts of the Apostles.

For text see above, page 621.

GOSPEL (Short or long reading)   John 14.8–17, (25–27)

Hear the gospel of our Lord Jesus Christ according to John.

Philip said to Jesus, 'Lord, show us the Father, and we will be satisfied.' Jesus
said to him, 'Have I been with you all this time, Philip, and you still do not
know me? Whoever has seen me has seen the Father. How can you say,
"Show us the Father"? Do you not believe that I am in the Father and the
Father is in me? The words that I say to you I do not speak on my own; but

the Father who dwells in me does his works. Believe me that I am in the Father and the Father is in me; but if you do not, then believe me because of the works themselves. Very truly, I tell you, the one who believes in me will also do the works that I do and, in fact, will do greater works than these, because I am going to the Father. I will do whatever you ask in my name, so that the Father may be glorified in the Son. If in my name you ask me for anything, I will do it.

If you love me, you will keep my commandments. And I will ask the Father, and he will give you another Advocate, to be with you for ever. This is the Spirit of truth, whom the world cannot receive, because it neither sees him nor knows him. You know him, because he abides with you, and he will be in you.

[I have said these things to you while I am still with you. But the Advocate, the Holy Spirit, whom the Father will send in my name, will teach you everything, and remind you of all that I have said to you. Peace I leave with you; my peace I give to you. I do not give to you as the world gives. Do not let your hearts be troubled, and do not let them be afraid.']

TRINITY SUNDAY   YEAR C

FIRST READING   Proverbs 8.1–4, 22–31

A reading from the book of Proverbs.

Thus says the wisdom of God:
Does not wisdom call,
and does not understanding raise her voice?
On the heights, beside the way,
at the crossroads she takes her stand;
beside the gates in front of the town,
at the entrance of the portals she cries out:
'To you, O people, I call, and my cry is to all that live.

The LORD created me at the beginning of his work,
the first of his acts of long ago.
Ages ago I was set up,
at the first, before the beginning of the earth.
When there were no depths I was brought forth,
when there were no springs abounding with water.
Before the mountains had been shaped,

before the hills, I was brought forth –
when he had not yet made earth and fields,
or the world's first bits of soil.
When he established the heavens, I was there,
when he drew a circle on the face of the deep,
when he made firm the skies above,
when he established the fountains of the deep,
when he assigned to the sea its limit,
so that the waters might not transgress his command,
when he marked out the foundations of the earth,
then I was beside him, like a master worker;
and I was daily his delight,
rejoicing before him always,
rejoicing in his inhabited world
and delighting in the human race.'

PSALM

Psalm 8

℟ **How exalted is your name in all the world!**

O Lord our governor,
how exalted is your name in all the world!
Out of the mouths of infants and children
your majesty is praised above the heavens.
You have set up a stronghold against your adversaries,
to quell the enemy and the avenger. ℟

When I consider your heavens, the work of your fingers,
the moon and the stars you have set in their courses,
What are mortals, that you should be mindful of them?
mere human beings, that you should seek them out?
You have made them little lower than the angels;
you adorn them with glory and honour. ℟

You give them mastery over the works of your hands;
and put all things under their feet,
All sheep and oxen,
even the wild beasts of the field,
The birds of the air, the fish of the sea,
and whatsoever walks in the paths of the sea.
O Lord our governor,
how exalted is your name in all the world! ℟

SECOND READING   **Romans 5.1-5**

A reading from the letter of Paul to the Romans.

Since we are justified by faith, we have peace with God through our Lord
Jesus Christ, through whom we have obtained access to this grace in which
we stand; and we boast in our hope of sharing the glory of God. And not
only that, but we also boast in our sufferings, knowing that suffering
produces endurance, and endurance produces character, and character
produces hope, and hope does not disappoint us, because God's love has
been poured into our hearts through the Holy Spirit that has been given to
us.

GOSPEL   **John 16.12-15**

Hear the gospel of our Lord Jesus Christ according to John.

Jesus said to his disciples: 'I still have many things to say to you, but you
cannot bear them now. When the Spirit of truth comes, he will guide you
into all the truth; for he will not speak on his own, but will speak whatever
he hears, and he will declare to you the things that are to come. He will
glorify me, because he will take what is mine and declare it to you. All that
the Father has is mine. For this reason I said that he will take what is mine
and declare it to you.'

THANKSGIVING FOR HOLY COMMUNION YEARS A B C
(CORPUS CHRISTI)

For text see Year A, pages 180–181.

† SUNDAY BETWEEN 24 AND 28 MAY   YEAR C
(if after Trinity Sunday)
PROPER 3

The Revised Common Lectionary provision for Epiphany 8 (above, pages 564–567) is used.

SUNDAYS AFTER TRINITY

The Church of England names the Sundays after Trinity Sunday 'Sundays after Trinity'.
The readings are provided by calendar date.
On most Sundays the First Reading and Psalm follow two tracks.
One track must be followed through the whole sequence.

† SUNDAY BETWEEN 29 MAY AND 4 JUNE   YEAR C
(if after Trinity Sunday)
PROPER 4

TRACK 1

FIRST READING (Short or long reading)
1 Kings 18:20–21, (22–29), 30–39

A reading from the first book of Kings.

Ahab sent to all the Israelites, and assembled the prophets at Mount Carmel. Elijah then came near to all the people, and said, 'How long will you go limping with two different opinions? If the LORD is God, follow him; but if Baal, then follow him.' The people did not answer him a word. [Then Elijah said to the people, 'I, even I only, am left a prophet of the LORD; but Baal's prophets number four hundred and fifty. Let two bulls be given to us; let them choose one bull for themselves, cut it in pieces, and lay it on the wood, but put no fire to it; I will prepare the other bull and lay it on the wood, but put no fire to it. Then you call on the name of your god and I will call on the name of the LORD; the god who answers by fire is indeed God.' All the people answered, 'Well spoken!' Then Elijah said to the prophets of Baal, 'Choose for yourselves one bull and prepare it first, for you are many; then call on the name of your god, but put no fire to it.' So they took the bull that was given them, prepared it, and called on the name of Baal from morning until noon, crying, 'O Baal, answer us!' But there was no voice, and no answer. They limped about the altar that they had made. At noon Elijah mocked them, saying, 'Cry aloud! Surely he is a god; either he is meditating, or he has wandered away, or he is on a journey, or perhaps he is asleep and must be awakened.' Then they cried aloud and, as was their custom, they cut themselves with swords and lances until the blood gushed out over them. As midday passed, they raved on until the time of the offering of the oblation, but there was no voice, no answer, and no response.]

Then Elijah said to all the people, 'Come closer to me'; and all the people came closer to him. First he repaired the altar of the LORD that had been thrown down; Elijah took twelve stones, according to the number of the tribes of the sons of Jacob, to whom the word of the LORD came, saying, 'Israel shall be your name'; with the stones he built an altar in the name of the LORD. Then he made a trench around the altar, large enough to contain two measures of seed. Next he put the wood in order, cut the bull in pieces, and laid it on the wood. He said, 'Fill four jars with water and pour it on the burnt-offering and on the wood.'
Then he said, 'Do it a second time'; and they did it a second time. Again he said, 'Do it a third time'; and they did it a third time, so that the water ran all around the altar, and filled the trench also with water.

At the time of the offering of the oblation, the prophet Elijah came near and said, 'O LORD, God of Abraham, Isaac, and Israel, let it be known this day that you are God in Israel, that I am your servant, and that I have done all these things at your bidding. Answer me, O LORD, answer me, so that this people may know that you, O LORD, are God, and that you have turned their hearts back.' Then the fire of the LORD fell and consumed the burnt-offering, the wood, the stones, and the dust, and even licked up the water that was in the trench. When all the people saw it, they fell on their faces and said, 'The LORD indeed is God; the LORD indeed is God.'

PSALM
Psalm 96

℟ **Worship the Lord in the beauty of holiness**
[let the whole earth tremble before him].

Sing to the Lord a new song;
sing to the Lord, all the whole earth.
Sing to the Lord and bless his name;
proclaim the good news of his salvation from day to day.
Declare his glory among the nations
and his wonders among all peoples. ℟

For great is the Lord and greatly to be praised;
he is more to be feared than all gods.
As for all the gods of the nations, they are but idols;
but it is the Lord who made the heavens.
O the majesty and magnificence of his presence!
O the power and the splendour of his sanctuary! ℞

Ascribe to the Lord, you families of the peoples;
ascribe to the Lord honour and power.
Ascribe to the Lord the honour due to his name;
bring offerings and come into his courts.
Worship the Lord in the beauty of holiness;
let the whole earth tremble before him. ℞

Tell it out among the nations: 'The Lord is king!
he has made the world so firm that it cannot be moved;
he will judge the peoples with equity.'
Let the heavens rejoice and let the earth be glad;
let the sea thunder and all that is in it;
let the field be joyful and all that is therein. ℞

Then shall all the trees of the wood shout for joy
before the Lord when he comes,
when he comes to judge the earth.
He will judge the world with righteousness
and the peoples with his truth. ℞

Or   TRACK 2

FIRST READING   **1 Kings 8.22–23, 41–43**

A reading from the first book of Kings.

Solomon stood before the altar of the LORD in the presence of all the
assembly of Israel, and spread out his hands to heaven. He said, 'O LORD,
God of Israel, there is no God like you in heaven above or on earth beneath,
keeping covenant and steadfast love for your servants who walk before you
with all their heart,

'Likewise when a foreigner, who is not of your people Israel, comes from a
distant land because of your name – for they shall hear of your great name,
your mighty hand, and your outstretched arm – when a foreigner comes and
prays towards this house, then hear in heaven your dwelling-place, and do

according to all that the foreigner calls to you, so that all the peoples of the earth may know your name and fear you, as do your people Israel, and so that they may know that your name has been invoked on this house that I have built.'

PSALM   Psalm 96.1–9

℟ **Ascribe to the Lord honour and power.**

Sing to the Lord a new song;
sing to the Lord, all the whole earth.
Sing to the Lord and bless his name;
proclaim the good news of his salvation from day to day.
Declare his glory among the nations
and his wonders among all peoples. ℟

For great is the Lord and greatly to be praised;
he is more to be feared than all gods.
As for all the gods of the nations, they are but idols;
but it is the Lord who made the heavens.
O the majesty and magnificence of his presence!
O the power and the splendour of his sanctuary! ℟

Ascribe to the Lord, you families of the peoples;
ascribe to the Lord honour and power.
Ascribe to the Lord the honour due to his name;
bring offerings and come into his courts.
Worship the Lord in the beauty of holiness;
let the whole earth tremble before him. ℟

SECOND READING   Galatians 1.1–12

A reading from the letter of Paul to the Galatians.

From Paul an apostle – sent neither by human commission nor from human authorities, but through Jesus Christ and God the Father, who raised him from the dead – and all the members of God's family who are with me, To the churches of Galatia:

Grace to you and peace from God our Father and the Lord Jesus Christ, who gave himself for our sins to set us free from the present evil age, according to the will of our God and Father, to whom be the glory for ever and ever. Amen.

I am astonished that you are so quickly deserting the one who called you in the grace of Christ and are turning to a different gospel – not that there is another gospel, but there are some who are confusing you and want to pervert the gospel of Christ. But even if we or an angel from heaven should proclaim to you a gospel contrary to what we proclaimed to you, let that one be accursed! As we have said before, so now I repeat, if anyone proclaims to you a gospel contrary to what you received, let that one be accursed!

Am I now seeking human approval, or God's approval? Or am I trying to please people? If I were still pleasing people, I would not be a servant of Christ. For I want you to know, brothers and sisters, that the gospel that was proclaimed by me is not of human origin; for I did not receive it from a human source, nor was I taught it, but I received it through a revelation of Jesus Christ.

GOSPEL   Luke 7.1b–10

Hear the gospel of our Lord Jesus Christ according to Luke.

Jesus entered Capernaum. A centurion there had a slave whom he valued highly, and who was ill and close to death. When he heard about Jesus, he sent some Jewish elders to him, asking him to come and heal his slave. When they came to Jesus, they appealed to him earnestly, saying, 'He is worthy of having you do this for him, for he loves our people, and it is he who built our synagogue for us.' And Jesus went with them, but when he was not far from the house, the centurion sent friends to say to him, 'Lord, do not trouble yourself, for I am not worthy to have you come under my roof; therefore I did not presume to come to you. But only speak the word, and let my servant be healed. For I also am a man set under authority, with soldiers under me; and I say to one, "Go," and he goes, and to another, "Come," and he comes, and to my slave, "Do this," and the slave does it.' When Jesus heard this he was amazed at him, and turning to the crowd that followed him, he said, 'I tell you, not even in Israel have I found such faith.' When those who had been sent returned to the house, they found the slave in good health.

† SUNDAY BETWEEN 5 AND 11 JUNE

YEAR C

(if after Trinity Sunday)

PROPER 5

TRACK 1

FIRST READING (Short or long reading)

1 Kings 17.8–16, (17–24)

A reading from the first book of Kings.

The word of the LORD came to Elijah, saying, 'Go now to Zarephath, which belongs to Sidon, and live there; for I have commanded a widow there to feed you.' So he set out and went to Zarephath. When he came to the gate of the town, a widow was there gathering sticks; he called to her and said, 'Bring me a little water in a vessel, so that I may drink.' As she was going to bring it, he called to her and said, 'Bring me a morsel of bread in your hand.' But she said, 'As the LORD your God lives, I have nothing baked, only a handful of meal in a jar, and a little oil in a jug; I am now gathering a couple of sticks, so that I may go home and prepare it for myself and my son, that we may eat it, and die.' Elijah said to her, 'Do not be afraid; go and do as you have said; but first make me a little cake of it and bring it to me, and afterwards make something for yourself and your son. For thus says the LORD the God of Israel: The jar of meal will not be emptied and the jug of oil will not fail until the day that the LORD sends rain on the earth.' She went and did as Elijah said, so that she as well as he and her household ate for many days. The jar of meal was not emptied, neither did the jug of oil fail, according to the word of the LORD that he spoke by Elijah.

[After this the son of the woman, the mistress of the house, became ill; his illness was so severe that there was no breath left in him. She then said to Elijah, 'What have you against me, O man of God? You have come to me to bring my sin to remembrance, and to cause the death of my son!' But he said to her, 'Give me your son.' He took him from her bosom, carried him up into the upper chamber where he was lodging, and laid him on his own bed. He cried out to the LORD, 'O LORD my God, have you brought calamity even upon the widow with whom I am staying, by killing her son?' Then he stretched himself upon the child three times, and cried out to the LORD, 'O LORD my God, let this child's life come into him again.' The LORD listened to the voice of Elijah; the life of the child came into him again, and he revived.

Elijah took the child, brought him down from the upper chamber into the house, and gave him to his mother; then Elijah said, 'See, your son is alive.' So the woman said to Elijah, 'Now I know that you are a man of God, and that the word of the LORD in your mouth is truth.']

PSALM   Psalm 146

℟ **The Lord gives food to those who hunger.**

Alleluia!
Praise the Lord, O my soul!
I will praise the Lord as long as I live;
I will sing praises to my God while I have my being.
Put not your trust in rulers,
nor in any child of earth,
for there is no help in them.
When they breathe their last, they return to earth,
and in that day their thoughts perish. ℟

Happy are they who have the God of Jacob
for their help!
whose hope is in the Lord their God;
Who made heaven and earth, the seas,
and all that is in them;
who keeps his promise for ever;
Who gives justice to those who are oppressed,
and food to those who hunger. ℟

The Lord sets the prisoners free;
the Lord opens the eyes of the blind;
the Lord lifts up those who are bowed down;
The Lord loves the righteous;
the Lord cares for the stranger;
he sustains the orphan and widow,
but frustrates the way of the wicked.
The Lord shall reign for ever,
your God, O Zion, throughout all generations.
Alleluia! ℟

Or TRACK 2

FIRST READING 1 Kings 17.17–24

A reading from the first book of Kings.

While Elijah was living in Zarephath; The son of the woman, the mistress of the house, became ill; his illness was so severe that there was no breath left in him. She then said to Elijah, 'What have you against me, O man of God? You have come to me to bring my sin to remembrance, and to cause the death of my son!' But he said to her, 'Give me your son.' He took him from her bosom, carried him up into the upper chamber where he was lodging, and laid him on his own bed. He cried out to the LORD, 'O LORD my God, have you brought calamity even upon the widow with whom I am staying, by killing her son?' Then he stretched himself upon the child three times, and cried out to the LORD, 'O LORD my God, let this child's life come into him again.' The LORD listened to the voice of Elijah; the life of the child came into him again, and he revived. Elijah took the child, brought him down from the upper chamber into the house, and gave him to his mother; then Elijah said, 'See, your son is alive.' So the woman said to Elijah, 'Now I know that you are a man of God, and that the word of the LORD in your mouth is truth.'

PSALM Psalm 30

℟ **The Lord has changed my mourning into dance.**
or
℟ **I will exalt you, O Lord,**
because you have restored my life.

I will exalt you, O Lord,
because you have lifted me up
and have not let my enemies triumph over me.
O Lord my God, I cried out to you,
and you restored me to health.
You brought me up, O Lord, from the dead;
you restored my life as I was going down to the grave. ℟

Sing to the Lord, you servants of his;
give thanks for the remembrance of his holiness.
For his wrath endures but the twinkling of an eye,
his favour for a lifetime.

Weeping may spend the night,
but joy comes in the morning. ℟

While I felt secure, I said,
'I shall never be disturbed.
You, Lord, with your favour,
made me as strong as the mountains.'
Then you hid your face,
and I was filled with fear. ℟

I cried to you, O Lord;
I pleaded with the Lord, saying,
'What profit is there in my blood,
if I go down to the Pit?
will the dust praise you or declare your faithfulness?
Hear, O Lord, and have mercy upon me;
O Lord, be my helper.' ℟

You have turned my wailing into dancing;
you have put off my sack-cloth and clothed me with joy;
Therefore my heart sings to you without ceasing;
O Lord my God, I will give you thanks for ever. ℟

SECOND READING   Galatians 1.11–24

A reading from the letter of Paul to the Galatians.

I want you to know, brothers and sisters, that the gospel that was proclaimed by me is not of human origin; for I did not receive it from a human source, nor was I taught it, but I received it through a revelation of Jesus Christ.

You have heard, no doubt, of my earlier life in Judaism. I was violently persecuting the church of God and was trying to destroy it. I advanced in Judaism beyond many among my people of the same age, for I was far more zealous for the traditions of my ancestors. But when God, who had set me apart before I was born and called me through his grace, was pleased to reveal his Son to me, so that I might proclaim him among the Gentiles, I did not confer with any human being, nor did I go up to Jerusalem to those who were already apostles before me, but I went away at once into Arabia, and afterwards I returned to Damascus.

Then after three years I did go up to Jerusalem to visit Cephas and stayed with him fifteen days; but I did not see any other apostle except James the

Lord's brother. In what I am writing to you, before God, I do not lie! Then I went into the regions of Syria and Cilicia, and I was still unknown by sight to the churches of Judea that are in Christ; they only heard it said, 'The one who formerly was persecuting us is now proclaiming the faith he once tried to destroy.' And they glorified God because of me.

GOSPEL   Luke 7.11–17

Hear the gospel of our Lord Jesus Christ according to Luke.

Jesus went to a town called Nain, and his disciples and a large crowd went with him. As he approached the gate of the town, a man who had died was being carried out. He was his mother's only son, and she was a widow; and with her was a large crowd from the town. When the Lord saw her, he had compassion for her and said to her, 'Do not weep.' Then he came forward and touched the bier, and the bearers stood still. And he said, 'Young man, I say to you, rise!' The dead man sat up and began to speak, and Jesus gave him to his mother. Fear seized all of them; and they glorified God, saying, 'A great prophet has risen among us!' and 'God has looked favourably on his people!' This word about him spread throughout Judea and all the surrounding country.

† SUNDAY BETWEEN 12 AND 18 JUNE   YEAR C
(if after Trinity Sunday)
PROPER 6

TRACK 1

FIRST READING (Short or long reading)
1 Kings 21.1b–10, (11–14), 15–21a

A reading from the first book of Kings.

Naboth the Jezreelite had a vineyard in Jezreel, beside the palace of King Ahab of Samaria. And Ahab said to Naboth, 'Give me your vineyard, so that I may have it for a vegetable garden, because it is near my house; I will give you a better vineyard for it; or, if it seems good to you, I will give you its value in money.' But Naboth said to Ahab, 'The LORD forbid that I should give you my ancestral inheritance.' Ahab went home resentful and sullen because of what Naboth the Jezreelite had said to him; for he had said, 'I will not give you my ancestral inheritance.' He lay down on his bed, turned away his face, and would not eat.

His wife Jezebel came to him and said, 'Why are you so depressed that you will not eat?' He said to her, 'Because I spoke to Naboth the Jezreelite and said to him, "Give me your vineyard for money; or else, if you prefer, I will give you another vineyard for it"; but he answered, "I will not give you my vineyard."' His wife Jezebel said to him, 'Do you now govern Israel? Get up, eat some food, and be cheerful; I will give you the vineyard of Naboth the Jezreelite.'

So she wrote letters in Ahab's name and sealed them with his seal; she sent the letters to the elders and the nobles who lived with Naboth in his city. She wrote in the letters, 'Proclaim a fast, and seat Naboth at the head of the assembly; seat two scoundrels opposite him, and have them bring a charge against him, saying, "You have cursed God and the king." Then take him out, and stone him to death.' [The men of his city, the elders and the nobles who lived in his city, did as Jezebel had sent word to them. Just as it was written in the letters that she had sent to them, they proclaimed a fast and seated Naboth at the head of the assembly. The two scoundrels came in and sat opposite him; and the scoundrels brought a charge against Naboth, in the presence of the people, saying, 'Naboth cursed God and the king.' So they took him outside the city, and stoned him to death. Then they sent to Jezebel, saying, 'Naboth has been stoned; he is dead.']

As soon as Jezebel heard that Naboth had been stoned and was dead, Jezebel said to Ahab, 'Go, take possession of the vineyard of Naboth the Jezreelite, which he refused to give you for money; for Naboth is not alive, but dead.' As soon as Ahab heard that Naboth was dead, Ahab set out to go down to the vineyard of Naboth the Jezreelite, to take possession of it.

Then the word of the LORD came to Elijah the Tishbite, saying: Go down to meet King Ahab of Israel, who rules in Samaria; he is now in the vineyard of Naboth, where he has gone to take possession. You shall say to him, 'Thus says the LORD: Have you killed, and also taken possession?' You shall say to him, 'Thus says the LORD: In the place where dogs licked up the blood of Naboth, dogs will also lick up your blood.'

Ahab said to Elijah, 'Have you found me, O my enemy?' He answered, 'I have found you. Because you have sold yourself to do what is evil in the sight of the LORD, I will bring disaster on you; I will consume you, and will cut off from Ahab every male, bond or free, in Israel.'

PSALM   **Psalm 5.1–8**

℟ **You are not a God who takes pleasure in wickedness.**

Give ear to my words, O Lord;
consider my meditation.
Hearken to my cry for help, my King and my God,
for I make my prayer to you. ℟

In the morning, Lord, you hear my voice;
early in the morning I make my appeal
and watch for you.
For you are not a God who takes pleasure in wickedness
and evil cannot dwell with you. ℟

Braggarts cannot stand in your sight;
you hate all those who work wickedness.
You destroy those who speak lies;
the bloodthirsty and deceitful, O Lord, you abhor. ℟

But as for me, through the greatness of your mercy, I will go into your house;
I will bow down towards your holy temple in awe of you.
Lead me, O Lord, in your righteousness,
because of those who lie in wait for me;
make your way straight before me. ℟

Or   TRACK 2

FIRST READING   **2 Samuel 11.26 – 12.10, 13–15**

A reading from the second book of Samuel.

When the wife of Uriah heard that her husband was dead, she made
lamentation for him. When the mourning was over, David sent and brought
her to his house, and she became his wife, and bore him a son.

But the thing that David had done displeased the LORD, and the LORD sent
Nathan to David. He came to him, and said to him, 'There were two men in a
certain city, the one rich and the other poor. The rich man had very many
flocks and herds; but the poor man had nothing but one little ewe lamb,
which he had bought. He brought it up, and it grew up with him and with
his children; it used to eat of his meagre fare, and drink from his cup, and lie
in his bosom, and it was like a daughter to him. Now there came a traveller

to the rich man, and he was loath to take one of his own flock or herd to prepare for the wayfarer who had come to him, but he took the poor man's lamb, and prepared that for the guest who had come to him.' Then David's anger was greatly kindled against the man. He said to Nathan, 'As the LORD lives, the man who has done this deserves to die; he shall restore the lamb fourfold, because he did this thing, and because he had no pity.'

Nathan said to David, 'You are the man! Thus says the LORD, the God of Israel: I anointed you king over Israel, and I rescued you from the hand of Saul; I gave you your master's house, and your master's wives into your bosom, and gave you the house of Israel and of Judah; and if that had been too little, I would have added as much more. Why have you despised the word of the LORD, to do what is evil in his sight? You have struck down Uriah the Hittite with the sword, and have taken his wife to be your wife, and have killed him with the sword of the Ammonites. Now therefore the sword shall never depart from your house, for you have despised me, and have taken the wife of Uriah the Hittite to be your wife.'

David said to Nathan, 'I have sinned against the LORD.' Nathan said to David, 'Now the LORD has put away your sin; you shall not die. Nevertheless, because by this deed you have utterly scorned the LORD, the child that is born to you shall die.' Then Nathan went to his house. The LORD struck the child that Uriah's wife bore to David, and it became very ill.

PSALM   **Psalm 32**

℟ **Forgive, O Lord, the guilt of my sin.**

Happy are they whose transgressions are forgiven,
and whose sin is put away!
Happy are they to whom the Lord imputes no guilt,
and in whose spirit there is no guile! ℟

While I held my tongue, my bones withered away,
because of my groaning all day long.
For your hand was heavy upon me day and night;
my moisture was dried up as in the heat of summer.
Then I acknowledged my sin to you,
and did not conceal my guilt.
I said, 'I will confess my transgressions to the Lord';
then you forgave me the guilt of my sin. ℟

Therefore all the faithful will make their prayers to you
in time of trouble;
when the great waters overflow, they shall not reach them.
You are my hiding-place;
you preserve me from trouble;
you surround me with shouts of deliverance. ℞

'I will instruct you and teach you
in the way that you should go;
I will guide you with my eye.
Do not be like horse or mule,
which have no understanding;
who must be fitted with bit and bridle,
or else they will not stay near you.' ℞

Great are the tribulations of the wicked;
but mercy embraces those who trust in the Lord.
Be glad, you righteous, and rejoice in the Lord;
shout for joy, all who are true of heart. ℞

SECOND READING   Galatians 2.15–21

A reading from the letter of Paul to the Galatians.

We ourselves are Jews by birth and not Gentile sinners; yet we know that a
person is justified not by the works of the law but through faith in Jesus
Christ. And we have come to believe in Christ Jesus, so that we might be
justified by faith in Christ, and not by doing the works of the law, because no
one will be justified by the works of the law. But if, in our effort to be
justified in Christ, we ourselves have been found to be sinners, is Christ then
a servant of sin? Certainly not! But if I build up again the very things that I
once tore down, then I demonstrate that I am a transgressor. For through the
law I died to the law, so that I might live to God. I have been crucified with
Christ; and it is no longer I who live, but it is Christ who lives in me. And the
life I now live in the flesh I live by faith in the Son of God, who loved me
and gave himself for me. I do not nullify the grace of God; for if justification
comes through the law, then Christ died for nothing.

GOSPEL   **Luke 7.36 – 8.3**

Hear the gospel of our Lord Jesus Christ according to Luke.

One of the Pharisees asked Jesus to eat with him, and he went into the Pharisee's house and took his place at the table. And a woman in the city, who was a sinner, having learned that he was eating in the Pharisee's house, brought an alabaster jar of ointment. She stood behind him at his feet, weeping, and began to bathe his feet with her tears and to dry them with her hair. Then she continued kissing his feet and anointing them with the ointment. Now when the Pharisee who had invited him saw it, he said to himself, 'If this man were a prophet, he would have known who and what kind of woman this is who is touching him – that she is a sinner.' Jesus spoke up and said to him, 'Simon, I have something to say to you.' 'Teacher,' he replied, 'Speak.' 'A certain creditor had two debtors; one owed five hundred denarii, and the other fifty. When they could not pay, he cancelled the debts for both of them. Now which of them will love him more?' Simon answered, 'I suppose the one for whom he cancelled the greater debt.' And Jesus said to him, 'You have judged rightly.' Then turning towards the woman, he said to Simon, 'Do you see this woman? I entered your house; you gave me no water for my feet, but she has bathed my feet with her tears and dried them with her hair.

You gave me no kiss, but from the time I came in she has not stopped kissing my feet. You did not anoint my head with oil, but she has anointed my feet with ointment. Therefore, I tell you, her sins, which were many, have been forgiven; hence she has shown great love. But the one to whom little is forgiven, loves little.'

Then he said to her, 'Your sins are forgiven.' But those who were at the table with him began to say among themselves, 'Who is this who even forgives sins?' And he said to the woman, 'Your faith has saved you; go in peace.'

Soon afterwards he went on through cities and villages, proclaiming and bringing the good news of the kingdom of God. The twelve were with him, as well as some women who had been cured of evil spirits and infirmities: Mary, called Magdalene, from whom seven demons had gone out, and Joanna, the wife of Herod's steward Chuza, and Susanna, and many others, who provided for them out of their resources.

† SUNDAY BETWEEN 19 AND 25 JUNE   YEAR C
(if after Trinity Sunday)
PROPER 7

TRACK 1

FIRST READING (Short or long reading)
1 Kings 19.1–4, (5–7), 8–15a

A reading from the first book of Kings.

Ahab told Jezebel all that Elijah had done, and how he had killed all the prophets with the sword. Then Jezebel sent a messenger to Elijah, saying, 'So may the gods do to me, and more also, if I do not make your life like the life of one of them by this time tomorrow.' Then he was afraid; he got up and fled for his life, and came to Beer-sheba, which belongs to Judah; he left his servant there.

But he himself went a day's journey into the wilderness, and came and sat down under a solitary broom tree. He asked that he might die: 'It is enough; now, O LORD, take away my life, for I am no better than my ancestors.'

[Then he lay down under the broom tree and fell asleep. Suddenly an angel touched him and said to him, 'Get up and eat.' He looked, and there at his head was a cake baked on hot stones, and a jar of water. He ate and drank, and lay down again. The angel of the LORD came a second time, touched him, and said, 'Get up and eat, otherwise the journey will be too much for you.'] He got up, and ate and drank; then he went in the strength of that food forty days and forty nights to Horeb the mount of God. At that place he came to a cave, and spent the night there.

Then the word of the LORD came to him, saying, 'What are you doing here, Elijah?' He answered, 'I have been very zealous for the LORD, the God of hosts; for the Israelites have forsaken your covenant, thrown down your altars, and killed your prophets with the sword. I alone am left, and they are seeking my life, to take it away.'

He said, 'Go out and stand on the mountain before the LORD, for the LORD is about to pass by.' Now there was a great wind, so strong that it was splitting mountains and breaking rocks in pieces before the LORD, but the LORD was not in the wind; and after the wind an earthquake, but the LORD was not in the earthquake; and after the earthquake a fire, but the LORD was not in the fire; and after the fire a sound of sheer silence. When Elijah heard it, he wrapped his face in his mantle and went out and stood at the entrance of the cave. Then there came a voice to him that said, 'What are you doing here, Elijah?' He answered, 'I have been very zealous for the LORD, the God of hosts; for the Israelites have forsaken your covenant, thrown down your altars, and killed your prophets with the sword. I alone am left, and they are seeking my life, to take it away.' Then the LORD said to him, 'Go, return on your way to the wilderness of Damascus; when you arrive, you shall anoint Hazael as king over Aram.'

PSALM   **Psalms 42 and 43**

℟ I will yet give thanks to him
   who is the help of my countenance, and my God.

As the deer longs for the water-brooks,
so longs my soul for you, O God.
My soul is athirst for God, athirst for the living God;
when shall I come to appear before the presence of God?
My tears have been my food day and night,
while all day long they say to me,
'Where now is your God?' ℟

I pour out my soul when I think on these things:
how I went with the multitude
and led them into the house of God,
With the voice of praise and thanksgiving,
among those who keep holy-day.
Why are you so full of heaviness, O my soul?
and why are you so disquieted within me? ℟

[Put your trust in God;
for I will yet give thanks to him,
who is the help of my countenance, and my God.]
My soul is heavy within me;
therefore I will remember you from the land of Jordan,
and from the peak of Mizar among the heights of Hermon.
One deep calls to another in the noise of your cataracts;
all your rapids and floods have gone over me.
The Lord grants his loving-kindness in the daytime;
in the night season his song is with me,
a prayer to the God of my life. ℟

I will say to the God of my strength,
'Why have you forgotten me?
and why do I go so heavily
while the enemy oppresses me?'
While my bones are being broken,
my enemies mock me to my face;
All day long they mock me,
say to me, 'Where now is your God?'
Why are you so full of heaviness, O my soul?
and why are you so disquieted within me? ℞

[Put your trust in God;
for I will yet give thanks to him,
who is the help of my countenance, and my God.]
Give judgement for me, O God,
and defend my cause against an ungodly people;
deliver me from the deceitful and the wicked.
For you are the God of my strength;
why have you put me from you?
and why do I go so heavily
while the enemy oppresses me? ℞

Send out your light and your truth,
that they may lead me,
and bring me to your holy hill
and to your dwelling;
That I may go to the altar of God,
to the God of my joy and gladness;
and on the harp I will give thanks to you,
O God my God.
Why are you so full of heaviness, O my soul?
and why are you so disquieted within me? ℞

[Put your trust in God;
for I will yet give thanks to him,
who is the help of my countenance, and my God.]

Or TRACK 2

FIRST READING **Isaiah 65.1–9**

A reading from the book of the prophet Isaiah.

The word of the Lord through the prophet:
I was ready to be sought out by those who did not ask,
to be found by those who did not seek me.
I said, 'Here I am, here I am,'
to a nation that did not call on my name.
I held out my hands all day long to a rebellious people,
who walk in a way that is not good, following their own devices;
a people who provoke me to my face continually,
sacrificing in gardens and offering incense on bricks;
who sit inside tombs, and spend the night in secret places;
who eat swine's flesh, with broth of abominable things in their vessels;
who say,
'Keep to yourself, do not come near me,
for I am too holy for you.'
These are a smoke in my nostrils,
a fire that burns all day long.
See, it is written before me:
I will not keep silent, but I will repay;
I will indeed repay into their laps
their iniquities and their ancestors' iniquities together, says the LORD;
because they offered incense on the mountains and reviled me on the hills,
I will measure into their laps full payment for their actions.
Thus says the LORD:
As the wine is found in the cluster, and they say,
'Do not destroy it, for there is a blessing in it,'
so I will do for my servants' sake, and not destroy them all.
I will bring forth descendants from Jacob,
and from Judah inheritors of my mountains;
my chosen shall inherit it, and my servants shall settle there.

PSALM

Psalm 22.18–27

℟ **All the ends of the earth shall bow before him.**

Be not far away, O, Lord;
You are my strength; hasten to help me.
Save me from the sword,
my life from the power of the dog.
Save me from the lion's mouth,
my wretched body from the horns of wild bulls. ℟

I will declare your name to my people;
in the midst of the congregation I will praise you.
Praise the Lord, you that fear him;
stand in awe of him, O offspring of Israel;
all you of Jacob's line, give glory. ℟

For he does not despise nor abhor
the poor in their poverty;
neither does he hide his face from them;
but when they cry to him he hears them.
My praise is of him in the great assembly;
I will perform my vows
in the presence of those who worship him. ℟

The poor shall eat and be satisfied,
and those who seek the Lord shall praise him:
'May your heart live for ever!'
All the ends of the earth
shall remember and turn to the Lord,
and all the families of the nations
shall bow before him.
For kingship belongs to the Lord;
he rules over the nations. ℟

SECOND READING

Galatians 3.23–29

A reading from the letter of Paul to the Galatians.

Before faith came, we were imprisoned and guarded under the law until faith would be revealed. Therefore the law was our disciplinarian until Christ came, so that we might be justified by faith. But now that faith has come, we are no longer subject to a disciplinarian, for in Christ Jesus you are all children of God through faith. As many of you as were baptized into Christ have clothed yourselves with Christ; There is no longer Jew or Greek, there is no longer slave or free, there is no longer male and female; for all of you are one in Christ Jesus. And if you belong to Christ, then you are Abraham's offspring, heirs according to the promise.

GOSPEL   Luke 8.26–39

Hear the gospel of our Lord Jesus Christ according to Luke.

Jesus and his disciples arrived at the country of the Gerasenes, which is opposite Galilee. As he stepped out on land, a man of the city who had demons met him. For a long time he had worn no clothes, and he did not live in a house but in the tombs. When he saw Jesus, he fell down before him and shouted at the top of his voice, 'What have you to do with me, Jesus, Son of the Most High God? I beg you, do not torment me' – for Jesus had commanded the unclean spirit to come out of the man. (For many times it had seized him; he was kept under guard and bound with chains and shackles, but he would break the bonds and be driven by the demon into the wilds.) Jesus then asked him, 'What is your name?' He said, 'Legion'; for many demons had entered him. They begged him not to order them to go back into the abyss.

Now there on the hillside a large herd of swine was feeding; and the demons begged Jesus to let them enter these. So he gave them permission. Then the demons came out of the man and entered the swine, and the herd rushed down the steep bank into the lake and was drowned. When the swineherds saw what had happened, they ran off and told it in the city and in the country. Then people came out to see what had happened, and when they came to Jesus, they found the man from whom the demons had gone sitting at the feet of Jesus, clothed and in his right mind. And they were afraid. Those who had seen it told them how the one who had been possessed by demons had been healed. Then all the people of the surrounding country of the Gerasenes asked Jesus to leave them; for they were seized with great fear. So he got into the boat and returned. The man from whom the demons had gone begged that he might be with him; but Jesus sent him away, saying, 'Return to your home, and declare how much God has done for you.' So he went away, proclaiming throughout the city how much Jesus had done for him.

† SUNDAY BETWEEN 26 JUNE AND 2 JULY   YEAR C
PROPER 8

TRACK 1

FIRST READING   2 Kings 2.1–2, 6–14

A reading from the second book of Kings.

When the LORD was about to take Elijah up to heaven by a whirlwind, Elijah and Elisha were on their way from Gilgal. Elijah said to Elisha, 'Stay here; for the LORD has sent me as far as Bethel.' But Elisha said, 'As the LORD lives, and as you yourself live, I will not leave you.' So they went down to Bethel.

Then Elijah said to him, 'Stay here; for the LORD has sent me to the Jordan.' But Elisha said, 'As the LORD lives, and as you yourself live, I will not leave you.' So the two of them went on. Fifty men of the company of prophets also went, and stood at some distance from them, as they both were standing by the Jordan. Then Elijah took his mantle and rolled it up, and struck the water; the water was parted to the one side and to the other, until the two of them crossed on dry ground.

When they had crossed, Elijah said to Elisha, 'Tell me what I may do for you, before I am taken from you.' Elisha said, 'Please let me inherit a double share of your spirit.' He responded, 'You have asked a hard thing; yet, if you see me as I am being taken from you, it will be granted you; if not, it will not.' As they continued walking and talking, a chariot of fire and horses of fire separated the two of them, and Elijah ascended in a whirlwind into heaven. Elisha kept watching and crying out, 'Father, father! The chariots of Israel and its horsemen!' But when he could no longer see him, he grasped his own clothes and tore them in two pieces.

He picked up the mantle of Elijah that had fallen from him, and went back and stood on the bank of the Jordan. He took the mantle of Elijah that had fallen from him, and struck the water, saying, 'Where is the LORD, the God of Elijah?' When he had struck the water, the water was parted to the one side and to the other, and Elisha went over.

PSALM

℞ **Your footsteps, O God, were not seen.**

I will cry aloud to God;
I will cry aloud and he will hear me.
In the day of my trouble I sought the Lord;
my hands were stretched out by night and did not tire;
I refused to be comforted.
I will remember the works of the Lord,
and call to mind your wonders of old time. ℞

I will meditate on all your acts
and ponder your mighty deeds.
Your way, O God, is holy;
who is so great a god as our God?
You are the God who works wonders
and have declared your power among the peoples.
By your strength you have redeemed your people,
the children of Jacob and Joseph. ℞

The waters saw you, O God;
the waters saw you and trembled;
the very depths were shaken.
The clouds poured out water; the skies thundered;
your arrows flashed to and fro;
The sound of your thunder was in the whirlwind;
your lightnings lit up the world;
the earth trembled and shook. ℞

Your way was in the sea,
and your paths in the great waters,
yet your footsteps were not seen.
You led your people like a flock
by the hand of Moses and Aaron. ℞

Or   TRACK 2

FIRST READING   1 Kings 19.15–16, 19–21

A reading from the first book of Kings.

The LORD said to Elijah, 'Go, return on your way to the wilderness of Damascus; when you arrive, you shall anoint Hazael as king over Aram. Also you shall anoint Jehu son of Nimshi as king over Israel; and you shall anoint Elisha son of Shaphat of Abel-meholah as prophet in your place.

So he set out from there, and found Elisha son of Shaphat, who was ploughing There were twelve yoke of oxen ahead of him, and he was with the twelfth. Elijah passed by him and threw his mantle over him. He left the oxen, ran after Elijah, and said, 'Let me kiss my father and my mother, and then I will follow you.' Then Elijah said to him, 'Go back again; for what have I done to you?' He returned from following him, took the yoke of oxen, and slaughtered them; using the equipment from the oxen, he boiled their flesh, and gave it to the people, and they ate. Then he set out and followed Elijah, and became his servant.

PSALM   Psalm 16

℞ O Lord, you are my portion and my cup.

Protect me, O God, for I take refuge in you;
I have said to the Lord, 'You are my Lord,
my good above all other.'
All my delight is upon the godly that are in the land,
upon those who are noble among the people. ℞

But those who run after other gods
shall have their troubles multiplied.
Their libations of blood I will not offer,
nor take the names of their gods upon my lips. ℞

O Lord, you are my portion and my cup;
it is you who uphold my lot.
My boundaries enclose a pleasant land;
indeed, I have a goodly heritage.
I will bless the Lord who gives me counsel;
my heart teaches me, night after night. ℞

I have set the Lord always before me;
because he is at my right hand I shall not fall.
My heart, therefore, is glad and my spirit rejoices;
my body also shall rest in hope. ℟

For you will not abandon me to the grave,
nor let your holy one see the Pit.
You will show me the path of life;
in your presence there is fullness of joy,
and in your right hand are pleasures for evermore. ℟

SECOND READING   Galatians 5.1, 13–25

A reading from the letter of Paul to the Galatians.

For freedom Christ has set us free. Stand firm, therefore, and do not submit
again to a yoke of slavery.

For you were called to freedom, brothers and sisters; only do not use your
freedom as an opportunity for self-indulgence, but through love become
slaves to one another. For the whole law is summed up in a single
commandment, 'You shall love your neighbour as yourself.' If, however, you
bite and devour one another, take care that you are not consumed by one
another.

Live by the Spirit, I say, and do not gratify the desires of the flesh. For what
the flesh desires is opposed to the Spirit, and what the Spirit desires is
opposed to the flesh; for these are opposed to each other, to prevent you
from doing what you want. But if you are led by the Spirit, you are not
subject to the law. Now the works of the flesh are obvious: fornication,
impurity, licentiousness, idolatry, sorcery, enmities, strife, jealousy, anger,
quarrels, dissensions, factions,
envy, drunkenness, carousing, and things like these. I am warning you, as I
warned you before: those who do such things will not inherit the kingdom of
God.

By contrast, the fruit of the Spirit is love, joy, peace, patience, kindness,
generosity, faithfulness, gentleness, and self-control. There is no law against
such things. And those who belong to Christ Jesus have crucified the flesh
with its passions and desires. If we live by the Spirit, let us also be guided by
the Spirit.

GOSPEL   **Luke 9.51–62**

Hear the gospel of our Lord Jesus Christ according to Luke.

When the days drew near for him be taken up, he set his face to go to
Jerusalem. And he sent messengers ahead of him. On their way they entered
a village of the Samaritans to make ready for him; but they did not receive
him, because his face was set towards Jerusalem. When his disciples James
and John saw it, they said, 'Lord, do you want us to command fire to come
down from heaven and consume them?' But he turned and rebuked them.
Then they went on to another village.

As they were going along the road, someone said to him, 'I will follow you
wherever you go.' And Jesus said to him, 'Foxes have holes, and birds of the
air have nests; but the Son of Man has nowhere to lay his head.' To another
Jesus said, 'Follow me.' But he said, 'Lord, first let me go and bury my father.'
But Jesus said to him, 'Let the dead bury their own dead; but as for you, go
and proclaim the kingdom of God.' Another said, 'I will follow you, Lord; but
let me first say farewell to those at my home.' Jesus said to him, 'No one who
puts a hand to the plough and looks back is fit for the kingdom of God.'

† SUNDAY BETWEEN 3 AND 9 JULY   YEAR C
PROPER 9

TRACK 1

FIRST READING   **2 Kings 5.1–14**

A reading from the first book of Kings.

Naaman, commander of the army of the king of Aram, was a great man and
in high favour with his master, because by him the LORD had given victory
to Aram. The man, though a mighty warrior, suffered from leprosy. Now the
Arameans on one of their raids had taken a young girl captive from the land
of Israel, and she served Naaman's wife. She said to her mistress, 'If only my
lord were with the prophet who is in Samaria! He would cure him of his
leprosy.' So Naaman went in and told his lord just what the girl from the
land of Israel had said. And the king of Aram said, 'Go then, and I will send
along a letter to the king of Israel.'

He went, taking with him ten talents of silver, six thousand shekels of gold, and ten sets of garments. He brought the letter to the king of Israel, which read, 'When this letter reaches you, know that I have sent to you my servant Naaman, that you may cure him of his leprosy.' When the king of Israel read the letter, he tore his clothes and said, 'Am I God, to give death or life, that this man sends word to me to cure a man of his leprosy? Just look and see how he is trying to pick a quarrel with me.'

But when Elisha the man of God heard that the king of Israel had torn his clothes, he sent a message to the king, 'Why have you torn your clothes? Let him come to me, that he may learn that there is a prophet in Israel.' So Naaman came with his horses and chariots, and halted at the entrance of Elisha's house. Elisha sent a messenger to him, saying, 'Go, wash in the Jordan seven times, and your flesh shall be restored and you shall be clean.' But Naaman became angry and went away, saying, 'I thought that for me he would surely come out, and stand and call on the name of the LORD his God, and would wave his hand over the spot, and cure the leprosy! Are not Abana and Pharpar, the rivers of Damascus, better than all the waters of Israel? Could I not wash in them, and be clean?' He turned and went away in a rage. But his servants approached and said to him, 'Father, if the prophet had commanded you to do something difficult, would you not have done it? How much more, when all he said to you was, "Wash, and be clean"?' So he went down and immersed himself seven times in the Jordan, according to the word of the man of God; his flesh was restored like the flesh of a young boy, and he was clean.

PSALM   Psalm 30

℞ **The Lord has changed my mourning into dance.**
  or
℞ **I will exalt you, O Lord,**
  because you have restored my life.

I will exalt you, O Lord,
because you have lifted me up
and have not let my enemies triumph over me.
O Lord my God, I cried out to you,
and you restored me to health.
You brought me up, O Lord, from the dead;
you restored my life as I was going down to the grave. ℞

Sing to the Lord, you servants of his;
give thanks for the remembrance of his holiness.
For his wrath endures but the twinkling of an eye,
his favour for a lifetime.
Weeping may spend the night,
but joy comes in the morning. ℟

While I felt secure, I said,
'I shall never be disturbed.
You, Lord, with your favour,
made me as strong as the mountains.'
Then you hid your face,
and I was filled with fear. ℟

I cried to you, O Lord;
I pleaded with the Lord, saying,
'What profit is there in my blood,
if I go down to the Pit?
will the dust praise you or declare your faithfulness?
Hear, O Lord, and have mercy upon me;
O Lord, be my helper.' ℟

You have turned my wailing into dancing;
you have put off my sack-cloth and clothed me with joy;
Therefore my heart sings to you without ceasing;
O Lord my God, I will give you thanks for ever. ℟

Or   TRACK 2

FIRST READING   Isaiah 66.10–14

A reading from the book of the prophet Isaiah.

Rejoice with Jerusalem,
and be glad for her,
all you who love her;
rejoice with her in joy,
all you who mourn over her –
that you may nurse and be satisfied
from her consoling breast;
that you may drink deeply with delight
from her glorious bosom.

For thus says the LORD:
I will extend prosperity to her like a river,
and the wealth of the nations like an overflowing stream;
and you shall nurse and be carried on her arm,
and dandled on her knees.
As a mother comforts her child,
so I will comfort you;
you shall be comforted in Jerusalem.

You shall see, and your heart shall rejoice;
your bodies shall flourish like the grass;
and it shall be known
that the hand of the LORD is with his servants,
and his indignation is against his enemies.

PSALM   Psalm 66.1–8

℟ **Be joyful in God, all you lands.**
   or
℟ **Bless our God, you peoples,**
   make the voice of his praise be heard.

Be joyful in God, all you lands;
sing the glory of his name;
sing the glory of his praise.
Say to God, 'How awesome are your deeds!
because of your great strength
your enemies cringe before you.
All the earth bows down before you,
sings to you, sings out your name.' ℟

Come now and see the works of God,
how wonderful he is in his doing towards all people.
He turned the sea into dry land,
so that they went through the water on foot,
and there we rejoiced in him. ℟

In his might he rules for ever;
his eyes keep watch over the nations;
let no rebel rise up against him.
Bless our God, you peoples;
make the voice of his praise to be heard;
Who holds our souls in life,
and will not allow our feet to slip. ℟

SECOND READING (Short or long reading)

Galatians 6.(1–6), 7–16

A reading from the letter of Paul to the Galatians.

[My friends, if anyone is detected in a transgression, you who have received the Spirit should restore such a one in a spirit of gentleness. Take care that you yourselves are not tempted. Bear one another's burdens, and in this way you will fulfil the law of Christ. For if those who are nothing think they are something, they deceive themselves. All must test their own work; then that work, rather than their neighbour's work, will become a cause for pride. For all must carry their own loads.

Those who are taught the word must share in all good things with their teacher.]

Do not be deceived; God is not mocked, for you reap whatever you sow. If you sow to your own flesh, you will reap corruption from the flesh; but if you sow to the Spirit, you will reap eternal life from the Spirit. So let us not grow weary in doing what is right, for we will reap at harvest time, if we do not give up. So then, whenever we have an opportunity, let us work for the good of all, and especially for those of the family of faith.

See what large letters I make when I am writing in my own hand! It is those who want to make a good showing in the flesh that try to compel you to be circumcised – only that they may not be persecuted for the cross of Christ. Even the circumcised do not themselves obey the law, but they want you to be circumcised so that they may boast about your flesh. May I never boast of anything except the cross of our Lord Jesus Christ, by which the world has been crucified to me, and I to the world. For neither circumcision nor uncircumcision is anything; but a new creation is everything! As for those who will follow this rule – peace be upon them, and mercy, and upon the Israel of God.

GOSPEL   Luke 10.1–11, 16–20

Hear the gospel of our Lord Jesus Christ according to Luke.

The Lord appointed seventy others and sent them on ahead of him in pairs to every town and place where he himself intended to go. He said to them, 'The harvest is plentiful, but the labourers are few; therefore ask the Lord of the harvest to send out labourers into his harvest. Go on your way. See, I am sending you out like lambs into the midst of wolves. Carry no purse, no bag, no sandals; and greet no one on the road. Whatever house you enter, first say, "Peace to this house!" And if anyone is there who shares in peace, your peace will rest on that person; but if not, it will return to you. Remain in the same house, eating and drinking whatever they provide, for the labourer deserves to be paid. Do not move about from house to house. Whenever you enter a town and its people welcome you, eat what is set before you; cure the sick who are there, and say to them, "The kingdom of God has come near to you." But whenever you enter a town and they do not welcome you, go out into its streets and say, "Even the dust of your town that clings to our feet, we wipe off in protest against you. Yet know this: the kingdom of God has come near."

Whoever listens to you listens to me, and whoever rejects you rejects me, and whoever rejects me rejects the one who sent me.'

The seventy returned with joy, saying, 'Lord, in your name even the demons submit to us!' He said to them, 'I watched Satan fall from heaven like a flash of lightning. See, I have given you authority to tread on snakes and scorpions, and over all the power of the enemy; and nothing will hurt you. Nevertheless, do not rejoice at this, that the spirits submit to you, but rejoice that your names are written in heaven.'

† SUNDAY BETWEEN 10 AND 16 JULY   YEAR C
PROPER 10

TRACK 1

FIRST READING   Amos 7.7–17

A reading from the book of the prophet Amos.

This is what the LORD showed me:
the Lord was standing beside a wall built with a plumb-line,
with a plumb-line in his hand.
And the LORD said to me,
'Amos, what do you see?'
And I said, 'A plumb-line.'
Then the Lord said,
'See, I am setting a plumb-line in the midst of my people Israel;
I will never again pass them by;
the high places of Isaac shall be made desolate,
and the sanctuaries of Israel shall be laid waste,
and I will rise against the house of Jeroboam with the sword.'

Then Amaziah, the priest of Bethel, sent to King Jeroboam of Israel, saying, 'Amos has conspired against you in the very centre of the house of Israel; the land is not able to bear all his words. For thus Amos has said,
"Jeroboam shall die by the sword,
and Israel must go into exile away from his land."'

And Amaziah said to Amos, 'O seer, go, flee away to the land of Judah, earn your bread there, and prophesy there; but never again prophesy at Bethel, for it is the king's sanctuary, and it is a temple of the kingdom.'

Then Amos answered Amaziah, 'I am no prophet, nor a prophet's son; but I am a herdsman, and a dresser of sycamore trees, and the LORD took me from following the flock, and the LORD said to me, "Go, prophesy to my people Israel."

Now therefore hear the word of the LORD.
You say, "Do not prophesy against Israel,
and do not preach against the house of Isaac."
Therefore thus says the LORD:
"Your wife shall become a prostitute in the city,
and your sons and your daughters shall fall by the sword,
and your land shall be parcelled out by line;
you yourself shall die in an unclean land,
and Israel shall surely go into exile away from its land."'

PSALM   Psalm 82

℟ **Arise, O God, and rule the earth.**

God takes his stand in the council of heaven;
he gives judgement in the midst of the gods:
'How long will you judge unjustly,
and show favour to the wicked? ℟

Save the weak and the orphan;
defend the humble and needy;
Rescue the weak and the poor;
deliver them from the power of the wicked. ℟

They do not know, neither do they understand;
they go about in darkness;
all the foundations of the earth are shaken. ℟

Now I say to you, "You are gods,
and all of you children of the Most High;
Nevertheless, you shall die like mortals,
and fall like any prince."'
Arise, O God, and rule the earth,
for you shall take all nations for your own. ℟

Or   TRACK 2

FIRST READING   **Deuteronomy 30.9–14**

A reading from the book of Deuteronomy.

Moses spoke to the people, saying,
The LORD your God will make you abundantly prosperous in all your
undertakings, in the fruit of your body, in the fruit of your livestock, and in
the fruit of your soil. For the LORD will again take delight in prospering you,
just as he delighted in prospering your ancestors, when you obey the LORD
your God by observing his commandments and decrees that are written in
this book of the law, because you turn to the LORD your God with all your
heart and with all your soul.

Surely, this commandment that I am commanding you today is not too hard
for you, nor is it too far away. It is not in heaven, that you should say, 'Who
will go up to heaven for us, and get it for us so that we may hear it and
observe it?' Neither is it beyond the sea, that you should say, 'Who will cross
to the other side of the sea for us, and get it for us so that we may hear it and
observe it?' No, the word is very near to you; it is in your mouth and in your
heart for you to observe.

PSALM   **Psalm 25.1–10**

℟ **Show me your ways, O Lord,**
   and teach me your paths.

To you, O Lord, I lift up my soul;
my God, I put my trust in you;
let me not be humiliated,
nor let my enemies triumph over me.
Let none who look to you be put to shame;
let the treacherous be disappointed in their schemes. ℟

Show me your ways, O Lord,
and teach me your paths.
Lead me in your truth and teach me,
for you are the God of my salvation;
in you have I trusted all the day long. ℟

Remember, O Lord, your compassion and love,
for they are from everlasting.
Remember not the sins of my youth
and my transgressions;
remember me according to your love
and for the sake of your goodness, O Lord. ℟

Gracious and upright is the Lord;
therefore he teaches sinners in his way.
He guides the humble in doing right
and teaches his way to the lowly. ℟

All the paths of the Lord are love and faithfulness
to those who keep his covenant and his testimonies.
For your name's sake, O Lord,
forgive my sin, for it is great. ℟

SECOND READING   Colossians 1.1–14

A reading from the letter of Paul to the Colossians.

Paul, an apostle of Christ Jesus by the will of God, and Timothy our brother,
To the saints and faithful brothers and sisters in Christ in Colossae: Grace to
you and peace from God our Father.

In our prayers for you we always thank God, the Father of our Lord Jesus
Christ, for we have heard of your faith in Christ Jesus and of the love that
you have for all the saints, because of the hope laid up for you in heaven.
You have heard of this hope before in the word of the truth,
the gospel that has come to you. Just as it is bearing fruit and growing in the
whole world, so it has been bearing fruit among yourselves from the day you
heard it and truly comprehended the grace of God. This you learned from
Epaphras, our beloved fellow-servant. He is a faithful minister of Christ on
your behalf, and he has made known to us your love in the Spirit.

For this reason, since the day we heard it, we have not ceased praying for you and asking that you may be filled with the knowledge of God's will in all spiritual wisdom and understanding, so that you may lead lives worthy of the Lord, fully pleasing to him, as you bear fruit in every good work and as you grow in the knowledge of God. May you be made strong with all the strength that comes from his glorious power, and may you be prepared to endure everything with patience, while joyfully giving thanks to the Father, who has enabled you to share in the inheritance of the saints in the light. He has rescued us from the power of darkness and transferred us into the kingdom of his beloved Son, in whom we have redemption, the forgiveness of sins.

GOSPEL

Luke 10.25–37

Hear the gospel of our Lord Jesus Christ according to Luke.

A lawyer stood up to test Jesus. 'Teacher,' he said, 'what must I do to inherit eternal life?' He said to him, 'What is written in the law? What do you read there?' He answered, 'You shall love the Lord your God with all your heart, and with all your soul, and with all your strength, and with all your mind; and your neighbour as yourself.' And he said to him, 'You have given the right answer; do this, and you will live.'

But wanting to justify himself, he asked Jesus, 'And who is my neighbour?' Jesus replied, 'A man was going down from Jerusalem to Jericho, and fell into the hands of robbers, who stripped him, beat him, and went away, leaving him half dead. Now by chance a priest was going down that road; and when he saw him, he passed by on the other side. So likewise a Levite, when he came to the place and saw him, passed by on the other side. But a Samaritan while travelling came near him; and when he saw him, he was moved with pity. He went to him and bandaged his wounds, having poured oil and wine on them. Then he put him on his own animal, brought him to an inn, and took care of him. The next day he took out two denarii, gave them to the innkeeper, and said, "Take care of him; and when I come back, I will repay you whatever more you spend." Which of these three, do you think, was a neighbour to the man who fell into the hands of the robbers?' He said, 'The one who showed him mercy.' Jesus said to him, 'Go and do likewise.'

† SUNDAY BETWEEN 17 AND 23 JULY   YEAR C
PROPER 11

TRACK 1

FIRST READING   Amos 8.1-12

A reading from the book of the prophet Amos.

This is what the Lord GOD showed me –
a basket of summer fruit.
He said, 'Amos, what do you see?'
And I said, 'A basket of summer fruit.'
Then the LORD said to me,
'The end has come upon my people Israel;
I will never again pass them by.
The songs of the temple shall become wailings in that day,' says the Lord
GOD;
'the dead bodies shall be many, cast out in every place.
Be silent!'
Hear this, you that trample on the needy,
and bring to ruin the poor of the land,
saying, 'When will the new moon be over so that we may sell grain;
and the sabbath, so that we may offer wheat for sale?
We will make the ephah small and the shekel great,
and practise deceit with false balances,
buying the poor for silver
and the needy for a pair of sandals,
and selling the sweepings of the wheat.'

The LORD has sworn by the pride of Jacob:
Surely I will never forget any of their deeds.
Shall not the land tremble on this account,
and everyone mourn who lives in it,
and all of it rise like the Nile, and be tossed about and sink again,
like the Nile of Egypt?

On that day, says the Lord GOD,
I will make the sun go down at noon,
and darken the earth in broad daylight.
I will turn your feasts into mourning,

and all your songs into lamentation;
I will bring sackcloth on all loins,
and baldness on every head;
I will make it like the mourning for an only son,
and the end of it like a bitter day.

The time is surely coming, says the Lord GOD,
when I will send a famine on the land;
not a famine of bread, or a thirst for water,
but of hearing the words of the LORD.
They shall wander from sea to sea,
and from north to east; they shall run to and fro,
seeking the word of the LORD,
but they shall not find it.

PSALM   Psalm 52

℟ **You tyrant, why do you boast of wickedness?**

You tyrant, why do you boast of wickedness
against the godly all day long?
You plot ruin; your tongue is like a sharpened razor,
O worker of deception.
You love evil more than good
and lying more than speaking the truth.
You love all words that hurt,
O you deceitful tongue. ℟

O that God would demolish you utterly,
topple you and snatch you from your dwelling
and root you out of the land of the living!
The righteous shall see and tremble,
and they shall laugh, saying,
'This is the one who did not take God for a refuge,
but trusted in great wealth and relied upon wickedness.' ℟

But I am like a green olive tree in the house of God;
I trust in the mercy of God for ever and ever.
I will give you thanks for what you have done
and declare the goodness of your name
in the presence of the godly. ℟

Or TRACK 2

FIRST READING

Genesis 18.1–10a

A reading from the book of Genesis.

The LORD appeared to Abraham by the oaks of Mamre, as he sat at the entrance of his tent in the heat of the day. He looked up and saw three men standing near him. When he saw them, he ran from the tent entrance to meet them, and bowed down to the ground. He said, 'My lord, if I find favour with you, do not pass by your servant. Let a little water be brought, and wash your feet, and rest yourselves under the tree. Let me bring a little bread, that you may refresh yourselves, and after that you may pass on – since you have come to your servant.' So they said, 'Do as you have said.' And Abraham hastened into the tent to Sarah, and said, 'Make ready quickly three measures of choice flour, knead it, and make cakes.' Abraham ran to the herd, and took a calf, tender and good, and gave it to the servant, who hastened to prepare it. Then he took curds and milk and the calf that he had prepared, and set it before them; and he stood by them under the tree while they ate.

They said to him, 'Where is your wife Sarah?' And he said, 'There, in the tent.' Then one said, 'I will surely return to you in due season, and your wife Sarah shall have a son.'

PSALM

Psalm 15

℟ **Those who do what is right**
will dwell in the presence of the Lord.

Lord, who may dwell in your tabernacle?
who may abide upon your holy hill?
Whoever leads a blameless life and does what is right,
who speaks the truth from his heart. ℟

There is no guile upon his tongue;
he does no evil to his friend;
he does not heap contempt upon his neighbour.
In his sight the wicked are rejected,
but he honours those who fear the Lord. ℟

He has sworn to do no wrong
and does not take back his word.
He does not give his money in hope of gain,

nor does he take a bribe against the innocent.
Whoever does these things
shall never be overthrown. ℟

SECOND READING   Colossians 1.15–28

A reading from the letter of Paul to the Colossians.

Christ is the image of the invisible God, the firstborn of all creation; for in
him all things in heaven and on earth were created, things visible and
invisible, whether thrones or dominions or rulers or powers – all things have
been created through him and for him. He himself is before all things, and in
him all things hold together. He is the head of the body, the church; he is the
beginning, the firstborn from the dead, so that he might come to have first
place in everything. For in him all the fullness of God was pleased to dwell,
and through him God was pleased to reconcile to himself all things, whether
on earth or in heaven, by making peace through the blood of his cross.

And you who were once estranged and hostile in mind, doing evil deeds, he
has now reconciled in his fleshly body through death, so as to present you
holy and blameless and irreproachable before him – provided that you
continue securely established and steadfast in the faith, without shifting from
the hope promised by the gospel that you heard, which has been proclaimed
to every creature under heaven. I, Paul, became a servant of this gospel.

I am now rejoicing in my sufferings for your sake, and in my flesh I am
completing what is lacking in Christ's afflictions for the sake of his body,
that is, the church. I became its servant according to God's commission that
was given to me for you, to make the word of God fully known, the mystery
that has been hidden throughout the ages and generations but has now been
revealed to his saints. To them God chose to make known how great among
the Gentiles are the riches of the glory of this mystery, which is Christ in
you, the hope of glory. It is he whom we proclaim, warning everyone and
teaching everyone in all wisdom, so that we may present everyone mature
in Christ.

GOSPEL   Luke 10.38–42

Hear the gospel of our Lord Jesus Christ according to Luke.

Now as Jesus and his disciples went on their way, he entered a certain village,
where a woman named Martha welcomed him into her home. She had a

sister named Mary, who sat at the Lord's feet and listened to what he was saying. But Martha was distracted by her many tasks; so she came to Jesus and asked, 'Lord, do you not care that my sister has left me to do all the work by myself? Tell her then to help me.' But the Lord answered her, 'Martha, Martha, you are worried and distracted by many things; there is need of only one thing. Mary has chosen the better part, which will not be taken away from her.'

† SUNDAY BETWEEN 24 AND 30 JULY   YEAR C
PROPER 12

TRACK 1

FIRST READING   **Hosea 1.2–10**

A reading from the book of the prophet Hosea.

When the LORD first spoke through Hosea, the LORD said to Hosea, 'Go, take for yourself a wife of whoredom and have children of whoredom, for the land commits great whoredom by forsaking the LORD.' So he went and took Gomer daughter of Diblaim, and she conceived and bore him a son. And the LORD said to him, 'Name him Jezreel; for in a little while I will punish the house of Jehu for the blood of Jezreel, and I will put an end to the kingdom of the house of Israel. On that day I will break the bow of Israel in the valley of Jezreel.' She conceived again and bore a daughter. Then the LORD said to him, 'Name her Lo-ruhamah, for I will no longer have pity on the house of Israel or forgive them. But I will have pity on the house of Judah, and I will save them by the LORD their God; I will not save them by bow, or by sword, or by war, or by horses, or by horsemen.' When she had weaned Lo-ruhamah, she conceived and bore a son. Then the LORD said, 'Name him Lo-ammi, for you are not my people and I am not your God.'

Yet the number of the people of Israel shall be like the sand of the sea, which can be neither measured nor numbered; and in the place where it was said to them, 'You are not my people,' it shall be said to them, 'Children of the living God.'

PSALM   **Psalm 85**

℟ **Show us your mercy, O Lord**
  [and grant us your salvation].

You have been gracious to your land, O Lord,
you have restored the good fortune of Jacob.
You have forgiven the iniquity of your people
and blotted out all their sins.
You have withdrawn all your fury
and turned yourself from your wrathful indignation. ℟

Restore us then, O God our Saviour;
let your anger depart from us.
Will you be displeased with us for ever?
will you prolong your anger from age to age?
Will you not give us life again,
that your people may rejoice in you?
Show us your mercy, O Lord,
and grant us your salvation. ℟

I will listen to what the Lord God is saying,
for he is speaking peace to his faithful people
and to those who turn their hearts to him.
Truly, his salvation is very near to those who fear him,
that his glory may dwell in our land. ℟

Mercy and truth have met together;
righteousness and peace have kissed each other.
Truth shall spring up from the earth,
and righteousness shall look down from heaven. ℟

The Lord will indeed grant prosperity,
and our land will yield its increase.
Righteousness shall go before him,
and peace shall be a pathway for his feet. ℟

Or   TRACK 2

FIRST READING   **Genesis 18.20–32**

A reading from the book of Genesis.

The LORD appeared to Abraham by the oaks of Mamre and said, 'How great is the outcry against Sodom and Gomorrah and how very grave their sin! I must go down and see whether they have done altogether according to the outcry that has come to me; and if not, I will know.'

So the men turned from there, and went towards Sodom, while Abraham remained standing before the LORD. Then Abraham came near and said, 'Will you indeed sweep away the righteous with the wicked? Suppose there are fifty righteous within the city; will you then sweep away the place and not forgive it for the fifty righteous who are in it? Far be it from you to do such a thing, to slay the righteous with the wicked, so that the righteous fare as the wicked! Far be that from you! Shall not the Judge of all the earth do what is just?' And the LORD said, 'If I find at Sodom fifty righteous in the city, I will forgive the whole place for their sake.' Abraham answered, 'Let me take it upon myself to speak to the Lord, I who am but dust and ashes. Suppose five of the fifty righteous are lacking? Will you destroy the whole city for lack of five?' And he said, 'I will not destroy it if I find forty-five there.' Again Abraham spoke to the LORD, 'Suppose forty are found there.' He answered, 'For the sake of forty I will not do it.' Then Abraham said, 'Oh do not let the Lord be angry if I speak. Suppose thirty are found there.' The LORD answered, 'I will not do it, if I find thirty there.' Abraham said, 'Let me take it upon myself to speak to the Lord. Suppose twenty are found there.' The LORD answered, 'For the sake of twenty I will not destroy it.' Then he said, 'Oh do not let the Lord be angry if I speak just once more. Suppose ten are found there.' The LORD answered, 'For the sake of ten I will not destroy it.'

PSALM   **Psalm 138**

℟ **When I called, you answered me, O Lord.**

I will give thanks to you, O Lord, with my whole heart;
before the gods I will sing your praise.
I will bow down towards your holy temple
and praise your name,
because of your love and faithfulness;

For you have glorified your name
and your word above all things. ℟

When I called, you answered me;
you increased my strength within me.
All the kings of the earth will praise you, O Lord,
when they have heard the words of your mouth.
They will sing of the ways of the Lord,
that great is the glory of the Lord.
Though the Lord be high, he cares for the lowly;
he perceives the haughty from afar. ℟

Though I walk in the midst of trouble,
you keep me safe;
you stretch forth your hand
against the fury of my enemies;
your right hand shall save me.
The Lord will make good his purpose for me;
O Lord, your love endures for ever;
do not abandon the works of your hands. ℟

SECOND READING (Short or long reading)

Colossians 2.6–15, (16–19)

A reading from the letter of Paul to the Colossians.

Brothers and sisters, as you have received Christ Jesus the Lord, continue to live your lives in him, rooted and built up in him and established in the faith, just as you were taught, abounding in thanksgiving.

See to it that no one takes you captive through philosophy and empty deceit, according to human tradition, according to the elemental spirits of the universe, and not according to Christ. For in him the whole fullness of deity dwells bodily, and you have come to fullness in him, who is the head of every ruler and authority. In him also you were circumcised with a spiritual circumcision, by putting off the body of the flesh in the circumcision of Christ; when you were buried with him in baptism, you were also raised with him through faith in the power of God, who raised him from the dead. And when you were dead in trespasses and the uncircumcision of your flesh, God made you alive together with him, when he forgave us all our trespasses, erasing the record that stood against us with its legal demands. He set this aside, nailing it to the cross.

669

He disarmed the rulers and authorities and made a public example of them, triumphing over them in it. [Therefore do not let anyone condemn you in matters of food and drink or of observing festivals, new moons, or sabbaths. These are only a shadow of what is to come, but the substance belongs to Christ.

Do not let anyone disqualify you, insisting on self-abasement and worship of angels, dwelling on visions, puffed up without cause by a human way of thinking, and not holding fast to the head, from whom the whole body, nourished and held together by its ligaments and sinews, grows with a growth that is from God.]

GOSPEL   Luke 11.1–13

Hear the gospel of our Lord Jesus Christ according to Luke.

Jesus was praying in a certain place, and after he had finished, one of his disciples said to him, 'Lord, teach us to pray, as John taught his disciples.' He said to them, 'When you pray, say:
Father, hallowed be your name.
Your kingdom come.
Give us each day our daily bread.
And forgive us our sins,
for we ourselves forgive everyone indebted to us.
And do not bring us to the time of trial.'

And he said to them, 'Suppose one of you has a friend, and you go to him at midnight and say to him, "Friend, lend me three loaves of bread; for a friend of mine has arrived, and I have nothing to set before him." And he answers from within, "Do not bother me; the door has already been locked, and my children are with me in bed; I cannot get up and give you anything." I tell you, even though he will not get up and give him anything because he is his friend, at least because of his persistence he will get up and give him whatever he needs.

So I say to you, Ask, and it will be given to you; search, and you will find; knock, and the door will be opened for you. For everyone who asks receives, and everyone who searches finds, and for everyone who knocks, the door will be opened. Is there anyone among you who, if your child asks for a fish, will give a snake instead of a fish? Or if the child asks for an egg, will give a scorpion? If you then, who are evil, know how to give good gifts to your children, how much more will the heavenly Father give the Holy Spirit to those who ask him!'

† SUNDAY BETWEEN 31 JULY AND 6 AUGUST   YEAR C
PROPER 13

TRACK 1

FIRST READING   Hosea 11.1–11

A reading from the book of the prophet Hosea.

Hear the word of the LORD, O people.
When Israel was a child, I loved him,
and out of Egypt I called my son.
The more I called them,
the more they went from me;
they kept sacrificing to the Baals,
and offering incense to idols.

Yet it was I who taught Ephraim to walk,
I took them up in my arms;
but they did not know that I healed them.
I led them with cords of human kindness,
with bands of love.
I was to them like those
who lift infants to their cheeks.
I bent down to them and fed them.

They shall return to the land of Egypt,
and Assyria shall be their king,
because they have refused to return to me.
The sword rages in their cities,
it consumes their oracle-priests,
and devours because of their schemes.
My people are bent on turning away from me.
To the Most High they call, but he does not raise them up at all.

How can I give you up, Ephraim?
How can I hand you over, O Israel?
How can I make you like Admah?
How can I treat you like Zeboiim?
My heart recoils within me;
my compassion grows warm and tender.
I will not execute my fierce anger;

I will not again destroy Ephraim;
for I am God and no mortal,
the Holy One in your midst,
and I will not come in wrath.

They shall go after the LORD,
who roars like a lion;
when he roars, his children shall come trembling from the west.
They shall come trembling like birds from Egypt,
and like doves from the land of Assyria;
and I will return them to their homes, says the LORD.

PSALM

Psalm 107.1–9, 43

℟ Give thanks to the Lord for his mercy
   [and the wonders he does for his children].

Give thanks to the Lord, for he is good,
and his mercy endures for ever.
Let all those whom the Lord has redeemed proclaim
that he redeemed them from the hand of the foe.
He gathered them out of the lands;
from the east and from the west,
from the north and from the south. ℟

Some wandered in desert wastes;
they found no way to a city where they might dwell.
They were hungry and thirsty;
their spirits languished within them.
Then they cried to the Lord in their trouble,
and he delivered them from their distress. ℟

He put their feet on a straight path
to go to a city where they might dwell.

[Let them give thanks to the Lord for his mercy
and the wonders he does for his children.]

For he satisfies the thirsty
and fills the hungry with good things.
Whoever is wise will ponder these things,
and consider well the mercies of the Lord. ℟

Or   TRACK 2

FIRST READING   **Ecclesiastes 1.2, 12–14; 2.18–23**

A reading from the book of Ecclesiastes.

Vanity of vanities, says the Teacher,
vanity of vanities! All is vanity.

I, the Teacher, when king over Israel in Jerusalem, applied my mind to seek
and to search out by wisdom all that is done under heaven; it is an unhappy
business that God has given to human beings to be busy with. I saw all the
deeds that are done under the sun; and see, all is vanity and a chasing after
wind.

I hated all my toil in which I had toiled under the sun, seeing that I must
leave it to those who come after me – and who knows whether they will be
wise or foolish? Yet they will be master of all for which I toiled and used my
wisdom under the sun. This also is vanity. So I turned and gave my heart up
to despair concerning all the toil of my labours under the sun, because
sometimes one who has toiled with wisdom and knowledge and skill must
leave all to be enjoyed by another who did not toil for it. This also is vanity
and a great evil. What do mortals get from all the toil and strain with which
they toil under the sun? For all their days are full of pain, and their work is a
vexation; even at night their minds do not rest. This also is vanity.

PSALM   **Psalm 49.1–12**

℟ **My mouth, O Lord, shall speak of wisdom.**

Hear this, all you peoples;
hearken, all you who dwell in the world,
you of high degree and low, rich and poor together.
My mouth shall speak of wisdom,
and my heart shall meditate on understanding. ℟

I will incline my ear to a proverb
and set forth my riddle upon the harp.
Why should I be afraid in evil days,
when the wickedness of those at my heels surrounds me,
The wickedness of those
who put their trust in their goods,
and boast of their great riches? ℟

We can never ransom ourselves,
or deliver to God the price of our life;
For the ransom of our life is so great,
that we should never have enough to pay it,
In order to live for ever and ever,
and never see the grave. ℟

For we see that the wise die also;
like the dull and stupid they perish
and leave their wealth to those who come after them.
Their graves shall be their homes for ever,
their dwelling places from generation to generation,
though they call the lands after their own names. ℟

Even though honoured, they cannot live for ever;
they are like the beasts that perish.
Such is the way of those
who foolishly trust in themselves,
and the end of those who delight in their own words. ℟

SECOND READING   Colossians 3.1–11

A reading from the letter of Paul to the Colossians.

If you have been raised with Christ, seek the things that are above, where
Christ is, seated at the right hand of God. Set your minds on things that are
above, not on things that are on earth, for you have died, and your life is
hidden with Christ in God. When Christ who is your life is revealed, then
you also will be revealed with him in glory.

Put to death, therefore, whatever in you is earthly: fornication, impurity,
passion, evil desire, and greed (which is idolatry). On account of these the
wrath of God is coming on those who are disobedient. These are the ways
you also once followed, when you were living that life. But now you must get
rid of all such things – anger, wrath, malice, slander, and abusive language
from your mouth. Do not lie to one another, seeing that you have stripped
off the old self with its practices and have clothed yourselves with the new
self, which is being renewed in knowledge according to the image of its
creator. In that renewal there is no longer Greek and Jew, circumcised and
uncircumcised, barbarian, Scythian, slave and free; but Christ is all and in all!

GOSPEL   Luke 12.13–21

Hear the gospel of our Lord Jesus Christ according to Luke.

Someone in the crowd said to Jesus, 'Teacher, tell my brother to divide the family inheritance with me.' But he said to him, 'Friend, who set me to be a judge or arbitrator over you?' And he said to the crowd, 'Take care! Be on your guard against all kinds of greed; for one's life does not consist in the abundance of possessions.' Then he told them a parable: 'The land of a rich man produced abundantly. And he thought to himself, "What should I do, for I have no place to store my crops?" Then he said, "I will do this: I will pull down my barns and build larger ones, and there I will store all my grain and my goods. And I will say to my soul, 'Soul, you have ample goods laid up for many years; relax, eat, drink, be merry.'" But God said to him, "You fool! This very night your life is being demanded of you. And the things you have prepared, whose will they be?" So it is with those who store up treasures for themselves but are not rich towards God.'

† SUNDAY BETWEEN 7 AND 13 AUGUST   YEAR C
PROPER 14

TRACK 1

FIRST READING   Isaiah 1.1, 10–20

A reading from the book of the prophet Isaiah.

The vision of Isaiah son of Amoz, which he saw concerning Judah and Jerusalem in the days of Uzziah, Jotham, Ahaz, and Hezekiah, kings of Judah.

Hear the word of the LORD, you rulers of Sodom!
Listen to the teaching of our God, you people of Gomorrah!
What to me is the multitude of your sacrifices? says the LORD;
I have had enough of burnt-offerings of rams and the fat of fed beasts;
I do not delight in the blood of bulls, or of lambs, or of goats.

When you come to appear before me,
who asked this from your hand?
Trample my courts no more;
bringing offerings is futile;
incense is an abomination to me.
New moon and sabbath and calling of convocation –
I cannot endure solemn assemblies with iniquity.

Your new moons and your appointed festivals my soul hates;
they have become a burden to me,
I am weary of bearing them.
When you stretch out your hands,
I will hide my eyes from you;
even though you make many prayers, I will not listen;
your hands are full of blood.
Wash yourselves;
make yourselves clean;
remove the evil of your doings from before my eyes;
cease to do evil,
learn to do good;
seek justice, rescue the oppressed,
defend the orphan, plead for the widow.

Come now, let us argue it out, says the LORD:
though your sins are like scarlet, they shall be like snow;
though they are red like crimson, they shall become like wool.
If you are willing and obedient,
you shall eat the good of the land;
but if you refuse and rebel,
you shall be devoured by the sword;
for the mouth of the LORD has spoken.

PSALM   **Psalm 50.1-8, 23-24**

℟ **Our God will come, and will not keep silence.**
　or
℟ **The heavens declare the rightness of God's cause.**

The Lord, the God of gods, has spoken;
he has called the earth
from the rising of the sun to its setting.
Out of Zion, perfect in its beauty,
God reveals himself in glory. ℟

Our God will come and will not keep silence;
before him there is a consuming flame,
and round about him a raging storm.
He calls the heavens and the earth from above
to witness the judgement of his people. ℟

'Gather before me my loyal followers,
those who have made a covenant with me
and sealed it with sacrifice.'
Let the heavens declare the rightness of his cause;
for God himself is judge. ℟

Hear, O my people, and I will speak:
'O Israel, I will bear witness against you;
for I am God, your God.
I do not accuse you because of your sacrifices;
your offerings are always before me. ℟

Consider this well, you who forget God,
lest I rend you and there be none to deliver you.
Whoever offers me the sacrifice of thanksgiving honours me;
but to those who keep in my way
will I show the salvation of God.' ℟

Or   TRACK 2

FIRST READING   **Genesis 15.1–6**

A reading from the book of Genesis.

The word of the LORD came to Abram in a vision, 'Do not be afraid, Abram, I
am your shield; your reward shall be very great.' But Abram said, 'O Lord
GOD, what will you give me, for I continue childless, and the heir of my
house is Eliezer of Damascus?' And Abram said, 'You have given me no
offspring, and so a slave born in my house is to be my heir.' But the word of
the LORD came to him, 'This man shall not be your heir; no one but your
very own issue shall be your heir.' The Lord brought Abraham outside and
said, 'Look toward heaven and count the stars, if you are able to count them.'
Then he said to him, 'So shall your descendants be.' And he believed the
LORD; and the LORD reckoned it to him as righteousness.

PSALM   **Psalm 33.12–22**

℟ **Happy the people the Lord has chosen as his own!**

Happy is the nation whose God is the Lord!
happy the people he has chosen to be his own!
The Lord looks down from heaven,
and beholds all the people in the world.
From where he sits enthroned he turns his gaze
on all who dwell on the earth. ℟

He fashions all the hearts of them
and understands all their works.
There is no king that can be saved by a mighty army;
the strong are not delivered by great strength.
The horse is a vain hope for deliverance;
for all its strength it cannot save. ℟

Behold, the eye of the Lord
is upon those who fear him,
on those who wait upon his love,
To pluck their lives from death,
and to feed them in time of famine. ℟

Our soul waits for the Lord;
he is our help and our shield.
Indeed, our heart rejoices in him,
for in his holy name we put our trust.
Let your loving-kindness, O Lord, be upon us,
as we have put our trust in you. ℟

SECOND READING   **Hebrews 11.1–3, 8–16**

A reading from the letter to the Hebrews.

Faith is the assurance of things hoped for, the conviction of things not seen.
Indeed, by faith our ancestors received approval. By faith we understand that
the worlds were prepared by the word of God, so that what is seen was made
from things that are not visible.

By faith Abraham obeyed when he was called to set out for a place that he
was to receive as an inheritance; and he set out, not knowing where he was
going. By faith he stayed for a time in the land he had been promised, as in a
foreign land, living in tents, as did Isaac and Jacob, who were heirs with him
of the same promise. For he looked forward to the city that has foundations,
whose architect and builder is God. By faith he received power of
procreation, even though he was too old – and Sarah herself was barren –
because he considered him faithful who had promised. Therefore from one
person, and this one as good as dead, descendants were born, 'as many as the
stars of heaven and as the innumerable grains of sand by the seashore.'

All of these died in faith without having received the promises, but from a
distance they saw and greeted them. They confessed that they were strangers
and foreigners on the earth, for people who speak in this way make it clear

that they are seeking a homeland. If they had been thinking of the land that they had left behind, they would have had opportunity to return. But as it is, they desire a better country, that is, a heavenly one. Therefore God is not ashamed to be called their God; indeed, he has prepared a city for them.

GOSPEL   **Luke 12.32–40**

Hear the gospel of our Lord Jesus Christ according to Luke.

Jesus said to his disciples,
'Do not be afraid, little flock, for it is your Father's good pleasure to give you the kingdom. Sell your possessions, and give alms. Make purses for yourselves that do not wear out, an unfailing treasure in heaven, where no thief comes near and no moth destroys. For where your treasure is, there your heart will be also.

Be dressed for action and have your lamps lit; be like those who are waiting for their master to return from the wedding banquet, so that they may open the door for him as soon as he comes and knocks. Blessed are those slaves whom the master finds alert when he comes; truly I tell you, he will fasten his belt and have them sit down to eat, and he will come and serve them. If he comes during the middle of the night, or near dawn, and finds them so, blessed are those slaves.

But know this: if the owner of the house had known at what hour the thief was coming, he would not have let his house be broken into. You also must be ready, for the Son of Man is coming at an unexpected hour.'

† SUNDAY BETWEEN 14 AND 20 AUGUST   YEAR C
PROPER 15

TRACK 1

FIRST READING   **Isaiah 5.1–7**

A reading from the book of the prophet Isaiah.

Let me sing for my beloved
my love-song concerning his vineyard:
My beloved had a vineyard on a very fertile hill.
He dug it and cleared it of stones,

and planted it with choice vines;
he built a watch-tower in the midst of it,
and hewed out a wine vat in it;
he expected it to yield grapes,
but it yielded wild grapes.

And now, inhabitants of Jerusalem and people of Judah,
judge between me and my vineyard.
What more was there to do for my vineyard
that I have not done in it?
When I expected it to yield grapes,
why did it yield wild grapes?

And now I will tell you what I will do to my vineyard.
I will remove its hedge, and it shall be devoured;
I will break down its wall, and it shall be trampled down.
I will make it a waste;
it shall not be pruned or hoed,
and it shall be overgrown with briers and thorns;
I will also command the clouds
that they rain no rain upon it.
For the vineyard of the LORD of hosts is the house of Israel,
and the people of Judah are his pleasant planting;
he expected justice, but saw bloodshed;
righteousness, but heard a cry!

PSALM   **Psalm 80.1–2, 8–18**

℟ **Show the light of your countenance
and we shall be saved.**
   or
℟ **O God of hosts, look down from heaven;
behold and tend this vine.**

Hear, O Shepherd of Israel, leading Joseph like a flock;
shine forth, you that are enthroned upon the cherubim.
In the presence of Ephraim, Benjamin and Manasseh,
stir up your strength and come to help us. ℟

You have brought a vine out of Egypt;
you cast out the nations and planted it.
You prepared the ground for it;

it took root and filled the land.
The mountains were covered by its shadow
and the towering cedar trees by its boughs.
You stretched out its tendrils to the Sea
and its branches to the River. ℟

Why have you broken down its wall,
so that all who pass by pluck off its grapes?
The wild boar of the forest has ravaged it,
and the beasts of the field have grazed upon it.
Turn now, O God of hosts, look down from heaven;
behold and tend this vine;
preserve what your right hand has planted. ℟

They burn it with fire like rubbish;
at the rebuke of your countenance let them perish.
Let your hand be upon the man of your right hand,
the son of man you have made so strong for yourself. ℟

And so will we never turn away from you;
give us life, that we may call upon your name.
Restore us, O Lord God of hosts;
show the light of your countenance
and we shall be saved. ℟

Or   TRACK 2

FIRST READING   Jeremiah 23.23–29

A reading from the book of the prophet Jeremiah.

Am I a God near by, says the LORD, and not a God far off? Who can hide in secret places so that I cannot see them? says the LORD. Do I not fill heaven and earth? says the LORD. I have heard what the prophets have said who prophesy lies in my name, saying, 'I have dreamed, I have dreamed!' How long? Will the hearts of the prophets ever turn back – those who prophesy lies, and who prophesy the deceit of their own heart? They plan to make my people forget my name by their dreams that they tell one another, just as their ancestors forgot my name for Baal. Let the prophet who has a dream tell the dream, but let the one who has my word speak my word faithfully. What has straw in common with wheat? says the LORD. Is not my word like fire, says the LORD, and like a hammer that breaks a rock in pieces?

PSALM   Psalm 82

℞ **Arise, O God, and rule the earth.**

God takes his stand in the council of heaven;
he gives judgement in the midst of the gods:
'How long will you judge unjustly,
and show favour to the wicked? ℞

Save the weak and the orphan;
defend the humble and needy;
Rescue the weak and the poor
deliver them from the power of the wicked. ℞

They do not know, neither do they understand;
they go about in darkness;
all the foundations of the earth are shaken. ℞

Now I say to you, "You are gods,
and all of you children of the Most High;
Nevertheless, you shall die like mortals,
and fall like any prince."'
Arise, O God, and rule the earth,
for you shall take all nations for you own. ℞

SECOND READING   Hebrews 11.29 – 12.2

A reading from the letter to the Hebrews.

By faith the people passed of Israel through the Red Sea as if it were dry land,
but when the Egyptians attempted to do so they were drowned. By faith the
walls of Jericho fell after they had been encircled for seven days. By faith
Rahab the prostitute did not perish with those who were disobedient, because
she had received the spies in peace.

And what more should I say? For time would fail me to tell of Gideon, Barak,
Samson, Jephthah, of David and Samuel and the prophets – who through
faith conquered kingdoms, administered justice, obtained promises, shut the
mouths of lions, quenched raging fire, escaped the edge of the sword, won
strength out of weakness, became mighty in war, put foreign armies to flight.
Women received their dead by resurrection. Others were tortured, refusing to
accept release, in order to obtain a better resurrection. Others suffered

mocking and flogging, and even chains and imprisonment. They were stoned to death, they were sawn in two, they were killed by the sword; they went about in skins of sheep and goats, destitute, persecuted, tormented – of whom the world was not worthy. They wandered in deserts and mountains, and in caves and holes in the ground.

Yet all these, though they were commended for their faith, did not receive what was promised, since God had provided something better so that they would not, apart from us, be made perfect.

Therefore, since we are surrounded by so great a cloud of witnesses, let us also lay aside every weight and the sin that clings so closely, and let us run with perseverance the race that is set before us, looking to Jesus the pioneer and perfecter of our faith, who for the sake of the joy that was set before him endured the cross, disregarding its shame, and has taken his seat at the right hand of the throne of God.

GOSPEL   **Luke 12.49–56**

Hear the gospel of our Lord Jesus Christ according to Luke.

Jesus said to his disciples: 'I came to bring fire to the earth, and how I wish it were already kindled! I have a baptism with which to be baptized, and what stress I am under until it is completed! Do you think that I have come to bring peace to the earth? No, I tell you, but rather division! From now on five in one household will be divided, three against two and two against three; they will be divided:
father against son and son against father,
mother against daughter and daughter against mother,
mother-in-law against her daughter-in-law
and daughter-in-law against mother-in-law.'

He also said to the crowds, 'When you see a cloud rising in the west, you immediately say, "It is going to rain"; and so it happens. And when you see the south wind blowing, you say, "There will be scorching heat"; and it happens. You hypocrites! You know how to interpret the appearance of earth and sky, but why do you not know how to interpret the present time?'

† SUNDAY BETWEEN 21 AND 27 AUGUST   YEAR C
PROPER 16

TRACK 1

FIRST READING   Jeremiah 1.4–10

A reading from the book of the prophet Jeremiah.

The word of the LORD came to me saying,
'Before I formed you in the womb I knew you,
and before you were born I consecrated you;
I appointed you a prophet to the nations.'
Then I said, 'Ah, Lord GOD!
Truly I do not know how to speak,
for I am only a boy.'
But the LORD said to me,
'Do not say, "I am only a boy";
for you shall go to all to whom I send you,
and you shall speak whatever I command you,
Do not be afraid of them,
for I am with you to deliver you,
says the LORD.'
Then the LORD put out his hand and touched my mouth;
and the LORD said to me,
'Now I have put my words in your mouth.
See, today I appoint you over nations and over kingdoms,
to pluck up and to pull down,
to destroy and to overthrow,
to build and to plant.'

PSALM   Psalm 71.1–6

℞ **You are my hope, O Lord God,**
   [my confidence since I was young].

In you, O Lord, have I taken refuge;
let me never be ashamed.
In your righteousness, deliver me and set me free;
incline your ear to me and save me. ℞

Be my strong rock, a castle to keep me safe;
you are my crag and my stronghold.
Deliver me, my God, from the hand of the wicked,
from the clutches of the evildoer and the oppressor. ℟

For you are my hope, O Lord God,
my confidence since I was young.
I have been sustained by you ever since I was born;
from my mother's womb you have been my strength;
my praise shall be always of you. ℟

Or   TRACK 2

FIRST READING   Isaiah 58.9–14

A reading from the book of the prophet Isaiah.

You shall call, and the LORD will answer;
you shall cry for help, and he will say, Here I am.

If you remove the yoke from among you,
the pointing of the finger, the speaking of evil,
if you offer your food to the hungry
and satisfy the needs of the afflicted,
then your light shall rise in the darkness
and your gloom be like the noonday.
The LORD will guide you continually,
and satisfy your needs in parched places,
and make your bones strong;
and you shall be like a watered garden,
like a spring of water, whose waters never fail.
Your ancient ruins shall be rebuilt;
you shall raise up the foundations of many generations;
you shall be called the repairer of the breach,
the restorer of streets to live in.

If you refrain from trampling the sabbath,
from pursuing your own interests on my holy day;
if you call the sabbath a delight
and the holy day of the LORD honourable;
if you honour it, not going your own ways,
serving your own interests, or pursuing your own affairs;

then you shall take delight in the LORD,
and I will make you ride upon the heights of the earth;
I will feed you with the heritage of your ancestor Jacob,
for the mouth of the LORD has spoken.

PSALM   Psalm 103.1–8

℟ **Bless the Lord, O my soul!**

Bless the Lord, O my soul,
and all that is within me, bless his holy name.
Bless the Lord, O my soul,
and forget not all his benefits. ℟

He forgives all your sins
and heals all your infirmities;
He redeems your life from the grave
and crowns you with mercy and loving-kindness; ℟

He satisfies you with good things,
and your youth is renewed like an eagle's.
The Lord executes righteousness
and judgement for all who are oppressed. ℟

He made his ways known to Moses
and his works to the children of Israel.
The Lord is full of compassion and mercy,
slow to anger and of great kindness. ℟

SECOND READING   Hebrews 12.18–29

A reading from the letter to the Hebrews.

You have not come to something that can be touched, a blazing fire, and
darkness, and gloom, and a tempest, and the sound of a trumpet, and a voice
whose words made the hearers beg that not another word be spoken to them.
(For they could not endure the order that was given, 'If even an animal
touches the mountain, it shall be stoned to death.' Indeed, so terrifying was
the sight that Moses said, 'I tremble with fear.') But you have come to Mount
Zion and to the city of the living God, the heavenly Jerusalem, and to
innumerable angels in festal gathering, and to the assembly of the firstborn

who are enrolled in heaven, and to God the judge of all, and to the spirits of the righteous made perfect, and to Jesus, the mediator of a new covenant, and to the sprinkled blood that speaks a better word than the blood of Abel.

See that you do not refuse the one who is speaking; for if they did not escape when they refused the one who warned them on earth, how much less will we escape if we reject the one who warns from heaven! At that time his voice shook the earth; but now he has promised, 'Yet once more I will shake not only the earth but also the heaven.' This phrase, 'Yet once more,' indicates the removal of what is shaken – that is, created things – so that what cannot be shaken may remain. Therefore, since we are receiving a kingdom that cannot be shaken, let us give thanks, by which we offer to God an acceptable worship with reverence and awe; for indeed our God is a consuming fire.

GOSPEL   Luke 13.10-17

Hear the gospel of our Lord Jesus Christ according to Luke.

Now he was teaching in one of the synagogues on the sabbath. And just then there appeared a woman with a spirit that had crippled her for eighteen years. She was bent over and was quite unable to stand up straight. When Jesus saw her, he called her over and said, 'Woman, you are set free from your ailment.' When he laid his hands on her, immediately she stood up straight and began praising God. But the leader of the synagogue, indignant because Jesus had cured on the sabbath, kept saying to the crowd, 'There are six days on which work ought to be done; come on those days and be cured, and not on the sabbath day.' But the Lord answered him and said, 'You hypocrites! Does not each of you on the sabbath untie his ox or his donkey from the manger, and lead it away to give it water? And ought not this woman, a daughter of Abraham whom Satan bound for eighteen long years, be set free from this bondage on the sabbath day?' When he said this, all his opponents were put to shame; and the entire crowd was rejoicing at all the wonderful things that he was doing.

† SUNDAY BETWEEN 28 AUGUST AND 3 SEPTEMBER PROPER 17

YEAR C

TRACK 1

FIRST READING

Jeremiah 2.4-13

A reading from the book of the prophet Jeremiah.

Hear the word of the LORD, O house of Jacob, and all the families of the house of Israel. Thus says the LORD: What wrong did your ancestors find in me that they went far from me, and went after worthless things, and became worthless themselves? They did not say, 'Where is the LORD who brought us up from the land of Egypt, who led us in the wilderness, in a land of deserts and pits, in a land of drought and deep darkness, in a land that no one passes through, where no one lives?' I brought you into a plentiful land to eat its fruits and its good things. But when you entered you defiled my land, and made my heritage an abomination. The priests did not say, 'Where is the LORD?' Those who handle the law did not know me; the rulers transgressed against me; the prophets prophesied by Baal, and went after things that do not profit. Therefore once more I accuse you, says the LORD, and I accuse your children's children. Cross to the coasts of Cyprus and look, send to Kedar and examine with care; see if there has ever been such a thing. Has a nation changed its gods, even though they are no gods? But my people have changed their glory for something that does not profit. Be appalled, O heavens, at this, be shocked, be utterly desolate, says the LORD,

for my people have committed two evils: they have forsaken me, the fountain of living water, and dug out cisterns for themselves, cracked cisterns that can hold no water.

PSALM

Psalm 81.1, 10-16

℟ **Oh, that my people would listen [that Israel would walk in my ways]!**

Sing with joy to God our strength
and raise a loud shout to the God of Jacob.
I am the Lord your God,
who brought you out of the land of Egypt and said,
'Open your mouth wide and I will fill it.' ℟

And yet my people did not hear my voice,
and Israel would not obey me.
So I gave them over to the stubbornness of their hearts,
to follow their own devices. ℟

O that my people would listen to me!
that Israel would walk in my ways!
I should soon subdue their enemies
and turn my hand against their foes. ℟

Those who hate the Lord would cringe before him,
and their punishment would last for ever.
But Israel would I feed with the finest wheat
and satisfy him with honey from the rock. ℟

Or   TRACK 2

FIRST READING (Alternative readings)

Either   **Ecclesiasticus 10.12–18**

A reading from the book of Ecclesiasticus.

The beginning of human pride is to forsake the Lord;
the heart has withdrawn from its Maker.
For the beginning of pride is sin,
and the one who clings to it pours out abominations.
Therefore the Lord brings upon them unheard-of calamities,
and destroys them completely.
The Lord overthrows the thrones of rulers,
and enthrones the lowly in their place.
The Lord plucks up the roots of the nations,
and plants the humble in their place.
The Lord lays waste the lands of the nations,
and destroys them to the foundations of the earth.
He removes some of them and destroys them,
and erases the memory of them from the earth.
Pride was not created for human beings,
or violent anger for those born of women.

Or   Proverbs 25.6–7

A reading from the book of Proverbs.

Do not put yourself forward in the king's presence
or stand in the place of the great;
for it is better to be told, 'Come up here,'
than to be put lower in the presence of a noble.

PSALM   Psalm 112

℞ **Light shines in the darkness for the upright.**

Alleluia!
Happy are they who fear the Lord
and have great delight in his commandments!
Their descendants will be mighty in the land;
the generation of the upright will be blessed.
Wealth and riches will be in their house,
and their righteousness will last for ever. ℞

Light shines in the darkness for the upright;
the righteous are merciful and full of compassion.
It is good for them to be generous in lending
and to manage their affairs with justice.
For they will never be shaken;
the righteous will be kept in everlasting remembrance. ℞

They will not be afraid of any evil rumours;
their heart is right;
they put their trust in the Lord.
Their heart is established and will not shrink,
until they see their desire upon their enemies. ℞

They have given freely to the poor,
and their righteousness stands fast for ever;
they will hold up their head with honour.
The wicked will see it and be angry;
they will gnash their teeth and pine away;
the desires of the wicked will perish. ℞

SECOND READING   **Hebrews 13.1-8, 15-16**

A reading from the letter to the Hebrews.

Let mutual love continue. Do not neglect to show hospitality to strangers, for by doing that some have entertained angels without knowing it. Remember those who are in prison, as though you were in prison with them; those who are being tortured, as though you yourselves were being tortured. Let marriage be held in honour by all, and let the marriage bed be kept undefiled; for God will judge fornicators and adulterers. Keep your lives free from the love of money, and be content with what you have; for he has said, 'I will never leave you or forsake you.' So we can say with confidence,
'The Lord is my helper;
I will not be afraid.
What can anyone do to me?'
Remember your leaders, those who spoke the word of God to you; consider the outcome of their way of life, and imitate their faith. Jesus Christ is the same yesterday and today and for ever.

Through him, then, let us continually offer a sacrifice of praise to God, that is, the fruit of lips that confess his name. Do not neglect to do good and to share what you have, for such sacrifices are pleasing to God.

GOSPEL   **Luke 14.1, 7-14**

Hear the gospel of our Lord Jesus Christ according to Luke.

On one occasion when Jesus was going to the house of a leader of the Pharisees to eat a meal on the sabbath, they were watching him closely.

When he noticed how the guests chose the places of honour, he told them a parable. 'When you are invited by someone to a wedding banquet, do not sit down at the place of honour, in case someone more distinguished than you has been invited by your host; and the host who invited both of you may come and say to you, "Give this person your place," and then in disgrace you would start to take the lowest place. But when you are invited, go and sit down at the lowest place, so that when your host comes, he may say to you, "Friend, move up higher"; then you will be honoured in the presence of all who sit at the table with you. For all who exalt themselves will be humbled, and those who humble themselves will be exalted.' He said also to the one who had invited him, 'When you give a luncheon or a dinner, do not invite your friends or your brothers or your relatives or rich neighbours, in case they may invite you in return, and you would be repaid.

But when you give a banquet, invite the poor, the crippled, the lame, and the blind. And you will be blessed, because they cannot repay you, for you will be repaid at the resurrection of the righteous.'

† SUNDAY BETWEEN 4 AND 10 SEPTEMBER   YEAR C
PROPER 18

TRACK 1

FIRST READING   Jeremiah 18.1–11

A reading from the book of the prophet Jeremiah.

The word that came to Jeremiah from the LORD:
'Come, go down to the potter's house, and there I will let you hear my words.' So I went down to the potter's house, and there he was working at his wheel. The vessel he was making of clay was spoiled in the potter's hand, and he reworked it into another vessel, as seemed good to him.

Then the word of the LORD came to me: Can I not do with you, O house of Israel, just as this potter has done? says the LORD. Just like the clay in the potter's hand, so are you in my hand, O house of Israel. At one moment I may declare concerning a nation or a kingdom, that I will pluck up and break down and destroy it, but if that nation, concerning which I have spoken, turns from its evil, I will change my mind about the disaster that I intended to bring on it. And at another moment I may declare concerning a nation or a kingdom that I will build and plant it, but if it does evil in my sight, not listening to my voice, then I will change my mind about the good that I had intended to do to it. Now, therefore, say to the people of Judah and the inhabitants of Jerusalem: Thus says the LORD: Look, I am a potter shaping evil against you and devising a plan against you. Turn now, all of you from your evil way, and amend your ways and your doings.

PSALM   Psalm 139.1–5, 12–17

℟ **You, O Lord, created my inward parts;**
[you knit me together in my mother's womb].

Lord, you have searched me out and known me;
you know my sitting down and my rising up;

you discern my thoughts from afar.
You trace my journeys and my resting-places
and are acquainted with all my ways. ℟

Indeed, there is not a word on my lips,
but you, O Lord, know it altogether.
You press upon me behind and before
and lay your hand upon me.
Such knowledge is too wonderful for me;
it is so high that I cannot attain to it. ℟

For you yourself created my inmost parts;
you knit me together in my mother's womb.
I will thank you because I am marvellously made;
your works are wonderful and I know it well. ℟

My body was not hidden from you,
while I was being made in secret
and woven in the depths of the earth.
Your eyes beheld my limbs, yet unfinished in the womb;
all of them were written in your book;
they were fashioned day by day,
when as yet there was none of them. ℟

How deep I find your thoughts, O God!
how great is the sum of them!
If I were to count them,
they would be more in number than the sand;
to count them all,
my life span would need to be like yours. ℟

Or   TRACK 2

FIRST READING   **Deuteronomy 30.15–20**

A reading from the book of Deuteronomy.

See, I have set before you today life and prosperity, death and adversity. If
you obey the commandments of the LORD your God that I am commanding
you today, by loving the LORD your God, walking in his ways, and observing
his commandments, decrees, and ordinances, then you shall live and become
numerous, and the LORD your God will bless you in the land that you are
entering to possess. But if your heart turns away and you do not hear, but are

led astray to bow down to other gods and serve them, I declare to you today that you shall perish; you shall not live long in the land that you are crossing the Jordan to enter and possess. I call heaven and earth to witness against you today that I have set before you life and death, blessings and curses. Choose life so that you and your descendants may live, loving the LORD your God, obeying him, and holding fast to him; for that means life to you and length of days, so that you may live in the land that the LORD swore to give to your ancestors, to Abraham, to Isaac, and to Jacob.

PSALM   Psalm 1

℟ **Lord, my delight is in your law.**

Happy are they who have not walked
in the counsel of the wicked,
nor lingered in the way of sinners,
nor sat in the seats of the scornful!
Their delight is in the law of the Lord,
and they meditate on his law day and night. ℟

They are like trees planted by streams of water,
bearing fruit in due season,
with leaves that do not wither;
everything they do shall prosper.
It is not so with the wicked:
they are like chaff which the wind blows away; ℟

Therefore the wicked shall not stand upright
when judgement comes,
nor the sinner in the council of the righteous.
For the Lord knows the way of the righteous,
but the way of the wicked is doomed. ℟

SECOND READING   Philemon 1–21

A reading from the letter of Paul to Philemon.

Paul, a prisoner of Christ Jesus, and Timothy our brother, To Philemon our dear friend and co-worker, to Apphia our sister, to Archippus our fellow-soldier, and to the church in your house:

Grace to you and peace from God our Father and the Lord Jesus Christ.

When I remember you in my prayers, I always thank my God because I hear of your love for all the saints and your faith towards the Lord Jesus. I pray that the sharing of your faith may become effective when you perceive all the good that we may do for Christ. I have indeed received much joy and encouragement from your love, because the hearts of the saints have been refreshed through you, my brother.

For this reason, though I am bold enough in Christ to command you to do your duty, yet I would rather appeal to you on the basis of love – and I, Paul, do this as an old man, and now also as a prisoner of Christ Jesus. I am appealing to you for my child, Onesimus, whose father I have become during my imprisonment. Formerly he was useless to you, but now he is indeed useful both to you and to me. I am sending him, that is, my own heart, back to you. I wanted to keep him with me, so that he might be of service to me in your place during my imprisonment for the gospel; but I preferred to do nothing without your consent, in order that your good deed might be voluntary and not something forced. Perhaps this is the reason he was separated from you for a while, so that you might have him back for ever, no longer as a slave but more than a slave, a beloved brother – especially to me but how much more to you, both in the flesh and in the Lord.

So if you consider me your partner, welcome him as you would welcome me. If he has wronged you in any way, or owes you anything, charge that to my account. I, Paul, am writing this with my own hand: I will repay it. I say nothing about your owing me even your own self. Yes, brother, let me have this benefit from you in the Lord! Refresh my heart in Christ. Confident of your obedience, I am writing to you, knowing that you will do even more than I say.

GOSPEL   Luke 14.25–33

Hear the gospel of our Lord Jesus Christ according to Luke.

Large crowds were travelling with Jesus; and he turned and said to them, 'Whoever comes to me and does not hate father and mother, wife and children, brothers and sisters, yes, and even life itself, cannot be my disciple. Whoever does not carry the cross and follow me cannot be my disciple. For which of you, intending to build a tower, does not first sit down and estimate the cost, to see whether he has enough to complete it? Otherwise, when he has laid a foundation and is not able to finish, all who see it will begin to ridicule him, saying, "This fellow began to build and was not able to finish." Or what king, going out to wage war against another king, will not sit down first and consider whether he is able with ten thousand to oppose the one who comes against him with twenty thousand? If he cannot, then, while the other is still far away, he sends a delegation and asks for the terms of peace. So therefore, none of you can become my disciple if you do not give up all your possessions.'

† SUNDAY BETWEEN 11 AND 17 SEPTEMBER YEAR C
PROPER 19

TRACK 1

FIRST READING Jeremiah 4.11–12, 22–28

A reading from the book of the prophet Jeremiah.

At that time it will be said to this people and to Jerusalem: A hot wind comes from me out of the bare heights in the desert towards my poor people, not to winnow or cleanse – a wind too strong for that. Now it is I who speak in judgement against them.

'For my people are foolish, they do not know me;
they are stupid children, they have no understanding.
They are skilled in doing evil, but do not know how to do good.'

I looked on the earth,
and lo, it was waste and void;
and to the heavens, and they had no light.
I looked on the mountains,
and lo, they were quaking,
and all the hills moved to and fro.
I looked, and lo,
there was no one at all,
and all the birds of the air had fled.
I looked, and lo,
the fruitful land was a desert,
and all its cities were laid in ruins before the LORD,
before his fierce anger.
For thus says the LORD:
The whole land shall be a desolation;
yet I will not make a full end.
Because of this the earth shall mourn,

and the heavens above grow black;
for I have spoken, I have purposed;
I have not relented nor will I turn back.

PSALM

Psalm 14

℟ **Is there any who is wise
and who seeks after God?**

The fool has said in his heart, 'There is no God.'
All are corrupt and commit abominable acts;
there is none who does any good.
The Lord looks down from heaven upon us all,
to see if there is any who is wise,
if there is one who seeks after God. ℟

Everyone has proved faithless;
all alike have turned bad;
there is none who does good; no, not one.
Have they no knowledge, all those evildoers
who eat up my people like bread
and do not call upon the Lord? ℟

See how they tremble with fear,
because God is in the company of the righteous.
Their aim is to confound the plans of the afflicted,
but the Lord is their refuge.
O that Israel's deliverance would come out of Zion!
when the Lord restores the fortunes of his people,
Jacob will rejoice and Israel be glad. ℟

Or

TRACK 2

FIRST READING

Exodus 32.7–14

A reading from the book of Exodus.

At the top of Mount Sinai, the LORD said to Moses, 'Go down at once! Your
people, whom you brought up out of the land of Egypt, have acted
perversely; they have been quick to turn aside from the way that I
commanded them; they have cast for themselves an image of a calf, and have
worshipped it and sacrificed to it, and said, "These are your gods, O Israel,

who brought you up out of the land of Egypt!"' The LORD said to Moses, 'I have seen this people, how stiff-necked they are. Now let me alone, so that my wrath may burn hot against them and I may consume them; and of you I will make a great nation.'

But Moses implored the LORD his God, and said, 'O LORD, why does your wrath burn hot against your people, whom you brought out of the land of Egypt with great power and with a mighty hand? Why should the Egyptians say, "It was with evil intent that he brought them out to kill them in the mountains, and to consume them from the face of the earth"? Turn from your fierce wrath; change your mind and do not bring disaster on your people. Remember Abraham, Isaac, and Israel, your servants, how you swore to them by your own self, saying to them, "I will multiply your descendants like the stars of heaven, and all this land that I have promised I will give to your descendants, and they shall inherit it for ever."' And the LORD changed his mind about the disaster that he planned to bring on his people.

PSALM   Psalm 51.1–10

℟ **Father, I have sinned against heaven and before you.**
   or
℟ **Hide your face from my sins, O God.**

Have mercy on me, O God,
according to your loving-kindness;
in your great compassion blot out my offences.
Wash me through and through from my wickedness
and cleanse me from my sin. ℟

For I know my transgressions,
and my sin is ever before me.
Against you only have I sinned
and done what is evil in your sight.
And so you are justified when you speak
and upright in your judgement. ℟

Indeed, I have been wicked from my birth,
a sinner from my mother's womb.
For behold, you look for truth deep within me,
and will make me understand wisdom secretly.
Purge me from my sin and I shall be pure;
wash me and I shall be clean indeed. ℟

Make me hear of joy and gladness,
that the body you have broken may rejoice.
Hide your face from my sins
and blot out all my iniquities. ℟

SECOND READING   1 Timothy 1.12–17

A reading from the first letter of Paul to Timothy.

I am grateful to Christ Jesus our Lord, who has strengthened me, because he
judged me faithful and appointed me to his service, even though I was
formerly a blasphemer, a persecutor, and a man of violence. But I received
mercy because I had acted ignorantly in unbelief, and the grace of our Lord
overflowed for me with the faith and love that are in Christ Jesus. The saying
is sure and worthy of full acceptance, that Christ Jesus came into the world to
save sinners – of whom I am the foremost. But for that very reason I received
mercy, so that in me, as the foremost, Jesus Christ might display the utmost
patience, making me an example to those who would come to believe in him
for eternal life. To the King of the ages, immortal, invisible, the only God, be
honour and glory for ever and ever. Amen.

GOSPEL   Luke 15.1–10

Hear the gospel of our Lord Jesus Christ according to Luke.

All the tax-collectors and sinners were coming near to listen to Jesus.
And the Pharisees and the scribes were grumbling and saying, 'This fellow
welcomes sinners and eats with them.' So he told them this parable: 'Which
one of you, having a hundred sheep and losing one of them, does not leave
the ninety-nine in the wilderness and go after the one that is lost until he
finds it? When he has found it, he lays it on his shoulders and rejoices. And
when he comes home, he calls together his friends and neighbours, saying to
them, "Rejoice with me, for I have found my sheep that was lost."
Just so, I tell you, there will be more joy in heaven over one sinner who
repents than over ninety-nine righteous persons who need no repentance.

Or what woman having ten silver coins, if she loses one of them, does not
light a lamp, sweep the house, and search carefully until she finds it? When
she has found it, she calls together her friends and neighbours, saying,
"Rejoice with me, for I have found the coin that I had lost." Just so, I tell you,
there is joy in the presence of the angels of God over one sinner who
repents.'

† SUNDAY BETWEEN 18 AND 24 SEPTEMBER   YEAR C
PROPER 20

TRACK 1

FIRST READING   Jeremiah 8.18 – 9.1

A reading from the book of the prophet Jeremiah.

The word of the LORD through the prophet:
My joy is gone, grief is upon me,
my heart is sick.
Hark, the cry of my poor people from far and wide in the land:
'Is the LORD not in Zion?
Is her King not in her?'
('Why have they provoked me to anger with their images,
with their foreign idols?')
'The harvest is past, the summer is ended,
and we are not saved.'
For the hurt of my poor people I am hurt,
I mourn, and dismay has taken hold of me.

Is there no balm in Gilead?
Is there no physician there?
Why then has the health of my poor people not been restored?
O that my head were a spring of water,
and my eyes a fountain of tears,
so that I might weep day and night
for the slain of my poor people!

PSALM   Psalm 79.1-9

℟ **Help us, O God our Saviour,**
  for the glory of your name.

O God, the heathen have come into your inheritance;
they have profaned your holy temple;
they have made Jerusalem a heap of rubble.
They have given the bodies of your servants
as food for the birds of the air,
and the flesh of your faithful ones
to the beasts of the field. ℟

They have shed their blood like water
on every side of Jerusalem,
and there was no one to bury them.
We have become a reproach to our neighbours,
an object of scorn and derision to those around us. ℟

How long will you be angry, O Lord?
will your fury blaze like fire for ever?
Pour out your wrath upon the heathen
who have not known you
and upon the kingdoms
that have not called upon your name. ℟

For they have devoured Jacob
and made his dwelling a ruin.
Remember not our past sins;
let your compassion be swift to meet us;
for we have been brought very low.
Help us, O God our Saviour, for the glory of your name;
deliver us and forgive us our sins, for your name's sake. ℟

Or   TRACK 2

FIRST READING   **Amos 8.4–7**

A reading from the book of the prophet Amos.

Hear this, you that trample on the needy,
and bring to ruin the poor of the land,
saying, 'When will the new moon be over so that we may sell grain;
and the sabbath, so that we may offer wheat for sale?
We will make the ephah small and the shekel great,
and practise deceit with false balances,
buying the poor for silver
and the needy for a pair of sandals,
and selling the sweepings of the wheat.'

The LORD has sworn by the pride of Jacob:
Surely I will never forget any of their deeds.

PSALM

℞ **Give praise to the Lord who lifts up the poor.**

Alleluia!
Give praise, you servants of the Lord;
praise the name of the Lord.
Let the name of the Lord be blessed,
from this time forth for evermore. ℞

From the rising of the sun to its going down
let the name of the Lord be praised.
The Lord is high above all nations,
and his glory above the heavens. ℞

Who is like the Lord our God,
who sits enthroned on high,
but stoops to behold the heavens and the earth?
He takes up the weak out of the dust
and lifts up the poor from the ashes. ℞

He sets them with the princes,
with the princes of his people.
He makes the woman of a childless house
to be a joyful mother of children. ℞

SECOND READING

A reading from the first letter of Paul to Timothy.

My dearly beloved, I urge that supplications, prayers, intercessions, and
thanksgivings be made for everyone, for kings and all who are in high
positions, so that we may lead a quiet and peaceable life in all godliness and
dignity. This is right and is acceptable in the sight of God our Saviour, who
desires everyone to be saved and to come to the knowledge of the truth. For
there is one God; there is also one mediator between God and humankind,
Christ Jesus, himself human, who gave himself a ransom for all – this was
attested at the right time. For this I was appointed a herald and an apostle
(I am telling the truth, I am not lying), a teacher of the Gentiles in faith
and truth.

GOSPEL   Luke 16.1-13

Hear the gospel of our Lord Jesus Christ according to Luke.

Jesus said to the disciples, 'There was a rich man who had a manager, and charges were brought to him that this man was squandering his property. So he summoned him and said to him, "What is this that I hear about you? Give me an account of your management, because you cannot be my manager any longer." Then the manager said to himself, "What will I do, now that my master is taking the position away from me? I am not strong enough to dig, and I am ashamed to beg. I have decided what to do so that, when I am dismissed as manager, people may welcome me into their homes."

So, summoning his master's debtors one by one, he asked the first, "How much do you owe my master?" He answered, "A hundred jugs of olive oil." He said to him, "Take your bill, sit down quickly, and make it fifty." Then he asked another, "And how much do you owe?" He replied, "A hundred containers of wheat." He said to him, "Take your bill and make it eighty." And his master commended the dishonest manager because he had acted shrewdly; for the children of this age are more shrewd in dealing with their own generation than are the children of light. And I tell you, make friends for yourselves by means of dishonest wealth so that when it is gone, they may welcome you into the eternal homes. Whoever is faithful in a very little is faithful also in much; and whoever is dishonest in a very little is dishonest also in much. If then you have not been faithful with the dishonest wealth, who will entrust to you the true riches? And if you have not been faithful with what belongs to another, who will give you what is your own? No slave can serve two masters; for a slave will either hate the one and love the other, or be devoted to the one and despise the other. You cannot serve God and wealth.'

† SUNDAY BETWEEN 25 SEPTEMBER AND 1 OCTOBER PROPER 21

YEAR C

TRACK 1

FIRST READING   **Jeremiah 32.1–3a, 6–15**

A reading from the book of the prophet Jeremiah.

The word that came to Jeremiah from the LORD in the tenth year of King Zedekiah of Judah, which was the eighteenth year of Nebuchadnezzar. At that time the army of the king of Babylon was besieging Jerusalem, and the prophet Jeremiah was confined in the court of the guard that was in the palace of the king of Judah, where King Zedekiah of Judah had confined him.

Jeremiah said, The word of the LORD came to me: Hanamel son of your uncle Shallum is going to come to you and say, 'Buy my field that is at Anathoth, for the right of redemption by purchase is yours.' Then my cousin Hanamel came to me in the court of the guard, in accordance with the word of the LORD, and said to me, 'Buy my field that is at Anathoth in the land of Benjamin, for the right of possession and redemption is yours; buy it for yourself.' Then I knew that this was the word of the LORD.

And I bought the field at Anathoth from my cousin Hanamel, and weighed out the money to him, seventeen shekels of silver. I signed the deed, sealed it, got witnesses, and weighed the money on scales. Then I took the sealed deed of purchase, containing the terms and conditions, and the open copy; and I gave the deed of purchase to Baruch son of Neriah son of Mahseiah, in the presence of my cousin Hanamel, in the presence of the witnesses who signed the deed of purchase, and in the presence of all the Judeans who were sitting in the court of the guard. In their presence I charged Baruch, saying, Thus says the LORD of hosts, the God of Israel: Take these deeds, both this sealed deed of purchase and this open deed, and put them in an earthenware jar, in order that they may last for a long time. For thus says the LORD of hosts, the God of Israel: Houses and fields and vineyards shall again be bought in this land.

PSALM   **Psalm 91.1-6, 14-16**

℟ **You are my refuge [and my stronghold], O Lord.**

He who dwells in the shelter of the Most High,
abides under the shadow of the Almighty.
He shall say to the Lord,
'You are my refuge and my stronghold,
my God in whom I put my trust.'
He shall deliver you from the snare of the hunter
and from the deadly pestilence. ℟

He shall cover you with his pinions,
and you shall find refuge under his wings;
his faithfulness shall be a shield and buckler.
You shall not be afraid of any terror by night,
nor of the arrow that flies by day;
Of the plague that stalks in the darkness,
nor of the sickness that lays waste at midday. ℟

Because he is bound to me in love,
therefore will I deliver him;
I will protect him, because he knows my name.
He shall call upon me and I will answer him;
I am with him in trouble,
I will rescue him and bring him to honour.
With long life will I satisfy him,
and show him my salvation. ℟

Or   **TRACK 2**

FIRST READING   **Amos 6.1a, 4-7**

A reading from the book of the prophet Amos.

Thus says the LORD, the God of hosts:

Alas for those who are at ease in Zion,
and for those who feel secure on Mount Samaria!

Alas for those who lie on beds of ivory,
and lounge on their couches,
and eat lambs from the flock,
and calves from the stall;

who sing idle songs to the sound of the harp,
and like David improvise on instruments of music;
who drink wine from bowls,
and anoint themselves with the finest oils,
but are not grieved over the ruin of Joseph!
Therefore they shall now be the first to go into exile,
and the revelry of the loungers shall pass away.

PSALM   **Psalm 146**

℞ **Praise the Lord, O my soul!**

Alleluia!
Praise the Lord, O my soul!
I will praise the Lord as long as I live;
I will sing praises to my God while I have my being.
Put not your trust in rulers,
nor in any child of earth,
for there is no help in them.
When they breathe their last, they return to earth,
and in that day their thoughts perish. ℞

Happy are they who have the God of Jacob
for their help!
whose hope is in the Lord their God;
Who made heaven and earth, the seas,
and all that is in them;
who keeps his promise for ever;
Who gives justice to those who are oppressed,
and food to those who hunger. ℞

The Lord sets the prisoners free;
the Lord opens the eyes of the blind;
the Lord lifts up those who are bowed down;
The Lord loves the righteous;
the Lord cares for the stranger;
he sustains the orphan and widow,
but frustrates the way of the wicked.
The Lord shall reign for ever,
your God, O Zion, throughout all generations.
Alleluia! ℞

SECOND READING   1 Timothy 6.6–19

A reading from the first letter of Paul to Timothy.

There is great gain in godliness combined with contentment; for we brought nothing into the world, so that we can take nothing out of it; but if we have food and clothing, we will be content with these. But those who want to be rich fall into temptation and are trapped by many senseless and harmful desires that plunge people into ruin and destruction. For the love of money is a root of all kinds of evil, and in their eagerness to be rich some have wandered away from the faith and pierced themselves with many pains.

But as for you, man of God, shun all this; pursue righteousness, godliness, faith, love, endurance, gentleness. Fight the good fight of the faith; take hold of the eternal life, to which you were called and for which you made the good confession in the presence of many witnesses. In the presence of God, who gives life to all things, and of Christ Jesus, who in his testimony before Pontius Pilate made the good confession, I charge you to keep the commandment without spot or blame until the manifestation of our Lord Jesus Christ, which he will bring about at the right time – he who is the blessed and only Sovereign, the King of kings and Lord of lords. It is he alone who has immortality and dwells in unapproachable light, whom no one has ever seen or can see; to him be honour and eternal dominion. Amen.

As for those who in the present age are rich, command them not to be haughty, or to set their hopes on the uncertainty of riches, but rather on God who richly provides us with everything for our enjoyment. They are to do good, to be rich in good works, generous, and ready to share, thus storing up for themselves the treasure of a good foundation for the future, so that they may take hold of the life that really is life.

GOSPEL   Luke 16.19–31

Hear the gospel of our Lord Jesus Christ according to Luke.

Jesus told this parable to those among the Pharisees who loved money: 'There was a rich man who was dressed in purple and fine linen and who feasted sumptuously every day. And at his gate lay a poor man named Lazarus, covered with sores, who longed to satisfy his hunger with what fell from the rich man's table; even the dogs would come and lick his sores. The poor man died and was carried away by the angels to be with Abraham. The rich man also died and was buried. In Hades, where he was being tormented, he looked up and saw Abraham far away with Lazarus by his side. He called out, "Father Abraham, have mercy on me, and send Lazarus to dip the tip of his finger in water and cool my tongue; for I am in agony in these flames." But Abraham said, "Child, remember that during your lifetime you received your good things, and Lazarus in like manner evil things; but now he is comforted here, and you are in agony. Besides all this, between you and us a great chasm has been fixed, so that those who might want to pass from here to you cannot do so, and no one can cross from there to us." The man who had been rich said, "Then, father, I beg you to send him to my father's house – for I have five brothers – that he may warn them, so that they will not also come into this place of torment." Abraham replied, "They have Moses and the prophets; they should listen to them." He said, "No, father Abraham; but if someone goes to them from the dead, they will repent." Abraham said to him, "If they do not listen to Moses and the prophets, neither will they be convinced even if someone rises from the dead."'

† SUNDAY BETWEEN 2 AND 8 OCTOBER YEAR C
PROPER 22

TRACK 1

FIRST READING   **Lamentations 1.1–6**

A reading from the book of Lamentations.

How lonely sits the city that once was full of people!
How like a widow she has become,
she that was great among the nations!
She that was a princess among the provinces has become a vassal.

She weeps bitterly in the night,
with tears on her cheeks;
among all her lovers she has no one to comfort her;
all her friends have dealt treacherously with her,
they have become her enemies.

Judah has gone into exile with suffering and hard servitude;
she lives now among the nations, and finds no resting-place;
her pursuers have all overtaken her in the midst of her distress.

The roads to Zion mourn,
for no one comes to the festivals;

all her gates are desolate, her priests groan;
her young girls grieve, and her lot is bitter.

Her foes have become the masters, her enemies prosper,
because the LORD has made her suffer for the multitude of her transgressions;
her children have gone away,
captives before the foe.

From daughter Zion has departed all her majesty.
Her princes have become like stags that find no pasture;
they fled without strength before the pursuer.

CANTICLE OR PSALM

Either   **Lamentations 3.19–26**

℟ **The steadfast love of the Lord never ceases.**

The thought of my affliction
and my homelessness is wormwood and gall!
My soul continually thinks of it and is bowed down within me.
But this I call to mind, and therefore I have hope: ℟

The steadfast love of the LORD never ceases,
his mercies never come to an end;
they are new every morning;
great is your faithfulness. ℟

'The LORD is my portion,'
says my soul, 'therefore I will hope in him.'
The LORD is good to those who wait for him,
to the soul that seeks him.
It is good that one should wait quietly
for the salvation of the LORD. ℟

Or   **Psalm 137**

℟ **By the waters of Babylon we sat down and wept.**

By the waters of Babylon we sat down and wept,
when we remembered you, O Zion.
As for our harps, we hung them up
on the trees in the midst of that land. ℟

For those who led us away captive asked us for a song,
and our oppressors called for mirth:
'Sing us one of the songs of Zion.'
How shall we sing the Lord's song
upon an alien soil? ℞

If I forget you, O Jerusalem,
let my right hand forget its skill.
Let my tongue cleave to the roof of my mouth
if I do not remember you,
if I do not set Jerusalem above my highest joy. ℞

Remember the day of Jerusalem, O Lord,
against the people of Edom,
who said, 'Down with it! down with it!
even to the ground!'
O Daughter of Babylon, doomed to destruction,
happy the one who pays you back
for what you have done to us!
Happy shall he be who takes your little ones,
and dashes them against the rock! ℞

Or   TRACK 2

FIRST READING   **Habakkuk 1.1–4; 2.1–4**

A reading from the book of the prophet Habakkuk.

The oracle that the prophet Habakkuk saw.
O LORD, how long shall I cry for help,
and you will not listen?
Or cry to you 'Violence!'
and you will not save?
Why do you make me see wrongdoing
and look at trouble?
Destruction and violence are before me;
strife and contention arise.
So the law becomes slack and justice never prevails.
The wicked surround the righteous –
therefore judgement comes forth perverted.

I will stand at my watch-post,
and station myself on the rampart;
I will keep watch to see what he will say to me,

and what he will answer concerning my complaint.
Then the LORD answered me and said:
Write the vision;
make it plain on tablets,
so that a runner may read it.
For there is still a vision for the appointed time;
it speaks of the end, and does not lie.
If it seems to tarry, wait for it;
it will surely come, it will not delay.
Look at the proud!
Their spirit is not right in them,
but the righteous live by their faith.

PSALM

Psalm 37.1–10

℟ **Put your trust in the Lord,**
  take your delight in him.
    or
℟ **Wait patiently for the Lord.**

Do not fret yourself because of evildoers;
do not be jealous of those who do wrong.
For they shall soon wither like the grass,
and like the green grass fade away.
Put your trust in the Lord and do good;
dwell in the land and feed on its riches. ℟

Take delight in the Lord,
and he shall give you your heart's desire.
Commit your way to the Lord
and put your trust in him,
and he will bring it to pass.
He will make your righteousness as clear as the light
and your just dealing as the noonday. ℟

Be still before the Lord
and wait patiently for him.
Do not fret yourself over the one who prospers,
the one who succeeds in evil schemes.
Refrain from anger, leave rage alone;
do not fret yourself; it leads only to evil.
For evildoers chall be cut off,
but those who wait upon the Lord shall possess the land. ℟

SECOND READING   2 Timothy 1.1–14

A reading from the second letter of Paul to Timothy.

Paul, an apostle of Christ Jesus by the will of God, for the sake of the promise of life that is in Christ Jesus, To Timothy, my beloved child: Grace, mercy, and peace from God the Father and Christ Jesus our Lord.

I am grateful to God – whom I worship with a clear conscience, as my ancestors did – when I remember you constantly in my prayers night and day. Recalling your tears, I long to see you so that I may be filled with joy. I am reminded of your sincere faith, a faith that lived first in your grandmother Lois and your mother Eunice and now, I am sure, lives in you. For this reason I remind you to rekindle the gift of God that is within you through the laying on of my hands; for God did not give us a spirit of cowardice, but rather a spirit of power and of love and of self-discipline.

Do not be ashamed, then, of the testimony about our Lord or of me his prisoner, but join with me in suffering for the gospel, relying on the power of God, who saved us and called us with a holy calling, not according to our works but according to his own purpose and grace. This grace was given to us in Christ Jesus before the ages began, but it has now been revealed through the appearing of our Saviour Christ Jesus, who abolished death and brought life and immortality to light through the gospel. For this gospel I was appointed a herald and an apostle and a teacher, and for this reason I suffer as I do. But I am not ashamed, for I know the one in whom I have put my trust, and I am sure that he is able to guard until that day what I have entrusted to him. Hold to the standard of sound teaching that you have heard from me, in the faith and love that are in Christ Jesus. Guard the good treasure entrusted to you, with the help of the Holy Spirit living in us.

GOSPEL   Luke 17.5–10

Hear the gospel of our Lord Jesus Christ according to Luke.

The apostles said to the Lord, 'Increase our faith!' The Lord replied, 'If you had faith the size of a mustard seed, you could say to this mulberry tree, "Be uprooted and planted in the sea," and it would obey you.

Who among you would say to your slave who has just come in from ploughing or tending sheep in the field, "Come here at once and take your place at the table"? Would you not rather say to him, "Prepare supper for me, put on your apron and serve me while I eat and drink; later you may eat and drink"? Do you thank the slave for doing what was commanded? So you also, when you have done all that you were ordered to do, say, "We are worthless slaves; we have done only what we ought to have done!"'

† SUNDAY BETWEEN 9 AND 15 OCTOBER   YEAR C
PROPER 23

TRACK 1

FIRST READING   Jeremiah 29.1, 4–7

A reading from the book of the prophet Jeremiah.

These are the words of the letter that the prophet Jeremiah sent from Jerusalem to the remaining elders among the exiles, and to the priests, the prophets, and all the people, whom Nebuchadnezzar had taken into exile from Jerusalem to Babylon.

Thus says the LORD of hosts, the God of Israel, to all the exiles whom I have sent into exile from Jerusalem to Babylon: Build houses and live in them; plant gardens and eat what they produce. Take wives and have sons and daughters; take wives for your sons, and give your daughters in marriage, that they may bear sons and daughters; multiply there, and do not decrease. But seek the welfare of the city where I have sent you into exile, and pray to the LORD on its behalf, for in its welfare you will find your welfare.

PSALM   Psalm 66.1–11

℞ **Come now and see the works of God**
  [who holds our souls in life].

Be joyful in God, all you lands;
sing the glory of his name;
sing the glory of his praise.
Say to God, 'How awesome are your deeds!
because of your great strength
your enemies cringe before you. ℞

All the earth bows down before you,
sings to you, sings out your name.'
Come now and see the works of God,
how wonderful he is in his doing towards all people. ℞

He turned the sea into dry land,
so that they went through the water on foot,
and there we rejoiced in him.
In his might he rules for ever;
his eyes keep watch over the nations;
let no rebel rise up against him. ℞

Bless our God, you peoples;
make the voice of his praise to be heard;
Who holds our souls in life,
and will not allow our feet to slip.
For you, O God, have proved us;
you have tried us just as silver is tried. ℞

You brought us into the snare;
you laid heavy burdens upon our backs.
You let enemies ride over our heads;
we went through fire and water;
but you brought us out into a place of refreshment. ℞

Or   TRACK 2

FIRST READING   **2 Kings 5.1–3, 7–15b**

A reading from the second book of Kings.

Naaman, commander of the army of the king of Aram, was a great man and in high favour with his master, because by him the LORD had given victory to Aram. The man, though a mighty warrior, suffered from leprosy. Now the Arameans on one of their raids had taken a young girl captive from the land of Israel, and she served Naaman's wife. She said to her mistress, 'If only my lord were with the prophet who is in Samaria! He would cure him of his leprosy.'

When the king of Israel read the letter, he tore his clothes and said, 'Am I God, to give death or life, that this man sends word to me to cure a man of his leprosy? Just look and see how he is trying to pick a quarrel with me.' But when Elisha the man of God heard that the king of Israel had torn his clothes, he sent a message to the king, 'Why have you torn your clothes? Let him come to me, that he may learn that there is a prophet in Israel.' So Naaman came with his horses and chariots, and halted at the entrance of Elisha's house. Elisha sent a messenger to him, saying, 'Go, wash in the

Jordan seven times, and your flesh shall be restored and you shall be clean.'
But Naaman became angry and went away, saying, 'I thought that for me he
would surely come out, and stand and call on the name of the LORD his
God, and would wave his hand over the spot, and cure the leprosy! Are not
Abana and Pharpar, the rivers of Damascus, better than all the waters of
Israel? Could I not wash in them, and be clean?' He turned and went away in
a rage. But his servants approached and said to him, 'Father, if the prophet
had commanded you to do something difficult, would you not have done it?
How much more, when all he said to you was, "Wash, and be clean"?' So he
went down and immersed himself seven times in the Jordan, according to
the word of the man of God; his flesh was restored like the flesh of a young
boy, and he was clean.

Then he returned to the man of God, he and all his company; Naaman came
and stood before him and said, 'Now I know that there is no God in all the
earth except in Israel.'

PSALM   Psalm 111

℟ **The works of the Lord stand fast for ever.**
   or
℟ **Great are the deeds of the Lord,**
   [full of majesty and splendour].

Alleluia!
I will give thanks to the Lord with my whole heart,
in the assembly of the upright, in the congregation.
Great are the deeds of the Lord!
they are studied by all who delight in them.
His work is full of majesty and splendour,
and his righteousness endures for ever. ℟

He makes his marvellous works to be remembered;
the Lord is gracious and full of compassion.
He gives food to those who fear him;
he is ever mindful of his covenant. ℟

He has shown his people the power of his works
in giving them the lands of the nations.
The works of his hands are faithfulness and justice;
all his commandments are sure.
They stand fast for ever and ever,
because they are done in truth and equity. ℟

He sent redemption to his people;
he commanded his covenant for ever;
holy and awesome is his name.
The fear of the Lord is the beginning of wisdom;
those who act accordingly have a good understanding;
his praise endures for ever. ℞

SECOND READING   2 Timothy 2.8–15

A reading from the second letter of Paul to Timothy.

Remember Jesus Christ, raised from the dead, a descendant of David – that is
my gospel, for which I suffer hardship, even to the point of being chained
like a criminal. But the word of God is not chained. Therefore I endure
everything for the sake of the elect, so that they may also obtain the
salvation that is in Christ Jesus, with eternal glory.
The saying is sure:
If we have died with him,
we will also live with him;
if we endure,
we will also reign with him;
if we deny him,
he will also deny us;
if we are faithless,
he remains faithful –
for he cannot deny himself.
Remind them of this, and warn them before God that they are to avoid
wrangling over words, which does no good but only ruins those who are
listening. Do your best to present yourself to God as one approved by him, a
worker who has no need to be ashamed, rightly explaining the word of truth.

GOSPEL   Luke 17.11–19

Hear the gospel of our Lord Jesus Christ according to Luke.

On the way to Jerusalem Jesus was going through the region between Samaria
and Galilee. As he entered a village, ten lepers approached him. Keeping their
distance, they called out, saying, 'Jesus, Master, have mercy on us!' When he
saw them, he said to them, 'Go and show yourselves to the priests.' And as
they went, they were made clean. Then one of them, when he saw that he

was healed, turned back, praising God with a loud voice. He prostrated himself at Jesus' feet and thanked him. And he was a Samaritan. Then Jesus asked, 'Were not ten made clean? But the other nine, where are they? Was none of them found to return and give praise to God except this foreigner?' Then he said to the Samaritan, 'Get up and go on your way; your faith has made you well.'

† SUNDAY BETWEEN 16 AND 22 OCTOBER   YEAR C
PROPER 24

TRACK 1

FIRST READING   Jeremiah 31.27–34

A reading from the book of the prophet Jeremiah.

The days are surely coming, says the LORD, when I will sow the house of Israel and the house of Judah with the seed of humans and the seed of animals. And just as I have watched over them to pluck up and break down, to overthrow, destroy, and bring evil, so I will watch over them to build and to plant, says the LORD.
In those days they shall no longer say:
'The parents have eaten sour grapes,
and the children's teeth are set on edge.'
But all shall die for their own sins;
the teeth of everyone who eats sour grapes shall be set on edge.

The days are surely coming, says the LORD, when I will make a new covenant with the house of Israel and the house of Judah. It will not be like the covenant that I made with their ancestors when I took them by the hand to bring them out of the land of Egypt – a covenant that they broke, though I was their husband, says the LORD. But this is the covenant that I will make with the house of Israel after those days, says the LORD: I will put my law within them, and I will write it on their hearts; and I will be their God, and they shall be my people. No longer shall they teach one another, or say to each other, 'Know the LORD,' for they shall all know me, from the least of them to the greatest, says the LORD; for I will forgive their iniquity, and remember their sin no more.

PSALM   Psalm 119.97–104

℟ **You yourself have taught me, O Lord.**

O how I love your law!
all the day long it is in my mind.
Your commandment has made me wiser
than my enemies,
and it is always with me. ℟

I have more understanding than all my teachers,
for your decrees are my study.
I am wiser than the elders,
because I observe your commandments. ℟

I restrain my feet from every evil way,
that I may keep your word.
I do not shrink from your judgements,
because you yourself have taught me. ℟

How sweet are your words to my taste!
they are sweeter than honey to my mouth.
Through your commandments I gain understanding;
therefore I hate every lying way. ℟

Or   TRACK 2

FIRST READING   Genesis 32.22–31

A reading from the book of Genesis.

At night Jacob got up and took his two wives, his two maids, and his eleven
children, and crossed the ford of the Jabbok. He took them and sent them
across the stream, and likewise everything that he had. Jacob was left alone;
and a man wrestled with him until daybreak. When the man saw that he did
not prevail against Jacob, he struck him on the hip socket; and Jacob's hip
was put out of joint as he wrestled with him. Then he said, 'Let me go, for
the day is breaking.' But Jacob said, 'I will not let you go, unless you bless
me.' So he said to him, 'What is your name?' And he said, 'Jacob.' Then the
man said, 'You shall no longer be called Jacob, but Israel, for you have striven
with God and with humans, and have prevailed.' Then Jacob asked him,
'Please tell me your name?' But he said, 'Why is it that you ask my name?'
And there he blessed him. So Jacob called the place Peniel, saying, 'For I have

seen God face to face, and yet my life is preserved.' The sun rose upon him as
he passed Penuel, limping because of his hip.

PSALM   Psalm 121

℟ **My help comes from the Lord,
    the maker of heaven and earth.**

I lift up my eyes to the hills;
from where is my help to come?
My help comes from the Lord,
the maker of heaven and earth. ℟

He will not let your foot be moved
and he who watches over you will not fall asleep.
Behold, he who keeps watch over Israel
shall neither slumber nor sleep; ℟

The Lord himself watches over you;
the Lord is your shade at your right hand,
So that the sun shall not strike you by day,
nor the moon by night. ℟

The Lord shall preserve you from all evil;
it is he who shall keep you safe.
The Lord shall watch over your going out
and your coming in,
from this time forth for evermore. ℟

SECOND READING   2 Timothy 3.14 – 4.5

A reading from the second letter of Paul to Timothy.

Continue in what you have learned and firmly believed, knowing from
whom you learned it, and how from childhood you have known the sacred
writings that are able to instruct you for salvation through faith in Christ
Jesus. All scripture is inspired by God and is useful for teaching, for reproof,
for correction, and for training in righteousness, so that everyone who
belongs to God may be proficient, equipped for every good work.

In the presence of God and of Christ Jesus, who is to judge the living and the
dead, and in view of his appearing and his kingdom, I solemnly urge you:
proclaim the message; be persistent whether the time is favourable or

unfavourable; convince, rebuke, and encourage, with the utmost patience in teaching. For the time is coming when people will not put up with sound doctrine, but having itching ears, they will accumulate for themselves teachers to suit their own desires, and will turn away from listening to the truth and wander away to myths. As for you, always be sober, endure suffering, do the work of an evangelist, carry out your ministry fully.

GOSPEL   Luke 18.1-8

Hear the gospel of our Lord Jesus Christ according to Luke.

Jesus told his disciples a parable about their need to pray always and not to lose heart. He said, 'In a certain city there was a judge who neither feared God nor had respect for people. In that city there was a widow who kept coming to him and saying, "Grant me justice against my opponent." For a while he refused; but later he said to himself, "Though I have no fear of God and no respect for anyone, yet because this widow keeps bothering me, I will grant her justice, so that she may not wear me out by continually coming."' And the Lord said, 'Listen to what the unjust judge says. And will not God grant justice to his chosen ones who cry to him day and night? Will he delay long in helping them? I tell you, he will quickly grant justice to them. And yet, when the Son of Man comes, will he find faith on earth?'

† SUNDAY BETWEEN 23 AND 29 OCTOBER   YEAR C
PROPER 25

Provision for Proper 25 is identical in the Revised Common Lectionary and the Church of England provision, but the Church of England adds alternative readings for Bible Sunday (see pages 726–727).

TRACK 1

FIRST READING   Joel 2.23-32

A reading from the book of the prophet Joel.

O children of Zion,
be glad and rejoice in the LORD your God;
for he has given the early rain for your vindication,
he has poured down for you abundant rain,
the early and the later rain, as before.

The threshing-floors shall be full of grain,
the vats shall overflow with wine and oil.

I will repay you
for the years that the swarming locust has eaten,
the hopper, the destroyer, and the cutter,
my great army, which I sent against you.

You shall eat in plenty and be satisfied,
and praise the name of the LORD your God,
who has dealt wondrously with you.
And my people shall never again be put to shame.
You shall know that I am in the midst of Israel,
and that I, the LORD,
am your God and there is no other.
And my people shall never again be put to shame.

Then afterwards I will pour out my spirit on all flesh;
your sons and your daughters shall prophesy,
your old men shall dream dreams,
and your young men shall see visions.
Even on the male and female slaves,
in those days, I will pour out my spirit.

I will show portents in the heavens and on the earth, blood and fire and
columns of smoke. The sun shall be turned to darkness, and the moon to
blood, before the great and terrible day of the LORD comes. Then everyone
who calls on the name of the LORD shall be saved; for in Mount Zion and in
Jerusalem there shall be those who escape, as the LORD has said, and among
the survivors shall be those whom the LORD calls.

PSALM   Psalm 65

℟ **To you, O God, shall all flesh come,**
   [and you will blot out their sins].
   or
℟ **You crown the year with your goodness, O Lord.**

You are to be praised, O God, in Zion;
to you shall vows be performed in Jerusalem.
To you that hear prayer shall all flesh come,
because of their transgressions.
Our sins are stronger than we are,
but you will blot them out. ℟

Happy are they whom you choose
and draw to your courts to dwell there!
they will be satisfied by the beauty of your house,
by the holiness of your temple.
Awesome things will you show us in your righteousness,
O God of our salvation,
O Hope of all the ends of the earth
and of the seas that are far away. ℟

You make fast the mountains by your power;
they are girded about with might.
You still the roaring of the seas,
the roaring of their waves,
and the clamour of the peoples.
Those who dwell at the ends of the earth
will tremble at your marvellous signs;
you make the dawn and the dusk to sing for joy. ℟

You visit the earth and water it abundantly;
you make it very plenteous;
the river of God is full of water.
You prepare the grain,
for so you provide for the earth.
You drench the furrows and smooth out the ridges;
with heavy rain you soften the ground
and bless its increase. ℟

You crown the year with your goodness,
and your paths overflow with plenty.
May the fields of the wilderness be rich for grazing,
and the hills be clothed with joy.
May the meadows cover themselves with flocks
and the valleys cloak themselves with grain;
let them shout for joy and sing. ℟

Or   TRACK 2

FIRST READING (Alternative readings)

Either   Ecclesiasticus 35.12–17

A reading from the book of Ecclesiasticus.

Give to the Most High as he has given to you,
and as generously as you can afford.
For the Lord is the one who repays,
and he will repay you sevenfold.
Do not offer him a bribe,
for he will not accept it;
and do not rely on a dishonest sacrifice;
for the Lord is the judge,
and with him there is no partiality.
He will not show partiality to the poor;
but he will listen to the prayer of one who is wronged.
He will not ignore the supplication of the orphan,
or the widow when she pours out her complaint.

Or   Jeremiah 14.7–10, 19–22

A reading from the book of the prophet Jeremiah.

Although our iniquities testify against us,
act, O LORD, for your name's sake;
our apostasies indeed are many,
and we have sinned against you.
O hope of Israel, its saviour in time of trouble,
why should you be like a stranger in the land,
like a traveller turning aside for the night?
Why should you be like someone confused,
like a mighty warrior who cannot give help?
Yet you, O LORD, are in the midst of us,
and we are called by your name;
do not forsake us!

Thus says the LORD concerning this people:
Truly they have loved to wander,
they have not restrained their feet;

therefore the LORD does not accept them,
now he will remember their iniquity and punish their sins.

Have you completely rejected Judah?
Does your heart loathe Zion?
Why have you struck us down
so that there is no healing for us?
We look for peace, but find no good;
for a time of healing, but there is terror instead.
We acknowledge our wickedness, O LORD,
the iniquity of our ancestors,
for we have sinned against you.
Do not spurn us, for your name's sake;
do not dishonour your glorious throne;
remember and do not break your covenant with us.
Can any idols of the nations bring rain?
Or can the heavens give showers?
Is it not you, O LORD our God?
We set our hope on you,
for it is you who do all this.

PSALM

Psalm 84.1–7

℟ **Happy are they who dwell in your house!**

How dear to me is your dwelling, O Lord of hosts!
My soul has a desire and longing
for the courts of the Lord;
my heart and my flesh rejoice in the living God.
The sparrow has found her a house
and the swallow a nest
where she may lay her young;
by the side of your altars, O Lord of hosts,
my King and my God. ℟

Happy are they who dwell in your house!
they will always be praising you.
Happy are the people whose strength is in you!
whose hearts are set on the pilgrims' way. ℟

Those who go through the desolate valley
will find it a place of springs,
for the early rains have covered it with pools of water.
They will climb from height to height,
and the God of gods will reveal himself in Zion.
Lord God of hosts, hear my prayer;
hearken, O God of Jacob. ℟

SECOND READING   **2 Timothy 4.6–8, 16–18**

A reading from the second letter of Paul to Timothy.

As for me, I am already being poured out as a libation, and the time of my
departure has come. I have fought the good fight, I have finished the race, I
have kept the faith. From now on there is reserved for me the crown of
righteousness, which the Lord, the righteous judge, will give to me on that
day, and not only to me but also to all who have longed for his appearing.

At my first defence no one came to my support, but all deserted me. May it
not be counted against them! But the Lord stood by me and gave me
strength, so that through me the message might be fully proclaimed and all
the Gentiles might hear it. So I was rescued from the lion's mouth.
The Lord will rescue me from every evil attack and save me for his heavenly
kingdom. To him be the glory for ever and ever. Amen.

GOSPEL   **Luke 18.9–14**

Hear the gospel of our Lord Jesus Christ according to Luke.

Jesus also told this parable to some who trusted in themselves that they were
righteous and regarded others with contempt: 'Two men went up to the
temple to pray, one a Pharisee and the other a tax-collector. The Pharisee,
standing by himself, was praying thus, "God, I thank you that I am not like
other people: thieves, rogues, adulterers, or even like this tax-collector. I fast
twice a week; I give a tenth of all my income." But the tax-collector, standing
far off, would not even look up to heaven, but was beating his breast and
saying, "God, be merciful to me, a sinner!" I tell you, this man went down to
his home justified rather than the other; for all who exalt themselves will be
humbled, but all who humble themselves will be exalted.'

Or

† BIBLE SUNDAY

YEAR C

FIRST READING

Isaiah 45.22–25

A reading from the book of the prophet Isaiah.

Thus says the LORD:
Turn to me and be saved, all the ends of the earth!
For I am God, and there is no other.
By myself I have sworn,
from my mouth has gone forth in righteousness a word that shall not return:
'To me every knee shall bow, every tongue shall swear.'

Only in the LORD, it shall be said of me,
are righteousness and strength;
all who were incensed against him shall come to him and be ashamed.
In the LORD all the offspring of Israel shall triumph and glory.

PSALM

Psalm 119.129–136

℟ **When your word goes forth it gives light.**

Your decrees are wonderful;
therefore I obey them with all my heart.
When your word goes forth it gives light;
it gives understanding to the simple. ℟

I open my mouth and pant;
I long for your commandments.
Turn to me in mercy,
as you always do to those who love your name. ℟

Steady my footsteps in your word;
let no iniquity have dominion over me.
Rescue me from those who oppress me,
and I will keep your commandments. ℟

Let your countenance shine upon your servant
and teach me your statutes.
My eyes shed streams of tears,
because people do not keep your law. ℟

SECOND READING   Romans 15.1–6

A reading from the letter of Paul to the Romans.

We who are strong ought to put up with the failings of the weak, and not to please ourselves. Each of us must please our neighbour for the good purpose of building up the neighbour. For Christ did not please himself; but, as it is written, 'The insults of those who insult you have fallen on me.' For whatever was written in former days was written for our instruction, so that by steadfastness and by the encouragement of the scriptures we might have hope. May the God of steadfastness and encouragement grant you to live in harmony with one another, in accordance with Christ Jesus, so that together you may with one voice glorify the God and Father of our Lord Jesus Christ.

GOSPEL   Luke 4.16–24

Hear the gospel of our Lord Jesus Christ according to Luke.

When Jesus came to Nazareth, where he had been brought up, he went to the synagogue on the sabbath day, as was his custom. He stood up to read, and the scroll of the prophet Isaiah was given to him. He unrolled the scroll and found the place where it was written:
'The Spirit of the Lord is upon me,
because he has anointed me
to bring good news to the poor.
He has sent me to proclaim release to the captives
and recovery of sight to the blind,
to let the oppressed go free,
to proclaim the year of the Lord's favour.'
And he rolled up the scroll, gave it back to the attendant, and sat down. The eyes of all in the synagogue were fixed on him. Then he began to say to them, 'Today this scripture has been fulfilled in your hearing.' All spoke well of him and were amazed at the gracious words that came from his mouth. They said, 'Is not this Joseph's son?' He said to them, 'Doubtless you will quote to me this proverb, "Doctor, cure yourself!" And you will say, "Do here also in your home town the things that we have heard you did at Capernaum."' And he said, 'Truly I tell you, no prophet is accepted in the prophet's home town.'

† DEDICATION FESTIVAL   YEAR C

First Sunday in October or Last Sunday after Trinity

FIRST READING   1 Chronicles 29.6–19

A reading from the first book of Chronicles.

The leaders of ancestral houses made their freewill-offerings, as did also the leaders of the tribes, the commanders of the thousands and of the hundreds, and the officers over the king's work. They gave for the service of the house of God five thousand talents and ten thousand darics of gold, ten thousand talents of silver, eighteen thousand talents of bronze, and one hundred thousand talents of iron. Whoever had precious stones gave them to the treasury of the house of the LORD, into the care of Jehiel the Gershonite. Then the people rejoiced because these had given willingly, for with single mind they had offered freely to the LORD; King David also rejoiced greatly.

Then David blessed the LORD in the presence of all the assembly; David said: 'Blessed are you, O LORD, the God of our ancestor Israel, for ever and ever. Yours, O LORD, are the greatness, the power, the glory, the victory, and the majesty; for all that is in the heavens and on the earth is yours; yours is the kingdom, O LORD, and you are exalted as head above all. Riches and honour come from you, and you rule over all. In your hand are power and might; and it is in your hand to make great and to give strength to all. And now, our God, we give thanks to you and praise your glorious name.

But who am I, and what is my people, that we should be able to make this freewill-offering? For all things come from you, and of your own have we given you. For we are aliens and transients before you, as were all our ancestors; our days on the earth are like a shadow, and there is no hope. O LORD our God, all this abundance that we have provided for building you a house for your holy name comes from your hand and is all your own. I know, my God, that you search the heart, and take pleasure in uprightness; in the uprightness of my heart I have freely offered all these things, and now I have seen your people, who are present here, offering freely and joyously to you. O LORD, the God of Abraham, Isaac, and Israel, our ancestors, keep for ever such purposes and thoughts in the hearts of your people, and direct their hearts towards you. Grant to my son Solomon that with single mind he may keep your commandments, your decrees, and your statutes, performing all of them, and that he may build the temple for which I have made provision.'

PSALM   Psalm 122

℟ I was glad when they said to me,
   'Let us go to the house of the Lord'.

I was glad when they said to me,
'Let us go to the house of the Lord.'
Now our feet are standing
within your gates, O Jerusalem. ℟

Jerusalem is built as a city
that is at unity with itself.
To which the tribes go up, the tribes of the Lord,
the assembly of Israel, to praise the name of the Lord.
For there are the thrones of judgement,
the thrones of the house of David. ℟

Pray for the peace of Jerusalem:
'May they prosper who love you.
Peace be within your walls
and quietness within your towers. ℟

For my family and companions' sake,
I pray for your prosperity.
Because of the house of the Lord our God,
I will seek to do you good.' ℟

SECOND READING   Ephesians 2.19–22

A reading from the letter of Paul to the Ephesians.

You are no longer strangers and aliens, but you are citizens with the saints
and also members of the household of God, built upon the foundation of the
apostles and prophets, with Christ Jesus himself as the cornerstone. In him
the whole structure is joined together and grows into a holy temple in the
Lord; in whom you also are built together spiritually into a dwelling-place
for God.

GOSPEL   John 2.13–22

Hear the gospel of our Lord Jesus Christ according to John.

The Passover of the Jews was near, and Jesus went up to Jerusalem. In the
temple he found people selling cattle, sheep, and doves, and the money-

changers seated at their tables. Making a whip of cords, he drove all of them out of the temple, both the sheep and the cattle. He also poured out the coins of the money-changers and overturned their tables. He told those who were selling the doves, 'Take these things out of here! Stop making my Father's house a market-place!' His disciples remembered that it was written, 'Zeal for your house will consume me.' The Jews then said to him, 'What sign can you show us for doing this?' Jesus answered them, 'Destroy this temple, and in three days I will raise it up.' They then said, 'This temple has been under construction for forty-six years, and will you raise it up in three days?' But he was speaking of the temple of his body. After he was raised from the dead, his disciples remembered that he had said this; and they believed the scripture and the word that Jesus had spoken.

SUNDAYS BEFORE ADVENT

> *In the weeks after All Saints' Day the Church of England provision designates Sundays 'Sundays before Advent', while the Revised Common Lectionary continues with 'Propers' designated by calendar dates.*

4 BEFORE ADVENT   YEAR C
PROPER 26

> *In Church of England provision this Sunday may be kept as All Saints' Sunday (see pages 734–737) or else the provision below is used. The Revised Common Lectionary continues to provide two tracks for the First Reading and Psalms. Church of England provision allows only Track 2.*

TRACK 1

Revised Common Lectionary only

FIRST READING   Habakkuk 1.1–4; 2.1–4

A reading from the book of the prophet Habakkuk.

The oracle that the prophet Habakkuk saw.

O LORD, how long shall I cry for help,
and you will not listen?
Or cry to you 'Violence!'
and you will not save?

Why do you make me see wrongdoing
and look at trouble?
Destruction and violence are before me;
strife and contention arise.
So the law becomes slack and justice never prevails.
The wicked surround the righteous –
therefore judgement comes forth perverted.

I will stand at my watch-post,
and station myself on the rampart;
I will keep watch to see what he will say to me,
and what he will answer concerning my complaint.
Then the LORD answered me and said:
Write the vision;
make it plain on tablets,
so that a runner may read it.
For there is still a vision for the appointed time;
it speaks of the end, and does not lie.
If it seems to tarry, wait for it;
it will surely come, it will not delay.
Look at the proud!
Their spirit is not right in them,
but the righteous live by their faith.

PSALM   Psalm 119.137–144

℟ Your justice is an everlasting justice.

You are righteous, O Lord,
and upright are your judgements.
You have issued your decrees
with justice and in perfect faithfulness. ℟

My indignation has consumed me,
because my enemies forget your words.
Your word has been tested to the uttermost,
and your servant holds it dear. ℟

I am small and of little account,
yet I do not forget your commandments.
Your justice is an everlasting justice
and your law is the truth. ℟

Trouble and distress have come upon me,
yet your commandments are my delight.
The righteousness of your decrees is everlasting;
grant me understanding, that I may live. ℟

Or   TRACK 2

FIRST READING   **Isaiah 1.10–18**

A reading from the book of the prophet Isaiah.

Hear the word of the LORD, you rulers of Sodom!
Listen to the teaching of our God, you people of Gomorrah!
What to me is the multitude of your sacrifices? says the LORD;
I have had enough of burnt-offerings of rams and the fat of fed beasts;
I do not delight in the blood of bulls, or of lambs, or of goats.

When you come to appear before me,
who asked this from your hand?
Trample my courts no more;
bringing offerings is futile;
incense is an abomination to me.
New moon and sabbath and calling of convocation –
I cannot endure solemn assemblies with iniquity.
Your new moons and your appointed festivals my soul hates;
they have become a burden to me,
I am weary of bearing them.
When you stretch out your hands,
I will hide my eyes from you;
even though you make many prayers, I will not listen;
your hands are full of blood.
Wash yourselves;
make yourselves clean;
remove the evil of your doings from before my eyes;
cease to do evil,
learn to do good;
seek justice, rescue the oppressed,
defend the orphan, plead for the widow.

Come now, let us argue it out, says the LORD:
though your sins are like scarlet, they shall be like snow;
though they are red like crimson, they shall become like wool.

PSALM   **Psalm 32.1–8**

℟ **Happy are they whose sins are forgiven.**

Happy are they whose transgressions are forgiven,
and whose sin is put away!
Happy are they to whom the Lord imputes no guilt,
and in whose spirit there is no guile! ℟

While I held my tongue, my bones withered away,
because of my groaning all day long.
For your hand was heavy upon me day and night;
my moisture was dried up as in the heat of summer. ℟

Then I acknowledged my sin to you,
and did not conceal my guilt.
I said, 'I will confess my transgressions to the Lord';
then you forgave me the guilt of my sin. ℟

Therefore all the faithful will make their prayers to you
in time of trouble;
when the great waters overflow, they shall not reach them.
You are my hiding-place;
you preserve me from trouble;
you surround me with shouts of deliverance. ℟

SECOND READING (Short or long reading)
                        2 Thessalonians 1.1–4, (5–10), 11–12

The Revised Common Lectionary gives the short version, the Church of England the longer one.

A reading from the second letter of Paul to the Thessalonians.

Paul, Silvanus, and Timothy, To the church of the Thessalonians in God our
Father and the Lord Jesus Christ: Grace to you and peace from God our
Father and the Lord Jesus Christ.

We must always give thanks to God for you, brothers and sisters, as is right,
because your faith is growing abundantly, and the love of everyone of you for
one another is increasing. Therefore we ourselves boast of you among the
churches of God for your steadfastness and faith during all your persecutions
and the afflictions that you are enduring. [This is evidence of the righteous
judgement of God, and is intended to make you worthy of the kingdom of
God, for which you are also suffering. For it is indeed just of God to repay
with affliction those who afflict you, and to give relief to the afflicted as well

as to us, when the Lord Jesus is revealed from heaven with his mighty angels in flaming fire, inflicting vengeance on those who do not know God and on those who do not obey the gospel of our Lord Jesus. These will suffer the punishment of eternal destruction, separated from the presence of the Lord and from the glory of his might, when he comes to be glorified by his saints and to be marvelled at on that day among all who have believed, because our testimony to you was believed.]

To this end we always pray for you, asking that our God will make you worthy of his call and will fulfil by his power every good resolve and work of faith, so that the name of our Lord Jesus may be glorified in you, and you in him, according to the grace of our God and the Lord Jesus Christ.

GOSPEL   Luke 19.1–10

Hear the gospel of our Lord Jesus Christ according to Luke.

Jesus entered Jericho and was passing through it. A man was there named Zacchaeus; he was a chief tax-collector and was rich. He was trying to see who Jesus was, but on account of the crowd he could not, because he was short in stature. So he ran ahead and climbed a sycamore tree to see Jesus, because he was going to pass that way. When Jesus came to the place, he looked up and said to him, 'Zacchaeus, hurry and come down; for I must stay at your house today.' So he hurried down and was happy to welcome Jesus. All who saw it began to grumble and said, 'He has gone to be the guest of one who is a sinner.' Zacchaeus stood there and said to the Lord, 'Look, half of my possessions, Lord, I will give to the poor; and if I have defrauded anyone of anything, I will pay back four times as much.' Then Jesus said to him, 'Today salvation has come to this house, because he too is a son of Abraham. For the Son of Man came to seek out and to save the lost.'

† ALL SAINTS' SUNDAY   YEAR C

Sunday between 30 October and 5 November (or, if this is not kept as All Saints' Sunday, 1 November itself)

FIRST READING   Daniel 7.1–3, 15–18

A reading from the book of Daniel.

In the first year of King Belshazzar of Babylon, Daniel had a dream and visions of his head as he lay in bed. Then he wrote down the dream: I,

Daniel, saw in my vision by night the four winds of heaven stirring up the great sea, and four great beasts came up out of the sea, different from one another.

As for me, Daniel, my spirit was troubled within me, and the visions of my head terrified me. I approached one of the attendants to ask him the truth concerning all this. So he said that he would disclose to me the interpretation of the matter: 'As for these four great beasts, four kings shall arise out of the earth. But the holy ones of the Most High shall receive the kingdom and possess the kingdom for ever – for ever and ever.'

PSALM   Psalm 149

℟ **My mouth, O God, shall speak of wisdom**
 [and my heart shall meditate on understanding].

Alleluia!
Sing to the Lord a new song;
sing his praise in the congregation of the faithful.
Let Israel rejoice in his maker;
let the children of Zion be joyful in their king.
Let them praise his name in the dance;
let them sing praise to him with timbrel and harp. ℟

For the Lord takes pleasure in his people
and adorns the poor with victory.
Let the faithful rejoice in triumph;
let them be joyful on their beds. ℟

Let the praises of God be in their throat
and a two-edged sword in their hand;
To wreak vengeance on the nations
and punishment on the peoples;
To bind their kings in chains
and their nobles with links of iron;
To inflict on them the judgement decreed;
this is glory for all his faithful people.
Alleluia! ℟

SECOND READING   Ephesians 1.11–23

A reading from the letter of Paul to the Ephesians.

In Christ we have also obtained an inheritance, having been destined according to the purpose of him who accomplishes all things according to his counsel and will, so that we, who were the first to set our hope on Christ, might live for the praise of his glory. In him you also, when you had heard the word of truth, the gospel of your salvation, and had believed in him, were marked with the seal of the promised Holy Spirit; this is the pledge of our inheritance towards redemption as God's own people, to the praise of his glory. I have heard of your faith in the Lord Jesus and your love towards all the saints, and for this reason

I do not cease to give thanks for you as I remember you in my prayers. I pray that the God of our Lord Jesus Christ, the Father of glory, may give you a spirit of wisdom and revelation as you come to know him, so that, with the eyes of your heart enlightened, you may know what is the hope to which he has called you, what are the riches of his glorious inheritance among the saints, and what is the immeasurable greatness of his power for us who believe, according to the working of his great power. God put this power to work in Christ when he raised him from the dead and seated him at his right hand in the heavenly places, far above all rule and authority and power and dominion, and above every name that is named, not only in this age but also in the age to come. And he has put all things under his feet and has made him the head over all things for the church, which is his body, the fullness of him who fills all in all.

GOSPEL   Luke 6.20–31

Hear the gospel of our Lord Jesus Christ according to Luke.

Jesus looked up at his disciples and said:

'Blessed are you who are poor,
for yours is the kingdom of God.
Blessed are you who are hungry now,
for you will be filled.
Blessed are you who weep now,
for you will laugh.
Blessed are you when people hate you, and when they exclude you, revile you, and defame you on account of the Son of Man. Rejoice in that day and

leap for joy, for surely your reward is great in heaven; for that is what their ancestors did to the prophets.
But woe to you who are rich,
for you have received your consolation.
Woe to you who are full now,
for you will be hungry.
Woe to you who are laughing now,
for you will mourn and weep.

Woe to you when all speak well of you, for that is what their ancestors did to the false prophets.

But I say to you that listen, Love your enemies, do good to those who hate you, bless those who curse you, pray for those who abuse you. If anyone strikes you on the cheek, offer the other also; and from anyone who takes away your coat do not withhold even your shirt. Give to everyone who begs from you; and if anyone takes away your goods, do not ask for them again. Do to others as you would have them do to you.'

ALL SAINTS' DAY   YEARS A B C

For use on 1 November if the material for All Saints' Sunday is used on the Sunday.
See Year A, pages 290–292.

3 BEFORE ADVENT   YEAR C
PROPER 27

The Revised Common Lectionary continues to provide two tracks. Church of England provision allows only Track 2.

TRACK 1

Revised Common Lectionary only

FIRST READING   Haggai 1.15b – 2.9

A reading from the book of the prophet Haggai.

In the second year of King Darius, in the seventh month, on the twenty-first day of the month, the word of the LORD came by the prophet Haggai, saying: Speak now to Zerubbabel son of Shealtiel, governor of Judah, and to Joshua son of Jehozadak, the high priest, and to the remnant of the people, and say, Who is left among you that saw this house in its former glory? How does it look to you now? Is it not in your sight as nothing? Yet now take courage, O Zerubbabel, says the LORD; take courage, O Joshua, son of Jehozadak, the high priest; take courage, all you people of the land, says the LORD; work, for I am with you, says the LORD of hosts, according to the promise that I made you when you came out of Egypt. My spirit abides among you; do not fear. For thus says the LORD of hosts: Once again, in a little while, I will shake the heavens and the earth and the sea and the dry land; and I will shake all the nations, so that the treasure of all nations shall come, and I will fill this house with splendour, says the LORD of hosts. The silver is mine, and the gold is mine, says the LORD of hosts. The latter splendour of this house shall be greater than the former, says the LORD of hosts; and in this place I will give prosperity, says the LORD of hosts.

PSALM

Either

Psalm 145.1–5, 18–22

℟ **You open wide your hand, O Lord,
and satisfy our needs.**

I will exalt you, O God my King,
and bless your name for ever and ever.
Every day will I bless you
and praise your name for ever and ever. ℟

Great is the Lord and greatly to be praised;
there is no end to his greatness.
One generation shall praise your works to another
and shall declare your power.
I will ponder the glorious splendour of your majesty
and all your marvellous works. ℟

The Lord is righteous in all his ways
and loving in all his works.
The Lord is near to those who call upon him,
to all who call upon him faithfully.
He fulfils the desire of those who fear him,
he hears their cry and helps them. ℟

The Lord preserves all those who love him,
but he destroys all the wicked.
My mouth shall speak the praise of the Lord;
let all flesh bless his holy name for ever and ever. ℟

Or   **Psalm 98**

℟ **The Lord comes to judge the earth**
   [and the peoples with equity].

Sing to the Lord a new song,
   for he has done marvellous things.
With his right hand and his holy arm
   has he won for himself the victory.
The Lord has made known his victory;
   his righteousness has he openly shown
   in the sight of the nations. ℟

He remembers his mercy and faithfulness
   to the house of Israel,
   and all the ends of the earth have seen
   the victory of our God.
Shout with joy to the Lord, all you lands;
   lift up your voice, rejoice and sing. ℟

Sing to the Lord with the harp,
   with the harp and the voice of song.
With trumpets and the sound of the horn
   shout with joy before the King, the Lord. ℟

Let the sea make a noise and all that is in it,
   the lands and those who dwell therein.
Let the rivers clap their hands,
   and let the hills ring out with joy before the Lord,
   when he comes to judge the earth.
In righteousness shall he judge the world,
   and the peoples with equity. ℟

Or   TRACK 2

FIRST READING   **Job 19.23–27a**

A reading from the book of Job.

Job said to his companions:
'O that my words were written down!
O that they were inscribed in a book!
O that with an iron pen and with lead
they were engraved on a rock for ever!

For I know that my Redeemer lives,
and that at the last he will stand upon the earth;
and after my skin has been thus destroyed,
then in my flesh I shall see God,
whom I shall see on my side,
and my eyes shall behold, and not another.'

PSALM

Psalm 17.1-9

℞ **Show me, O Lord, your loving-kindness.**

Hear my plea of innocence, O Lord;
give heed to my cry;
listen to my prayer,
which does not come from lying lips.
Let my vindication come forth from your presence;
let your eyes be fixed on justice.
Weigh my heart, summon me by night,
melt me down; you will find no impurity in me. ℞

I give no offence with my mouth as others do;
I have heeded the words of your lips.
My footsteps hold fast to the ways of your law;
in your paths my feet shall not stumble.
I call upon you, O God, for you will answer me;
incline your ear to me and hear my words. ℞

Show me your marvellous loving-kindness,
O Saviour of those who take refuge at your right hand
from those who rise up against them.
Keep me as the apple of your eye;
hide me under the shadow of your wings,
From the wicked who assault me,
from my deadly enemies who surround me. ℞

SECOND READING

2 Thessalonians 2.1-5, 13-17

A reading from the second letter of Paul to the Thessalonians.

As to the coming of our Lord Jesus Christ and our being gathered together to
him, we beg you, brothers and sisters, not to be quickly shaken in mind or
alarmed, either by spirit or by word or by letter, as though from us, to the

effect that the day of the Lord is already here. Let no one deceive you in any way; for that day will not come unless the rebellion comes first and the lawless one is revealed, the one destined for destruction. He opposes and exalts himself above every so-called god or object of worship, so that he takes his seat in the temple of God, declaring himself to be God. Do you not remember that I told you these things when I was still with you?

But we must always give thanks to God for you, brothers and sisters beloved by the Lord, because God chose you as the first fruits for salvation through sanctification by the Spirit and through belief in the truth. For this purpose he called you through our proclamation of the good news, so that you may obtain the glory of our Lord Jesus Christ. So then, brothers and sisters, stand firm and hold fast to the traditions that you were taught by us, either by word of mouth or by our letter. Now may our Lord Jesus Christ himself and God our Father, who loved us and through grace gave us eternal comfort and good hope, comfort your hearts and strengthen them in every good work and word.

GOSPEL   Luke 20.27–38

Hear the gospel of our Lord Jesus Christ according to Luke.

Some Sadducees, those who say there is no resurrection, came to Jesus, and asked him a question, 'Teacher, Moses wrote for us that if a man's brother dies, leaving a wife but no children, the man shall marry the widow and raise up children for his brother. Now there were seven brothers; the first married, and died childless; then the second and the third married her, and so in the same way all seven died childless. Finally the woman also died. In the resurrection, therefore, whose wife will the woman be? For the seven had married her.'

Jesus said to them, 'Those who belong to this age marry and are given in marriage; but those who are considered worthy of a place in that age and in the resurrection from the dead neither marry nor are given in marriage. Indeed they cannot die any more, because they are like angels and are children of God, being children of the resurrection. And the fact that the dead are raised Moses himself showed, in the story about the bush, where he speaks of the Lord as the God of Abraham, the God of Isaac, and the God of Jacob. Now he is God not of the dead, but of the living; for to him all of them are alive.'

2 BEFORE ADVENT
PROPER 28

YEAR C

The Revised Common Lectionary continues to provide two tracks. Church of England provision allows only Track 2.

TRACK 1

Revised Common Lectionary only

FIRST READING   Isaiah 65.17–25

A reading from the book of the prophet Isaiah.

Thus says the LORD:

For I am about to create new heavens and a new earth;
the former things shall not be remembered or come to mind.
But be glad and rejoice for ever in what I am creating;
for I am about to create Jerusalem as a joy,
and its people as a delight.
I will rejoice in Jerusalem, and delight in my people;
no more shall the sound of weeping be heard in it,
or the cry of distress.
No more shall there be in it an infant that lives but a few days,
or an old person who does not live out a lifetime;
for one who dies at a hundred years will be considered a youth,
and one who falls short of a hundred will be considered accursed.
They shall build houses and inhabit them;
they shall plant vineyards and eat their fruit.
They shall not build and another inhabit;
they shall not plant and another eat;
for like the days of a tree shall the days of my people be,
and my chosen shall long enjoy the work of their hands.
They shall not labour in vain,
or bear children for calamity;
for they shall be offspring blessed by the LORD –
and their descendants as well.
Before they call I will answer,
while they are yet speaking I will hear.
The wolf and the lamb shall feed together,
the lion shall eat straw like the ox;

but the serpent –
its food shall be dust!
They shall not hurt or destroy on all my holy mountain,
says the LORD.

CANTICLE   Isaiah 12

℟ **With joy you will draw water
from the wells of salvation.**

I will give thanks to you, O LORD,
for though you were angry with me,
your anger turned away, and you comforted me.
Surely God is my salvation;
I will trust, and will not be afraid,
for the LORD GOD is my strength and my might;
he has become my salvation. ℟

[With joy you will draw water from the wells of salvation.]
And you will say in that day:
Give thanks to the LORD, call on his name;
make known his deeds among the nations;
proclaim that his name is exalted. ℟

Sing praises to the LORD,
for he has done gloriously;
let this be known in all the earth.
Shout aloud and sing for joy, O royal Zion,
for great in your midst is the Holy One of Israel. ℟

Or   TRACK 2

FIRST READING   Malachi 4.1–2a

A reading from the book of the prophet Malachi.

See, the day is coming, burning like an oven, when all the arrogant and all
evildoers will be stubble; the day that comes shall burn them up, says the
LORD of hosts, so that it will leave them neither root nor branch. But for
you who revere my name the sun of righteousness shall rise, with healing in
its wings.

PSALM

℟ **The Lord comes to judge the earth**
   [and the peoples with equity].

Sing to the Lord a new song,
for he has done marvellous things.
With his right hand and his holy arm
has he won for himself the victory.
The Lord has made known his victory;
his righteousness has he openly shown
in the sight of the nations. ℟

He remembers his mercy and faithfulness
to the house of Israel,
and all the ends of the earth have seen
the victory of our God.
Shout with joy to the Lord, all you lands;
lift up your voice, rejoice and sing. ℟

Sing to the Lord with the harp,
with the harp and the voice of song.
With trumpets and the sound of the horn
shout with joy before the King, the Lord. ℟

Let the sea make a noise and all that is in it,
the lands and those who dwell therein.
Let the rivers clap their hands,
and let the hills ring out with joy before the Lord,
when he comes to judge the earth.
In righteousness shall he judge the world,
and the peoples with equity. ℟

SECOND READING

2 Thessalonians 3.6–13

A reading from the second letter of Paul to the Thessalonians.

We command you, beloved, in the name of our Lord Jesus Christ, to keep away from believers who are living in idleness and not according to the tradition that they received from us. For you yourselves know how you ought to imitate us; we were not idle when we were with you, and we did not eat anyone's bread without paying for it; but with toil and labour we worked night and day, so that we might not burden any of you. This was not because we do not have that right, but in order to give you an example to imitate. For even when we were with you, we gave you this command: Anyone unwilling to work should not eat. For we hear that some of you are living in idleness, mere busybodies, not doing any work. Now such persons we command and exhort in the Lord Jesus Christ to do their work quietly and to earn their own living. Brothers and sisters, do not be weary in doing what is right.

GOSPEL   Luke 21.5–19

Hear the gospel of our Lord Jesus Christ according to Luke.

When some were speaking about the temple, how it was adorned with beautiful stones and gifts dedicated to God, Jesus said, 'As for these things that you see, the days will come when not one stone will be left upon another; all will be thrown down.'

They asked him, 'Teacher, when will this be, and what will be the sign that this is about to take place?' And Jesus said, 'Beware that you are not led astray; for many will come in my name and say, "I am he!" and, "The time is near!" Do not go after them.

When you hear of wars and insurrections, do not be terrified; for these things must take place first, but the end will not follow immediately.' Then he said to them, 'Nation will rise against nation, and kingdom against kingdom; there will be great earthquakes, and in various places famines and plagues; and there will be dreadful portents and great signs from heaven.

But before all this occurs, they will arrest you and persecute you; they will hand you over to synagogues and prisons, and you will be brought before kings and governors because of my name. This will give you an opportunity to testify. So make up your minds not to prepare your defence in advance; for I will give you words and a wisdom that none of your opponents will be able to withstand or contradict. You will be betrayed even by parents and brothers, by relatives and friends; and they will put some of you to death. You will be hated by all because of my name. But not a hair of your head will perish. By your endurance you will gain your souls.'

CHRIST THE KING   YEAR C

*Revised Common Lectionary provides an alternative Canticle. Church of England provision
allows only Psalm 46.*

FIRST READING   Jeremiah 23.1–6

A reading from the book of the prophet Jeremiah.

Woe to the shepherds who destroy and scatter the sheep of my pasture! says
the LORD. Therefore thus says the LORD, the God of Israel, concerning the
shepherds who shepherd my people: It is you who have scattered my flock,
and have driven them away, and you have not attended to them. So I will
attend to you for your evil doings, says the LORD. Then I myself will gather
the remnant of my flock out of all the lands where I have driven them, and I
will bring them back to their fold, and they shall be fruitful and multiply. I
will raise up shepherds over them who will shepherd them, and they shall
not fear any longer, or be dismayed, nor shall any be missing, says the LORD.

The days are surely coming, says the LORD, when I will raise up for David a
righteous Branch, and he shall reign as king and deal wisely, and shall
execute justice and righteousness in the land. In his days Judah will be saved
and Israel will live in safety. And this is the name by which he will be called:
'The LORD is our righteousness.'

CANTICLE OR PSALM

Either (Revised Common Lectionary only)   Luke 1.68–79

℟ **Blessed be the Lord who sets his people free.**

Blessèd be the Lord, the God of Israel, for he has come to his people and set
them free.
He has raised up for us a mighty Saviour,
born of the house of his servant, David. ℟

Through his holy prophets he promised of old,
that he would save us from our enemies,
from the hands of all that hate us.
He promised to show mercy to our forebears
and to remember his holy covenant. ℟

This was the oath he swore to our father Abraham:
to set us free from the hands of our enemies,

free to worship him without fear,
holy and righteous in his sight,
all the days of our life. ℟

You, my child,
shall be called the prophet of the Most High,
for you will go before the Lord to prepare his way,
To give his people knowledge of salvation,
by the forgiveness of all their sins. ℟

In the tender compassion of our God,
the dawn from on high shall break upon us,
To shine on those who dwell in darkness
and the shadow of death,
and to guide our feet into the way of peace. ℟

Or

PSALM   **Psalm 46**

℟ **The Lord of hosts is with us:**
  the God of Jacob is our stronghold.

God is our refuge and strength,
a very present help in trouble;
Therefore we will not fear, though the earth be moved,
and though the mountains be toppled
into the depths of the sea;
Though its waters rage and foam,
and though the mountains tremble at its tumult. ℟

[The Lord of hosts is with us;
the God of Jacob is our stronghold.]

There is a river whose streams
make glad the city of God,
the holy habitation of the Most High.
God is in the midst of her;
she shall not be overthrown;
God shall help her at the break of day.
The nations make much ado
and the kingdoms are shaken;
God has spoken and the earth shall melt away. ℟

[The Lord of hosts is with us;
the God of Jacob is our stronghold.]

Come now and look upon the works of the Lord,
what awesome things he has done on earth.
It is he who makes war to cease in all the world;
he breaks the bow and shatters the spear
and burns the shields with fire.
'Be still, then, and know that I am God;
I will be exalted among the nations;
I will be exalted in the earth.' ℟

[The Lord of hosts is with us;
the God of Jacob is our stronghold.]

SECOND READING   Colossians 1.11–20

A reading from the letter of Paul to the Colossians.

Brothers and sisters: May you be made strong with all the strength that
comes from his glorious power, and may you be prepared to endure
everything with patience, while joyfully giving thanks to the Father, who has
enabled you to share in the inheritance of the saints in the light. He has
rescued us from the power of darkness and transferred us into the kingdom of
his beloved Son, in whom we have redemption, the forgiveness of sins.

He is the image of the invisible God, the firstborn of all creation; for in him
all things in heaven and on earth were created, things visible and invisible,
whether thrones or dominions or rulers or powers – all things have been
created through him and for him. He himself is before all things, and in him
all things hold together. He is the head of the body, the church; he is the
beginning, the firstborn from the dead, so that he might come to have first
place in everything. For in him all the fullness of God was pleased to dwell,
and through him God was pleased to reconcile to himself all things, whether
on earth or in heaven, by making peace through the blood of his cross.

GOSPEL   Luke 23.33–43

Hear the gospel of our Lord Jesus Christ according to Luke.

When they came to the place that is called The Skull, they crucified Jesus
there with the criminals, one on his right and one on his left. Then Jesus

said, 'Father, forgive them; for they do not know what they are doing.' And they cast lots to divide his clothing. And the people stood by, watching; but the leaders scoffed at him, saying, 'He saved others; let him save himself if he is the Messiah of God, his chosen one!' The soldiers also mocked him, coming up and offering him sour wine, and saying, 'If you are the King of the Jews, save yourself!' There was also an inscription over him, 'This is the King of the Jews.'

One of the criminals who were hanged there kept deriding him and saying, 'Are you not the Messiah? Save yourself and us!' But the other rebuked him, saying, 'Do you not fear God, since you are under the same sentence of condemnation? And we indeed have been condemned justly, for we are getting what we deserve for our deeds, but this man has done nothing wrong.' Then he said, 'Jesus, remember me when you come into your kingdom.' Jesus replied, 'Truly I tell you, today you will be with me in Paradise.'

FESTIVALS

† THE NAMING AND CIRCUMCISION OF JESUS
HOLY NAME OF JESUS   YEARS A B C

1 January

> *Both the Revised Common Lectionary and Church of England provide for this day.*
> *The Revised Common Lectionary allows an alternative Second Reading.*

FIRST READING Numbers 6.22–27

A reading from the book of Numbers.

The LORD spoke to Moses, saying
'Speak to Aaron and his sons, saying, "Thus you shall bless the Israelites: You shall say to them,
The LORD bless you and keep you;
the LORD make his face to shine upon you
and be gracious to you;
the LORD lift up his countenance upon you,
and give you peace."
So they shall put my name on the Israelites, and I will bless them.'

PSALM   Psalm 8

℟ **Your name, O Lord, is exalted in all the world!**

O Lord our governor,
how exalted is your name in all the world!
Out of the mouths of infants and children
your majesty is praised above the heavens.
You have set up a stronghold against your adversaries,
to quell the enemy and the avenger. ℟

When I consider your heavens, the work of your fingers,
the moon and the stars you have set in their courses,
What are mortals, that you should be mindful of them?
mere human beings, that you should seek them out?
You have made them little lower than the angels;
you adorn them with glory and honour. ℟

You give them mastery over the works of your hands;
and put all things under their feet,
All sheep and oxen,
even the wild beasts of the field,
The birds of the air, the fish of the sea,
and whatsoever walks in the paths of the sea.
O Lord our governor,
how exalted is your name in all the world! ℟

SECOND READING (Alternative readings)

Either   Galatians 4.4–7

A reading from the letter of Paul to the Galatians.

When the fullness of time had come, God sent his Son, born of a woman,
born under the law, in order to redeem those who were under the law, so that
we might receive adoption as children. And because you are children, God
has sent the Spirit of his Son into our hearts, crying, 'Abba! Father!' So you
are no longer a slave but a child, and if a child then also an heir, through
God.

Or (Revised Common Lectionary only)   Philippians 2.5–11

A reading from the letter of Paul to the Philippians.

Let the same mind be in you that was in Christ Jesus,
who, though he was in the form of God,
did not regard equality with God
as something to be exploited,
but emptied himself,
taking the form of a slave,
being born in human likeness.
And being found in human form,
he humbled himself
and became obedient to the point of death,
even death on a cross.

Therefore God also highly exalted him
and gave him the name that is above every name,
so that at the name of Jesus every knee should bend,

in heaven and on earth and under the earth,
and every tongue should confess that Jesus Christ is Lord,
to the glory of God the Father.

GOSPEL   Luke 2.15–21

Hear the gospel of our Lord Jesus Christ according to Luke.

When the angels had left them and gone into heaven, the shepherds said to one another, 'Let us go now to Bethlehem and see this thing that has taken place, which the Lord has made known to us.' So they went with haste and found Mary and Joseph, and the child lying in the manger. When they saw this, they made known what had been told them about this child; and all who heard it were amazed at what the shepherds told them. But Mary treasured all these words and pondered them in her heart. The shepherds returned, glorifying and praising God for all they had heard and seen, as it had been told them.

After eight days had passed, it was time to circumcise the child; and he was called Jesus, the name given by the angel.

† THE CONVERSION OF ST PAUL   YEARS A B C

25 January

Acts 9.1–22 must be read as either the First or the Second Reading.

FIRST READING (Alternative readings)

Either   Jeremiah 1.4–10

A reading from the book of the prophet Jeremiah.

The word of the LORD came to me saying,
'Before I formed you in the womb I knew you,
and before you were born I consecrated you;
I appointed you a prophet to the nations.'
Then I said, 'Ah, Lord GOD! Truly I do not know how to speak, for I am only a boy.'
But the LORD said to me,
'Do not say, "I am only a boy";
for you shall go to all to whom I send you,

and you shall speak whatever I command you,
Do not be afraid of them,
for I am with you to deliver you, says the LORD.'
Then the LORD put out his hand and touched my mouth; and the LORD said to me,
'Now I have put my words in your mouth.
See, today I appoint you over nations and over kingdoms,
to pluck up and to pull down, to destroy
and to overthrow, to build and to plant.'

Or

Acts 9.1–22

A reading from the Acts of the Apostles.

Saul, still breathing threats and murder against the disciples of the Lord, went to the high priest and asked him for letters to the synagogues at Damascus, so that if he found any who belonged to the Way, men or women, he might bring them bound to Jerusalem. Now as he was going along and approaching Damascus, suddenly a light from heaven flashed around him. He fell to the ground and heard a voice saying to him, 'Saul, Saul, why do you persecute me?' He asked, 'Who are you, Lord?' The reply came, 'I am Jesus, whom you are persecuting. But get up and enter the city, and you will be told what you are to do.' The men who were travelling with him stood speechless because they heard the voice but saw no one. Saul got up from the ground, and though his eyes were open, he could see nothing; so they led him by the hand and brought him into Damascus. For three days he was without sight, and neither ate nor drank.

Now there was a disciple in Damascus named Ananias. The Lord said to him in a vision, 'Ananias.' He answered, 'Here I am, Lord.' The Lord said to him, 'Get up and go to the street called Straight, and at the house of Judas look for a man of Tarsus named Saul. At this moment he is praying, and he has seen in a vision a man named Ananias come in and lay his hands on him so that he might regain his sight.' But Ananias answered, 'Lord, I have heard from many about this man, how much evil he has done to your saints in Jerusalem; and here he has authority from the chief priests to bind all who invoke your name.' But the Lord said to him, 'Go, for he is an instrument whom I have chosen to bring my name before Gentiles and kings and before the people of Israel; I myself will show him how much he must suffer for the sake of my name.' So Ananias went and entered the house. He laid his hands on Saul and said, 'Brother Saul, the Lord Jesus, who appeared to you on your way here, has sent me so that you may regain your sight and be filled with the Holy Spirit.' And immediately something like scales fell from his eyes, and his sight was restored. Then he got up and was baptized, and after taking some food, he regained his strength. For several days he was with the disciples in Damascus, and immediately he began to proclaim Jesus in the synagogues, saying, 'He is the Son of God.' All who heard him were amazed and said, 'Is not this the man who made havoc in Jerusalem among those who invoked this name? And has he not come here for the purpose of bringing them bound before the chief priests?' Saul became increasingly more powerful and confounded the Jews who lived in Damascus by proving that Jesus was the Messiah.

PSALM   Psalm 67

℟ **Let the peoples praise you, O God;**
   let all the peoples praise you.

May God be merciful to us and bless us,
show us the light of his countenance and come to us.
Let your ways be known upon earth,
your saving health among all nations. ℟

[Let the peoples praise you, O God;
let all the peoples praise you.]

Let the nations be glad and sing for joy,
for you judge the peoples with equity
and guide all the nations upon earth. ℟

[Let the peoples praise you, O God;
let all the peoples praise you.]

The earth has brought forth her increase;
may God, our own God, give us his blessing.
May God give us his blessing,
and may all the ends of the earth stand in awe of him. ℟

SECOND READING (Alternative readings)

Either   **Acts 9.1–22**

A reading from the Acts of the Apostles.

See above, page 754.

Or   **Galatians 1.11–16a**

A reading from the letter of Paul to the Galatians.

I want you to know, brothers and sisters, that the gospel that was proclaimed by me is not of human origin; for I did not receive it from a human source, nor was I taught it, but I received it through a revelation of Jesus Christ.

You have heard, no doubt, of my earlier life in Judaism. I was violently persecuting the church of God and was trying to destroy it. I advanced in Judaism beyond many among my people of the same age, for I was far more zealous for the traditions of my ancestors. But when God, who had set me apart before I was born and called me through his grace, was pleased to reveal his Son to me, so that I might proclaim him among the Gentiles, I did not confer with any human being.

GOSPEL   **Matthew 19.27–30**

Hear the gospel of our Lord Jesus Christ according to Matthew.

Peter said to Jesus: 'Look, we have left everything and followed you. What then will we have?' Jesus said to them, 'Truly I tell you, at the renewal of all things, when the Son of Man is seated on the throne of his glory, you who have followed me will also sit on twelve thrones, judging the twelve tribes of Israel. And everyone who has left houses or brothers or sisters or father or mother or children or fields, for my name's sake, will receive a hundredfold, and will inherit eternal life. But many who are first will be last, and the last will be first.'

† ST JOSEPH   YEARS A B C

19 March

FIRST READING   2 Samuel 7.1–16

A reading from the second book of Samuel.

Now when David was settled in his house, and the LORD had given him rest from all his enemies around him, the king said to the prophet Nathan, 'See now, I am living in a house of cedar, but the ark of God stays in a tent.' Nathan said to the king, 'Go, do all that you have in mind; for the LORD is with you.'

But that same night the word of the LORD came to Nathan: Go and tell my servant David: Thus says the LORD: Are you the one to build me a house to live in? I have not lived in a house since the day I brought up the people of Israel from Egypt to this day, but I have been moving about in a tent and a tabernacle. Wherever I have moved about among all the people of Israel, did I ever speak a word with any of the tribal leaders of Israel, whom I commanded to shepherd my people Israel, saying, 'Why have you not built me a house of cedar?' Now therefore thus you shall say to my servant David: Thus says the LORD of hosts: I took you from the pasture, from following the sheep to be prince over my people Israel; and I have been with you wherever you went, and have cut off all your enemies from before you; and I will make for you a great name, like the name of the great ones of the earth. And I will appoint a place for my people Israel and will plant them, so that they may live in their own place, and be disturbed no more; and evildoers shall afflict them no more, as formerly, from the time that I appointed judges over my people Israel; and I will give you rest from all your enemies. Moreover the LORD declares to you, David, that the LORD will make you a house. When your days are fulfilled and you lie down with your ancestors, I will raise up your offspring after you, who shall come forth from your body, and I will establish his kingdom. He shall build a house for my name, and I will establish the throne of his kingdom for ever. I will be a father to him, and he shall be a son to me.

But I will not take my steadfast love from him, as I took it from Saul, whom I put away from before you. Your house and your kingdom shall be made sure for ever before me; your throne shall be established for ever.

PSALM   Psalm 89.27–36

℟ **I will be a father to him,
    and he shall be a son to me.**

'I will make him my first-born
and higher than the kings of the earth.
I will keep my love for him for ever,
and my covenant will stand firm for him.
I will establish his line for ever
and his throne as the days of heaven. ℟

If his children forsake my law
and do not walk according to my judgements;
If they break my statutes
and do not keep my commandments;
I will punish their transgressions with a rod
and their iniquities with the lash;
But I will not take my love from him,
nor let my faithfulness prove false. ℟

I will not break my covenant,
nor change what has gone out of my lips.
Once for all I have sworn by my holiness:
"I will not lie to David.
His line shall endure for ever
and his throne as the sun before me."' ℟

SECOND READING   Romans 4.13–18

A reading from the letter of Paul to the Romans.

The promise that Abraham would inherit the world did not come to
Abraham or to his descendants through the law but through the
righteousness of faith. If it is the adherents of the law who are to be the heirs,
faith is null and the promise is void. For the law brings wrath; but where
there is no law, neither is there violation. For this reason the promise
depends on faith, in order that the promise may rest on grace and be
guaranteed to all his descendants, not only to the adherents of the law but
also to those who share the faith of Abraham He is the father of all of us, as it
is written, 'I have made you the father of many nations.' Abraham believed
in the presence of the God who gives life to the dead and calls into existence

the things that do not exist. Hoping against hope, he believed that he would become 'the father of many nations,' according to what was said, 'So numerous shall your descendants be.'

GOSPEL   Matthew 1.18–25

Hear the gospel of our Lord Jesus Christ according to Matthew.

The birth of Jesus the Messiah took place in this way. When his mother Mary had been engaged to Joseph, but before they lived together, she was found to be with child from the Holy Spirit. Her husband Joseph, being a righteous man and unwilling to expose her to public disgrace, planned to dismiss her quietly. But just when he had resolved to do this, an angel of the Lord appeared to him in a dream and said, 'Joseph, son of David, do not be afraid to take Mary as your wife, for the child conceived in her is from the Holy Spirit. She will bear a son, and you are to name him Jesus, for he will save his people from their sins.' All this took place to fulfil what had been spoken by the Lord through the prophet: 'Look, the virgin shall conceive and bear a son, and they shall name him Emmanuel,' which means, 'God is with us.' When Joseph awoke from sleep, he did as the angel of the Lord commanded him; he took her as his wife, but had no marital relations with her until she had borne a son; and he named him Jesus.

THE ANNUNCIATION   YEARS A B C

25 March

Revised Common Lectionary and Church of England provision.

FIRST READING   Isaiah 7.10–14

A reading from the book of the prophet Isaiah.

The LORD spoke to Ahaz, saying, 'Ask a sign of the LORD your God; let it be deep as Sheol or high as heaven.' But Ahaz said, 'I will not ask, and I will not put the LORD to the test.' Then Isaiah said: 'Hear then, O house of David! Is it too little for you to weary mortals, that you weary my God also? Therefore the Lord himself will give you a sign. Look, the young woman is with child and shall bear a son, and shall name him Immanuel.'

PSALM   Psalm 40.5–10

℟ **We have come to do your will, O God,**
   [for it is by your will that we are sanctified].

Great things are they that you have done, O Lord my God!
how great your wonders and your plans for us!
there is none who can be compared with you.
O that I could make them known and tell them!
but they are more than I can count. ℟

In sacrifice and offering you take no pleasure
you have given me ears to hear you;
Burnt-offering and sin-offering you have not required,
and so I said, 'Behold, I come.
In the roll of the book it is written concerning me:
"I love to do your will, O my God;
your law is deep in my heart."' ℟

I proclaimed righteousness in the great congregation;
behold, I did not restrain my lips;
and that, O Lord, you know. ℟

SECOND READING   Hebrews 10.4–10

A reading from the letter to the Hebrews.

It is impossible for the blood of bulls and goats to take away sins.
Consequently, when Christ came into the world, he said,
'Sacrifices and offerings you have not desired,
but a body you have prepared for me;
in burnt-offerings and sin-offerings
you have taken no pleasure.
Then I said,
"See, God, I have come to do your will, O God"
(in the scroll of the book it is written of me).'
When Christ said, 'You have neither desired nor taken pleasure in sacrifices
and offerings and burnt-offerings and sin-offerings' (these are offered
according to the law), then he added, 'See, I have come to do your will.' He
abolishes the first in order to establish the second. And it is by God's will that
we have been sanctified through the offering of the body of Jesus Christ once
for all.

GOSPEL   **Luke 1.26–38**

Hear the gospel of our Lord Jesus Christ according to Luke.

In the sixth month the angel Gabriel was sent by God to a town in Galilee
called Nazareth, to a virgin engaged to a man whose name was Joseph, of the
house of David. The virgin's name was Mary. And he came to her and said,
'Greetings, favoured one! The Lord is with you.' But she was much perplexed
by his words and pondered what sort of greeting this might be. The angel
said to her, 'Do not be afraid, Mary, for you have found favour with God. And
now, you will conceive in your womb and bear a son, and you will name him
Jesus. He will be great, and will be called the Son of the Most High, and the
Lord God will give to him the throne of his ancestor David. He will reign
over the house of Jacob for ever, and of his kingdom there will be no end.'
Mary said to the angel, 'How can this be, since I am a virgin?' The angel said
to her, 'The Holy Spirit will come upon you, and the power of the Most High
will overshadow you; therefore the child to be born will be holy; he will be
called Son of God. And now, your relative Elizabeth in her old age has also
conceived a son; and this is the sixth month for her who was said to be
barren. For nothing will be impossible with God.' Then Mary said, 'Here am I,
the servant of the Lord; let it be with me according to your word.' Then the
angel departed from her.

† ST GEORGE   YEARS A B C

23 April

FIRST READING (Alternative readings)

Either   **1 Maccabees 2.59–64**

A reading from the first book of Maccabees.

Hananiah, Azariah, and Mishael believed and were saved from the flame.
Daniel, because of his innocence, was delivered from the mouth of the lions.

And so observe, from generation to generation, that none of those who put
their trust in him will lack strength. Do not fear the words of sinners, for
their splendour will turn into dung and worms. Today they will be exalted,
but tomorrow they will not be found, because they will have returned to the
dust, and their plans will have perished. My children, be courageous and
grow strong in the law, for by it you will gain honour.

Or   **Revelation 12.7–12**

A reading from the book of Revelation.

War broke out in heaven; Michael and his angels fought against the dragon. The dragon and his angels fought back, but they were defeated, and there was no longer any place for them in heaven. The great dragon was thrown down, that ancient serpent, who is called the Devil and Satan, the deceiver of the whole world – he was thrown down to the earth, and his angels were thrown down with him. Then I heard a loud voice in heaven, proclaiming, 'Now have come the salvation and the power and the kingdom of our God and the authority of his Messiah, for the accuser of our comrades has been thrown down, who accuses them day and night before our God. But they have conquered him by the blood of the Lamb and by the word of their testimony, for they did not cling to life even in the face of death. Rejoice then, you heavens and those who dwell in them! But woe to the earth and the sea, for the devil has come down to you with great wrath, because he knows that his time is short!'

PSALM   **Psalm 126**

℟ **Those who sowed with tears**
   will reap with songs of joy.

When the Lord restored the fortunes of Zion,
then were we like those who dream.
Then was our mouth filled with laughter,
and our tongue with shouts of joy. ℟

Then they said among the nations,
'The Lord has done great things for them.'
The Lord has done great things for us,
and we are glad indeed. ℟

Restore our fortunes, O Lord,
like the watercourses of the Negev.
Those who sowed with tears
will reap with songs of joy.
Those who go out weeping, carrying the seed,
will come again with joy, shouldering their sheaves. ℟

SECOND READING   **2 Timothy 2.3–13**

A reading from the second letter of Paul to Timothy.

Share in suffering like a good soldier of Christ Jesus. No one serving in the army gets entangled in everyday affairs; the soldier's aim is to please the enlisting officer. And in the case of an athlete, no one is crowned without competing according to the rules. It is the farmer who does the work who ought to have the first share of the crops. Think over what I say, for the Lord will give you understanding in all things.

Remember Jesus Christ, raised from the dead, a descendant of David – that is my gospel, for which I suffer hardship, even to the point of being chained like a criminal. But the word of God is not chained. Therefore I endure everything for the sake of the elect, so that they may also obtain the salvation that is in Christ Jesus, with eternal glory. The saying is sure: If we have died with him, we will also live with him; if we endure, we will also reign with him; if we deny him, he will also deny us; if we are faithless, he remains faithful – for he cannot deny himself.

GOSPEL   **John 15.18–21**

Hear the gospel of our Lord Jesus Christ according to John.

Jesus said to his disciples:

'If the world hates you, be aware that it hated me before it hated you. If you belonged to the world, the world would love you as its own. Because you do not belong to the world, but I have chosen you out of the world – therefore the world hates you. Remember the word that I said to you, "Servants are not greater than their master." If they persecuted me, they will persecute you; if they kept my word, they will keep yours also. But they will do all these things to you on account of my name, because they do not know him who sent me.'

† ST MARK   YEARS A B C

25 April

FIRST READING (Alternative readings)

Either   Proverbs 15.28–33

A reading from the book of Proverbs.

The mind of the righteous ponders how to answer, but the mouth of the wicked pours out evil. The LORD is far from the wicked, but he hears the prayer of the righteous. The light of the eyes rejoices the heart, and good news refreshes the body. The ear that heeds wholesome admonition will lodge among the wise. Those who ignore instruction despise themselves, but those who heed admonition gain understanding. The fear of the LORD is instruction in wisdom, and humility goes before honour.

Or   Acts 15.35–41

A reading from the Acts of the Apostles.

Paul and Barnabas remained in Antioch, and there, with many others, they taught and proclaimed the word of the Lord. After some days Paul said to Barnabas, 'Come, let us return and visit the believers in every city where we proclaimed the word of the Lord and see how they are doing.' Barnabas wanted to take with them John called Mark. But Paul decided not to take with them one who had deserted them in Pamphylia and had not accompanied them in the work. The disagreement became so sharp that they parted company; Barnabas took Mark with him and sailed away to Cyprus. But Paul chose Silas and set out, the believers commending him to the grace of the Lord. He went through Syria and Cilicia, strengthening the churches.

PSALM   Psalm 119.9–16

℟ **My delight is in your statutes;**
   I will not forget your word.

How shall the young cleanse their way?
By keeping to your words.
With my whole heart I seek you;
let me not stray from your commandments. ℟

I treasure your promise in my heart,
that I may not sin against you.
Blessèd are you, O Lord;
instruct me in your statutes. ℞

With my lips will I recite
all the judgements of your mouth.
I have taken greater delight in the way of your decrees
than in all manner of riches. ℞

I will meditate on your commandments
and give attention to your ways.
My delight is in your statutes;
I will not forget your word. ℞

SECOND READING   Ephesians 4.7–16

A reading from the letter of Paul to the Ephesians.

Each of us was given grace according to the measure of Christ's gift. Therefore it is said,
'When he ascended on high he made captivity itself a captive;
he gave gifts to his people.'
(When it says, 'He ascended,' what does it mean but that he had also descended into the lower parts of the earth? He who descended is the same one who ascended far above all the heavens, so that he might fill all things.)

The gifts he gave were that some would be apostles, some prophets, some evangelists, some pastors and teachers, to equip the saints for the work of ministry, for building up the body of Christ, until all of us come to the unity of the faith and of the knowledge of the Son of God, to maturity, to the measure of the full stature of Christ. We must no longer be children, tossed to and fro and blown about by every wind of doctrine, by people's trickery, by their craftiness in deceitful scheming. But speaking the truth in love, we must grow up in every way into him who is the head, into Christ, from whom the whole body, joined and knit together by every ligament with which it is equipped, as each part is working properly, promotes the body's growth in building itself up in love.

GOSPEL   Mark 13.5–13

Hear the gospel of our Lord Jesus Christ according to Mark.

Jesus began to say to the disciples, 'Beware that no one leads you astray. Many will come in my name and say, "I am he!" and they will lead many astray. When you hear of wars and rumours of wars, do not be alarmed; this must take place, but the end is still to come. For nation will rise against nation, and kingdom against kingdom; there will be earthquakes in various places; there will be famines. This is but the beginning of the birth pangs.

As for yourselves, beware; for they will hand you over to councils; and you will be beaten in synagogues; and you will stand before governors and kings because of me, as a testimony to them. And the good news must first be proclaimed to all nations. When they bring you to trial and hand you over, do not worry beforehand about what you are to say; but say whatever is given you at that time, for it is not you who speak, but the Holy Spirit. Brother will betray brother to death, and a father his child, and children will rise against parents and have them put to death; and you will be hated by all because of my name. But the one who endures to the end will be saved.'

† ST PHILIP AND ST JAMES   YEARS A B C

1 May

FIRST READING   Isaiah 30.15–21

A reading from the book of the prophet Isaiah.

Thus said the Lord GOD, the Holy One of Israel:
In returning and rest you shall be saved;
in quietness and in trust shall be your strength.
But you refused
and said, 'No!
We will flee upon horses' –
therefore you shall flee! and,
'We will ride upon swift steeds' –
therefore your pursuers shall be swift!
A thousand shall flee at the threat of one,
at the threat of five you shall flee,
until you are left like a flagstaff on the top of a mountain,
like a signal on a hill.

Therefore the LORD waits to be gracious to you;
therefore he will rise up to show mercy to you.
For the LORD is a God of justice;
blessed are all those who wait for him.
Truly, O people in Zion, inhabitants of Jerusalem, you shall weep no more.
He will surely be gracious to you at the sound of your cry; when he hears it,
he will answer you. Though the Lord may give you the bread of adversity and
the water of affliction, yet your Teacher will not hide himself any more, but
your eyes shall see your Teacher. And when you turn to the right or when
you turn to the left, your ears shall hear a word behind you, saying, 'This is
the way; walk in it.'

PSALM   **Psalm 119.1–8**

℞ **My delight is in your statutes;**
  I will not forget your word.

Happy are they whose way is blameless,
who walk in the law of the Lord!
Happy are they who observe his decrees
and seek him with all their hearts! ℞

Who never do any wrong,
but always walk in his ways.
You laid down your commandments,
that we should fully keep them. ℞

O that my ways were made so direct
that I might keep your statutes!
Then I should not be put to shame,
when I regard all your commandments. ℞

I will thank you with an unfeigned heart,
when I have learned your righteous judgements.
I will keep your statutes;
do not utterly forsake me. ℞

SECOND READING   **Ephesians 1.3–10**

A reading from the letter of Paul to the Ephesians.

Blessed be the God and Father of our Lord Jesus Christ, who has blessed us in
Christ with every spiritual blessing in the heavenly places, just as he chose us

in Christ before the foundation of the world to be holy and blameless before him in love. He destined us for adoption as his children through Jesus Christ, according to the good pleasure of God's will, to the praise of his glorious grace that he freely bestowed on us in the Beloved. In him we have redemption through his blood, the forgiveness of our trespasses, according to the riches of his grace that he lavished on us. With all wisdom and insight he has made known to us the mystery of his will, according to his good pleasure that he set forth in Christ, as a plan for the fullness of time, to gather up all things in Christ, things in heaven and things on earth.

GOSPEL   John 14.1–14

Hear the gospel of our Lord Jesus Christ according to John.

Jesus said to his disciples:

'Do not let your hearts be troubled. Believe in God, believe also in me. In my Father's house there are many dwelling-places. If it were not so, would I have told you that I go to prepare a place for you? And if I go and prepare a place for you, I will come again and will take you to myself, so that where I am, there you may be also. And you know the way to the place where I am going.' Thomas said to him, 'Lord, we do not know where you are going. How can we know the way?' Jesus said to him, 'I am the way, and the truth, and the life. No one comes to the Father except through me. If you know me, you will know my Father also. From now on you do know him and have seen him.'

Philip said to him, 'Lord, show us the Father, and we will be satisfied.' Jesus said to him, 'Have I been with you all this time, Philip, and you still do not know me? Whoever has seen me has seen the Father. How can you say, "Show us the Father"? Do you not believe that I am in the Father and the Father is in me? The words that I say to you I do not speak on my own; but the Father who dwells in me does his works. Believe me that I am in the Father and the Father is in me; but if you do not, then believe me because of the works themselves. Very truly, I tell you, the one who believes in me will also do the works that I do and, in fact, will do greater works than these, because I am going to the Father. I will do whatever you ask in my name, so that the Father may be glorified in the Son. If in my name you ask me for anything, I will do it.'

† ST MATTHIAS YEARS A B C

14 May

Acts 11.15–26 must be read as either the First or the Second Reading.

FIRST READING (Alternative readings)

Either Isaiah 22.15–25

A reading from the book of the prophet Isaiah.

Thus says the Lord GOD of hosts: Come, go to this steward, to Shebna, who is master of the household, and say to him: What right do you have here? Who are your relatives here, that you have cut out a tomb here for yourself, cutting a tomb on the height, and carving a habitation for yourself in the rock? The LORD is about to hurl you away violently, my man. He will seize firm hold on you, whirl you round and round, and throw you like a ball into a wide land; there you shall die, and there your splendid chariots shall lie, O you disgrace to your master's house! I will thrust you from your office, and you will be pulled down from your post.

On that day I will call my servant Eliakim son of Hilkiah, and will clothe him with your robe and bind your sash on him. I will commit your authority to his hand, and he shall be a father to the inhabitants of Jerusalem and to the house of Judah. I will place on his shoulder the key of the house of David; he shall open, and no one shall shut; he shall shut, and no one shall open. I will fasten him like a peg in a secure place, and he will become a throne of honour to his ancestral house. And they will hang on him the whole weight of his ancestral house, the offspring and issue, every small vessel, from the cups to all the flagons. On that day, says the LORD of hosts, the peg that was fastened in a secure place will give way; it will be cut down and fall, and the load that was on it will perish, for the LORD has spoken.

Or Acts 1.15–26

A reading from the Acts of the Apostles.

In those days Peter stood up among the believers; (together the crowd numbered about one hundred and twenty people) and said, 'Friends, the scripture had to be fulfilled, which the Holy Spirit through David foretold concerning Judas, who became a guide for those who arrested Jesus – for he was numbered among us and was allotted his share in this ministry.' (Now

this man acquired a field with the reward of his wickedness; and falling headlong, he burst open in the middle and all his bowels gushed out. This became known to all the residents of Jerusalem, so that the field was called in their language Hakeldama, that is, Field of Blood.) 'For it is written in the book of Psalms,
"Let his homestead become desolate,
and let there be no one to live in it";
and "Let another take his position of overseer."
So one of the men who have accompanied us throughout the time that the Lord Jesus went in and out among us, beginning from the baptism of John until the day when he was taken up from us – one of these must become a witness with us to his resurrection.' So they proposed two, Joseph called Barsabbas, who was also known as Justus, and Matthias. Then they prayed and said, 'Lord, you know everyone's heart. Show us which one of these two you have chosen to take the place in this ministry and apostleship from which Judas turned aside to go to his own place.' And they cast lots for them, and the lot fell on Matthias; and he was added to the eleven apostles.

PSALM   Psalm 15

℟ **Behold, whoever does these things**
  shall never be overthrown.

Lord, who may dwell in your tabernacle?
who may abide upon your holy hill?
Whoever leads a blameless life and does what is right,
who speaks the truth from his heart. ℟

There is no guile upon his tongue;
he does no evil to his friend;
he does not heap contempt upon his neighbour.
In his sight the wicked are rejected,
but he honours those who fear the Lord. ℟

He has sworn to do no wrong
and does not take back his word.
He does not give his money in hope of gain,
nor does he take a bribe against the innocent.
Whoever does these things
shall never be overthrown. ℟

SECOND READING

Either   **Acts 1.15–26**

A reading from the Acts of the Apostles.

See above, page 769.

Or   **1 Corinthians 4.1–7**

A reading from the first letter of Paul to the Corinthians.

My brothers and sisters: Think of us in this way, as servants of Christ and stewards of God's mysteries. Moreover, it is required of stewards that they be found trustworthy. But with me it is a very small thing that I should be judged by you or by any human court. I do not even judge myself. I am not aware of anything against myself, but I am not thereby acquitted. It is the Lord who judges me. Therefore do not pronounce judgement before the time, before the Lord comes, who will bring to light the things now hidden in darkness and will disclose the purposes of the heart. Then each one will receive commendation from God.

I have applied all this to Apollos and myself for your benefit, brothers and sisters, so that you may learn through us the meaning of the saying, 'Nothing beyond what is written,' so that none of you will be puffed up in favour of one against another. For who sees anything different in you? What do you have that you did not receive? And if you received it, why do you boast as if it were not a gift?

GOSPEL   **John 15.9–17**

Hear the gospel of our Lord Jesus Christ according to John.

Jesus said to his disciples: 'As the Father has loved me, so I have loved you; abide in my love. If you keep my commandments, you will abide in my love, just as I have kept my Father's commandments and abide in his love. I have said these things to you so that my joy may be in you, and that your joy may be complete.

This is my commandment, that you love one another as I have loved you. No one has greater love than this, to lay down one's life for one's friends. You are my friends if you do what I command you. I do not call you servants any longer, because the servant does not know what the master is doing; but I have called you friends, because I have made known to you everything that I have heard from my Father. You did not choose me but I chose you. And I appointed you to go and bear fruit, fruit that will last, so that the Father will give you whatever you ask him in my name. I am giving you these commands so that you may love one another.'

THE VISIT OF MARY TO ELIZABETH   YEARS A B C

31 May

Revised Common Lectionary and Church of England provision.

FIRST READING (Alternative readings)

Either (Revised Common Lectionary only)   1 Samuel 2.1–10

A reading from the first book of Samuel.

Hannah prayed and said, 'My heart exults in the LORD;
my strength is exalted in my God.
My mouth derides my enemies,
because I rejoice in my victory.

There is no Holy One like the LORD,
no one besides you;
there is no Rock like our God.
Talk no more so very proudly,
let not arrogance come from your mouth;
for the LORD is a God of knowledge,
and by him actions are weighed.
The bows of the mighty are broken,
but the feeble gird on strength.
Those who were full have hired themselves out for bread,
but those who were hungry are fat with spoil.
The barren has borne seven,
but she who has many children is forlorn.
The LORD kills and brings to life;
he brings down to Sheol and raises up.
The LORD makes poor and makes rich;
he brings low, he also exalts.
He raises up the poor from the dust;

he lifts the needy from the ash heap,
to make them sit with princes and inherit a seat of honour.
For the pillars of the earth are the Lord's,
and on them he has set the world.
He will guard the feet of his faithful ones,
but the wicked shall be cut off in darkness;
for not by might does one prevail.
The LORD!
His adversaries shall be shattered;
the Most High will thunder in heaven.
The LORD will judge the ends of the earth;
he will give strength to his king,
and exalt the power of his anointed.'

† Or   **Zephaniah 3.14–18**

A reading from the book of the prophet Zephaniah.

Sing aloud, O daughter Zion; shout, O Israel!
Rejoice and exult with all your heart,
O daughter Jerusalem!
The LORD has taken away the judgements against you,
he has turned away your enemies.
The king of Israel, the LORD, is in your midst;
you shall fear disaster no more.
On that day it shall be said to Jerusalem:
Do not fear, O Zion;
do not let your hands grow weak.
The LORD, your God, is in your midst,
a warrior who gives victory;
he will rejoice over you with gladness,
he will renew you in his love;
he will exult over you with loud singing
as on a day of festival.
I will remove disaster from you,
so that you will not bear reproach for it.

PSALM

Psalm 113

℟ **He makes the woman of a childless house
to be a joyful mother of children. Alleluia!**

Alleluia!
Give praise, you servants of the Lord;
praise the name of the Lord.
Let the name of the Lord be blessed,
from this time forth for evermore. ℟

From the rising of the sun to its going down
let the name of the Lord be praised.
The Lord is high above all nations,
and his glory above the heavens. ℟

Who is like the Lord our God,
who sits enthroned on high,
but stoops to behold the heavens and the earth?
He takes up the weak out of the dust
and lifts up the poor from the ashes. ℟

He sets them with the princes,
with the princes of his people.
He makes the woman of a childless house
to be a joyful mother of children. ℟

SECOND READING

Romans 12.9–16

A reading from the letter of Paul to the Romans.

Let love be genuine; hate what is evil, hold fast to what is good; love one another with mutual affection; outdo one another in showing honour. Do not lag in zeal, be ardent in spirit, serve the Lord. Rejoice in hope, be patient in suffering, persevere in prayer. Contribute to the needs of the saints; extend hospitality to strangers. Bless those who persecute you; bless and do not curse them. Rejoice with those who rejoice, weep with those who weep. Live in harmony with one another; do not be haughty, but associate with the lowly; do not claim to be wiser than you are.

GOSPEL (Short or long reading)   Luke 1.39–49, (50–56)

Hear the gospel of our Lord Jesus Christ according to Luke.

Mary set out and went with haste to a Judean town in the hill country, where she entered the house of Zechariah and greeted Elizabeth. When Elizabeth heard Mary's greeting, the child leapt in her womb. And Elizabeth was filled with the Holy Spirit and exclaimed with a loud cry, 'Blessed are you among women, and blessed is the fruit of your womb. And why has this happened to me, that the mother of my Lord comes to me? For as soon as I heard the sound of your greeting, the child in my womb leapt for joy. And blessed is she who believed that there would be a fulfilment of what was spoken to her by the Lord.'

And Mary said, 'My soul magnifies the Lord, and my spirit rejoices in God my Saviour, for he has looked with favour on the lowliness of his servant. Surely, from now on all generations will call me blessed; for the Mighty One has done great things for me, and holy is his name. [His mercy is for those who fear him from generation to generation. He has shown strength with his arm; he has scattered the proud in the thoughts of their hearts. He has brought down the powerful from their thrones, and lifted up the lowly; he has filled the hungry with good things, and sent the rich away empty. He has helped his servant Israel, in remembrance of his mercy, according to the promise he made to our ancestors, to Abraham and to his descendants for ever.'

And Mary remained with her for about three months and then returned to her home.]

† ST BARNABAS   YEARS A B C

11 June

Acts 11.19–30 must be read as either the First or the Second Reading.

FIRST READING (Alternative readings)

Either   Job 29.11–16

A reading from the book of Job.

Job said to his companions:
'When the ear heard, it commended me,
and when the eye saw, it approved;

because I delivered the poor who cried,
and the orphan who had no helper.
The blessing of the wretched came upon me,
and I caused the widow's heart to sing for joy.
I put on righteousness, and it clothed me;
my justice was like a robe and a turban.
I was eyes to the blind, and feet to the lame.
I was a father to the needy,
and I championed the cause of the stranger.'

Or   **Acts 11.19–30**

A reading from the Acts of the Apostles.

Those who were scattered because of the persecution that took place over
Stephen travelled as far as Phoenicia, Cyprus, and Antioch, and they spoke
the word to no one except Jews. But among them were some men of Cyprus
and Cyrene who, on coming to Antioch, spoke to the Hellenists also,
proclaiming the Lord Jesus. The hand of the Lord was with them, and a great
number became believers and turned to the Lord. News of this came to the
ears of the church in Jerusalem, and they sent Barnabas to Antioch. When he
came and saw the grace of God, he rejoiced, and he exhorted them all to
remain faithful to the Lord with steadfast devotion; for he was a good man,
full of the Holy Spirit and of faith. And a great many people were brought to
the Lord. Then Barnabas went to Tarsus to look for Saul, and when he had
found him, he brought him to Antioch. So it was that for an entire year they
met with the church and taught a great many people, and it was in Antioch
that the disciples were first called 'Christians.'

At that time prophets came down from Jerusalem to Antioch. One of them
named Agabus stood up and predicted by the Spirit that there would be a
severe famine over all the world; and this took place during the reign of
Claudius. The disciples determined that according to their ability, each would
send relief to the believers living in Judea; this they did, sending it to the
elders by Barnabas and Saul.

PSALM   **Psalm 112**

℟ **They have given freely to the poor,**
    and their righteousness stands fast for ever.

Alleluia!
Happy are they who fear the Lord
and have great delight in his commandments!
Their descendants will be mighty in the land;
the generation of the upright will be blessed. ℟

Wealth and riches will be in their house,
and their righteousness will last for ever.
Light shines in the darkness for the upright;
the righteous are merciful and full of compassion. ℟

It is good for them to be generous in lending
and to manage their affairs with justice.
For they will never be shaken;
the righteous will be kept in everlasting remembrance. ℟

They will not be afraid of any evil rumours;
their heart is right;
they put their trust in the Lord.
Their heart is established and will not shrink,
until they see their desire upon their enemies. ℟

They have given freely to the poor,
and their righteousness stands fast for ever;
they will hold up their head with honour.
The wicked will see it and be angry;
they will gnash their teeth and pine away;
the desires of the wicked will perish. ℟

SECOND READING (Alternative readings)

Either   **Acts 11.19–30**

A reading from the Acts of the Apostles.

See above, page 776.

Or   **Galatians 2.1-10**

A reading from the letter of Paul to the Galatians.

After fourteen years I went up again to Jerusalem with Barnabas, taking Titus along with me. I went up in response to a revelation. Then I laid before them (though only in a private meeting with the acknowledged leaders) the gospel that I proclaim among the Gentiles, in order to make sure that I was not running, or had not run, in vain. But even Titus, who was with me, was not compelled to be circumcised, though he was a Greek. But because of false believers secretly brought in, who slipped in to spy on the freedom we have in Christ Jesus, so that they might enslave us – we did not submit to them even for a moment, so that the truth of the gospel might always remain with you. And from those who were supposed to be acknowledged leaders (what they actually were makes no difference to me; God shows no partiality) – those leaders contributed nothing to me. On the contrary, when they saw that I had been entrusted with the gospel for the uncircumcised, just as Peter had been entrusted with the gospel for the circumcised (for he who worked through Peter making him an apostle to the circumcised also worked through me in sending me to the Gentiles), and when James and Cephas and John, who were acknowledged pillars, recognized the grace that had been given to me, they gave to Barnabas and me the right hand of fellowship, agreeing that we should go to the Gentiles and they to the circumcised. They asked only one thing, that we remember the poor, which was actually what I was eager to do.

GOSPEL   **John 15.12-17**

Hear the gospel of our Lord Jesus Christ according to John.

Jesus said to his disciples:

'This is my commandment, that you love one another as I have loved you. No one has greater love than this, to lay down one's life for one's friends. You are my friends if you do what I command you. I do not call you servants any longer, because the servant does not know what the master is doing; but I have called you friends, because I have made known to you everything that I have heard from my Father. You did not choose me but I chose you. And I appointed you to go and bear fruit, fruit that will last, so that the Father will give you whatever you ask him in my name. I am giving you these commands so that you may love one another.'

† THE BIRTH OF ST JOHN THE BAPTIST   YEARS A B C

24 June

FIRST READING   Isaiah 40.1–11

A reading from the book of the prophet Isaiah.

Comfort, O comfort my people,
says your God.
Speak tenderly to Jerusalem,
and cry to her
that she has served her term,
that her penalty is paid,
that she has received from the LORD's hand
double for all her sins.

A voice cries out:
'In the wilderness prepare the way of the LORD,
make straight in the desert a highway for our God.
Every valley shall be lifted up,
and every mountain and hill be made low;
the uneven ground shall become level,
and the rough places a plain.
Then the glory of the LORD shall be revealed,
and all people shall see it together,
for the mouth of the LORD has spoken.'

A voice says, 'Cry out!'
And I said, 'What shall I cry?'
All people are grass,
their constancy is like the flower of the field.
The grass withers, the flower fades,
when the breath of the LORD blows upon it;
surely the people are grass.
The grass withers, the flower fades;
but the word of our God will stand for ever.
Get you up to a high mountain,
O Zion, herald of good tidings;
lift up your voice with strength,
O Jerusalem, herald of good tidings,
lift it up, do not fear;
say to the cities of Judah,

'Here is your God!'
See, the Lord GOD comes with might,
and his arm rules for him;
his reward is with him,
and his recompense before him.
He will feed his flock like a shepherd;
he will gather the lambs in his arms,
and carry them in his bosom,
and gently lead the mother sheep.

PSALM

Psalm 85.7–13

℟ **The Lord will indeed grant prosperity,
and our land will yield its increase.**

Show us your mercy, O Lord,
and grant us your salvation.
I will listen to what the Lord God is saying,
for he is speaking peace to his faithful people
and to those who turn their hearts to him. ℟

Truly, his salvation is very near to those who fear him,
that his glory may dwell in our land.
Mercy and truth have met together;
righteousness and peace have kissed each other.
Truth shall spring up from the earth,
and righteousness shall look down from heaven. ℟

The Lord will indeed grant prosperity,
and our land will yield its increase.
Righteousness shall go before him,
and peace shall be a pathway for his feet. ℟

SECOND READING (Alternative readings)

Either

Acts 13.14b–26

A reading from the Acts of the Apostles.

On the sabbath day Paul and his companions went into the synagogue and
sat down. After the reading of the law and the prophets, the officials of the
synagogue sent them a message, saying, 'Brothers, if you have any word of

exhortation for the people, give it.' So Paul stood up and with a gesture began to speak: 'You Israelites, and others who fear God, listen. The God of this people Israel chose our ancestors and made the people great during their stay in the land of Egypt, and with uplifted arm he led them out of it. For about forty years he put up with them in the wilderness. After he had destroyed seven nations in the land of Canaan, he gave them their land as an inheritance for about four hundred and fifty years. After that he gave them judges until the time of the prophet Samuel. Then they asked for a king; and God gave them Saul son of Kish, a man of the tribe of Benjamin, who reigned for forty years. When he had removed him, he made David their king. In his testimony about him he said, "I have found David, son of Jesse, to be a man after my heart, who will carry out all my wishes." Of this man's posterity God has brought to Israel a Saviour, Jesus, as he promised; before his coming John had already proclaimed a baptism of repentance to all the people of Israel. And as John was finishing his work, he said, "What do you suppose that I am? I am not he. No, but one is coming after me; I am not worthy to untie the thong of the sandals on his feet." My brothers, you descendants of Abraham's family, and others who fear God, to us the message of this salvation has been sent.'

Or   **Galatians 3.23–29**

A reading from the letter of Paul to the Galatians.

Before faith came, we were imprisoned and guarded under the law until faith would be revealed. Therefore the law was our disciplinarian until Christ came, so that we might be justified by faith. But now that faith has come, we are no longer subject to a disciplinarian, for in Christ Jesus you are all children of God through faith. As many of you as were baptized into Christ have clothed yourselves with Christ;

There is no longer Jew or Greek, there is no longer slave or free, there is no longer male and female; for all of you are one in Christ Jesus. And if you belong to Christ, then you are Abraham's offspring, heirs according to the promise.

GOSPEL   **Luke 1.57–66, 80**

Hear the gospel of our Lord Jesus Christ according to Luke.

The time came for Elizabeth to give birth, and she bore a son. Her neighbours and relatives heard that the Lord had shown his great mercy to her, and they rejoiced with her. On the eighth day they came to circumcise the child, and they were going to name him Zechariah after his father. But his mother said, 'No; he is to be called John.' They said to her, 'None of your relatives has this name.' Then they began motioning to his father to find out what name he wanted to give him. He asked for a writing-tablet and wrote, 'His name is John.' And all of them were amazed. Immediately his mouth was opened and his tongue freed, and he began to speak, praising God. Fear came over all their neighbours, and all these things were talked about throughout the entire hill country of Judea. All who heard them pondered them and said, 'What then will this child become?' For, indeed, the hand of the Lord was with him.

The child grew and became strong in spirit, and he was in the wilderness until the day he appeared publicly to Israel.

† ST PETER AND ST PAUL   YEARS A B C

29 June

Acts 12.1–11 must be read as either the First or the Second Reading.
See below, pages 785–787, for provision for St Peter alone.

FIRST READING   Zechariah 4.1–6a, 10b–14

A reading from the book of the prophet Zechariah.

The angel who talked with me came again, and wakened me, as one is wakened from sleep. He said to me, 'What do you see?' And I said, 'I see a lampstand all of gold, with a bowl on the top of it; there are seven lamps on it, with seven lips on each of the lamps that are on the top of it. And by it there are two olive trees, one on the right of the bowl and the other on its left.' I said to the angel who talked with me, 'What are these, my lord?' Then the angel who talked with me answered me, 'Do you not know what these are?' I said, 'No, my lord.' He said to me,

'These seven are the eyes of the LORD, which range through the whole earth.' Then I said to him, 'What are these two olive trees on the right and the left of the lampstand?' And a second time I said to him, 'What are these two branches of the olive trees, which pour out the oil through the two golden pipes?' He said to me, 'Do you not know what these are?' I said, 'No, my lord.' Then he said, 'These are the two anointed ones who stand by the Lord of the whole earth.'

Or   **Acts 12.1–11**

A reading from the Acts of the Apostles.

About that time King Herod laid violent hands upon some who belonged to the church. He had James, the brother of John, killed with the sword. After he saw that it pleased the Jews, he proceeded to arrest Peter also. (This was during the festival of Unleavened Bread.) When he had seized him, he put him in prison and handed him over to four squads of soldiers to guard him, intending to bring him out to the people after the Passover. While Peter was kept in prison, the church prayed fervently to God for him.

The very night before Herod was going to bring him out, Peter, bound with two chains, was sleeping between two soldiers, while guards in front of the door were keeping watch over the prison. Suddenly an angel of the Lord appeared and a light shone in the cell. He tapped Peter on the side and woke him, saying, 'Get up quickly.' And the chains fell off his wrists. The angel said to him, 'Fasten your belt and put on your sandals.' He did so. Then he said to him, 'Wrap your cloak around you and follow me.' Peter went out and followed him; he did not realize that what was happening with the angel's help was real; he thought he was seeing a vision. After they had passed the first and the second guard, they came before the iron gate leading into the city. It opened for them of its own accord, and they went outside and walked along a lane, when suddenly the angel left him. Then Peter came to himself and said, 'Now I am sure that the Lord has sent his angel and rescued me from the hands of Herod and from all that the Jewish people were expecting.'

PSALM   **Psalm 125**

℟ **Show your goodness, O Lord, to those who are good
   [and to those who are true of heart].**

Those who trust in the Lord are like Mount Zion,
which cannot be moved, but stands fast for ever.
The hills stand about Jerusalem;
so does the Lord stand round about his people,
from this time forth for evermore. ℟

The sceptre of the wicked shall not hold sway
over the land allotted to the just,
so that the just shall not put their hands to evil.
Show your goodness, O Lord, to those who are good
and to those who are true of heart.
As for those who turn aside to crooked ways,
the Lord will lead them away with the evildoers;
but peace be upon Israel. ℟

SECOND READING (Alternative readings)

Either

Acts 12.1–11

A reading from the Acts of the Apostles.

See above, page 783.

Or

2 Timothy 4.6–8, 17–18

A reading from the second letter of Paul to Timothy.

As for me, I am already being poured out as a libation, and the time of my departure has come. I have fought the good fight, I have finished the race, I have kept the faith. From now on there is reserved for me the crown of righteousness, which the Lord, the righteous judge, will give to me on that day, and not only to me but also to all who have longed for his appearing.

But the Lord stood by me and gave me strength, so that through me the message might be fully proclaimed and all the Gentiles might hear it. So I was rescued from the lion's mouth. The Lord will rescue me from every evil attack and save me for his heavenly kingdom. To him be the glory for ever and ever. Amen.

GOSPEL

Matthew 16.13–19

Hear the gospel of our Lord Jesus Christ according to Matthew.

When Jesus came into the district of Caesarea Philippi, he asked his disciples, 'Who do people say that the Son of Man is?' And they said, 'Some say John the Baptist, but others Elijah, and still others Jeremiah or one of the prophets.' He said to them, 'But who do you say that I am?' Simon Peter answered, 'You are the Messiah, the Son of the living God.' And Jesus answered him, 'Blessed are you, Simon son of Jonah! For flesh and blood has not revealed this to you, but my Father in heaven. And I tell you, you are Peter, and on this rock I will build my church, and the gates of Hades will not prevail against it. I will give you the keys of the kingdom of heaven, and whatever you bind on earth will be bound in heaven, and whatever you loose on earth will be loosed in heaven.'

† ST PETER   YEARS A B C

29 June

> *Acts 12.1–11 must be read as either the First or the Second Reading.*
> *See also St Peter and St Paul, pages 782–785.*

FIRST READING (Alternative readings)

Either   Ezekiel 3.22–27

A reading from the book of the prophet Ezekiel.

The hand of the LORD was upon me there; and he said to me, Rise up, go out into the valley, and there I will speak with you. So I rose up and went out into the valley; and the glory of the LORD stood there, like the glory that I had seen by the river Chebar; and I fell on my face. The spirit entered into me, and set me on my feet; and he spoke with me and said to me: Go, shut yourself inside your house. As for you, mortal, cords shall be placed on you, and you shall be bound with them, so that you cannot go out among the people; and I will make your tongue cling to the roof of your mouth, so that you shall be speechless and unable to reprove them; for they are a rebellious house. But when I speak with you, I will open your mouth, and you shall say to them, 'Thus says the Lord GOD'; let those who will hear, hear; and let those who refuse to hear, refuse; for they are a rebellious house.

Or   Acts 12.1–11

A reading from the Acts of the Apostles.

See above, page 783.

PSALM

℞ **Show your goodness, O Lord, to those who are good
   [and to those who are true of heart].**

Those who trust in the Lord are like Mount Zion,
which cannot be moved, but stands fast for ever.
The hills stand about Jerusalem;
so does the Lord stand round about his people,
from this time forth for evermore. ℞

The sceptre of the wicked shall not hold sway
over the land allotted to the just,
so that the just shall not put their hands to evil.
Show your goodness, O Lord, to those who are good
and to those who are true of heart.
As for those who turn aside to crooked ways,
the Lord will lead them away with the evildoers;
but peace be upon Israel. ℞

SECOND READING (Alternative readings)

Either

Acts 12.1–11

A reading from the Acts of the Apostles.

See above, page 988.

Or

1 Peter 2.19–25

A reading from the first letter of Peter.

It is a credit to you if, being aware of God, you endure pain while suffering
unjustly. If you endure when you are beaten for doing wrong, what credit is
that? But if you endure when you do right and suffer for it, you have God's
approval. For to this you have been called, because Christ also suffered for
you, leaving you an example, so that you should follow in his steps.
'He committed no sin,
and no deceit was found in his mouth.'

When he was abused, he did not return abuse; when he suffered, he did not
threaten; but he entrusted himself to the one who judges justly. He himself
bore our sins in his body on the cross, so that, free from sins, we might live
for righteousness; by his wounds you have been healed. For you were going

astray like sheep, but now you have returned to the shepherd and guardian of your souls.

GOSPEL   Matthew 16.13–19

Hear the gospel of our Lord Jesus Christ according to Matthew.

See above, page 784.

† ST THOMAS   YEARS A B C

3 July

FIRST READING   Habakkuk 2.1–4

A reading from the book of the prophet Habakkuk.

I will stand at my watch-post,
and station myself on the rampart;
I will keep watch to see what he will say to me,
and what he will answer concerning my complaint.
Then the LORD answered me and said:
Write the vision;
make it plain on tablets,
so that a runner may read it.
For there is still a vision for the appointed time;
it speaks of the end, and does not lie.
If it seems to tarry, wait for it;
it will surely come, it will not delay.
Look at the proud!
Their spirit is not right in them,
but the righteous live by their faith.

PSALM   Psalm 31.1–6

℟ **The Lord has done great things indeed,**
  [whereof we rejoice and sing].

In you, O Lord, have I taken refuge;
let me never be put to shame;
deliver me in your righteousness.
Incline your ear to me;
make haste to deliver me. ℟

Be my strong rock, a castle to keep me safe,
for you are my crag and my stronghold;
for the sake of your name, lead me and guide me.
Take me out of the net
that they have secretly set for me,
for you are my tower of strength. ℟

Into your hands I commend my spirit,
for you have redeemed me,
O Lord, O God of truth.
I hate those who cling to worthless idols,
and I put my trust in the Lord. ℟

SECOND READING   Ephesians 2.19–22

A reading from the letter of Paul to the Ephesians.

You are no longer strangers and aliens, but you are citizens with the saints
and also members of the household of God, built upon the foundation of the
apostles and prophets, with Christ Jesus himself as the cornerstone. In him
the whole structure is joined together and grows into a holy temple in the
Lord; in whom you also are built together spiritually into a dwelling-place for
God.

GOSPEL   John 20.24–29

Hear the gospel of our Lord Jesus Christ according to John.

Thomas (who was called the Twin), one of the twelve, was not with them
when Jesus came. So the other disciples told him, 'We have seen the Lord.'
But he said to them, 'Unless I see the mark of the nails in his hands, and put
my finger in the mark of the nails and my hand in his side, I will not
believe.'

A week later his disciples were again in the house, and Thomas was with
them. Although the doors were shut, Jesus came and stood among them and
said, 'Peace be with you.' Then he said to Thomas, 'Put your finger here and
see my hands. Reach out your hand and put it in my side. Do not doubt but
believe.' Thomas answered him, 'My Lord and my God!' Jesus said to him,
'Have you believed because you have seen me? Blessed are those who have
not seen and yet have come to believe.'

† ST MARY MAGDALENE   YEARS A B C

22 July

FIRST READING   Song of Solomon 3.1-4

A reading from the book of the Song of Solomon.

Upon my bed at night I sought him whom my soul loves;
I sought him, but found him not;
I called him, but he gave no answer.
'I will rise now and go about the city,
in the streets and in the squares;
I will seek him whom my soul loves.'
I sought him, but found him not.
The sentinels found me, as they went about in the city.
'Have you seen him whom my soul loves?'
Scarcely had I passed them, when I found him whom my soul loves.
I held him, and would not let him go
until I brought him into my mother's house,
and into the chamber of her that conceived me.

PSALM   Psalm 42.1-7

℟ **Then was our mouth filled with laughter,
and our tongue with shouts of joy.**

As the deer longs for the water-brooks,
so longs my soul for you, O God.
My soul is athirst for God, athirst for the living God;
when shall I come to appear before the presence of God? ℟

My tears have been my food day and night,
while all day long they say to me,
'Where now is your God?'
I pour out my soul when I think on these things:
how I went with the multitude
and led them into the house of God,
With the voice of praise and thanksgiving,
among those who keep holy-day. ℟

Why are you so full of heaviness, O my soul?
and why are you so disquieted within me?
Put your trust in God;
for I will yet give thanks to him,
who is the help of my countenance, and my God. ℟

SECOND READING   2 Corinthians 5.14–17

A reading from the second letter of Paul to the Corinthians.

The love of Christ urges us on, because we are convinced that one has died for all; therefore all have died. And he died for all, so that those who live might live no longer for themselves, but for him who died and was raised for them.

From now on, therefore, we regard no one from a human point of view; even though we once knew Christ from a human point of view, we know him no longer in that way. So if anyone is in Christ, there is a new creation: everything old has passed away; see, everything has become new!

GOSPEL   John 20.1–2, 11–18

Hear the gospel of our Lord Jesus Christ according to John.

Early on the first day of the week, while it was still dark, Mary Magdalene came to the tomb and saw that the stone had been removed from the tomb. So she ran and went to Simon Peter and the other disciple, the one whom Jesus loved, and said to them, 'They have taken the Lord out of the tomb, and we do not know where they have laid him.'

But Mary stood weeping outside the tomb. As she wept, she bent over to look into the tomb; and she saw two angels in white, sitting where the body of Jesus had been lying, one at the head and the other at the feet. They said to her, 'Woman, why are you weeping?' She said to them, 'They have taken away my Lord, and I do not know where they have laid him.' When she had said this, she turned around and saw Jesus standing there, but she did not know that it was Jesus. Jesus said to her, 'Woman, why are you weeping? For whom are you looking?' Supposing him to be the gardener, she said to him, 'Sir, if you have carried him away, tell me where you have laid him, and I will take him away.' Jesus said to her, 'Mary!' She turned and said to him in Hebrew, 'Rabbouni!' (which means Teacher). Jesus said to her, 'Do not hold on to me, because I have not yet ascended to the Father. But go to my brothers and say to them, "I am ascending to my Father and your Father, to my God and your God."' Mary Magdalene went and announced to the disciples, 'I have seen the Lord'; and she told them that he had said these things to her.

† ST JAMES   YEARS A B C

25 July

Acts 11.27 – 12.2 must be read as either the First or the Second Reading.

FIRST READING (Alternative readings)

Either   Jeremiah 45.1-5

A reading from the book of the prophet Jeremiah.

The word that the prophet Jeremiah spoke to Baruch son of Neriah, when he wrote these words in a scroll at the dictation of Jeremiah, in the fourth year of King Jehoiakim son of Josiah of Judah: Thus says the LORD, the God of Israel, to you, O Baruch: You said, 'Woe is me! The LORD has added sorrow to my pain; I am weary with my groaning, and I find no rest.' Thus you shall say to him, 'Thus says the LORD: I am going to break down what I have built, and pluck up what I have planted – that is, the whole land. And you, do you seek great things for yourself? Do not seek them; for I am going to bring disaster upon all flesh, says the LORD; but I will give you your life as a prize of war in every place to which you may go.'

Or   Acts 11.27 – 12.2

A reading from the Acts of the Apostles.

At that time prophets came down from Jerusalem to Antioch. One of them named Agabus stood up and predicted by the Spirit that there would be a severe famine over all the world; and this took place during the reign of Claudius. The disciples determined that according to their ability, each would send relief to the believers living in Judea; this they did, sending it to the elders by Barnabas and Saul. About that time King Herod laid violent hands upon some who belonged to the church. He had James, the brother of John, killed with the sword.

PSALM Psalm 126

℟ **Those who go out weeping, carrying the seed,**
   will come again with joy, shouldering their sheaves.

When the Lord restored the fortunes of Zion,
then were we like those who dream.
Then was our mouth filled with laughter,
and our tongue with shouts of joy. ℟

Then they said among the nations,
'The Lord has done great things for them.'
The Lord has done great things for us,
and we are glad indeed. ℟

Restore our fortunes, O Lord,
like the watercourses of the Negev.
Those who sowed with tears
will reap with songs of joy.
Those who go out weeping, carrying the seed,
will come again with joy, shouldering their sheaves. ℟

SECOND READING (Alternative readings)

Either   Acts 11.27 – 12.2

A reading from the Acts of the Apostles.

See above, page 791.

Or   2 Corinthians 4.7–15

A reading from the second letter of Paul to the Corinthians.

We have this treasure in clay jars, so that it may be made clear that this extraordinary power belongs to God and does not come from us. We are afflicted in every way, but not crushed; perplexed, but not driven to despair; persecuted, but not forsaken; struck down, but not destroyed; always carrying in the body the death of Jesus, so that the life of Jesus may also be made visible in our bodies. For while we live, we are always being given up to death for Jesus' sake, so that the life of Jesus may be made visible in our mortal flesh. So death is at work in us, but life in you. But just as we have the same spirit of faith that is in accordance with scripture – 'I believed, and so I spoke' – we also believe, and so we speak, because we know that the one who raised the Lord Jesus will raise us also with Jesus, and will bring us with you into his presence. Yes, everything is for your sake, so that grace, as it extends to more and more people, may increase thanksgiving, to the glory of God.

GOSPEL   **Matthew 20.20–28**

Hear the gospel of our Lord Jesus Christ according to Matthew.

The mother of the sons of Zebedee came to him with her sons, and kneeling before him, she asked a favour of him. And he said to her, 'What do you want?' She said to him, 'Declare that these two sons of mine will sit, one at your right hand and one at your left, in your kingdom.' But Jesus answered, 'You do not know what you are asking. Are you able to drink the cup that I am about to drink?' They said to him, 'We are able.' He said to them, 'You will indeed drink my cup, but to sit at my right hand and at my left, this is not mine to grant, but it is for those for whom it has been prepared by my Father.'

When the ten heard it, they were angry with the two brothers. But Jesus called them to him and said, 'You know that the rulers of the Gentiles lord it over them, and their great ones are tyrants over them. It will not be so among you; but whoever wishes to be great among you must be your servant, and whoever wishes to be first among you must be your slave; just as the Son of Man came not to be served but to serve, and to give his life a ransom for many.'

† THE TRANSFIGURATION   YEARS A B C

6 August

FIRST READING   **Daniel 7.9–10, 13–14**

A reading from the book of Daniel.

As I watched,
thrones were set in place,
and an Ancient One took his throne,
his clothing was white as snow,
and the hair of his head like pure wool;
his throne was fiery flames,
and its wheels were burning fire.
A stream of fire issued
and flowed out from his presence.

A thousand thousand served him,
and ten thousand times ten thousand stood attending him.
The court sat in judgement, and the books were opened.

As I watched in the night visions,
I saw one like a human being coming with the clouds of heaven.
And he came to the Ancient One
and was presented before him.
To him was given dominion and glory and kingship,
that all peoples, nations, and languages should serve him.
His dominion is an everlasting dominion
that shall not pass away,
and his kingship is one that shall never be destroyed.

PSALM   Psalm 97

℞ Rejoice in the Lord, you righteous,
    and give thanks to his holy name.

The Lord is king; let the earth rejoice;
let the multitude of the isles be glad.
Clouds and darkness are round about him,
righteousness and justice
are the foundations of his throne.
A fire goes before him
and burns up his enemies on every side. ℞

His lightnings light up the world;
the earth sees it and is afraid.
The mountains melt like wax
at the presence of the Lord,
at the presence of the Lord of the whole earth.
The heavens declare his righteousness,
and all the peoples see his glory. ℞

Confounded be all who worship carved images
and delight in false gods!
Bow down before him, all you gods.
Zion hears and is glad and the cities of Judah rejoice,
because of your judgements, O Lord.
For you are the Lord: most high over all the earth;
you are exalted far above all gods. ℞

The Lord loves those who hate evil;
he preserves the lives of his saints
and delivers them from the hand of the wicked.
Light has sprung up for the righteous,
and joyful gladness for those who are true-hearted.
Rejoice in the Lord, you righteous,
and give thanks to his holy name. ℟

SECOND READING   2 Peter 1.16-19

A reading from the second letter of Peter.

We did not follow cleverly devised myths when we made known to you the
power and coming of our Lord Jesus Christ, but we had been eyewitnesses of
his majesty. For he received honour and glory from God the Father when that
voice was conveyed to him by the Majestic Glory, saying, 'This is my Son, my
Beloved, with whom I am well pleased.' We ourselves heard this voice come
from heaven, while we were with him on the holy mountain. So we have the
prophetic message more fully confirmed. You will do well to be attentive to
this as to a lamp shining in a dark place, until the day dawns and the
morning star rises in your hearts.

GOSPEL   Luke 9.28b–36

Hear the gospel of our Lord Jesus Christ according to Luke.

Jesus took with him Peter and John and James, and went up on the mountain
to pray. And while he was praying, the appearance of his face changed, and
his clothes became dazzling white. Suddenly they saw two men, Moses and
Elijah, talking to him. They appeared in glory and were speaking of his
departure, which he was about to accomplish at Jerusalem. Now Peter and his
companions were weighed down with sleep; but since they had stayed awake,
they saw his glory and the two men who stood with him. Just as they were
leaving him, Peter said to Jesus, 'Master, it is good for us to be here; let us
make three dwellings, one for you, one for Moses, and one for Elijah.' Peter
did not know what he said. While he was saying this, a cloud came and
overshadowed them; and they were terrified as they entered the cloud. Then
from the cloud came a voice that said, 'This is my Son, my Chosen; listen to
him!' When the voice had spoken, Jesus was found alone. And they kept
silent and in those days told no one any of the things they had seen.

† THE BLESSED VIRGIN MARY   YEARS A B C

15 August

FIRST READING (Alternative readings)

Either   Isaiah 61.10–11

A reading from the book of the prophet Isaiah.

I will greatly rejoice in the LORD,
my whole being shall exult in my God;
for he has clothed me with the garments of salvation,
he has covered me with the robe of righteousness,
as a bridegroom decks himself with a garland,
and as a bride adorns herself with her jewels.
For as the earth brings forth its shoots,
and as a garden causes what is sown in it to spring up,
so the Lord GOD will cause righteousness
and praise to spring up before all the nations.

Or   Revelation 11.19 – 12.6

A reading from the book of Revelation.

God's temple in heaven was opened, and the ark of his covenant was seen within his temple; and there were flashes of lightning, rumblings, peals of thunder, an earthquake, and heavy hail.

A great portent appeared in heaven: a woman clothed with the sun, with the moon under her feet, and on her head a crown of twelve stars. She was pregnant and was crying out in birth pangs, in the agony of giving birth.

Then another portent appeared in heaven: a great red dragon, with seven heads and ten horns, and seven diadems on his heads. His tail swept down a third of the stars of heaven and threw them to the earth. Then the dragon stood before the woman who was about to bear a child, so that he might devour her child as soon as it was born. And she gave birth to a son, a male child, who is to rule all the nations with a rod of iron. But her child was snatched away and taken to God and to his throne; and the woman fled into the wilderness, where she has a place prepared by God, so that there she can be nourished for one thousand two hundred and sixty days.

PSALM

℟ **Sing praises to God, sing praises;**
  [sing praises to our king, sing praises].

'Hear, O daughter; consider and listen closely;
forget your people and your family's house.
The king will have pleasure in your beauty;
he is your master; therefore do him honour. ℟

The people of Tyre are here with a gift;
the rich among the people seek your favour.'
All glorious is the princess as she enters;
her gown is cloth-of-gold. ℟

In embroidered apparel she is brought to the king;
after her the bridesmaids follow in procession.
With joy and gladness they are brought,
and enter into the palace of the king. ℟

'In place of fathers, O king, you shall have sons;
you shall make them princes over all the earth.
I will make your name to be remembered
from one generation to another;
therefore nations will praise you for ever and ever.' ℟

SECOND READING

A reading from the letter of Paul to the Galatians.

When the fullness of time had come, God sent his Son, born of a woman,
born under the law, in order to redeem those who were under the law, so that
we might receive adoption as children. And because you are children, God
has sent the Spirit of his Son into our hearts, crying, 'Abba! Father!' So you
are no longer a slave but a child, and if a child then also an heir, through
God.

GOSPEL

Hear the gospel of our Lord Jesus Christ according to Luke.

Mary said,
'My soul magnifies the Lord,
and my spirit rejoices in God my Saviour,

FESTIVALS

for he has looked with favour on the lowliness of his servant.
Surely, from now on all generations will call me blessed;
for the Mighty One has done great things for me,
and holy is his name.
His mercy is for those who fear him
from generation to generation.
He has shown strength with his arm;
he has scattered the proud in the thoughts of their hearts.
He has brought down the powerful from their thrones,
and lifted up the lowly;
he has filled the hungry with good things,
and sent the rich away empty.
He has helped his servant Israel,
in remembrance of his mercy,
according to the promise he made to our ancestors,
to Abraham and to his descendants for ever.'

† ST BARTHOLOMEW   YEARS A B C

24 August

FIRST READING (Alternative readings)

Either   Isaiah 43.8–13

A reading from the book of the prophet Isaiah.

Bring forth the people who are blind, yet have eyes,
who are deaf, yet have ears!
Let all the nations gather together,
and let the peoples assemble.
Who among them declared this,
and foretold to us the former things?
Let them bring their witnesses to justify them,
and let them hear and say, 'It is true.'
You are my witnesses, says the LORD,
and my servant whom I have chosen,
so that you may know and believe me and understand that I am he.
Before me no god was formed,
nor shall there be any after me.
I, I am the LORD, and besides me there is no saviour.

798

I declared and saved and proclaimed,
when there was no strange god among you;
and you are my witnesses, says the LORD.
I am God, and also henceforth I am He;
there is no one who can deliver from my hand;
I work and who can hinder it?

Or   **Acts 5.12–16**

A reading from the Acts of the Apostles.

Many signs and wonders were done among the people through the apostles.
And they were all together in Solomon's Portico. None of the rest dared to
join them, but the people held them in high esteem. Yet more than ever
believers were added to the Lord, great numbers of both men and women, so
that they even carried out the sick into the streets, and laid them on cots and
mats, in order that Peter's shadow might fall on some of them as he came by.
A great number of people would also gather from the towns around
Jerusalem, bringing the sick and those tormented by unclean spirits, and they
were all cured.

PSALM   **Psalm 145.1–7**

℟ **The Lord is loving to everyone,**
   [and his compassion is over all his works].

I will exalt you, O God my King,
and bless your name for ever and ever.
Every day will I bless you
and praise your name for ever and ever. ℟

Great is the Lord and greatly to be praised;
there is no end to his greatness.
One generation shall praise your works to another
and shall declare your power.
I will ponder the glorious splendour of your majesty
and all your marvellous works. ℟

They shall speak of the might of your wondrous acts,
and I will tell of your greatness.
They shall publish the remembrance
of your great goodness;
they shall sing of your righteous deeds. ℟

SECOND READING (Alternative readings)

Either

Acts 5.12–16

A reading from the Acts of the Apostles.

See above, page 799.

Or

1 Corinthians 4.9–15

A reading from the first letter from Paul to the Corinthians.

I think that God has exhibited us apostles as last of all, as though sentenced to death, because we have become a spectacle to the world, to angels and to mortals. We are fools for the sake of Christ, but you are wise in Christ. We are weak, but you are strong. You are held in honour, but we in disrepute. To the present hour we are hungry and thirsty, we are poorly clothed and beaten and homeless, and we grow weary from the work of our own hands. When reviled, we bless; when persecuted, we endure; when slandered, we speak kindly. We have become like the rubbish of the world, the dregs of all things, to this very day.

I am not writing this to make you ashamed, but to admonish you as my beloved children. For though you might have ten thousand guardians in Christ, you do not have many fathers. Indeed, in Christ Jesus I became your father through the gospel.

GOSPEL

Luke 22.24–30

Hear the gospel of our Lord Jesus Christ according to Luke.

A dispute also arose among the twelve as to which one of them was to be regarded as the greatest. But he said to them, 'The kings of the Gentiles lord it over them; and those in authority over them are called benefactors. But not so with you; rather the greatest among you must become like the youngest, and the leader like one who serves. For who is greater, the one who is at the table or the one who serves? Is it not the one at the table? But I am among you as one who serves.

You are those who have stood by me in my trials; and I confer on you, just as my Father has conferred on me, a kingdom, so that you may eat and drink at my table in my kingdom, and you will sit on thrones judging the twelve tribes of Israel.'

HOLY CROSS DAY   YEARS A B C

14 September

Revised Common Lectionary and Church of England provision.

FIRST READING   Numbers 21.4–9

A reading from the book of Numbers.

The Israelites set out by the way to the Red Sea, to go around the land of Edom; but the people became impatient on the way. The people spoke against God and against Moses, 'Why have you brought us up out of Egypt to die in the wilderness? For there is no food and no water, and we detest this miserable food.' Then the LORD sent poisonous serpents among the people, and they bit the people, so that many Israelites died. The people came to Moses and said, 'We have sinned by speaking against the LORD and against you; pray to the LORD to take away the serpents from us.' So Moses prayed for the people. And the LORD said to Moses, 'Make a poisonous serpent, and set it on a pole; and everyone who is bitten shall look at it and live.' So Moses made a serpent of bronze, and put it upon a pole; and whenever a serpent bit someone, that person would look at the serpent of bronze and live.

PSALM   Psalm 22.22–27

℞ **You are the Holy One, O God,
[enthroned on the praises of Israel].**

Praise the Lord, you that fear him;
stand in awe of him, O offspring of Israel;
all you of Jacob's line, give glory.
For he does not despise nor abhor
the poor in their poverty;
neither does he hide his face from them;
but when they cry to him he hears them. ℞

My praise is of him in the great assembly;
I will perform my vows
in the presence of those who worship him.
The poor shall eat and be satisfied,
and those who seek the Lord shall praise him:
'May your heart live for ever!' ℞

All the ends of the earth
shall remember and turn to the Lord,
and all the families of the nations
shall bow before him.
For kingship belongs to the Lord;
he rules over the nations. ℟

SECOND READING (Alternative readings)

Either (Revised Common Lectionary)   1 Corinthians 1.18–24

A reading from the first letter of Paul to the Corinthians.

For the message about the cross is foolishness to those who are perishing, but to us who are being saved it is the power of God. For it is written,
'I will destroy the wisdom of the wise,
and the discernment of the discerning I will thwart.'
Where is the one who is wise? Where is the scribe? Where is the debater of this age? Has not God made foolish the wisdom of the world? For since, in the wisdom of God, the world did not know God through wisdom, God decided, through the foolishness of our proclamation, to save those who believe. For Jews demand signs and Greeks desire wisdom, but we proclaim Christ crucified, a stumbling-block to Jews and foolishness to Gentiles, but to those who are the called, both Jews and Greeks, Christ the power of God and the wisdom of God.

† Or

                                                 Philippians 2.6–11

A reading from the letter of Paul to the Philippians.

Christ Jesus, though he was in the form of God,
did not regard equality with God
as something to be exploited,
but emptied himself,
taking the form of a slave,
being born in human likeness.
And being found in human form,
he humbled himself
and became obedient to the point of death –
even death on a cross.

Therefore God also highly exalted him
and gave him the name that is above every name,
so that at the name of Jesus every knee should bend,
in heaven and on earth and under the earth,
and every tongue should confess that Jesus Christ is Lord,
to the glory of God the Father.

GOSPEL   John 3.13–17

Hear the gospel of our Lord Jesus Christ according to John.

Jesus said to Nicodemus: 'No one has ascended into heaven except the one
who descended from heaven, the Son of Man. And just as Moses lifted up the
serpent in the wilderness, so must the Son of Man be lifted up, that whoever
believes in him may have eternal life.

For God so loved the world that he gave his only Son, so that everyone who
believes in him may not perish but may have eternal life.

Indeed, God did not send the Son into the world to condemn the world, but
in order that the world might be saved through him.'

† ST MATTHEW   YEARS A B C

21 September

FIRST READING   Proverbs 3.13–18

A reading from the book of Proverbs.

Happy are those who find wisdom,
and those who get understanding,
for her income is better than silver,
and her revenue better than gold.
She is more precious than jewels,
and nothing you desire can compare with her.
Long life is in her right hand;
in her left hand are riches and honour.
Her ways are ways of pleasantness,
and all her paths are peace.
She is a tree of life to those who lay hold of her;
those who hold her fast are called happy.

PSALM

Psalm 119.65-72

℟ **Happy are those who find holy wisdom,
[she is the tree of life].**

O Lord, you have dealt graciously with your servant,
according to your word.
Teach me discernment and knowledge,
for I have believed in your commandments. ℟

Before I was afflicted I went astray,
but now I keep your word.
You are good and you bring forth good;
instruct me in your statutes. ℟

The proud have smeared me with lies,
but I will keep your commandments
with my whole heart.
Their heart is gross and fat,
but my delight is in your law. ℟

It is good for me that I have been afflicted,
that I might learn your statutes.
The law of your mouth is dearer to me
than thousands in gold and silver. ℟

SECOND READING

2 Corinthians 4.1-6

A reading from the second letter of Paul to the Corinthians.

Since it is by God's mercy that we are engaged in this ministry, we do not lose heart. We have renounced the shameful things that one hides; we refuse to practise cunning or to falsify God's word; but by the open statement of the truth we commend ourselves to the conscience of everyone in the sight of God. And even if our gospel is veiled, it is veiled to those who are perishing. In their case the god of this world has blinded the minds of the unbelievers, to keep them from seeing the light of the gospel of the glory of Christ, who is the image of God. For we do not proclaim ourselves; we proclaim Jesus Christ as Lord and ourselves as your slaves for Jesus' sake. For it is the God who said, 'Let light shine out of darkness,' who has shone in our hearts to give the light of the knowledge of the glory of God in the face of Jesus Christ.

GOSPEL — Matthew 9.9–13

Hear the gospel of our Lord Jesus Christ according to Matthew.

As Jesus was walking along, he saw a man called Matthew sitting at the tax booth; and he said to him, 'Follow me.' And he got up and followed him.

And as he sat at dinner in the house, many tax-collectors and sinners came and were sitting with him and his disciples. When the Pharisees saw this, they said to his disciples, 'Why does your teacher eat with tax-collectors and sinners?' But when he heard this, he said, 'Those who are well have no need of a physician, but those who are sick. Go and learn what this means, "I desire mercy, not sacrifice." For I have come to call not the righteous but sinners.'

† MICHAELMAS — YEARS A B C

29 September

FIRST READING (Alternative readings)

Either — Genesis 28.10–17

A reading from the book of Genesis.

Jacob left Beer-sheba and went towards Haran. He came to a certain place and stayed there for the night, because the sun had set. Taking one of the stones of the place, he put it under his head and lay down in that place. And he dreamed that there was a ladder set up on the earth, the top of it reaching to heaven; and the angels of God were ascending and descending on it. And the LORD stood beside him and said, 'I am the LORD, the God of Abraham your father and the God of Isaac; the land on which you lie I will give to you and to your offspring; and your offspring shall be like the dust of the earth, and you shall spread abroad to the west and to the east and to the north and to the south; and all the families of the earth shall be blessed in you and in your offspring. Know that I am with you and will keep you wherever you go, and will bring you back to this land; for I will not leave you until I have done what I have promised you.' Then Jacob woke from his sleep and said, 'Surely the LORD is in this place – and I did not know it!' And he was afraid, and said, 'How awesome is this place! This is none other than the house of God, and this is the gate of heaven.'

Or **Revelation 12.7–12**

A reading from the book of Revelation.

War broke out in heaven; Michael and his angels fought against the dragon. The dragon and his angels fought back, but they were defeated, and there was no longer any place for them in heaven. The great dragon was thrown down, that ancient serpent, who is called the Devil and Satan, the deceiver of the whole world – he was thrown down to the earth, and his angels were thrown down with him. Then I heard a loud voice in heaven, proclaiming, 'Now have come the salvation and the power and the kingdom of our God and the authority of his Messiah, for the accuser of our comrades has been thrown down, who accuses them day and night before our God. But they have conquered him by the blood of the Lamb and by the word of their testimony, for they did not cling to life even in the face of death. Rejoice then, you heavens and those who dwell in them! But woe to the earth and the sea, for the devil has come down to you with great wrath, because he knows that his time is short!'

PSALM **Psalm 103.19–22**

℟ **Bless the Lord, you angels of his.**

The Lord has set his throne in heaven,
and his kingship has dominion over all.
Bless the Lord, you angels of his,
you mighty ones who do his bidding,
and hearken to the voice of his word. ℟

Bless the Lord, all you his hosts,
you ministers of his who do his will.
Bless the Lord, all you works of his,
in all places of his dominion;
bless the Lord, O my soul. ℟

SECOND READING (Alternative readings)

Either   **Hebrews 1.5–14**

A reading from the letter to the Hebrews.

To which of the angels did God ever say, 'You are my Son; today I have begotten you'? Or again, 'I will be his Father, and he will be my Son'? And again, when he brings the firstborn into the world, he says, 'Let all God's angels worship him.' Of the angels he says, 'He makes his angels winds, and his servants flames of fire.' But of the Son he says, 'Your throne, O God, is for ever and ever, and the righteous sceptre is the sceptre of your kingdom. You have loved righteousness and hated wickedness; therefore God, your God, has anointed you with the oil of gladness beyond your companions.' And, 'In the beginning, Lord, you founded the earth, and the heavens are the work of your hands; they will perish, but you remain; they will all wear out like clothing; like a cloak you will roll them up, and like clothing they will be changed. But you are the same, and your years will never end.' But to which of the angels has he ever said, 'Sit at my right hand until I make your enemies a footstool for your feet'? Are not all angels spirits in the divine service, sent to serve for the sake of those who are to inherit salvation?

Or   **Revelation 12.7–12**

A reading from the book of Revelation.

See above, page 806.

GOSPEL   **John 1.47–51**

Hear the gospel of our Lord Jesus Christ according to John.

When Jesus saw Nathanael coming towards him, he said of him, 'Here is truly an Israelite in whom there is no deceit!' Nathanael asked him, 'Where did you come to know me?' Jesus answered, 'I saw you under the fig tree before Philip called you.' Nathanael replied, 'Rabbi, you are the Son of God! You are the King of Israel!' Jesus answered, 'Do you believe because I told you that I saw you under the fig tree? You will see greater things than these.' And he said to him, 'Very truly, I tell you, you will see heaven opened and the angels of God ascending and descending upon the Son of Man.'

† ST LUKE   YEARS A B C

18 October

FIRST READING (Alternative readings)

Either   Isaiah 35.3-6

A reading from the book of the prophet Isaiah.

Strengthen the weak hands,
and make firm the feeble knees.
Say to those who are of a fearful heart,
'Be strong, do not fear!
Here is your God.
He will come with vengeance, with terrible recompense.
He will come and save you.'

Then the eyes of the blind shall be opened,
and the ears of the deaf unstopped;
then the lame shall leap like a deer,
and the tongue of the speechless sing for joy.
For waters shall break forth in the wilderness,
and streams in the desert.

Or   Acts 16.6-12a

A reading from the Acts of the Apostles.

Paul and Timothy went through the region of Phrygia and Galatia, having
been forbidden by the Holy Spirit to speak the word in Asia.
When they had come opposite Mysia, they attempted to go into Bithynia,
but the Spirit of Jesus did not allow them; so, passing by Mysia, they went
down to Troas. During the night Paul had a vision: there stood a man of
Macedonia pleading with him and saying, 'Come over to Macedonia and
help us.' When he had seen the vision, we immediately tried to cross over to
Macedonia, being convinced that God had called us to proclaim the good news
to them.

We set sail from Troas and took a straight course to Samothrace, the
following day to Neapolis, and from there to Philippi, which is a leading city
of the district of Macedonia and a Roman colony.

PSALM Psalm 147.1–7

℞ **The Lord heals the brokenhearted
[and binds up their wounds].**

Alleluia!
How good it is to sing praises to our God!
how pleasant it is to honour him with praise!
The Lord rebuilds Jerusalem;
he gathers the exiles of Israel. ℞

He heals the brokenhearted
and binds up their wounds.
He counts the number of the stars
and calls them all by their names. ℞

Great is our Lord and mighty in power;
there is no limit to his wisdom.
The Lord lifts up the lowly,
but casts the wicked to the ground.
Sing to the Lord with thanksgiving;
make music to our God upon the harp. ℞

SECOND READING 2 Timothy 4.5–17

A reading from the second letter of Paul to Timothy.

As for you, always be sober, endure suffering, do the work of an evangelist,
carry out your ministry fully.

As for me, I am already being poured out as a libation, and the time of my
departure has come. I have fought the good fight, I have finished the race, I
have kept the faith. From now on there is reserved for me the crown of
righteousness, which the Lord, the righteous judge, will give to me on that
day, and not only to me but also to all who have longed for his appearing.

Do your best to come to me soon, for Demas, in love with this present world,
has deserted me and gone to Thessalonica; Crescens has gone to Galatia,
Titus to Dalmatia. Only Luke is with me. Get Mark and bring him with you,
for he is useful in my ministry. I have sent Tychicus to Ephesus. When you
come, bring the cloak that I left with Carpus at Troas, also the books, and
above all the parchments. Alexander the coppersmith did me great harm; the
Lord will pay him back for his deeds. You also must beware of him, for he
strongly opposed our message. At my first defence no one came to my

support, but all deserted me. May it not be counted against them! But the Lord stood by me and gave me strength, so that through me the message might be fully proclaimed and all the Gentiles might hear it. So I was rescued from the lion's mouth.

GOSPEL
Luke 10.1–9

Hear the gospel of our Lord Jesus Christ according to Luke.

The Lord appointed seventy others and sent them on ahead of him in pairs to every town and place where he himself intended to go.
He said to them, 'The harvest is plentiful, but the labourers are few; therefore ask the Lord of the harvest to send out labourers into his harvest. Go on your way. See, I am sending you out like lambs into the midst of wolves. Carry no purse, no bag, no sandals; and greet no one on the road. Whatever house you enter, first say, "Peace to this house!" And if anyone is there who shares in peace, your peace will rest on that person; but if not, it will return to you. Remain in the same house, eating and drinking whatever they provide, for the labourer deserves to be paid. Do not move about from house to house. Whenever you enter a town and its people welcome you, eat what is set before you; cure the sick who are there, and say to them, "The kingdom of God has come near to you."'

† ST SIMON AND ST JUDE
YEARS A B C

28 October

FIRST READING
Isaiah 28.14–16

A reading from the book of the prophet Isaiah.

Hear the word of the LORD,
you scoffers who rule this people in Jerusalem.
Because you have said,
'We have made a covenant with death,
and with Sheol we have an agreement;
when the overwhelming scourge passes through it will not come to us;
for we have made lies our refuge, and in falsehood we have taken shelter';
therefore thus says the Lord GOD,
See, I am laying in Zion a foundation stone,
a tested stone, a precious cornerstone, a sure foundation:
'One who trusts will not panic.'

PSALM   Psalm 119.89–96

℟ **Bless the Lord, you servants of the Lord,**
   [you that stand in the house of the Lord].

O Lord, your word is everlasting;
it stands firm in the heavens.
Your faithfulness remains
from one generation to another;
you established the earth and it abides. ℟

By your decree these continue to this day,
for all things are your servants.
If my delight had not been in your law,
I should have perished in my affliction. ℟

I will never forget your commandments,
because by them you give me life.
I am yours; O that you would save me!
for I study your commandments. ℟

Though the wicked lie in wait for me to destroy me,
I will apply my mind to your decrees.
I see that all things come to an end,
but your commandment has no bounds. ℟

SECOND READING   Ephesians 2.19–22

A reading from the letter of Paul to the Ephesians.

You are no longer strangers and aliens, but you are citizens with the saints
and also members of the household of God, built upon the foundation of
the apostles and prophets, with Christ Jesus himself as the cornerstone. In
him the whole structure is joined together and grows into a holy temple in
the Lord; in whom you also are built together spiritually into a dwelling-place
for God.

GOSPEL   John 15.17–27

Hear the gospel of our Lord Jesus Christ according to John.

Jesus said to his disciples: 'I am giving you these commands so that you may
love one another.

If the world hates you, be aware that it hated me before it hated you. If you belonged to the world, the world would love you as its own. Because you do not belong to the world, but I have chosen you out of the world – therefore the world hates you. Remember the word that I said to you, "Servants are not greater than their master." If they persecuted me, they will persecute you; if they kept my word, they will keep yours also. But they will do all these things to you on account of my name, because they do not know him who sent me. If I had not come and spoken to them, they would not have sin; but now they have no excuse for their sin. Whoever hates me hates my Father also. If I had not done among them the works that no one else did, they would not have sin. But now they have seen and hated both me and my Father. It was to fulfil the word that is written in their law, "They hated me without a cause." When the Advocate comes, whom I will send to you from the Father, the Spirit of truth who comes from the Father, he will testify on my behalf.

You also are to testify because you have been with me from the beginning.'

† ALL SAINTS' DAY   YEARS A B C

1 November if the material for All Saints' Sunday is used on the Sunday

See Year A, pages 290–292.

† ST ANDREW   YEARS A B C

30 November

FIRST READING   Isaiah 52.7–10

A reading from the book of the prophet Isaiah.

How beautiful upon the mountains
are the feet of the messenger who announces peace,
who brings good news,
who announces salvation,
who says to Zion, 'Your God reigns.'
Listen! Your sentinels lift up their voices,
together they sing for joy;
for in plain sight they see
the return of the LORD to Zion.
Break forth together into singing,

you ruins of Jerusalem;
for the LORD has comforted his people,
he has redeemed Jerusalem.
The LORD has bared his holy arm
before the eyes of all the nations;
and all the ends of the earth shall see the salvation of our God.

PSALM   Psalm 19.1–6

℟ **The heavens declare the glory of God,**
  [and the firmament shows his handiwork].

The heavens declare the glory of God,
and the firmament shows his handiwork.
One day tells its tale to another,
and one night imparts knowledge to another. ℟

Although they have no words or language,
and their voices are not heard,
Their sound has gone out into all lands,
and their message to the ends of the world. ℟

In the deep has he set a pavilion for the sun;
it comes forth like a bridegroom out of his chamber;
it rejoices like a champion to run its course.
It goes forth from the uttermost edge of the heavens
and runs about to the end of it again;
nothing is hidden from its burning heat. ℟

SECOND READING   Romans 10.12–18

A reading from the letter of Paul to the Romans.

There is no distinction between Jew and Greek; the same Lord is Lord of all
and is generous to all who call on him. For, 'Everyone who calls on the name
of the Lord shall be saved.'

But how are they to call on one in whom they have not believed? And how
are they to believe in one of whom they have never heard? And how are they
to hear without someone to proclaim him? And how are they to proclaim
him unless they are sent? As it is written, 'How beautiful are the feet of those
who bring good news!' But not all have obeyed the good news; for Isaiah

says, 'Lord, who has believed our message?' So faith comes from what is heard, and what is heard comes through the word of Christ. But I ask, have they not heard? Indeed they have;
for 'Their voice has gone out to all the earth,
and their words to the ends of the world.'

GOSPEL
Matthew 4.18–22

Hear the gospel of our Lord Jesus Christ according to Matthew.

As he walked by the Sea of Galilee, Jesus saw two brothers, Simon, who is called Peter, and Andrew his brother, casting a net into the lake – for they were fishermen. And he said to them, 'Follow me, and I will make you fish for people.' Immediately they left their nets and followed him. As he went from there, he saw two other brothers, James son of Zebedee and his brother John, in the boat with their father Zebedee, mending their nets, and he called them. Immediately they left the boat and their father, and followed him.

† ST STEPHEN   YEARS A B C

26 December

Acts 7.51–60 must be read as either the First or Second Reading.

FIRST READING (Alternative readings)

Either   2 Chronicles 24.20–24

A reading from the second book of Chronicles.

The spirit of God took possession of Zechariah son of the priest Jehoiada; he stood above the people and said to them, 'Thus says God: Why do you transgress the commandments of the LORD, so that you cannot prosper? Because you have forsaken the LORD, he has also forsaken you.' But they conspired against him, and by command of the king they stoned him to death in the court of the house of the LORD. King Joash did not remember the kindness that Jehoiada, Zechariah's father, had shown him, but killed his son. As he was dying, he said, 'May the LORD see and avenge!' At the end of the year the army of Aram came up against Joash. They came to Judah and Jerusalem, and destroyed all the officials of the people from among them, and sent all the booty they took to the king of Damascus. Although the army of Aram had come with few men, the LORD delivered into their hand a very great army, because they had abandoned the LORD, the God of their ancestors. Thus they executed judgement on Joash.

Or   **Acts 7.51–60**

A reading from the Acts of the Apostles.

Stephen said to the high priest and the council: 'You stiff-necked people, uncircumcised in heart and ears, you are for ever opposing the Holy Spirit, just as your ancestors used to do. Which of the prophets did your ancestors not persecute? They killed those who foretold the coming of the Righteous One, and now you have become his betrayers and murderers. You are the ones that received the law as ordained by angels, and yet you have not kept it.' When they heard these things, they became enraged and ground their teeth at Stephen. Stephen, filled with the Holy Spirit, gazed into heaven and saw the glory of God and Jesus standing at the right hand of God. 'Look,' he said, 'I see the heavens opened and the Son of Man standing at the right hand of God!' But they covered their ears, and with a loud shout all rushed together against him. Then they dragged him out of the city and began to stone him; and the witnesses laid their coats at the feet of a young man named Saul. While they were stoning Stephen, he prayed, 'Lord Jesus, receive my spirit.' Then he knelt down and cried out in a loud voice, 'Lord, do not hold this sin against them.' When he had said this, he died.

PSALM   **Psalm 119.161–168**

℟ **Our help is in the name of the Lord,**
   [the maker of heaven and earth].

Rulers have persecuted me without a cause,
but my heart stands in awe of your word.
I am as glad because of your promise
as one who finds great spoils. ℟

As for lies, I hate and abhor them,
but your law is my love.
Seven times a day do I praise you,
because of your righteous judgements. ℟

Great peace have they who love your law;
for them there is no stumbling block.
I have hoped for your salvation, O Lord,
and I have fulfilled your commandments. ℞

I have kept your decrees
and I have loved them deeply.
I have kept your commandments and decrees,
for all my ways are before you. ℞

SECOND READING

Either   Acts 7.51–60

A reading from the Acts of the Apostles.

See above, page 815.

Or   Galatians 2.16b–20

A reading from the letter of Paul to the Galatians.

We have come to believe in Christ Jesus, so that we might be justified by
faith in Christ, and not by doing the works of the law, because no one will be
justified by the works of the law. But if, in our effort to be justified in Christ,
we ourselves have been found to be sinners, is Christ then a servant of sin?
Certainly not! But if I build up again the very things that I once tore down,
then I demonstrate that I am a transgressor. For through the law I died to the
law, so that I might live to God. I have been crucified with Christ; and it is no
longer I who live, but it is Christ who lives in me. And the life I now live in
the flesh I live by faith in the Son of God, who loved me and gave himself for
me.

GOSPEL   Matthew 10.17–22

Hear the gospel of our Lord Jesus Christ according to Matthew.

Jesus said to the twelve:
'Beware of them, for they will hand you over to councils and flog you in their
synagogues; and you will be dragged before governors and kings because of
me, as a testimony to them and the Gentiles. When they hand you over, do

not worry about how you are to speak or what you are to say; for what you are to say will be given to you at that time; for it is not you who speak, but the Spirit of your Father speaking through you. Brother will betray brother to death, and a father his child, and children will rise against parents and have them put to death; and you will be hated by all because of my name. But the one who endures to the end will be saved.'

† ST JOHN   YEARS A B C

27 December

FIRST READING   Exodus 33.7–11a

A reading from the book of Exodus.

Moses used to take the tent and pitch it outside the camp, far off from the camp; he called it the tent of meeting. And everyone who sought the LORD would go out to the tent of meeting, which was outside the camp. Whenever Moses went out to the tent, all the people would rise and stand, each of them, at the entrance of their tents and watch Moses until he had gone into the tent. When Moses entered the tent, the pillar of cloud would descend and stand at the entrance of the tent, and the LORD would speak with Moses. When all the people saw the pillar of cloud standing at the entrance of the tent, all the people would rise and bow down, all of them, at the entrance of their tents. Thus the LORD used to speak to Moses face to face, as one speaks to a friend.

PSALM   Psalm 117

℟ **The Lord spoke to him face to face
[as one speaks to a friend].**

Praise the Lord, all you nations;
laud him, all you peoples.
For his loving-kindness towards us is great,
and the faithfulness of the Lord endures for ever.
Alleluia! ℟

SECOND READING   1 John 1

A reading from the first letter of John.

We declare to you what was from the beginning, what we have heard, what we have seen with our eyes, what we have looked at and touched with our hands, concerning the word of life – this life was revealed, and we have seen it and testify to it, and declare to you the eternal life that was with the Father and was revealed to us – we declare to you what we have seen and heard so that you also may have fellowship with us; and truly our fellowship is with the Father and with his Son Jesus Christ. We are writing these things so that our joy may be complete.

This is the message we have heard from him and proclaim to you, that God is light and in him there is no darkness at all. If we say that we have fellowship with him while we are walking in darkness, we lie and do not do what is true; but if we walk in the light as he himself is in the light, we have fellowship with one another, and the blood of Jesus his Son cleanses us from all sin. If we say that we have no sin, we deceive ourselves, and the truth is not in us. If we confess our sins, he who is faithful and just will forgive us our sins and cleanse us from all unrighteousness. If we say that we have not sinned, we make him a liar, and his word is not in us.

GOSPEL   John 21.19b–25

Hear the gospel of our Lord Jesus Christ according to John.

After this Jesus said to Peter, 'Follow me.'

Peter turned and saw the disciple whom Jesus loved following them; he was the one who had reclined next to Jesus at the supper and had said, 'Lord, who is it that is going to betray you?' When Peter saw him, he said to Jesus, 'Lord, what about him?' Jesus said to him, 'If it is my will that he remain until I come, what is that to you? Follow me!' So the rumour spread in the community that this disciple would not die. Yet Jesus did not say to him that he would not die, but, 'If it is my will that he remain until I come, what is that to you?'

This is the disciple who is testifying to these things and has written them, and we know that his testimony is true. But there are also many other things that Jesus did; if every one of them were written down, I suppose that the world itself could not contain the books that would be written.

† HOLY INNOCENTS   YEARS A B C

28 December

FIRST READING   Jeremiah 31.15–17

A reading from the book of the prophet Jeremiah.

Thus says the LORD:
A voice is heard in Ramah, lamentation and bitter weeping.
Rachel is weeping for her children;
she refuses to be comforted for her children, because they are no more.
Thus says the LORD:
Keep your voice from weeping, and your eyes from tears;
for there is a reward for your work, says the LORD:
they shall come back from the land of the enemy;
there is hope for your future, says the LORD:
your children shall come back to their own country.

PSALM   Psalm 124

℞ **Our help is in the name of the Lord,**
   [the maker of heaven and earth].

If the Lord had not been on our side,
let Israel now say;

If the Lord had not been on our side,
when enemies rose up against us; ℞

Then would they have swallowed us up alive
in their fierce anger towards us;
Then would the waters have overwhelmed us
and the torrent gone over us. ℞

Then would the raging waters
have gone right over us.
Blessèd be the Lord!
he has not given us over to be a prey for their teeth.
We have escaped like a bird from the snare of the fowler;
the snare is broken and we have escaped. ℞

[Our help is in the name of the Lord,
the maker of heaven and earth.]

SECOND READING   1 Corinthians 1.26–29

A reading from the first letter of Paul to the Corinthians.

Consider your own call, brothers and sisters: not many of you were wise by human standards, not many were powerful, not many were of noble birth. But God chose what is foolish in the world to shame the wise; God chose what is weak in the world to shame the strong; God chose what is low and despised in the world, things that are not, to reduce to nothing things that are, so that no one might boast in the presence of God.

GOSPEL   Matthew 2.13–18

Hear the gospel of our Lord Jesus Christ according to Matthew.

After the wise men had left, an angel of the Lord appeared to Joseph in a dream and said, 'Get up, take the child and his mother, and flee to Egypt, and remain there until I tell you; for Herod is about to search for the child, to destroy him.' Then Joseph got up, took the child and his mother by night, and went to Egypt,
and remained there until the death of Herod. This was to fulfil what had been spoken by the Lord through the prophet, 'Out of Egypt I have called my son'. When Herod saw that he had been tricked by the wise men, he was infuriated, and he sent and killed all the children in and around Bethlehem who were two years old or under, according to the time that he had learned from the wise men.
Then was fulfilled what had been spoken through the prophet Jeremiah:
'A voice was heard in Ramah,
wailing and loud lamentation,
Rachel weeping for her children;
she refused to be consoled, because they are no more.'

HARVEST   YEAR A

Revised Common Lectionary and Church of England provision.

FIRST READING (Alternative readings)

Either   **Deuteronomy 8.7–18**

A reading from the book of Deuteronomy.

The LORD your God is bringing you into a good land, a land with flowing streams, with springs and underground waters welling up in valleys and hills, a land of wheat and barley, of vines and fig trees and pomegranates, a land of olive trees and honey, a land where you may eat bread without scarcity, where you will lack nothing, a land whose stones are iron and from whose hills you may mine copper. You shall eat your fill and bless the LORD your God for the good land that he has given you.

Take care that you do not forget the LORD your God, by failing to keep his commandments, his ordinances, and his statutes, which I am commanding you today. When you have eaten your fill and have built fine houses and live in them, and when your herds and flocks have multiplied, and your silver and gold is multiplied, and all that you have is multiplied, then do not exalt yourself, forgetting the LORD your God, who brought you out of the land of Egypt, out of the house of slavery, who led you through the great and terrible wilderness, an arid waste-land with poisonous snakes and scorpions. He made water flow for you from flint rock, and fed you in the wilderness with manna that your ancestors did not know, to humble you and to test you, and in the end to do you good. Do not say to yourself, 'My power and the might of my own hand have gained me this wealth.' But remember the LORD your God, for it is he who gives you power to get wealth, so that he may confirm his covenant that he swore to your ancestors, as he is doing today.

† Or   **Deuteronomy 28.1–14**

If you will only obey the LORD your God, by diligently observing all his commandments that I am commanding you today, the LORD your God will set you high above all the nations of the earth; all these blessings shall come upon you and overtake you, if you obey the LORD your God: Blessed shall you be in the city, and blessed shall you be in the field. Blessed shall be the fruit of your womb, the fruit of your ground, and the fruit of your livestock,

both the increase of your cattle and the issue of your flock. Blessed shall be
your basket and your kneading-bowl. Blessed shall you be when you come in,
and blessed shall you be when you go out. The LORD will cause your enemies
who rise against you to be defeated before you; they shall come out against
you one way, and flee before you seven ways. The LORD will command the
blessing upon you in your barns, and in all that you undertake; he will bless
you in the land that the LORD your God is giving you. The LORD will
establish you as his holy people, as he has sworn to you, if you keep the
commandments of the LORD your God and walk in his ways. All the peoples
of the earth shall see that you are called by the name of the LORD, and they
shall be afraid of you. The LORD will make you abound in prosperity, in the
fruit of your womb, in the fruit of your livestock, and in the fruit of your
ground in the land that the LORD swore to your ancestors to give you. The
LORD will open for you his rich storehouse, the heavens, to give the rain of
your land in its season and to bless all your undertakings. You will lend to
many nations, but you will not borrow. The LORD will make you the head,
and not the tail; you shall be only at the top, and not at the bottom – if you
obey the commandments of the LORD your God, which I am commanding
you today, by diligently observing them, and if you do not turn aside from
any of the words that I am commanding you today, either to the right or to
the left, following other gods to serve them.

PSALM

Psalm 65

℟ **You crown the year with goodness.**

You are to be praised, O God, in Zion;
to you shall vows be performed in Jerusalem.
To you that hear prayer shall all flesh come,
because of their transgressions.
Our sins are stronger than we are,
but you will blot them out. ℟

Happy are they whom you choose
and draw to your courts to dwell there!
they will be satisfied by the beauty of your house,
by the holiness of your temple.
Awesome things will you show us in your righteousness,
O God of our salvation,
O Hope of all the ends of the earth
and of the seas that are far away. ℟

You make fast the mountains by your power;
they are girded about with might.
You still the roaring of the seas,
the roaring of their waves,
and the clamour of the peoples. ℞

Those who dwell at the ends of the earth
will tremble at your marvellous signs;
you make the dawn and the dusk to sing for joy.
You visit the earth and water it abundantly;
you make it very plenteous;
the river of God is full of water. ℞

You prepare the grain,
for so you provide for the earth.
You drench the furrows and smooth out the ridges;
with heavy rain you soften the ground
and bless its increase.
You crown the year with your goodness,
and your paths overflow with plenty. ℞

May the fields of the wilderness be rich for grazing,
and the hills be clothed with joy.
May the meadows cover themselves with flocks
and the valleys cloak themselves with grain;
let them shout for joy and sing. ℞

SECOND READING   **2 Corinthians 9.6–15**

A reading from the second letter of Paul to the Corinthians.

The one who sows sparingly will also reap sparingly, and the one who sows
bountifully will also reap bountifully. Each of you must give as you have
made up your mind, not reluctantly or under compulsion, for God loves a
cheerful giver. And God is able to provide you with every blessing in
abundance, so that by always having enough of everything, you may share
abundantly in every good work.
As it is written, 'He scatters abroad, he gives to the poor;
his righteousness endures for ever.'
He who supplies seed to the sower and bread for food will supply and
multiply your seed for sowing and increase the harvest of your righteousness.
You will be enriched in every way for your great generosity, which will

produce thanksgiving to God through us; for the rendering of this ministry not only supplies the needs of the saints but also overflows with many thanksgivings to God. Through the testing of this ministry you glorify God by your obedience to the confession of the gospel of Christ and by the generosity of your sharing with them and with all others, while they long for you and pray for you because of the surpassing grace of God that he has given you. Thanks be to God for his indescribable gift!

GOSPEL (Alternative readings)

† Either   Luke 12.16–30

Hear the gospel of our Lord Jesus Christ according to Luke.

Jesus told the people a parable: 'The land of a rich man produced abundantly. And he thought to himself, "What should I do, for I have no place to store my crops?" Then he said, "I will do this: I will pull down my barns and build larger ones, and there I will store all my grain and my goods. And I will say to my soul, 'Soul, you have ample goods laid up for many years; relax, eat, drink, be merry.'" But God said to him, "You fool! This very night your life is being demanded of you. And the things you have prepared, whose will they be?" So it is with those who store up treasures for themselves but are not rich towards God.'

He said to his disciples, 'Therefore I tell you, do not worry about your life, what you will eat, or about your body, what you will wear. For life is more than food, and the body more than clothing. Consider the ravens: they neither sow nor reap, they have neither storehouse nor barn, and yet God feeds them. Of how much more value are you than the birds! And can any of you by worrying add a single hour to your span of life? If then you are not able to do so small a thing as that, why do you worry about the rest? Consider the lilies, how they grow: they neither toil nor spin; yet I tell you, even Solomon in all his glory was not clothed like one of these. But if God so clothes the grass of the field, which is alive today and tomorrow is thrown into the oven, how much more will he clothe you – you of little faith! And do not keep striving for what you are to eat and what you are to drink, and do not keep worrying. For it is the nations of the world that strive after all these things, and your Father knows that you need them.'

Or   **Luke 17.11–19**

Hear the gospel of our Lord Jesus Christ according to Luke.

On the way to Jerusalem Jesus was going through the region between Samaria and Galilee. As he entered a village, ten lepers approached him. Keeping their distance, they called out, saying, 'Jesus, Master, have mercy on us!' When he saw them, he said to them, 'Go and show yourselves to the priests.' And as they went, they were made clean. Then one of them, when he saw that he was healed, turned back, praising God with a loud voice. He prostrated himself at Jesus' feet and thanked him. And he was a Samaritan. Then Jesus asked, 'Were not ten made clean? But the other nine, where are they? Was none of them found to return and give praise to God except this foreigner?' Then he said to the Samaritan, 'Get up and go on your way; your faith has made you well.'

HARVEST   YEAR B

FIRST READING   Joel 2.21–27

A reading from the book of the prophet Joel.

Do not fear, O soil;
be glad and rejoice, for the LORD has done great things!
Do not fear, you animals of the field,
for the pastures of the wilderness are green;
the tree bears its fruit,
the fig tree and vine give their full yield.

O children of Zion, be glad and rejoice in the LORD your God;
for he has given the early rain for your vindication,
he has poured down for you abundant rain,
the early and the later rain, as before.
The threshing-floors shall be full of grain,
the vats shall overflow with wine and oil.
I will repay you for the years that the swarming locust has eaten,
the hopper, the destroyer, and the cutter,
my great army, which I sent against you.

You shall eat in plenty and be satisfied,
and praise the name of the LORD your God,
who has dealt wondrously with you.

And my people shall never again be put to shame.
You shall know that I am in the midst of Israel,
and that I, the LORD, am your God and there is no other.
And my people shall never again be put to shame.

PSALM   Psalm 126

℟ **Those who sowed with tears
   will reap with songs of joy.**

When the Lord restored the fortunes of Zion,
then were we like those who dream.
Then was our mouth filled with laughter,
and our tongue with shouts of joy. ℟

Then they said among the nations,
'The Lord has done great things for them.'
The Lord has done great things for us,
and we are glad indeed. ℟

Restore our fortunes, O Lord,
like the watercourses of the Negev.
Those who sowed with tears
will reap with songs of joy.
Those who go out weeping, carrying the seed,
will come again with joy, shouldering their sheaves. ℟

SECOND READING (Alternative readings)

Either   1 Timothy 2.1–7

A reading from the first letter of Paul to Timothy.

My dearly beloved, I urge that supplications, prayers, intercessions, and
thanksgivings be made for everyone, for kings and all who are in high
positions, so that we may lead a quiet and peaceable life in all godliness and
dignity. This is right and is acceptable in the sight of God our Saviour, who
desires everyone to be saved and to come to the knowledge of the truth.
For there is one God;
there is also one mediator between God and humankind,
Christ Jesus, himself human,

who gave himself a ransom for all –
this was attested at the right time. For this I was appointed a herald and an apostle (I am telling the truth, I am not lying), a teacher of the Gentiles in faith and truth.

† Or   1 Timothy 6.6–10

A reading from the first letter of Paul to Timothy.

There is great gain in godliness combined with contentment; for we brought nothing into the world, so that we can take nothing out of it; but if we have food and clothing, we will be content with these. But those who want to be rich fall into temptation and are trapped by many senseless and harmful desires that plunge people into ruin and destruction. For the love of money is a root of all kinds of evil, and in their eagerness to be rich some have wandered away from the faith and pierced themselves with many pains.

GOSPEL   Matthew 6.25–33

Hear the gospel of our Lord Jesus Christ according to Matthew.

Jesus said to his disciples: 'Do not worry about your life, what you will eat or what you will drink, or about your body, what you will wear. Is not life more than food, and the body more than clothing? Look at the birds of the air; they neither sow nor reap nor gather into barns, and yet your heavenly Father feeds them. Are you not of more value than they? And can any of you by worrying add a single hour to your span of life? And why do you worry about clothing? Consider the lilies of the field, how they grow; they neither toil nor spin, yet I tell you, even Solomon in all his glory was not clothed like one of these. But if God so clothes the grass of the field, which is alive today and tomorrow is thrown into the oven, will he not much more clothe you – you of little faith? Therefore do not worry, saying, "What will we eat?" or "What will we drink?" or "What will we wear?" For it is the Gentiles who strive for all these things; and indeed your heavenly Father knows that you need all these things. But strive first for the kingdom of God and his righteousness, and all these things will be given to you as well.'

HARVEST   YEAR C

FIRST READING   Deuteronomy 26.1–11

A reading from the book of Deuteronomy.

Moses spoke to the people, saying:
When you have come into the land that the LORD your God is giving you as an inheritance to possess, and you possess it, and settle in it, you shall take some of the first of all the fruit of the ground, which you harvest from the land that the LORD your God is giving you, and you shall put it in a basket and go to the place that the LORD your God will choose as a dwelling for his name. You shall go to the priest who is in office at that time, and say to him, 'Today I declare to the LORD your God that I have come into the land that the LORD swore to our ancestors to give us.' When the priest takes the basket from your hand and sets it down before the altar of the LORD your God, you shall make this response before the LORD your God: 'A wandering Aramean was my ancestor; he went down into Egypt and lived there as an alien, few in number, and there he became a great nation, mighty and populous. When the Egyptians treated us harshly and afflicted us, by imposing hard labour on us, we cried to the LORD, the God of our ancestors; the LORD heard our voice and saw our affliction, our toil, and our oppression. The LORD brought us out of Egypt with a mighty hand and an outstretched arm, with a terrifying display of power, and with signs and wonders; and he brought us into this place and gave us this land, a land flowing with milk and honey. So now I bring the first of the fruit of the ground that you, O LORD, have given me.' You shall set it down before the LORD your God and bow down before the LORD your God. Then you, together with the Levites and the aliens who reside among you, shall celebrate with all the bounty that the LORD your God has given to you and to your house.

PSALM   Psalm 100

℞ **Give thanks to the Lord**
and call upon his name.

Be joyful in the Lord, all you lands;
serve the Lord with gladness
and come before his presence with a song.
Know this: The Lord himself is God;
he himself has made us and we are his;
we are his people and the sheep of his pasture. ℞

Enter his gates with thanksgiving;
go into his courts with praise;
give thanks to him and call upon his name.
For the Lord is good; his mercy is everlasting;
and his faithfulness endures from age to age. ℞

SECOND READING (Alternative readings)

Either   Philippians 4.4–9

A reading from the letter of Paul to the Philippians.

Rejoice in the Lord always; again I will say, Rejoice. Let your gentleness be
known to everyone. The Lord is near. Do not worry about anything, but in
everything by prayer and supplication with thanksgiving let your requests be
made known to God. And the peace of God, which surpasses all
understanding, will guard your hearts and your minds in Christ Jesus.

Finally, beloved, whatever is true, whatever is honourable, whatever is just,
whatever is pure, whatever is pleasing, whatever is commendable, if there is
any excellence and if there is anything worthy of praise, think about these
things. Keep on doing the things that you have learned and received and
heard and seen in me, and the God of peace will be with you.

† Or   Revelation 14.14–18

A reading from the book of Revelation.

I, John, looked, and there was a white cloud, and seated on the cloud was
one like the Son of Man, with a golden crown on his head, and a sharp sickle
in his hand! Another angel came out of the temple, calling with a loud voice
to the one who sat on the cloud, 'Use your sickle and reap, for the hour to
reap has come, because the harvest of the earth is fully ripe.' So the one who
sat on the cloud swung his sickle over the earth, and the earth was reaped.

Then another angel came out of the temple in heaven, and he too had a
sharp sickle. Then another angel came out from the altar, the angel who has
authority over fire, and he called with a loud voice to him who had the sharp
sickle, 'Use your sharp sickle and gather the clusters of the vine of the earth,
for its grapes are ripe.'

GOSPEL   **John 6.25–35**

Hear the gospel of our Lord Jesus Christ according to John.

When they found Jesus on the other side of the sea, the crowd said to him, 'Rabbi, when did you come here?' Jesus answered them, 'Very truly, I tell you, you are looking for me, not because you saw signs, but because you ate your fill of the loaves. Do not work for the food that perishes, but for the food that endures for eternal life, which the Son of Man will give you. For it is on him that God the Father has set his seal.' Then they said to Jesus, 'What must we do to perform the works of God?' Jesus answered them, 'This is the work of God, that you believe in him whom he has sent.' So they said to him, 'What sign are you going to give us then, so that we may see it and believe you? What work are you performing? Our ancestors ate the manna in the wilderness; as it is written, "He gave them bread from heaven to eat."' Then Jesus said to them, 'Very truly, I tell you, it was not Moses who gave you the bread from heaven, but it is my Father who gives you the true bread from heaven. For the bread of God is that which comes down from heaven and gives life to the world.' They said to him, 'Sir, give us this bread always.'

Jesus said to them, 'I am the bread of life. Whoever comes to me will never be hungry, and whoever believes in me will never be thirsty.'

SUPPLEMENT

ALTERNATIVE FIRST READINGS FOR SUNDAYS IN EASTERTIDE

CHURCH OF ENGLAND

These alternative First Readings are authorized in the Church of England.

THE SECOND SUNDAY OF EASTER   YEAR A

FIRST READING   **Exodus 14.10–31; 15.20–21**

A reading from the book of Exoduss.

As Pharaoh drew near, the Israelites looked back, and there were the
Egyptians advancing on them. In great fear the Israelites cried out to the
LORD. They said to Moses, 'Was it because there were no graves in Egypt that
you have taken us away to die in the wilderness? What have you done to us,
bringing us out of Egypt? Is this not the very thing we told you in Egypt,
"Let us alone and let us serve the Egyptians"? For it would have been better
for us to serve the Egyptians than to die in the wilderness.' But Moses said to
the people, 'Do not be afraid, stand firm, and see the deliverance that the
LORD will accomplish for you today; for the Egyptians whom you see today
you shall never see again. The LORD will fight for you, and you have only to
keep still.'

Then the LORD said to Moses, 'Why do you cry out to me? Tell the Israelites
to go forward. But you lift up your staff, and stretch out your hand over the
sea and divide it, that the Israelites may go into the sea on dry ground. Then
I will harden the hearts of the Egyptians so that they will go in after them;
and so I will gain glory for myself over Pharaoh and all his army, his chariots,
and his chariot drivers. And the Egyptians shall know that I am the LORD,
when I have gained glory for myself over Pharaoh, his chariots, and his
chariot drivers.'

The angel of God who was going before the Israelite army moved and went
behind them; and the pillar of cloud moved from in front of them and took
its place behind them. It came between the army of Egypt and the army of
Israel. And so the cloud was there with the darkness, and it lit up the night;
one did not come near the other all night.

Then Moses stretched out his hand over the sea. The LORD drove the sea back by a strong east wind all night, and turned the sea into dry land; and the waters were divided. The Israelites went into the sea on dry ground, the waters forming a wall for them on their right and on their left. The Egyptians pursued, and went into the sea after them, all of Pharaoh's horses, chariots, and chariot drivers. At the morning watch the LORD in the pillar of fire and cloud looked down upon the Egyptian army, and threw the Egyptian army into panic. He clogged their chariot wheels so that they turned with difficulty. The Egyptians said, 'Let us flee from the Israelites, for the LORD is fighting for them against Egypt.'

Then the LORD said to Moses, 'Stretch out your hand over the sea, so that the water may come back upon the Egyptians, upon their chariots and chariot drivers.' So Moses stretched out his hand over the sea, and at dawn the sea returned to its normal depth. As the Egyptians fled before it, the LORD tossed the Egyptians into the sea. The waters returned and covered the chariots and the chariot drivers, the entire army of Pharaoh that had followed them into the sea; not one of them remained. But the Israelites walked on dry ground through the sea, the waters forming a wall for them on their right and on their left.

Thus the LORD saved Israel that day from the Egyptians; and Israel saw the Egyptians dead on the seashore. Israel saw the great work that the LORD did against the Egyptians. So the people feared the LORD and believed in the LORD and in his servant Moses. Then the prophet Miriam, Aaron's sister, took a tambourine in her hand; and all the women went out after her with tambourines and with dancing. And Miriam sang to them: 'Sing to the LORD, for he has triumphed gloriously; horse and rider he has thrown into the sea.'

THE THIRD SUNDAY OF EASTER   YEAR A

FIRST READING   Zephaniah 3.14–20

A reading from the book of the prophet Zephaniah.

Sing aloud, O daughter Zion; shout, O Israel!
Rejoice and exult with all your heart,
O daughter Jerusalem!
The LORD has taken away the judgements against you,
he has turned away your enemies.
The king of Israel, the LORD, is in your midst;

you shall fear disaster no more.
On that day it shall be said to Jerusalem:
Do not fear, O Zion;
do not let your hands grow weak.
The LORD, your God, is in your midst,
a warrior who gives victory;
he will rejoice over you with gladness,
he will renew you in his love;
he will exult over you with loud singing
as on a day of festival.
I will remove disaster from you,
so that you will not bear reproach for it.
I will deal with all your oppressors at that time.
And I will save the lame and gather the outcast,
and I will change their shame into praise and renown in all the earth.
At that time I will bring you home, at the time when I gather you;
for I will make you renowned
and praised among all the peoples of the earth,
when I restore your fortunes before your eyes, says the LORD.

THE FOURTH SUNDAY OF EASTER   YEAR A

FIRST READING   Genesis 7

A reading from the book of Genesis.

The LORD said to Noah, 'Go into the ark, you and all your household, for I have seen that you alone are righteous before me in this generation. Take with you seven pairs of all clean animals, the male and its mate; and a pair of the animals that are not clean, the male and its mate; and seven pairs of the birds of the air also, male and female, to keep their kind alive on the face of all the earth. For in seven days I will send rain on the earth for forty days and forty nights; and every living thing that I have made I will blot out from the face of the ground.' And Noah did all that the LORD had commanded him.

Noah was six hundred years old when the flood of waters came on the earth. And Noah with his sons and his wife and his sons' wives went into the ark to escape the waters of the flood. Of the clean animals, and of animals that are not clean, and of birds, and of everything that creeps on the ground, two and two, male and female, went into the ark with Noah, as God had commanded Noah. And after seven days the waters of the flood came on the earth.

In the six-hundredth year of Noah's life, in the second month, on the seventeenth day of the month, on that day all the fountains of the great deep burst forth, and the windows of the heavens were opened. The rain fell on the earth for forty days and forty nights. On the very same day Noah with his sons, Shem and Ham and Japheth, and Noah's wife and the three wives of his sons, entered the ark, they and every wild animal of every kind, and all domestic animals of every kind, and every creeping thing that creeps on the earth, and every bird of every kind – every bird, every winged creature. They went into the ark with Noah, two and two of all flesh in which there was the breath of life. And those that entered, male and female of all flesh, went in as God had commanded him; and the LORD shut him in.

The flood continued for forty days on the earth; and the waters increased, and bore up the ark, and it rose high above the earth. The waters swelled and increased greatly on the earth; and the ark floated on the face of the waters. The waters swelled so mightily on the earth that all the high mountains under the whole heaven were covered; the waters swelled above the mountains, covering them fifteen cubits deep. And all flesh died that moved on the earth, birds, domestic animals, wild animals, all swarming creatures that swarm on the earth, and all human beings; everything on dry land in whose nostrils was the breath of life died. He blotted out every living thing that was on the face of the ground, human beings and animals and creeping things and birds of the air; they were blotted out from the earth. Only Noah was left, and those that were with him in the ark.And the waters swelled on the earth for one hundred and fifty days.

THE FIFTH SUNDAY OF EASTER   YEAR A

FIRST READING   **Genesis 8.1–19**

A reading from the book of Genesis.

God remembered Noah and all the wild animals and all the domestic animals that were with him in the ark. And God made a wind blow over the earth, and the waters subsided; the fountains of the deep and the windows of the heavens were closed, the rain from the heavens was restrained, and the waters gradually receded from the earth. At the end of one hundred and fifty days the waters had abated; and in the seventh month, on the seventeenth day of the month, the ark came to rest on the mountains of Ararat. The waters continued to abate until the tenth month; in the tenth month, on the first day of the month, the tops of the mountains appeared.

At the end of forty days Noah opened the window of the ark that he had made and sent out the raven; and it went to and fro until the waters were dried up from the earth. Then he sent out the dove from him, to see if the waters had subsided from the face of the ground; but the dove found no place to set its foot, and it returned to him to the ark, for the waters were still on the face of the whole earth. So he put out his hand and took it and brought it into the ark with him. He waited another seven days, and again he sent out the dove from the ark; and the dove came back to him in the evening, and there in its beak was a freshly plucked olive leaf; so Noah knew that the waters had subsided from the earth. Then he waited another seven days, and sent out the dove; and it did not return to him any more.

In the six hundred and first year, in the first month, on the first day of the month, the waters were dried up from the earth; and Noah removed the covering of the ark, and looked, and saw that the face of the ground was drying. In the second month, on the twenty-seventh day of the month, the earth was dry. Then God said to Noah, 'Go out of the ark, you and your wife, and your sons and your sons' wives with you. Bring out with you every living thing that is with you of all flesh – birds and animals and every creeping thing that creeps on the earth – so that they may abound on the earth, and be fruitful and multiply on the earth.' So Noah went out with his sons and his wife and his sons' wives. And every animal, every creeping thing, and every bird, everything that moves on the earth, went out of the ark by families.

THE SIXTH SUNDAY OF EASTER   YEAR A

FIRST READING   Genesis 8.20 – 9.17

A reading from the book of Genesis.

Noah built an altar to the LORD, and took of every clean animal and of every clean bird, and offered burnt-offerings on the altar. And when the LORD smelt the pleasing odour, the LORD said in his heart, 'I will never again curse the ground because of humankind, for the inclination of the human heart is evil from youth; nor will I ever again destroy every living creature as I have done.
As long as the earth endures,
seedtime and harvest, cold and heat,
summer and winter, day and night,
shall not cease.'

God blessed Noah and his sons, and said to them, 'Be fruitful and multiply, and fill the earth. The fear and dread of you shall rest on every animal of the earth, and on every bird of the air, on everything that creeps on the ground, and on all of the fish of the sea; into your hand they are delivered. Every moving thing that lives shall be food for you; and just as I gave you the green plants, I give you everything. Only, you shall not eat flesh with its life, that is, its blood. For your own lifeblood I will surely require a reckoning: from every animal I will require it and from human beings, each one for the blood of another, I will require a reckoning for human life.

Whoever sheds the blood of a human,
by a human shall that person's blood be shed;
for in his own image God made humankind.
And you, be fruitful and multiply,
abound on the earth and multiply in it.'

Then God said to Noah and to his sons with him, 'As for me, I am establishing my covenant with you and your descendants after you, and with every living creature that is with you, the birds, the domestic animals, and every animal of the earth with you, as many as came out of the ark. I establish my covenant with you, that never again shall all flesh be cut off by the waters of a flood, and never again shall there be a flood to destroy the earth.' God said, 'This is the sign of the covenant that I make between me and you and every living creature that is with you, for all future generations: I have set my bow in the clouds, and it shall be a sign of the covenant between me and the earth. When I bring clouds over the earth and the bow is seen in the clouds, I will remember my covenant that is between me and you and every living creature of all flesh; and the waters shall never again become a flood to destroy all flesh. When the bow is in the clouds, I will see it and remember the everlasting covenant between God and every living creature of all flesh that is on the earth.' God said to Noah, 'This is the sign of the covenant that I have established between me and all flesh that is on the earth.'

THE SEVENTH SUNDAY OF EASTER   YEAR A

FIRST READING   Ezekiel 36.24–28

A reading from the book of the prophet Ezekiel.

The word of the LORD came to me: I will take you from the nations, and gather you from all the countries, and bring you into your own land. I will sprinkle clean water upon you, and you shall be clean from all your uncleannesses, and from all your idols I will cleanse you. A new heart I will give you, and a new spirit I will put within you; and I will remove from your body the heart of stone and give you a heart of flesh.

I will put my spirit within you, and make you follow my statutes and be careful to observe my ordinances. Then you shall live in the land that I gave to your ancestors; and you shall be my people, and I will be your God.

THE SECOND SUNDAY OF EASTER   YEAR B

FIRST READING   **Exodus 14.10–31; 15.20–21**

A reading from the book of Exodus.

For text see Year A above, p. 831.

THE THIRD SUNDAY OF EASTER   YEAR B

FIRST READING   **Zephaniah 3.14–20**

A reading from the book of the prophet Zephaniah.

For text see Year A above, p. 832.

THE FOURTH SUNDAY OF EASTER   YEAR B

FIRST READING   **Genesis 7.1–5, 11–18; 8.6–18; 9.8–13**

A reading from the book of Genesis.

The LORD said to Noah, 'Go into the ark, you and all your household, for I have seen that you alone are righteous before me in this generation. Take with you seven pairs of all clean animals, the male and its mate; and a pair of the animals that are not clean, the male and its mate; and seven pairs of the birds of the air also, male and female, to keep their kind alive on the face of all the earth. For in seven days I will send rain on the earth for forty days and forty nights; and every living thing that I have made I will blot out from the face of the ground.' And Noah did all that the LORD had commanded him.

In the six-hundredth year of Noah's life, in the second month, on the seventeenth day of the month, on that day all the fountains of the great deep burst forth, and the windows of the heavens were opened. The rain fell on the earth forty days and forty nights. On the very same day Noah with his sons, Shem and Ham and Japheth, and Noah's wife and the three wives of his sons entered the ark, they and every wild animal of every kind, and all domestic animals of every kind, and every creeping thing that creeps on the earth, and every bird of every kind – every bird, every winged creature. They went into the ark with Noah, two and two of all flesh in which there was the breath of life. And those that entered, male and female of all flesh, went in as God had commanded him; and the LORD shut him in.

The flood continued for forty days on the earth; and the waters increased, and bore up the ark, and it rose high above the earth. The waters swelled and increased greatly on the earth; and the ark floated on the face of the waters.

At the end of forty days Noah opened the window of the ark that he had made and sent out the raven; and it went to and fro until the waters were dried up from the earth. Then he sent out the dove from him, to see if the waters had subsided from the face of the ground; but the dove found no place to set its foot, and it returned to him to the ark, for the waters were still on the face of the whole earth. So he put out his hand and took it and brought it into the ark with him. He waited another seven days, and again he sent out the dove from the ark; and the dove came back to him in the evening, and there in its beak was a freshly plucked olive leaf; so Noah knew that the waters had subsided from the earth. Then he waited another seven days, and sent out the dove; and it did not return to him any more.

In the six hundred and first year, in the first month, the first day of the month, the waters were dried up from the earth; and Noah removed the covering of the ark, and looked, and saw that the face of the ground was drying. In the second month, on the twenty-seventh day of the month, the earth was dry. Then God said to Noah,

'Go out of the ark, you and your wife, and your sons and your sons' wives with you. Bring out with you every living thing that is with you of all flesh – birds and animals and every creeping thing that creeps on the earth – so that they may abound on the earth, and be fruitful and multiply on the earth.' So Noah went out with his sons and his wife and his sons' wives.

Then God said to Noah and to his sons with him, 'As for me, I am establishing my covenant with you and your descendants after you, and with every living creature that is with you, the birds, the domestic animals, and every animal of the earth with you, as many as came out of the ark. I establish my covenant with you, that never again shall all flesh be cut off by the waters of a flood, and never again shall there be a flood to destroy the earth.' God said, 'This is the sign of the covenant that I make between me and you and every living creature that is with you, for all future generations: I have set my bow in the clouds, and it shall be a sign of the covenant between me and the earth.'

THE FIFTH SUNDAY OF EASTER   YEAR B

FIRST READING (Alternative readings)

Either   **Baruch 3.9–15, 32–36; 4.1–4**

A reading from the book of the prophet Baruch.

Hear the commandments of life, O Israel;
give ear, and learn wisdom!
Why is it, O Israel,
why is it that you are in the land of your enemies,
that you are growing old in a foreign country,
that you are defiled with the dead,
that you are counted among those in Hades?
You have forsaken the fountain of wisdom.
If you had walked in the way of God,
you would be living in peace for ever.
Learn where there is wisdom,
where there is strength,
where there is understanding,
so that you may at the same time discern
where there is length of days, and life,
where there is light for the eyes, and peace.

Who has found her place?
And who has entered her storehouses?

But the one who knows all things knows her,
he found her by his understanding.
The one who prepared the earth for all time
filled it with four-footed creatures;
the one who sends forth the light, and it goes;
he called it, and it obeyed him, trembling;
the stars shone in their watches, and were glad;
he called them, and they said, 'Here we are!'
They shone with gladness for him who made them.
This is our God;
no other can be compared to him.
He found the whole way to knowledge,
and gave her to his servant Jacob
and to Israel, whom he loved.

She is the book of the commandments of God,
the law that endures for ever.
All who hold her fast will live,
and those who forsake her will die.
Turn, O Jacob, and take her;
walk towards the shining of her light.
Do not give your glory to another,
or your advantages to an alien people.
Happy are we, O Israel,
for we know what is pleasing to God.

Or   **Genesis 22.1–18**

A reading from the book of Genesis.

God tested Abraham. He said to him, 'Abraham!' And Abraham said, 'Here I
am.' God said, 'Take your son, your only son Isaac, whom you love, and go to
the land of Moriah, and offer him there as a burnt-offering on one of the
mountains that I shall show you.' So Abraham rose early in the morning,
saddled his donkey, and took two of his young men with him, and his son
Isaac; he cut the wood for the burnt-offering, and set out and went to the
place in the distance that God had shown him. On the third day Abraham
looked up and saw the place far away. Then Abraham said to his young men,
'Stay here with the donkey; the boy and I will go over there; we will worship,
and then we will come back to you.' Abraham took the wood of the burnt-
offering and laid it on his son Isaac, and he himself carried the fire and the
knife. So the two of them walked on together. Isaac said to his father
Abraham, 'Father!' And Abraham said, 'Here I am, my son.' Isaac said, 'The fire
and the wood are here, but where is the lamb for a burnt-offering?' Abraham
said, 'God himself will provide the lamb for a burnt-offering, my son.' So the
two of them walked on together.

When they came to the place that God had shown him, Abraham built an
altar there and laid the wood in order. He bound his son Isaac, and laid him
on the altar, on top of the wood. Then Abraham reached out his hand and
took the knife to kill his son. But the angel of the LORD called to him from
heaven, and said, 'Abraham, Abraham!' And he said, 'Here I am.' The angel
said, 'Do not lay your hand on the boy or do anything to him; for now I
know that you fear God, since you have not withheld your son, your only
son, from me.' And Abraham looked up and saw a ram, caught in a thicket
by its horns. Abraham went and took the ram and offered it up as a

burnt-offering instead of his son. So Abraham called that place 'The LORD will provide'; as it is said to this day, 'On the mount of the LORD it shall be provided.'

The angel of the LORD called to Abraham a second time from heaven, and said, 'By myself I have sworn, says the LORD: Because you have done this, and have not withheld your son, your only son, I will indeed bless you, and I will make your offspring as numerous as the stars of heaven and as the sand that is on the seashore. And your offspring shall possess the gate of their enemies, and by your offspring shall all the nations of the earth gain blessing for themselves, because you have obeyed my voice.'

THE SIXTH SUNDAY OF EASTER   YEAR B

FIRST READING   **Isaiah 55.1–11**

A reading from the book of the prophet Isaiah.

The LORD says this:
Everyone who thirsts,
come to the waters;
and you that have no money,
come, buy and eat!
Come, buy wine and milk
without money and without price.
Why do you spend your money for that which is not bread,
and your labour for that which does not satisfy?
Listen carefully to me, and eat what is good,
and delight yourselves in rich food.
Incline your ear, and come to me;
listen, so that you may live.
I will make with you an everlasting covenant,
my steadfast, sure love for David.
See, I made him a witness to the peoples,
a leader and commander for the peoples.
See, you shall call nations that you do not know,
and nations that do not know you shall run to you,
because of the LORD your God, the Holy One of Israel,
for he has glorified you.

Seek the LORD while he may be found,
call upon him while he is near;

let the wicked forsake their way,
and the unrighteous their thoughts;
let them return to the LORD, that he may have mercy on them,
and to our God, for he will abundantly pardon.
For my thoughts are not your thoughts,
nor are your ways my ways, says the LORD.
For as the heavens are higher than the earth,
so are my ways higher than your ways
and my thoughts than your thoughts.

For as the rain and the snow come down from heaven,
and do not return there until they have watered the earth,
making it bring forth and sprout,
giving seed to the sower and bread to the eater,
so shall my word be that goes out from my mouth;
it shall not return to me empty,
but it shall accomplish that which I purpose
and succeed in the thing for which I sent it.

THE SEVENTH SUNDAY OF EASTER   YEAR B

FIRST READING   **Ezekiel 36.24–28**

A reading from the book of the prophet Ezekiel.

For text see Year A above, p. 836.

THE SECOND SUNDAY OF EASTER   YEAR C

FIRST READING   **Exodus 14.10–31; 15.20–21**

A reading from the book of Exodus.

For text see Year A above, p. 831.

THE THIRD SUNDAY OF EASTER   YEAR C

FIRST READING   **Zephaniah 3.14–20**

A reading from the book of the prophet Zephaniah.

For text see Year A above, p. 832.

THE FOURTH SUNDAY OF EASTER   YEAR C

FIRST READING   Genesis 7.1–5, 11–18; 8.6–18; 9.8–13

A reading from the book of Genesis.

For text see Year B above, p. 837.

THE FIFTH SUNDAY OF EASTER   YEAR C

FIRST READING (Alternative readings)

Either   Baruch 3.9–15, 32–36; 4.1–4

A reading from the book of the prophet Baruch.

For text see Year B above, p. 839.

Or   Genesis 22.1–18

A reading from the book of Genesis.

For text see Year B above, p. 840.

THE SIXTH SUNDAY OF EASTER   YEAR C

FIRST READING   Ezekiel 37.1–14

A reading from the book of the prophet Ezekiel.

The hand of the LORD came upon me, and he brought me out by the spirit
of the LORD and set me down in the middle of a valley; it was full of bones.
He led me all around them; there were very many lying in the valley, and
they were very dry. He said to me, 'Mortal, can these bones live?' I answered,
'O Lord GOD, you know.' Then he said to me, 'Prophesy to these bones, and
say to them: O dry bones, hear the word of the LORD. Thus says the Lord
GOD to these bones: I will cause breath to enter you, and you shall live.
I will lay sinews on you, and will cause flesh to come upon you, and cover
you with skin, and put breath in you, and you shall live; and you shall know
that I am the LORD.'

So I prophesied as I had been commanded; and as I prophesied, suddenly
there was a noise, a rattling, and the bones came together, bone to its bone.

I looked, and there were sinews on them, and flesh had come upon them, and skin had covered them; but there was no breath in them. Then he said to me, 'Prophesy to the breath, prophesy, mortal, and say to the breath: Thus says the Lord GOD: Come from the four winds, O breath, and breathe upon these slain, that they may live.' I prophesied as he commanded me, and the breath came into them, and they lived, and stood on their feet, a vast multitude.

Then he said to me, 'Mortal, these bones are the whole house of Israel. They say, "Our bones are dried up, and our hope is lost; we are cut off completely." Therefore prophesy, and say to them, Thus says the Lord GOD: I am going to open your graves, and bring you up from your graves, O my people; and I will bring you back to the land of Israel. And you shall know that I am the LORD, when I open your graves, and bring you up from your graves, O my people. I will put my spirit within you, and you shall live, and I will place you on your own soil; then you shall know that I, the LORD, have spoken and will act, says the LORD.'

THE SEVENTH SUNDAY OF EASTER   YEAR C

FIRST READING   **Ezekiel 36.24–28**

A reading from the book of the prophet Ezekiel.

For text see Year A above, p. 836.

CHURCH OF IRELAND/CHURCH IN WALES

These alternative First Readings are authorized in the Church of Ireland and in the Church in Wales.

THE SECOND SUNDAY OF EASTER   YEAR A

FIRST READING   **Genesis 8.6–16; 9.8–16**

A reading from the book of Genesis.

At the end of forty days Noah opened the window of the ark that he had made and sent out the raven; and it went to and fro until the waters were dried up from the earth. Then he sent out the dove from him, to see if the waters had subsided from the face of the ground; but the dove found no place to set its foot, and it returned to him to the ark, for the waters were still on the face of the whole earth. So he put out his hand and took it and brought it into the ark with him. He waited another seven days, and again he sent out the dove from the ark; and the dove came back to him in the evening, and there in its beak was a freshly plucked olive leaf; so Noah knew that the waters had subsided from the earth. Then he waited another seven days, and sent out the dove; and it did not return to him any more.

In the six hundred and first year, in the first month, on the first day of the month, the waters were dried up from the earth; and Noah removed the covering of the ark, and looked, and saw that the face of the ground was drying. In the second month, on the twenty-seventh day of the month, the earth was dry. Then God said to Noah, 'Go out of the ark, you and your wife, and your sons and your sons' wives with you.'

Then God said to Noah and to his sons with him. 'As for me, I am establishing my covenant with you and your descendants after you, and with every living creature that is with you, the birds, the domestic animals, and every animal of the earth with you, as many as came out of the ark. I establish my covenant with you, that never again shall all flesh be cut off by the waters of a flood, and never again shall there be a flood to destroy the earth.' God said, 'This is the sign of the covenant that I make between me and you and every living creature that is with you, for all future generations: I have set my bow in the clouds, and it shall be a sign of the covenant between me and the earth. When I bring clouds over the earth and the bow is seen in the clouds, I will remember my covenant that is between me and you and every living creature of all flesh; and the waters shall never again become a flood to destroy all flesh. When the bow is in the clouds, I will see it and remember the everlasting covenant between God and every living creature of all flesh that is on the earth.'

THE THIRD SUNDAY OF EASTER   YEAR A

FIRST READING   Isaiah 43.1-12

A reading from the book of the prophet Isaiah.

Thus says the LORD,
he who created you, O Jacob,
he who formed you, O Israel:
Do not fear for I have redeemed you;
I have called you by name, you are mine.
When you pass through the waters, I will be with you;

and through the rivers, they shall not overwhelm you;
when you walk through fire you shall not be burned,
and the flame shall not consume you.
For I am the LORD your God,
the Holy One of Israel, your Saviour.
I give Egypt as your ransom,
Ethiopia and Seba in exchange for you.
Because you are precious in my sight, and honoured, and I love you,
I give people in return for you, nations in exchange for your life.
Do not fear, for I am with you;
I will bring your offspring from the east,
and from the west I will gather you;
I will say to the north, 'Give them up',
and to the south, 'Do not withhold;
bring my sons from far away
and my daughters from the end of the earth –
everyone who is called by my name,
whom I created for my glory,
whom I formed and made.'
Bring forth the people who are blind, yet have eyes,
who are deaf, yet have ears!
Let all the nations gather together, and let the peoples assemble.
Who among them declared this,
and foretold to us the former things?
Let them bring their witnesses to justify them,
and let them hear and say, 'It is true.'
You are my witnesses, says the LORD,
and my servant whom I have chosen,
so that you may know and believe me
and understand that I am he.
Before me no god was formed,
nor shall there be any after me.
I, I am the LORD,
and besides me there is no saviour.
I declared and saved and proclaimed,
when there was no strange god among you;
and you are my witnesses, says the LORD.

THE FOURTH SUNDAY OF EASTER   YEAR A

FIRST READING   **Nehemiah 9.6–15**

A reading from the book of Nehemiah.

When the people of Israel were assembled, Ezra said: 'You are the LORD, you alone; you have made heaven, the heaven of heavens, with all their host, the earth and all that is on it, the seas and all that is in them. To all of them you give life, and the host of heaven worships you. You are the LORD, the God who chose Abram and brought him out of Ur of the Chaldeans and gave him the name Abraham; and you found his heart faithful before you and made with him a covenant to give to his descendants the land of the Canaanite, the Hittite, the Amorite, the Perizzite, the Jebusite, and the Girgashite; and you have fulfilled your promise, for you are righteous.

And you saw the distress of our ancestors in Egypt and heard their cry at the Red Sea. You performed signs and wonders against Pharaoh and all his servants and all the people of his land, for you knew that they acted insolently against our ancestors. You made a name for yourself, which remains to this day. And you divided the sea before them, so that they passed through the sea on dry land, but you threw their pursuers into the depths, like a stone into mighty waters. Moreover, you led them by day with a pillar of cloud, and by night with a pillar of fire, to give them light on the way in which they should go. You came down also upon Mount Sinai, and spoke with them from heaven, and gave them right ordinances and true laws, good statutes and commandments, and you made known your holy sabbath to them and gave them commandments and statutes and a law through your servant Moses. For their hunger you gave them bread from heaven, and for their thirst you brought water for them out of the rock, and you told them to go in to possess the land that you swore to give them.'

THE FIFTH SUNDAY OF EASTER   YEAR A

FIRST READING   **Deuteronomy 6.20–25**

A reading from the book of Deuteronomy.

Moses said to the people: When your children ask you in time to come, 'What is the meaning of the decrees and the statutes and the ordinances that the LORD our God has commanded you?' then you shall say to your children, 'We were Pharaoh's slaves in Egypt, but the LORD brought us out of

Egypt with a mighty hand. The LORD displayed before our eyes great and awesome signs and wonders against Egypt, against Pharaoh and all his household. He brought us out from there in order to bring us in, to give us the land that he promised on oath to our ancestors. Then the LORD commanded us to observe all these statutes, to fear the LORD our God, for our lasting good so as to keep us alive, as is now the case. If we diligently observe this entire commandment before the LORD our God, as he has commanded us, we will be in the right.'

THE SIXTH SUNDAY OF EASTER   YEAR A

FIRST READING   Isaiah 41.17–20

A reading from the book of the prophet Isaiah.

The word of the LORD through the prophet:
When the poor and needy seek water, and there is none,
and their tongue is parched with thirst,
I the LORD will answer them,
I the God of Israel will not forsake them.
I will open rivers on the bare heights,
and fountains in the midst of the valleys;
I will make the wilderness a pool of water,
and the dry land springs of water.
I will put in the wilderness the cedar,
the acacia, the myrtle, and the olive:
I will set in the desert the cypress,
the plane and the pine together,
so that all may see and know,
all may consider and understand,
that the hand of the LORD has done this,
the Holy One of Israel has created it.

THE SEVENTH SUNDAY OF EASTER   YEAR A

FIRST READING   Ezekiel 39.21–29

A reading from the book of the prophet Ezekiel.

Thus says the Lord GOD: I will display my glory among the nations; and all the nations shall see my judgement that I have executed, and my hand that I have laid on them. The house of Israel shall know that I am the LORD their

God, from that day forward. And the nations shall know that the house of Israel went into captivity for their iniquity, because they dealt treacherously with me. So I hid my face from them and gave them into the hand of their adversaries, and they all fell by the sword. I dealt with them according to their uncleanness and their transgressions, and hid my face from them.

Therefore, thus says the Lord GOD: Now I will restore the fortunes of Jacob, and have mercy on the whole house of Israel; and I will be jealous for my holy name. They shall forget their shame, and all the treachery they have practised against me, when they live securely in their land with no one to make them afraid,
when I have brought them back from the peoples
and gathered them from their enemies' lands,
and through them have displayed my holiness in the sight of many nations.
Then they shall know that I am the LORD their God
because I sent them into exile among the nations,
and then gathered them into their own land.
I will leave none of them behind;
and I will never again hide my face from them,
when I pour out my spirit upon the house of Israel,
says the Lord GOD.

THE SECOND SUNDAY OF EASTER   YEAR B

FIRST READING   **Isaiah 26.2-9, 19**

A reading from the book of the prophet Isaiah.

On that day this song will be sung in the land of Judah:
Open the gates,
so that the righteous nation that keeps faith may enter in.
Those of steadfast mind you keep in peace –
in peace because they trust in you.
Trust in the LORD for ever,
for in the LORD GOD you have an everlasting rock.
For he has brought low the inhabitants of the height;
the lofty city he lays low.
He lays it low to the ground, casts it to the dust.
The foot tramples it, the feet of the poor, the steps of the needy.

The way of the righteous is level;
O Just One, you make smooth the path of the righteous.

In the path of your judgements, O LORD, we wait for you;
your name and your renown are the soul's desire.
My soul yearns for you in the night,
my spirit within me earnestly seeks you.
For when your judgements are in the earth,
the inhabitants of the world learn righteousness.
Your dead shall live, their corpses shall rise.
O dwellers in the dust, awake and sing for joy!
For your dew is a radiant dew,
and the earth will give birth to those long dead.

THE THIRD SUNDAY OF EASTER   YEAR B

FIRST READING   Micah 4.1–5

A reading from the book of the prophet Micah.

In days to come
the mountain of the LORD's house
shall be established as the highest of the mountains,
and shall be raised up above the hills.
Peoples shall stream to it,
and many nations shall come and say:
'Come, let us go up to the mountain of the LORD,
to the house of the God of Jacob:
that he may teach us his ways
and that we may walk in his paths.'
For out of Zion shall go forth instruction,
and the word of the LORD from Jerusalem.
He shall judge between many peoples,
and shall arbitrate between strong nations far away;
they shall beat their swords into ploughshares,
and their spears into pruning hooks;
nation shall not lift up sword against nation,
neither shall they learn war any more;
but they shall all sit under their own vines and under their own fig trees,
and no one shall make them afraid;
for the mouth of the LORD of hosts has spoken.
For all the peoples walk, each in the name of its god,
but we will walk in the name of the LORD our God for ever and ever.

THE FOURTH SUNDAY OF EASTER   YEAR B

FIRST READING   **Ezekiel 34.1–10**

A reading from the book of the prophet Ezekiel.

The word of the LORD came to me: Mortal, prophesy against the shepherds of Israel: prophesy, and say to them – to the shepherds: Thus says the Lord GOD: Ah, you shepherds of Israel who have been feeding yourselves! Should not shepherds feed the sheep? You eat the fat, you clothe yourselves with the wool, you slaughter the fatlings; but you do not feed the sheep. You have not strengthened the weak, you have not healed the sick, you have not bound up the injured, you have not brought back the strayed, you have not sought the lost, but with force and harshness you have ruled them. So they were scattered, because there was no shepherd; and scattered, they became food for all the wild animals. My sheep were scattered, they wandered over all the mountains and on every high hill; my sheep were scattered over all the face of the earth, with no one to search or seek for them.

Therefore, you shepherds, hear the word of the LORD: As I live, says the Lord GOD, because my sheep have become a prey, and my sheep have become food for all the wild animals, since there was no shepherd; and because my shepherds have not searched for my sheep, but the shepherds have fed themselves, and have not fed my sheep; therefore, you shepherds, hear the word of the LORD: Thus says the Lord GOD, I am against the shepherds; and I will demand my sheep at their hand, and put a stop to their feeding the sheep; no longer shall the shepherds feed themselves. I will rescue my sheep from their mouths, so that they may not be food for them.

THE FIFTH SUNDAY OF EASTER   YEAR B

FIRST READING   **Deuteronomy 4.32–40**

A reading from the book of Deuteronomy.

Moses said to the people: Ask now about former ages long before your own, ever since the day that God created human beings on the earth; ask from one end of heaven to the other: has anything so great as this ever happened or has its like ever been heard of? Has any people ever heard the voice of a god speaking out of a fire, as you have heard and lived? Or has any god ever attempted to go and take a nation for himself from the midst of another nation, by trials, by signs and wonders, by war, by a mighty hand and an outstretched arm, and by terrifying displays of power as the LORD your God did for you in Egypt before your very eyes? To you it was shown so that you would acknowledge that the LORD is God; there is no other besides him. From heaven he made you hear his voice to discipline you. On earth he showed you his great fire, while you heard his words coming out of the fire. And because he loved your ancestors, he chose their descendants after them. He brought you out of Egypt with his own presence, by his great power, driving out before you nations greater and mightier than yourselves, to bring you in, giving you their land for a possession, as it is still today. So acknowledge today and take to heart that the LORD is God in heaven above and on the earth beneath; there is no other. Keep his statutes and his commandments, which I am commanding you today for your own well-being and that of your descendants after you, so that you may long remain in the land that the LORD your God is giving you for all time.

THE SIXTH SUNDAY OF EASTER   YEAR B

FIRST READING   **Isaiah 45.11–13, 18–19**

A reading from the book of the prophet Isaiah.

Thus says the LORD,
the Holy One of Israel, and its Maker:
Will you question me about my children,
or command me concerning the work of my hands?
I made the earth, and created humankind upon it;
it was my hands that stretched out the heavens,
and I commanded all their host.
I have aroused Cyrus in righteousness,
and I will make all his paths straight;
he shall build my city and set my exiles free,
not for price or reward, says the LORD of hosts.
For thus says the LORD, who created the heavens (he is God!),
who formed the earth and made it (he established it;
he did not create it a chaos, he formed it to be inhabited!):
I am the LORD and there is no other.
I did not speak in secret, in a land of darkness;
I did not say to the offspring of Jacob, 'Seek me in chaos.'
I the LORD speak the truth,
I declare what is right.

THE SEVENTH SUNDAY OF EASTER   YEAR B

FIRST READING   **Exodus 28.1–4, 9–10, 29–30**

A reading from the book of Exodus.

The LORD said to Moses: Bring near to you your brother Aaron, and his sons with him, from among the Israelites, to serve me as priests – Aaron and Aaron's sons, Nadal and Abihu, Eleazar and Ithamar. You should make sacred vestments for the glorious adornment of your brother Aaron. And you shall speak to all who have ability, whom I have endowed with skill, that they make Aaron's vestments to consecrate him for my priesthood. These are the vestments that they shall make: a breastpiece, an ephod, a robe, a chequered tunic, a turban, and a sash.

You shall take two onyx stones, and engrave on them the names of the sons of Israel, six of their names on one stone, and the names of the remaining six on the other stone, in the order of their birth.

So Aaron shall bear the names of the sons of Israel in the breastpiece of judgement on his heart when he goes into the holy place, for a continual remembrance before the LORD. In the breastpiece of judgement you shall put the Urim and the Thummim, and they shall be on Aaron's heart when he goes in before the LORD; thus Aaron shall bear the judgement of the Israelites on his heart before the LORD continually.

THE SECOND SUNDAY OF EASTER   YEAR C

FIRST READING   **Job 42.1–6**

A reading from the book of Job.

Job answered the LORD:
'I know that you can do all things,
and that no purpose of yours can be thwarted.
"Who is this that hides counsel without knowledge?"
Therefore I have uttered what I did not understand,
things too wonderful for me, which I did not know.
"Hear, and I will speak:
I will question you, and you declare to me."
I had heard of you by the hearing of the ear,
but now my eye sees you;
therefore I despise myself,
and repent in dust and ashes.'

THE THIRD SUNDAY OF EASTER   YEAR C

FIRST READING   **Jeremiah 32.36–41**

A reading from the book of the prophet Jeremiah.

Thus says the LORD, the God of Israel, concerning this city of which you say,
'It is being given into the hand of the king of Babylon by the sword, by
famine, and by pestilence': See, I am going to gather them from all the lands
to which I drove them in my anger and my wrath and in great indignation; I
will bring them back to this place, and I will settle them in safety. They shall
be my people, and I will be their God. I will give them one heart and one
way, that they may fear me for all time, for their own good and the good of
their children after them. I will make an everlasting covenant with them,
never to draw back from doing good to them; and I will put the fear of me in
their hearts, so that they may not turn from me. I will rejoice in doing good
to them, and I will plant them in this land in faithfulness, with all my heart
and all my soul.

THE FOURTH SUNDAY OF EASTER   YEAR C

FIRST READING   **Numbers 27.12–23**

A reading from the book of Numbers.

The LORD said to Moses, 'Go up this mountain of the Abarim range, and see
the land that I have given to the Israelites. When you have seen it, you also
shall be gathered to your people, as your brother Aaron was, because you
rebelled against my word in the wilderness of Zin when the congregation
quarrelled with me. You did not show my holiness before their eyes at the
waters.' (These are the waters of Meribath-kadesh in the wilderness of Zin.)
Moses spoke to the LORD, saying, 'Let the LORD, the God of the spirits of all
flesh, appoint someone over the congregation who shall go out before them
and come in before them, who shall lead them out and bring them in, so
that the congregation of the LORD may not be like sheep without a
shepherd.' So the LORD said to Moses, 'Take Joshua son of Nun, a man in
whom is the spirit, and lay your hand upon him; have him stand before
Eleazar the priest and all the congregation, and commission him in their
sight. You shall give him some of your authority, so that all the congregation
of the Israelites may obey. But he shall stand before Eleazar the priest, who
shall inquire for him by the decision of the Urim before the LORD: at his

word they shall go out, and at his word they shall come in, both he and all the Israelites with him, the whole congregation.' So Moses did as the LORD commanded him. He took Joshua and had him stand before Eleazar the priest and the whole congregation; he laid his hands on him and commissioned him – as the LORD had directed through Moses.

THE FIFTH SUNDAY OF EASTER   YEAR C

FIRST READING   Leviticus 19.1–2, 9–18

A reading from the book of Leviticus.

The LORD spoke to Moses, saying: Speak to all the congregation of the people of Israel and say to them: You shall be holy, for I the LORD your God am holy.

When you reap the harvest of your land, you shall not reap to the very edges of your field, or gather the gleanings of your harvest. You shall not strip your vineyard bare, or gather the fallen grapes of your vineyard; you shall leave them for the poor and the alien: I am the LORD your God.

You shall not steal; you shall not deal falsely; and you shall not lie to one another. And you shall not swear falsely by my name, profaning the name of your God: I am the LORD.

You shall not defraud your neighbour; you shall not steal; and you shall not keep for yourself the wages of a labourer until morning. you shall not revile the deaf or put a stumbling-block before the blind; you shall fear your God: I am the LORD.

You shall not render an unjust judgement; you shall not be partial to the poor or defer to the great: with justice you shall judge your neighbour. You shall not go around as a slanderer among your people, and you shall not profit by the blood of your neighbour: I am the LORD.

You shall not hate in your heart anyone of your kin; you shall reprove your neighbour, or you will incur guilt yourself. You shall not take vengeance or bear a grudge against any of your people, but you shall love your neighbour as yourself: I am the LORD.

THE SIXTH SUNDAY OF EASTER   YEAR C

FIRST READING   Joel 2.21–27

A reading from the book of the prophet Joel.

The word of the LORD through the prophet:
Do not fear, O soil;
be glad and rejoice, for the LORD has done great things!
Do not fear, you animals of the field,
for the pastures of the wilderness are green;
the tree bears its fruit,
the fig tree and vine give their full yield.

O children of Zion, be glad
and rejoice in the LORD your God;
for he has given the early rain for your vindication,
he has poured down for you abundant rain,
the early and the later rain, as before.
The threshing-floors shall be full or grain,
the vats shall overflow with wine and oil.

I will repay you for the years
that the swarming locust has eaten,
the hopper, the destroyer, and the cutter,
my great army, which I sent against you.

You shall eat in plenty and be satisfied,
and praise the name of the LORD your God,
who has dealt wondrously with you.
And my people shall never again be put to shame.
You shall know that I am in the midst of Israel,
and that I, the LORD, am your God and there is no other.
And my people shall never again be put to shame.

THE SEVENTH SUNDAY OF EASTER   YEAR C

FIRST READING   1 Samuel 12.19–24

A reading from the first book of Samuel.

All the people said to Samuel, 'Pray to the LORD your God for your servants,
so that we may not die; for we have added to all our sins the evil of
demanding a king for ourselves.' And Samuel said to the people, 'Do not be

afraid: you have done all this evil, yet do not turn aside from following the LORD, but serve the LORD with all your heart; and do not turn aside after useless things that cannot profit or save, for they are useless. For the LORD will not cast away his people, for his great name's sake, because it has pleased the LORD to make you a people for himself. Moreover as for me, far be it from me that I should sin against the LORD by ceasing to pray for you: and I will instruct you in the good and the right way. Only fear the LORD, and serve him faithfully with all your heart; for consider what great things he has done for you.'

SAINTS FOR IRELAND, SCOTLAND AND WALES

Readings authorized for use in the Church of Ireland, the Scottish Episcopal Church or the Church in Wales.

ST KENTIGERN (MUNGO)	YEARS A B C	SCOTLAND ONLY

13 January

FIRST READING   Isaiah 52.7–10

A reading from the book of the prophet Isaiah.

How beautiful upon the mountains
are the feet of the messenger who announces peace,
who brings good news, who announces salvation,
who says to Zion, 'Your God reigns.'
Listen! Your sentinels lift up their voices,
together they sing for joy;
for in plain sight they see the return of the LORD to Zion.
Break forth together into singing, you ruins of Jerusalem;
for the LORD has comforted his people,
he has redeemed Jerusalem,
The LORD has bared his holy arm before the eyes of all the nations;
and all the ends of the earth shall see the salvation of our God.

PSALM   Psalm 16.5–11

℞ **My heart is glad and my spirit rejoices.**

O Lord, you are my portion and my cup;
it is you who uphold my lot.
My boundaries enclose a pleasant land;
indeed, I have a goodly heritage.
I will bless the Lord who gives me counsel;
my heart teaches me, night after night. ℞

I have set the Lord always before me;
because he is at my right hand I shall not fall.
My heart, therefore, is glad and my spirit rejoices;
my body also shall rest in hope. ℞

For you will not abandon me to the grave,
nor let your holy one see the Pit.
You will show me the path of life;
in your presence there is fullness of joy,
and in your right hand are pleasures for evermore. ℞

SECOND READING (Alternative readings)

Either   1 Corinthians 9.16–19, 22–23

A reading from the first letter of Paul to the Corinthians.

If I proclaim the gospel, this gives me no ground for boasting, for an
obligation is laid on me, and woe betide me if I do not proclaim
the gospel! For if I do this of my own will, I have a reward; but if not of my
own will, I am entrusted with a commission. What then is my reward? Just
this: that in my proclamation I may make the gospel free of charge, so as not
to make full use of my rights in the gospel.

For though I am free with respect to all, I have made myself a slave to all, so
that I might win more of them. To the weak I became weak, so that I might
win the weak. I have become all things to all people, so that I might by any
means save some. I do it all for the sake of the gospel, so that I may share in
its blessings.

Or   **1 Thessalonians 2.2b–12**

A reading from the first letter of Paul to the Thessalonians.

We had courage in our God to declare to you the gospel of God in spite of great opposition. For our appeal does not spring from deceit or impure motives or trickery, but just as we have been approved by God to be entrusted with the message of the gospel, even so we speak, not to please mortals, but to please God who tests our hearts. As you know and as God is our witness, we never came with words of flattery or with a pretext for greed; nor did we seek praise from mortals, whether from you or from others, though we might have made demands as apostles of Christ. But we were gentle among you, like a nurse tenderly caring for her own children. So deeply do we care for you that we are determined to share with you not only the gospel of God but also our own selves, because you have become very dear to us.

You remember our labour and toil, brothers and sisters; we worked night and day, so that we might not burden any of you while we proclaimed to you the gospel of God. You are witnesses, and God also, how pure, upright, and blameless our conduct was towards you believers. As you know, we dealt with each one of you like a father with his children, urging and encouraging you and pleading that you should lead a life worthy of God, who calls you into his own kingdom and glory.

GOSPEL   **Matthew 28.16–20**

Hear the gospel of our Lord Jesus Christ according to Matthew.

The eleven disciples went to Galilee, to the mountain to which Jesus had directed them. When they saw him, they worshipped him; but some doubted. And Jesus came and said to them, 'All authority in heaven and on earth has been given to me. Go therefore and make disciples of all nations, baptizing them in the name of the Father and of the Son and of the Holy Spirit, and teaching them to obey everything that I have commanded you. And remember, I am with you always, to the end of the age.'

ST BRIGID   YEARS A B C   IRELAND ONLY

1 February

FIRST READING   Hosea 6.1–4

A reading from the book of the prophet Hosea.

'Come, let us return to the LORD;
for it is he who has torn, and he will heal us;
he has struck down, and he will bind us up.
After two days he will revive us;
on the third day he will raise us up,
that we may live before him.
Let us know, let us press on to know the LORD;
his appearing is as sure as the dawn;
he will come to us like the showers,
like the spring rains that water the earth.'
What shall I do with you, O Ephraim?
What shall I do with you, O Judah?
Your love is like a morning cloud,
like the dew that goes away early.

PSALM   Psalm 134

℟ **Bless the Lord, all you servants of the Lord.**

Behold now, bless the Lord,
all you servants of the Lord,
you that stand by night in the house of the Lord. ℟

Lift up your hands in the holy place
and bless the Lord;
the Lord who made heaven and earth
bless you out of Zion. ℟

SECOND READING   1 John 1.1–4

A reading from the first letter of John.

We declare to you what was from the beginning, what we have heard, what
we have seen with our eyes, what we have looked at and touched with our
hands, concerning the word of life – this life was revealed, and we have seen

it and testify to it, and declare to you the eternal life that was with the Father and was revealed to us – we declare to you what we have seen and heard so that you also may have fellowship with us; and truly our fellowship is with the Father and with his Son Jesus Christ. We are writing these things so that our joy may be complete.

GOSPEL   John 10.7–16

Hear the gospel of our Lord Jesus Christ according to John.

Jesus said to the Jews: 'Very truly, I tell you, I am the gate for the sheep. All who came before me are thieves and bandits; but the sheep did not listen to them. I am the gate. Whoever enters by me will be saved, and will come in and go out and find pasture. The thief comes only to steal and kill and destroy. I came that they may have life, and have it abundantly. I am the good shepherd. The good shepherd lays down his life for the sheep. The hired hand, who is not the shepherd and does not own the sheep, sees the wolf coming and leaves the sheep and runs away – and the wolf snatches them and scatters them. The hired hand runs away because a hired hand does not care for the sheep. I am the good shepherd. I know my own and my own know me, just as the Father knows me and I know the Father. And I lay down my life for the sheep. I have other sheep that do not belong to this fold. I must bring them also, and they will listen to my voice. So there will be one flock, one shepherd.'

ST DAVID   YEARS A B C   WALES ONLY

1 March

FIRST READING (Alternative readings)

Either   Ecclesiasticus 15.1–6

A reading from the book of Ecclesiasticus.

Whoever fears the Lord will do this,
and whoever holds to the law will obtain wisdom.
She will come to meet him like a mother,
and like a young bride she will welcome him.
She will feed him with the bread of learning,
and give him the water of wisdom to drink.

He will lean on her and not fall,
and he will rely on her and not be put to shame.
She will exalt him above his neighbours,
and will open his mouth in the midst of the assembly.
He will find gladness and a crown of rejoicing,
and will inherit an everlasting name.

Or   **Jeremiah 1.4–10**

A reading from the book of the prophet Jeremiah.

The word of the LORD came to me, saying:
'Before I formed you in the womb I knew you,
and before you were born I consecrated you;
I appointed you a prophet to the nations.'
Then I said, 'Ah, Lord GOD! Truly I do not know how to speak, for I am only
a boy.'
But the LORD said to me,
'Do not say, "I am only a boy";
for you shall go to all to whom I send you,
and you shall speak whatever I command you.
Do not be afraid of them,
for I am with you to deliver you, says the LORD.'
Then the LORD put out his hand and touched my mouth; and the LORD said
to me,
'Now, I have put my words in your mouth.
See, today I appoint you over nations and over kingdoms,
to pluck up and to pull down, to destroy and to overthrow,
to build and to plant.'

PSALM   **Psalm 16.2, 5–8**

℟ **You are my portion and my cup.**

All my delight is upon the godly that are in the land,
upon those who are noble among the people.
O Lord, you are my portion and my cup;
it is you who uphold my lot.
My boundaries enclose a pleasant land;
indeed, I have a goodly heritage. ℟

I will bless the Lord who gives me counsel;
my heart teaches me, night after night.
I have set the Lord always before me;
because he is at my right hand I shall not fall. ℟

SECOND READING   1 Thessalonians 2.2b–12

A reading from the first letter of Paul to the Thessalonians.

We had courage in our God to declare to you the gospel of God in spite of great opposition. For our appeal does not spring from deceit or impure motives or trickery, but just as we have been approved by God to be entrusted with the message of the gospel, even so we speak, not to please mortals, but to please God who tests our hearts. As you know and as God is our witness, we never came with words of flattery or with a pretext for greed; nor did we seek praise from mortals, whether from you or from others, though we might have made demands as apostles of Christ. But we were gentle among you, like a nurse tenderly caring for her own children. So deeply do we care for you that we are determined to share with you not only the gospel of God but also our own selves, because you have become very dear to us.

You remember our labour and toil, brothers and sisters; we worked night and day, so that we might not burden any of you while we proclaimed to you the gospel of God. You are witnesses, and God also, how pure, upright, and blameless our conduct was towards you believers. As you know, we dealt with each one of you like a father with his children, urging and encouraging you and pleading that you should lead a life worthy of God, who calls you into his own kingdom and glory.

GOSPEL   Matthew 16.24–27

Hear the gospel of our Lord Jesus Christ according to Matthew.

Jesus told his disciples, 'If any want to become my followers, let them deny themselves and take up their cross and follow me. For those who want to save their life will lose it, and those who lose their life for my sake will find it. For what will it profit them if they gain the whole world but forfeit their life? Or what will they give in return for their life? For the Son of Man is to come with his angels in the glory of his Father, and then he will repay everyone for what has been done.'

ST PATRICK   YEARS A B C   IRELAND ONLY

17 March

SET A

FIRST READING (Alternative readings)

Either   **Tobit 13.1b–7**

A reading from the book of Tobit.

'Blessed be God who lives for ever, because his kingdom lasts throughout all ages. For he afflicts, and he shows mercy; he leads down to Hades in the lowest regions of the earth, and he brings up from the great abyss, and there is nothing that can escape his hand. Acknowledge him before the nations, O children of Israel; for he has scattered you among them. He has shown you his greatness even there. Exalt him in the presence of every living being, because he is our Lord and he is our God; he is our Father and he is God for ever. He will afflict you for your iniquities, but he will again show mercy on all of you. He will gather you from all the nations among whom you have been scattered. If you turn to him with all your heart and with all your soul, to do what is true before him, then he will turn to you and will no longer hide his face from you. So now see what he has done for you; acknowledge him at the top of your voice. Bless the Lord of righteousness, and exalt the King of the ages. In the land of my exile I acknowledge him, and show his power and majesty to a nation of sinners: "Turn back, you sinners, and do what is right before him; perhaps he may look with favour upon you and show you mercy." As for me, I exalt my God, and my soul rejoices in the King of heaven.'

Or   **Deuteronomy 32.1–9**

A reading from the book of Deuteronomy.

Give ear, O heavens, and I will speak;
let the earth hear the words of my mouth.
May my teaching drop like the rain,
my speech condense like the dew; like gentle rain on grass,
like showers on new growth.
For I will proclaim the name of the LORD;
ascribe greatness to our God!

The Rock, his work is perfect, and all his ways are just,
A faithful God, without deceit, just and upright is he;
yet his degenerate children have dealt falsely with him,
a perverse and crooked generation.
Do you thus repay the LORD,
O foolish and senseless people?
Is not he your father, who created you,
who made you and established you?
Remember the days of old,
consider the years long past;
ask your father, and he will inform you;
your elders, and they will tell you.
When the Most High apportioned the nations,
when he divided humankind,
he fixed the boundaries of the peoples
according to the number of the gods;
the LORD's own portion was his people,
Jacob his allotted share.

PSALM   Psalm 145.1–13

℟ [All your works praise you,] O Lord,
    your faithful servants bless you.

I will exalt you, O God my King,
and bless your name for ever and ever.
Every day will I bless you
and praise your name for ever and ever.
Great is the Lord and greatly to be praised;
there is no end to his greatness. ℟

One generation shall praise your works to another
and shall declare your power.
I will ponder the glorious splendour of your majesty
and all your marvellous works. ℟

They shall speak of the might of your wondrous acts,
and I will tell of your greatness.
They shall publish the remembrance
 of your great goodness;
they shall sing of your righteous deeds. ℟

The Lord is gracious and full of compassion,
slow to anger and of great kindness.
The Lord is loving to everyone
and his compassion is over all his works. ℟

All your works praise you, O Lord,
and your faithful servants bless you.
They make known the glory of your kingdom
and speak of your power; ℟

That the peoples may know of your power
and the glorious splendour of your kingdom.
Your kingdom is an everlasting kingdom;
your dominion endures throughout all ages. ℟

SECOND READING   **2 Corinthians 4.1–12**

A reading from the second letter of Paul to the Corinthians.

Since it is by God's mercy that we are engaged in this ministry, we do not lose
heart. We have renounced the shameful things that one hides; we refuse to
practise cunning or to falsify God's word; but by the open statement of the
truth we commend ourselves to the conscience of everyone in the sight of
God. And even if our gospel is veiled, it is veiled to those who are perishing.
In their case the god of this world has blinded the minds of the unbelievers,
to keep them from seeing the light of the gospel of the glory of Christ, who is
the image of God. For we do not proclaim ourselves; we proclaim Jesus Christ
as Lord and ourselves as your slaves for Jesus' sake.

For it is the God who said, 'Let light shine out of darkness', who has shone in
our hearts to give the light of the knowledge of the glory of God in the face
of Jesus Christ. But we have this treasure in clay jars, so that it may be made
clear that this extraordinary power belongs to God and does not come from
us.

We are afflicted in every way, but not crushed; perplexed, but not driven to
despair; persecuted, but not forsaken; struck down, but not destroyed; always
carrying in the body the death of Jesus, so that the life of Jesus may also be
made visible in our bodies. For while we live, we are always being given up to
death for Jesus' sake, so that the life of Jesus may be made visible in our
mortal flesh. So death is at work in us, but life in you.

GOSPEL · John 4.31–38

Hear the gospel of our Lord Jesus Christ according to John.

The disciples were urging Jesus, 'Rabbi, eat something.' But he said to them, 'I have food to eat that you do not know about.' So the disciples said to one another, 'Surely no one has brought him something to eat?' Jesus said to them, 'My food is to do the will of him who sent me and to complete his work. Do you not say, "Four months more, then comes the harvest"? But I tell you, look around you, and see how the fields are ripe for harvesting. The reaper is already receiving wages and is gathering fruit for eternal life, so that sower and reaper may rejoice together. For here the saying holds true, "One sows and another reaps." I sent you to reap that for which you did not labour. Others have laboured, and you have entered into their labour.'

SET B

FIRST READING · Isaiah 51.1–11

A reading from the book of the prophet Isaiah.

The word of the LORD through the prophet:
Listen to me, you that pursue righteousness,
you that seek the LORD.
Look to the rock from which you were hewn,
and to the quarry from which you were dug.
Look to Abraham your father and to Sarah who bore you;
for he was but one when I called him,
but I blessed him and made him many.
For the LORD will comfort Zion;
he will comfort all her waste places,
and will make her wilderness like Eden,
her desert like the garden of the LORD:
joy and gladness will be found in her,
thanksgiving and the voice of song.

Listen to me, my people,
and give heed to me, my nation:
for a teaching will go out from me,
and my justice for a light to the peoples.
I will bring near my deliverance swiftly,

my salvation has gone out
and my arms will rule the peoples;
the coastlands wait for me,
and for my arm they hope.
Lift up your eyes to the heavens,
and look at the earth beneath;
for the heavens will vanish like smoke,
the earth will wear out like a garment,
and those who live on it will die like gnats;
but my salvation will be for ever,
and my deliverance will never be ended.

Listen to me, you who know righteousness,
you people who have my teaching in your hearts;
do not fear the reproach of others,
and do not be dismayed when they revile you.
For the moth will eat them up like a garment,
and the worm will eat them like wool:
but my deliverance will be for ever,
and my salvation to all generations.

Awake, awake, put on strength,
O arm of the LORD!
Awake, as in days of old,
the generations of long ago!
Was it not you who cut Rahab in pieces,
who pierced the dragon?
Was it not you who dried up the sea,
the waters of the great deep;
who made the depths of the sea a way
for the redeemed to cross over?
So the ransomed of the LORD shall return,
and come to Zion with singing;
everlasting joy shall be upon their heads;
they shall obtain joy and gladness,
and sorrow and sighing shall flee away.

PSALM   **Psalm 96**

℞ **Proclaim the good news of salvation from day to day.**

Sing to the Lord a new song;
sing to the Lord, all the whole earth.
Sing to the Lord and bless his name;
proclaim the good news of his salvation from day to day.
Declare his glory among the nations
and his wonders among all peoples. ℞

For great is the Lord and greatly to be praised;
he is more to be feared than all gods.
As for all the gods of the nations, they are but idols;
but it is the Lord who made the heavens.
O the majesty and magnificence of his presence!
O the power and the splendour of his sanctuary! ℞

Ascribe to the Lord, you families of the peoples;
ascribe to the Lord honour and power.
Ascribe to the Lord the honour due to his name;
bring offerings and come into his courts.
Worship the Lord in the beauty of holiness;
let the whole earth tremble before him. ℞

Tell it out among the nations: 'The Lord is king!
he has made the world so firm that it cannot be moved;
he will judge the peoples with equity.'
Let the heavens rejoice and let the earth be glad;
let the sea thunder and all that is in it;
let the field be joyful and all that is therein. ℞

Then shall all the trees of the wood shout for joy
before the Lord when he comes,
when he comes to judge the earth.
He will judge the world with righteousness
and the peoples with his truth. ℞

SECOND READING   Revelation 22.1-5

A reading from the book of Revelation.

The angel showed me the river of the water of life, bright as crystal, flowing from the throne of God and of the Lamb through the middle of the street of the city. On either side of the river is the tree of life with its twelve kinds of fruit, producing its fruit each month; and the leaves of the tree are for the healing of the nations. Nothing accursed will be found there any more. But the throne of God and of the Lamb will be in it, and his servants will worship him; they will see his face, and his name will be on their foreheads. And there will be no more night; they need no light of lamp or sun, for the Lord God will be their light, and they will reign for ever and ever.

GOSPEL   Matthew 10.16-23

Hear the gospel of our Lord Jesus Christ according to Matthew.

Jesus said to his disciples, 'See, I am sending you out like sheep into the midst of wolves; so be wise as serpents and innocent as doves. Beware of them, for they will hand you over to councils and flog you in their synagogues; and you will be dragged before governors and kings because of me, as a testimony to them and the Gentiles. When they hand you over, do not worry about how you are to speak or what you are to say; for what you are to say will be given to you at that time; for it is not you who speak, but the Spirit of your Father speaking through you. Brother will betray brother to death, and a father his child, and children will rise against parents and have them put to death; and you will be hated by all because of my name. But the one who endures to the end will be saved. When they persecute you in one town, flee to the next; for truly I tell you, you will not have gone through all the towns of Israel before the Son of Man comes.'

ST COLUMBA   YEARS A B C   IRELAND ONLY

(Scottish provision below, pages 873–877.)

9 June

FIRST READING   Micah 4.1-5

A reading from the book of the prophet Micah.

In days to come the mountain of the Lord's house
shall be established as the highest of the mountains,
and shall be raised up above the hills.
Peoples shall stream to it,
and many nations shall come and say:
'Come, let us go up to the mountain of the LORD,
to the house of the God of Jacob;
that he may teach us his ways
and that we may walk in his paths.'
For out of Zion shall go forth instruction,
and the word of the LORD from Jerusalem.
He shall judge between many peoples,
and shall arbitrate between strong nations far away;
they shall beat their swords into ploughshares,
and their spears into pruning-hooks;
nation shall not lift up sword against nation,
neither shall they learn war any more;
but they shall all sit under their own vines and under their own fig trees,
and no one shall make them afraid;
for the mouth of the LORD of hosts has spoken.

For all the peoples walk, each in the name of its god,
but we will walk in the name of the LORD our God for ever and ever.

PSALM   Psalm 34.9-15

℟ [Come, children, and listen to me.]
   I will teach you to fear the Lord.

Fear the Lord, you that are his saints,
for those who fear him lack nothing.
The young lions lack and suffer hunger,
but those who seek the Lord
lack nothing that is good. ℟

Come, children, and listen to me;
I will teach you the fear of the Lord.
Who among you loves life
and desires long life to enjoy prosperity?
Keep your tongue from evil-speaking
and your lips from lying words. ℟

Turn from evil and do good;
seek peace and pursue it.
The eyes of the Lord are upon the righteous,
and his ears are open to their cry. ℟

SECOND READING   **Romans 15.1–6**

A reading from the letter of Paul to the Romans.

We who are strong ought to put up with the failings of the weak, and not to
please ourselves. Each of us must please our neighbour for the good purpose
of building up the neighbour. For Christ did not please himself; but, as it is
written, 'The insults of those who insult you have fallen on me.' For
whatever was written in former days was written for our instruction, so that
by steadfastness and by the encouragement of the scriptures we might have
hope. May the God of steadfastness and encouragement grant you to live in
harmony with one another, in accordance with Christ Jesus, so that together
you may with one voice glorify the God and Father of our Lord Jesus Christ.

GOSPEL   **John 12.20–26**

Hear the gospel of our Lord Jesus Christ according to John.

Among those who went up to worship at the festival were some Greeks. They
came to Philip, who was from Bethsaida in Galilee, and said to him, 'Sir, we
wish to see Jesus.' Philip went and told Andrew; then Andrew and Philip
went and told Jesus. Jesus answered them, 'The hour has come for the Son of
Man to be glorified. Very truly, I tell you, unless a grain of wheat falls into
the earth and dies, it remains just a single grain; but if it dies, it bears much
fruit. Those who love their life lose it, and those who hate their life in this
world will keep it for eternal life. Whoever serves me must follow me, and
where I am, there will my servant be also. Whoever serves me, the Father
will honour.'

ST COLUMBA **YEARS A B C** **SCOTLAND ONLY**

(Irish provision above, pages 871–872.)

FIRST READING Isaiah 61.1-3

A reading from the book of the prophet Isaiah.

The spirit of the Lord GOD is upon me,
because the LORD has anointed me:
he has sent me to bring good news to the oppressed,
to bind up the broken-hearted,
to proclaim liberty to the captives,
and release to the prisoners;
to proclaim the year of the LORD's favour,
and the day of vengeance of our God;
to comfort all who mourn;
to provide for those who mourn in Zion –
to give them a garland instead of ashes,
the oil of gladness instead of mourning,
the mantle of praise instead of a faint spirit.
They will be called oaks of righteousness,
the planting of the LORD to display his glory.

PSALM

Either Psalm 34.1-8

℟ **O taste and see that the Lord is good.**

I will bless the Lord at all times;
his praise shall ever be in my mouth.
I will glory in the Lord;
let the humble hear and rejoice. ℟

Proclaim with me the greatness of the Lord;
let us exalt his name together.
I sought the Lord and he answered me
and delivered me out of all my terror. ℟

Look upon him and be radiant,
and let not your faces be ashamed.
I called in my affliction and the Lord heard me
and saved me from all my troubles. ℟

The angel of the Lord encompasses those who fear him,
and he will deliver them.
Taste and see that the Lord is good;
happy are they who trust in him! ℟

Or   **Psalm 34.9–22**

℟ **[Come, children, and listen to me.]**
   I will teach you to fear the Lord.

Fear the Lord, you that are his saints,
for those who fear him lack nothing.
The young lions lack and suffer hunger,
but those who seek the Lord
lack nothing that is good. ℟

Come, children, and listen to me;
I will teach you the fear of the Lord.
Who among you loves life
and desires long life to enjoy prosperity?
Keep your tongue from evil-speaking
and your lips from lying words.
Turn from evil and do good;
seek peace and pursue it. ℟

The eyes of the Lord are upon the righteous,
and his ears are upon to their cry.
The face of the Lord is against those who do evil,
to root out the remembrance of them from the earth.
The righteous cry and the Lord hears them
and delivers them from all their troubles. ℟

The Lord is near to the brokenhearted
and will save those whose spirits are crushed.
Many are the troubles of the righteous,
but the Lord will deliver him out of them all.
He will keep safe all his bones;
not one of them shall be broken. ℟

Evil shall slay the wicked,
and those who hate the righteous will be punished.
The Lord ransoms the life of his servants,
and none will be punished who trust in him. ℟

SECOND READING (Alternative readings)

Either   **1 Thessalonians 2.2b–12**

A reading from the first letter of Paul to the Thessalonians.

We had courage in our God to declare to you the gospel of God in spite of
great opposition. For our appeal does not spring from deceit or impure
motives or trickery, but just as we have been approved by God to be
entrusted with the message of the gospel, even so we speak, not to please
mortals, but to please God who tests our hearts. As you know and as God is
our witness, we never came with words of flattery or with a pretext for greed;
nor did we seek praise from mortals, whether from you or from others,
though we might have made demands as apostles of Christ. But we were
gentle among you, like a nurse tenderly caring for her own children. So
deeply do we care for you that we are determined to share with you not only
the gospel of God but also our own selves, because you have become very
dear to us.

You remember our labour and toil, brothers and sisters; we worked night and
day, so that we might not burden any of you while we proclaimed to you the
gospel of God. You are witnesses, and God also, how pure, upright, and
blameless our conduct was towards you believers. As you know, we dealt with
each one of you like a father with his children, urging and encouraging you
and pleading that you should lead a life worthy of God, who calls you into
his own kingdom and glory.

Or   **Ephesians 4.14–19**

We must no longer be children, tossed to and fro and blown about by every
wind of doctrine, by people's trickery, by their craftiness in deceitful
scheming. But speaking the truth in love, we must grow up in every way into
him who is the head, into Christ, from whom the whole body, joined and
knitted together by every ligament with which it is equipped, as each part is
working properly, promotes the body's growth in building itself up in love.

875

Now this I affirm and insist on in the Lord: you must no longer live as the Gentiles live, in the futility of their minds. They are darkened in their understanding, alienated from the life of God because of their ignorance and hardness of heart. They have lost all sensitivity and have abandoned themselves to licentiousness, greedy to practise every kind of impurity.

GOSPEL (Alternative readings)

Either   **Matthew 5.13–16**

Hear the gospel of our Lord Jesus Christ according to Matthew.

Jesus said to the crowd: 'You are the salt of the earth; but if salt has lost its taste, how can its saltiness be restored? It is no longer good for anything, but is thrown out and trampled under foot.

You are the light of the world, a city built on a hill cannot be hidden. No one after lighting a lamp puts it under the bushel basket, but on the lampstand, and it gives light to all in the house. In the same way, let your light shine before others, so that they may see your good works and give glory to your Father in heaven.'

Or   **Matthew 28.16–20**

Hear the gospel of our Lord Jesus Christ according to Matthew.

The eleven disciples went to Galilee, to the mountain to which Jesus had directed them. When they saw him, they worshipped him; but some doubted. And Jesus came and said to them, 'All authority in heaven and on earth has been given to me. Go therefore and make disciples of all nations, baptizing them in the name of the Father and of the Son and of the Holy Spirit, and teaching them to obey everything that I have commanded you. And remember, I am with you always, to the end of the age.'

Or   **Luke 12.32–37**

Hear the gospel of our Lord Jesus Christ according to Luke.

Jesus said to his disciples: 'Do not be afraid, little flock, for it is your Father's good pleasure to give you the kingdom. Sell your possessions, and give alms. Make purses for yourselves that do not wear out, an unfailing treasure in heaven, where no thief comes near andno moth destroys. For where your treasure is, there your heart will be also.

Be dressed for action and have your lamps lit; be like those who are waiting for their master to return from the wedding banquet, so that they may open the door for him as soon as he comes and knocks. Blessed are those slaves whom the master finds alert when he comes; truly I tell you, he will fasten his belt and have them sit down to eat, and he will come and serve them.'

ST NINIAN   YEARS A B C   SCOTLAND ONLY

16 September

FIRST READING   Jeremiah 1.4–9

A reading from the book of the prophet Jeremiah.

The word of the LORD came to me, saying,
'Before I formed you in the womb I knew you,
and before you were born I consecrated you;
I appointed you a prophet to the nations.'
Then I said, 'Ah, Lord GOD! Truly I do not know how to speak, for I am only a boy.'
But the LORD said to me,
'Do not say, "I am only a boy";
for you shall go to all to whom I send you,
and you shall speak whatever I command you.
Do not be afraid of them,
for I am with you to deliver you, says the LORD.'
Then the LORD put out his hand and touched my mouth; and the LORD said to me,
'Now I have put my words in your mouth.'

PSALM   Psalm 67

℟ **Let the peoples praise you, O God;**
  let all the peoples praise you.

May God be merciful to us and bless us,
show us the light of his countenance and come to us.
Let your ways be known upon earth,
your saving health among all nations. ℟

Let the peoples praise you, O God;
let all the peoples praise you.]

Let the nations be glad and sing for joy,
for you judge the peoples with equity
and guide all the nations upon earth. ℟

[Let the peoples praise you, O God;
let all the peoples praise you.]

The earth has brought forth her increase;
may God, our own God, give us his blessing.
May God give us his blessing,
and may all the ends of the earth stand in awe of him. ℟

SECOND READING

Either   2 Corinthians 5.17 – 6.2

A reading from the second letter of Paul to the Corinthians.

If anyone is in Christ, there is a new creation: everything old has passed
away; see, everything has become new! All this is from God, who reconciled
us to himself through Christ and has given us the ministry of reconciliation;
that is, in Christ God was reconciling the world to himself, not counting
their trespasses against them, and entrusting the message of reconciliation to
us. So we are ambassadors for Christ, since God is making his appeal through
us; we entreat you on behalf of Christ, be reconciled to God. For our sake he
made him to be sin who knew no sin, so that in him we might become the
righteousness of God.

As we work together with him, we urge you also not to accept the grace of
God in vain. For he says,
'At an acceptable time I have listened to you,
and on a day of salvation I have helped you.'
See, now is the acceptable time; see, now is the day of salvation!

Or   1 Thessalonians 2.2b–12

A reading from the first letter of Paul to the Thessalonians.

We had courage in our God to declare to you the gospel of God in spite of
great opposition. For our appeal does not spring from deceit or impure motives

or trickery, but just as we have been approved by God to be entrusted with the message of the gospel, even so we speak, not to please mortals, but to please God who tests our hearts. As you know and as God is our witness, we never came with words of flattery or with a pretext for greed; nor did we seek praise from mortals, whether from you or from others, though we might have made demands as apostles of Christ. But we were gentle among you, like a nurse tenderly caring for her own children. So deeply do we care for you that we are determined to share with you not only the gospel of God but also our own selves, because you have become very dear to us.

You remember our labour and toil, brothers and sisters; we worked night and day, so that we might not burden any of you while we proclaimed to you the gospel of God. You are witnesses, and God also, how pure, upright, and blameless our conduct was towards you believers. As you know, we dealt with each one of you like a father with his children, urging and encouraging you and pleading that you should lead a life worthy of God, who calls you into his own kingdom and glory.

GOSPEL (Alternative readings)

Either   Matthew 9.35–38

Hear the gospel of our Lord Jesus Christ according to Matthew.

Jesus went about all the cities and villages, teaching in their synagogues, and proclaiming the good news of the kingdom, and curing every disease and every sickness. When he saw the crowds, he had compassion for them, because they were harassed and helpless, like sheep without a shepherd. Then he said to his disciples. 'The harvest is plentiful, but the labourers are few; therefore ask the Lord of the harvest to send out labourers into his harvest.'

Or   Matthew 28.16–20

Hear the gospel of our Lord Jesus Christ according to Matthew.

The eleven disciples went to Galilee, to the mountain to which Jesus had directed them. When they saw him, they worshipped him; but some doubted. And Jesus came and said to them, 'All authority in heaven and on earth has been given to me. Go therefore and make disciples of all nations, baptizing them in the name of the Father and of the Son and of the Holy Spirit, and teaching them to obey everything that I have commanded you. And remember, I am with you always, to the end of the age.'

ST MARGARET OF SCOTLAND

YEARS A B C   **SCOTLAND ONLY**

16 November

FIRST READING   Proverbs 31.10–13, (14–24), 25–31

A reading from the book of Proverbs.

A capable wife who can find?
She is far more precious than jewels.
The heart of her husband trusts in her,
and he will have no lack of gain.
She does him good, and not harm,
all the days of her life.
She seeks wool and flax,
and works with willing hands.
[She is like the ships of the merchant,
she brings her food from far away.
She rises while it is still night
and provides food for her household
and tasks for her servant-girls.
She considers a field and buys it;
with the fruit of her hands she plants a vineyard.
She girds herself with strength,
and makes her arms strong.
She perceives that her merchandise is profitable.
Her lamp does not go out at night.
She puts her hands to the distaff,
and her hands hold the spindle.
She opens her hand to the poor,
and reaches out her hands to the needy.
She is not afraid for her household when it snows,
for all her household are clothed in crimson.
She makes herself coverings;
her clothing is fine linen and purple.
Her husband is known in the city gates,
taking his seat among the elders of the land.
She makes linen garments and sells them;
she supplies the merchant with sashes.]
Strength and dignity are her clothing,
and she laughs at the time to come.

She opens her mouth with wisdom,
and the teaching of kindness is on her tongue.
She looks well to the ways of her household,
and does not eat the bread of idleness,
Her children rise up and call her happy;
her husband too, and he praises her:
'Many women have done excellently,
but you surpass them all.'
Charm is deceitful, and beauty is vain,
but a woman who fears the LORD is to be praised.
Give her a share in the fruit of her hands,
and let her works praise her in the city gates.

PSALM   Psalm 112

℟ **The righteous are merciful and full of compassion.**

Alleluia!
Happy are they who fear the Lord
and have great delight in his commandments!
Their descendants will be mighty in the land;
the generation of the upright will be blessed.
Wealth and riches will be in their house,
and their righteousness will last for ever. ℟

Light shines in the darkness for the upright;
the righteous are merciful and full of compassion.
It is good for them to be generous in lending
and to manage their affairs with justice.
For they will never be shaken;
the righteous will be kept in everlasting remembrance. ℟

They will not be afraid of any evil rumours;
their heart is right;
they put their trust in the Lord.
Their heart is established and will not shrink,
until they see their desire upon their enemies. ℟

They have given freely to the poor,
and their righteousness stands fast for ever;
they will hold up their head with honour.
The wicked will see it and be angry;
they will gnash their teeth and pine away;
the desires of the wicked will perish. ℟

SECOND READING   **2 Timothy 1.1–7**

A reading from the second letter of Paul to Timothy.

Paul, an apostle of Christ Jesus by the will of God, for the sake of the promise of life that is in Christ Jesus, To Timothy, my beloved child: Grace, mercy, and peace from God the Father and Christ Jesus our Lord.

I am grateful to God – whom I worship with a clear conscience, as my ancestors did – when I remember you constantly in my prayers night and day. Recalling your tears, I long to see you so that I may be filled with joy. I am reminded of your sincere faith, a faith that lived first in your grandmother Lois and your mother Eunice and now, I am sure, lives in you. For this reason I remind you to rekindle the gift of God that is within you through the laying on of my hands; for God did not give us a spirit of cowardice, but rather a spirit of power and of love and of self-discipline.

GOSPEL (Alternative readings)

Either   **Matthew 13.44–46**

Hear the gospel of our Lord Jesus Christ according to Matthew.

Jesus said to his disciples: 'The kingdom of heaven is like treasure hidden in a field, which someone found and hid; then in his joy he goes and sells all that he has and buys that field.

Again, the kingdom of heaven is like a merchant in search of fine pearls; on finding one pearl of great value, he went and sold all that he had and bought it.'

Or   **Luke 11.33–36**

Hear the gospel of our Lord Jesus Christ according to Luke.

Jesus said to the crowds, 'No one after lighting a lamp puts it in a cellar, but on the lampstand so that those who enter may see the light. Your eye is the lamp of your body. If your eye is healthy, your whole body is full of light; but if it is not healthy, your body is full of darkness. Therefore consider whether the light in you is not darkness. If then your whole body is full of light, with no part of it in darkness, it will be as full of light as when a lamp gives you light with its rays.'

COLLECTS AND POST COMMUNION PRAYERS

ADVENT 1

COLLECT

Almighty God,
give us grace to cast away the works of darkness
and to put on the armour of light,
now in the time of this mortal life,
in which your Son Jesus Christ
    came to us in great humility;
that on the last day,
when he shall come again in his glorious majesty
    to judge the living and the dead,
we may rise to the life immortal;
through him who is alive and reigns with you,
in the unity of the Holy Spirit,
one God, now and for ever.

*This Collect may be used as the Post Communion on any day from the Second Sunday of
Advent until Christmas Eve instead of the Post Communion provided.*

POST COMMUNION

O Lord our God,
make us watchful and keep us faithful
as we await the coming of your Son our Lord;
that, when he shall appear,
he may not find us sleeping in sin
but active in his service
and joyful in his praise;
through Jesus Christ our Lord.

ADVENT 2

COLLECT

O Lord, raise up, we pray, your power
and come among us,
and with great might succour us;
that whereas, through our sins and wickedness
we are grievously hindered
in running the race that is set before us,
your bountiful grace and mercy
may speedily help and deliver us;
through Jesus Christ your Son our Lord,
to whom with you and the Holy Spirit,
be honour and glory, now and for ever.

POST COMMUNION

Father in heaven,
who sent your Son to redeem the world
and will send him again to be our judge:
give us grace so to imitate him
    in the humility and purity of his first coming
that, when he comes again,
we may be ready to greet him
with joyful love and firm faith;
through Jesus Christ our Lord.

ADVENT 3

COLLECT

O Lord Jesus Christ,
who at your first coming sent your messenger
to prepare your way before you:
grant that the ministers and stewards of your mysteries
may likewise so prepare and make ready your way
by turning the hearts of the disobedient
    to the wisdom of the just,
that at your second coming to judge the world

we may be found an acceptable people in your sight;
for you are alive and reign with the Father
in the unity of the Holy Spirit,
one God, now and for ever.

POST COMMUNION

We give you thanks, O Lord, for these heavenly gifts;
kindle in us the fire of your Spirit
that when your Christ comes again
we may shine as lights before his face;
who is alive and reigns now and for ever.

ADVENT 4

COLLECT

God our redeemer,
who prepared the Blessed Virgin Mary
to be the mother of your Son:
grant that, as she looked for his coming as our saviour,
so we may be ready to greet him
when he comes again as our judge;
who is alive and reigns with you,
in the unity of the Holy Spirit,
one God, now and for ever.

POST COMMUNION

Heavenly Father,
who chose the Blessed Virgin Mary
to be the mother of the promised saviour:
fill us your servants with your grace,
that in all things we may embrace your holy will
and with her rejoice in your salvation;
through Jesus Christ our Lord.

CHRISTMAS NIGHT

25 December

COLLECT

Eternal God,
who made this most holy night
to shine with the brightness of your one true light:
bring us, who have known the revelation
    of that light on earth,
to see the radiance of your heavenly glory;
through Jesus Christ your Son our Lord,
who is alive and reigns with you,
in the unity of the Holy Spirit,
one God, now and for ever.

POST COMMUNION

God our Father,
in this night you have made known to us again
the coming of our Lord Jesus Christ:
confirm our faith and fix our eyes on him
until the day dawns
and Christ the Morning Star rises in our hearts.
To him be glory both now and for ever.

CHRISTMAS DAY

25 December

COLLECT

Almighty God,
you have given us your only-begotten Son
to take our nature upon him
and as at this time to be born of a pure virgin:
grant that we, who have been born again
and made your children by adoption and grace,
may daily be renewed by your Holy Spirit;

through Jesus Christ your Son our Lord,
who is alive and reigns with you,
in the unity of the Holy Spirit,
one God, now and for ever.

POST COMMUNION

God our Father,
whose Word has come among us
in the Holy Child of Bethlehem:
may the light of faith illumine our hearts
and shine in our words and deeds;
through him who is Christ the Lord.

CHRISTMAS 1

COLLECT

Almighty God,
who wonderfully created us in your own image
and yet more wonderfully restored us
through your Son Jesus Christ:
grant that, as he came to share in our humanity,
so we may share the life of his divinity;
who is alive and reigns with you,
in the unity of the Holy Spirit,
one God, now and for ever.

POST COMMUNION

Heavenly Father,
whose blessed Son shared at Nazareth
the life of an earthly home:
help your Church to live as one family,
united in love and obedience,
and bring us all at last to our home in heaven;
through Jesus Christ our Lord.

CHRISTMAS 2

COLLECT

Almighty God,
in the birth of your Son
you have poured on us the new light of your incarnate Word,
and shown us the fullness of your love:
help us to walk in his light and dwell in his love
that we may know the fullness of his joy;
who is alive and reigns with you,
in the unity of the Holy Spirit,
one God, now and for ever.

POST COMMUNION

All praise to you,
almighty God and heavenly King,
who sent your Son into the world
to take our nature upon him
and to be born of a pure virgin:
grant that, as we are born again in him,
so he may continually dwell in us
and reign on earth as he reigns in heaven,
now and for ever.

EPIPHANY OF THE LORD

6 January

COLLECT

O God,
who by the leading of a star
manifested your only Son to the peoples of the earth:
mercifully grant that we,
who know you now by faith,
may at last behold your glory face to face;
through Jesus Christ your Son our Lord,
who is alive and reigns with you,

in the unity of the Holy Spirit,
one God, now and for ever.

POST COMMUNION

Lord God,
the bright splendour whom the nations seek:
may we who with the wise men
    have been drawn by your light
discern the glory of your presence in your Son,
the Word made flesh, Jesus Christ our Lord.

THE BAPTISM OF CHRIST

COLLECT

Eternal Father,
who at the baptism of Jesus
revealed him to be your Son,
anointing him with the Holy Spirit:
grant to us, who are born again by water and the Spirit,
that we may be faithful to our calling
    as your adopted children;
through Jesus Christ your Son our Lord,
who is alive and reigns with you,
in the unity of the Holy Spirit,
one God, now and for ever.

POST COMMUNION

Lord of all time and eternity,
you opened the heavens
    and revealed yourself as Father
in the baptism of Jesus your beloved Son:
by the power of your Spirit
complete the heavenly work of our rebirth
through the waters of the new creation;
through Jesus Christ our Lord.

EPIPHANY 2

COLLECT

Almighty God,
in Christ you make all things new:
transform the poverty of our nature
    by the riches of your grace,
and in the renewal of our lives
make known your heavenly glory;
through Jesus Christ your Son our Lord,
who is alive and reigns with you,
in the unity of the Holy Spirit,
one God, now and for ever.

POST COMMUNION

God of glory,
you nourish us with your Word
who is the bread of life:
fill us with your Holy Spirit
that through us the light of your glory
may shine in all the world.
We ask this in the name of Jesus Christ our Lord.

EPIPHANY 3

COLLECT

Almighty God,
whose Son revealed in signs and miracles
the wonder of your saving presence:
renew your people with your heavenly grace,
and in all our weakness
sustain us by your mighty power;
through Jesus Christ your Son our Lord,
who is alive and reigns with you,
in the unity of the Holy Spirit,
one God, now and for ever.

POST COMMUNION

Almighty Father,
whose Son our Saviour Jesus Christ
   is the light of the world:
may your people, ·
illumined by your word and sacraments,
shine with the radiance of his glory,
that he may be known, worshipped, and obeyed
   to the ends of the earth;
for he is alive and reigns, now and for ever.

EPIPHANY 4

COLLECT

God our creator,
who in the beginning
commanded the light to shine out of darkness:
we pray that the light of the glorious gospel of Christ
may dispel the darkness of ignorance and unbelief,
shine into the hearts of all your people,
and reveal the knowledge of your glory
   in the face of Jesus Christ your Son our Lord,
who is alive and reigns with you,
in the unity of the Holy Spirit,
one God, now and for ever.

POST COMMUNION

Generous Lord,
in word and eucharist we have proclaimed
   the mystery of your love:
help us so to live out our days
that we may be signs of your wonders in the world;
through Jesus Christ our Saviour.

PRESENTATION OF CHRIST

2 February

COLLECT

Almighty and ever-living God,
clothed in majesty,
whose beloved Son
    was this day presented in the Temple,
in substance of our flesh:
grant that we may be presented to you
with pure and clean hearts,
by your Son Jesus Christ our Lord,
who is alive and reigns with you,
in the unity of the Holy Spirit,
one God, now and for ever.

POST COMMUNION

Lord, you fulfilled the hope of Simeon and Anna,
who lived to welcome the Messiah:
may we, who have received these gifts beyond words,
prepare to meet Christ Jesus when he comes
    to bring us to eternal life;
for he is alive and reigns, now and for ever.

FIFTH SUNDAY BEFORE LENT

COLLECT

Almighty God,
by whose grace alone we are accepted
    and called to your service:
strengthen us by your Holy Spirit
and make us worthy of our calling;
through Jesus Christ your Son our Lord,
who is alive and reigns with you,
in the unity of the Holy Spirit,
one God, now and for ever.

POST COMMUNION

God of truth,
we have seen with our eyes
    and touched with our hands the bread of life:
strengthen our faith
that we may grow in love for you and for each other;
through Jesus Christ our Lord.

FOURTH SUNDAY BEFORE LENT

COLLECT

O God,
you know us to be set
in the midst of so many and great dangers,
that by reason of the frailty of our nature
we cannot always stand upright:
grant to us such strength and protection
as may support us in all dangers
and carry us through all temptations;
through Jesus Christ your Son our Lord,
who is alive and reigns with you,
in the unity of the Holy Spirit,
one God, now and for ever.

POST COMMUNION

Go before us, Lord, in all we do
with your most gracious favour,
and guide us with your continual help,
that in all our works
begun, continued and ended in you,
we may glorify your holy name,
and finally by your mercy receive everlasting life;
through Jesus Christ our Lord.

THIRD SUNDAY BEFORE LENT

COLLECT

Almighty God,
who alone can bring order
to the unruly wills and passions of sinful humanity:
give your people grace
so to love what you command
and to desire what you promise,
that, among the many changes of this world,
our hearts may surely there be fixed
where true joys are to be found;
through Jesus Christ your Son our Lord,
who is alive and reigns with you,
in the unity of the Holy Spirit,
one God, now and for ever.

POST COMMUNION

Merciful Father,
who gave Jesus Christ to be for us the bread of life,
that those who come to him should never hunger:
draw us to the Lord in faith and love,
that we may eat and drink with him
at his table in the kingdom,
where he is alive and reigns, now and for ever.

SECOND SUNDAY BEFORE LENT

COLLECT

Almighty God,
you have created the heavens and the earth
and made us in your own image:
teach us to discern your hand in all your works
and your likeness in all your children;
through Jesus Christ your Son our Lord,

who with you and the Holy Spirit
　　reigns supreme over all things,
now and for ever.

POST COMMUNION

God our creator,
by your gift
the tree of life was set at the heart of the earthly paradise,
and the bread of life at the heart of your Church:
may we who have been nourished at your table on earth
be transformed by the glory of the Saviour's cross
and enjoy the delights of eternity;
through Jesus Christ our Lord.

SUNDAY NEXT BEFORE LENT

COLLECT

Almighty Father,
whose Son was revealed in majesty
before he suffered death upon the cross:
give us grace to perceive his glory,
that we may be strengthened to suffer with him
and be changed into his likeness, from glory to glory;
who is alive and reigns with you,
in the unity of the Holy Spirit,
one God, now and for ever.

POST COMMUNION

Holy God,
we see your glory in the face of Jesus Christ:
may we who are partakers at his table
reflect his life in word and deed,
that all the world may know
　　his power to change and save.
This we ask through Jesus Christ our Lord.

ASH WEDNESDAY

COLLECT

Almighty and everlasting God,
you hate nothing that you have made
and forgive the sins of all those who are penitent:
create and make in us new and contrite hearts
that we, worthily lamenting our sins
and acknowledging our wretchedness,
may receive from you, the God of all mercy,
perfect remission and forgiveness;
through Jesus Christ your Son our Lord,
who is alive and reigns with you,
in the unity of the Holy Spirit,
one God, now and for ever.

This Collect may be used as the Post Communion on any day from the First Sunday of Lent until the Saturday after the Fourth Sunday of Lent instead of the Post Communion provided.

POST COMMUNION

Almighty God,
you have given your only Son to be for us
both a sacrifice for sin
and also an example of godly life:
give us grace
that we may always most thankfully receive
these his inestimable gifts,
and also daily endeavour to follow
    the blessed steps of his most holy life;
through Jesus Christ our Lord.

LENT 1

COLLECT

Almighty God,
whose Son Jesus Christ fasted forty days in the wilderness,
and was tempted as we are, yet without sin:

give us grace to discipline ourselves
    in obedience to your Spirit;
and, as you know our weakness,
so may we know your power to save;
through Jesus Christ your Son our Lord,
who is alive and reigns with you,
in the unity of the Holy Spirit,
one God, now and for ever.

POST COMMUNION

Lord God,
you have renewed us with the living bread from heaven;
by it you nourish our faith,
increase our hope,
and strengthen our love:
teach us always to hunger for him
    who is the true and living bread,
and enable us to live by every word
    that proceeds from out of your mouth;
through Jesus Christ our Lord.

LENT 2

COLLECT

Almighty God,
you show to those who are in error the light of your truth,
that they may return to the way of righteousness:
grant to all those who are admitted
    into the fellowship of Christ's religion,
that they may reject those things
    that are contrary to their profession,
and follow all such things as are agreeable to the same;
through our Lord Jesus Christ,
who is alive and reigns with you,
in the unity of the Holy Spirit,
one God, now and for ever.

POST COMMUNION

Almighty God,
you see that we have no power of ourselves to help ourselves:
keep us both outwardly in our bodies,
and inwardly in our souls;
that we may be defended from all adversities
    which may happen to the body,
and from all evil thoughts
    which may assault and hurt the soul;
through Jesus Christ our Lord.

LENT 3

COLLECT

Almighty God,
whose most dear Son went not up to joy
    but first he suffered pain,
and entered not into glory before he was crucified:
mercifully grant that we, walking in the way of the cross,
may find it none other than the way of life and peace;
through Jesus Christ your Son our Lord,
who is alive and reigns with you,
in the unity of the Holy Spirit,
one God, now and for ever.

POST COMMUNION

Merciful Lord,
grant your people grace to withstand the temptations
    of the world, the flesh and the devil,
and with pure hearts and minds to follow you,
    the only God;
through Jesus Christ our Lord.

LENT 4

COLLECT

Merciful Lord,
absolve your people from their offences,
that through your bountiful goodness
we may all be delivered from the chains of those sins
which by our frailty we have committed;
grant this, heavenly Father,
for Jesus Christ's sake, our blessed Lord and Saviour,
who is alive and reigns with you,
in the unity of the Holy Spirit,
one God, now and for ever.

POST COMMUNION

Lord God,
whose blessed Son our Saviour
gave his back to the smiters
and did not hide his face from shame:
give us grace to endure the sufferings of this present time
with sure confidence in the glory that shall be revealed;
through Jesus Christ our Lord.

Mothering Sunday may be celebrated in preference to the provision for the
Fourth Sunday of Lent.

MOTHERING SUNDAY

COLLECT

God of compassion,
whose Son Jesus Christ, the child of Mary,
shared the life of a home in Nazareth,
and on the cross drew the whole human family to himself:
strengthen us in our daily living
that in joy and in sorrow
we may know the power of your presence
   to bind together and to heal;

through Jesus Christ your Son our Lord,
who is alive and reigns with you,
in the unity of the Holy Spirit,
one God, now and for ever.

POST COMMUNION

Loving God,
as a mother feeds her children at the breast
you feed us in this sacrament
    with the food and drink of eternal life:
help us who have tasted your goodness
to grow in grace within the household of faith;
through Jesus Christ our Lord.

*Mothering Sunday may be celebrated in preference to the provision for the
Fourth Sunday of Lent.*

LENT 5

COLLECT

Most merciful God,
who by the death and resurrection of your Son Jesus Christ
delivered and saved the world:
grant that by faith in him who suffered on the cross
we may triumph in the power of his victory;
through Jesus Christ your Son our Lord,
who is alive and reigns with you,
in the unity of the Holy Spirit,
one God, now and for ever.

POST COMMUNION

Lord Jesus Christ,
you have taught us
that what we do for the least of our brothers and sisters
we do also for you:
give us the will to be the servant of others
as you were the servant of all,

and gave up your life and died for us,
but are alive and reign, now and for ever.

PALM SUNDAY

Use this Collect until Maundy Thursday.

COLLECT

Almighty and everlasting God,
who in your tender love towards the human race
　　sent your Son our Saviour Jesus Christ
to take upon him our flesh
and to suffer death upon the cross:
grant that we may follow the example
　　of his patience and humility,
and also be made partakers of his resurrection;
through Jesus Christ your Son our Lord,
who is alive and reigns with you,
in the unity of the Holy Spirit,
one God, now and for ever.

POST COMMUNION

Lord Jesus Christ,
you humbled yourself in taking the form of a servant,
and in obedience died on the cross for our salvation:
give us the mind to follow you
and to proclaim you as Lord and King,
to the glory of God the Father.

MAUNDY THURSDAY

COLLECT

God our Father,
you have invited us to share in the supper
which your Son gave to his Church
to proclaim his death until he comes:
may he nourish us by his presence,

and unite us in his love;
who is alive and reigns with you,
in the unity of the Holy Spirit,
one God, now and for ever.

POST COMMUNION

Lord Jesus Christ,
we thank you that in this wonderful sacrament
you have given us the memorial of your passion:
grant us so to reverence the sacred mysteries
    of your body and blood
that we may know within ourselves
and show forth in our lives
the fruit of your redemption,
for you are alive and reign, now and for ever.

GOOD FRIDAY

COLLECT

Almighty Father,
look with mercy on this your family
for which our Lord Jesus Christ
    was content to be betrayed
    and given up into the hands of sinners
    and to suffer death upon the cross;
who is alive and glorified
    with you and the Holy Spirit,
one God, now and for ever.

EASTER EVE

COLLECT

Grant, Lord,
that we who are baptized into the death
    of your Son our Saviour Jesus Christ
may continually put to death our evil desires
    and be buried with him;

and that through the grave and gate of death
we may pass to our joyful resurrection;
through his merits, who died and was buried
   and rose again for us,
your Son Jesus Christ our Lord.

EASTER VIGIL

Use the Collect and Post Communion Prayer for Easter Day.

EASTER DAY

COLLECT

Lord of all life and power,
who through the mighty resurrection of your Son
overcame the old order of sin and death
to make all things new in him:
grant that we, being dead to sin
and alive to you in Jesus Christ,
may reign with him in glory;
to whom with you and the Holy Spirit
be praise and honour, glory and might,
now and in all eternity.

POST COMMUNION

God of Life,
who for our redemption gave your only-begotten Son
   to the death of the cross,
and by his glorious resurrection
have delivered us from the power of our enemy:
grant us so to die daily to sin,
that we may evermore live with him
   in the joy of his risen life;
through Jesus Christ our Lord.

EASTER 2

COLLECT

Almighty Father,
you have given your only Son to die for our sins
and to rise again for our justification:
grant us so to put away the leaven of malice and wickedness
that we may always serve you
in pureness of living and truth;
through the merits of your Son Jesus Christ our Lord,
who is alive and reigns with you,
in the unity of the Holy Spirit,
one God, now and for ever.

POST COMMUNION

Lord God our Father,
through our Saviour Jesus Christ
you have assured your children of eternal life
and in baptism have made us one with him:
deliver us from the death of sin
and raise us to new life in your love,
in the fellowship of the Holy Spirit,
by the grace of our Lord Jesus Christ.

EASTER 3

COLLECT

Almighty Father,
who in your great mercy gladdened the disciples
    with the sight of the risen Lord:
give us such knowledge of his presence with us,
that we may be strengthened and sustained
    by his risen life
and serve you continually in righteousness and truth;
through Jesus Christ your Son our Lord,
who is alive and reigns with you,
in the unity of the Holy Spirit,
one God, now and for ever.

POST COMMUNION

Living God,
your Son made himself known to his disciples
in the breaking of bread:
open the eyes of our faith,
that we may see him in all his redeeming work;
who is alive and reigns, now and for ever.

EASTER 4

COLLECT

Almighty God,
whose Son Jesus Christ is the resurrection and the life:
raise us, who trust in him,
from the death of sin to the life of righteousness,
that we may seek those things which are above,
where he reigns with you
in the unity of the Holy Spirit,
one God, now and for ever.

POST COMMUNION

Merciful Father,
you gave your Son Jesus Christ to be the good shepherd,
and in his love for us to lay down his life and rise again:
keep us always under his protection,
and give us grace to follow in his steps;
through Jesus Christ our Lord.

EASTER 5

COLLECT

Almighty God,
who through your only-begotten Son Jesus Christ
have overcome death and opened to us
   the gate of everlasting life:

grant that, as by your grace going before us
    you put into our minds good desires,
so by your continual help
we may bring them to good effect;
through Jesus Christ our risen Lord,
who is alive and reigns with you,
in the unity of the Holy Spirit,
one God, now and for ever.

POST COMMUNION

Eternal God,
whose Son Jesus Christ is the way, the truth, and the life:
grant us to walk in his way,
to rejoice in his truth,
and to share his risen life;
who is alive and reigns, now and for ever.

EASTER 6

COLLECT

God our redeemer,
you have delivered us from the power of darkness
and brought us into the kingdom of your Son:
grant, that as by his death he has recalled us to life,
so by his continual presence in us he may raise us
    to eternal joy;
through Jesus Christ your Son our Lord,
who is alive and reigns with you,
in the unity of the Holy Spirit,
one God, now and for ever.

POST COMMUNION

God our Father,
whose Son Jesus Christ gives the water of eternal life:
may we thirst for you,
the spring of life and source of goodness,
through him who is alive and reigns, now and for ever.

ASCENSION DAY

COLLECT

Grant, we pray, almighty God,
that as we believe your only-begotten Son
    our Lord Jesus Christ
to have ascended into the heavens,
so we in heart and mind may also ascend
and with him continually dwell;
who is alive and reigns with you,
in the unity of the Holy Spirit,
one God, now and for ever.

POST COMMUNION

God our Father,
you have raised our humanity in Christ
and have fed us with the bread of heaven:
mercifully grant that, nourished with such spiritual blessings,
we may set our hearts in the heavenly places;
through Jesus Christ our Lord.

EASTER 7

COLLECT

O God the king of glory,
you have exalted your only Son Jesus Christ
with great triumph to your kingdom in heaven:
we beseech you, leave us not comfortless,
but send your Holy Spirit to strengthen us
and exalt us to the place
    where our Saviour Christ is gone before,
who is alive and reigns with you,
in the unity of the Holy Spirit,
one God, now and for ever.

POST COMMUNION

Eternal God, giver of love and power,
your Son Jesus Christ has sent us into all the world
to preach the gospel of his kingdom:
confirm us in this mission,
and help us to live the good news we proclaim;
through Jesus Christ our Lord.

PENTECOST

COLLECT

God, who as at this time
taught the hearts of your faithful people
by sending to them the light of your Holy Spirit:
grant us by the same Spirit
to have a right judgement in all things
and evermore to rejoice in his holy comfort;
through the merits of Christ Jesus our Saviour,
who is alive and reigns with you,
in the unity of the Holy Spirit,
one God, now and for ever.

POST COMMUNION

Faithful God,
who fulfilled the promises of Easter
by sending us your Holy Spirit
and opening to every race and nation
the way of life eternal:
open our lips by your Spirit,
that every tongue may tell of your glory;
through Jesus Christ our Lord.

TRINITY SUNDAY

COLLECT

Almighty and everlasting God,
you have given us your servants grace,
by the confession of a true faith,
to acknowledge the glory of the eternal Trinity
and in the power of the divine majesty to worship the Unity:
keep us steadfast in this faith,
that we may evermore be defended from all adversities;
through Jesus Christ your Son our Lord,
who is alive and reigns with you,
in the unity of the Holy Spirit,
one God, now and for ever.

POST COMMUNION

Almighty and eternal God,
you have revealed yourself as Father, Son and Holy Spirit,
and live and reign in the perfect unity of love:
hold us firm in this faith,
that we may know you in all your ways
and evermore rejoice in your eternal glory,
who are three Persons yet one God,
now and for ever.

THANKSGIVING FOR HOLY COMMUNION

COLLECT

Lord Jesus Christ,
we thank you that in this wonderful sacrament
you have given us the memorial of your passion:
grant us so to reverence the sacred mysteries
    of your body and blood
that we may know within ourselves
and show forth in our lives
the fruits of your redemption;
for you are alive and reign with the Father
in the unity of the Holy Spirit,
one God, now and for ever.

POST COMMUNION

All praise to you, our God and Father,
for you have fed us with the bread of heaven
and quenched our thirst from the true vine:
hear our prayer that, being grafted into Christ,
we may grow together in unity
and feast with him in his kingdom;
through Jesus Christ our Lord.

FIRST SUNDAY AFTER TRINITY

COLLECT

O God,
the strength of all those who put their trust in you,
mercifully accept our prayers
and, because through the weakness of our mortal nature
we can do no good thing without you,
grant us the help of your grace,
that in the keeping of your commandments
we may please you both in will and deed;
through Jesus Christ your Son our Lord,
who is alive and reigns with you,
in the unity of the Holy Spirit,
one God, now and for ever.

POST COMMUNION

Eternal Father,
we thank you for nourishing us
with these heavenly gifts:
may our communion strengthen us in faith,
build us up in hope,
and make us grow in love;
for the sake of Jesus Christ our Lord.

SECOND SUNDAY AFTER TRINITY

COLLECT

Lord, you have taught us
that all our doings without love are nothing worth:
send your Holy Spirit
and pour into our hearts that most excellent gift of love,
the true bond of peace and of all virtues,
without which whoever lives is counted dead before you.
Grant this for your only Son Jesus Christ's sake,
who is alive and reigns with you,
in the unity of the Holy Spirit,
one God, now and for ever.

POST COMMUNION

Loving Father,
we thank you for feeding us at the supper of your Son:
sustain us with your Spirit,
that we may serve you here on earth
until our joy is complete in heaven,
and we share in the eternal banquet
with Jesus Christ our Lord.

THIRD SUNDAY AFTER TRINITY

COLLECT

Almighty God,
you have broken the tyranny of sin
and have sent the Spirit of your Son into our hearts
    whereby we call you Father:
give us grace to dedicate our freedom to your service,
that we and all creation may be brought
    to the glorious liberty of the children of God;
through Jesus Christ your Son our Lord,
who is alive and reigns with you,
in the unity of the Holy Spirit,
one God, now and for ever.

POST COMMUNION

O God, whose beauty is beyond our imagining
and whose power we cannot comprehend:
show us your glory as far as we can grasp it,
and shield us from knowing more than we can bear
until we may look upon you without fear;
through Jesus Christ our Saviour.

FOURTH SUNDAY AFTER TRINITY

COLLECT

O God, the protector of all who trust in you,
without whom nothing is strong, nothing is holy:
increase and multiply upon us your mercy;
that with you as our ruler and guide
we may so pass through things temporal
that we lose not our hold on things eternal;
grant this, heavenly Father,
for our Lord Jesus Christ's sake,
who is alive and reigns with you,
in the unity of the Holy Spirit,
one God, now and for ever.

POST COMMUNION

Eternal God,
comfort of the afflicted and healer of the broken,
you have fed us at the table of life and hope:
teach us the ways of gentleness and peace,
that all the world may acknowledge
the kingdom of your Son Jesus Christ our Lord.

FIFTH SUNDAY AFTER TRINITY

COLLECT

Almighty and everlasting God,
by whose Spirit the whole body of the Church
   is governed and sanctified:
hear our prayer which we offer for all your faithful people,
that in their vocation and ministry
they may serve you in holiness and truth
to the glory of your name;
through our Lord and Saviour Jesus Christ,
who is alive and reigns with you,
in the unity of the Holy Spirit,
one God, now and for ever.

POST COMMUNION

Grant, O Lord, we beseech you,
that the course of this world may be so peaceably ordered
   by your governance,
that your Church may joyfully serve you
   in all godly quietness;
through Jesus Christ our Lord.

SIXTH SUNDAY AFTER TRINITY

COLLECT

Merciful God,
you have prepared for those who love you
such good things as pass our understanding:
pour into our hearts such love toward you
that we, loving you in all things and above all things,
may obtain your promises,
which exceed all that we can desire;
through Jesus Christ your Son our Lord,
who is alive and reigns with you,
in the unity of the Holy Spirit,
one God, now and for ever.

POST COMMUNION

God of our pilgrimage,
you have led us to the living water:
refresh and sustain us
as we go forward on our journey,
in the name of Jesus Christ our Lord.

SEVENTH SUNDAY AFTER TRINITY

COLLECT

Lord of all power and might,
the author and giver of all good things:
graft in our hearts the love of your name,
increase in us true religion,
nourish us with all goodness,
and of your great mercy keep us in the same;
through Jesus Christ your Son our Lord,
who is alive and reigns with you,
in the unity of the Holy Spirit,
one God, now and for ever.

POST COMMUNION

Lord God, whose Son is the true vine and the source of life,
ever giving himself that the world may live:
may we so receive within ourselves
    the power of his death and passion
that, in his saving cup,
    we may share his glory and be made perfect in his love;
for he is alive and reigns, now and for ever.

EIGHTH SUNDAY AFTER TRINITY

COLLECT

Almighty Lord and everlasting God,
we beseech you to direct, sanctify and govern
    both our hearts and bodies

in the ways of your laws
    and the works of your commandments;
that through your most mighty protection, both here and ever,
we may be preserved in body and soul;
through our Lord and Saviour Jesus Christ,
who is alive and reigns with you,
in the unity of the Holy Spirit,
one God, now and for ever.

POST COMMUNION

Strengthen for service, Lord,
the hands that have taken holy things;
may the ears which have heard your word
    be deaf to clamour and dispute;
may the tongues which have sung your praise
    be free from deceit;
may the eyes which have seen the tokens of your love
    shine with the light of hope;
and may the bodies which have been fed with your body
    be refreshed with the fullness of your life;
glory to you for ever.

NINTH SUNDAY AFTER TRINITY

COLLECT

Almighty God,
who sent your Holy Spirit
to be the life and light of your Church:
open our hearts to the riches of your grace,
that we may bring forth the fruit of the Spirit
in love and joy and peace;
through Jesus Christ your Son our Lord,
who is alive and reigns with you,
in the unity of the Holy Spirit,
one God, now and for ever.

POST COMMUNION

Holy Father,
who gathered us here around the table of your Son
to share this meal with the whole household of God:
in that new world
    where you reveal the fullness of your peace,
gather people of every race and language
    to share in the eternal banquet
    of Jesus Christ our Lord.

TENTH SUNDAY AFTER TRINITY

COLLECT

Let your merciful ears, O Lord,
be open to the prayers of your humble servants;
and that they may obtain their petitions
make them to ask such things as shall please you;
through Jesus Christ your Son our Lord,
who is alive and reigns with you,
in the unity of the Holy Spirit,
one God, now and for ever.

POST COMMUNION

God of our pilgrimage,
you have willed that the gate of mercy
should stand open for those who trust in you:
look upon us with your favour
that we who follow the path of your will
may never wander from the way of life;
through Jesus Christ our Lord.

ELEVENTH SUNDAY AFTER TRINITY

COLLECT

O God, you declare your almighty power
most chiefly in showing mercy and pity:
mercifully grant to us such a measure of your grace,
that we, running the way of your commandments,
may receive your gracious promises,
and be made partakers of your heavenly treasure;
through Jesus Christ your Son our Lord,
who is alive and reigns with you,
in the unity of the Holy Spirit,
one God, now and for ever.

POST COMMUNION

Lord of all mercy,
we your faithful people have celebrated that one true sacrifice
    which takes away our sins and brings pardon and peace:
by our communion
keep us firm on the foundation of the gospel
and preserve us from all sin;
through Jesus Christ our Lord.

TWELFTH SUNDAY AFTER TRINITY

COLLECT

Almighty and everlasting God,
you are always more ready to hear than we to pray
and to give more than either we desire or deserve:
pour down upon us the abundance of your mercy,
forgiving us those things of which our conscience is afraid
and giving us those good things
    which we are not worthy to ask
but through the merits and mediation
of Jesus Christ your Son our Lord,
who is alive and reigns with you,
in the unity of the Holy Spirit,
one God, now and for ever.

POST COMMUNION

God of all mercy,
in this eucharist you have set aside our sins
and given us your healing:
grant that we who are made whole in Christ
may bring that healing to this broken world,
in the name of Jesus Christ our Lord.

THIRTEENTH SUNDAY AFTER TRINITY

COLLECT

Almighty God,
who called your Church to bear witness
that you were in Christ reconciling the world to yourself:
help us to proclaim the good news of your love,
that all who hear it may be drawn to you;
through him who was lifted up on the cross,
and reigns with you in the unity of the Holy Spirit,
one God, now and for ever.

POST COMMUNION

God our creator,
you feed your children with the true manna,
the living bread from heaven:
let this holy food sustain us through our earthly pilgrimage
until we come to that place
    where hunger and thirst are no more;
through Jesus Christ our Lord.

FOURTEENTH SUNDAY AFTER TRINITY

COLLECT

Almighty God,
whose only Son has opened for us
a new and living way into your presence:

give us pure hearts and steadfast wills
to worship you in spirit and in truth;
through Jesus Christ your Son our Lord,
who is alive and reigns with you,
in the unity of the Holy Spirit,
one God, now and for ever.

POST COMMUNION

Lord God, the source of truth and love,
keep us faithful to the apostles' teaching and fellowship,
united in prayer and the breaking of bread,
and one in joy and simplicity of heart,
in Jesus Christ our Lord.

FIFTEENTH SUNDAY AFTER TRINITY

COLLECT

God, who in generous mercy sent the Holy Spirit
    upon your Church in the burning fire of your love:
grant that your people may be fervent
    in the fellowship of the gospel
that, always abiding in you,
they may be found steadfast in faith and active in service;
through Jesus Christ your Son our Lord,
who is alive and reigns with you,
in the unity of the Holy Spirit,
one God, now and for ever.

POST COMMUNION

Keep, O Lord, your Church,
    with your perpetual mercy;
and, because without you our human frailty cannot but fall,
keep us ever by your help from all things hurtful,
and lead us to all things profitable to our salvation;
through Jesus Christ our Lord.

SIXTEENTH SUNDAY AFTER TRINITY

COLLECT

O Lord, we beseech you mercifully to hear the prayers
    of your people who call upon you;
and grant that they may both perceive and know
what things they ought to do,
and also may have grace and power
    faithfully to fulfil them;
through Jesus Christ your Son our Lord,
who is alive and reigns with you,
in the unity of the Holy Spirit,
one God, now and for ever.

POST COMMUNION

Almighty God,
you have taught us through your Son
that love is the fulfilling of the law:
grant that we may love you with our whole heart
and our neighbours as ourselves;
through Jesus Christ our Lord.

SEVENTEENTH SUNDAY AFTER TRINITY

COLLECT

Almighty God,
you have made us for yourself,
and our hearts are restless till they find their rest in you:
pour your love into our hearts and draw us to yourself,
and so bring us at last to your heavenly city
where we shall see you face to face;
through Jesus Christ your Son our Lord,
who is alive and reigns with you,
in the unity of the Holy Spirit,
one God, now and for ever.

POST COMMUNION

Lord, we pray that your grace
may always precede and follow us,
and make us continually to be given to all good works;
through Jesus Christ our Lord.

EIGHTEENTH SUNDAY AFTER TRINITY

COLLECT

Almighty and everlasting God,
increase in us your gift of faith
that, forsaking what lies behind
and reaching out to that which is before,
we may run the way of your commandments
and win the crown of everlasting joy;
through Jesus Christ your Son our Lord,
who is alive and reigns with you,
in the unity of the Holy Spirit,
one God, now and for ever.

POST COMMUNION

We praise and thank you, O Christ, for this sacred feast:
for here we receive you,
here the memory of your passion is renewed,
here our minds are filled with grace,
and here a pledge of future glory is given,
when we shall feast at that table where you reign
with all your saints for ever.

NINETEENTH SUNDAY AFTER TRINITY

COLLECT

O God, forasmuch as without you
we are not able to please you;
mercifully grant that your Holy Spirit
may in all things direct and rule our hearts;
through Jesus Christ your Son our Lord,
who is alive and reigns with you,
in the unity of the Holy Spirit,
one God, now and for ever.

POST COMMUNION

Holy and blessed God,
you have fed us with the body and blood of your Son
and filled us with your Holy Spirit:
may we honour you,
not only with our lips
but in lives dedicated to the service
   of Jesus Christ our Lord.

TWENTIETH SUNDAY AFTER TRINITY

COLLECT

God, the giver of life,
whose Holy Spirit wells up within your Church:
by the Spirit's gifts equip us to live the gospel of Christ
   and make us eager to do your will,
that we may share with the whole creation
   the joys of eternal life;
through Jesus Christ your Son our Lord,
who is alive and reigns with you,
in the unity of the Holy Spirit,
one God, now and for ever.

POST COMMUNION

God our Father,
whose Son, the light unfailing,
has come from heaven to deliver the world
    from the darkness of ignorance:
let these holy mysteries open the eyes of our understanding
that we may know the way of life,
and walk in it without stumbling;
through Jesus Christ our Lord.

TWENTY-FIRST SUNDAY AFTER TRINITY

COLLECT

Grant, we beseech you, merciful Lord,
to your faithful people pardon and peace,
that they may be cleansed from all their sins
and serve you with a quiet mind;
through Jesus Christ your Son our Lord,
who is alive and reigns with you,
in the unity of the Holy Spirit,
one God, now and for ever.

POST COMMUNION

Father of light,
in whom is no change or shadow of turning,
you give us every good and perfect gift
and have brought us to birth by your word of truth:
may we be a living sign of that kingdom
where your whole creation will be made perfect
    in Jesus Christ our Lord.

LAST SUNDAY AFTER TRINITY

COLLECT

Blessed Lord,
who caused all holy scriptures
   to be written for our learning:
help us so to hear them,
to read, mark, learn and inwardly digest them
that, through patience, and the comfort of your holy word,
we may embrace and for ever hold fast
   the hope of everlasting life,
which you have given us in our Saviour Jesus Christ,
who is alive and reigns with you,
in the unity of the Holy Spirit,
one God, now and for ever.

POST COMMUNION

God of all grace,
your Son Jesus Christ fed the hungry
with the bread of his life
and the word of his kingdom:
renew your people with your heavenly grace,
and in all our weakness
sustain us by your true and living bread;
who is alive and reigns, now and for ever.

ALL SAINTS' DAY

1 November

For use also on All Saints' Sunday.

COLLECT

Almighty God,
you have knit together your elect
in one communion and fellowship
   in the mystical body of your Son Christ our Lord:
grant us grace so to follow your blessed saints
in all virtuous and godly living

that we may come to those inexpressible joys
that you have prepared for those who truly love you;
through Jesus Christ your Son our Lord,
who is alive and reigns with you,
in the unity of the Holy Spirit,
one God, now and for ever.

POST COMMUNION

God, the source of all holiness
    and giver of all good things:
may we who have shared at this table
    as strangers and pilgrims here on earth
be welcomed with all your saints
    to the heavenly feast on the day of your kingdom;
through Jesus Christ our Lord.

FOURTH SUNDAY BEFORE ADVENT

COLLECT

Almighty and eternal God,
you have kindled the flame of love
    in the hearts of the saints:
grant to us the same faith and power of love,
that, as we rejoice in their triumphs,
we may be sustained by their example and fellowship;
through Jesus Christ your Son our Lord,
who is alive and reigns with you,
in the unity of the Holy Spirit,
one God, now and for ever.

POST COMMUNION

Lord of heaven,
in this eucharist you have brought us near
    to an innumerable company of angels
    and to the spirits of the saints made perfect:
as in this food of our earthly pilgrimage
    we have shared their fellowship,
so may we come to share their joy in heaven;
through Jesus Christ our Lord.

THIRD SUNDAY BEFORE ADVENT

COLLECT

Almighty Father,
whose will is to restore all things
in your beloved Son, the king of all:
govern the hearts and minds of those in authority,
and bring the families of the nations,
divided and torn apart by the ravages of sin,
to be subject to his just and gentle rule;
who is alive and reigns with you,
in the unity of the Holy Spirit,
one God, now and for ever.

POST COMMUNION

God of peace,
whose Son Jesus Christ proclaimed the kingdom
and restored the broken to wholeness of life:
look with compassion on the anguish of the world,
and by your healing power
make whole both people and nations;
through our Lord and Saviour Jesus Christ.

SECOND SUNDAY BEFORE ADVENT

COLLECT

Heavenly Father,
whose blessed Son was revealed
   to destroy the works of the devil
and to make us the children of God and heirs of eternal life:
grant that we, having this hope,
may purify ourselves even as he is pure;
that when he shall appear in power and great glory
we may be made like him
   in his eternal and glorious kingdom;
where he is alive and reigns with you,
in the unity of the Holy Spirit,
one God, now and for ever.

POST COMMUNION

Gracious Lord,
in this holy sacrament
you give substance to our hope:
bring us at the last
to that fullness of life for which we long;
through Jesus Christ our Saviour.

CHRIST THE KING

COLLECT

Eternal Father,
whose Son Jesus Christ ascended to the throne of heaven
    that he might rule over all things as Lord and King:
keep the Church in the unity of the Spirit
and in the bond of peace,
and bring the whole created order to worship at his feet;
who is alive and reigns with you,
in the unity of the Holy Spirit,
one God, now and for ever.

POST COMMUNION

Stir up, O Lord,
the wills of your faithful people;
that they, plenteously bringing forth the fruit of good works,
may by you be plenteously rewarded;
through Jesus Christ our Lord.

DEDICATION FESTIVAL

COLLECT

Almighty God,
to whose glory we celebrate the dedication
    of this house of prayer:
we praise you for the many blessings
you have given to those who worship you here:
and we pray that all who seek you in this place
    may find you,
and, being filled with the Holy Spirit,
may become a living temple acceptable to you;
through Jesus Christ your Son our Lord,
who is alive and reigns with you,
in the unity of the Holy Spirit,
one God, now and for ever.

POST COMMUNION

Father in heaven,
whose Church on earth is a sign of your heavenly peace,
an image of the new and eternal Jerusalem:
grant to us in the days of our pilgrimage
that, fed with the living bread of heaven,
and united in the body of your Son,
we may be the temple of your presence,
the place of your glory on earth,
and a sign of your peace in the world;
through Jesus Christ our Lord.

THE NAMING AND CIRCUMCISION OF JESUS

1 January

COLLECT

Almighty God,
whose blessed Son was circumcised
in obedience to the law for our sake
and given the Name that is above every name:

give us grace faithfully to bear his Name,
to worship him in the freedom of the Spirit,
and to proclaim him as the Saviour of the world;
who is alive and reigns with you,
in the unity of the Holy Spirit,
one God, now and for ever.

POST COMMUNION

Eternal God,
whose incarnate Son was given the Name of Saviour:
grant that we who have shared
    in this sacrament of our salvation
may live out our years in the power
    of the Name above all other names,
Jesus Christ our Lord.

CONVERSION OF ST PAUL

25 January

COLLECT

Almighty God,
who caused the light of the gospel
to shine throughout the world
through the preaching of your servant Saint Paul:
grant that we who celebrate his wonderful conversion
may follow him in bearing witness to your truth;
through Jesus Christ your Son our Lord,
who is alive and reigns with you,
in the unity of the Holy Spirit,
one God, now and for ever.

POST COMMUNION

Almighty God,
who on the day of Pentecost
sent your Holy Spirit to the apostles
with the wind from heaven and in tongues of flame,
filling them with joy and boldness to preach the gospel:

by the power of the same Spirit
strengthen us to witness to your truth
and to draw everyone to the fire of your love;
through Jesus Christ our Lord.

or

Lord God, the source of truth and love,
keep us faithful to the apostles' teaching and fellowship,
united in prayer and the breaking of bread,
and one in joy and simplicity of heart,
in Jesus Christ our Lord.

ST JOSEPH

19 March

COLLECT

God our Father,
who from the family of your servant David
raised up Joseph the carpenter
to be the guardian of your incarnate Son
and husband of the Blessed Virgin Mary:
give us grace to follow him
in faithful obedience to your commands;
through Jesus Christ your Son our Lord,
who is alive and reigns with you,
in the unity of the Holy Spirit,
one God, now and for ever.

POST COMMUNION

Heavenly Father,
whose Son grew in wisdom and stature
in the home of Joseph the carpenter of Nazareth
and on the wood of the cross perfected the work
    of the world's salvation:
help us, strengthened by this sacrament of his passion,
to count the wisdom of the world as foolishness,
and to walk with him in simplicity and trust;
through Jesus Christ our Lord.

THE ANNUNCIATION

25 March

COLLECT

We beseech you, O Lord,
pour your grace into our hearts,
that as we have known the incarnation
    of your Son Jesus Christ
by the message of an angel,
so by his cross and passion
we may be brought to the glory of his resurrection;
through Jesus Christ your Son our Lord,
who is alive and reigns with you,
in the unity of the Holy Spirit,
one God, now and and for ever.

POST COMMUNION

God most high
whose handmaid bore the Word made flesh:
we thank you that in this sacrament of our redemption
you visit us with your Holy Spirit
and overshadow us by your power;
strengthen us to walk with Mary the joyful path of obedience
and so to bring forth the fruits of holiness;
through Jesus Christ our Lord.

ST GEORGE

23 April

COLLECT

God of hosts,
who so kindled the flame of love
in the heart of your servant George
that he bore witness to the risen Lord
by his life and by his death:
give us the same faith and power of love
that we who rejoice in his triumphs

may come to share with him the fullness of the resurrection;
through Jesus Christ your Son our Lord,
who is alive and reigns with you,
in the unity of the Holy Spirit,
one God, now and for ever.

POST COMMUNION

Eternal God,
who gave us this holy meal
in which we have celebrated the glory of the cross
and the victory of your martyr George:
by our communion with Christ
in his saving death and resurrection,
give us with all your saints the courage to conquer evil
and so to share the fruit of the tree of life;
through Jesus Christ our Lord.

or

God our redeemer,
whose Church was strengthened
    by the blood of your martyr George:
so bind us, in life and death, to Christ's sacrifice
that our lives, broken and offered with his,
may carry his death and proclaim his resurrection in the world;
through Jesus Christ our Lord.

ST MARK

25 April

COLLECT

Almighty God,
who enlightened your holy Church
through the inspired witness
    of your evangelist Saint Mark:
grant that we, being firmly grounded
    in the truth of the gospel,
may be faithful to its teaching both in word and deed;

through Jesus Christ your Son our Lord,
who is alive and reigns with you,
in the unity of the Holy Spirit,
one God, now and for ever.

POST COMMUNION

Almighty God,
who on the day of Pentecost
sent your Holy Spirit to the apostles
with the wind from heaven and in tongues of flame,
filling them with joy and boldness to preach the gospel:
by the power of the same Spirit
strengthen us to witness to your truth
and to draw everyone to the fire of your love;
through Jesus Christ our Lord.

or

Lord God, the source of truth and love,
keep us faithful to the apostles' teaching and fellowship,
united in prayer and the breaking of bread,
and one in joy and simplicity of heart,
in Jesus Christ our Lord.

ST PHILIP AND ST JAMES

1 May

COLLECT

Almighty Father,
whom truly to know is eternal life:
teach us to know your Son Jesus Christ
as the way, the truth, and the life;
that we may follow the steps
    of your holy apostles Philip and James,
and walk steadfastly in the way that leads to your glory;
through Jesus Christ your Son our Lord,
who is alive and reigns with you,
in the unity of the Holy Spirit,
one God, now and for ever

POST COMMUNION

Almighty God,
who on the day of Pentecost
sent your Holy Spirit to the apostles
with the wind from heaven and in tongues of flame,
filling them with joy and boldness to preach the gospel:
by the power of the same Spirit
strengthen us to witness to your truth
and to draw everyone to the fire of your love;
through Jesus Christ our Lord.

or

Lord God, the source of truth and love,
keep us faithful to the apostles' teaching and fellowship,
united in prayer and the breaking of bread,
and one in joy and simplicity of heart,
in Jesus Christ our Lord.

ST MATTHIAS

14 May

COLLECT

Almighty God,
who in the place of the traitor Judas
chose your faithful servant Matthias
to be of the number of the Twelve:
preserve your Church from false apostles
and, by the ministry of faithful pastors and teachers,
keep us steadfast in your truth;
through Jesus Christ your Son our Lord,
who is alive and reigns with you,
in the unity of the Holy Spirit,
one God, now and for ever.

POST COMMUNION

Almighty God,
who on the day of Pentecost
sent your Holy Spirit to the apostles
with the wind from heaven and in tongues of flame,
filling them with joy and boldness to preach the gospel:
by the power of the same Spirit
strengthen us to witness to your truth
and to draw everyone to the fire of your love;
through Jesus Christ our Lord.

or

Lord God, the source of truth and love,
keep us faithful to the apostles' teaching and fellowship,
united in prayer and the breaking of bread,
and one in joy and simplicity of heart,
in Jesus Christ our Lord.

THE VISIT OF MARY TO ELIZABETH

31 May

COLLECT

Mighty God,
by whose grace Elizabeth rejoiced with Mary
and greeted her as the mother of the Lord:
look with favour on your lowly servants
that, with Mary, we may magnify your holy name
and rejoice to acclaim her Son our Saviour,
who is alive and reigns with you,
in the unity of the Holy Spirit,
one God, now and for ever.

POST COMMUNION

Gracious God,
who gave joy to Elizabeth and Mary
as they recognized the signs of redemption
    at work within them:
help us, who have shared in the joy of this eucharist,

to know the Lord deep within us
and his love shining out in our lives,
that the world may rejoice in your salvation;
through Jesus Christ our Lord.

ST BARNABAS

11 June

COLLECT

Bountiful God, giver of all gifts,
who poured your Spirit upon your servant Barnabas
and gave him grace to encourage others:
help us, by his example,
to be generous in our judgements
and unselfish in our service;
through Jesus Christ your Son our Lord,
who is alive and reigns with you,
in the unity of the Holy Spirit,
one God, now and for ever.

POST COMMUNION

Almighty God,
who on the day of Pentecost
sent your Holy Spirit to the apostles
with the wind from heaven and in tongues of flame,
filling them with joy and boldness to preach the gospel:
by the power of the same Spirit
strengthen us to witness to your truth
and to draw everyone to the fire of your love;
through Jesus Christ our Lord.

or

Lord God, the source of truth and love,
keep us faithful to the apostles' teaching and fellowship,
united in prayer and the breaking of bread,
and one in joy and simplicity of heart,
in Jesus Christ our Lord.

THE BIRTH OF ST JOHN THE BAPTIST

24 June

COLLECT

Almighty God,
by whose providence your servant John the Baptist
was wonderfully born,
and sent to prepare the way of your Son our Saviour
by the preaching of repentance:
lead us to repent according to his preaching
and, after his example,
constantly to speak the truth, boldly to rebuke vice,
and patiently to suffer for the truth's sake;
through Jesus Christ your Son our Lord,
who is alive and reigns with you,
in the unity of the Holy Spirit,
one God, now and for ever.

POST COMMUNION

Merciful Lord,
whose prophet John the Baptist
proclaimed your Son as the Lamb of God
    who takes away the sin of the world:
grant that we who in this sacrament have known
    your forgiveness and your life-giving love
may ever tell of your mercy and your peace;
through Jesus Christ our Lord.

ST PETER AND ST PAUL
ST PETER

29 June

COLLECT

Almighty God,
whose blessed apostles Peter and Paul
glorified you in their death as in their life:

grant that your Church,
inspired by their teaching and example,
and made one by your Spirit,
may ever stand firm upon the one foundation,
Jesus Christ your Son our Lord,
who is alive and reigns with you,
in the unity of the Holy Spirit,
one God, now and for ever.

or, where Peter is celebrated alone

Almighty God,
who inspired your apostle Saint Peter
to confess Jesus as Christ and Son of the living God:
build up your Church upon this rock,
that in unity and peace it may proclaim one truth
and follow one Lord, your Son our Saviour Christ,
who is alive and reigns with you,
in the unity of the Holy Spirit,
one God, now and for ever.

POST COMMUNION

Almighty God,
who on the day of Pentecost
sent your Holy Spirit to the apostles
with the wind from heaven and in tongues of flame,
filling them with joy and boldness to preach the gospel:
by the power of the same Spirit
strengthen us to witness to your truth
and to draw everyone to the fire of your love;
through Jesus Christ our Lord.

or

Lord God, the source of truth and love,
keep us faithful to the apostles' teaching and fellowship,
united in prayer and the breaking of bread,
and one in joy and simplicity of heart,
in Jesus Christ our Lord.

ST THOMAS

3 July

COLLECT

Almighty and eternal God,
who, for the firmer foundation of our faith,
allowed your holy apostle Thomas
    to doubt the resurrection of your Son
till word and sight convinced him:
grant to us, who have not seen, that we also may believe
and so confess Christ as our Lord and our God;
who is alive and reigns with you,
in the unity of the Holy Spirit,
one God, now and for ever.

POST COMMUNION

Almighty God,
who on the day of Pentecost
sent your Holy Spirit to the apostles
with the wind from heaven and in tongues of flame,
filling them with joy and boldness to preach the gospel:
by the power of the same Spirit
strengthen us to witness to your truth
and to draw everyone to the fire of your love;
through Jesus Christ our Lord.

or

Lord God, the source of truth and love,
keep us faithful to the apostles' teaching and fellowship,
united in prayer and the breaking of bread,
and one in joy and simplicity of heart,
in Jesus Christ our Lord.

ST MARY MAGDALENE

22 July

COLLECT

Almighty God,
whose Son restored Mary Magdalene
    to health of mind and body
and called her to be a witness to his resurrection:
forgive our sins and heal us by your grace,
that we may serve you in the power of his risen life;
who is alive and reigns with you,
in the unity of the Holy Spirit,
one God, now and for ever.

POST COMMUNION

God of life and love,
whose risen Son called Mary Magdalene by name
and sent her to tell of his resurrection to his apostles:
in your mercy, help us,
who have been united with him in this eucharist,
to proclaim the good news
    that he is alive and reigns, now and for ever.

ST JAMES

25 July

COLLECT

Merciful God,
whose holy apostle Saint James,
leaving his father and all that he had,
was obedient to the calling of your Son Jesus Christ
and followed him even to death:
help us, forsaking the false attractions of the world,
to be ready at all times to answer your call without delay;
through Jesus Christ your Son our Lord,

who is alive and reigns with you,
in the unity of the Holy Spirit,
one God, now and for ever.

POST COMMUNION

Almighty God,
who on the day of Pentecost
sent your Holy Spirit to the apostles
with the wind from heaven and in tongues of flame,
filling them with joy and boldness to preach the gospel:
by the power of the same Spirit
strengthen us to witness to your truth
and to draw everyone to the fire of your love;
through Jesus Christ our Lord.

or

Lord God, the source of truth and love,
keep us faithful to the apostles' teaching and fellowship,
united in prayer and the breaking of bread,
and one in joy and simplicity of heart,
in Jesus Christ our Lord.

THE TRANSFIGURATION

6 August

COLLECT

Father in heaven,
whose Son Jesus Christ was wonderfully transfigured
before chosen witnesses upon the holy mountain,
and spoke of the exodus he would accomplish at Jerusalem:
give us strength so to hear his voice and bear our cross
that in the world to come we may see him as he is;
who is alive and reigns with you,
in the unity of the Holy Spirit,
one God, now and for ever.

POST COMMUNION

Holy God,
we see your glory in the face of Jesus Christ:
may we who are partakers at his table
reflect his life in word and deed,
that all the world may know
 his power to change and save.
This we ask through Jesus Christ our Lord.

THE BLESSED VIRGIN MARY

15 August

COLLECT

Almighty God,
who looked upon the lowliness of the Blessed Virgin Mary
and chose her to be the mother of your only Son:
grant that we who are redeemed by his blood
may share with her in the glory of your eternal kingdom;
through Jesus Christ your Son our Lord,
who is alive and reigns with you,
in the unity of the Holy Spirit,
one God, now and for ever.

POST COMMUNION

God most high,
whose handmaid bore the Word made flesh:
we thank you that in this sacrament of our redemption
you visit us with your Holy Spirit
and overshadow us by your power;
strengthen us to walk with Mary the joyful path of obedience
and so to bring forth the fruits of holiness;
through Jesus Christ our Lord.

ST BARTHOLOMEW

24 August

COLLECT

Almighty and everlasting God,
who gave to your apostle Bartholomew grace
    truly to believe and to preach your word:
grant that your Church
may love that word which he believed
and may faithfully preach and receive the same;
through Jesus Christ your Son our Lord,
who is alive and reigns with you,
in the unity of the Holy Spirit,
one God, now and for ever.

POST COMMUNION

Almighty God,
who on the day of Pentecost
sent your Holy Spirit to the apostles
with the wind from heaven and in tongues of flame,
filling them with joy and boldness to preach the gospel:
by the power of the same Spirit
strengthen us to witness to your truth
and to draw everyone to the fire of your love;
through Jesus Christ our Lord.

or

Lord God, the source of truth and love,
keep us faithful to the apostles' teaching and fellowship,
united in prayer and the breaking of bread,
and one in joy and simplicity of heart,
in Jesus Christ our Lord.

HOLY CROSS DAY

14 September

COLLECT

Almighty God,
who in the passion of your blessed Son
made an instrument of painful death
to be for us the means of life and peace:
grant us so to glory in the cross of Christ
that we may gladly suffer for his sake;
who is alive and reigns with you,
in the unity of the Holy Spirit,
one God, now and for ever.

POST COMMUNION

Faithful God,
whose Son bore our sins in his body on the tree
and gave us this sacrament to show forth his death
    until he comes:
give us grace to glory in the cross of our Lord Jesus Christ,
for he is our salvation, our life and our hope,
who reigns as Lord, now and for ever.

ST MATTHEW

21 September

COLLECT

O Almighty God,
whose blessed Son called Matthew the tax-collector
to be an apostle and evangelist:
give us grace to forsake the selfish pursuit of gain
    and the possessive love of riches
that we may follow in the way of your Son Jesus Christ,
who is alive and reigns with you,
in the unity of the Holy Spirit,
one God, now and for ever.

POST COMMUNION

Almighty God,
who on the day of Pentecost
sent your Holy Spirit to the apostles
with the wind from heaven and in tongues of flame,
filling them with joy and boldness to preach the gospel:
by the power of the same Spirit
strengthen us to witness to your truth
and to draw everyone to the fire of your love;
through Jesus Christ our Lord.

or

Lord God, the source of truth and love,
keep us faithful to the apostles' teaching and fellowship,
united in prayer and the breaking of bread,
and one in joy and simplicity of heart,
in Jesus Christ our Lord.

MICHAELMAS

29 September

COLLECT

Everlasting God,
you have ordained and constituted the ministries
    of angels and mortals in a wonderful order:
grant that as your holy angels
    always serve you in heaven,
so, at your command,
they may help and defend us on earth;
through Jesus Christ your Son our Lord,
who is alive and reigns with you,
in the unity of the Holy Spirit,
one God, now and for ever.

POST COMMUNION

Lord of heaven,
in this eucharist you have brought us near
    to an innumerable company of angels
    and to the spirits of the saints made perfect:
as in this food of our earthly pilgrimage
    we have shared their fellowship,
so may we come to share their joy in heaven;
through Jesus Christ our Lord.

ST LUKE

18 October

COLLECT

Almighty God,
you called Luke the physician,
whose praise is in the gospel,
to be an evangelist and physician of the soul:
by the grace of the Spirit
and through the wholesome medicine of the gospel,
give your Church the same love and power to heal;
through Jesus Christ your Son our Lord,
who is alive and reigns with you,
in the unity of the Holy Spirit,
one God, now and for ever.

POST COMMUNION

Almighty God,
who on the day of Pentecost
sent your Holy Spirit to the apostles
with the wind from heaven and in tongues of flame,
filling them with joy and boldness to preach the gospel:
by the power of the same Spirit
strengthen us to witness to your truth
and to draw everyone to the fire of your love;
through Jesus Christ our Lord.

or

Lord God, the source of truth and love,
keep us faithful to the apostles' teaching and fellowship,
united in prayer and the breaking of bread,
and one in joy and simplicity of heart,
in Jesus Christ our Lord.

ST SIMON AND ST JUDE

28 October

COLLECT

Almighty God,
who built your Church upon the foundation
    of the apostles and prophets,
with Jesus Christ himself as the chief corner-stone:
so join us together in unity of spirit by their doctrine,
that we may be made a holy temple acceptable to you;
through Jesus Christ your Son our Lord,
who is alive and reigns with you,
in the unity of the Holy Spirit,
one God, now and for ever.

POST COMMUNION

Almighty God,
who on the day of Pentecost
sent your Holy Spirit to the apostles
with the wind from heaven and in tongues of flame,
filling them with joy and boldness to preach the gospel:
by the power of the same Spirit
strengthen us to witness to your truth
and to draw everyone to the fire of your love;
through Jesus Christ our Lord.

or

Lord God, the source of truth and love,
keep us faithful to the apostles' teaching and fellowship,
united in prayer and the breaking of bread,
and one in joy and simplicity of heart,
in Jesus Christ our Lord.

ST ANDREW

30 November

COLLECT

Almighty God,
who gave such grace to your apostle Saint Andrew
that he readily obeyed the call of your Son Jesus Christ
   and brought his brother with him:
call us by your holy word,
and give us grace to follow you without delay
   and to tell the good news of your kingdom;
through Jesus Christ your Son our Lord,
who is alive and reigns with you,
in the unity of the Holy Spirit,
one God, now and for ever.

POST COMMUNION

Almighty God,
who on the day of Pentecost
sent your Holy Spirit to the apostles
with the wind from heaven and in tongues of flame,
filling them with joy and boldness to preach the gospel:
by the power of the same Spirit
strengthen us to witness to your truth
and to draw everyone to the fire of your love;
through Jesus Christ our Lord.

or

Lord God, the source of truth and love,
keep us faithful to the apostles' teaching and fellowship,
united in prayer and the breaking of bread,
and one in joy and simplicity of heart,
in Jesus Christ our Lord.

ST STEPHEN

26 December

COLLECT

Gracious Father,
who gave the first martyr Stephen
grace to pray for those who took up stones against him:
grant that in all our sufferings for the truth
we may learn to love even our enemies
and to seek forgiveness for those who desire our hurt,
looking up to heaven to him who was crucified for us,
Jesus Christ, our mediator and advocate,
who is alive and reigns with you,
in the unity of the Holy Spirit,
one God, now and for ever.

POST COMMUNION

Merciful Lord,
we thank you for the signs of your mercy
revealed in birth and death:
save us by the coming of your Son,
and give us joy in honouring Stephen,
first martyr of the new Israel;
through Jesus Christ our Lord.

ST JOHN

27 December

COLLECT

Merciful Lord,
cast your bright beams of light upon the Church:
that, being enlightened by the teaching
of your blessed apostle and evangelist Saint John,
we may so walk in the light of your truth
that we may at last attain to the light of everlasting life;
through Jesus Christ
your incarnate Son our Lord,

who is alive and reigns with you,
in the unity of the Holy Spirit,
one God, now and for ever.

POST COMMUNION

Grant, O Lord, we pray,
that the Word made flesh
proclaimed by your apostle John
may, by the celebration of these holy mysteries,
ever abide and live within us;
through Jesus Christ our Lord.

HOLY INNOCENTS

28 December

COLLECT

Heavenly Father,
whose children suffered at the hands of Herod,
though they had done no wrong:
by the suffering of your Son
and by the innocence of our lives
frustrate all evil designs
and establish your reign of justice and peace;
through Jesus Christ your Son our Lord,
who is alive and reigns with you,
in the unity of the Holy Spirit,
one God, now and for ever.

POST COMMUNION

Lord Jesus Christ,
in your humility you have stooped to share our human life
with the most defenceless of your children:
may we who have received these gifts of your passion
rejoice in celebrating the witness of the holy innocents

to the purity of your sacrifice

made once for all upon the cross;
for you are alive and reign, now and for ever.

HARVEST

COLLECT

Eternal God,
you crown the year with your goodness
and you give us the fruits of the earth in their season:
grant that we may use them to your glory,
    for the relief of those in need
    and for our own well-being;
through Jesus Christ your Son our Lord,
who is alive and reigns with you,
in the unity of the Holy Spirit,
one God, now and for ever.

POST COMMUNION

Lord of the harvest,
with joy we have offered thanksgiving
    for your love in creation
and have shared in the bread and the wine of the kingdom:
by your grace plant within us a reverence for all that you give us
and make us generous and wise stewards
of the good things we enjoy;
through Jesus Christ our Lord.

ST KENTIGERN (MUNGO)

13 January

COLLECT

Almighty God,
the light of the faithful and shepherd of souls,
who set your servant Kentigern (Mungo) to be a bishop in the Church,
to feed your sheep by the word of Christ
and to guide them by good example:
give us grace to keep the faith of the Church
and to follow in the footsteps
of Jesus Christ your Son our Lord,
who is alive and reigns with you,
in the unity of the Holy Spirit,
one God, now and for ever,

POST COMMUNION

Holy Father,
who gathered us here around the table of your Son
to share this meal with the whole household of God:
in that new world where you reveal
    the fullness of your peace,
gather people of every race and language
to share with Kentigern (Mungo) and all your saints
in the eternal banquet of Jesus Christ our Lord.

ST BRIGID

1 February

COLLECT

Father,
by the leadership of your blessed servant Brigid
you strengthened the Church in this land:
as we give you thanks for her life of devoted service,
inspire us with new life and light,
and give us perseverance to serve you all our days;
through Jesus Christ our Lord.

POST COMMUNION

God of truth,
whose Wisdom set her table
    and invited us to eat the bread and drink the wine of the kingdom:
help us to lay aside all foolishness
and to live and walk in the way of insight,
that we may come in fellowship with Brigid
to the eternal feast of heaven;
through Jesus Christ our Lord.

ST DAVID

1 March

COLLECT

Almighty God,
who called your servant David
to be a faithful and wise steward of your mysteries
for the people of Wales:
in your mercy, grant that,
following his purity of life and zeal for the gospel of Christ,
we may with him receive the crown of everlasting life;
through Jesus Christ your Son our Lord,
who is alive and reigns with you,
in the unity of the Holy Spirit,
one God, now and for ever.

POST COMMUNION

God, shepherd of your people,
whose servant david revealed the loving service of Christ
in his ministry as a pastor of your people:
by this eucharist in which we share
awaken within us the love of Christ
and keep us faithful to our Christian calling;
through him who laid down his life for us,
but is alive and reigns with you, now and for ever.

ST PATRICK

17 March

COLLECT

Almighty God,
in your providence you chose your servant Patrick,
to be the apostle of the Irish people,
to baptize those who were wandering
in darkness and error
and to bring them to the true light

and knowledge of your Word:
keep us in that light
and bring us to everlasting life;
through Jesus Christ our Lord.

POST COMMUNION

Hear us, most merciful God, for that part of the Church
which through your servant Patrick you planted in our land:
that it may hold fast the faith entrusted to the saints
and in the end bear much fruit to eternal life:
through Jesus Christ our Lord.

ST COLUMBA   Ireland

9 June

COLLECT

O God, you called your servant Columba
from among the princes of this land
to be a herald and evangelist of your kingdom:
grant that your Church,
remembering his faith and courage,
may so proclaim the gospel,
that people everywhere will come to know your Son as their Saviour,
and serve him as their King;
who lives and reigns with you and the Holy Spirit,
one God, now and for ever.

POST COMMUNION

Lord Jesus, King of Saints,
in the solemn rollcall of your sons we name Columba:
mould us who have tasted your goodness at this table
    to your perfection
so we may come as guests to the Royal banquet
    of your kingdom in heaven;
where with the Father and the Son, you reign, for ever.

ST COLUMBA   Scotland

9 June

COLLECT

O God, you called your servant Columba
from amond the princes of his land
to be a herald and evangelist of your kingdom:
grant that your Church,
remembering his faith and courage,
may so proclaim the gospel
that people everywhere will come
to know your Son as their saviour,
and serve him as their king;
who is alive and reigns with you and the Holy Spirit,
one God, now and for ever.

POST COMMUNION

Holy Father,
who gathered us here around the table of your Son
to share this meal with the whole household of God:
in that new world where your reveal
    the fullness of your peace,
gather people of every race and language
to share with Columba and all your saints
in the eternal banquet of Jesus Christ our Lord.

ST NINIAN

16 September

COLLECT

Almighty and everlasting God,
who called your servant Ninian to preach the gospel
    to the people of northern Britain:
raise up in this and every land
heralds and evangelists of your kingdom,
that your Church may make known the immeasurable riches
    of your Son our Saviour Jesus Christ,
who is alive and reigns with you,
in the unity of the Holy Spirit,
one God, now and for ever.

POST COMMUNION

Holy Father,
who gathered us here around the table of your Son
to share this meal with the whole household of God:
in that new world where you reveal
    the fullness of your peace,
gather people of every race and language
to share with Ninian and all your saints
in the eternal banquet of Jesus Christ our Lord.

ST MARGARET OF SCOTLAND

16 November

COLLECT

God, the ruler of all,
who called your servant Margaret to an earthly throne
and gave her zeal for your Church and love for your people
that she might advance your heavenly kingdom:
mercifully grant that we who commemorate her example
may be fruitful in good works
and attain to the glorious crown of your saints;
through Jesus Christ your Son our Lord,
who is alive and reigns with you,
in the unity of the Holy Spirit,
one God, now and for ever.

POST COMMUNION

God our redeemer,
who inspired Margaret to witness to your love
and to work for the coming of your kingdom:
may we, who in this sacrament share the bread of heaven,
be fired by your Spirit to proclaim the gospel in our daily living
and never to rest content until your kingdom come,
on earth as it is in heaven;
through Jesus Christ our Lord.

INDEX